Reader's Digest

GREAT
BIOGRAPHIES

Reader's Digest
Great Biographies

THE AUTOBIOGRAPHY OF MARK TWAIN

edited by Charles Neider

Printer, silver prospector, riverboat pilot, newspaperman, lecturer, world traveler, and undoubtedly America's most beloved humorist, Mark Twain crammed enough experience for several lives into the nearly eight decades he lived. His life, so full of adventure and dazzling triumphs, was marred by financial troubles and devastating personal tragedies; but nothing could quench the wit, the sardonic humor and the great human warmth that illuminate every page of his autobiography.

Charles Neider edited a number of other volumes of Twain's work, including *The Complete Humorous Sketches and Tales of Mark Twain*.

"*I know how inviting a prize watermelon looks when it is cooling itself in a tub of water, waiting, the children gathered for the sacrifice, their mouths watering; I know the crackling sound it makes when the carving knife enters its end; I can see its halves fall apart and display the rich red meat and the black seeds; I know how a boy looks behind a yard-long slice of that melon, and I know how he feels, for I have been there.*"
—from The Autobiography of Mark Twain

ELIZABETH THE GREAT

by Elizabeth Jenkins

At the death of King Henry VIII, his redheaded, high-spirited daughter Elizabeth was third in line for the crown of England, after her brother Edward and her sister Mary Tudor. She survived a stormy childhood to mount the throne in 1558, borne there by a rejoicing people. Her reign, riddled with plots and counterplots, peopled with great adventurers, statesmen and writers, was one of the most exciting and truly majestic in all history.

Elizabeth Jenkins is a novelist as well as a biographer. In this splendid book, considered her masterpiece, she has made the unforgettable figures of the Elizabethan Age come alive like the characters in a good novel.

MARTIN LUTHER
Oak of Saxony

by Edwin P. Booth

To his followers he was God's avenging angel; to his enemies he was the devil dressed in priestly robes. Yet Martin Luther, the fiery reformer, was also very human, as this compelling portrait shows.

Edwin P. Booth was especially qualified to evaluate Luther's achievement—he was a Methodist clergyman and educator, specializing in the field of church history.

DARWIN AND THE BEAGLE

by Alan Moorehead

When Charles Darwin, age 22, lightheartedly set sail aboard H.M.S. *Beagle* to study the flora and fauna of the New World, he had no thought that the evidence he found would lead him to a revolutionary concept of the origin of species. From the events of that voyage, Alan Moorehead has shaped an absorbing narrative with an engaging hero—a young scientist who changed the course of human thought.

Moorehead, recognized as one of the most talented correspondents who covered World War II, later turned his attention to history and biography, with special emphasis on exploration and discovery. Two of his other books, *The White Nile* and *The Blue Nile*, have as their subject the 19th Century explorers of Egypt's great river.

*Reader's
Digest*

GREAT
BIOGRAPHIES

*selected
and
condensed by
the editors
of
Reader's
Digest*

The Reader's Digest Association, Inc.
Pleasantville, New York
Cape Town, Hong Kong, London, Montreal, Sydney

READER'S DIGEST CONDENSED BOOKS

Editor-in-Chief: John S. Zinsser, Jr.

Executive Editor: Barbara J. Morgan

Managing Editors: Anne H. Atwater, Ann Berryman, Tanis H. Erdmann,
Thomas Froncek, Marjorie Palmer

Senior Staff Editors: Jean E. Aptakin, Virginia Rice (Rights), Ray Sipherd, Angela Weldon

Senior Editors: M. Tracy Brigden, Linn Carl, Joseph P. McGrath,
James J. Menick, Margery D. Thorndike

Associate Editors: Thomas S. Clemmons, Alice Jones-Miller, Maureen A. Mackey

Senior Copy Editors: Claire A. Bedolis, Jeane Garment, Jane F. Neighbors

Associate Copy Editors: Maxine Bartow, Rosalind H. Campbell, Jean S. Friedman

Assistant Copy Editors: Ainslie Gilligan, Jeanette Gingold, Marilyn J. Knowlton

Art Director: William Gregory

Executive Art Editors: Soren Noring, Angelo Perrone

Associate Art Editors, Research: George Calas, Jr., Katherine Kelleher

CB PROJECTS

Executive Editor: Herbert H. Lieberman

Senior Editors: Dana Adkins, Catherine T. Brown, John R. Roberson

CB INTERNATIONAL EDITIONS

Executive Editor: Francis Schell

Senior Editor: Gary Q. Arpin

FIRST EDITION

All rights reserved. Unauthorized reproduction, in any manner, is prohibited.
Library of Congress Cataloging-in-Publication Data
Reader's digest great biographies.
Contents: v. 1. The Spirit of St. Louis / by Charles A. Lindbergh.
Florence Nightingale / by Cecil Woodham-Smith.
Edison / by Matthew Josephson.
Hans Christian Andersen / by Rumer Godden—[etc.]
1. Biography—Collected works. I. Reader's Digest Association.
II. Reader's digest. III. Title: Great biographies.
CT101.R42 1987 920'.02 86-29816 ISBN 0-89577-261-2 (v.3)

Printed in the United States of America

Contents

A CONDENSATION OF

ELIZABETH THE GREAT
by
ELIZABETH
JENKINS

ILLUSTRATED BY
CHARLES RAYMOND

Elizabeth I of England was perhaps the most regal queen ever to grace a throne. She was also a fascinating woman whose life was filled with conflict and paradox. When she was only three her mother, Anne Boleyn, was beheaded by order of her father, Henry VIII, who thereafter banished Elizabeth from his presence for long periods. Her youth was lonely and threatened; more than once she was a prisoner in the Tower, until at last, in her twenty-fifth year, she was crowned Queen.

Making up for a childhood of neglect, as a ruler she was resplendent in rich fabrics and laces and precious gems. Though she never married, she played political cat-and-mouse with the crowned heads of Europe who sought her hand, while at home she demanded total devotion from the gallant courtiers she raised to high office. Outwardly self-indulgent, her first concern was unfailingly for her subjects, to whom she said: "And though God has raised me high, yet this I count the glory of my crown, that I have reigned with your loves." She was indeed beloved of her people.

In *Elizabeth the Great* Miss Jenkins has painted a vivid personal portrait of the "Virgin Queen." This fine and highly readable biography enables the reader to enter into the mystery of the extraordinary woman who gave her name to the tumultuous age in which she lived.

Chapter 1

WHEN HENRY VIII DIED in January 1547, the most remarkable beings left in the realm were three pale and close-lipped children. One was his daughter Elizabeth by his second wife Anne Boleyn, another was his son Edward by his third wife Jane Seymour, the third was his great-niece Jane, granddaughter of his sister Mary and eldest child of Lord Henry Grey, marquess of Dorset. Elizabeth was almost fourteen, Edward and Jane both nine.

The children bore considerable resemblance to one another, but the faces of the king's son and daughter were stamped with a look at once repressed and preternaturally vigilant. They were not robust, but their intellects were remarkable, and the greatest scholars had been employed to stimulate them into a state of alarming precocity.

The second generation of the king's family circle was completed by a figure very different in age and outlook. The princess Mary, only child of his first wife, Catherine of Aragon, was thirty at the time of her father's death. For the past fifteen years her life had been very unhappy. She had most dearly loved her mother, and had seen her divorced so that the king could marry Catherine's lady-in-waiting, the disagreeable and dazzling Anne Boleyn. An ardent member of the Roman Church, she had seen the English government throw off papal authority and her father style himself the Church's supreme head. She had vowed passionately she would never call him so, and a fearful dispute was joined in which the king banished her from his presence and left her to the mercy of his ministers. On her mother's death she succumbed to his will, avowing her own birth illegitimate and accepting the king as supreme head of the Church. These sufferings had made her old before her time and had given a twist to her unselfish and affectionate nature.

The king's obsessive desire for the son whom his first twenty years of marriage had not given him was the source of the energy with which he shouldered through the breach with Rome; its immediate inspiration was his passion for Elizabeth's mother. Black-eyed, excitable, tart and witty, Anne Boleyn made gentleness and amiability appear insipid. For six years she refused to gratify the king's passion, keeping the lustful and domineering king in a white heat of desire. When the divorce was all but accomplished she yielded to him, and the marriage was performed secretly in January 1533 so that the coming child might be the heir to its father's throne.

Anne's coronation procession was made in brilliant weather on the last day of May. In her ruby wreath and her robes of glittering silver, "a woman clothed with the sun," she was borne on her way to be crowned Queen already five months gone with child. Her long-sustained effort had resulted in an enormous triumph.

Her child proved to be a girl, and from that hour her influence began to wane. Two miscarriages diminished it further. The hysterical shrewishness to which she was driven by the dreadful sense of failure paved the way for a successor of meek, adoring tenderness. When Anne discovered the king making love to her lady-in-waiting, Jane Seymour, she burst into furious denunciation; the rage brought on a premature labor and she was delivered of a dead boy. In Sir John Neale's words, "She had miscarried of her saviour."

Her reckless behavior had provided ample means to destroy

her. She was at Greenwich after the fatal miscarriage, where she was suddenly arrested and brought to the Tower in the month of May. The only description of the queen with her child Elizabeth belongs to the days immediately before the arrest. A Protestant refugee to whom the Protestant Anne had seemed a being of angelic virtue, writing to congratulate Queen Elizabeth on her accession, exclaimed: "Alas I shall never forget the sorrow I felt when I saw the sainted Queen your mother, carrying you, still a little baby, in her arms, and entreating the most serene King your father in Greenwich Palace, from the open window of which he was looking into the courtyard where she brought you to him. The faces and gestures of the speakers plainly showed the King was angry, though he concealed his anger wonderfully well."

The queen was charged with having committed adultery with five men, of whom one was her brother, and condemned on a verdict of high treason to be beheaded or burned alive at the king's pleasure. Some mercy was shown to her by the bringing over from Calais of a notably skillful headsman who used a sword instead of an axe. The lieutenant of the Tower assured her she would feel no pain. "I have a little neck," she said, and putting her hand around it, she shrieked with laughter.

On May 19, 1536, she was beheaded on Tower Green, a few minutes before noon. The guns of the Tower were fired to mark the act and the king, who was hunting in Richmond Park, paused to catch the sound. That night he was at the Seymours' house in Wiltshire, whence he married Jane Seymour the next morning. Meanwhile the head and body of Anne Boleyn had been put into a chest made for arrows and carried a few paces from the scaffold into the chapel of St. Peter ad Vincula, where she was buried. Her daughter was not three years old.

The child was a lively little creature with reddish-golden hair, a very white skin, and eyes of golden brown with brows and lashes so fair as to be almost invisible. Though headstrong, she was remarkably teachable. Her excellent governess, Lady Bryan, said that she was spoiling the child at present because she was in pain with cutting her double teeth, but once this was over, Lady Bryan meant to have her behaving very differently.

The question of how the king would now regard her was an anxious one to those in charge of Elizabeth. Lady Bryan wrote with pathetic eagerness to the great minister Thomas Cromwell, saying she was sure that when the princess had got over her teething, the king would be delighted with his little girl. Meanwhile, she was in dire need of clothes.

Her mother had dressed her beautifully, and included in the lists of Anne Boleyn's dresses for the last year of her life are the kirtles made for "my Lady Princess": orange velvet, russet velvet, yellow satin, white damask. Now, a year later, Elizabeth had outworn and outgrown almost everything she had. "I have driven it off as best I can," Lady Bryan wrote, "that by my troth I can drive it off no longer; beseeching you, my Lord, that ye will see that her Grace hath that which is needful for her."

That her father had killed her mother was no doubt concealed from her for the time being, but the fact that her governess was very anxious about her and they had not clothes to put on her could not fail to make a deep impression on so young a child, and a year or so later Elizabeth proved capable of asking a disconcerting question. When Jane Seymour was pregnant, she asked to have the princess Mary recalled to court, as a companion. "She shall come to thee, darling," said the king; and as Mary was now reinstated in her honors it was decided that Elizabeth must no longer be called princess. The decision was communicated to the governor of her household and he repeated it to Elizabeth. She listened carefully, and then asked: "How haps it, Governor, yesterday my Lady Princess, and to-day but my Lady Elizabeth?"

The third queen fulfilled the king's hopes and was brought to bed of a son in October 1537; he was christened when he was three days old, the ceremony taking place at night in the chapel of Hampton Court Palace. In the great procession which took the baby from his mother's bedchamber to the chapel, Elizabeth carried the chrisom, the cloth in which the child was received after his immersion in the font. As she was so very small, she herself was carried by the queen's brother, Edward Seymour, the earl of Hertford. The ceremony was not over till after midnight, and as the procession re-formed Princess Mary disregarded the prescribed order and took her little sister by the hand.

Jane Seymour had been raised to almost supernatural importance by her situation. She had endured agonies in a labor of thirty hours, but this was her moment of supreme triumph. Because they had failed of it, Catherine of Aragon had been divorced and Anne Boleyn beheaded. While the king exulted beside her, the invaluable baby was laid in her arms that she might bless him and call him by his baptismal name. Within a week she was dead, and with letters announcing the king's loss and grief were mingled inquiries about the beauty and other marriageable qualities of French princesses.

Before the little prince could speak, he showed an affection for his sister Elizabeth. The children formed a natural alliance: each was motherless, with a splendid, ominous father whom they scarcely saw. The value of his sister's companionship to the frail, precocious little boy was recognized by everyone; that her exceedingly important brother loved her and wanted her society increased Elizabeth's own importance, a fact no child was likely to overlook, but that she felt for him a genuine natural fondness was never in doubt by those who saw them. On New Year's Day in 1539, when Edward was not yet two, the king gave him a superb equipage of silver-gilt plate, while his sister Mary presented him with a beautiful crimson satin coat and cap embroidered with gold and pearl. Elizabeth gave him a cambric shirt that she had sewed herself.

The king owned many palaces, and as the lack of sanitation made it necessary for houses with a large number of inmates to be vacated from time to time to be "aired and sweetened," the king's own establishment and that of each of his children progressed regularly from one abode to another. With this movement and with no family circle, Elizabeth's existence owed such stability as it had to the governess who was appointed when she was four. This was a young woman called Katherine Champernowne. She not only recognized the child's remarkable abilities, she loved her. When Katherine Champernowne had been with Elizabeth eight years she married a Mr. John Ashley, who was related to the Boleyns.

13

No one knows when Elizabeth found out what had happened to her mother. A dead silence involves the whole matter. Once, when she was twenty, she hinted to the Spanish ambassador that her sister's hostility to her was due to injuries that Mary and her mother had received from Anne Boleyn, and once she told the Venetian ambassador that her mother would never have cohabited with the king except by a marriage declared legal by the primate of England. Apart from these instances there is no record of her having uttered her mother's name. But with this determined silence there went a marked kindness toward her mother's connections—to Careys, Howards, Knollys, the humble Ashleys, and to that Henry Norris whose father had been put to death as her mother's lover and had died declaring her mother's innocence. In her kindness to these, she paid a mute tribute where she would not speak.

The King's fourth marriage, his farcical union with the uncouth but sensible Anne of Cleves, was dissolved in June 1540 and left him free to contract his fifth marriage with the girl who inspired the second great passion of his life, the nineteen-year-old Catherine Howard.

The French ambassador wrote: "The King is so greatly enamored, he knows not how to show enough affection for her." Her power to charm Henry recalled her cousin Anne Boleyn, but Catherine would never have refused him for six years, as Anne had done. A sweet-natured wanton, it turned out, indeed, that she had refused nobody. She was particularly kind to Elizabeth as her own relation. The first time the new queen dined in public, the seven-year-old Elizabeth had a place of honor opposite to her.

Kindness always made an impression on Elizabeth. Her young, sweet stepmother, who was so powerful with her great father, went out of her way to be good to her, and might, in time, have laid the past; but a hideous repetition called up the specter from the grave. Within eighteen months the intrigues in which Catherine had indulged since the age of twelve were uncovered, and she was charged with having committed adultery since her marriage with her cousin Culpepper. During the investigations she escaped from her apartment in Hampton Court and rushed down the gallery toward the chapel where the king was at mass. The guards caught her before she could reach him and she was dragged back, shrieking. On the morning of February 13, 1542, she was beheaded on the spot where her cousin had died before her, and her head and body, wrapped together in a cloth, were carried into the chapel of St. Peter ad Vincula and buried near her cousin's grave.

Twenty years later, when England and the courts of Europe were agog with the idea that Queen Elizabeth might marry the earl of Leicester, Lord Leicester told the French ambassador that he had known Elizabeth since she was a child of eight, and from that very time she had always said: "I will never marry." Little notice was paid to the words. It did not occur to anyone, it seems, to look back and recall that when Elizabeth was eight years and five months old Catherine Howard was beheaded.

Had she disliked or despised her father the impression would have been less dreadful, but she admired him with her whole heart. It was indeed impossible to know the king and remain indifferent to him, for in every aspect of his personality Henry displayed overwhelming force: engrossingly affectionate where his feelings were engaged, severe and cruel when his confidence was betrayed. The people as a whole were not affected by his treacheries, his ruthless acts; they saw in this splendid figure, with his power, his energy, his personal authority, a man who identified them with the modern world, and whose firm establishment on the throne was a reassurance against the horror and ruin of the past.

Elizabeth was only thirteen when her father died, and her admiration for his genius and pride in his relationship were the instinctive emotions of childhood. The one execution which she had been too young to understand, and the second which had taught her, at the age of eight, everything she had not known about the first—these events could not be judged from any point of view unfavorable to the glorious king, but the effect they made went the deeper for that. To the child of her own age she said what she might not have said to an older person: "I will never marry." It was her comment on her mother and her mother's cousin, who had married her father and were lying headless in their graves.

Though terribly bereaved, Elizabeth was never without affection. Katherine Ashley, whose name the princess shortened to Kat, supplied the doting fondness that could see no fault, and her sister Mary would always be kind to her as long as she was a good girl. Mary's account books show that she made Elizabeth numerous presents.

In 1543 the king contracted his last marriage. It seemed at first as if the whole royal family must benefit by the king's choice. Catherine Parr was thirty years old; she had been twice widowed and was very rich. Her disposition was one of radiant kindness, she was intelligent and cheerful, and she possessed mature but still youthful good looks.

The king was now fifty-two, but appeared much older. It was noticed that after the death of Catherine Howard his deterioration had been rapid. He had an ulcer in his leg which gave him savage pain, and his once handsome body was a pitiable and disgusting ruin. His will, decreeing that in the succession his children by Catherine Parr were to take precedence over Mary and Elizabeth, showed that the marriage was to be no mere companionship.

The new queen fulfilled her duties with inspired goodwill. She was allowed to have Edward and Elizabeth in her household, and for the first time in their lives the king's younger children had a home. Their stepmother encouraged them in their lessons and continued her own reading under the guidance of their tutors. Unknown to the king, she also encouraged their interest in the teaching of the Reformed Church. Elizabeth held the unquestioning belief in the Christian faith which was universal in Europe, but her mind was incapable of religious fanaticism. The famous saying of her later years, "There is only one Christ Jesus and one faith: the rest is a dispute about trifles," is an expression not of experience but of temperament.

Cautious beyond her years and of exemplary behavior as a rule, at the age of twelve Elizabeth's discretion was not entirely perfect: in this year she offended the king. Nothing is known of the offense, only of its consequence. She was banished from his household, and it was a year before her humble entreaties and the queen's good offices brought her back to the family circle. Henceforward the attitude of respectful worship was maintained unblemished. Her gratitude to the queen was ardent. As a New Year's gift for 1545 she wrote out in a small vellum book her own translation of a French poem called *The Mirror, or Glass, of the Sinful Soul*, and bound it in a cover she had embroidered in blue silk and silver twist, with clusters of hearts-ease in purple and yellow. The dedication said: *To Our most Noble and Virtuous Queen Catherine, Elizabeth, her humble daughter, wisheth perpetual felicity and everlasting joy.*

In Queen Catherine's household, Elizabeth and Edward were companions and friends, but Edward was also on good terms with his cousin Jane Grey, who joined them at the age of nine. Jane's mother Frances was the eldest daughter of the king's sister Mary, and had therefore inherited royal blood, which she passed on to her children with consequences to them which were very serious. Her marriage to Lord Henry Grey had produced three daughters: Jane, Catherine and Mary. The two younger were unremarkable; all the moral and intellectual endowments and all the graces of the family were concentrated in the eldest daughter. Like her cousins, she had been very carefully taught. A young Cambridge scholar, John Aylmer, had been appointed as the family tutor when Jane was four years old. He had given her a thorough education in Greek and Latin, but his chief concern was with her spiritual development, over which he watched with anxious devotion.

Although she was now under the same roof with her cousin Elizabeth, nothing is heard of any intercourse between the two of them. There was perhaps some instinctive lack of sympathy, in spite of cousinship, nearness in years and great fondness for reading. Elizabeth's ability at her lessons was now generally recognized as something unusual; she was learning history, geography, mathematics, the elements of architecture and astronomy and four modern languages: French, Italian, Spanish and Flemish. Her Greek and Latin had been entrusted to another young Cambridge scholar, William Grindal; he was considered to have brought the princess on very well, the more so as he had had the help and advice of his master, the celebrated Roger Ascham.

Ascham's book, *The Scholemaster*, shows that he was a teacher so enlightened that he would be considered progressive even today. The amount of work he expected would now be looked at askance, but within the framework of sixteenth-century usage his sympathy with the childish mind was that of a first-rate teacher. Through Grindal, Ascham was now brought into contact with his famous pupil. He advised Grindal on books and method; on the question of the princess's preparation he addressed himself to Mrs. Ashley, who had some degree of education herself. She still supervised the princess's private study, for Ascham speaks of her "diligent overseeing." He was of two minds as to how to exhort the governess; he wanted energy used, that the pupil's brilliant promise might be fulfilled. "Good mistress," he wrote, "I would have you in any case to labor and not give yourself to ease." But then came the dread of seeing the young mind injured by too much severity, and he begged Mrs. Ashley "to favour somewhat" this rare intelligence; for, he said, "the younger, the more tender, the quicker, the easier to break." The process should be like pouring water into a goblet: too much at once would dash out, but slowly it might be filled to the brim.

While her education in classical and European languages was being carried on by teachers of this distinction, Elizabeth acquired another language from a homelier source. One of her attendants was a Welshwoman, Blanche Parry, who had been with her even longer than Mrs. Ashley, for Blanche Parry said that she had seen the princess rocked in her cradle. This lady was surprisingly knowledgeable, and it is assumed that it was she who taught the great-granddaughter of Owen Tudor to speak Welsh.

To this period, when she was thirteen, is ascribed the portrait of Elizabeth at Windsor Castle. The smooth red-gold hair is worn hanging straight down her back, she holds a book with hands whose fingers are so long and delicate they look inhuman, and her expression is watchful and disillusioned. The unchildlike wariness on the youthful face shows the effect of what had happened to her from the age of three. But despite the caution that appeared in her countenance, an inherent haughtiness sometimes showed itself to those whom the princess neither liked nor saw any reason to conciliate.

In November of 1546 Edward and Elizabeth were together at Hatfield, the brick palace whose remains still stand in the beautiful wooded park. Their companionship was in its closest phase, and when it was abruptly broken by orders from the Privy Council directing the prince to Hertford and the princess to Enfield, Elizabeth wrote to Edward immediately, consoling him as best she could for their being driven from their favorite place and suggesting an exchange of letters as the next best thing to being with each other. Edward's reply, dated December 5, 1546, written in Latin, showed not only his affection but a pitiable sense of insecurity: "Change of place did not vex me so much, dearest sister, as your going from me. Now there can be nothing pleasanter than a letter from you. . . . It is some comfort in my grief that my chamberlain tells me I may hope to visit you soon, (if nothing happens to either of us in the mean-time). Farewell dearest sister."

The visit was made before they expected it and in impressive circumstances. Henry VIII was sinking fast, and early in the morning of January 28, holding the hand of the archbishop of Canterbury, Thomas Cranmer, he died. No sooner was the breath out of his body than Edward Seymour, Lord Hertford, whose ambitions had been cautiously advanced during the ten years since the king had married his sister, broke from cover and outdistanced all competitors.

Henry's will left the succession first to Edward; then, in default of heirs, to Mary; then, in default of heirs, to Elizabeth. Should Elizabeth die childless, it was to devolve on the family of his sister Mary: her daughter Frances, and the latter's daughters, Jane, Catherine and Mary Grey. Hertford had been appointed one of sixteen guardians to the young king, but he rapidly assumed a supreme authority. His nephew was instructed to make him duke of Somerset, and Parliament acquiesced in his becoming lord protector with powers to act independently of the council's advice. His first action, however, was to secure the person of the child who was king. He and Sir Anthony Brown rode to Hatfield, where they told Edward merely that he was to visit his sister at Enfield. When the children were brought face-to-face, Hertford announced to them their father's death. The shock was succeeded by fits of uncontrolled crying in both of them, which went on so long that the onlookers were filled not only with pity but with awe. Hertford's maneuver had had a double purpose: Edward, allowed to cry with his sister to his heart's content, was less of a burden to his guardians than he would have been without her, and by bringing the children together Hertford could thenceforward ensure the safe custody of Elizabeth. From the moment her father's will became known, her doings would take on an importance which, though not enough to put them in the forefront of events, no one could afford to overlook.

Two days later Hertford rode with the king rapidly to London. Delighted by the thunderous salute of cannon, with Hertford riding before him and his retinue behind him, Edward entered the precincts of the Tower, where the archbishop of Canterbury, the lord chancellor and the other lords of the council were waiting to do him homage.

Fifteen miles separated Elizabeth from her brother, but there was a distance between them now that miles could not measure; nevertheless she kept their relationship a living one by such means as she had. She wrote continually to Edward and she adopted without effort the adoring and respectful attitude which in Henry VIII's daughter was natural toward a king, even though he were a small boy nearly four years younger than herself.

With the publication of the late king's will, some information became known concerning the princesses besides their claims to the succession. The claim of either princess was to be canceled should she, during her brother's lifetime, marry without the consent of the council. By inference, any man who attempted to marry either sister without the necessary permission would involve himself and her in a most serious charge. This was an obvious precaution to take with regard to heiresses to the Crown. There was indeed only one matter in the will which caused surprise. The late king's elder sister Margaret had married

Elizabeth, Mary and Edward beneath a portrait of their father, Henry VIII.

James IV of Scotland, but her conduct had caused scandal, and her family had been entirely left out of the succession. The Stuarts, therefore, though by primogeniture their claim was superior to the Greys', were, it seemed, to have no chance of succeeding to the English throne.

Chapter 2

WHEN HERTFORD had himself created duke of Somerset, his brother Thomas Seymour was made Lord Seymour of Sudeley and lord high admiral. Somerset, though arrogant, grasping and unscrupulous, had some enlightened ideas of government. Seymour, on the other hand, had the total selfishness and irresponsibility of a criminal. He bitterly resented the fact that the office of protector was not shared equally between Somerset and himself.

On the king's death, Seymour proposed to the council that he should marry Elizabeth, but he received an unequivocal rebuff from the council, and immediately renewed his old suit to Queen Catherine, whom he had courted before her marriage to Henry. The queen dowager, released from the sufferings of her marriage to Henry VIII, behaved like an enamored girl. She married Seymour secretly, and received his clandestine visits at her house in Chelsea, where her porteress let him in at five in the morning. The situation was full of submerged danger, for by the council's permission Elizabeth was now living with her stepmother. Seymour, for all his geniality, was a man of ruthless ambition. He was twenty-five years older than Elizabeth, but as he was in his prime this meant only that he had the maturity a very young girl admires, and his attractions were of the kind to which she was susceptible all her life. He had been put into her head already as a possible husband, and now he was coming and going in romantic secrecy as the husband of her still-youthful stepmother.

Had Seymour left Elizabeth alone, no harm would have come of it; but one of his reasons for marrying the queen dowager was that Elizabeth had been consigned to her care. His brother had control of the king; he himself would have control of the king's enigmatic sister. It was true that if she were drawn into any entanglement it might be regarded as high treason, and that the penalty for this was, for a woman, beheading or burning alive. Seymour knew these facts, but he preferred to disregard them.

Elizabeth's household formed a unit within the queen dowager's; it included Mrs. Ashley, William Grindal and several ladies-in-waiting. There was also attached to it a man who would seem to have had more sense than all the rest put together: this was Kat Ashley's husband John, the princess's distant cousin. In the months after the king's death he gave his wife a warning "to take heed for he did fear that the Lady Elizabeth did bear some affection to my Lord Admiral."

Seymour went openly to work. He began romping with the princess, and his wife did what many women do in such a case: to prove to herself and everybody else that there was no harm in the romp, she joined it herself. There was no doubt as to Elizabeth's state of mind—Ashley had recognized it at once; but with the passion there was considerable fear. Seymour's boisterous approaches were liable to be alarming to a girl of fourteen, and one with who knows what buried dread of men? Seymour would come into her bedchamber in the mornings. If she were up "he would strike her familiarly on the back and buttocks." If she were in bed he would open the bed-curtain "and make as though he would come at her," while she "would go further into the bed." One morning he tried to kiss her in her bed, at which Mrs. Ashley, who slept in the princess's room, "bade him go away for shame." The queen dowager took to coming with her husband on his morning visits and one morning they both tickled the princess as she lay in her bed. In the garden one day there was some startling horseplay: the queen dowager held Elizabeth so that she could not run away, while Seymour cut her black cloth gown into a hundred pieces. The cowering under bedclothes, the struggling and running away culminated in a scene of classical nightmare, that of helplessness in the power of a smiling ogre. Seymour had possessed himself of a master key, and early one morning at Chelsea Elizabeth heard the privy lock undo, and, "knowing he would come in"—Seymour, smiling in his long red beard—"she ran out of her bed to her maidens and then went behind the curtains of the bed, the maidens being there; and my Lord tarried a long time in hopes she would come out." Afterward, "she was commonly up and at her book" by the time Seymour came, and then he would merely look in at the door and say good-morning. But he had overcome her initial resistance; the queen dowager, who was undergoing an uncomfortable pregnancy, could not bring herself to make her husband angry by protesting about his conduct, but she began to realize that he and Elizabeth were very often together; then one day in May, she went into a room unexpectedly and found Elizabeth in his arms.

There was no public appearance of her being sent away in disgrace, but it was decided that Elizabeth should remove with her establishment to the house of Sir Anthony Denny at Cheshunt. She and her train arrived there just after Whitsun, and Elizabeth wrote to her stepmother to say that at their parting she had been too much moved to thank her properly for her kindness, so sad was she to go away, leaving her "in doubtful health," and, she said, "albeit I answered little, I weighed it the more, when you said you would warn me of all evils you should hear of me, for if your Grace had not a good opinion of me, you would not have offered friendship to me that way."

The abrupt parting from Seymour, the disgrace and the contrition, and the warring of sexual excitement with deep-buried dread—all this coming upon her at the critical age of fourteen and a half coincided with, if it did not bring on, an illness.

For the next few years the princess suffered from intermittent ill health; she developed migraine attacks and pains in the eyes, and by the time she was twenty it was a matter of common rumor, of particular interest to ambassadors, that her monthly periods were very few or none, a condition often accounted for by shock and emotional strain. In Elizabeth's history, the events of her mother's death, and that of her mother's cousin, and the engaging of her own affections by Seymour's outrageous siege, seem to have done her nervous system and her sexual development an injury from which they never recovered. But her loyalty in her affections remained unshaken.

In August 1548 the queen dowager's daughter was born, and in the delirium of fever Catherine complained that those she had meant well to, and tried to be good to, stood around her bed laughing at her pain. She died within a week, and was buried in the small chapel of Sudeley Castle. The chief mourner was Lady Jane Grey, in deepest mourning, with a long train upheld by another young lady.

Her parents now wished Lady Jane to return to them, but Seymour did not intend to let her go. He held out a dazzling prospect: "If I can get the king at liberty, I dare warrant you he shall marry none other than Jane." The Dorsets were elated, and that Seymour might have complete authority in negotiating their daughter's marriage, Dorset sold him her wardship for two thousand pounds, of which Seymour gave him five hundred pounds on account immediately.

While these matters were transacting, it was understood that Seymour was in deep distress over his wife's death. One person, however, did not believe it. When Mrs. Ashley told the princess that she should write him a letter of condolence, Elizabeth refused the disagreeable suggestion. In her own words: "I said I would not do it for he needed it not." Meanwhile she was very anxious to come to London to see her brother, but a practical difficulty prevented her. Durham House, in London, had been left to her in her father's will, but Somerset had appropriated it and turned it into a mint. She was now without a town house, and as her household numbered one hundred and twenty persons, she could not remove without ample accommodation. Seymour heard of her lack, and meeting her treasurer Thomas Parry in London, he sent a message offering the princess the loan of Seymour Place with all its "household stuff" for as long as she cared to make use of it. Parry returned to the princess, who was at Hatfield, and here, on December 11, he had a long conversation with his young mistress. He saw that she was much pleased with the offer of Seymour Place, and he made a bold push. He asked her whether, if the council liked it, she would be willing to marry his lordship. The question was a most dangerous one, but it was perhaps not caution only that made Elizabeth reply: "When that time comes, I will do as God shall put in my mind." Parry went on to relate the searching examination Seymour had put him through, as to the details of Elizabeth's property, and the suggestion Seymour had made that the princess's lands should be exchanged for others which lay beside his own property in the west. The significance of this was clear, but all her life Elizabeth liked to hear of people who wanted to marry her, and now she insisted on the explanation from Parry's own lips. Parry said he could not tell what the lord admiral meant by the suggestion "unless he go about to have you also." Then he told her of Seymour's plan for getting the exchange accomplished; it was none other than that Elizabeth should make herself pleasant to the duchess of Somerset. An unscrupulous man of the world saw nothing wrong in the proposal; to a high-spirited child it was anathema. Not only had the duchess shown great insolence to the queen dowager; she had interfered when Kat Ashley allowed the princess to go to a party on the Thames at night. "Not fit to have the governance of a king's daughter," she had said. Make suit to *her* indeed! Elizabeth was first incredulous, then very angry. " 'Well!' quoth she, 'I will not do so, and so tell him!' " Then she showed how much superior her discretion was to that of her elders. She told Parry to let Mrs. Ashley know at once what the lord admiral had said to him, for, she said, "I will know nothing but she shall know it." Parry went to Mrs. Ashley, who assured him he could tell her nothing she did not know already, and declared: "I would wish her his wife before all men living," adding that "he could bring it to pass at the Council's hands well enough." Parry demurred, saying that the admiral had used his late wife badly. "Tush, tush," said Mrs. Ashley, "I know him better than you do. . . . I know he will make but too much of her and that she knows well enough." Then she told him, for the first time, the cause of their removal to Cheshunt. He exclaimed in amazement. She sighed and said, "I will tell you more another time."

More—the word covered an unknown quantity of very great importance, but it had not yet come to examination.

Meanwhile Seymour was rapidly spreading the web in which he meant to take all the royal children. He had gained Elizabeth's affections and had the charge of Jane Grey; now he concentrated on the young king. He saw that Somerset kept Edward far too short of money, and he sent him some privately. Edward was pleased with this, but when Seymour tried to tamper seriously with the protector's authority, in Edward's words, "I desired him to let me alone." The eleven-year-old king was obedient not from docility but from unchildlike common sense; he understood what his position required of him. Nevertheless when Seymour said, "Your uncle is not likely to live long," Edward answered: "It were better he should die." The abnormal coldness, like that of a fairy changeling, misled Seymour; he thought it meant hostility to the protector, and he made his plans to abduct Edward accordingly.

His possession of master keys seemed to put the royal children at his mercy; he had one that opened all the gates in the palace garden, and at dead of night on January 18 he came with some confederates to the antechamber of the king's bedroom. While he was groping at the bedroom door, the king's spaniel barked. Seymour killed the dog instantly but it was too late. An officer of the guard appeared, demanding angrily to know what he did there at that time of night. At daybreak he was arrested and taken to the Tower.

The news of the arrest spread quickly, and when one of Edward's guardians, Sir Anthony Denny, and his train appeared at the gates of Hatfield Palace, Parry needed no explanation of their arrival. He turned pale as death and said he wished he had never been born. Denny interviewed the princess and asked for the details of her intercourse with the lord admiral. She related some innocuous episodes. Denny did not press her: he went another way to work. He arrested Parry and Mrs. Ashley and was on the way to London with his prisoners before the princess knew what had happened to them. Of the two, Parry at least understood the acuteness of the peril. If the council could prove that the lord admiral had proposed marriage to Elizabeth, he was as good as dead already, since according to Henry's will the princesses could not marry without the council's consent. If they could prove that Elizabeth had accepted Seymour's proposal, then she herself was standing in the shadow of the scaffold. The council sent their commissioner Sir Robert Tyrwhit down to Hatfield to interrogate the princess and to extract the confession that might prove a death warrant.

When it was disclosed to her that her governess and the treasurer were in jail, she burst out crying and wept "for a long time." When she had recovered herself Tyrwhit held his first interrogation, which he began with the extremely ominous reminder that "she was but a subject." He tried to get her to dissociate herself from Mrs. Ashley, saying that if she would confess everything the council would exonerate her and lay the blame on her elders; but here he met with implacable resistance. "She will not," he wrote, "confess any practice by Mrs. Ashley or the cofferer . . . and yet I do see it in her face that she is guilty. . . . I do assure your Grace," he added, "she hath a very good wit and nothing is gotten of her but by great policy." Meanwhile he had been looking at Parry's accounts and was shocked to find that in addition to his other drawbacks the treasurer could not keep his books straight. "So indiscreetly made," they were, "it doth appear that he had little understanding to execute his office."

In the meantime Elizabeth was told of rumors that were spreading about her, that she was herself in the Tower, with child by the lord admiral. She wrote to Somerset, "My lord, these are shameful slanders, for which, besides the great desire I have to see the King's Majesty, I shall most heartily desire your Lordship, that I may come to the court . . . that I may show myself there as I am." Her words had the boldness of truth; she was not secretly betrothed to the lord admiral, she was not with child by him. But in the first week in February the council ordered the interrogation of the two prisoners in the Tower. In the garrulity of deathly fright they tumbled out the whole story of Seymour's behavior with Elizabeth from the time of his coming under her stepmother's roof.

The depositions were sent down to Tyrwhit, who laid them before her. She read them, aghast and half breathless, and studied the prisoners' signatures at the bottom of each page, although, said Tyrwhit, "she knew them with half a sight." Two days later he had her confession to send to the council, but he said regretfully that even so, "she will in no way confess that our mistress Ashley or Parry willed her to any practise with my Lord Admiral either by message or writing." The confession indeed added nothing to the depositions of the prisoners, and dreadful as it was to read Kat Ashley's revelations there was nothing in them that contradicted what Elizabeth had originally said. The disclosures were painful and damaging but they were not what the council were looking for. It could hardly be expected, however, that they would take no action. With a governess who lacked elementary discretion and a treasurer who could not balance his books, it was not surprising that the council should think the princess's household arrangements in need of some revision. They decided that a responsible lady must replace Mrs. Ashley and they fixed upon the unfortunate Lady Tyrwhit. The latter was most unwilling to undertake the task, and Elizabeth's reception of her justified her fears. The princess exclaimed that Mrs. Ashley was her mistress, and that she had not so demeaned herself that the council needed to appoint other mistresses to her.

After stormy interchange, Elizabeth cried all night, and "lowered" all the next day; but she collected herself to write to Somerset a letter which showed the unmistakable evidence of a master passion: the desire that the people should think well of her and take her part. The council had offered to punish anyone she could point out who had slandered her. She could name them, she said, but she feared she might seem glad to punish them and so get the ill will of the people, "which thing I would be loth to have." But she suggested that the council themselves should issue a proclamation forbidding the detraction of the king's sisters; so practical a suggestion could hardly be refused, and the proclamation was issued according to the princess's draft.

On March 4 a bill of attainder was passed condemning Seymour to death. The news was known at Hatfield within three days, for on the seventh Elizabeth wrote to Somerset again. A plea for Seymour would have been useless and worse, but there was someone for whom she must intercede at once, for Seymour's condemnation meant that the situation of his associates was now critical. Mrs. Ashley was enduring great hardship in a prison cell, lamenting "my great folly that would either talk or speak of marriage to such as her." Elizabeth implored the protector's mercy for Mrs. Ashley, because she had been with her so long and brought her up in learning and honesty; and then the ruling instinct showed itself: "And because it doth make men think I am not clear of the deed myself, but that it is pardoned to me because of my youth, because she I loved so well is in such a place."

The council released Mrs. Ashley but forbade her to return to the princess; and now Elizabeth had thirteen days to wait for the news of Seymour's death. When the word came, she made the comment which she had doubtless prepared: "This day died a man of much wit and very little judgment." No one who saw her doubted the intensity of her emotion; they merely admired the fortitude with which she restrained it. But she had now made the greatest effort of which she was capable. The results of nervous strain began to show themselves almost immediately in increasing weakness. For days at a time she could not leave her bed. By midsummer she was a helpless invalid.

Lady Tyrwhit had at first seemed odious because she was not Kat Ashley, but in her state of exhaustion, and receptive as she always was to kindness, Elizabeth now found that Lady Tyrwhit was not unacceptable. One memento of their present intercourse Elizabeth was to retain for the rest of her life. Lady Tyrwhit had a collection of mottoes and one took strong hold of Elizabeth's mind. *Be always one*, it said. Turned into Latin it became her own motto, identified with her like some favorite jewel. William Camden, the historian, says: "She took this device unto herself: SEMPER EADEM."

She was now looked on more favorably by the council; she had not been discovered in any intrigue against them, she had been the victim of a scoundrel, and her state of health was alarming. Somerset sent Dr. Bill to prescribe for her, and Elizabeth, in a grateful letter, said that she owed her recovery to him. He may have been responsible for the most effective prescription of allowing Mrs. Ashley to return to her. This had been brought about by August, for on August 2, 1549, Mrs. Ashley wrote a letter for the princess to which Elizabeth added one line of postscript. The letter was written to the protector's secretary, William Cecil, a lawyer, grave, quiet, immensely able and thirty years old. Mrs. Ashley said the princess had asked her to write to him "because she is so much assured of your willingness to set forth her causes to my Lord Protector's grace." This cause concerned the exchange of a poor man, the father of several children, who was lying a prisoner with the Scots, for a Scotsman imprisoned in Colchester. The postscript in Elizabeth's own hand is the earliest known of her writings to her future great minister: "I pray you, further this poor man's suit. Your friend Elizabeth."

In September Parry himself had been allowed to return to her. Elizabeth had both her friends again, but the recent commotion had taught her one thing among many. Her household account books for the years after 1549 show that she audited them herself, signing her name at the bottom of every page.

A principal step in her rehabilitation was the appointment of Ascham as her tutor. Grindal had died of the plague the previous year, and Ascham at last had his professional ambition realized. He had had experience of many learned young ladies, but the princess Elizabeth was unique; to teach her was the supreme experience of his career. His view of her is the first one gained at close quarters by a trained observer. Her mind, he said, seemed to be free from female weakness, and her power of application was like a man's. He had never seen a quicker apprehension or a more retentive memory. She had a grasp already of several languages, speaking French, Italian and Spanish as fluently as English, Latin easily and Greek moderately well; and under his guidance she quickly developed a critical appreciation of the use of words. They began the day by reading the New Testament in Greek, and then passages from Sophocles, which Ascham had chosen not only for their beauty but because they contained ideas which he thought would strengthen her mind against misfortune. She spent hours translating works from one foreign language into another and conversing with

Ascham on intellectual topics in all the languages in turn; her favorite study, however, was history. She liked to spend three hours a day reading it, and would study the same period in all the different books she could get hold of. Also, her handwriting was now of exquisite beauty. The sight of letters written in its prime gives a pang of esthetic pleasure. Besides the clerkly hand she had a rapid longhand for private use, whose curved and pointed shapes looked like the print of birds' feet.

Ascham's regime soothed Elizabeth's mind and was invaluable to her reputation, but it was not calculated to relieve a tendency to eyestrain and headaches. These were sometimes so severe that she could not write or even dictate anything, and she asked Edward to put down her neglect of letter writing "not to my slothful hand but to my aching head." But when a long spell of migraine attacks had abated, she wrote to him, in Latin, that he might be sure she never altered in her love and her respect, "I, who from your tender infancy have ever been your fondest sister."

Edward well remembered that she had, and his enforced separation from her did not mitigate his dislike of Somerset. The king was now thirteen; with admirable sense he made no attempt at an independent use of his power, but he coldly resented Somerset's domination. The latter was on treacherous ground and within sight of an evil end. He had discontented the council and Parliament by a combination of arrogance and failure, and in January 1550 he was deprived of his office, although readmitted to a place on the council in April. John Dudley, earl of Warwick, a worse man than himself but a capable soldier, succeeded Somerset as protector.

In August Dudley had himself created duke of Northumberland, and he took over his rival's secretary, Mr. Cecil. This was very convenient for the princess when she wanted to approach the new protector. She was ill again in September and wrote to Northumberland with a shaky hand to ask if she might come to court to see her brother.

The opportunity for coming to court presented itself a few months later. The king, with his precocity and intensity, his starry eyes and air of supernatural brightness, was not then diagnosed as a tuberculous subject, but some observers had gained the idea that his life might not be a long one. Northumberland's conduct showed that he himself recognized this possibility. If Edward died without children, his successor by Henry VIII's will would be Mary, and Mary, harassed but indomitable, had shown that she would be no pawn in the council's hands. Under her, the restoration of Catholicism was certain. They had not been able to coerce her while she was a subject; what could they hope to do if she were queen? Their fortunes, so far as these were bound up with the maintenance of Protestantism, would founder altogether. But the heir after Mary was Elizabeth, a Protestant by education and still very young, seventeen and a half this March. It would be useful to gain a closer view of her and estimate her qualities.

On March 17 the princess Elizabeth entered London and rode with a retinue of two hundred persons to St. James's Palace. The opportunity had come at last. The personal magnetism that Henry VIII had never lost, even when corpulent and old, was present in the pale, erect young woman, and it was emphasized by a plainness of dress that was dramatic in contrast to the rich and elaborate costumes of the court. Curling and double curling was the fashion, but the princess's red-blond hair was smooth. Aylmer, Lady Jane Grey's tutor, who saw Elizabeth with rapture, described her unadorned head and "her pure hands."

There were no mistakes now, no indiscretions. Edward was enthusiastic in his welcome; he called her "his dearest, sweetest sister," "his sweet sister Temperance." The events of eighteen months ago seemed to have vanished without a stain; yet there was one conversation that recalled the past. Between March and October, when Somerset was finally committed to the Tower, he spoke, if not privately to Elizabeth, at least in her presence, of Thomas Seymour. He said that had his brother been able to speak to him, he would have been spared. The council feared this and saw to it that the lord admiral was not allowed access to the protector, and that the latter had understood this only when it was too late. Such words could not be spoken or listened to without emotion, but their importance lay in the lesson they conveyed. Elizabeth did not forget it.

In October the Scottish queen mother, Mary of Guise, on her way back to Scotland from France, was entertained with her ladies at the English court. The French ladies, fresh from Paris, electrified the English ladies by their elegance and fashion, and the latter could think of nothing but new dresses and new methods of hairdressing—all of them except one. "The Princess Elizabeth," said Aylmer, "altered nothing but kept her old maiden shame-fastness." So lovely did she seem to him in manners and appearance, he was astonished that other women, with their frizzled hair and gaudy clothes, could not see how much they would be improved by following her example.

Quietness, simple clothes and the interest of a very clever mind in the theology of the Reformation were captivating to a scholar, but Northumberland was looking for something else. During the months of her stay at St. James's he decided that the younger princess, though a Protestant, carried about her something as dangerous to his plans as the militant Catholicism of the elder sister. She was sent back to the country before the end of the year, but she did not go empty-handed. Edward conveyed Hatfield Palace to her; it was a gracious as well as a valuable gift, for the late Gothic, red brick pile in the lovely fields and woods of Hertfordshire had been, after Greenwich, her earliest home, and in it she and her brother had spent some of their happiest times. It was an expression of his love, and the last.

Somerset was beheaded in January without Edward's lifting a finger to save him. His nephew recorded the execution in his journal: "The Duke of Somerset had his head cut off upon Tower Hill between eight and nine in the morning." Henry VIII had taken the death of those once intimately connected with him with a similar matter-of-factness.

Northumberland was now in complete control of the king, but the spring showed that his ascendancy might be short-lived. In April Edward fell ill with smallpox followed by an attack of measles. He made a surprising recovery and wrote to tell Elizabeth he was better; but toward Christmas he developed a cough, whose paroxysms were frightful. Elizabeth determined to see him; but Northumberland had no intention of allowing the brother and sister to meet. He had seen all too plainly how

Edward delighted in her society. Northumberland's animosity toward her was now well known, but not known, unhappily, to her brother. For the next six months, all that remained of Edward's life, Northumberland bent every effort to destroy Edward's affection and confidence in her.

Northumberland's only unmarried son was the nineteen-year-old Guildford Dudley, and he had arranged with Lord Henry Grey, who had now inherited the dukedom of Suffolk, that Jane Grey should be married to Guildford and should claim the Crown on Edward's death. When matters had been brought to this point, Jane Grey's unwillingness to be married to Guildford Dudley could not be allowed to interfere. Her mother assailed her with furious reproaches and her father with blows; between them she was reduced to acquiescence and the marriage was celebrated on Whitsunday of 1553.

Meanwhile Edward, shut off from all influence except Northumberland's, and in the throes of a galloping consumption whose effect upon his mind was to increase its fanaticism to a fearful pitch, had prepared what he called "My device for the Succession," in which he struck out the claims of his sisters and settled the crown upon Lady Jane and her male heirs. It was now absolutely essential to Northumberland's success to make certain that Elizabeth and her brother did not see each other, for Elizabeth would have answered Edward's purpose better than Jane Grey. He wished to protect the realm against a return to Catholicism, and Elizabeth was a Protestant. She was also, if Mary were excluded, the heir nominated by Henry VIII; all his life her brother had recognized her abilities and loved her dearly. Northumberland had done his work well, but he knew that at the eleventh hour Elizabeth might undo it at her brother's bedside. When she set out on a journey to London Northumberland had her stopped halfway and given a message, supposedly from the king, telling her she had better go home. On her return to Hatfield she wrote to Edward at once, of her fears for his health, her longing to see him. Nothing but a message from himself, she said, would have prevented her from finishing her journey. But not only had the king been deprived of her visit; her letter was not allowed to reach him either.

Edward was now very near death. On July 6 a fearful storm blew up and the summer afternoon was as black as night. Edward, lying in his bed, thought no one was within earshot and spoke aloud the prayer he had composed for himself: "Lord, thou knowest how happy I shall be may I live with thee for ever, yet would I might live and be well for thine elect's sake," and he implored God's protection for the realm and the Protestant religion. (Elizabeth afterward wore at her waist a gold replica of a book, two inches square, in which was transcribed this prayer.) Edward now opened his eyes and saw Dr. Owen sitting by him. "I had not thought you had been so near," he said. Three hours later, at six in the evening, he died.

Chapter 3

NORTHUMBERLAND KNEW that his success largely depended on his getting hold of both princesses and shutting them up while he proclaimed Jane Grey Queen. He sent messages to them in their brother's name calling them to London. Mary was warned in mid-journey and made off to Framlingham Castle, where she raised her standard and proclaimed her accession. Elizabeth too was prevented from running into the snare. Someone, deep in Northumberland's counsels, had a lively interest in her safety. It is assumed that the warning to stay where she was came from William Cecil.

Ten days were enough to rally public support to Mary, and Northumberland was brought back to the Tower in abject defeat. Jane Grey, who had been lodged in the White Tower to await her coronation, was now taken to the Yeoman Gaoler's House, a timbered dwelling-house fronting Tower Green. Beside it stood the stone-built Beauchamp Tower, and here her husband was shut up with his brothers John, Ambrose, Henry and Robert.

Elizabeth was told to meet Mary at Wanstead on July 30, that they might enter London together. She received the kindest welcome. Mary kissed her and held her by the hand as she spoke. At seven in the evening, they entered Aldgate riding side by side. Over the heads of the wildly shouting crowds, the church bells were ringing.

The first public appearance of Elizabeth in her sister's reign was watched by Simon Renard, ambassador from the queen's cousin, Emperor Charles V. His business was to secure the alliance with England for the emperor, by the marriage of Mary with his son Philip, the prince of Spain. From the first, Renard regarded Elizabeth as his master's enemy. Her heretical taint was of course obnoxious to him, but her chief and indelible offense was her extraordinary popularity with the people. This first sight of Elizabeth, riding through the streets on a summer evening, told Renard almost everything he needed to know about her. Happiness had given Mary an appearance almost of beauty, but it was the momentary transfiguration of a sickly woman of thirty-seven. Riding beside her, it was Elizabeth who drew the eye. An extremely good horsewoman, she was always seen to advantage on horseback, while the way she looked and bore herself, no less than her aquiline nose and the tint of her hair, were immediately recognized by anyone who had seen Henry VIII. It was said at once how much more like him the younger daughter was than the elder, and as she passed, white and smiling, the vital current of personal popularity magnetized the shouting crowds.

The procession made its way to the Tower, where the queen was greeted by a group of released prisoners on their knees. Among them were the marchioness of Exeter and her son Edward Courtenay, who had been imprisoned by Henry VIII because of the fatal nobility of his birth. His father had been the grandson of the princess Katherine Plantagenet, and Courtenay was therefore the great-grandson of Edward IV. The queen cordially welcomed him and his mother and withdrew with them into the White Tower.

In every direction except that of religious fanaticism, Mary was unusually merciful. To Renard's alarm she declared that Jane Grey, a girl of sixteen, was not to blame for the affairs of the past month, and though not formally pardoning her and Guildford Dudley, she allowed them to remain in easy conditions of imprisonment; Northumberland's execution even she could not avoid, though she would have spared him if she could. But the restoring of Catholicism as the national religion, and the reestablishing of papal authority—these ends were to be pushed on with eager and fierce determination.

In the first flush of happiness the queen looked at her sister with warmth and tolerance; provided her reconciliation to the Church could be brought about, Mary was ready, not entirely to trust her, but to treat her with sisterly kindness.

Renard strongly disapproved of this attitude; he pointed out that Elizabeth's almost magical popularity was a threat on account of French support. The emperor wanted the English resources to use in the Hapsburgs' struggle with France; Henry II wanted the same thing for France. The emperor meant to acquire the control of England through the marriage of Mary with his son; but Henry II had in his court, betrothed to the dauphin, the eleven-year-old Mary Stuart, Queen of Scotland, who, though omitted from the will of Henry VIII, was one of the lineal heiresses to the English crown, the granddaughter of Henry's sister Margaret. Through her, if Mary Tudor were disposed of, France might acquire a controlling interest in the combined realms of England and Scotland. What, in that case, was to happen to Elizabeth, the French king had not entirely made up his mind: a marriage, possibly, with some ally of France. Meanwhile, Elizabeth was to be encouraged as the readiest means of injuring Mary Tudor, and the French ambassador, Antoine de Noailles, relentlessly inquisitive but consummately agreeable and discreet, was soon on confidential terms with the princess.

Elizabeth declined to go to the requiem mass held for her brother, or to any mass whatsoever, and by the time the court removed to Whitehall, Mary refused to grant her an interview when she asked for one. At last an audience was granted her, in which Elizabeth wept and asked if it were her fault that she could not believe? Mary spoke kindly and told her that if she went to mass, belief would come. Elizabeth went to mass in the Chapel Royal, but on the way she complained of a bad pain and made one of the queen's ladies rub her stomach for her. It was thus seen by many that the princess had not gone to mass in any cheerful spirit. Mary, however, was pathetically pleased by her obedience, and gave her a diamond-and-ruby brooch and a rosary of white coral. On a second interview, when the queen had questioned her about her state of mind, Renard heard that she had trembled and looked pale, but he did not believe it. "*We* maintain that she appears quite composed and proud."

The first Parliament of the reign, in which Stephen Gardiner as lord chancellor was the leading spirit, revoked the divorce of Mary's parents, thereby stating Elizabeth to be illegitimate; but so far from diminishing her importance, the work of the session brought her into perilous prominence. Mary's announcement of her intended marriage to Philip of Spain was greeted with widespread, furious dismay. The reformers were alarmed at the idea of a powerful Catholic alliance, but also the nation as a whole was united in a thorough detestation of foreigners. The queen had rejected a suggestion that she herself should marry Courtenay, and now there was a clamorous demand that he should be married to Elizabeth. The direct Plantagenet descent of the one, the claim to the succession through Henry VIII's will of the other, made the suggestion a menacing one. There was no evidence of treason against Elizabeth, but Gardiner and Renard openly and shamelessly assured the queen that her sister would be better dead: both as a heretic whose accession would defeat the Catholic revival, and as an object of the people's love who might provoke a rebellion against the betrothed wife of the prince of Spain.

Courtenay himself was terrified at the prospect of marrying Elizabeth. If he were to marry, he besought the queen it might be "to some simple girl," not to Elizabeth, who was a heretic and "too proud." It was not surprising. In her early twenties Elizabeth showed something indescribably strange—a cold, eerie brightness. Though it faded from her face when other aspects developed, it looks out in the portrait of her in coronation robes at Warwick Castle, and a last gleam of it touches a miniature painted in 1572. Renard described it in a sentence of unusual felicity: "The Princess Elizabeth is greatly to be feared; she has a spirit full of incantation."

The kindness of the older sister to the younger, persevered in for so long a time, was disappearing before the evidence of Elizabeth's heretical taint and her popularity. The first, if incurable, would make the queen fear that her sister was not fit to live; the second showed a temper in the nation that wounded and angered her. She now admitted to Renard that she would do her best to prevent Elizabeth from ever succeeding her, even should she herself prove childless.

The act annulling Henry VIII's divorce had not injured Elizabeth's claim to the throne, which depended on Henry's Act of Succession, but it had drastically altered her social position. She was now required to give place to two of her cousins: one was the duchess of Suffolk, and this in spite of the fact that she was the mother of Lady Jane Grey, who was in the Tower on a charge of high treason in which she was at least as much implicated as her daughter. The other was the countess of Lennox, the daughter of Margaret Tudor, who had been Queen of Scotland by her second marriage. Elizabeth did not now find it amusing to walk out of rooms after these female relatives, one discredited, the other outlandish. At the beginning of December she asked permission to go down to her house at Ashridge. Renard thought it a good thing she should go—properly spied upon. Away from the court she might be tempted into some incriminating step and then . . . they would profit by their opportunity. But, he said, the queen must say good-by to her sister affectionately, so that she should suspect nothing. Mary acquiesced. Elizabeth begged her passionately that whatever she might hear about her, the queen would not condemn her without giving her a chance to speak for herself. This Mary promised. Perhaps some of the old kindness remained; at all events, the old custom was kept of giving her younger sister presents. She now gave Elizabeth some pearls and a beautiful sable hood, and the princess rode away into Hertfordshire.

She left behind her an air murmuring with conspiracy. De Noailles believed that if she and Courtenay were married and appeared in the southwest, they would provoke such a rising that the queen and the Spanish influence would be overthrown. He was all for the thing's being attempted, at whatever risk to the protagonists. He saw only one obstacle to the plan, and that was Courtenay's faintheartedness; that there might be objection on Elizabeth's side does not seem to have occurred to him. Elizabeth had in fact a powerful reason for refraining from any conspiracy: in the event of failure, it meant a charge of high treason. This implied almost certain death, but also a verdict of high treason was the only thing understood to cancel a claim to the succession. No one who knew Elizabeth could believe that she would take this enormous risk.

But to those who saw them only from a distance it seemed that the marriage of these fair young creatures of the blood royal would be a heaven-sent alternative to the queen, who persisted in her odious match. In the middle of January a rebellion burst out with alarming force. Its avowed object was to break off the Spanish match and put Elizabeth and Courtenay on the throne. The leader, Sir Thomas Wyatt, was to advance on London from Kent, Courtenay was expected to join a contingent from the west, and the duke of Suffolk to bring forces from the midlands. Courtenay lost heart and stayed at home, Suffolk was ignominiously rounded up, and Wyatt, after a series of mishaps, was cut off in the London streets and taken to the Tower. A rising that with a run of luck might have been very serious was quickly extinguished.

When the news of the rebellion reached her, the queen had written to Elizabeth to come to London at once; but Elizabeth could see that a rebellion which announced as its object the setting of herself and Courtenay on the throne was an excuse for putting her into prison that could scarcely be improved on. If she returned to London while Wyatt was advancing on it, she would go to the Tower and never leave it alive. She sent back the answer that she was too ill to travel and could not obey the queen's command.

Wyatt's confession at first implicated Elizabeth and Courtenay, and although he afterward withdrew it, Gardiner felt that Elizabeth might be beheaded out of hand. First, however, there was something else to do. The rebellion had made the execution of Lady Jane and her husband inevitable, and it was carried out on February 12, 1554. Guildford Dudley was beheaded outside the Tower, and his wife, who had refused a farewell interview with him lest it should uselessly agitate their minds, was standing at the window of the Yeoman Gaoler's House when the cart crossed the green beneath bearing the corpse to the chapel; she looked down into it and saw the head by itself and the body wrapped in a bloody sheet. Her supernatural tranquillity was unshaken, and though she had firmly resisted all the efforts of the abbot of Westminster to persuade her to renounce her faith, the old man's goodness, his intense compassion and concern had been gratefully felt. On the scaffold she turned to him and said with childlike simplicity, "Shall I say this psalm?" It was the Miserere. When she had repeated it she kissed him. Her head was cut off with one blow, and de Noailles heard that the torrent of blood was extraordinary.

Meanwhile the queen had turned her attention to her sister. If Elizabeth were indeed ill, Mary had no wish to act inhumanly. She sent a commission to Ashridge headed by Lord William Howard the lord admiral, who was Elizabeth's great-uncle. Two of the queen's physicians, Dr. Owen and Dr. Wendy, had been sent on before, taking with them the queen's own litter as the most comfortable means of transporting an invalid; but the commission had orders to bring the princess to London immediately if the doctors said she might be moved.

Both doctors found that the princess was undoubtedly ill: "replenished with watery humours," suffering from what is now supposed to have been nephritis; but they said she could make the journey. Elizabeth exclaimed that she was willing, she only feared her weakness was too great.

Throughout her life she had moments of collapse, in which some man took charge of her and told her what she must do. Lord William Howard did so now. He told her that since the doctors said she could travel she must come at once: to do anything else would be acutely dangerous. Preparations were made, therefore, and on February 12 the journey began that was to bring the princess to London.

Elizabeth was brought toward the litter in a half-fainting condition. The party had to travel slowly, and in five days' time they reached Highgate, where they halted. Below them London was lying, in whose streets the passersby were terrified and sickened by the sight of corpses hanging upon gibbets. The corpses had been men whose leader had told the King of France that he would put Elizabeth and Courtenay on the throne of England.

On February 23 the last stage of the journey was begun. The cortege descended from Highgate, and as it entered the London streets, Elizabeth's spirit rose to the occasion. She had the curtains of the litter pulled back that everyone in the streets might see her. She was taken to Whitehall, and her fears were confirmed when all but a handful of her servants were parted from her and she learned that the queen would not see her.

For three weeks Elizabeth remained under the same roof with her sister and barred from her presence. Her fate now hinged on whether it could be proved that she had known of Wyatt's plans.

Gardiner examined the princess and threatened her with the severest punishment if she did not throw herself on the queen's mercy. Elizabeth denied all communication with Wyatt and said that she could not ask mercy for a fault she had not committed. While matters remained at this impasse, the queen expected to leave London to hold a Parliament at Oxford. It was necessary that Elizabeth should be in absolute safekeeping during the absence of queen and council, and it was decided to put her into the Tower.

On March 18 the marquess of Winchester and the earl of Sussex, two of the queen's staunchest supporters, came to the princess and told her where she was to go. The news turned Elizabeth almost frantic. She exclaimed that the queen did not know what was being done—it was Gardiner's doing, and she implored to be allowed to write a letter to her sister.

Winchester replied harshly that she neither could nor ought to have permission, but Sussex paused; something in the look of the desperate young woman made a strange impression on him. He went down on his knee and declared that she should write her mind and he himself would deliver the letter.

Elizabeth there and then wrote in her exquisite hand a letter of passionate entreaty. She was panic-stricken that once inside the Tower she would perish for lack of the personal interview that would save her; but even in this extremity she showed her concern at what the people would think if they saw her put into "a place more wonted for a false traitor than a true subject, which, though I know I deserve it not, yet in face of all this realm appears that it is proved." She reminded her sister of her promise not to condemn her unheard, and she gave the terrible example that only desperation would have prompted: "In late days I heard my Lord of Somerset say that if his brother had been suffered to speak with him, he had never suffered." The use twice over of the latter word shows the mind too rapt to notice repetition, and the writing of this passage is larger and less even than the rest. The closing words are written with the greatest beauty. Indeed, it was an object to write them as slowly as possible, for all the time the tide was going down, and at low water, the river, racing through the piers, was not navigable under London Bridge. Sussex carried the letter to the queen but Mary angrily refused to read it and demanded to know why her orders had not been immediately carried out. She wished her father were alive again and among them but for a month! she said. This tide was lost and the one at midnight must go by, for the council were afraid that someone might attempt a rescue of the princess under darkness, while the fear of public indignation made it too risky to take her through the streets. It was decided that she should go by water at nine o'clock next morning, which was Palm Sunday; and at that hour Sussex and other members of the council led the princess from her apartments across the garden to the river stairs. It was raining.

In the covered cabin of the barge, Elizabeth sat with six ladies, a gentleman and a gentleman usher. When the barge stayed, she came out of the cabin and saw she had landed at the Traitor's Gate. The sight of the archway with its overhanging grating aroused her vehement indignation. She cried that such a gate was not fit for her to enter, that she would not use it. One of the nobles told her she could not choose. As it was still raining he offered her his cloak, but she dashed it impatiently aside. Stepping out over the shoes in water she exclaimed: "Here lands as true a subject as ever landed at these stairs. Before

A prisoner in the Tower of London at age 21, Elizabeth strolls in the garden with the jailer's son.

Thee, O God, do I speak it, having no other friend than Thee alone!" She mounted the stairs, and the arch yawned above her head. Like an animal that smells the blood of the slaughter-house, she made a last effort at resistance; she sat down on a damp stone and declared that she would go no farther.

Left to himself, the lieutenant of the Tower might have ordered the use of force, but in the presence of the earl of Sussex this straightforward method was not open to him; nor were the results certain even if he tried it: there was a posse of yeomen warders drawn up inside the gate and at the sight of the princess some of them had broken rank and knelt down, shouting: "God preserve your Grace!"

The lieutenant tried persuasion. "You had best come in, Madam," he said, "for here you sit unwholesomely." "Better sit here than in a worse place," she said; and the gentleman usher broke down and sobbed aloud.

The response was unfailing. Elizabeth stood up. She berated the man for giving way when he should be supporting her by his firmness. Her truth, she said, was such, she thanked God her friends had no cause to weep for her. She entered the gateway and was led to the left, where the Bell Tower rose on an angle of the curtain wall. On the first floor of the tower was a large, vaulted, stone-walled chamber with a great fireplace, opposite to which were three pointed windows with stone hoods and deep stone window seats. The rest of the floor consisted of a small passage and three latrines in tall and narrow niches. Into this chamber the princess and her ladies were shut and the door was bolted behind them. When she had disappeared from view, Sussex said uneasily to the rest: "Let us take heed, my Lords, that we go not beyond our commission, for she was our King's daughter."

Gardiner had achieved part of his aim in that the princess was now under lock and key; the next object was to extract a confession from her that she had been in Wyatt's confidence. He and nine lords of the council repaired to the Tower and conducted a vigorous examination of the prisoner. How, she was asked, did she explain the coincidence that Wyatt had written her a letter advising her to remove to Donnington Castle, and that she had actually made preparations to move there? In a moment of blinding panic, she made a futile pretense of knowing nothing even of the existence of Donnington, one of her own properties. The moment passed, and she recollected herself. She replied haughtily that she had received no letter from Wyatt, as the council knew, for they had intercepted it, and as to her meaning to go to Donnington, she said: "Might I not, my Lords, go to mine own houses at all times?"

And now occurred another strange capitulation. Henry Fitzalan, twelfth earl of Arundel, a Catholic of long descent, not only supported the queen but had been one of those who urged her to put Elizabeth to death; but the sight of the princess with her back to the wall affected him as it had affected Sussex. He went down on his knee and said: "Her Grace spoke the truth, and for his part he was sorry to see her troubled about such vain matters." Gardiner was obliged to end the interview without having achieved anything.

On April 11 Wyatt was executed; it was both claimed and denied that on the scaffold he had exonerated Courtenay and Elizabeth. If he had, his words carried no weight. Courtenay indeed was released and went abroad, but Elizabeth remained in the Bell Tower.

She grew so weak and exhausted from confinement that in the middle of April she was allowed to walk on the leads. This walk, about three feet wide, extends some seventy feet from a door in the Bell Tower to one in the Beauchamp Tower, and lies in a trough between the battlements on one hand and the gables of the King's House and the Yeoman Gaoler's House on the other. Even in this strait path she was not allowed to walk without two persons in front of her and two behind, but it at least had movement, light and air, and presently she was allowed to walk in the Tower garden. This liberty took off the worst edge of her imprisonment, for it brought her into touch again with some of the common people, a contact that renewed her. The son of one of the jailers, a child three years old, was attracted by the lady who walked in the garden. He used to watch for her coming and bring her little bunches of flowers. As soon as this was noticed it was suspected that the boy was being used to convey messages, and his father was sternly ordered to keep him away from the princess. The child came to the locked garden gate and called through it: "Mistress, I can bring you no more flowers now."

Gardiner had got his heresy bill through the Houses of Parliament. The church lands were to remain in the hands of their present owners, but the bishops were to have the power of examination of religious opinions and putting to death for heresy. Few people who heard the bill passed forsaw its dire consequences. Meanwhile, preparations were made for the prince of Spain's arrival and it was thought wise to convey Elizabeth out of the capital. It was decided that she should be removed as a prisoner to the palace of Woodstock in Oxfordshire, and Sir Henry Bedingfield was appointed as her jailer. On May 20 she was led out of the Tower and taken by water as far as Richmond.

Bedingfield had been given a charge extremely onerous to his conscientious mind. He was to keep the princess in strict custody and to manage her removal with as little stir as possible. The first was within his power; the second was like trying to catch and cover up the reflections of light. His difficulties began with the first moments of embarkation. Seeing the princess's barge on its way upstream, the gunners in the shoreside marketplace fired a thunderous salute, to the indignation of the queen, the chancellor and the Spanish ambassador when the matter was reported. The difficulty of transporting her secretly increased as they proceeded; by some means the identity of the closely guarded lady was known in the villages through which they passed, and as the retinue appeared, the church bells were set ringing. Bedingfield had the ringers put in the stocks.

Inside the domain of Woodstock Elizabeth's imprisonment began once more. The palace was solitary in its great park, and though the town was not far distant, bad weather made the roads impassable. She was not lodged in the royal apartments but in four rooms in the gatehouse.

Bedingfield was both admiring and apprehensive of his prisoner, of whom he spoke in his reports to the council as "that great Lady." She was perpetually demanding something, and he told them: "I am marvelously perplexed to grant her desire or to say her nay." He allowed the princess to walk in the upper and lower orchard, and though she complained to her gentlewomen that she had been promised she could walk in the park and this was not allowed, he was thankful to say she had not so far raised the matter with himself.

Elizabeth's mental disquiet grew as the summer came on; she feared that out of sight at Woodstock was out of mind, and that she might be left to languish there indefinitely. She demanded that Bedingfield should send a message from her to the council and was fretted beyond bearing when he replied merely: "I shall do for your Grace what I am able to do."

Elizabeth at last gained permission to write to the queen. She could not write without it, for Bedingfield doled out ink, pens, rough paper for a draft and smaller sheets of writing paper for a fair copy, and when the writing was finished, took away again the material that had not been used.

But the letter, protesting loyalty, had no effect. The queen replied to Bedingfield that the traitors would not have made Elizabeth the object of their conspiracy "unless they had more certain knowledge of her favour . . . than is yet confessed by her," and ended by saying she wanted no more such letters. Elizabeth was appalled; she begged him to let her send a reply to the council. This he refused to do. The next morning, the third of July, at ten o'clock, she called him up to her as she was walking in the little garden and told him that if he would not allow her to appeal to the council, she was worse off than the worst prisoners in Newgate, "for they are never gainsaid, in the time of their imprisonment, by one friend or another, to have their cause opened and sued for." The refusal meant that she "must continue this life without all worldly hope." She could only leave her cause to God, determining that whatever should happen to her, she would remain, as she had been all her life, the queen's true subject. As she spoke, the summer rain came on. " 'It waxes wet,' she said, 'and therefore I will depart to my lodging again.' And so she did."

On July 25, 1554, the marriage of Philip and Mary took place in Winchester Cathedral. This great event was celebrated with-

out any word to the queen's sister, who remained in imprisonment, wearing herself down by agitation and restless repining.
She wrote with a diamond on a windowpane:

> Much suspected by me,
> Nothing proved can be,
> Quoth Elizabeth, prisoner.

The long strain was telling on her nerves. One day in the
garden the sight of Bedingfield unlocking and locking six pairs
of gates after her was too much. She burst out into vehement
reproaches, calling him her jailer. Like Sussex and Arundel
before him, Bedingfield was deeply moved by her passion. He
knelt and begged her not to call him by that harsh name; he was
her officer, appointed to take care of her and protect her from
any injury.

In October the princess said that she wanted to be bled, and
the council were asked to send Dr. Owen, Dr. Wendy and
Dr. Huick to her. Dr. Owen and Dr. Wendy came, bringing
a surgeon to perform the bleeding, and Bedingfield was present
while they bled Elizabeth from the arm in the morning and
from the foot in the afternoon. "Since which time," he said,
"she does reasonably well."

A new danger now loomed, beyond the Spanish emperor's
desire to deport her and Gardiner's to cut off her head. The
queen's marriage and her supposed pregnancy had given her
confidence, and the extirpation of heresy by burning alive was
to be put in hand forthwith. The punishment of death by fire
had been used against heresy for centuries, and it was not the
burning itself but the choice and number of the victims that
made the persecution appear abominable to its own time. The
stubborn determination of the queen, so merciful in every other
matter, showed not only the strength of her feelings but the
outrage they had suffered in the treatment of her mother and
herself. The force of her nature had hitherto shown itself in
courage and patience; now it was seen in another aspect.

The burnings began in February 1555, but someone, it would
seem, had conveyed a warning to Elizabeth, for in the previous

September she took Communion according to the Roman Catholic rites. The capitulation was of extreme urgency, because, as the case of Cranmer was to show, once the queen's morbid ferocity was aroused, recantation did not mean a reprieve from the fire.

MARY, WHO HAD MISTAKEN the symptoms of ovarian dropsy for those of pregnancy, expected to be confined early in May. Parliament had refused Philip the Crown Matrimonial and had scouted Mary's attempt to put him into the succession. If the queen were now to die, his hold on the kingdom would depend on his either marrying Elizabeth or controlling her as his protégée. Renard had told him that he must on no account leave the country without seeing the princess and giving her a severe and threatening lecture.

Thus Elizabeth's release from Woodstock came about unexpectedly, and on April 30 she arrived at Hampton Court, still as a prisoner. She was not allowed to see the queen, but Mary sent a message to say the king would see her, adding the ingenuous command that Elizabeth was to put on her richest clothes for the occasion. A time was appointed and the two beings who for forty years were to represent the struggles of opposing worlds met face-to-face: one was a short, fair, phlegmatic man of twenty-eight, the other a pale young woman of twenty-two with a weird brightness like sea fire. Nothing transpired from their conversation, but it was said years afterward that Philip was heard to reproach himself because he had entertained a passion for his sister-in-law, while on her part, it amused Queen Elizabeth to say that her brother-in-law had been in love with her.

The imprisonment continued none the less; Gardiner and some of the lords of the council now came to examine her once more with a view to forcing a confession, and Elizabeth greeted them by saying, "My Lords, I am glad to see you, for methinks I have been kept a great while from you, desolately alone," but when Gardiner said that if she wanted her liberty she must confess her guilt and beg the queen's mercy, the words were scarcely out of his mouth before she exclaimed that rather than confess a fault she had not committed, she was prepared to stay in prison for the rest of her life. This outburst was reported to the queen, who sent word back again by Gardiner that she was astonished at such brazen defiance and that Elizabeth "must tell another tale ere she were set at liberty."

By the third week in May, there were still no signs that Mary's confinement was to take place; she feared that she had offended Heaven because she had not sufficiently persecuted the heretics, and issued a circular to the bishops, commanding them to increase their efforts to detect and punish the offenders, but the disappointment inspired Philip to more practical measures. If the queen died without a child, he himself might not only lose control of the country, he might lose it to the King of France; for many people believed that succession could not be settled by will, even the will of Henry VIII, but only by descent, and since all Catholics believed Elizabeth to be illegitimate, on the death of Henry's daughter Mary the legitimate heir was the descendant of his elder sister Margaret—and this heir was none other than the future Queen of France. To a Spaniard such a prospect was intolerable; therefore Philip was determined to support Elizabeth's claims against those of Mary Stuart.

At the end of May, at ten o'clock at night, Elizabeth was sent for by the queen. She was led across the garden and brought up the privy stair to the queen's bedroom. She had not seen Mary for over a year. She knelt, and in a burst of tears declared that she was and always had been her sister's loyal subject. Mary turned away and said aloud, in Spanish, "God knoweth." She did not speak to empty air. Behind some hangings, with his eye to a hole, Philip had watched the scene.

When even the queen was convinced that she was not carrying a child, Philip's impatience could no longer be restrained. In August he left his wretched, despairing wife, impressing on her that her policy toward Elizabeth must be one of conciliation. Mary did not find the command wholly uncongenial, and now she was kind to Elizabeth. Bedingfield had been discharged and the queen then appointed Sir Thomas Pope, a rich and amiable gentleman, to be the princess's governor.

Elizabeth withdrew to Hatfield in October. The route out of London from Fleet Street to the north led through the parish of Shoreditch, and the parishioners were among those who had the habit of welcoming the princess's approach with a peal of bells. She loved to hear the loud, sweet ringing that spoke affection for her, and as she came and went on the Hatfield road, "she would pause and listen attentively and commend the bells."

At Hatfield, old friends were gathered: Kat Ashley and Parry were in residence, and Ascham, now Latin reader to the queen, had permission to visit Hatfield and resume his reading with the princess.

The unhappy queen, deprived both of her husband and of her subjects' love, now received a fresh proof of her unpopularity. Sir Henry Dudley, with a band of refugees, malcontents and pirates, was in France, planning, with the unconcealed help of the French government, an invasion once again to set Elizabeth and Courtenay on the throne. The queen sent a message assuring Elizabeth that no suspicion attached to her, and when a young man who bore a remarkable likeness to the Plantagenet family appeared in Essex and announced that he was Courtenay, and his followers proclaimed, "The Lady Elizabeth Queen and her beloved bed-fellow Lord Courtenay, King," this also the queen accepted as having nothing to do with her sister. The strain of endurance had gone on for a very long time, and Elizabeth was in weak health again; she had an attack of jaundice, and spasms of breathlessness. Some point of exhaustion had been reached at which she was prepared to give up the struggle. De Noailles had never ceased assuring her that if she would confide herself to the King of France she would find eager and chivalrous support; she now prepared to avail herself of the promise. She sent Lady Sussex, incognito, to the French ambassador.

Another occasion now arose on which, in a state of collapse, she was saved by the decision and guidance of a man. Had the ambassador been de Noailles himself, there would have been but one outcome of Lady Sussex's mission—before Elizabeth had come to herself she would have been halfway across the Channel; but by inestimable good fortune de Noailles had been recalled and his place taken by his brother, the bishop of Acqs. The bishop stood her friend in the most unexpected manner. He told Lady Sussex that such a flight would be disastrous, and that if Elizabeth meant to be queen she must in no circumstances leave the country; if she did, she would never come back.

Mary's wretchedness was temporarily relieved by the return of Philip in March 1557. His objects were two: to bring about the marriage of Elizabeth to his cousin Emmanuel Philibert of Savoy, and to bring the English into his war against the French. Elizabeth was summoned to court to meet Philip but she refused the proposed marriage with calm resolution. Philip blamed Mary for her sister's intransigence; in vain the unfortunate queen assured him that anything she could do for him should be done, but it was not in her power to force her sister into a marriage against Elizabeth's own wishes and those of the realm.

In his second object, Philip was unhappily successful. An attempt at invasion by Sir Thomas Stafford, sponsored by the French, irritated the government into promising aid to the Spanish forces. Having gained this end, Philip left the country. The misery of his wife at his departure was extreme, but the summer months were marked by an intercourse of the sisters that appeared to have almost the cordiality of earlier times. At midsummer Elizabeth was invited to Richmond, and a barge was sent to convey her and her ladies which had an awning of green silk embroidered with gold, and was garlanded with fresh flowers. The queen returned the visit at Hatfield.

A relic of the sisters' sympathy remains, of peculiar interest. Mary again imagined herself pregnant, and Elizabeth made baby linen for her. Needlework is favorable to reflection, and the head bent over these exquisite pieces can seldom have known more disturbing and complicated thoughts.

For herself, Elizabeth it seemed had already determined that no such preparations were ever to be needed. Gustavus of Sweden sent a letter to her, asking if she would consider a proposal from his son, Prince Eric. Elizabeth replied, much to the satisfaction of the queen, that she could consider no proposal that did not come to her through her sister. She stated, further, that she had always wished to live unmarried. Sir Thomas Pope, incredulous and gallant, suggested that she would scarcely persevere in this attitude if some suitable wooer approached her with the queen's consent.

Elizabeth's reply was impressive: "What I shall do hereafter I know not, but I assure you . . . I am not at this time otherwise minded than I have declared unto you." Words could scarcely speak plainer, but however plainly and however often she was to make this declaration, she could not get men to believe it.

It was clear now that Mary had once again been disappointed and that she was very ill. The miseries of the last months of her life were of a concentrated bitterness. The English intervention in France had drawn the French attack on the crumbling stronghold of Calais. Though the English had never had a shadow of right to it in the first place, the loss of the last remains of the conquests of Edward III and Henry V was bitterly resented by the nation, whose anger redounded on the queen. The desertion by her husband and the loss of her hope of a child had produced a keenness of suffering that had driven her almost beside herself.

At Hatfield, Elizabeth had not let go of caution. She had told Sir Nicholas Throckmorton that he was to bring her the black-and-gold betrothal ring that would never leave Mary's hand till she was dead. Meanwhile Cecil came and went, with drafted plans to take over the government in the new queen's name. While Elizabeth waited, one thing forced itself on her attention that she was never to forget: it was the sight of the road from London, thronged with horses and their riders, all streaming away from the capital of the dying queen, agog to establish themselves with her successor. The grim moral it conveyed remained with her for the rest of her life.

At daybreak on November 17, 1558, Mary died and Throckmorton set out for Hatfield with the ring, but he was outdistanced on the road by the lords of the council. When they arrived, Elizabeth was walking in the park and they came up with her as she stood beneath a leafless oak. At their words she knelt on the grass and exclaimed: *"A domino factum est . . . mirabile in oculis nostris!"* ("This is the Lord's doing; it is marvelous in our eyes.")

The passion of joy for the new reign, and of love for the young queen who had captured the imagination before she had been seen, echoes still in nameless popular verse:

> *Then God sent us your noble Grace*
> *As indeed it was high time . . .*
> *For whom we are all bound to pray, Lady, Lady,*
> *Long life to reign! Both night and day, most dear Lady!*

Chapter 4

THE NEW QUEEN was just twenty-five, "indifferent tall, slender and straight." On public occasions her slow, stately movement was much admired, but it was noticed that "she walked apace for her pleasure, or to catch her a heat in the cold mornings." She loved to ride fast, to dance, and to watch other people dancing.

Her appearance was still very young and fragile, with an unselfconscious intensity. Her skin, more than white, was "candidus," of a glowing paleness; her hair was variously described as "redder than yellow" and "tawny inclining to gold." Her eyes, golden and large-pupiled from short sight, had eyebrows arched but faint. Her face was a long oval like her mother's, but her coloring was her father's and her likeness to him in the aquiline nose and the shape of the brow is shown in the miniatures of the young king. Her father's ability and his physical magnetism, infused with something of her mother's fascination, had distilled themselves into a personal magic that was admitted even by those who distrusted and disliked her. She had also inherited from her mother a strain of hysteria, and while her mental power and nervous energy were equal to excessive demands, brainstorms and fainting fits were sure signs of a nervous system that was overstrung.

The immediate impression she made was one of remarkable intelligence. Elizabeth's claim to wisdom was formally made three days after her accession; at her first council meeting, held in the great hall of Hatfield Palace, she announced the appointment of William Cecil as her chief secretary of state, "to take pains" for her and her realm. She told him that she knew him to be faithful and incorruptible, and that he would advise her, regardless of her private wishes, and she herself made a promise: "If you shall know anything necessary to be declared to me of secrecy, you shall show it to myself only, and assure yourself I will not fail to keep taciturnity therein." Her words were the seal on a bond of lifelong partnership.

Cecil was now thirty-eight, quiet, formidable, with a spare frame and clear, pale eyes in a forehead oppressed by care. His talents were extraordinary not so much in kind as in degree; he had the abilities of the professional man, raised to a pitch far beyond mere ability. Camden said: "Of all men of genius he was the most a drudge; of all men of business, the most a genius." Though he had conformed under Mary, he had a personal devotion to the Protestant creed, and in his private life he much resembled the present-day Quakers.

In many ways Elizabeth was his opposite. Though formidable, she was not quiet; she had a keen instinct for the dramatic. A natural elegance of mind led her to prefer the ritual of the Catholic Church, and she would have found no difficulty in adopting its tenets if every consideration connected with the great end of her existence had not pointed in the contrary direction. But she and her secretary had an absolute community of aim. They wanted, beyond anything, to make a success of governing the country, and on three major points they were agreed as to how this was to be done. They saw the nation's future as bound up with the Reformation, and they abhorred the ruinous waste of war. Cecil's maxim was: "A realm gains more in one year's peace than by ten years of war," and "No war, my lords!" in the queen's vehement and ringing tones was to cut across many an argument at the council table. Thirdly, they agreed that a reestablishment of the national credit was a step without which nothing else could be done, and that this itself could not be achieved without vigilant economy. There was a further point of similarity between them: in their life's business, the art of government, they recognized no distinction between work and pleasure.

Of the appointments announced at Hatfield, Cecil's was the one of supreme importance, but others were interesting. Kat Ashley was made first lady of the bedchamber, and her husband, keeper of the queen's jewels. Parry was knighted and made treasurer of the household, an office in which the arithmetical drudgery could be performed by clerks, and Blanche Parry, elderly, learned and wise, was made keeper of the royal books in the library of Windsor Castle. The earl of Arundel and Lord William Howard were created privy councillors.

Before the council meeting on November 20, Lord Robert Dudley had arrived posthaste from London to tender his allegiance. Dudley's emergence in the new reign was altogether in character: a splendid appearance and a promptness and energy of devotion. He had known Elizabeth since they were both eight years old, at a time when his father Northumberland was master of the horse to Anne of Cleves. In 1550, when he and Elizabeth were seventeen, he had married an heiress, Amy Robsart. However long his passion for his wife lasted, it did not prevent Dudley from showing considerable friendship for Elizabeth during her sister's reign. The Venetian ambassador had noted that in spite of her talent for economy the princess was in debt, and according to Elizabeth herself, Dudley at some time between 1553 and 1558 sold part of his property and gave her the proceeds. The transaction was a secret one at the time, and Elizabeth, who was much moved by personal kindness to herself, spoke of it afterward when saying that Dudley had a claim on her affections.

When she was allowed, during her imprisonment in the Tower, to walk on the leads, her promenade behind the battlements had led directly toward the narrow door of the Beauchamp Tower, behind which was the great stone-walled chamber in which Robert Dudley was shut up with his surviving brothers. Guarded as she had been, the nearness of the door had availed nothing; but the situation, romantic and desperate, was of a kind to make the two prisoners even more interesting to each other. Dudley, like all Northumberland's sons, was tall; his portrait at full length shows the striking elegance of his legs. "Of a tall personage and manly countenance," said the Venetian ambassador, adding that he was "somewhat brown of visage," and Sussex, who hated and distrusted him, called him "the gipsy." His face, with its round, hard eyes and short, beaklike nose, was that of a handsome and not unamiable bird of prey. His strong qualities were physical: he rode, jousted and danced with perfection, and he had an inborn knack of managing horses. Made master of the horse by Elizabeth, he was responsible not only for the queen's riding horses and hunters, but for all the horses used in the royal transport for riders, coaches and baggage wagons, for buying them, maintaining them and making them available. He could do the practical work of the office efficiently, and he was eminently suited to its decorative function, which required him to make a splendid public appearance in close attendance on the queen.

As Elizabeth's fondness for him was the source of wealth and influence which he could never have gained without it, any just assessment of him by his peers was next to impossible. The charge brought against him was, and has always been, that his show of devotion to her was an odious sham. No doubt he would have betrayed her had it ever been to his interest to do so, but his interest was served by attaching himself as closely to her as possible; the advantages his attachment brought him were so great that he could not escape the accusation of self-interest and hypocrisy. But his devotion was unequivocal. In the dawn of the reign he was at the queen's feet. Everyone knew he was a married man, but his wife, at whose wedding Elizabeth had stood by as an onlooker, remained in the country.

Six days after her accession, the queen and her retinue, followed by a great crowd of ladies and gentlemen on horseback, took the road from Hatfield to London. Her destination was Lord North's town house at the end of the Barbican. Here she stayed a fortnight and here, at a large assembly, the Spanish ambassador, de Feria, had his first sight of her as queen.

He had sent the queen, in Philip's name, two precious rings that Philip had originally given to her sister, and had taken it on himself to tell her that the king would be glad for her to take a box of Spanish jewels left in Whitehall, and anything else of his she fancied, "as a good brother should." This was a successful move, he reported, for "she is very fond of having things given to her." At the party the queen treated him most graciously; as soon as she saw him making his way toward her, she began taking off her glove that he might kiss her hand. Amidst expressions of friendship and encouragement, Feria said his master hoped that she would be extremely careful in her handling of religious matters. The queen answered that it would be very bad of her to forget God, who had been so good to her: "Which," said Feria, "seemed to me rather an equivocal reply."

She presented to the Spaniard's penetrating eye an appearance that was far from reassuring, but to the English themselves she had already shown an earnestness of singular force. The daily council meetings were continued at Lord North's house, and at one of these she spoke to a deputation of judges. Cecil was a lawyer: he cared deeply for the efficiency and good name of the legal profession, and he got the queen to raise the salaries of the Queen's Bench judges. It was clear that he had told her his view of the state to which the administration of the courts had fallen. Bishop Jewel heard the queen say to the judges, with the repetition that marked her speech when she was deeply moved: "Have a care over my people . . . they are *my* people. Every man oppresseth them and spoileth them without mercy. They cannot revenge their quarrel nor help themselves. See unto them, see unto them, for they are my charge."

On Monday, November 28, the queen took possession of the Tower. She went in a chariot to Cripplegate, but there she mounted, and began the first of her great processions. First rode the lord mayor carrying her scepter, with garter king-of-arms beside him; next came Lord Pembroke, bearing the sword of state in a gold scabbard loaded with pearls. Then came the sergeants-at-arms, surrounding the queen. Behind her, on a black horse, came Lord Robert Dudley.

At fixed stages along the route, bursts of music greeted her; choirs of children poured their sweet, shrill notes, schoolboys stood forward to make orations. As the procession reached Mark Lane, the Tower guns began to sound. The roar of cannon filled the narrow streets. It ceased as the queen drew rein on Tower Hill.

Below them, girdled by its curtain wall, the great fortress lay on the river strand, the pinnacles of the White Tower rising into the wintry air. Those in earshot around her heard her say that some had fallen from being princes of the land to being prisoners in that place. The ghosts of the Plantagenets rose thronging at her words. She herself, she said, had risen from being a prisoner there to be a prince of the land. She ended: "Let me show myself to God thankful and to men merciful."

She remained a week in the state apartments of the White Tower, holding councils daily. Before the court left Hatfield, the pressing problems confronting the government had been analyzed and the work of resolving them had begun. A peace treaty between France and Spain with her English ally was being discussed at Le Cateau-Cambrésis; a religious settlement had to be devised which would satisfy the Protestants without being more offensive to the Catholics than could be helped; three bad harvests had spread poverty and labor unrest; the coinage, which had been debased by Henry VIII, Edward VI and Mary, was now so worthless that trade was very seriously affected; above all there was a threat more ominous than all the other troubles put together: on the death of Mary Tudor, Henry II of France had added the arms of England to the coat of arms of his son and his daughter-in-law, Mary Queen of Scots.

These matters of extreme weight and urgency meant that the Privy Council were sitting day in, day out, and the queen with them. From the first hours of the reign, and to Cecil's private knowledge long before, she had shown herself to have the memory and penetration that goes with a mind of uncommon ability, and an inexhaustible interest in the theory and practice of government. The element she lacked was experience. Cecil had had practical experience in three reigns. Like a man riding some high-spirited horse whom he guides but without whom he cannot cover the ground, he was now advising and instructing the remarkable being without whose signature he and his colleagues could, in the last resort, do nothing. The collaboration was the closest sort of professional relationship; but there was about to be revealed one serious discrepancy in which the personal factors were brought into spectacular prominence. Everyone assumed that the queen's coronation would be

Sir William Cecil. Elizabeth's chief secretary of state.

followed speedily by the announcement of her marriage; and everyone regarded the potential alliance as of the greatest importance in the European balance of power. To Cecil, the marriage and the children of it were more than a matter of European importance; they were a guarantee of personal safety. If this frail-looking young woman were to die without a child, a Catholic revival under Mary Stuart would mean not only his political eclipse but his execution.

It was taken for granted that this urgency felt by the government was felt no less acutely by the queen. If the threat represented by Mary Stuart became a fact, the first victim would be Elizabeth herself. Her strongest defenses would be a powerful husband and a male infant. It was fully believed that she would take steps to gain them as soon as possible. Nor was it unreasonable for Philip to assume that Elizabeth would eagerly accept his hand and his great alliance if he offered it. He was not personally averse to the match, but it was necessary to approach the matter with extreme circumspection. He told Feria to make it clear among other stipulations that if the marriage took place Elizabeth must become a Catholic, so that it would be seen that he was sacrificing himself for the sake of religion; and that it must be understood that he could spend very little time with her "whether he left her pregnant or not."

Elizabeth received the Spanish approaches in a manner both sharp-tongued and evasive. She said she had been told that the king would marry her and go off to Spain immediately. Then she gave a peal of laughter. Feria's memorandum of the interview says: "It looks as if she had seen His Majesty's letter. This should be taken good note of." The suspicion was disconcerting; and her conduct in concealing her intentions in sparkling ambiguities, instead of snatching at the proposal, seemed to the ambassador reckless, improper and extraordinary.

There was, in fact, something mysterious about her altogether. A belief in astrology and clairvoyance, though widely held at the time, was an unexpected trait in her clear and practical intelligence. Blanche Parry had a cousin, Dr. John Dee, of great cultivation. He had been a university lecturer in mathematics, he was a geographer, an astronomer and the promoter of an early system of shorthand. Dee was also an astrologer. He had drawn Elizabeth's horoscope during her sister's reign, and the result was, not surprisingly, a sentence of imprisonment from the Court of Star Chamber.

Elizabeth sent Lord Robert Dudley to Dee privately, to ask him to cast a date that would be fortunate for her coronation. Dee chose Sunday, January 15, 1559, and the achievements of the reign appeared to justify the doctor's advice.

Chapter 5

THE SATURDAY before the coronation was the day of the recognition procession through London, of very great importance when those who did not see the queen with their own eyes could gain no idea of what she looked like. She had returned to the Tower the previous Thursday, and at two in the afternoon she set out from Tower Hill to make the journey through the streets to Westminster. Her retinue went before and behind her, and she herself was seated in a chariot draped with crimson velvet, over which four knights, walking beside it, held a canopy.

The English are fond of their sovereign and fond of a spectacle, and the miseries of the immediate past and the present hopes would have ensured considerable success for the occasion; to this was added the magical quality of the central figure. The crowds lining the streets broke into exclamations at the sight of her. What they saw when they pressed up to the chariot was a straight and narrow figure in a cloth-of-gold dress under a cloth-of-gold mantle with an ermine cape. From a gold circlet, limp strands of red-gold hair fell down, framing the delicacy and strangeness of an oval, pale face, a face with faint brows spanned like Norman arches, and heavy-lidded golden eyes, smiling at them.

The route was studded with pageants and demonstrations, of which children recited the meaning in verse. In Gracechurch Street the cheers of the crowd drowned a child's voice: the queen, halting her chariot, begged for silence and then sat listening attentively. In Cheapside her brilliant smile was re-marked when a voice shouted: "Remember old King Harry the Eighth!" At the Little Conduit there were the statues of an old man and a girl. The queen asked who these were, and was told that they were Time and his daughter Truth. "Time!" she exclaimed, looking around on the sea of faces. "And Time hath brought me here!"

In the early dusk she arrived at Whitehall and was at last shut up from sight. The achievement of sustained responsiveness was over, going at a footpace along three crowded, tumultuous miles. The people had been prepared to welcome her: now they were wild about her. In all the excitement of the spectacle, two details had particularly struck the public imagination: the queen's smile at her father's name; and the fact that a branch of rosemary a poor woman had put into her hand was still in her chariot when she came to Westminster Bridge.

A long carpet of purple cloth had been spread for the queen to walk on into the abbey. She came wearing a crimson velvet robe high to the throat with a small ermine cape and a crimson velvet cap on her head. The earls of Shrewsbury and Pembroke walked each side of her, supporting her arms, and the duchess of Norfolk carried the long train of her crimson mantle.

When she had been anointed, the queen withdrew to a side chapel and changed her crimson robes for the gold ones she had worn the day before. Her nose was always sensitive and she complained to the ladies who were rerobing her that "the oil was grease and smelt ill."

In her gold robes the queen was crowned with St. Edward's crown, the state crown, and lastly with the beautiful little crown that had been made for her brother at nine years old: a wreath of pearls and diamonds with a large sapphire in front, and pearl hoops at whose intersection was mounted the great crimson gem, the Black Prince's ruby. She was then presented to the people, with trumpets sounding, pipes and drums playing, the organ pealing, and in the towers above, bells ringing, "as if," said the Venetian ambassador, "the world were coming to an end." When she had been dressed in a robe of purple velvet, she was led to the state banquet in Westminster Hall, and by three o'clock she had washed her hands and was sitting at table on the dais under the vast window. Below her, four tables seated two hundred persons each and a crowd of servitors attended, all dressed in red. The earl of Arundel and the duke of Norfolk were in charge of the banquet and they rode about the hall on horseback. Lord William Howard and the earl of Sussex stood one each side of the queen and served her with everything she ate and drank.

The banquet was not over till after one in the morning. A joust had been arranged for the coming day but this was put off, for the queen was exhausted. The fatigues of the Saturday and Sunday ended in a bad cold, and the opening of Parliament was postponed from January 23rd to the 25th.

The queen came to the opening soon after ten o'clock, "a most marvelous pendant" around her neck and a small cap of gold and pearls on her head. As she had been crowned according to Catholic rites, the government's policy was still in doubt, but one of the queen's unrehearsed symbolic gestures gave a strong indication. The abbot of Westminster met her with his monks holding lighted torches, and she exclaimed in carrying tones: "Away with those torches! We see very well."

Cecil's brother-in-law, Sir Nicholas Bacon, had been appointed lord keeper of the great seal. In his opening speech he said how fortunate they were in "a princess to whom nothing—what, nothing? no, no worldly thing—was so dear as the hearty love and goodwill of her subjects." The words were no oratorical flourish: they were literally true, and uttered as they were in the first Parliament, they expressed the one fact about a complex, paradoxical and mysterious character which, throughout a long reign, was never once in doubt.

The session's outstanding work, the evolving of the religious settlement in the acts of Supremacy and Uniformity, was a feat of distinguished statecraft, the work of the Privy Council and both Houses of Parliament, but not only was its spirit of tolerance and moderation in key with the queen's own attitude (she said she wished to open no window into men's consciences), but the Act of Uniformity contained a sign of her own handiwork. This act restored the first Prayer Book of Edward VI, but with two alterations meant to conciliate the Catholics: one was the putting together of two lines from the first and second of Edward VI's prayer books, so that the Communion service could be used both by those who believed in the Real Presence and those who regarded the rite as a commemoration; the other was a deletion made by the queen herself. The Litany of the first Prayer Book had prayed: "From the Bishop of Rome and his detestable enormities, Good Lord, deliver us." The queen removed this aspiration. She also crossed out "Roman Catholics" from the clause praying for the conversion of Jews and infidels.

The question next in importance with which the session dealt was the queen's marriage and childbearing. The urgency of this was underlined by a note in Cecil's diary: "On January 16, 1559, the Dauphin of France and the Queen of Scots his wife did, by the style and title of King & Queen of England and Ireland, grant to Lord Fleming certain things."

From the hour of Mary Tudor's death, Mary Stuart and her supporters considered that she was Queen of England. The English Catholics who could not admit that Elizabeth's birth was legitimate or that succession could be settled by law must always think that Mary Stuart's claim was superior to Elizabeth's; but large numbers of them were willing to be loyal to Elizabeth, provided that some concessions were made to them and, above all, provided that her government was a success.

The queen wanted toleration used: "Let it not be said that *our* reformation tendeth to cruelty," she said, and of the large proportion of the nation who were Catholics (estimated at something near half), the majority were prepared to be loyal, but she and they were the victims of an enormous European combination which was waiting to overpower England as a bastion of the Reformation. In the struggle the political and economic factors were to prove inseparable from the religious. Philip was determined to reduce the wealthy Netherlands, in the name of Catholicism. France was determined to gain control first of Scotland, then of England, in the name of Catholicism. In Mary Stuart's cause, the French might pour into Scotland and thence over the border, where in the northern shires the great Catholic families had still their almost feudal powers; they might gain control of half England in a week—and then Spain would rouse. Scotland and England in French hands would be intolerable to the Hapsburgs. Spanish forces from the Netherlands would land on the south coast, and the miseries which the English had endured in the Wars of the Roses would be as nothing to their fate while French and Spanish soldiers fought a savage war for the possession of English soil.

The sum of these possibilities was that the queen and her government had no margin for error. They must start to consolidate their position immediately, and the queen's marriage, as a means of defensive alliance and the establishment of the succession, was in everybody's mouth.

As a princess, Elizabeth had shown invariable resistance to the idea of marriage, and she maintained the attitude now. To a parliamentary deputation who waited on her in the Great Gallery at Whitehall on February 6, and begged her to set about marrying, she replied that she would act as God directed her. If God directed her not to marry, no doubt He would provide for the succession in other ways. From a long, delicate finger, she withdrew the coronation ring, and holding it up to them, she said: "I am already bound unto a husband, which is the Kingdom of England."

Her objections to marriage were varied and enclosed one within another like a Chinese puzzle, but the outer circles were legible enough. To marry and establish the succession would take away at once her immense importance as a matrimonial catch, and though a strong alliance would bring great advantages it would deprive her of an invaluable diplomatic weapon. It would also alter the character of that intense loyalty and solicitude that was centered upon her by men who knew that her single life stood between them and disaster.

Then, too, in the first delicious exhilaration of freedom and power, many could see that she repudiated the idea of a yoke. Marriage up till now had always been spoken of as a means of curtailing her. Sir James Melville, formerly a page to Mary Queen of Scots, put the impression in a nutshell. The queen had been telling him that she did not intend to marry unless she were driven to it—"I know the truth of that, Madam," exclaimed the Scotsman, "you need not tell me. Your Majesty thinks that if you were married you would be but Queen of England, and now you are both King and Queen. I know your spirit cannot endure a commander."

Melville thought that he knew something else. He had been asked to deliver a proposal to the Queen of England from the duke Casimir, the son of the elector palatine, but he had declined the commission. "I had ground to conjecture that she would never marry," he said, "because of that story one of the gentlemen of her chamber told me." Melville supposed that, "knowing herself incapable of children, she would never render herself subject to any man." Cecil, despite his ceaseless anxiety and care, always took the view that Elizabeth could and should bear a child. In drawing up a memorandum of arguments for and against a marriage, against the peril of childbirth he wrote merely: "In God's hands."

In the personal sphere Cecil and his colleagues had another anxiety. In March the King of Spain's proposals were transferred to Catherine de Médicis's beautiful daughter Elizabeth of Valois, and Philip's nephew the archduke Charles was put forward as a match for the queen, but by April it was a matter of public comment that she and Lord Robert Dudley were inseparable. Feria wrote on April 18: "During the last few days Lord Robert has come so much into favour that he does whatever he likes with affairs and it is even said that Her Majesty visits him in his chamber day and night." Feria had heard it said that Lady Dudley had a growth in one of her breasts and that her husband was only waiting for her death to marry the queen.

Chapter 6

No SAFETY FOR THE REALM was seen without heirs of the queen's body, and anxiety was now fanned by the march of affairs in Scotland. The Catholic Mary of Guise, queen regent for her daughter the Queen of Scots, was almost overborne by the reforming party, who called themselves Lords of the Congregation. The latter were determined to secure the Protestant religion and to oust the French. On the brink of open rebellion, they asked Elizabeth to help them. The chance to clear the French out of Scotland was extremely tempting; but open hostilities might result in a French invasion of England. Elizabeth sent money to pay the rebel army, but when, in October, the Scots lords deposed the queen regent, and the Privy Council with Cecil at their head urged open intervention, Elizabeth hung back. Her native caution, which had been increased by two near escapes from death, had come to the pass at which it had sometimes the effect of paralysis. She had begun to reign so straitened for men, ships, money, that to her mind almost anything was to be preferred to the risk of loss. There was not a soldier or a shilling to spare; the idea of being forced to expend either was an agony. To wait and see how things fell out, how others would commit themselves, and then to intervene at the last possible moment, was her method all her life.

Cecil was cautious, but he knew that poor as the kingdom was, the risk of financial loss must be balanced against the perils of inaction. The queen's refusal to unclose her hand drove him to the last resort. In December he addressed a minute to her, saying that if she would not permit open intervention in Scotland, he must retire from the government. He could not, he said, "serve your Majesty in anything that myself cannot allow." The upshot was that at the end of the month the queen allowed Admiral Winter to take fourteen ships up to the Firth of Forth with orders to destroy any French shipping that was bringing reinforcements to Leith. On January 23 Winter entered the Firth and destroyed ships of munition and supplies, and this naval success was followed by a great disaster to the French fleet from stormy weather. Encouraged by this, Elizabeth allowed an English army to cross the border in March. It was severely defeated by the French outside Leith, and Elizabeth, while ordering reinforcements with furious energy, at the same time rounded on Cecil for having urged intervention in the first place.

But fortune favored the English. The queen regent was dying and the French had their hands full with conspiracy at home. In June they sent to treat and in July Cecil went north to arrange the Treaty of Edinburgh. His work on the treaty was a masterpiece, and while it secured favorable terms for the Scots reformers, it gained three points of major importance for the English: Francis and Mary were to relinquish the royal arms of England, Elizabeth's title was to be recognized, and the French forces were to be withdrawn from Scotland. It was assumed that the next step would be the ratification of the treaty made on her behalf by Mary Queen of Scots; but Mary refused to ratify a treaty which renounced her own title as Queen of England and recognized that of Elizabeth. She had not ratified it when, twenty-seven years later, she went to the block.

The French government, however, accepted it, and the prestige of England soared. Sir Thomas Gresham, the financier, was in the Netherlands on transactions to repair the credit of the English Crown, and he saw the effects of the victory on the money market. The work had been Cecil's and the queen had, if anything, obstructed it; but it was inevitable that she was now hailed as the brilliant symbol of the nation's success.

An enterprise in which the queen ardently participated was the reform of the currency, in this year, as Camden says, "brought happily to a pass in a few months without making any stay." Perhaps nothing did more to gain the public confidence.

The queen had made an excellent beginning but those nearest to her who wished to gaze upon her with approval found their vision blocked by Lord Robert Dudley. Protective and adoring, the master of the horse fulfilled his office thoroughly to the queen's satisfaction. He wrote to the earl of Sussex in Ireland that the queen would like some Irish horses sent over, thinking that they might go faster than hers, "which," he said, "she spareth not to try as fast as they can go. And I fear them much, yet she will prove them." But to the anxious councillors the satisfaction he gave to the queen was far too great. The queen's youth and her glamorous appearance, and the fact that Dudley's young wife was living apart from her husband, gave their intimacy a scandalous air. Amy Dudley had no children and no proper establishment of her own; she and her servants occupied part of a house at Cumnor, near Oxford, belonging to a man called Forster. Horse transport and bad roads made every rural district secluded and remote, but a surprising number of people knew about Lady Dudley in her lonely situation. Then they heard that on September 8, a Sunday, she had been found at the bottom of a staircase with her neck broken.

The scandal was appalling. In France Mary Stuart said with a ringing laugh: "The Queen of England is going to marry her horsekeeper, who has killed his wife to make room for her."

Elizabeth sent Lord Robert away from Windsor at once, and he himself wrote begging his cousin Blount to go to Cumnor to take charge of everything. He urged Blount to make sure that the coroner's jury were "discreet and substantial persons," who would sift the matter to the bottom. The verdict at the inquest was accidental death, but in the general opinion it should have been murder, either at Dudley's instigation, or without his connivance but in his interest. The question, all-important though hardly to be framed, was whether the queen had been accessory before the fact.

Bishop de Quadra, the Spanish ambassador, told Philip that the queen had said to him as she came in from hunting that Lady Dudley had fallen down a staircase and broken her neck, and asked him to say nothing about it. He made out that the queen had said this before the news of the death was brought to Windsor on the 9th. Had Elizabeth connived at the murder, it may be safely asserted that she would not have been so grossly stupid as to tell de Quadra the death had occurred before she was supposed to know that it had.

When Elizabeth had dismissed Lord Robert from the court she had ordered him not to show himself there again till his wife was buried. A few weeks after the funeral, however, he returned; and Elizabeth had now to face the position that if she went on with the liaison she would be expected to marry her lover. The prospect of her wedding to Robert Dudley aroused general abhorrence. He was the son of a traitor, he was suspected of wife-murder, it was believed that he had dishonored the queen already: all those sound reasons reinforced the inevitable ones of envy and jealousy. Yet there was one voice prepared to speak in his favor, that of Sussex, whose chivalry toward Elizabeth was pure, tender and constant. He disliked Dudley to such an extent that their relationship was almost a standing quarrel, but he wrote to Cecil in October, saying that they were all agreed that a child of the queen's body was their greatest necessity. Therefore, said Sussex, let her choose after her own affection, for that was the way to bring them a blessed prince, and, he affirmed, "whomsoever she will choose, him will I love and honour and serve to the uttermost."

Whatever feelings were aroused at the idea of Robert Dudley's wearing the Crown Matrimonial, it was taken for granted that the queen must want him for her husband. The only question seemed to be, how far she would let I-dare-not wait upon I-would. It was not yet realized how keenly, how exquisitely Elizabeth enjoyed conducting courtships and marriage negotiations which she never intended to complete. To be the object of public and magnificent courtship, to be intensely desired in marriage, was to her a fascinating, an absorbing diversion. But when she came to the edge of the precipice, and it looked as if she might have to endure a hard struggle to avoid being pushed over it, then nervous strain began to show itself.

The urgent wish that Elizabeth should not make a ruinous marriage was paralleled by the anxiety that she should make a good one and as soon as possible. The pressure upon her to do this now received a sudden and painful impetus.

If Elizabeth died without heirs, her successor by Henry VIII's will was Catherine, the elder of the two surviving sisters of Jane Grey. This young woman was twenty-two years old. Though gentle and feminine she had a strong sense of her own importance; she was easily influenced by anyone who paid her attention and easily offended by the appearance of a slight.

Elizabeth's experience of how the heir is courted at the expense of the reigning monarch had made her determine never to recognize a successor. But Catherine Grey cared nothing for this; she resented the fact that Elizabeth had not at once accorded her the position of heiress presumptive to the Crown. She was heard to speak "very arrogant and unseemly words in the presence of the Queen." The duchess of Suffolk was in her last illness, and with disastrous irresponsibility she encouraged a clandestine courtship between Catherine and the young earl of

Hertford, son of the late protector Somerset. Hertford's sister, Lady Jane Seymour, a charming but delicate girl, was one of Elizabeth's favorite maids of honor; she was also Catherine Grey's best friend, and as Lord Hertford's dilatory and languid courtship caused Catherine much jealous misery, he was brought up to scratch by his frail but energetic sister. The wedding took place secretly in the winter of 1560, in Hertford's lodging. The clergyman whom Lady Jane had fetched in was unknown by name to the bride or bridegroom, and she herself was the sole witness.

In the following March Lady Jane died suddenly, and the queen, much distressed, ordered her a state funeral in Westminster Abbey. Soon afterward Hertford was appointed to go to France. He made no move to avoid the mission, but before he disappeared he gave his wife a deed of jointure, settling on her one thousand pounds a year. This document was not only her sole claim to her husband's support; as the clergyman was unknown and the single witness dead, it was the one and only proof that the marriage had taken place. It is hardly necessary to say what happened: Lady Catherine lost the deed, so completely that she never afterward "knew where it was become." This was the lady who was eager to take over the cares of government from Queen Elizabeth.

It was August and the queen was going on a progress through Suffolk and Norfolk. She had the look of someone greatly oppressed. The question of marriage, pressing heavily on her, sharpened her irritation at the sights which met her at Ipswich and Norwich, of the squalid and disordered state to which wives and children had reduced the cathedral and college precincts. The queen at once wrote out an ordinance and sent copies of it for publication to the archbishops of Canterbury and York, forbidding the presence of women in cathedral or college lodgings; it was an interruption of studies, she said, and contrary to the intentions of the founders.

Matthew Parker, archbishop of Canterbury, had once been chaplain to Anne Boleyn. Scholarly, grave, gentle and courageous, he had hoped to spend the rest of his life in a university. Elizabeth, with her remarkable insight in making appointments, offered him the see of Canterbury, and when he declined it, she positively refused to take no for an answer. When Dr. Parker at last submitted, he told Cecil that one of the considerations which influenced him was that he could never forget what Anne Boleyn had said to him about her child six weeks before her own death. He did not say what the words had been, but his tenderness for Elizabeth was obvious, in spite of the disapproval of some of her doings which he courageously expressed. She told him that she disapproved of married bishops and wished she had not appointed any. Dr. Parker, a married man, gently reminded her that the idea of a celibate clergy was a Catholic, not a Protestant, one; whereupon the queen's self-control gave way. "She took occasion to speak in that bitterness of the holy estate of matrimony . . ." that the archbishop in his own words to Cecil, "was in a horror to hear her." In this frame of mind, Elizabeth was visiting the great houses of Suffolk, with Lord Robert Dudley in attendance and Lady Catherine Grey among the ladies-in-waiting.

The latter was now in miserable plight: she was pregnant, her mother was dead and she could get no word from her husband in France. While the court was at Ipswich, she decided to make her case known to Lady Saintlow, a brisk matron who after several profitable marriages became known as the redoubtable Bess of Hardwick. Lady Saintlow's response was to call down curses on the wretched girl for making her party to such a secret. Lady Catherine's next bestowal of her confidence was even more unwelcome. At dead of night she glided to the bedchamber of her dead sister's brother-in-law, Lord Robert Dudley, and poured out at his bedside the story of her deplorable mishaps. The possibility of the queen's hearing of a woman in his bedroom electrified Lord Robert; he obliged Lady Catherine to remove herself, and the next morning he told Elizabeth the facts.

The mere unfounded suspicion of a secret marriage had once brought Elizabeth herself into extreme peril, so gravely was such an act regarded in anyone who claimed to be in succession to the throne. That Lady Catherine should be removed that afternoon from Ipswich to the Tower, and Lord Hertford sent for, was a matter of course. But Elizabeth's fury had another source beside the uncovering of potential treason. She had been urged by the Privy Council and by Parliament to marry and become a mother, and this was the thing she could neither face nor bring herself to say she could not do. It remained to be seen whether her brilliance, her hold on the public imagination would outweigh the lack of the one essential service of bearing a child. Meanwhile, the heiress presumptive was bearing one.

THAT AUGUST another submerged peril rose into sight. The husband of Mary Queen of Scots was dead, and there was no future for the young widow in France, where her hostile step-mother Catherine de Médicis was now regent for the boy Charles IX. Mary determined to return to Scotland, and her request for a passport to come through England had been refused because she herself had refused to ratify the Treaty of Edinburgh. "You see," said the English ambassador, "such as be noted usurpers of other folks' states, cannot patiently be borne withal for such doings." Mary had replied innocently that all this was not her fault; the treaty had been made by other people. She could not be expected to ratify it until she got back to Scotland and consulted her nobles. To disaffected Catholics she was the hope of a Catholic revival; to loyal Catholics she was, in theory at least, the Queen of England. On August 19 she arrived at Leith. Before, the Channel had lain between Elizabeth and her. Now she was on the other side of Hadrian's Wall.

The situation was full of menace: yet, intricate and perilous as the game was, Elizabeth knew, in the last resort, that she could play it; she was equal to the task.

Chapter 7

THE ABILITY ELIZABETH SHOWED in choosing men was uncom-mon, as uncommon as Mary's lack of it. Not only did the latter choose men who contributed largely to her ruin; when a man was before her who could have saved her, she fell out with him.

Her baseborn brother Lord James Stuart, earl of Murray, was a strong Protestant but ready to help his sister, and he would have made an invaluable link between her and the reformed party. That she should have antagonized and at last completely alienated Murray illustrates that Mary combined a lust for power with the utmost incapacity for ruling. She had always a certain body of Catholic supporters in Scotland, and those who saw her were apt to be melted by her loveliness and charm; but she made no appeal to the Scots nation as a whole. The difference between Mary and Elizabeth was summed up in their attitudes to their own kingdoms. Mary never troubled to conceal the fact that her ambition was to gain the throne of England; and to compass this she was ready to submit Scotland to invasion by French or Spanish soldiers and to destroy the Scottish Reformation. When Sir Thomas Randolph, the English ambassador at Holyrood, explained to her that Elizabeth would not name Mary as her successor until Elizabeth herself was married or had finally decided not to marry, Mary said bitterly that for the present she would content herself with her small portion, by which she meant her kingdom of Scotland and the Isles, and when better should come, by which she meant England, then she would give God thanks for it but nobody else. Elizabeth would never have spoken of a kingdom of hers in such slighting and contemptuous terms. Had she been Queen of Scotland, the Scots would have known that they had a queen who was as proud of them as they were proud of themselves.

Mary had two schemes in consideration, one open, one secret, to get the English Crown. One was by ceaseless demands to make Elizabeth and the English Parliament give her official recognition as Elizabeth's heir; with this the Scots were naturally in sympathy. The one secretly pursued was to make a marriage alliance with a Catholic power; this, with the presumed assistance of the English Catholics, would lead to a revolution in England on her behalf and get the Crown for her by force. This method would inevitably mean the murder of Elizabeth, and it would also mean that the Scots would be forced either to accept the mass, for which the Reformers had developed a maniacal hatred, or else to undergo such hideous sufferings as the

Spaniards were now inflicting on the Protestant Netherlanders. It was not surprising that Mary's marriage negotiations should be scanned with extreme distrust on both sides of the border. The relations of the two queens were, however, those of ceremonious cordiality: they exchanged affectionate letters and tokens made of diamonds.

The match Mary desired most was Philip's son Don Carlos, a criminal lunatic whom his father afterward had put to death like a mad dog; but though Philip entertained the negotiations, he was not eager for the marriage. His cautious view of the way the English Catholics were likely to behave was quite unshared by her. With the natural self-confidence of a beautiful woman, Mary felt that she had only to show herself on English soil, and the Catholics would rise to acclaim her. In her own view, she was the rightful queen and Elizabeth a bastard usurper, and she had another source of superiority. She had more beauty than Elizabeth and much more sexual magnetism; these qualities she had found of such advantage to her up till this time that she overlooked the fact that though, generally speaking, they are the most valuable gifts a woman can possess, in the exceptional case of personal sovereignty there are others that men will value even more.

Mary's contention that Elizabeth was not Queen of England was countered by that popular feeling among the English themselves that the Queen of Scots was never able to arouse in either Elizabeth's kingdom or her own. The ballad makers exulted in the queen's likeness to Henry VIII:

> *His daughter doth him so revive*
> *As if the father were alive.*

Not by temperament only, but in physical mold, Elizabeth was fitted to be a visible symbol, to be stared and wondered at. Her upright figure, her aquiline face, the amazing delicacy of the long, transparent, jeweled hand that she held out to be kissed, formed a magnet to the public gaze. Every phase of her self-presentation had been carried to dramatic extremes. The plainness of her dress and hair had once astonished and made an unforgettable impression; now, she both gratified her own love of jewels and made herself a brilliant spectacle to beholders.

Among the suitors who were entertained and rejected, one still kept the field. Lord Robert Dudley intended to marry the queen and was pursuing his quarry with steady determination. Once, at least, it was said that he had succeeded. In June 1562 de Quadra had told the queen point-blank that he heard everywhere she had been secretly married to Lord Robert. The queen admitted that the rumor had somehow got about, and that when she had come back that afternoon from the earl of Pembroke's house and entered her presence chamber with Lord Robert, her ladies had asked if they were to kiss his hand as well as hers. She had told them no, and that they must not believe everything they heard. The talk went on everywhere; only Lord Robert's ambition halted.

An English candidate now appeared for the hand of Mary Queen of Scots. Lady Lennox, to whom Elizabeth had once been obliged to give place, had two sons, of whom the elder, Henry Stuart, Lord Darnley, her darling, she had taught to regard himself as the heir to the English throne. The Lennox Stuarts, like Mary herself, had both been excluded by the terms of Henry VIII's will; but as Catholics they all disregarded Henry's Act of Succession. Lady Lennox had naturally disliked and resented Elizabeth, whom she viewed as an illegal supplanter of her boy's claims, and in Mary Tudor's reign she had taken no pains to disguise her ill will.

The doings of Lady Lennox did not, however, injure the surface of the cordial relations between Elizabeth and Mary Stuart, and Elizabeth was obliged to justify herself to the latter for an expedition of English troops on French soil. The long religious civil war in France between the Catholics and the Huguenot party had been closely watched by the English Privy Council, who dreaded a great accession of power to the party of Guise, the supporters of Mary Stuart and her English ambitions. The closely woven international considerations of each country's domestic politics were shown by the English decision to give the Huguenots some support in defending Havre. Elizabeth's own letter of explanation to Mary Stuart based the English interference on the need "to guard our houses from

Philip, prince of Spain.

spoil when our neighbours' are burning," to keep the ports on the Channel open to English trading vessels, and to check the violent cruelties practiced against the Huguenot victims. She ended her letter by saying: "My hot fever prevents my writing more." This was on October 15, 1562.

The queen, who was at Hampton Court, had found herself somewhat unwell five days before, and had thought a bath would make her feel better. Washing of the body was done in basins, and the queen's own expenses for linen towels, as well as the scale of the manufacture of soap, suggest that the well-to-do washed themselves with considerable thoroughness; but total immersion in a bath was regarded as a treatment for health or mere pleasure. Elizabeth was fond of it. On October 10 she took a bath and went out afterward. She shortly developed a temperature, and a German doctor was called in to see her. Dr. Burcot's skill in diagnosis was unusual: no sign was present on the skin, but at sight of the feverish queen, he said, "My liege, thou shalt have the pox." The dreadful sentence was too much for the patient's equanimity. "Have the knave away out of my sight!" she cried. Five days later there were still no spots, but the queen's illness had increased, and a raging temperature would not let her finish her letter to the Queen of Scots. That night the doctors sent for Cecil and told him they did not expect Elizabeth to live. The ghastly moment he, above others, had dreaded was upon them; the queen was about to die, leaving no successor. The Privy Council gathered at Hampton Court and discussed whether they should back Lord Huntingdon, who claimed Plantagenet descent, or Lady Catherine Grey; no one suggested the Queen of Scots; but it was agreed that a decision must be made before the King of Spain had time to interfere.

Meanwhile the queen, who had lain in a stupor, recovered consciousness. She saw the council standing around her bed, and thinking herself at the point of death she uttered some disconcerting words: she begged them to appoint Lord Robert Dudley protector of the realm with a salary of twenty thousand pounds a year, and to give his body servant Tamworth, who slept in his room, five hundred pounds a year. In a few words she asked the lords to be good to her cousin Lord Hunsdon and her household servants; and she called upon God to witness that though she loved and had always loved Lord Robert dearly, nothing improper had ever passed between them. The council soothed her by promising everything that she asked.

In the meantime two mounted messengers with a third horse between them had sought out Dr. Burcot; but the doctor had been professionally insulted, and when told that he must come to the queen at once, he replied with the independence of a foreigner: "By God's pestilence! If she be sick, let her die!" An old servant of the Carew family brought Burcot's cloak and boots, then drew his dagger and said that if the doctor did not dress and go immediately, he should be killed where he stood. In a furious passion, the doctor tore downstairs and without a word mounted and thundered away to Hampton.

As he was brought to the queen's bedside he said, "Almost too late, my liege." But he ordered a mattress to be put down in front of the fire, and having sent for a length of scarlet cloth, he wrapped her up in it, leaving one hand out, and then had her carried to the mattress. He put a bottle to her lips as she lay, and told her to drink as much as she liked. Elizabeth drank eagerly and said "it was very comfortable." Presently she saw red spots coming out on her hand and said fearfully, "What is this, Master Doctor?" " 'Tis the pox," he answered. The queen began to lament but the irascible doctor stood no nonsense. "God's pestilence!" he cried. "Which is better, to have the pox in the hands, in the face, or in the heart and kill the whole body?"

The bringing out of the eruptions saved the patient's life and the scabs left her face without permanent blemishes. The queen was soon out of bed and only keeping to her room, de Quadra said, till the marks on her face should be healed. She gave Dr. Burcot a grant of land and a pair of gold spurs that had belonged to Henry VII. The next month she was out and about again. On the afternoon of November 26, Lord Robert Dudley and Lord Windsor were having a shooting match in Windsor Park, and "the Queen's Majesty stole out upon them." Her young cousin Kate Carey, Lord Hunsdon's daughter, and two other ladies went first, and the queen followed them "as a maid." When they came up to the archers, the queen said to Lord Robert "that he was beholden to her, for she had passed the pikes for his sake."

The phrase meant overcoming danger, but in French, at least, it had a secondary meaning. In this sense, Elizabeth had not passed the pikes for him, nor would. When she swore on what she thought was her deathbed "that nothing improper had passed between Lord Robert and her," and at the same time asked for a lavish pension to be given to the servant who slept in his bedchamber, she indicated the nature of their relationship, that it was a sexual one which stopped short only of the sexual act. No one who saw her among men doubted her extreme susceptibility to male attraction; but it would seem that the harm which had been done to Elizabeth as a small child had resulted in an irremediable condition of nervous shock. In a creature of such intensity, the emotions connected with a vital instinct were, inevitably, of tremendous force. Held up in the arms of her imploring mother to her terrible father as he frowned down upon them, hearing that a sword had cut off her mother's head, that her young stepmother had been dragged shrieking down the gallery when she tried to reach the king to entreat his mercy—these experiences, it would appear, had built up a resistance that nothing could conquer.

Even the ostensible fears, the loss of liberty and submission of will, were so strong that they made the prospect of marriage seem an alienation of herself. Up to the point of capitulation, however, she enjoyed being made love to with an abnormal avidity; and as she never passed the point at which nature transforms the adoring suitor into the complacent lover, the element of worship that was incense to her vanity was perpetually prolonged.

Chapter 8

THE PARLIAMENT that met in January of 1563 were still aghast at the alarm of last October; to avoid another risk of civil war they determined the queen must be urged, forced even, to marry, and pending the birth of her own children, some candidates for the succession at least must be legally recognized. A deputation from the Commons waited on her in the Great Gallery at Whitehall, and made clear their dread of a Catholic revival under Mary Queen of Scots. "The papists," they said, "not only hope the woeful day of your death but also lie in wait to advance some title under which they may renew their late unspeakable cruelty."

The queen assured them that she viewed the outlook as seriously as they did. There was no need to tell her, she said, after her recent experience, that human life hangs by a thread. "I know now, as well as I did then, that I am mortal." As to marriage and the succession, how could they suppose that when she was so careful of other aspects of the common weal, she would neglect this one? She concluded: "I mean upon further advice to answer."

While Elizabeth was being harried, an event increased the calamity of her position. Lord Hertford, imprisoned in the Tower at a distance from Lady Catherine, persuaded a sympathetic jailer to let him into his wife's apartments, where he went to bed with her. After this, the lieutenant of the Tower allowed the prisoners to remain together, and on February 10, Lady Catherine was delivered of a second son.

The implied comment on the queen's obdurate virginity was damaging in the extreme; there were many people who sympathized strongly with the heiress presumptive who was already a mother of two boys. The queen and the Privy Council did what they could to neutralize the danger. A commission examined Lord Hertford; since he could produce neither clergyman, witness nor marriage settlement, the commission declared that it must be assumed that there had been no legal marriage. Lord Hertford was sentenced to a heavy fine for seducing a virgin of royal blood, and his children were pronounced illegitimate.

Whether legitimate or not, the birth of Catherine Grey's second son could but increase the disapproval with which many people regarded the queen's disastrous liaison with Lord Robert Dudley; but very shortly, Elizabeth caused the gossip about this relationship to take an altogether different turn.

The extreme danger to England inherent in a marriage of

Mary Stuart's was a matter of dread not only to the English themselves. Philip had dealt tepidly in her negotiations for Don Carlos because such a match involved a war with England, for which he was not ready. Now he heard that Catherine de Médicis was suggesting that Mary should marry her late husband's brother, the young King Charles IX. This, Philip told de Quadra, must be stopped at all costs. Such a marriage would end in a French invasion of England, which for his own sake he would be obliged to repel. "To be at war on account of other people's affairs is not at all to my liking," he wrote, "but in this case, seeing *whom* I should be obliging, it would be doubly disagreeable to me." While the English government were in a state of apprehension and strained vigilance, Maitland of Lethington, the cleverest of the Scots nobility, presented himself in London, and to him Elizabeth made a suggestion so unexpected that even Lethington was taken aback. She repeated to him her previous warning that any "mighty marriage" Mary made would cause England to regard her as an enemy. An English nobleman of sufficient distinction would, the queen felt, provide the solution. She suggested Lord Robert Dudley.

On the face of it, it seemed as if Elizabeth could not be sincere in making the proposal, but the hardheaded men at work on the negotiation thought that she was. Cecil warned Randolph, the English ambassador at Holyrood, "Of my knowledge of these fickle matters, I can affirm nothing that I can assure will continue," but Randolph was heart and soul in the affair; he was charmed by Mary, he thought well of Lord Robert, and the object of his life was to bring about a peaceful relationship between the two kingdoms. He welcomed the proposal and urged Lord Robert's suit with all his might.

At first it looked as if the offer ran no risk of acceptance. Mary, who on Amy Dudley's death had made the remark about the Queen of England's horsekeeper, was affronted by the suggestion; but she, who had been eager to marry Don Carlos, would have found no objection to Lord Robert's morals had he been a crowned head. Since he was a commoner, she was astonished at the presumption of anyone who offered him to her as a husband. But, said Randolph, the offer might bring certain advantages with it; if Queen Elizabeth were assured that Queen Mary was going to safeguard the interests of England by her marriage, then Elizabeth might consent to the official recognition of Mary as heiress presumptive to the English Crown. Mary's tone began to alter. Her brother Murray and Lethington both told Randolph that if suitable conditions were offered with the match, they would recommend Mary to accept it.

But one person at least was determined the marriage should not take place. Lord Robert Dudley meant to have the English Crown, and in his view the quickest way to it was not by posting off to Scotland after Mary, but by staying where he was and marrying Elizabeth. Some months later, when Randolph imagined that he had gained Mary's consent to the marriage, he was irritated and bewildered at the backwardness of the suitor. But here Dudley was on safe ground. He had allowed his name to be used in the negotiations; he could only gain, in Elizabeth's eyes, from his refusal to show eagerness in the match.

DE QUADRA DIED, and he was succeeded by the most charming and best liked of all the Spanish ambassadors to Elizabeth's court, Don Guzman de Silva. The latter began his embassy with a series of brilliant dispatches to Philip, depicting the queen as gay, courteous, talkative in the midst of her courtiers. Philip in his own dispatches sent his ambassador some guidance. "I avail myself of the occasion," he wrote, "to tell you my opinion of that Cecil. I am in the highest degree dissatisfied with him. He is a confirmed heretic and if with Lord Robert's assistance you can so inflame matters as to crush him down and deprive him of all further share in the administration, I shall be delighted to have it done." De Silva was shrewd enough to see at the very outset that it could not be done. His estimation of Cecil showed his own perception and integrity. "He is . . . lucid, modest and just, and although he is zealous in serving his queen, which is one of his best traits, yet he is amenable to reason. He knows the French, and like an Englishman he is their enemy. . . . With regard to his religion I say nothing except that I wish he were a Catholic."

Lucid, modest, just: the qualities, admirable in themselves, do not suggest fire, and yet burning energy there was, maintaining Cecil's supernormal tale of work. His labors as a minister would have been too much for most men, but they were not the whole of his undertakings. In August the queen was to visit Cambridge, and Cecil as chancellor of the university took all arrangements for the visit upon himself. He began by drawing up exhaustive notes for the guidance of the vice-chancellor and the masters. He planned where everyone was to sleep: the queen at King's in the Master's Lodge, her ladies and physicians in the Fellows' Lodgings; Lord Warwick and Lord Robert Dudley in Trinity, he himself in St. John's. There followed a consideration of what learned entertainments were to be devised for the queen, who, he reminded the university authorities, was extremely well educated. Stringent precautions were to be observed against the plague, which had struck London shortly before, but two points above all he desired the university to exhibit: namely, learning and *order*.

The queen and her entourage arrived in the afternoon; she came riding into the court of Queen's College, where everyone dismounted except herself. She remained on horseback listening to the long and stately welcome. She was wearing black velvet; her hair was drawn back into a gold net sewn with pearls and precious stones, and over this she wore a black hat spangled with gold, with a bush of feathers at the side. All her powers were engaged in listening, noticing and responding, and she never perhaps appeared more strikingly as a product of the Renaissance than on this visit.

King's College became the court, and its chapel was the centerpiece of the whole occasion. The lofty walls and exquisite fan-vaulted roof of dove-colored stone seem as if they existed to frame the astonishing height and range of the jeweled windows. On the pavement below these enormous fields of colored light the queen stood, "marvellously revising at the beauty of the chapel," gazing and gazing again, "and praising it above all the others within her realm."

On Sunday evening a stage was erected over the whole width of the nave, to take both actors and spectators of a Latin play.

At nine o'clock Cecil and the vice-chancellor came in and with them the queen's guard bearing lighted torches. The guard stood below the stage to give illumination, while high up above the windows, dimmed and scattered blots only of ruby and emerald, glowed with the evening sky.

WHEN THE COURT returned to London in September, Sir James Melville was sent down from Holyrood to discuss the negotiations for the marriage of the Queen of Scots and Lord Robert Dudley. Such at least was his ostensible commission, but he had another; it concerned Lady Lennox and her elder son. Lord Darnley was nineteen years old, very tall, and though slight, most beautifully proportioned. He was graceful and athletic, he could play the lute, and his mother had sedulously taught him everything in the way of good manners that he was capable of learning. His interest for his cousin Mary at present was that in Catholic eyes he had a claim to the English Crown nearly as good as her own, for while she was descended from Margaret Tudor by the latter's first husband, Lady Lennox was the child of Margaret's second marriage to the earl of Angus. Indeed, as Lord Darnley had been born in England, some people would argue that his claim was better than Mary's. Melville was instructed to see Lady Lennox secretly and tell her to use all her efforts to get leave for Darnley to join his father, the earl of Lennox, in Scotland, where he had gone to see about his Scottish estates.

The public part of Melville's mission resulted in dispatches describing the queen's behavior at first hand. Elizabeth's apprehensive curiosity about her rival caused her to question Melville minutely about Mary and also to challenge his admiration by a display of her own accomplishments. In reply to her questions about Mary's appearance, Melville said: "I said that she was whiter, but that my Queen was very lovely." When he told her about the different fashions in women's dress he had seen on his travels, Elizabeth said she had dresses in the fashions of all those countries, and she wore them for him to see, one after the other. He said he liked her best in the Italian dress, and this pleased her, because in that one she had worn her hair loose over her shoulders. Her hair, Melville said, was a reddish-yellow and looked as if it curled naturally. When he was asked if Mary was a good musician, he said she played "reasonably well, for a Queen." That day after dinner Lord Hunsdon told him he should hear some music and took him to the door of a gallery. Inside, someone was playing the virginals remarkably well. Melville pulled aside the portiere and went quietly in; the queen was playing, with her back toward him. He stood listening while she played, he was obliged to say, "excellently." She was indeed a most accomplished performer. His visit was, he believed, prolonged by two days that he might have an opportunity to see Elizabeth dancing. In the comparison that was inevitably demanded, he said that the Queen of Scots' dancing was less stately and elaborate than hers.

Melville's business was not with exhibitions but with what the queen might inadvertently show, and his shrewd, attentive observation was trained on her behavior to Lord Robert Dudley. He suggested that the earl of Bedford and Lord Robert should be sent to the border to confer with Murray and Lethington, and Elizabeth instantly exclaimed that he made small account of Lord Robert, naming the earl of Bedford before him; but before Melville went home he should see Lord Robert made the greater earl of the two.

Elizabeth had already thought of making Dudley a peer, but she had decided against it. He was her lover—but he was also the son of that Northumberland who had kept her from her dying brother and tried to deprive her of her crown. But now that it would make Dudley more useful in the political game, he was to receive the earldom of Leicester. The ceremony was performed at Westminster Palace in state, and at the queen's entry the sword of state in its pearl-studded scabbard was carried before her by the fair, extravagantly tall young Darnley.

Kneeling at Elizabeth's feet, Dudley received the title which was to become the most famous, most envied and best hated in the length and breadth of England. The Queen herself fastened the mantle on the earl's shoulders, and as she did so, Melville said, "she could not refrain from putting her hand in his neck, tickling him." She then asked Melville how he liked her new creation. Melville made a courteous reply; then, as a flash of lightning reveals an unfamiliar landscape, the queen showed that Lady Lennox's intrigues were not entirely secret from her. She pointed to Darnley: "And yet," she said, "you like better of yonder long lad!" The ambassador collected his wits; he said at once that any woman must prefer so proper a man as the earl of Leicester to a lady-faced boy.

On a subsequent evening, by candlelight, the queen took Melville into her bedchamber to show him some of her treasures. She opened a little cabinet and showed Melville some miniatures, each wrapped up in paper with her handwriting on it. She took out one labeled *My Lord's picture*. It was Leicester's portrait and he asked to be allowed to take it to Queen Mary. Elizabeth replied she could not spare it, she had no other. "Your Majesty has the original," said Melville. The queen then took out a picture of the Queen of Scots and kissed it, whereupon Melville seized her hand and pressed it to his lips. Then he spied an enormous ruby. Supposing she were to send Queen Mary that, or else Lord Leicester's picture, he suggested. The queen put her treasures away. She said that if the Queen of Scots followed her counsel, Mary would in time get all she had.

In spite of Elizabeth's public caress, and of her saying that she could not part even with Leicester's picture, Melville did not report that the queen was insincere in the matter of the marriage proposal. He seemed to have formed the view that she was willing that the marriage should take place, since "it would best remove out of her mind all fear and suspicion of being supplanted before her death." But he knew that the Queen of Scots was not interested in the match. It was true that, cleverly handled, it might bring with it the recognition by Parliament of her claim to succeed Elizabeth in default of the latter's heirs, but a marriage with Darnley might mean that they could together claim the English Crown immediately.

As Melville was leaving Hampton Court by water, Leicester came with him in the barge. The earl made a sort of apology for his presumption in appearing to seek the hand of the Queen of Scots. He said it was all the fault of Cecil, who was trying to ruin him in the eyes of both queens at once. The ostensible aim of Melville's mission had hung fire; the other one was a different story.

Mary Stuart, to conceal her interest in Darnley, was making Randolph believe that she was seriously considering the match with Leicester, and Randolph conveyed his hopeful impression to the English court. Cecil, to give what help he might, wrote to Lethington a testimonial to Leicester's virtues and claims. In the draft of the letter, he wrote that Leicester was a man "most dearly beloved of her Majesty"; then he crossed out "beloved" and wrote "esteemed" instead. But what dismayed Randolph was to see that Leicester himself was going to refuse the jump. Leicester's tepid behavior astonished him; the Queen of Scots had been lovely at her first coming, but her beauty had brightened until now, he wrote, she excelled any since the framing of mankind. Prudence came to his elbow and he added in brackets, "our own most worthy Queen alone excepted"; and now that Leicester might have this ravishing creature "in his naked arms" and a kingdom as well, he hung back. But Randolph was hoodwinked in believing that Mary was ready to accept Leicester; under cover of the feint, Lennox got permission for Darnley to come to Scotland, that Lennox might entail his Scots estates on him. In February Darnley went up to Edinburgh.

Chapter 9

MARY WAS NOW PROMISED the support for her darling project that she had been trying for ever since she came to Scotland. Lady Lennox had already assured her of the allegiance of both the English and the Scottish Catholics if she and Darnley would join their claims in marriage and come forward as the King and Queen of Great Britain; but more important still was the encouragement of the King of Spain. Philip had no ambassador in Scotland, but he told de Silva to tell Mary and Darnley: "If they will govern themselves by our advice and not be precipitate, but will patiently await a favorable juncture, when any attempt to frustrate their plans would be fruitless, I will assist and aid them with the end they have in view."

Mary had been prepared to marry Darnley as she had been prepared to marry Don Carlos, but when the young man appeared, with height, grace, boyish charm and on his best behavior, her policy chimed with an immediate infatuation; she announced that she would marry him and that he should be made King of Scotland. The significance of the marriage was clear to every politician.

The matter was now treated with the utmost seriousness. Sir Nicholas Throckmorton was sent posthaste to Holyrood to say that if Mary would marry either the duke of Norfolk, the earl of Arundel or the earl of Leicester, Parliament would recognize her as heiress presumptive to the English Crown. In this extremity Leicester felt obliged to safeguard himself. According to Mary, he sent her a private word, assuring her that as far as he himself was concerned, the offer was a sham. But had he in fact desired the match, it would have been of no interest to Mary, nor was the promise that she should become Queen of England on Elizabeth's death without children. An armed invasion of England with Spanish help was a far quicker method of realizing her wishes.

Throckmorton, a much sharper man than Randolph, picked up in a few days more information than the latter had gained in months. He saw that the forthcoming marriage was part of an international Catholic movement against the heretic queen. He warned Cecil to keep a vigilant watch on the Catholic families in the north of England, and told him at all costs to prevent Lady Lennox from any further communication with the Spanish ambassador. Lady Lennox was at once removed to the Tower, and peremptory orders were sent to Lennox and Darnley on their allegiance as English subjects to return immediately. Darnley replied with crude impertinence. The English queen was so envious of his good fortune, no doubt she would like to get him back again, but, he added, "I find myself very well where I am, and so purpose to keep."

The Protestant lords with Lord Murray at their head declared that to impose a Catholic king upon Scotland without consent of Parliament was illegal. Mary cared nothing for that. On July 28, 1565, Darnley was proclaimed King in Edinburgh. The next day she married him. This was Mary's hour of success; with the long-coveted Spanish alliance behind her, and the young husband with whom she was still infatuated at her side, she summoned Murray and his colleagues to meet her at Edinburgh, and when they did not comply she had them declared outlaws, and herself riding with her troops, she fought the action called the Chase-About-Raid and finally drove Murray across the border into England. In the rapturous excitement of successful action, she exclaimed that she would lead her troops to the walls of London.

With the state of affairs in Scotland and with private troubles, Elizabeth passed a summer of much disquiet. In the middle of June, Kat Ashley died, and the queen was in deep grief at her loss. Capricious and ungrateful as Elizabeth often proved, she was faithful to old friendships, and all her life she cried bitterly over losses by death.

The court was at Windsor in August and the queen, perhaps to leave care behind, rode so hard that she tired out her ladies. In this summer retreat the queen quarreled with her lover. Cecil told Sir Thomas Smith, "The Queen's Majesty is fallen into some misliking with my Lord of Leicester and therewith he is much dismayed." Negotiations for the queen's marriage with the archduke Charles had been revived, and this project was particularly dear to Cecil and to Sussex: both as a means of getting Elizabeth with child and, although the archduke himself was a Catholic, of making alliance with the German Protestants. The matter seemed progressing, and Cecil told Smith: "My Lord of Leicester hath behaved himself very wisely to allow of it." The words explain the abuse afterward heaped upon Leicester for having, it was said, prevented the queen from marrying, not only by engrossing her affections but actually interfering with negotiations.

Although Elizabeth's intellect was extremely subtle, her emotions were not; they were vivid and, it would have been supposed, easily predictable by someone who had known her well since she was eight; but Leicester, though he had great influence over her and saw farther into her mind than anyone else, occasionally made crass blunders in dealing with her. These extraordinary lapses showed a bumptious self-assertion, almost inexplicable until the overbearing arrogance of his father is remembered. With the new honors of his earldom upon him, he attempted to overpower Bowyer, the official whose business it was to deny entrance to everyone who had not the entrée to the privy chamber, the apartment beyond the presence chamber, which was the queen's private retreat. Bowyer having refused entrance to a protégée of Leicester's, the latter exclaimed that Bowyer was a knave and threatened him with loss of his place. Bowyer showed that knowledge of Elizabeth's character which Leicester had momentarily forgotten. Kneeling at the queen's feet he stated his case, and begged to know "whether my Lord of Leicester were King, or her Majesty Queen." The violence of the response was like a thunderclap. "God's death, my Lord!" she exclaimed. "I have wished you well, but my favour is not so locked up in you that others shall not participate thereof. . . . If you think to rule here, I will take a course to see you forthcoming. I will have here but one mistress and no master." Yet, so differently did she behave at other times, that even with a scene like this in his memory, Leicester still thought he was going to be able to marry her.

The summer's cloud between Elizabeth and Leicester had not removed by the autumn, and it may have been darkened by the queen's discovery of his private canceling of his proposal to Mary Stuart. At all events, their relationship was disturbed, and Elizabeth set up a strong flirtation with Sir Thomas Heneage, an able young courtier who became eventually vice-chamberlain and treasurer of her household. Heneage was one of the men who thought her personally attractive and was fond of her for her own sake. Thirty years later he left in his will a jewel to the queen, "who, above all other earthly creatures, I have thought most worthy of all my heart's love and reverence." Elizabeth's preoccupation with Heneage caused Leicester to try, for the first time, the strength of her affection for him. He set up a counterflirtation that was to have very far-reaching consequences. Its object was the queen's cousin Lettice, the daughter of Sir Francis Knollys; she was at present Lady Hereford, her husband afterward being created earl of Essex. Elizabeth was inclined to like all her relations on her mother's side;

the blank in her existence left by the absence of any family life made her ready to welcome attractive, affectionate cousins who understood what her position demanded. One of her favorite cousins had been Lettice Knollys, whose youthful good humor, combined with intelligence, had made her very pleasant, but ebbed to reveal the outlines of a character sensual, scheming and arrogant. Leicester's advances to the countess aroused a passion that bore fruit twelve years later in a secret marriage; for the present his interest in her was subsidiary to his main purpose and his ruse produced the desired result. The estrangement reached its climax in mutual reproaches of faithlessness and neglect. De Silva had heard that in the course of the scene, "both the Queen and Robert shed tears," but afterward, as he could see for himself, Leicester "returned to his former favour."

As the year drew to an end Leicester felt that the catch was very nearly in his net. He approached Cecil and said that as he thought the queen was making up her mind to marry him, he must ask Cecil to give up any other plans for her marriage; but, he added, he would always befriend Cecil and see to it that he received the promotion and encouragement which his usefulness deserved. Cecil thanked the earl for his good opinion, and drew up a table for and against Leicester as king consort; the latter considerations outweighed the former, but the desire to see Elizabeth the mother of an heir consumed him.

So the year ended. On Christmas Day the queen came to chapel in purple velvet embroidered all over with silver, very richly set with stones. New Year's Day was occupied by the giving her a treasury of clothes, jewels and precious things, and the Spanish ambassador was told by the French ambassador that Lord Leicester slept with her on New Year's night.

Chapter 10

THE YEAR 1566 was the one above all others when it seemed that the Crown Matrimonial was within Leicester's grasp. On April 12 a plan of the lovers went awry and passersby in the London streets could see strange doings to which they had not the clue. Lord Leicester came into London followed by seven hundred footmen, his own and the queen's, and went to the young earl of Oxford's house, but when he reached the rendez-vous no one was there. Meantime the queen came up secretly from Greenwich by river, attended by two ladies only, and was landed at the Three Cranes. There the queen entered a coach covered all in blue, and drove to the rendezvous; but she found no one, either. Lord Leicester had gone off in a huff. However, he halted his retinue at a spot he knew the queen must pass on her return to Greenwich. When she saw him there, "she came out of her coach in the highway and she embraced the Earl and kissed him three times." Then he climbed into the coach with her and they drove back to Greenwich. The follow-ing August Leicester repeated to de la Forêt, who had succeeded de Foix as French ambassador, that poignant, little-heeded remark Elizabeth had made as a child of eight. Leicester said: "I have known her since she was eight years of age, better than any man in the world. From that time she has always, invar-iably, declared that she would remain unmarried." He added, however, that the queen had done him the honor to tell him, in private, several times, that if she did marry an Englishman, it should be he.

Cecil was exceedingly anxious to allay rumors that Elizabeth had entirely given herself to her lover; he admitted the rumors were natural enough, but he wrote to Sir Thomas Smith at Paris: "Briefly I affirm that the Queen's Majesty may be by malicious tongues not well reported, but in truth she herself is blameless and hath no spot of evil intent." The opinion of a man singularly acute who saw her every day and frequently in the lover's company was that she had not.

It was extremely important to make this opinion carry weight at the French court. The Queen of Scots' marriage with Darn-ley had removed the fear of her marrying a foreign prince, but her understanding with Spain meant that an alliance between France and England was urgently desired by both countries. Catherine de Médicis hankered to see the Crown of England fall to one or other of her goblin brood; she tried to get it for three of her sons in turn and she began by proposing Charles IX as a husband for the English queen. The boy was seventeen and Elizabeth was now thirty-two, but the latter was still within the span of physical youth and charm, and the French king, his mother said, was already a man. The French court pushed the proposal with every show of earnestness, and though Elizabeth had assured de Silva that "she would not make the world laugh by seeing at the church door an old woman and a child," her replies to the French ambassador were more encouraging. The latter therefore thought it necessary to find out as far as he was able whether it was thought likely that Elizabeth would bear children.

One of the queen's physicians gave a member of the French embassy an unequivocal reply: "Your king," said the doctor, "is seventeen, and the queen is only thirty-two. . . . If the king marries her, I will answer for her having ten children, and no one knows her temperament better than I do." Cecil had always assumed that Elizabeth could bear children, and a professional opinion of such weight appeared to justify him. But another of the queen's physicians, Dr. Huick, though he did not contradict his colleague, gave the advice that marriage and childbearing had better not be attempted.

The news of the consultation and Huick's opinion got out, and council and Parliament were infuriated. Parliament "besought her to be joined by the sacred bond of marriage with whom she would, in what place she liked and as soon as she pleased, to the end to have children for help to the kingdom," for if she died childless, "England that breathed by her spirit, would expire with her."

Mary Queen of Scots, married and pregnant, seemed to be in a position immeasurably stronger than Elizabeth's; but her misfortunes were gathering over her. Marriage with a queen and one of the most beautiful of women had been too much for Darnley's weak head. His brainless arrogance had been so much increased that he did not treat even his wife with courtesy. Mary's passion was soon extinct, and her coldness and dislike roused him to the fatuous self-assertion that had been fostered by his mother. Mary's confidence was given to the Italian secretary, David Rizzio; this baseborn man's swaggering manners and his familiarity with the queen offended the nobles, but he was the object of much more serious disapproval, for he managed the whole of the queen's correspondence which carried on her negotiations with the Pope and the King of Spain. A group of the Protestant lords headed by Morton, Lethington and Ruthven planned Rizzio's murder for political ends, and by playing on Darnley's jealousy they made him the prime mover in the outrage; the hideous act was deliberately committed in the presence of the queen, who was seven months gone with child. Mary's caliber showed itself when instead of being prostrated by shock and a threatened miscarriage she collected herself and in twenty-four hours had seduced her husband to her side again and escaped with him at midnight from Holyrood. Horses were waiting for them and they rode wildly to Dunbar. By her heroic energy and courage Mary had regained command of the situation. Darnley denounced all the planners of the murder except himself. They were banished and in June the queen was safely delivered of a son.

Sir James Melville brought the news to London and gave it to Cecil, and Cecil at once took boat down the river to Greenwich. He arrived at the palace after supper and found the queen dancing with some courtiers. At a pause, the news was quietly repeated to her, and her ladies were alarmed to see her sit down suddenly in a chair, leaning her head upon her hand. They gathered around her and before she could prevent herself, the words escaped her: "The Queen of Scots is lighter of a fair son, and I am but a barren stock."

When Melville was received by her the following morning, she had recovered herself. She bounded forward, congratulating him on his news; she accepted Mary's invitation to stand godmother; as regards a proxy, she could not, she said, send an English lady northward at that time of year, but the duchess of Argyll must stand for her and she gave orders for a splendid silver-gilt font to be sent for her godson's christening.

Melville told her with unkind relish that Mary had been "so sore-handled" in her labor, she wished she had never married. He did this, he said, to give the English queen "a little scare of marrying." This was a strange statement from Melville, who, ten years before, had made up his mind that Elizabeth was incapable of bearing children.

The scare of marrying needed no encouragement. This issue between the queen and Parliament was about to take a formidable shape. Parliament reopened at the end of September, and its most urgent concern was to force the queen to agree to marry, and meanwhile to appoint her successor. At a council meeting in early October, the duke of Norfolk reminded her that in the last session of Parliament she had promised an answer to the petition as to marriage and succession. He begged that she would now sanction the discussion by the Houses of these matters, of such crucial importance to her well-being and the realm's.

That the queen had not expected such a speech at that moment was clear from the way she received it. She exclaimed that she had governed the country well up to now, and these matters she would keep in her own hands without submitting to interference. As to appointing a successor, she said passionately she had no desire to be buried alive like her sister! The last days of Mary rushed upon her mind, as well as the appearance that the London to Hatfield road had presented. She cried that she wanted no such journeyings in *her* reign! The Privy Council could do nothing with her. But Parliament had a weapon. A subsidy was absolutely necessary if the business of government were to be carried on. Among other expenses, the queen was daily spending large sums not only to maintain ships but to build new ones; it was moved therefore to revive the suit for the succession and make it clear that the granting of the subsidy depended on it. The debate in the Commons developed into unprecedented uproar. Some members said it was too late in the day to go on, whereupon others rushed to the doors and shut them. Blows were exchanged, and when patience was urged, there were cries of: "No! No! We have express charges to grant nothing before the queen gives a firm answer to our demands!" The House of Lords agreed with the Commons and the steady pressure on the queen to grant something that she could not grant was driving her almost beside herself. Norfolk, Pembroke, Northampton and Leicester sought an audience, and at the sight of them entering the presence chamber all together, Elizabeth behaved like a frantic animal at bay. She poured out a stream of reproaches in which she almost called Norfolk a traitor; she told Pembroke that he talked like a swaggering soldier, and as for Northampton, whose matrimonial entanglements had been such that his present marriage had required an act of Parliament to bring it about, if he wanted to talk about marriage, the queen said, let him talk about his own, instead of mincing words with her.

Leicester, who had no doubt believed that if the queen gave way to the insistence on marriage it would be in his favor, found himself as fiercely resisted as the rest. Elizabeth rounded on him, exclaiming she had thought if all the world abandoned her, he would not. Aghast, he swore that he would die at her feet. In passionate irritation she answered, that had nothing to do with the matter.

Cecil made a note: "Because it seemeth very uncomfortable to the Queen's Majesty to hear of this, at this time, and that it is hoped God will direct her heart to think more comfortable hereafter"—it would be as well, he thought, to prorogue Parliament, arrange the marriage meanwhile, and convene the members again when this was a *fait accompli*. But the temper of the Houses was dangerous, and the Crown's need of money was pressing. The queen, whose alarm was now reined in, prepared to do battle. A deputation of thirty members from each House waited on her, and she addressed them with a vehement, personal eloquence, using indeed the idiom she had used to Parry at fourteen: " 'Well,' she said, 'I will not, and so tell him.' " The passion of resistance and self-defense she had been thrown into in the presence chamber was still there, but it was now formed into a collected argument and put into words that flew like a pelting of flints. "So to aggravate the cause against me!" cried the ringing voice. "Was I not born in this realm? Were my parents born in any foreign country? . . . Is not my kingdom here? Whom have I oppressed? Whom have I enriched to other's harm? . . . How have I governed since my reign? I will be tried by enmity itself. I need not to use many words for my deeds do try me."

As for the marriage: "I say again, I will marry as soon as I can conveniently, if God take not away him whom I mind to marry, or myself, or else some other great [hindrance] happen. . . . And I hope to have children, otherwise I would never marry."

For the succession: she rehearsed the danger of appointing one successor among so many who thought they had a claim. It was the sure way to civil disorder. "If you have liberty to treat of it, there be so many competitors . . . some would speed for their master, some for their mistress and every man for his friend."

For any peril to herself, without a husband, or, childless, when her single life would tempt the assassin, she cared not. "Though I be a woman, yet I have as good a courage, answerable to my place, as ever my father had . . . I will never be by violence constrained to do anything. I thank God I am endued with such qualities, that if I were turned out of the realm in my petticoat, I were able to live in any place in Christendom."

Were it not for the danger to the realm, she would allow them to discuss the succession, notwithstanding the danger to her. "As soon as there may be a convenient time, and that it may be done with the least peril to you, although never without great danger to me, I will deal therein for your safety.

"This," she said in conclusion, "is my will and answer, which I would have to be showed to the two Houses." It was not the queen's habit to leave anything in which she was interested to the discretion of the officers of state. She proceeded to detailed instruction. "And for the doing thereof," she said, "you, my Lord Chief Justice, are meetest to do it in the Upper House, and you, Cecil, in the Nether House."

This rebuff, however, was not the whole; it was accompanied by a very bold and able stroke. The subsidy under review was to be paid in three parts. She told the Houses she would relinquish the third part, saying that the money was as good as in her exchequer if it were in her subjects' pockets. It was a gesture of the utmost value in her relations with Parliament, and she could not have made it but for the unsleeping carefulness and economy of her spending.

The concession was received with great enthusiasm but there was still one more attempt to coerce the queen. Bills that were made acts were published, and it was suggested that her promise to marry should be incorporated in the prologue to the published version of the Subsidy Bill, as a means of forcing the queen's hand by letting the nation read what she had actually said. When the draft was brought to Elizabeth for her signature and she saw what had been done, her indignation blazed up again. She wrote at the foot of the draft in her private scrawl: "I know no reason why any of my private answers to the realm should serve as a prologue to a subsidy book, neither yet do I understand why such audacity should be used to make without my license an Act of my words."

The prologue was reworded and in its published form contained merely a polite statement as to "the great hope and comfort" the members had felt on hearing a gracious promise from the queen to marry when it should be convenient.

Chapter 11

AFFAIRS IN SCOTLAND, though still alarming to the English, were taking an unexpected turn. The situation between Mary and Darnley had gone from bad to worse; Lethington told her ambassador in France that it was a "heart-break" to her to be tied to such a husband, with no prospect of an "outgait." By 1567 the Protestant lords had decided that some outgate must and should be found to release Mary and themselves. The matter was discussed at Craigmillar Castle between the queen and a representative body of nobles, including Lethington, Morton, Mar and Mary's evil genius, the earl of Bothwell. Murray was not present. Mary refused to consider divorce in case it threw doubts on the legitimacy of her son, and the lords told her to leave the matter to them; she agreed to do so.

THE TERRIFIC EXPLOSION that roused Edinburgh in the early hours of February 11, 1567, did more than blow up the house in which Darnley was lying ill with smallpox: it brought down Mary's ambition in ruins. The charges of promiscuous immorality brought against her derived merely from the Presbyterian terror

Mary Queen of Scots with Bothwell.

of gaiety, music and fine clothes; but once she had conceived a passion, her determination to gratify it was uncontrollable. Her first husband was a sickly child, her second was Darnley. She was infatuated with Bothwell, which was natural, but it was also disastrous. Had she merely accepted the help of the lords in freeing herself of Darnley, she could have begun afresh, secure in the tolerance of mutual blackmail; but the lords had not given their support to Bothwell in these compromising measures, to have him, rapacious, arrogant and detested, put over their heads and made their king. When Mary insisted upon doing this, they turned on her. They had discussed the murder, they knew who was to do it; but the wife's guilt was greater than the councillors', and, to Mary's endless anger, this was the aspect placed before the world.

The famous Casket Letters were found in a silver-gilt casket under Bothwell's bed; it was characteristic that the casket itself, with its chasing of F's crowned, had belonged to Mary's first husband. Of the letters apparently written by Mary, only two show a foreknowledge of the murder, and much effort has been spent in making out that these are forgeries; but the presumptive evidence against her is so strong that if all the letters were forgeries it would make no difference to the appearance of Mary's guilt. By a sudden reconciliation with her sick husband, she took him out of his father's protection at Glasgow and established him in the remote, half-ruined dwelling, Kirk o' Field. Here she had been sleeping in a room under his own, but on the night of the murder she left for Holyrood two hours before the explosion took place.

Suspicious as this was, her behavior after the murder was damning. That Bothwell had brought it about was universally accepted; Mary took no steps to have the crime investigated, and when urged to do so by Darnley's wretched father, she replied that Parliament would meet in the spring and they would look into the matter.

The news of the murder reached London on February 17. It at first caused a general panic; Elizabeth had the locks changed on the doors of her privy chamber and bedchamber.

The next reports said that after one week's retirement for

mourning the Queen of Scots had announced that her health was suffering from confinement, and she had gone to a house party at Lord Seton's castle, where the guests included Bothwell.

The whole course of Mary's doings caused Elizabeth a painful agitation of mingled feelings. Jealous, frightened as she was of Mary's power, she was not prepared to see it thrown away by actions which discredited monarchy and seemed likely, by plunging Scotland into civil war, either to encourage rebellion or to bring in the French. Elizabeth was Mary's enemy, but she was by no means incapable of sympathy with her. Now she wrote with urgency, imploring Mary to realize what people were saying, and not to "look through her fingers" at the murder but to have proper inquiries set on foot at once. "I should not do the office of a faithful cousin and friend if I did not urge you to preserve your honour," she wrote.

The advice was totally ignored. The farcical trial of Bothwell took place on April 12, at which, instead of his being prosecuted by the Crown, the prosecution was left to Lennox, who was forbidden to bring more than six retainers with him, while Bothwell's men, estimated at four thousand, thronged the streets surrounding the courthouse. Bothwell, mounted on Darnley's charger, rode out of the gates of Holyrood to stand his trial, and the queen waved to him from her window as he went. Lennox was too frightened to appear, and the verdict of "not guilty" was the prelude to Bothwell's staged abduction of the queen, a device which deceived nobody, and to the marriage which the abduction was supposed to render necessary. The marriage was performed with Protestant rites, Bothwell's divorce from his wife, Lady Jane, having been brought about in time for the ceremony.

Mary's reputation was so completely lost that, for the time being, her political importance in Europe had gone with it and she was now faced with stark ruin at home. The lords' fury against Bothwell reached its climax when Mary placed in his hands the fortresses of Edinburgh, Leith, Dumbarton and Dunbar. The risings against them began in June; Elizabeth, though she expressed herself freely on Mary's hasty marriage with a subject who was publicly said to be the murderer of

Mary's late husband, promised nonetheless to do what she could, in face of this insurrection, for Mary's comfort, her child's safety and the tranquillity of her realm.

But nothing could be done. At Carberry Hill Mary's forces disbanded without fighting, and at the end of the day Bothwell rode away leaving her on the field, proving once more how incapable Mary was of choosing men. She was brought back to Edinburgh, where the mob was kept off her with difficulty. After a night of raving hysteria she was taken to Loch Leven Castle, a beautiful solitude in the middle of a lake.

Elizabeth had wanted to see Mary's power curtailed by a Protestant council so that she would not be able to launch a Catholic invasion of England; she did not want to see a neighboring sovereign a prisoner in her subjects' hands. The English queen felt Mary's imprisonment as a personal affront.

Each party in Scotland now claimed her help. Elizabeth had said of the lords: "Though she were guilty of all they charge her with, I cannot assist them while their queen is imprisoned." To Mary she sent a message promising to help her to regain her rights, but saying that it was essential that the truth of the matter with which Mary was charged should be discovered and proclaimed, so that those responsible might be punished. But Mary was determined never to submit to any inquiry, and she had already made up her mind that England should be the scene of her next activities. It was the last place where Elizabeth wished to see her, and her going to France to bring French armies into Scotland would be nearly as bad. But what was to be done with her? Her refusal to give up Bothwell, with all that such a refusal implied, had closed any prospect of her return to the throne. There was a strong party among the Scots who wanted her put to death, and Elizabeth fiercely threatened an invasion to revenge the crime if it were perpetrated. She was savagely answered that any more such threats would lead to Mary's instant execution.

Murray now returned to Scotland, and going to Loch Leven saw his sister for the first time since the murder. He told her that her life could be saved only by her giving up Bothwell, making no attempt at escape and no effort to bring foreign soldiers into Scotland. He got the nearest of any living being to making her admit some of her actions. She told Murray she wanted him to act as regent and to take charge of her jewels. While she was still in bed after miscarrying of twin children, a deed of abdication was forced on her as the alternative to death, and in her weeping she exclaimed: "I am but twenty-five years old!" This was the age at which Elizabeth had assumed the Crown of England.

Though Mary afterward repudiated it, she wrote the signature by which James became King of Scotland at thirteen months old; but it had been prophesied that it would prove easier to catch her than to keep her, and her extraordinary charm, which left a nation unmoved but was irresistible to people at close quarters, got her the assistance she needed to escape out of Loch Leven. Her supporters made a stand against the regent's forces at Langside and were heavily defeated, and Mary made a long flight to Dundrennan on the shores of Solway Firth. On the other side of the narrow inlet rose the coast of Cumberland; the danger Elizabeth had so long dreaded was now very close. On Sunday, May 17, Mary, accompanied by twenty followers, boarded a fishing boat and crossed to the English shore at Workington.

Mary had always meant to come to England. She believed that her mere presence would arouse unlimited enthusiasm and she thought herself to have solid grounds for this optimism. Four years before, Cecil had been told by a spy that the Scottish queen had a list of the families all over England from whom she could expect support. England offered a fresh opportunity and a near prospect of a glorious future which would overpay the losses and humiliations of the past. The deputy governor, pending instructions from London, escorted her to Carlisle, and here the neighboring gentry streamed in to pay their respects. Meanwhile Mary wrote to Elizabeth telling her that she had no clothes except those she stood up in and adding: "Pray send for me as soon as you can."

Elizabeth was about to do this when Cecil managed to deflect the impulse. Mary, he said, considering "her appetite to the Crown," must be handled with extreme caution. To receive her would be tantamount to acknowledging her as Elizabeth's heir; and from every point of view, she could not be admitted to Elizabeth's presence until a full inquiry had been held into the murder of Elizabeth's cousin. The instincts of statecraft and of mere self-preservation were quickly revived, and Elizabeth heard that her deadly enemy was holding court among Elizabeth's subjects; then she had to consider Mary's letter. The Queen of Scots had come to take the kingdom; she began by demanding clothes from Elizabeth.

The demand's symbolic meaning was out of all proportion to the practical one. In her infancy Elizabeth had been deprived of her mother and declared a bastard by her father, and the medium through which she had understood her misfortunes was that her servants had not clothes to put on her. The importance she now attached to clothes and jewels sprang from the ruling passion of her existence; they were part of the apparatus of sovereignty, but they had an additional meaning for her. Elizabeth felt something more than the reluctance of a vain and greedy woman to part with her things; for her to send a present of clothes and jewels suitable to the Queen of Scots would have required an effort of which she was incapable.

Sir Francis Knollys, vice-chamberlain of the queen's household, was sent up to Carlisle to take charge of Mary and her establishment, and before he left, Elizabeth told him to tell one of her waiting-women to make up a parcel of clothes for the Queen of Scots. The maid collected some underlinen. The Spanish ambassador "heard" that the parcel contained two worn-out chemises, a length of black velvet and a pair of shoes. Mary's own version in a letter to France was: "The Queen of England has sent me a little linen."

Murray, meanwhile, who had taken possession of his sister's jewels, knew, it seemed, of Elizabeth's fondness for pearls. Of the great treasury now in his hands he chose out six ropes of extremely fine pearls strung on knotted thread and twenty-five separate pearls of enormous size whose tinge was "like that of black muscat grapes," and sent them by an agent to London. Elizabeth, with Leicester and Pembroke beside her, had examined the pearls and all three had been astonished at their beauty;

and Murray had directed that, to gratify the Queen of England, she was to be allowed to buy them at a price one-third less than their value.

That Mary had been meanly treated in matters where she would have behaved very well herself made her pitiable, but it did not alter the facts of how she had behaved in Scotland and how she meant to behave in England if she got the chance. She knew that she was a potential threat to the English queen and she flaunted the fact with wild indiscretion.

Lord Herries was her ambassador to Elizabeth and dealt in peremptory language. He demanded either that an armed force should be sent to Scotland to restore his mistress to the throne, or that she should be allowed to go to France to ask the help that was refused in England. To the English government the requests were equally impossible, but Mary followed them with a letter asking for a passport for Lord Fleming to go to France that he might negotiate for her with Catherine de Médicis. When this was refused, Mary's indignation was extreme. It was her firm conviction that she ought, with the armed help of friendly princes, to be replaced on her throne immediately; that nothing she had done deserved blame. The question of her guilt did not arise; the sin of her subjects in rebelling against her appeared so heinous, it canceled any trivial indiscretions of her own. Her attitude to Elizabeth was uncompromising: she demanded and expected to be received officially by the English queen, who was to chastise her rebels for her and to restore her crown. At the same time she had never ratified the Treaty of Edinburgh, she continued to demand the recognition by the English Parliament of her right to succeed Elizabeth on the latter's death and, as her words were soon to show, was secretly prepared to replace her without waiting for that event.

Elizabeth, at the time of Mary's imprisonment in Loch Leven, had made the fatal mistake of promising to help her to regain her throne. This Mary never allowed anyone to forget, and the Queen of England was forever branded as a treacherous hypocrite. Mary never acknowledged that Elizabeth had done her best to save her life. Whatever the Scots' answer to Elizabeth's threat had been, the fact remained that Elizabeth had threatened reprisals if they took Mary's life, and that Mary's life had, in fact, been spared. But the promise of help had been given; and everything that Mary demanded on the strength of it was impossible.

Every decision Elizabeth now took would be disapproved of by some influential party, and every course of action open to her would be fraught with some danger to herself. Since neither Mary's side nor Murray's could prevail without English help, the latter agreed to let the quarrel be judged by English commissioners.

Mary was at first highly indignant at the idea of submitting to any inquiry but she at last agreed, instructing Lord Herries and the bishop of Ross that they were to treat Murray and his party as defendants only, who were there to answer the charge of rebellion against her; she herself would admit nothing.

The inquiry opened in October 1567 at York, before the duke of Norfolk, the earl of Sussex, and Sir Ralph Sadler. Mary told the bishop of Ross that she hoped and expected they would be in her favor. Murray asked the commissioners whether, if he proved the charge of complicity in Darnley's murder against Mary, the English government would undertake to keep her a prisoner in England. He was told that question must be referred to the Privy Council in London. He therefore opened his case with the charge of Mary's having handed over the power of the realm to Bothwell; but privately, he showed the commissioners copies of the Casket Letters. Lethington had already shown copies to Mary, who had not said that the letters were forgeries; she had only told Lethington to do his best to suppress them. Now the commissioners had seen them, and Norfolk urged Murray most strongly not to put them in as evidence. He spoke of Mary as "our future queen," and he wanted the letters suppressed, not because he thought she had not written them but because he thought she had.

Norfolk's sister, Lady Scrope, had acted as hostess to Mary in her triumphant weeks at Carlisle, and here it is supposed that Norfolk must have seen, for the first and only time, the woman who was to prove his ruin. Mary had discerned him to be favorable to her cause. Though nominally a Protestant his connections were those of the ancient Catholic nobility; he had been married three times and at thirty-two was once again a widower. The urgent need to settle the succession, and Elizabeth's steady refusal to make an immediate marriage, were leading some people to say that whatever the rights or wrongs of the Scots, the English would be best served by recognizing, under suitable safeguards to the Protestant religion, Mary's claim as heiress presumptive, and marrying her to a distinguished Englishman. Norfolk, the premier duke of England and head of the great family of Howard, who called himself a Protestant and at the same time was acceptable to the Catholics, might answer the wishes of a very numerous party, to whom the idea of such a marriage and of Mary's recognition seemed the likeliest way of laying the specter of civil war. Norfolk was strongly drawn to the scheme, which gave a romantic and splendid turn to his own fortunes.

The duke had interesting and sympathetic qualities but ability was not among them. He first incurred the enmity of Leicester and then trusted and tried to make use of him. He had once threatened to strike Leicester in the face for his familiar behavior to the queen. Norfolk and his father-in-law Arundel one day addressed Leicester with great severity. They told him that he was a traitor to the realm, since it was his influence that prevented the queen from making a suitable marriage. They went on to say that an injury to the queen's reputation was an injury to themselves, and then gave a detailed explanation of what they found fault with in his behavior.

The sovereign's bedchamber was, by usage, a state apartment to which the chief officers of the realm had the entrée on occasion, but their access was through the ranks of gentlemen pensioners (the fifty picked men who were chosen, among other attributes, for height and appearance, and formed the queen's ceremonial bodyguard) outside the presence chamber, and the ladies of the privy chamber into which the bedchamber opened, so that there was no danger of the queen's privacy being disturbed. Leicester as master of the horse had the entrée with other officers of state, but Arundel and Norfolk told him that he used it most improperly. They had heard that he was there in the morning before the queen was out of bed, and that he was in the habit of handing her the shift she was to put on. They expressed their views on this matter in no uncertain terms. At the same time, if he could now tell them that the queen meant to marry him, then, so important did they think it that she should marry somebody, they would support his suit.

Leicester could be amazingly arrogant; he could also be unexpectedly supple and quiet. He was quiet now. He was not able to say that he expected the queen to marry him, but he made a courteous reply and thanked the peers for their advice, by which he promised to be guided. It seemed that he had taken it in excellent part; but soon afterward it was noticed that there was violent hostility between his servants and Norfolk's, and that they were wearing violet sashes and yellow sashes respectively, as the badges of their vendetta.

When affairs had been in this same state less than a year before, a sensible man would have been very cautious in laying himself open to injury from Leicester; but on the face of it, it appeared natural that Leicester should join any movement to gain the favor of the Queen of Scots. He was of course in favor of Elizabeth's remaining Queen of England, since no other arrangement was likely to suit him so well. He would not promote a rebellion to take away her life, but if someone else should, or if she were to die in the course of nature, he owed it to himself to stand well with whoever was to succeed her.

The details of a projected marriage between Mary and Norfolk were not immediately known to Elizabeth, but the unsatisfactory progress of the inquiry at York made her decide to have the seat of the conference moved to Westminster. Here Cecil and Sir Nicholas Bacon, Leicester and his brother Warwick were added to the commissioners, and a summons was sent to the earls of Northumberland and Westmorland to attend. These nobles were Catholic, and they were, after Norfolk, the most important of the ancient northern families. That they were sent for to attend an inquiry at which the evidence of adultery and murder was to be brought against Mary Queen of Scots, showed that someone in the government had an idea of which way the wind was blowing.

When the conference reopened at Westminster, a much stronger tone against Mary was obvious. Someone had given Murray confidence, for he now made the charge against her of complicity in Darnley's murder and supported it with a great deal of evidence.

Mary's commissioners had been instructed by her that they were to leave the court if Murray's party moved from defense to accusation, and the bishop of Ross therefore announced that the proceedings of the commission were null and void and that he and his colleagues would give no further attendance at it. In their absence, Murray produced the confessions of Bothwell's accomplices and at last, with a show of unwillingness, the Casket Letters.

In the face of evidence now produced by Murray, Elizabeth wrote to Mary to say that if Mary had any reply to these charges, let her make it in God's name, and not do herself the irreparable damage of declining to answer from any considerations of dignity. But since no answer was in Mary's power, she fell back on the effective method of haughty silence. Knollys reported that she would say nothing "unless your Council would take a short answer for a sufficient answer; that is to say, that the accusations of her adversaries are false because that she, on the word of a prince, will say that they are false."

Since Mary refused to answer Murray's accusations, Elizabeth was able to terminate the conference by saying that nothing had been brought forward to impair the honor of Murray, but that, on the other hand, the charges against the Queen of Scots were "not sufficiently proven." Murray, his regency for the infant James recognized, went back to Scotland, where he was urgently needed.

Since neither party had been declared guilty by the tribunal it was difficult to justify keeping Mary in captivity while Murray was allowed to return to Scotland, but this difficulty was academic, while the difficulty of releasing her was of the most serious practical kind. The prospect of letting her loose to collect Spanish or French troops to bring into Scotland could not be faced. She might have been allowed to return to Scotland for the Scots themselves to decide her fate, but since at the

Congress of Perth the following year the Scots flatly refused to have her back in Scotland either as queen, co-regent or private person, it is tolerably certain what that fate would have been, and Elizabeth had Mary established at Tutbury Castle in Staffordshire under the guardianship of the admiring earl of Shrewsbury, waited upon by her own ladies and gentlemen, secretaries and servants, allowed to hunt and hawk, the expenses of her miniature court defrayed by the English government while her dowry as Queen Dowager of France was paid into her own hands.

Had Mary acquiesced in this situation, her position with all the English parties would have strengthened, and had her ambition been merely to be recognized as Elizabeth's heir, she must, with patience, have gained it at last. But it was idle to hope that Mary would submit to any such arrangement.

Chapter 12

To the English court's regret, the charming de Silva was replaced by Don Guerau de Spes. He landed in England in the spirit of a crusader. He thought that the reclamation of England for Catholicism and the Spanish interest could and should be put in hand immediately. He established a rapport with the Queen of Scots at Tutbury, and he soon had his hands on a plot of which the aims were to restore Catholicism as the state religion, to remove Cecil and restore to the old nobility the powers and influence Cecil had assumed, and to seal the whole by the marriage of Mary to the duke of Norfolk. The earls of Northumberland and Westmorland were more positive in their views than Norfolk himself, and their countesses, particularly Lady Northumberland, were more positive even than the earls. De Spes equaled the ladies in sanguine enthusiasm. He thought it would be a simple matter for the duke of Alva to release a force of picked Spanish veterans from the Netherlands and throw them across the Channel to aid that host of English Catholics who were only waiting for an opportunity to rise and overthrow Queen Elizabeth.

Mary's aptitude for *grande passion* was such that she had already elevated the weak, uncertain Norfolk, who was barely known to her, to be the master of her affections and her fate. She was writing to him as "My own Lord," and promising to obey his lightest word. Had Norfolk been capable of playing the part Mary assigned to him, the situation would have been very dangerous, but now that he was considering a marriage with the heiress presumptive of the realm he had not the resolution to say so. He approached the queen in the garden of Richmond Palace. Elizabeth asked him if he had any news to give her of a marriage. He said no. Then she told him straight out she had heard he would marry the Queen of Scots.

Norfolk's nerve failed him; he exclaimed that his loyalty would not allow him to take such a step and added that he preferred to sleep on a safe pillow. A lady came up with some flowers and the queen dropped the topic. It was perhaps too much to say that Elizabeth's suspicion, once aroused, was forever entirely laid to sleep, but this pointed allusion to Darnley's fate seemed for the time being to convince her.

Meanwhile de Spes, in close touch with Mary, nursed his schemes, and the events of the next few months justified their optimism.

The English Channel was swarming with pirates whom Elizabeth tacitly encouraged by taking no steps against them. Cecil was against this toleration; it was Elizabeth's personal favor which supported them. The pirates maintained a fleet at their own expense which would augment the Royal Navy if called upon, their crews gained seamanship and the loot was of great value. The pirates also served another turn. The fearful onslaught of Spain on the freedom of the Netherland provinces was entering its fiercest phase under the duke of Alva, whose aim was to reduce them completely and to make them a seat of government from which Spain would dominate the rest of Europe. The nearness to England of this great hostile force was a continual menace, and that English pirates whose actions could be disclaimed by the Crown should obstruct Spanish communications through the Channel was a welcome situation.

In December 1568 four Spanish ships took refuge from pirates in Plymouth and Southampton. They were carrying between them eighty-five thousand pounds packed in chests, which were being sent to Alva to pay his troops. The contents of the chests and their destination became known to the Privy Council, and another fact also: that the money, which had been advanced by Genoese bankers, was the bankers' property until Alva had received it. The bankers' London agent, when sounded, said warmly that the English queen's credit was much better than that of the King of Spain, whereupon Elizabeth announced that she herself was borrowing the gold: the chests were disembarked and brought up to the Tower.

Alva was *in extremis* for the money, and with de Spes's strong approval, Alva imprisoned the English merchants then in the Netherlands and impounded their goods. The English government retaliated against the Spanish traders in England, put de Spes under house arrest and opened his correspondence. A threat of further Spanish reprisals had made the queen a prey to doubts and fears. It was a hard condition of working with her that when she had endorsed a policy that succeeded she took the credit to herself, and when she had endorsed a failure she laid the blame entirely on other shoulders. Now she was reported as saying she wished the devil might fly away with those who had advised her to appropriate the money.

To Mary, the situation looked bright, and she wrote a letter to de Spes which entirely explains the fear and hatred which the House of Commons showed in all its language about her and the anger that Elizabeth drew upon herself by her refusal, throughout seventeen years, to allow the Queen of Scots to be executed for high treason. In this letter Mary revealed not only "her appetite to the Crown" but that she was eager to do the one thing for which the English never forgive anybody: bring in a foreign army to coerce them. "Tell your master," she wrote to the Spanish ambassador, "that if he will help me, I shall be Queen of England in three months and mass shall be said all over the kingdom." But Alva saw that his own actions were causing such economic damage in the Netherlands, he must not keep up his reprisals. Two years before, Hamburg had been considered as an alternative trading center to Antwerp, and in

May an English fleet, convoyed by the Royal Navy, made a highly successful voyage there. Norfolk, Arundel and de Spes had exhorted Alva to stop this fleet, a step which would inflict enormous damage on the City of London and, by creating panic, would make conditions favorable for rebellion.

Cecil knew something of what was going on. He knew also that there was a coalition against himself whose objectives were to put down the new men, restore the national alliance with Spain and ultimately to restore Catholicism; and that the figurehead of this group was the ambivalent Norfolk.

Norfolk meanwhile thought Leicester was waiting for a favorable opportunity to speak to the queen in favor of his marriage with the Queen of Scots. The court was on its summer progress, and he came upon the queen and Leicester in the queen's lodging at Guildford. For coolness the cushions had been placed in an open doorway and here the queen sat, listening with one ear to a little child who was playing the lute and singing to her, and with the other to Lord Leicester who knelt beside her. Norfolk was about to withdraw but Leicester came up to him, leaving the queen listening to the child, and told Norfolk he had that moment been speaking to the queen about the marriage project. How had the queen received it? asked Norfolk eagerly. "Indifferent well," had been the answer. Norfolk's confidence cannot have been great, for when the court came to Thornham, the queen told him to sit down to dinner at her table, and after the meal, in his words, she gave him a nip, bidding him beware of his pillow. His delusion as to Leicester's support was soon dispelled. The queen had reached Hampshire in her progress. Here Leicester, slightly ill, took to his bed, and implored the queen to come to him. Elizabeth hurried to his bedside, and Leicester, with groans and bitter sighs, poured out all that he knew of Norfolk's project for marrying the Queen of Scots, the details of which his sensitive conscience would no longer allow him to keep to himself. Norfolk was unhinged by the exposure. Elizabeth summoned him and, asking him fiercely how he dared go about such a marriage behind her back, ordered him to give over the scheme at once. Norfolk vowed to obey the queen.

Suspicious and agitated, Elizabeth returned to Windsor in

117

September. Vague but disturbing reports came of doings in the north, and the truth was worse than the rumor. Northumberland and Westmorland were ready to lead a force southward. Hartlepool was to be invested so that Alva should have a landing place for his troops, and the Queen of Scots was to be released. These movements were to be supported by Norfolk's activity in the south; between them the two forces were to gain control of the government and Spanish soldiers were to put down all resistance. What then was to be Elizabeth's fate? "Tell your master that if he will help me, I shall be Queen of England in three months," Mary had said. There was only one way to make sure of that. Stone dead hath no fellow.

Norfolk had retired to his London house, and Elizabeth summoned him to Windsor. The duke replied that he did not feel well, but would come, God willing, in four days' time. "Which manner of answer we have not been accustomed to receive from any person," ran the draft of the queen's reply. Norfolk sent to tell the northern earls that the rising must be postponed, and he himself mounted and set off for Windsor, while his despairing followers clung to his stirrups in a last attempt to save him. As he came toward Windsor he was arrested and taken to London, where he was committed to the Tower.

Chapter 13

WHEN ELIZABETH ADDRESSED a deputation from the Houses of Parliament she spoke with a pointed decision; on public occasion she was completely in command of herself and of the situation, but to the men who worked in close association with her she seemed at times on the verge of nervous breakdown. Sir Francis Knollys, who had formed his opinion of Mary Stuart at close quarters, was shocked and astounded that Elizabeth should have allowed the conference at Westminster to break up without drastic action against her. With the freedom of a cousin and of one accustomed to speak his mind, he had written to Elizabeth the previous January: "It is not possible for your Majesty's

Four Spanish ships riding at anchor outside of Plymouth harbor.

faithful councillors to govern your estate unless you shall resolutely follow their opinion in weighty affairs." Cecil, on October 6, in a minute headed: "My advice to the Queen's Majesty in the Duke of Norfolk's Case," wrote that he wanted for various reasons to give her his opinion privately in writing rather than in council. He began by saying, "No true councillor to your Majesty can be without inward grief to behold this unfortunate case of the Queen of Scots to become so troublesome to your Majesty. . . . The Queen of Scots," he went on, "is and indeed always shall be, a dangerous person to your estate," but then he drew up a set of conditions which would reduce the danger: if Elizabeth were married, if Mary were kept in prison, if her divorce from Bothwell were not allowed, if she were publicly declared guilty of murder. To reduce Norfolk's power of injury, he should be encouraged to marry someone else, and he should not be charged with treason. If the charge were made but could not be proved, Norfolk would be more dangerous than before.

Two days later Norfolk entered the Tower, and he was examined before Bacon, Cecil, Northampton, Sadler and Bedford, all of whom confirmed that the facts, so far as they were known, did not bear out a charge of treason. Elizabeth heard this verdict with passionate repudiation. After eleven years of very hard-won success in giving the country stable government, the shock and affront of finding the head of the nobility in league against her with Mary Stuart had been dismaying; and to hear that the Privy Council did not regard his act as treasonable threw her into a hysterical passion. She exclaimed that she would have Norfolk's head off by her own authority. Then she fainted.

Norfolk had tried to postpone the movement in the north, but it was too late. Sussex, who was in York as lord president of the Council of the North, knew that disaffection was working but he did not know to what extent. He was averse from taking any aggressive step that might precipitate an outbreak, and could not bring himself to believe Norfolk a traitor. "I have always loved him above all others, her Majesty excepted." Nevertheless if Norfolk were found to be false, "which God forbid," Sussex would act the part of a true man, "and thereof her Majesty may be most assured."

Putting aside his own view of what the situation required, he summoned Norfolk's fellow conspirators, the earls of Northumberland and Westmorland, to York. The news of Norfolk's arrest had made them desperate and they refused to come.

Alva had told the rebels that before he sent them any help, they must first release the Queen of Scots. The earls made this their first object and they brought their forces south through Staffordshire, making for Tutbury; but the Privy Council had sent Lord Huntingdon and Sir Ralph Sadler to the castle, and they had removed Mary into Warwickshire, holding her at Coventry. Northumberland and Westmorland were disconcerted by this coup; but a more serious sign of failure was forced on their attention. In spite of de Spes's confident predictions, they had marched the length of four counties without attracting popular support.

Three bodies of the queen's forces were now on foot. The lord admiral, Clinton, led one from Lincolnshire, while Lord Warwick brought one from his own county and took a third contingent up to Hull, whence he and Hunsdon went over to join Sussex at York. By the beginning of January the rebellion was extinct.

It was now a question of reprisals, and Sussex had written to the Privy Council on January 1 that he proposed to "execute some for example, imprison principal offenders who might have great lands or wealth and extend her Majesty's mercy to the servingmen of meaner sort." Elizabeth, however, was wound up to a pitch of anger that spurned this suggestion. The harshness with which, on her personal authority, she treated the rebels showed the fear as well as the fury into which they had thrown her, and on her own reiterated orders to Sussex eight hundred of the earls' humble followers were hanged. What made her policy odious was that the well-to-do were spared that they might either buy their pardons or forfeit their lands.

Elizabeth had many causes for anger. The solid achievements of her twelve years' reign were so identified with her personal policy that the dissatisfaction disclosed by the rebels was felt

by her as a personal insult. They had also cost her a great deal
of money. With all the effort of which she was capable, she had
kept the Crown's finances on an even keel. Her sacrifices and
her sleepless vigilance in the service of economy had attained
their end, but only just attained it. Heavy unforeseen calls on
the exchequer would imperil it, and loss of credit meant loss
of independence, of power. So maddened was she by the enforced drain on her resources, so anxious not to incur the cost
of one unnecessary day, that she insisted on Sussex's disbanding
the greater part of his forces in January, while he and the other
generals still thought it most unsafe.

The queen was deeply angered and mortified that her religious policy, which in comparison with that pursued by any
other sovereign was exceptionally lenient and tolerant, should
have been spurned by the northern Catholics. In the height of
her indignation she declared to the bishop of Ross that Lady
Northumberland's guilt was so great she deserved to be burned.
Her most telling pronouncement, however, was reserved for
the person whom she knew to be the head and front of the disaffection. Elizabeth was not poetical, but she composed sixteen
lines describing her own distraught state of mind and the confidence which, nevertheless, she had in the people's satisfaction
with her reign, and prophesying that the Queen of Scots would
not be able to overthrow it. In the course of them, she bestowed
on Mary Stuart an imperishable soubriquet:

> The Daughter of Debate that eke discord doth sow,
> Shall reap no gain where former rule hath taught
> still peace to grow.

Peace was the great achievement: however precariously kept,
it meant developing trade, low taxes and energy used for prosperity instead of destruction. In the south, at least, Catholics
wanted civil security and freedom from crushing taxation as
much as the Protestants wanted them. If by a moderate monthly
fine they could contract out of going to the parish church, and
celebrate mass in secret at home, numbers of them were prepared to do that.

A royal proclamation that was sent around to parishes after

the putting down of the rebellion denied the claim the rebels had made that Catholics had been forced to take arms against the queen to preserve the practice of their religion. She declared that she intended no interference with anyone of the Christian faith "as long as they shall in their outward conversation show themselves quiet and not manifestly repugnant and obstinate to the laws of the realm which are established for frequenting of divine service in the ordinary churches of the realm."

The system was, in fact, working only too well. In the absence of direction from Rome, the English Catholics as a whole would continue to tolerate it indefinitely. Therefore, in February 1570, Pope Pius V issued his Bull of Excommunication against Elizabeth. This stated that "Peers, subjects and people of the said kingdom, and all others upon what terms soever bound unto her, are freed from their oath and all manner of duty, fidelity and obedience." This was dangerous enough, but it was nothing to the clause that followed: "commanding moreover and enjoining all and every, the nobles, subjects, people and others whatsoever *that they shall not once dare to obey her or any of her laws, directions or commands, binding under the same curse those who do anything to the contrary.*"

A copy of this document was found pinned to the door of the bishop of London's house in St. Paul's churchyard on the morning of May 1. Henceforward, English Catholics were disobedient to the pope if they were loyal to the queen, and traitors to the queen if they obeyed the pope.

England was not the only country in which the pope's Bull caused dismay. Philip and the emperor Maximilian were, by its implication, made violent enemies of Elizabeth, a position for which they were by no means ready. In England its publication was mistimed, since it was too late to hearten the northern rebels, and made the lot of fervent Catholics incomparably harder than before. But it did the one thing which presumably the pope intended it to do: it abruptly shattered the compromise which had made the majority of Catholics find Elizabeth's system tolerable.

The Protestant response to the Bull was instantaneous, and sermons, pamphlets and broadsheets poured out on a wave of enthusiasm and affection for the queen. Bishop Jewel's answer to the pope's Bull said much against the pope, but its most pregnant sentence was a simple one in praise of Elizabeth, that showed the rock on which the nation's love for her was based: "God gave us Queen Elizabeth, and with her, gave us peace, and so long a peace as England hath seldom seen before."

Elizabeth's passion for her kingdom has been celebrated gloriously, but never better than in the simple lines a ballad writer here put into her mouth:

> Here is my hand
> My dear lover England,
> I am thine both with mind and heart.
> For ever to endure,
> Thou mayst be sure,
> Until death we two do part.

Chapter 14

THE FIRST TWELVE YEARS of the reign were passed; Elizabeth was now thirty-seven. *Christian Prayers*, published in 1570, has for frontispiece an illumination of her kneeling, elbows raised and long hands joined. The slender figure, with the small head whose limp hair is dragged back under a jeweled net, appears on a ground of apple green.

Anyone who described Elizabeth always said that her skin was pure white. To preserve this paleness she used a cosmetic lotion made of white of egg, powdered eggshell, alum, borax and white poppyseeds. These ingredients were mixed with water and the milky fluid was beaten until a froth stood on it three fingers deep. The usual method of washing hair was with lye, a compound of wood ash and water. Teeth were cleaned by rubbing them with a cloth inside and out, and using a toothpick, and the queen's New Year's gifts included Holland tooth cloths edged with black and silver, and gold toothpicks. There were many favorite recipes for mouthwashes, whose ingredients included rosemary, myrrh, mastic and cinnamon.

The clothes in which Elizabeth's portraits were taken were

usually variations of black, white and gold, and the dresses in which ambassadors described her, as a rule black, violet, crimson or white. These colors, of striking visibility, were the obvious choice for ceremonial occasions, but as Edmund Bohun wrote, though she was splendid in public, "she loved a prudent and moderate habit in her own apartments," and the lists of clothes given to her as New Year's gifts reveal a charming choice of color for a pale woman with red hair. There were gowns of ash-colored satin embroidered in silver and black, straw-colored satin embroidered in silver and gold, dove color worked in gold and orange. Pink appears, though less often: a peach-colored satin doublet covered with white cutwork and lined with orange sarcenet, a mantle of pink-colored cobweb lawn striped with silver. In 1560 Mrs. Montagu, the queen's silkwoman, gave Elizabeth her first pair of knitted silk stockings. She was enchanted with them and asked Mrs. Montagu to set about making more at once: "I like silk stockings well," she exclaimed; "they are pleasant, fine and delicate. Henceforth I will wear no more cloth stockings."

Among the splendid presents of the wealthy courtiers, Leicester's make an interesting contrast with those of Cecil. The former's were almost always jewelry, of a personal kind; one was a ruby and diamond bracelet "with a clock in the clasp," one a diamond chain with "a round clock set with diamonds and a diamond pendant hanging from it"; once he gave her an amber scent bottle with his arms, a little gold bear and ragged staff on the stopper. These were lover's gifts. Cecil's presents were eminently suitable. One was a stand dish of silver gilt and mother-of-pearl with a crystal and silver-gilt ink bottle, and sandboxes and a penknife of silver gilt, a beautiful gift from Mr. Secretary.

The queen loved flowers as well as jewels. Their loveliness was not their only charm for her; her passion for her realm extended to its natural beauty, and on her summer progresses she would amuse herself with noticing and exclaiming at the variety of fruit England produced, and at the goodness of God in creating the variety of field, meadow, pasture and wood. In the first summer of de La Mothe-Fénelon's embassy the queen filled one of her little workbaskets with apricots and had it carried to him that he might see the fairness of English fruit. In a portrait in Jesus College, Oxford, the queen is wearing a double cherry as an earring, a strawberry and its flower are pinned to her breast, and a fern is fastened like a plume in her hair.

The winter season meant extreme cold for everyone outside the orbit of a blazing fire, no fresh meat except birds, no green vegetables and no fruit except stored apples and imported oranges. The queen did not suffer much from cold, though she dressed for it. One of her winter garments was a cloak of black silver tinsel lined with white plush; to put over her knees she had a "lap mantle" of white taffeta lined with orange plush, and one of her presents was "a warming-ball of gold."

The rigors of the winter months made the coming of spring and summer an ecstasy. The accounts of the Revels Office for the 1570's show this in the lavish use of flowers. For the festivities of winter artificial flowers were used, and the breath of vanished summer was supplied by scent and spice. In the Masque of January, the hailstones were musk comfits, clove comfits, cinnamon and ginger comfits, and the snowballs presented to the queen were scented with rose water.

The singing for entertainments was furnished by the Children of the Revels—who were recruited from the four choirs of singing boys paid by the royal household: those of St. Paul's, Westminster, St. George's, Windsor—and the Children of the Chapel Royal. Their exquisite notes, accompanied by strings and flutes, added their other-worldly beauty to a scene of congested richness and brilliance, in which the highest point of dramatic interest was not the presentation upon the stage, but the place where, in a half circle of famous faces, the pale and aquiline lady was sitting, with jewels winking on her long fingers.

IN FEBRUARY 1571 the queen made Cecil a peer with the title Baron Burghley of Stamford Burghley in Northamptonshire. The creation marked the end of the severe crisis which his government had weathered. He had had a great deal to put up with;

the queen, though an indefatigable, an inspiring colleague, was not an easy one. In spite of his enormous industry and a sober temperament, Cecil was capable of enjoyment in private life. He found energy for ambitious building. Of his two great country houses, Stamford Baron and Theobalds, the latter is the more famous because Hertfordshire is more accessible from London than Northamptonshire. Theobalds was originally a small house called Tongs, and the queen, who had spent much time in Hertfordshire as a child, continued to call it by the name she had first known. Cecil spent years enlarging it into a characteristic red brick erection, built around successive courtyards.

Burghley's relaxations were entirely domestic. His blue-stocking wife appeared somewhat forbidding to the world, but she was her husband's dearest companion. On her death he spoke of her to his son Robert as "thy matchless mother." He was profoundly anxious for the queen to marry someone who would give her children, but his view of marriage was a serious one. When he drew up a table of pros and cons for her possible marriages with Leicester and the archduke Charles, he included among the considerations of each man: "In likelihood to love his wife." To Burghley marriage with a woman meant consorting with her as well as sleeping with her.

Burghley's character being such, and so long known to her, Elizabeth never attempted to engage him in her favorite pastime of amorous amusement, nor did he ever adopt what became in time a recognized idiom for those who wanted to gain a near approach to the queen: a manner in which respect was colored by an appearance of romantic admiration.

Since it was known that this manner of approach was very successful, it was inevitable that Elizabeth's detractors should say that any expression of sexual feeling toward her was gross flattery merely. She was not, it was true, a woman whom men would die to possess; she was self-willed and dictatorial, and she had none of that capacity for sexual passion which, if it is strong enough, will, in a man's view, carry off these or any other failings. Yet she had qualities that aroused the admiration and emotion of men. She was brilliantly responsive; she met with comprehension and sympathy a wide range of interests;

anything, indeed, that interested the men about her, interested her. Pale and frail, glittering with jewels, in long, narrow bodice and inordinate skirts that looked fit only for a garden lawn, she rode so fast that it alarmed the master of the horse responsible for her safety, and danced and walked as if she could never get enough of rapid motion. But, active and domineering though she was, one of her strongest claims on men was her dependence on them. Her ministers groaned at the amount of work she exacted and at having to spend their own money in the public service; they exclaimed that they must retire, or at least take a holiday; but the queen could not spare them, and they were with her till they died or until she did. She might provoke anger, distrust or even hatred, but indifference never.

Leicester's passion, whatever its degree, had a smack of commonplace reality about it; he sometimes behaved like an offended lover. No one else behaved like this, and the only possible rival to himself was of very different caliber.

Christopher Hatton gave signs of an undoubted passion for her. He was tall, large-framed, graceful and gentle; he had caught Elizabeth's eye while dancing in a masque at Gray's Inn in 1564. He was made one of the gentlemen pensioners.

In 1571, when Hatton was M.P. for Higham Ferrers, he was thirty-one and Elizabeth thirty-eight. He had not displaced Leicester as confidential favorite, but he had overhauled him, and while every year produced gifts of lands, buildings and offices to Leicester and Hatton, during the years 1568 to 1571 the queen gave Leicester four benefactions only and Hatton eight. No one would ever entirely supplant Leicester in her affection, but Hatton's newness as an adorer and the vehemence of his passion made a strong appeal to her feelings, and for some years the relationship between them was one of the kind that was Elizabeth's nearest approach to sexual passion.

Hatton had encroached upon Leicester's preserves and in 1572 he himself became alarmed by the success of a rival who, though not a sharer of the intimate relationship that Hatton enjoyed, dazzled the queen. Edward de Vere, seventeenth earl of Oxford, was a young man of high birth, arresting presence and exceptionally disagreeable temper. His father had died nine years before, and since he was twelve years old, Oxford had been a royal ward brought up in Burghley's house. In 1571 the young man proposed for Burghley's favorite daughter, Ann. The girl was fifteen years old, and as she was not a beauty, surprise as well as bitterness was felt by her contemporaries. The Cecils were not highly born but Burghley's position made the match an eligible one; though Oxford was not the son-in-law he would have chosen, the connection brought distinction, and as Ann Cecil was in love with the young man, her father put a good face on it. The marriage was celebrated in Westminster Abbey and the queen herself was present.

The youthful countess of Oxford was not likely to shine at court, nor did her husband intend she should. Lord Shrewsbury's son, Gilbert Talbot, described to his father Lord Oxford's brilliance as a center of attraction: "The Queen's Majesty delighteth more in his personage and his dancing and valiantness than any other." Lady Burghley, said Talbot, was angry at Oxford's amusing the queen while his wife was left at home.

Another who felt injured was Hatton; and as his feelings contained some genuine affection he was in considerable danger of making a nuisance of himself. He sometimes wrote with the anger of a man in love. "Madame, in striving to withstand your violent course of evil opinion towards me"—he would, he wrote, have her to know that he was neither unthankful, covetous nor ambitious: nothing of the sort. But as regards the more intimate relationship, he returned to his strain of desperate but humble longing. In 1573 he was ill; it was decided that he must try the cure at Spa, and Elizabeth sent him off under the care of a court physician, Dr. Julio. On the journey and after his arrival at Spa he wrote to the queen describing the wreck to which love and suffering had reduced him: "Scarcely will you know your own, so much hath this disease dashed me." The torments of absence, he declared, were unbearable: "I love yourself, I cannot lack you." Never would he leave her again, on any consideration. "Bear with me, my most dear, sweet lady; passion overcometh me. I can write no more. Love me, for I love you."

He returned in October, and renewed his plea to be allowed the final privilege of a lover. In an undated letter, Elizabeth replied with serious and calm remonstrance. It had once been put to her, she said, in a game of Question and Answer: Should anything be denied to a friend? The proper answer was no. But who is a friend? "Friend leaves he to be, that doth demand more than the giver's grant with reason's leave may yield. And if so, then my friend no more—my foe." But if a true friend be found, then, "I bid myself farewell: I am but his."

The distinction was quite clear in her own mind, that to be unchaste meant to commit the sexual act; to display her naked beauty to the gaze of an adoring man did not deserve this term. The distinction explained her solemn declaration that "nothing wrong" had ever passed between herself and Leicester, and the gravity of her reply to Hatton, in a situation where most women would feel that it did not lie in their mouths to reproach the man who tried to possess them.

The adoration of the unobtainable may have been the form of lovemaking that suited Hatton best, for he never married. His lifelong attachment to Elizabeth was kind, comforting and true. He is painted holding a cameo of her, worn on a long chain around his neck.

One man of great abilities and complete devotion to the state seemed, unlike the rest, to have no personal liking for the queen. Francis Walsingham was a fervent Protestant, but he had the fanatical strain which would have made him, in other circumstances, an adviser more sympathetic to Mary Tudor than to her sister. Patriotic as he was, Walsingham felt that, in the last resort, creed was more important than nationality; Elizabeth wanted the English Catholics let alone, provided they conformed to what she thought the necessary minimum of state observance, but Walsingham wanted to see Protestant Germany and Protestant Scotland, Protestant rebels in France and the Low Countries, all united with England in a league against the Catholic powers. The warlike implications of such a course aroused the queen's alarm; but Walsingham said: "What juster cause can a Prince that maketh profession of the Gospel have, to enter into wars, than when he seeth confederacies made for rooting out of the Gospel and religion he professeth?"

In 1572 the queen had made Burghley lord treasurer; as such

he was responsible for public finance, and Walsingham succeeded him as secretary of state for all departments. They worked in the closest cooperation and their spheres overlapped: Burghley himself ran a widespread system of secret intelligence, but Walsingham became the grand master of espionage. He was "a watchful servant over the safety of his mistress," but he was not the more congenial to her for that, for it meant his attempting, with unrelenting pressure, to force her hand: he had early made up his mind that the safety of the Protestant religion, the country and the queen, demanded the death of Mary Queen of Scots.

Chapter 15

"Here is my hand my dear lover England!" The spring of love drew its source from the knowledge that the queen's policies were in the interests of economic prosperity. The English had peace and offered a refuge to hundreds of skilled workers from France and the Netherlands, who practiced in English towns, creating employment for English people. There was humming prosperity in the felt, thread, lace and silk-weaving industries, in parchment and papermaking, among engravers, glassmakers and makers of steel instruments. Alva had nearly ruined Antwerp as a seat of exchange, and Sir Thomas Gresham decided to set up one in London. He built an exchange on Cornhill, of three wings enclosing a courtyard, the upper story consisting of three rows of shops supported on pillars. He asked the queen to open it, and he gave some shopkeepers a year's lease free, to have the shops filled with goods and lit up with candles on the evening of her visit. On January 23, 1571, the queen came in state, glimmering through the murky air, and brought the French ambassador with her. They dined with Gresham in the City and then rode to Cornhill. The citizens who, because of outbreaks of the plague, had not seen her in their streets for two years now saw the queen there for the first time since the pope's Bull had appeared in St. Paul's churchyard. The exchange met them with a brilliant spectacle, its upper stories filled with a show of

rich things. The queen and her train of ladies and gentlemen examined every part of it; she congratulated Gresham and said the place should henceforth be called the Royal Exchange. At eight o'clock she began her homeward procession. Beneath the darkness of the sky the queen passed in a glow of light, and at the sight and sound of their welcome she could not restrain her exultation: she said to Fénelon that it did her heart good to see herself so much beloved and desired of her subjects.

But none of these implications made their way to the troubled, uncertain mind of the duke of Norfolk. To remove him from the neighborhood of the plague, he had been released from the Tower and was living in his town house under nominal supervision. Before he left the Tower he had signed a paper reaffirming his oath of loyalty to Queen Elizabeth and swearing to have no further dealings with the Queen of Scots; but at the same time he had sent a copy of the document to the bishop of Ross, explaining that he had felt obliged to sign it and that his signature did not mean anything.

Catherine de Médicis and the young Charles IX had just put a temporary stop to religious war in France by the Peace of St. Germain in 1570, and they were now anxious to get Prince Henry, duke of Anjou, off the scene, for as a dissolute and cross-grained youth, in the pocket of the Guise family, they foresaw that his presence would cause them endless trouble. They were therefore prepared to consider the plan now proposed by the Guises: that Anjou should marry the Queen of Scots. This suggestion, bringing back all the peril of the French reentering Scotland and using it as a base for a Catholic invasion of England in Mary's interest, was acutely alarming to everyone in England. To meet this desperate situation, Elizabeth began the first of those extraordinary stratagems against the House of Valois that made her a target for ridicule and abuse, and achieved exactly and precisely the end she had in view. She hinted that she herself might be brought to consider Anjou as a husband.

The mere possibility of such a marriage alliance caused the queen mother and the king to abandon all interest in Mary Queen of Scots. Elizabeth, having admitted the matter for discussion, now began the delaying tactics that were the essential feature of the negotiation; she said to Fénelon she feared the discrepancy in age was too great for happiness, for she was thirty-seven while the duke was barely twenty. Fénelon assured her that the duke's manliness and her own unimpaired youth made nonsense of such fears.

Elizabeth was very much in earnest in wishing to be thought in earnest, and Cecil and Walsingham supported the match. The scheme appeared, also, to have an unexpected supporter: Leicester was now an ally of Walsingham's, who was sent to Paris to open the marriage negotiations.

The queen mother was avidly eager for the English match—"Such a kingdom for one of my children!" she exclaimed to Fénelon—but Anjou himself was being awkward to a degree. "Obstinate, papistical and restive like a mule" was Sir Thomas Smith's description in a confidential letter. The English queen was in the eyes of contemporaries youthful, but she was seventeen years older than the young man, and in 1569 she had developed an ulcer on her shin. As she would not give it the proper rest but went on riding and dancing, it sometimes ached so much that she had to lie up with it. The Guises had told Anjou that if he wanted the English throne, he had better marry Mary Stuart and take it by force of arms, rather than marry an old woman with a sore leg who was no better than she should be.

By April Anjou had been brought around to acquiesce in the serious offer of his hand; he even seemed interested in the prospect himself; but the terms that accompanied the offer were ludicrous. They included a demand that he should be king and joint ruler of England, that he should be crowned, be given sixty thousand pounds a year for life, and rule the country for his children if the queen predeceased him.

The discussions went on, until they seemed to have come to a stop on the question of the prince's having liberty to go to mass in public. The French could hardly waive this point, nor the English allow it. The obstruction would have acted as a welcome brake on the proceedings, but for the fact of a rapprochement between the King of Spain and the queen mother, which turned it into a situation suddenly menacing to the English. Elizabeth instructed Walsingham to bring the proceedings forward again on any terms, and he replied that English stock was so low at the moment he must wait a better opportunity. The tide had turned suddenly and was running against the English queen, but in spite of this, the Spanish ambassador thought the negotiations so far forward that Elizabeth's marriage with Anjou was a settled thing. The prospect of the Anglo-French alliance was most alarming to Spanish interests, but so imminent did it seem that de Spes wrote: "The only remedy is that with which Ridolfi is charged." Roberto Ridolfi, a Florentine banker, had evolved a plan to seize the queen and council, liberate Mary Stuart and place her on the English throne and restore the Catholic religion. Through the bishop of Ross he brought Norfolk into touch with Mary once more, and Mary rekindled in his mind the fatal enthusiasm for her cause.

In the four major plots in which she was concerned during her eighteen years' imprisonment, the crucial question in each case was whether she had plotted or connived at the murder of Elizabeth. Her own story was that she never had. She had, naturally, and as she always said she would, used every means to gain her own freedom, but her plans, she swore most solemnly, had never included the murder of the English queen.

Ridolfi had received through Ross a paper of detailed instructions agreed on by Mary and Norfolk; these empowered him to ask the duke of Alva for guns, ammunition, armor and money, and ten thousand men. The instructions contained a clause that the most important part of Ridolfi's mission he would convey by word of mouth only.

Ridolfi went to Brussels, where the much-tried Alva heard him with mounting dismay. Alva was holding his position in the Netherlands only with difficulty, and the suggestion that he should send away ten thousand of his men took no account of what was to happen behind their backs. Ridolfi went on his way toward Madrid and Alva sent express to the Spanish ambassador at the papal court, urging him to give the pope a realistic account of the difficulties inherent in the scheme; otherwise, he feared that the pope's would be yet another voice, assuring him, at a great distance from the scene of action, that with the forces at his command the conquest of England might readily be undertaken. He then wrote to Philip; he said that to wage a serious war in England would be out of the question so long as Elizabeth were alive. "But," he wrote, "if the Queen of England should die, either a natural or any other death"— then he would feel justified in lending troops for a rapid operation to put Mary Stuart on the vacant throne. He arrived in Madrid and presented his written credentials. As he then stated that Elizabeth was to be murdered, it is assumed that this was the subject of the instructions that were too compromising to write down. Later in the day, the Council of State debated his mission. The invasion of England and the assassination of its queen were discussed as two parts of the same operation.

The most tepid member of the council was the king himself. His heavy commitments against the Moors in the southeast of Spain, the Turks in the Mediterranean, and the Netherland provinces, as well as his natural dislike of rash enterprises, made Philip fully agree with Alva that nothing expensive should be done for the plotters until they had done something for themselves. Let them seize the council and put the queen to death; then they should have help to maintain their position.

Ridolfi had failed to get help abroad; he now plunged the conspirators into ruin at home. He wrote full and compromising reports of his interviews with Alva to the Queen of Scots, Norfolk, the bishop of Ross and de Spes, and sent them in cipher to England by his agent Bailly. Burghley's watch on the ports was so close that Bailly was arrested at Dover. He was taken to the Tower and tortured on the rack, and the information wrung from him led to the arrest of the bishop of Ross. The latter, however, haughtily refused to answer questions; he said he was answerable for his actions to no one but the Queen of Scots. He was therefore put in charge of the bishop of Ely, who kept him under house arrest in his palace at Holborn.

The regent Murray had been assassinated in January 1570, and Mary Stuart, who had command of her French dowry, had bestowed a pension on the murderer of her half brother. He had been succeeded by the earl of Mar, who claimed the headship of the country in the name of the young King James and was now fighting those who wished to wrest it from him in the name of Mary. The French government, despite their conciliatory approaches to Elizabeth, were secretly sending money to the Queen of Scots' party, just as Elizabeth was supporting the Huguenots in La Rochelle. Fénelon had procured two thousand crowns for Mary to send to her Scots supporters, and Norfolk undertook to send it by his servants to Lord Herries. The duke's secretaries, Higford and Barker, gave the money to his steward Banister. The bags fell into the hands of Burghley, and with the money was found a letter in cipher to Mary's supporters which disclosed the main shape of the conspiracy.

Elizabeth had no reluctance toward the use of torture for getting information of vital importance. Her instructions were cold-blooded though not vindictive. She wrote to Sir Thomas Smith and to Dr. Wilson, master of the Court of Requests, who were responsible for interrogating Higford and Barker: "If they shall not seem to you to confess plainly their knowledge, then we warrant you to cause them both or either of them to be brought to the rack and first to move them with fear thereof to deal plainly in their answers."

At sight of the rack, Banister and Higford told all they knew. Barker dared the torture, but his resolution failed under it and he revealed an unsuspected hiding place in Howard House, among the tiles of the roof. Here were found a complete collection of the papers connected with Ridolfi's mission, and nineteen letters to Norfolk from the Queen of Scots and the bishop of Ross. The latter was now examined by members of the Privy Council, and at first he repeated his refusal, as an ambassador, to submit to interrogation; but Burghley had taken the opinion of eleven lawyers, who told him that no immunity could be claimed by anyone for acts of treason against the Crown. Ross, they said, by joining a conspiracy against the queen had forfeited an ambassador's privileges.

Burghley was not a man of great presence, but he was able to speak in a way that carried absolute conviction. He told Ross that if he would not answer the questions put to him where he was, they should be put to him on the rack.

The speed, the loquacity and above all the nature of Ross's communications almost overwhelmed Dr. Wilson, who was charged with taking them down. Ross poured out an account of the dealings between Mary and Norfolk from the time of the inquiry at York till Ridolfi's departure for the Continent. He went on to say that "the Queen, his mistress, was not fit for any husband . . . she poisoned her husband, the French King, as he credibly understood, she consented to the murder of her late husband, the Lord Darnley. Thirdly, she matched with the murderer and brought him to the field to be murdered. The Duke," he added, "should not have had the best days with her."

"Lord, what people are these!" wrote Wilson in his report. "What a Queen and what an Ambassador!" But the man who used the instrument of deadly fear should have been able to discriminate in its effects. Nonetheless, more than enough of solid evidence had been produced to convict the duke of Norfolk. Elizabeth was determined that the people should hear for themselves that he had asked for ten thousand Spaniards to be sent into England to cow them. The lord mayor and aldermen were summoned to the Court of Star Chamber, and there shown the documents found in Howard House.

The state trial of the sixteenth century was little more than a public justification of a verdict that had already been reached. In January 1572 Norfolk was pronounced guilty of high treason and condemned to death. He returned to the Tower to write letters of passionate repentance to the queen that he had dealt with her enemies, but denying that he had ever intended harm to her.

His life was inevitably forfeit. The jury of his peers demanded it, Burghley demanded it, the majority of the Privy Council demanded it, the House of Commons demanded it. Only Elizabeth wavered. Now that the law had decreed Norfolk's death, and all that was needed was her signature on a warrant, she was paralyzed. Hysterical subjects, it is said, are to an unusual degree dominated by their past; to be obliged to set in motion the machinery of axe and block, which had an awful significance for herself, produced a nervous resistance that was going to need very careful handling.

The warrant for the execution was drawn for Monday, February 8. "I cannot write," Burghley wrote to Walsingham, "what is the inward stay of the Duke of Norfolk's death; but suddenly on Sunday late in the night, the Queen's Majesty sent for me and entered into a great misliking that the Duke should die the next day; and she would have a new warrant made that night for the sheriffs to forbear until they should hear further. God's will be fulfilled and aid Her Majesty to do herself good."

Elizabeth's distress of mind culminated in a violent attack of nervous indigestion, of which the "heavy and vehement pains," which might well have been caused by poison, drove the council nearly frantic with anxiety. Burghley and Leicester sat up with her for three nights running.

The warrant was drawn a second time, for execution on April 9; but again the queen shrank. After midnight on the 8th, she wrote a note to Burghley, saying the sheriffs must be told the execution was postponed. "If they will need a warrant, let this suffice, all written with my own hand. Your most loving sovereign, Elizabeth R." The note was endorsed: "The Q. Majy: with her own hand for staying of the execution of the D.N. Received at 2 in the morning."

In May Parliament was to reassemble, and then not only would the duke of Norfolk's fate be discussed but that of the Queen of Scots also. Tempers were rising. As regards the immediate danger of a Franco-Scottish alliance, however, Elizabeth's entertainment of the duke of Anjou had done its work. Anjou had finally declared that he could not consider marrying the queen of a country that would not permit him full, public exercise of the Catholic religion, and his mother was already inquiring of the English envoys whether Queen Elizabeth could "fantasy" her younger son, the duke of Alençon? But behind these airy speculations, a most solid gain had been secured. Burghley and Walsingham had worked out with the French government the Treaty of Blois, which was signed in April. It laid down that if either country were invaded, "under any pretence or cause, none excepted," the other should send six thousand men to its assistance. Both countries agreed not to interfere in Scotland, but it should be lawful for the English queen to attack any Scots who were supporting English rebels in Scotland. In the whole course of the treaty, Mary Stuart was not mentioned once. The diplomatic triumph was complete.

Parliament reassembled in a mood of implacable determination. It was not only Norfolk's execution they wanted; the sinister statement was made, "This error has crept into the heads of a number: that there is a person in this land whom no law can touch." But treason was privileged in no one; and they asserted that the Queen of Scots was guilty of treason. She had declared herself Queen of England during the lifetime of the reigning queen, she had seduced the duke of Norfolk from his allegiance, she had encouraged rebellion in the north, she had conspired with Ridolfi to bring in foreign soldiers to overthrow the government. She had been warned before; now, "The ax must give the next warning," said one speaker. The House devised two bills: one to execute Mary Stuart for high treason, the other to say she was incapable of succession to the English throne. The first of these Elizabeth rejected out of hand; the second she promised to consider.

To the council the queen exclaimed: "Can I put to death the bird that, to escape the pursuit of the hawk, has fled to my feet for protection? Honour and conscience forbid!" The council saw that the matter was, for the time being, beyond them; but since the queen was immovable on this point, she could not hold out for the other. The warrant for Norfolk's execution was finally signed for June 2. Since she came to the throne, Elizabeth had ordered no execution by beheading. After fourteen years of disuse, the scaffold on Tower Hill was falling to pieces, and it was necessary to put up another. The duke's letters to his children, his letters to the queen, his perfect dignity and courage at his death, made his end moving in the extreme, and it could at least be said that no sovereign had ever put a subject to death with greater unwillingness.

Chapter 16

CATHERINE DE MÉDICIS, who had encouraged the Huguenot party as a counterpoise to the Guises, had then found them threatening her influence with the king. The plan to exterminate the heads of the party under pretense of treason on their part,

Elizabeth riding at Kenilworth.

while hundreds of Huguenots were in Paris for the wedding of the Protestant King of Navarre with the princess Margaret, succeeded with a completeness that took even the perpetrators aback. The frenzied hatred of the Parisians for the Protestants burst out into scenes of satanic cruelty. The Spanish ambassador at Paris wrote to Madrid: ". . . they are casting them out naked and dragging them through the streets, pillaging their houses and sparing not a babe. Blessed be God, who has converted the Princes of France to His purpose. May He inspire their hearts to go on as they have begun!" The pope had a medal struck to commemorate the event.

That the massacre spread from Paris to other cities made the English believe at first that it was the work of a revival of the Catholic League for the suppression of heresy. The accounts by refugees crowding into English ports increased the panic, and the national fury was turned upon the Queen of Scots.

THE QUEEN was on progress in August, and had spent a charming time at Warwick Castle, where Leicester's brother Warwick, Leicester himself, and her dear friend Lady Warwick had entertained her at a house party. After this she proceeded to Kenilworth to visit Leicester. She was out riding when dispatches were brought to her and she learned the first news of the Massacre of St. Bartholomew. She returned to the castle at once, and Fénelon, who was one of the guests, was not allowed to speak to her. Four days later, when the court had come to Woodstock, he was summoned to an audience.

The unhappy ambassador passed through antechambers where all the courtiers stood silent, staring at the ground. In the presence chamber, in a semicircle, were standing the queen, the chief ladies of her court and the privy councillors. All of them were dressed in black.

The queen, with a sad, stern face, withdrew with Fénelon to a window; he attempted to say that a conspiracy had been discovered against the French king and justice had demanded the most severe reprisals. No enmity, he declared, was entertained against the Protestant powers. The queen asked whether justice had demanded the murder of so many women and their children. She feared, she said, that those who had led the French king to abandon his natural subjects would lead him also to abandon his alliance with a foreign queen. She withdrew on a note of reserved but calm civility and left Fénelon to the severe reproaches of the councillors. Burghley opened the attack by saying that the massacre was the greatest crime since the Crucifixion.

Meanwhile the horror caused by the massacre had added formidable strength to the pressure exerted on Elizabeth to have Mary put to death. Elizabeth's objection was to the English Parliament's decreeing Mary's death, not to the death itself. Mary's coadjutors, Philip and Alva, had discussed the desirability of Elizabeth's death "by natural or by any other means," and Elizabeth pondered the desirability of Mary's death, not by assassination but by judicial process of the Scots themselves. This process she had once interfered to stop; since then Mary had been active in a conspiracy to murder Elizabeth and bring a foreign army into England. The English queen began to wonder if the step she had taken might be retracted.

On November 23, 1572, Sir Henry Killigrew was summoned to a private audience, at which no one was present except Burghley, Leicester and the queen herself. He was told to proceed to Scotland and talk to the regent Mar in such a manner that Mar should renew the suggestion that the Scots had already made, namely, that Mary should be given up to them for execution. Killigrew was to agree, but with the stipulation that the prisoner's head should be off within four hours. The mission must be undertaken in the most absolute secrecy; the queen herself told Killigrew that if anything of it transpired, he must be prepared to answer for it with his life. Killigrew found Mar very willing in the matter but demanding too high a price for his cooperation; he wanted, among other concessions, the presence of three thousand English soldiers to safeguard the execution, and that Elizabeth should thereafter pay to the Scots the annual sum she was spending on Mary's upkeep. Burghley was indignant; Killigrew, he felt, should not have allowed such terms even to be proposed to him. At almost the same moment news arrived of Mar's death. The plan was now out of the question, and Burghley could only hope that the queen would consent to a more direct method. He wrote to Leicester, who was with her at Windsor: "God send her Majesty strength of spirit to preserve God's cause, her own life and the lives of millions of good subjects."

The queen, who got up early and sometimes gave audiences at eight o'clock, used to lie down in the evening before the festivities or the labors of the night. Leicester replied to Burghley that his letter had come at six o'clock, but could not be taken immediately to her Majesty "for she was at her wonted repose." Before the arrival of the letter the possibility that Mary might, even at that hour, have met her death, had brought Elizabeth into a hysterical condition. Leicester knew this would get about and wrote to tell Walsingham the facts. It had not been raving hysteria: only a few fits, none of which lasted long.

Leicester, once his connection with Norfolk was severed, seemed to enter a new phase: responsible and industrious, the friend of Walsingham, the trusted colleague of Burghley, the support and comfort of the queen. His letters were those of a man of sense and a gentleman. Had modern means of communication been at their disposal, we should have known less about the people of the time, for they would have written fewer letters to each other, and they themselves would have known much more about each other than was often the case. Leicester, living in a relationship of affection and close intimacy with Elizabeth, acutely observant as she was, found it possible to conceal completely from her a most important part of his existence. The royal palaces out of London that lay in a string along the Thames—Greenwich, Richmond, Hampton Court, Windsor— were reached either by rowing on the river, by horse or by horse-drawn coach. Journeyings to and from them and the nobles' houses could go no faster than horses or oarsmen could move, and were impeded by heavy roads, bad weather and the falling of darkness. The traveler who had gone to the other side of the county from London was as much cut off from its inmates as if he had crossed the sea. Those from whom he parted could know little of his doings except what he chose to reveal.

Leicester, said the historian Francis Osborne, had seen "from the continued high-beating of her heart" that Elizabeth was not going to submit herself to a foreign husband, and had therefore "hoped to have her for himself." But this prospect was indefinitely receding, and he had found that, without marriage, he could rely on her affection to keep him in prosperity and power. The queen was not his mistress in the final sense of the word, and if she had been, she would not have been enough to satisfy him. Leicester had the reputation of a lecher who would expend fantastic sums to gratify himself. The queen may have known something of this and disregarded it; what she would not be likely to forgive was his making a second marriage.

In 1571 Leicester had been one of a house party that entertained the queen in Rutland, where, among the guests, was young Lady Sheffield. This girl, née Douglas Howard, and her sister Frances, were the daughters of Lord William Howard, the queen's great-uncle. Douglas Sheffield was "a star in the court for beauty and richness of apparel," and Leicester, suddenly and violently enamored, found her "an easy purchase." The party broke up, and when Douglas had returned to her husband's house the intrigue was discovered by her sister-in-law, who picked up and read a letter of Leicester's which Douglas had dropped upon the staircase. The former told her brother, who "parted beds" with his wife that night and went up to London, meaning to arrange a separation. Before he could thus publicly compromise Lord Leicester, he died, very suddenly. The narrator of the affair had no hesitation in saying that Leicester poisoned him.

On Lord Sheffield's death, Leicester plighted his troth secretly to the widow. He took no immediate steps legally to complete the marriage, and the young Lady Sheffield was in a miserable position: in the eyes of the world, a member of Leceister's circle but not able to claim her right to his attention.

In 1573, four days before the birth of his son, Leicester at last went through a form of marriage with the mother privately at Esher, the only witness being his confidential physician Dr. Julio. The utmost caution was necessary, and he fell out with his bride because, in the privacy of her own rooms, she had herself waited on with the ceremony due to a countess.

Chapter 17

THE SUMMER OF 1575 was that of the great entertainment at Kenilworth. Perhaps Leicester's secret marriage had made him anxious to give some flourishing demonstration of his devotion to the queen; at all events this historic house party for Elizabeth was held for eighteen days in July of that year. It was an exhibition, on epic scale, of Leicester's importance, his taste, his wealth, his adoration. He and Elizabeth were now forty-two, and while the queen was to retain a degree of youth for several years, Leicester was in the last phase of his superb handsomeness, before he turned red-faced, bald and too fat.

His preparations had been enormous, and if self-interest and treachery were the motive of this act of homage, at least the conception and all its details could not have been more in accordance with devoted love.

The earl had met the queen and her train seven miles away at Long Ichen, where he feasted her under a tent so vast that when dismantled it required seven carts to carry it away. Leicester brought the queen to the park gates of Kenilworth at eight in the evening of July 9. The castle, which the queen had given him ten years before, was filled with everything the age could attain to, of luxury and magnificence. There were hangings of scarlet leather stamped with gilt, and a Turkey carpet of a light blue ground, fifty feet long. The four-poster beds were most of them hung with scarlet or crimson, embroidered with silver and gold, but there was one of which the blue curtains were trimmed with gold and silver lace.

The queen's household was lodged in Warwick, where special arrangements had to be made for delivering her letters "which came very thick," and twenty horses at a time were in daily use for transport. She herself, with her ladies, was to be in the entire care of Leicester, the object of his devoted attention and ceremonious adoration. Thirty distinguished guests had been invited to meet her, including Leicester's brother-in-law and sister, Sir Henry and Lady Mary Sidney, and their son Philip, and with their servants and the household servants, the castle was like a small township put down in acres of gently falling green parkland studded with great trees. On one side, the windows looked onto the countryside across a wide ornamental water, and on another, a stretch of water lay like a moat against the curtain wall.

It was over the bridge that spanned it that the queen and her splendid entourage were conducted into the castle. As Elizabeth gained the bridge, an island sparkling with lights floated toward it, bearing a Nereid in silk robes, who in a boy's high voice told her: "I am the Lady of this pleasant lake," and assured her: "The Lake, the Lodge, the Lord, are yours for to command." The queen smiled and said: "We had thought the lake had been ours, and do you call it yours, now? Well, we will herein commune more with you hereafter."

A salute of guns greeted the queen's entry into the inner court, and when she was led to her chamber the tower clock was stopped. While the queen remained, time was to stand still. The twilight of a summer's day came on at last, and with darkness the castle in its fields and groves became a fairy palace: "so glittering by glass a'night by continual brightness of candle, fire and torchlight, transparent through the lightsome windows, as it were the Egyptian Pharaoh's, relucent unto all the Alexandrian coast."

The next day was Sunday. Queen and court went to church in the morning; in the afternoon the lords and ladies danced in the garden and in the evening there was a tremendous display of fireworks.

Monday was so hot, the queen stayed indoors till five o'clock, when she went out to hunt the hart. As her troop was returning in the evening, Sylvanus, a wild man of the woods, met them and ran beside the queen's horse, uttering reams of congratulatory verse. A close arbor stood in the way, and at the queen's approach the bushes shook, sweet airs sounded, and Deep Desire stepped out of a holly bush, expressing Lord Leicester's profound but respectful anguish. At the close of these utterances, Sylvanus in a final act of homage broke the sapling he carried and cast it away. Unhappily one half came down almost on the head of the queen's horse, which gave a frenzied plunge.

Several gentlemen rushed for its bridle, but before they could lay hand on it the queen had reined in the terrified beast and called out, "No hurt, no hurt!"

On Tuesday evening the queen, attended, went on foot over the bridge and into the tree-sprinkled meadows called the Chase. When she came back a barge was on the pool, filled with musicians playing and singing, and she stood on the bridge, listening in the evening light. During the next two days the heat abated and continuous showers refreshed the countryside. The castle had its indoor attractions, one of which was a great aviary filled with both familiar and exotic birds. The mesh was stretched between columns whose capitals were painted with a trompe l'oeil of rubies, diamonds, emeralds and sapphires of enormous size, in gold settings.

As the heat returned after the rain, the queen went out in the cool of the early evening, and on her return from one expedition at twilight a water pageant greeted her as she rode onto the bridge. While strains of music sounded, the Lady of the Lake advanced on her floating island, scintillating with lights. A mermaid drew a tail eighteen feet long through the waves beside her, and perched on the back of a gigantic dolphin, Arion prepared to address the awe-inspiring figure whose horse was reined to a standstill above his head. Some lines, indeed, he did bring out, but the occasion was too much for him; his memory failed, and pulling off his mask in exasperation, he shouted that "he was none of Arion, not he, but honest Harry Goldingham." The queen was in fits of laughter and said afterward that this had been the best part of the show.

The tremendous festival at Kenilworth was not a single event after which everyone retired to recuperate; it was merely the highlight of the summer progress. At its close, the queen was escorted by Leicester on a round of visits to other country houses, while a fine summer made traveling through deep country pleasant.

THE MARRIAGE NEGOTIATION between the queen and Catherine de Médicis' younger son Prince François, duke of Alençon, was now well under way. When Anjou became king in 1574,

Alençon's attitude was so hostile and mischievous that the king and the queen mother were eager to get him out of France. The prince was twenty-one, and though undersized and very ugly, he was lively and responsive. It was said that the impression he made in conversation was so good, it misled the hearer as to his real capacity. Unlike his brother, who was entirely Catholic in sympathy and had privately disdained the notion of marrying Elizabeth, Alençon appeared to entertain no such feelings. The king would probably have sons who would exclude Alençon [now the new duke of Anjou] from the French throne, and a marriage with the Queen of England would be, for him, exceptionally brilliant. Though the discrepancy of their ages was formidable, Elizabeth's achievement in keeping her realm free from foreign conflict and civil war, with its result of thriving prosperity, formed the economic basis of her high repute, while her intellect, elegance and grandeur surrounded it with a blaze of personal distinction.

Alençon had worked himself into a state of emotional as well as political eagerness for the match; in 1572 Walsingham had written from Paris to Burghley, "Touching the affection towards her Majesty, many ways I am given to understand that his affection is unfeigned and great." As for Elizabeth, at one moment she said she feared she was too old to retain the affections of so young a husband; at another she was making pointed inquiries into the degree of disfigurement Alençon had suffered from smallpox; but Alençon himself showed no wavering. His agent Maisonfleur gained the queen's confidence and he was allowed to tell her of his master's ardors. Maisonfleur, who wanted his master to come to England and propose like a private gentleman, could not tell him that Elizabeth had said the one word they wanted to hear from her: but she had said, "Let him come," and Maisonfleur had read her meaning in her eyes; or so he thought.

Alençon, weak and incompetent, was now nonetheless amazingly busy. In the complicated situation in the Netherlands, the resistance to Spanish tyranny was divided; for the Catholic states who wanted a degree of freedom did not want to join a Protestant movement of revolt; the Flemish therefore made advances to Alençon to accept their sovereignty, and the possibility of his being able to accept and maintain this position was disturbing to Spain, France and England alike. Philip was about to launch the concentrated attack on the Netherlands called "The Spanish Fury"; Catherine and Henry III foresaw that Alençon's doings might involve them in a war with Spain, and Elizabeth was alarmed at the idea of a strong French influence in the Netherlands, in which France should command the whole coastline opposite to the English shore of the Channel. This situation to which every burning issue, religious, political, commercial, contributed its own range of interlocking considerations, formed a puzzle of vast complexity in which the values of the pieces were perpetually changing and in which failure to find the solution meant, for the country, ruin, and for the queen and Burghley, death. The constant presence of extreme danger and the ceaseless weight of care had become the background of Elizabeth's daily life.

THE SITUATION in the Netherlands, apropos the movements of Alençon, was not only intricate but ceaselessly changing. Alençon's determination to enter the arena at once intensified the importance of every aspect for both Spain and England. Burghley's minute on this position of affairs, dated June 2, 1578, shows his conviction that England was always menaced by a potential attack of the concerted forces of Catholic Europe. He notes the great expense the queen "presently sustaineth to defend her estate against a navy set out by the Pope and succoured by the Kings of Spain, France and Portugal whereby her Majesty shall be forced to be at great charges and so more unable to give them aid." On the other hand, it was vitally necessary to consider, with the states, the dangers likely to ensue from their receiving French aid. Catherine and Henry III had shown themselves glad that Alençon should have occupation outside France; but for Alençon to operate in the Netherlands in firm alliance with his family would be a menace to the English government. Their aim was to encourage him to enter the Netherlands independently of France; they wished at the same time to send as much English help into the Netherlands as would prevent French preponderance there, without provoking Spain to retaliate. The instrument for this extremely delicate work was to be the entertaining of marriage negotiations between Alencon and Elizabeth.

No question of the queen's marriage could come up without bringing Leicester immediately to mind. He and Elizabeth no longer gave scandal by carrying on with the indiscreet eagerness of young lovers, but their relationship was recognized as one of deep intimacy. Leicester's marriage with Douglas Sheffield, or what Lady Sheffield had taken to be a marriage, remained a secret, though the child was thriving and lived to claim his father's earldom. The queen, whose overstrung nerves required management, was apt to treat Burghley, Sussex and Leicester, all three, with the abandonment of self-control of a patient in the hands of an experienced physician, but whereas her relationship with the first two was one of affection without even the idiom of romance, with Leicester it was romantic always. In 1578, the very year of the negotiations with Alençon, the queen gave Leicester a violin with her arms and his engraved on the silver fingerboard, and in May she came to his house at Wanstead. The visit was adorned by a masque, "The Lady of the May," which Philip Sidney had written for his uncle's house party.

A picture at Welbeck Abbey of Elizabeth at this period shows her standing in the garden of Wanstead; one of Leicester's oriental carpets is spread on the grass, and the queen is standing on it with the sword of state laid at her feet and her little dog sitting beside it. She wears a white dress, suitable to May, embroidered with sprays of flowers and leaves in natural colors. In spite of the painter's properties—a hanging with the royal arms behind the queen, and the great sword at her feet—there is an air of naturalness, of summer out of doors, in the picture. Elizabeth's face is moving; it is frail-looking, of transparent pallor and the expression is gentle, almost tranquil, as if she were in the house of a friend.

The nearness of Wanstead to London and its rural solitude, in the midst of which was found every luxury and comfort that romantic friendship could suggest, made it a retreat both convenient and very charming to the queen: some of the Privy Council meetings at which the Alençon match was most heatedly discussed were held at Wanstead during her visits.

Walsingham, accompanied by Lord Cobham, went over to Flanders to investigate the position of Alençon vis-à-vis the states. The difficulty of deciding what part the queen should take and how much she should pay was faithfully relayed by Burghley to his sympathizing colleague. The queen's preoccupation with money was never laid aside for a moment. Burghley wrote: "When she perceived that the States required more money, I will not write how greatly she misliked thereof." Walsingham, who was handling the negotiations with devoted energy and had thought it essential to the main purpose that the loan the queen had made to the states should not be called in, as she herself was asking that it should, wrote to Christopher Hatton: "It is an intolerable grief to me to receive so hard measure at her Majesty's hands as if I were some notorious offender . . . the greatest fault we may be charged withal is that we have had more regard to her Majesty's honour and safety than to her treasure." But as the queen saw it, honor and safety could be secured only on a solid basis of treasure.

Walsingham reported that Alencon was treating with the states independently of the French king, and this was the information needed to send the negotiations forward. The queen threw her glittering bait and the tug on the line was immediate. The duke's agent, de Bocqueville, said that "his master was determined to marry the Queen or the Netherlands," and Elizabeth set herself to play the fish.

De Bocqueville and his suite were received by her while she was on progress at Long Melford. She was bent on displaying her court to them in all possible splendor, but this was not easily done away from home. A certain amount of gold plate to be used at meals was carried in the sovereign's train, though not of course anything like as much as was used in a palace. When the Frenchmen were dining with her, the queen, like some deceitful creature in a fairy tale, attempted to conjure up an illusion of grandeur. She demanded of Sussex, the lord chamberlain, why there was so little gold plate in evidence.

Sussex was by nature incapable of playing these games. He answered that he had been on progress with Henry VIII himself, and had never seen so much plate carried as there was here. The queen flew into a passion, exclaiming that the more that was done for people like him, the worse they grew. How little her asperity to Sussex represented their actual relationship, he showed by the tone of his letter to her about the Alençon match, written ten days after her public and unjust berating. Sussex detailed the various arguments for and against the match, of which he himself was in favor, and he wrote a straightforward and beautifully sympathetic passage upon her personal feelings. The obstacles to the match from this point of view were, he said, "your own mislike to marriage which might breed a discontented life hereafter," and "the difficulty of the choice of a person that might in all respects content your mind." "These considerations," he went on, "receive not the counsel of others but must be decided by yourself. Whereby you be to follow only the counsel of your own heart, whereunto all men must leave you. For it is the judgment of your own heart that may make it ill to you, which no man can say . . . but to be quite good of itself, if your heart like it."

While Elizabeth was appearing to consider a marriage, Leicester made one. Two years before, in 1576, when the earl of Essex had died in Ireland of what was described as a flux, Leicester had been through a secret marriage ceremony with Essex's widow, Lettice Devereux, a cousin of the queen's. Leicester had long ago shown himself susceptible to Lettice's voluptuous attractions, and when the earl of Essex died, Leicester offered Douglas Sheffield seven hundred pounds a year to let him hear no more of her. When she refused the suggestion with angry dismay, Leicester attained his object and saved money by explaining to her that their marriage had been invalid and she was not his wife. This left him free to contract a marriage, or at least a connection with Lettice Devereux, which was at first kept profoundly secret. But Lettice's father was Sir Francis Knollys, a man of considerable experience of the world and a Puritan. Knollys heard of his daughter's stolen match, and he had also, by this time, heard of Leicester's doings with the miserable Douglas Sheffield. He told Leicester in uncompromising terms that whatever might have gone before, a marriage must be performed, at which he, Knollys, must be present, with witnesses chosen by himself. He carried all before him. The second ceremony was performed at Wanstead on September 20, in the presence of Sir Francis Knollys, the earl of Warwick, the earl of Lincoln and Lord North. Secrecy was enjoined on all the parties, but it was impossible to keep dark what was now known to so many. Yet still the queen did not hear what had happened. Her ordered and ceremonial existence, with its distractions and its intense preoccupations, stood like a screen between her and the doings at Wanstead. Leicester was at court when she expected him to be, and the countess of Leicester continued to call herself the countess of Essex.

In October the queen had attacks of toothache, and her plight distressed the men who were fond of her. Elizabeth in her own person represented security to every Englishman who wanted freedom from foreign invasion and from civil war so that he could go on with the concerns of daily life; her corporeal existence was his only guarantee of these conditions. Her ailments were anxiously reported and discussed.

In December the queen's toothache came to a raging climax that kept her without sleep for forty-eight hours. Elizabeth was forty-five, but she had never had a tooth pulled out, and combined with unwillingness to lose one was a shrinking from the operation itself. A meeting of the Privy Council was convened to deal with this emergency, at which the ministers listened to the opinion of a tooth-drawer called Fenatus. What he recommended was immediate extraction by the ordinary method.

The council, having heard him, decided upon extraction and a body of them, taking a surgeon with them, waited on the exhausted queen. They had the advantage that among their number was Elizabeth's lifelong admirer John Aylmer, the former tutor of Lady Jane Grey, who was now bishop of London. He said to her that he had not many teeth left in his head, but such as he had were entirely at her service. The surgeon should now pull one of them out, and she would see that it was no such great matter. The surgeon then drew one of the bishop's teeth, and the queen consented to have her own taken out.

To her intimate circle, her fearfulness perhaps endeared her as much as her heroic qualities. It made men regard her, not as an amazon who was their superior, but as a precious being to be guarded with their lives.

Chapter 18

ALENÇON'S ENVOY and confidential friend, Jehan de Simier, arrived in London on January 5, and according to the Spanish ambassador, Don Bernardino de Mendoza, a consultation of the queen's doctor was held a few days before, to decide if she could expect to bear a child. The doctors, said Mendoza, "foresaw no difficulty." The ambassador's words do not sound like those of doctors discussing the prospect of a first confinement after forty-five, but at least the gist of his report appears to confirm that the queen was not considered physically incapable of childbearing. This important matter being settled, the queen received Simier and his suite; and now opened the last, and the most dazzling of the interludes of Elizabeth's favorite pastime. It had everything to make it brilliant, except the person of the wooer, who for the time being, was out of sight. The queen was incomparably more important as a match than she had been in earlier courtships, and yet she still preserved an unusual measure of youth and looks for a woman of her years. "Her skin," said Bohun, "was pure white, and her beauty lasted to her middle age."

Elizabeth had enjoyed a good deal of amorous skirmishing, but the game had for the most part been played rather more stylishly by her than by the opponents. Now she was in the hand of a master. The French are considered to make love better than anybody else, and Simier was admitted by the French themselves to possess *une connaissance exquise des gaietés d'amour*. But his charm, his gallantry, his attentiveness would hardly have achieved their success if he had not felt some genuine admiration; the French value for esprit made her, in a purely amatory sense, perhaps more congenial to a Frenchman than to another.

Simier's task was to carry on a courtship by proxy for a dubious and grotesque young man and by this means to effect a complicated political maneuver; but the method gave him a chance to see at close quarters a most remarkable woman, and the opportunity was not thrown away on him. His response, in one kind, was genuine: he told the French king that her wit was admirable; and the eagerness with which he expressed his own admiration and assured her of his master's, the liveliness and ardor of his behavior, the amusement, the elegance of his courting, played on the surface of the queen's susceptible emotions with consummate skill.

The enjoyment was ravishing; but contrary to appearances, it was not all-engrossing. There was a spectacle of more absorbing interest still: a terrestrial globe, on which could be traced the vast possessions of Spain, the size of France with its extensive coastline, the Netherlands territory, complete conquest of which would give either Spain or France the undisputed mastery of Europe, and the smallness of England and Wales which made one kingdom, with an inimical Ireland in the west and to the north a Scotland which at any moment might become inimical.

The French match was scanned with the utmost narrowness by the council, whether for or against it. Sussex had always wanted to see Elizabeth married and a mother, and as he had already told her, he was in favor of this match, provided she could put up with the duke of Alençon. Burghley appeared also to be in favor of it but he was more doubtful than Sussex of its coming off. Hatton did not disapprove of the match, though he made it clear that should it take place his personal sufferings would be dreadful.

The one wholeheartedly against the affair was, not unnaturally, Leicester. The economic motive of his objection was unmistakable, but it is possible too that he was smarting from a sense of repudiated ownership. In huffing resentment, he put it about that Simier had caused Elizabeth to fall in love with Alençon by using "drinks and unlawful arts." Simier had at once recognized the chief enemy mission. He had been urgent, both with Alençon to come to England and with Elizabeth to promote his coming. He knew that the conditions Alençon was demanding—to be crowned immediately after marriage, to be associated with the queen in power, to have public exercise of the Catholic religion and a lifelong pension—would all be hardly digested by the government, while the people's view of the match was one of perfect abhorrence; but to overcome all this, in the last resort only one thing was necessary: the queen's signature on the marriage treaty. Simier wanted Alencon to come at once and strike while the iron was hot; then, in June, he learned that Leicester had persuaded the queen that out of regard to public dislike she should refuse Alençon a passport.

The secret of Leicester's marriage with Lettice Devereux was of the kind that Simier could have been relied on to detect, and the information gave him a weapon of extreme effectiveness. He urged the queen to understand that Leicester, in spite of the incalculable benefits he had received from her, was neither a faithful councillor nor a loyal friend. He was attempting to prevent her marriage—and by what right? He was married himself, and Simier related the facts of the secret wedding.

Elizabeth's rage was shattering. That she had repeatedly refused to marry Leicester herself was a straw against the torrential force of wounded affection, betrayed confidence, jealousy and anger. The court was at Greenwich, and she ordered Leicester's immediate arrest. In Greenwich Park there stood a tower that had been built by Henry VIII and called by him the Tower Mireflore, or Tower of the Wondrous Flower, because it had then given a lodging to Anne Boleyn. To this ill-omened place Leicester was sent to be out of the queen's sight; she declared that he should be committed to the Tower of London.

Again, a man saved her. As lord chamberlain, Sussex was in attendance at Greenwich. He disliked and distrusted Leicester, and most men in his position would at least have remained passive while the queen's vindictiveness took its course; but Sussex stepped in to save her from herself. It was true that she could send Leicester to the Tower although he had committed no legal offense; but Sussex told her that she must not do it. The damage to herself from such an act must be avoided at all costs. Under this strong-minded and sympathetic influence, the tempest spent itself harmlessly. The odious Lettice was given to understand that she must not show her face, but Leicester was released from the Mireflore and allowed to go quietly to Wanstead. Here he played the card he had found so successful once before. He became ill, very ill indeed. The terrific force of the queen's fury against Leicester had spent itself, and the alarm of hearing that he was ill in bed overcame the last of her anger. The two days she spent secretly at Wanstead gave Leicester the time, the opportunity he needed, and by throwing in the whole of his resources and summoning to his aid the experience of their past lives since eight years old, with everything it had taught him about her selfish passion and her unselfish loyalty, he managed to repair the injury and bridge the gulf.

Meanwhile a passport had been sent to Alencon, in the teeth of wide public disapproval. The duke arrived on the morning of August 16, so early that Simier was not out of bed. Travel-stained as he was, Alençon was all for starting to make love at once, and he ordered Simier to lead him to the queen immediately. Simier told him she could not be broken in upon at this hour of the morning; Alençon himself must first rest and be refreshed. The ambassador saw his master into bed, and then wrote a letter to be taken to the queen. In it he said: "At last I persuaded him to take some rest and soon got him between the sheets and I wish to God you were with him there as he could then with greater ease convey his thoughts to you."

The courtship was now carried on at first hand and the lovers appeared perfectly delighted with each other. People had supposed that Alençon's appearance would undo him, for he was not only puny and much pitted from smallpox, he had a nose so large it amounted to deformity. But he was ardent, civilized and a good talker; and if a young man of twenty-four could be found anywhere to make love convincingly to a woman who had talent, strangeness, elegance but not youth, he might, over-sophisticated and perverse, be found in the House of Valois. Elizabeth had the inveterate English habit of giving nicknames and Alençon was at once christened "Grenouille." The ancient Romans had used the frog as a charm for lovers, betokening mutual ardor and constancy.

Elizabeth with one of her suitors, the Frog Prince, who later became Charles IX of France.

All the while Alençon's presence was supposed to be secret, but it would not have amused the queen had it really been so. It was the public spectacle of his homage that she enjoyed most. At a court ball on August 23 Alençon was posted behind the arras; the queen danced, and in the pauses of the dance, she made gestures toward him as he craned out of his hiding place which those present pretended not to see. A crisis in his own affairs in France put an abrupt stop to these gay doings; the news that his friend Bussy d'Amboise had been killed in a duel caused Alençon to dash away on August 27. It was plain that the lover's absence was not to mean out of sight, out of mind. Elizabeth talked of her departed suitor continually, of his accomplishments and masculine graces, and wore upon her hand the superb diamond that Catherine de Médicis had chosen from her store as a betrothal ring.

The political situation which had given rise to the negotiations had now become acutely threatening. The religious war in France, which had so effectively acted as a brake on any hostile intentions of the French, was temporarily ended by the Treaty of Nérac, and Spain was about to annex Portugal on the death of its childless king. With France whole and disengaged, and Spain acquiring a substantial increase in territory and resources, alliance with a prince who, though bringing French friendship to England, would act in the Netherlands against Spain but independently of France was of extreme importance. To the success of the negotiations, it was essential that the queen should be believed to be in earnest—not that she had actually made up her mind to marry Alençon but that she was seriously considering the possibility and that French cooperation would bring about the desired result. It was amusing, it was delightful, but behind the pretense was stark, threatening reality. The pope had absolved her subjects from their allegiance to her; the King of Spain in open council had discussed her assassination as a prelude to the liberation and enthronement of the Queen of Scots; the wavering fortunes of the Netherland states might founder altogether beneath the Spanish power, and then the Spanish army would move across from the Low Countries to the shores of England. Should fortune favor France rather than

Spain, then the French would fulfill their long-cherished design of moving into Scotland, and streaming southward, join the disaffected Catholics in rescuing and exalting the Queen of Scots. The clue leading through this labyrinth to a position of temporary safety was the holding out to Alençon of the possibility of becoming King of England. So necessary was it that the game should be played exactly as the queen directed that for mere incautious gossiping Lady Derby and a friend had been shut up and not released till Alençon had gone; and then, no sooner had the duke left the shore, than John Stubbs, a high-minded, warmhearted, zealous Puritan, published a pamphlet called "The Discovery of a Gaping Gulf wherein England is like to be swallowed." The gulf was the French marriage.

The English dislike of foreign rule was now indissolubly connected with a fear of Catholic persecution. The idea of a French Catholic husband for the queen roused an abhorrence which, in the Puritans, reached almost to frenzy. The interesting feature of Stubbs's pamphlet is the warm, protective love it shows for the queen. He saw in the proposed alliance "the very foundation of our commonwealth dangerously digged at by the French, and our dear Queen Elizabeth (I shake to speak it) led blindfold as a poor lamb to the slaughter." The project was perilous to her in every way. He besought Heaven to grant her "honourable, healthful, joyful, peaceful, and long sovereignty, without any superior over-ruling commander, especially French, namely Monsieur."

The pamphlet was in every line an expression of loyalty and love but its appearance was inopportune to the last degree. By stating that Alençon could hardly be seriously considered as a suitor, and that if he were, he ought not to be, it cracked open that elaborate plan behind which the queen was manipulating a diplomatic course of extreme complexity. This offense was unforgivable and it was combined with another.

Elizabeth's marriage negotiations had been of great diplomatic value all through the reign, but now she was forty-five. This instrument would not be within her hold much longer, for though a foreigner would be willing to marry the Queen of England without prospect of children, the English Parliament would never sanction such a match except in hope of heirs. Such negotiations could not be carried on once the queen was obviously past the age of childbearing. Stubbs's words were kindness itself but they had the ruthless realism of family conversation. Stubbs had now put it in print for all to read, that the graceful and passionate lovemaking she had received from Alençon was a sham, and could not be anything else.

This serious attempt at interference with her diplomacy, edged as it was with a sexual insult, put Elizabeth almost beside herself. Stubbs, the publisher and the printer were put on trial in October on a charge of seditious libel.

The court exonerated the printer, but Stubbs and the publisher were found guilty, and a penalty was imposed on them which had been devised in Mary Tudor's reign to punish the libelers of her and Philip; it was that the convicted man should have his right hand cut off. This savage and odious sentence caused a great deal of public disapproval, from sympathy with Stubbs and his arguments, but Elizabeth was fiercely determined on it. She had no mercy on a loyal, warmhearted subject who said she was too old to marry and could not exert any genuine attraction over a man as young as her French suitor.

When the men's right hands were cut off by the executioner with a butcher's cleaver, the bleeding was stopped by searing the stump with a hot iron. Elizabeth was the more disgraced because when her sentence had been carried out, Stubbs pulled off his hat with his left hand and cried: "God save the Queen!" before he fell in a dead faint. The crowd were ominously silent.

Chapter 19

On New Year's Day, 1580, the earl of Leicester gave the queen fifteen large and thirty-six smaller gold buttons; his marriage notwithstanding, they were engraved with his arms and decorated with diamonds and rubies arranged in true-love knots.

While his uncle did his best by these charming improprieties to undermine Alençon's influence, Philip Sidney went more directly to work. Sidney, as a boy of eighteen, had been in

Walsingham's household in Paris during the Massacre of St. Bartholomew, and like Stubbs, he did not separate the religious from the political issue; his personal abhorrence of the match was inevitable. Sidney resolved to put the matter to the queen in a strong light, and he wrote her a letter, explaining to her that the French match would not do. "A Frenchman and a Papist, a son of the Jezebel of our age!" The English abhorred the very notion of such an alliance, and it would cause them to withdraw from her the affection which, Sidney could assure her, they had entertained for her up till now.

Sidney reminded her that she had always said she would never marry from personal inclination and he pointed out to her with solemn kindness that if she were to contract a marriage that was both disagreeable to her and disastrous for the realm, "it were a dear purchase of repentance." Then the young man who was so ready to instruct and guide the sharpest woman in the world disappeared, and for an unforgettable moment his place was taken by the poet. "Nothing can it add unto you but the bliss of children, which I confess were a most unspeakable comfort." But, Sidney continued, a marriage with Alençon was not the only means of getting children. The advantages of marrying him were no greater than those attached to marrying anybody else, and the disadvantages were exceptional. And this brought Sidney to another point. A marriage with such a man would give credence to those scandalous stories about the queen that Sidney himself, he said, always regarded as blasphemy. "No, no, excellent Lady, do not raze out the impression you have made in such a multitude of hearts."

In writing to the queen in such a strain Sidney showed courage. There was no fear of his meeting with a penalty such as Stubbs had suffered, for Stubbs's remonstrance was not only much more offensive in itself—it had been printed; while Sidney's was confined to a private letter. But it was plain speaking on a topic on which the queen did not invite plain speaking. It was not surprising that during this year Sidney left the court and spent much time at Wilton with his sister the young countess of Pembroke. Here, while she sat in the room with him, he wrote his chivalric romance, *Arcadia*.

AT THE END OF SEPTEMBER 1580 there occurred one of the great events in the history of the world. Francis Drake brought the *Golden Hind* into Plymouth after a voyage of three years in which he had sailed around the world. The effect of his achievement on national confidence and public imagination was indescribable. The exquisite Drake Cup, the bowl and cover two halves of a gold terrestrial globe, shows the desire to symbolize his achievement, and so, too, does the portrait of him wearing a doublet decorated with medallions formed by the world enclosed in a ring.

The political significance of Drake's exploit was, however, much narrower and of an urgent topical nature. The *Golden Hind*'s hold was crammed with silver, amounting in value to one and a half million ducats in money of the time, and with jewels whose value could scarcely be computed; this was loot from Spanish ships taken in the Pacific, whose vast emptiness the Spaniards had till then had entirely to themselves, and Mendoza, as the King of Spain's ambassador, demanded its return.

No one with a personal knowledge of the queen could have supposed that she would return it unless at the point of the sword. She herself had been among the investors in Drake's enterprise, and if the loot were retained they stood to gain one hundred percent on their outlay. Then, too, the splendor of Drake's success was a national asset; to allow the nation's enemy to take his spoils away from him would have been completely against the national feeling. The shares were paid out to the investors and to Drake himself, and the queen's commissioners were told that in making their inventory they were not to treat Drake with pettifogging exactitude. The captain was to be allowed to make his own dispositions. When all arrangements had been concluded, the great sum of bullion remaining was brought up to London and stowed away in the Tower.

Mendoza tried repeatedly to gain an audience of the queen, but he was told that her Majesty was at present looking into the question of Spanish interference in Ireland and would speak to him when she had been able to gain some insight into that situation. The infuriated ambassador was a little comforted by the actions of Burghley and Sussex. Drake had offered the former ten bars of gold and the latter a service of gold plate, but they had declined the presents, saying, according to Mendoza, that they did not feel they could accept things which had been stolen. Drake meanwhile had given a commission to some London jewelers for a present which he had no fear would be refused. From a quantity of diamonds and five enormous emeralds the jewelers fashioned a crown, and the queen wore it on New Year's Day, 1581.

AT THE FRENCH EMBASSY de La Mothe-Fénelon had been replaced by Mauvissière. The Alençon marriage was brought forward by the French with every show of willingness to meet the English queen's demands so far as this might be done. In April an embassy was to be sent from France to conclude the marriage treaty, and to house the festivities a banqueting pavilion was hurriedly built in the riverside garden of Whitehall.

While the pavilion was being built, the queen, on April 14, went to Deptford, where the *Golden Hind* had been laid up, and dined on board with Drake, on such a banquet as had not been seen, it was said, since the days of Henry VIII. She was attended by Alençon's confidential agent, Marchaumont, and as she entered the ship, her purple-and-gold garter came untied and trailed after her. Marchaumont besought the queen to give it to him to send to his master. Elizabeth said he could not have it for the time being as she had nothing else to keep up her stocking, and she made no ado about tying it again in front of him. She gave it to him when they got back to Westminster.

Meanwhile, after the banquet, the queen prepared to knight Drake. The Spanish demands for action against him were common hearing, and as he approached to kneel at her feet, she told him gaily she had a sword ready to cut off his head. She commanded Marchaumont to give the accolade, and as he did so, France was joined with England in honoring the man who had dealt such injuries to Spain.

Drake had a present ready for the queen to mark this occasion, and it was appropriately topical. Elizabeth already possessed among her ornaments "a little flower of gold with a frog thereon," and Drake now gave her, besides a large silver casket, a frog made all of diamonds. Nevertheless, or so Mendoza heard, the queen shortly thereafter summoned Burghley, Sussex, Leicester and Walsingham and told them that for some time past she had felt great repugnance at the prospect of the marriage.

At the end of April the French commissioners arrived, attended by five hundred followers. The queen, in a dress of gold tissue, wearing ornaments of diamonds and rubies, greeted the embassy in the great pavilion. The large and splendid reception appeared to confirm that the marriage would take place. The commissioners, after three days of banqueting, intimated that they would be glad to open their negotiation. They were summoned to Cecil House in the Strand, where Lord Burghley received them with much courtesy. Then, to the astonishment and dismay of the French, the first of the queen's delaying tactics was displayed. From notes prepared by Burghley, Walsingham made a speech to the effect that for the last eighteen months the mere rumor of this Catholic marriage for the English queen had heartened Catholic aggression. The pope had launched Jesuit missionaries into the kingdom and subsidized an invasion of Ireland; as to Alençon himself, he had entered into a treaty with the Flemish behind the queen's back. The queen had written to the prince about this matter, and Walsingham said the matter must halt until she received his reply. The commissioners were astounded and indignant. They said that now that the queen, by allowing Drake's depredations, had offended the King of Spain beyond repair, she needed the alliance with the Valois. The queen's ministers replied with stately reproof that her Majesty had no *need* of the alliance; the proposed marriage was one of affection only. They suggested that in the meantime a political treaty should be framed between France and England.

To such extraordinary statements the French had but one reply. They had come to make a marriage treaty, they had no authority to make one of any other kind. So far as they were concerned, it was that or nothing. Meanwhile the queen sent Alençon a letter, asking him to come to her. Alençon could not come immediately, for he had undertaken to raise the siege of

Cambrai, which was being beleaguered by Parma; but he declared that he would fly to England the moment he could and sent his fine clothes on in advance.

When Elizabeth received word that he was coming, her own attitude to the commissioners, which had been one of eager courtesy, underwent an alteration; she struck out from the proposed terms of the treaty the clause which granted Alençon the right to free exercise of his religion in England.

The sudden arrival of Alençon on June 2 exasperated the commissioners. They themselves were treating on behalf of his brother, King Henry III, and they felt that the unauthorized appearance of the bridegroom to treat over their heads could only darken counsel. Alençon remained, incognito, for two days, and during that time Elizabeth learned from him that the French king was forcibly disbanding his brother's levies. Alençon, therefore, was now dependent on English money to keep him in the field in the Netherlands, and henceforth his actions would be in the interests of England, not of France. So far as the position could be held, it was a triumph.

But the success barely gave time to draw breath. The position in Scotland had become very threatening. The young James, now fifteen years old, precocious, conceited, neurotic, had suffered keenly from an upbringing by severe Scots Puritans; and when a connection of the Lennox Stuarts, Esmé Stuart, Count d'Aubigny, was sent from France by the Guises to obtain a footing in the court of Scotland, the treacherous but charming young man made a complete conquest of his awkward, strange cousin. The only point on which Esmé Stuart met defeat was in attempting to convert James to Catholicism. With the young king so much under his influence, Stuart caused Morton, the Anglophile regent, to be arrested in the middle of a council meeting, and charged with complicity in the murder of Darnley. Morton confessed to having with others foreknown the deed, and said that nothing had been done to prevent it because it was known that the Queen of Scots desired it.

Honest but forbidding, he had never gained James's affection, and the latter lured him willingly to his death, treating him the day before his arrest with revolting deception, calling him his "father." News of this behavior aroused Elizabeth's disgust. Morton's condemnation and execution were a serious calamity, for they meant the eclipse of the English party in Scotland.

The Queen of Scots was filled with exultation at Morton's death. She wrote to Philip saying that James was abandoning the heretics who had brought him up and was planning to declare war on England to gain her release. All that was needed to implement the design was a promise of the Spanish king's support. It now seemed that the Catholic interest was to triumph once more in Scotland, bringing the old threat to England in its train. This gave to the negotiations with Alençon even more urgency. By the end of June it was understood that England would not consent to the marriage without a firm guarantee from Henry III of an Anglo-French alliance against Spain.

The French reply was: perform the marriage, and the alliance you desire will naturally follow. But Elizabeth would have repudiated this, even if she had meant to marry. The marriage would not necessarily bind the French king to join her and his brother in an alliance against Spain, but the protracting of the negotiations would prevent him from taking a step that could be construed as an act of hostility toward her. She wrote a letter to Alençon in July, in which she explained that she loved him tenderly, but it now seemed that the King of France would only move against Spain in conjunction with England after their marriage. She had always struggled to keep her realm at peace and this tying of her marriage to a war was something which for her people's sake she could not face. It would deprive her of their love. While matters remained at this pass, she could not see her way to marrying him.

Chapter 20

In August 1581 Alençon made the one successful feat of his military career and relieved Cambrai. In November he hastened over to England to gain another triumph.

Walsingham had written severe letters to the queen from Paris, blaming her for her irresolute conduct, and urging her once for all to make up her mind about the marriage; by this vacillation, he said, "you lose the benefit of time, which (your years considered) is not the least thing to be weighed."

It looked as if Elizabeth had taken his words to heart. On November 24 she was walking with Alençon in the gallery at Greenwich after dinner, when Mauvissière approached and asked if he might tell his master that the marriage would take place. The queen turned to Alençon and kissed him on the lips. She said: "You may tell his Majesty that the Prince will be my husband," and she withdrew a ring from her own hand and put it on Alençon.

Leicester and Hatton were aghast. It seemed that this time she had really gone too far to retreat. Hatton spoke to her with tears in his eyes; even the people's love for her, he said, would not be proof against this. To Leicester her conduct, particularly over the ring, seemed reckless to the verge of insanity.

But when Alençon's arrival had been announced the queen had sent to Burghley, who was laid up with gout. Her words were: "Let me know what you wish me to do." And when the news of the promise given at Greenwich was taken to him in his bed, Burghley had exclaimed: "God be thanked! Her Majesty has done her part. Now must Parliament do theirs."

The queen had done her part: she had gained time; she had for the present bound Alençon to her completely, and she had sown the seeds of discord between him and Henry III, for the English Parliament would be instructed to demand terms which the French king would refuse, thus infuriating his brother.

And now the unraveling of the web began. Elizabeth, after a wakeful night, sent a message to Alençon that she feared, if she married him, she would not have long to live; she hoped he did not want his love to prove fatal to her. She would be his friend, always, even more than if she had married him. Alençon was thunderstruck. He tore off the ring and pitched it on the ground, cursing the inconstancy of women and islanders.

At this inappropriate moment the envoy arrived from Henry III, bearing his congratulations; and so earnest was the French king to complete the matter, that every stipulation made by the English council was agreed to, one after another—until the queen said she must have Calais back again. This preposterous demand was taken as an insult, and Leicester, really alarmed, suggested raising two hundred thousand pounds and sending Alençon back to the Netherlands with it. Elizabeth, oblivious of what was plain to everybody else, namely, that the French in their indignation were on the verge of severing diplomatic relations, absolutely scoffed at the idea of giving away so much good money. She said if Alençon thought fit to forget her in exchange for her money, she would neither marry him nor give him any money, and he might do the best he could.

Though she had made up her mind to it, the actual process of dislodging the Frog Prince proved unexpectedly difficult. He declared that sooner than leave the queen without marrying her, he would rather they both perished. Elizabeth exclaimed that he must not threaten a poor old woman in her own kingdom. The young man, who had been pitiably tried, cried out: "No, no, Madame, you mistake. I meant no hurt to your blessed person. I meant only that I would sooner be cut in pieces than not marry you and so be laughed at by the world," and he burst into tears. The queen gave him her handkerchief.

At last, in return for substantial promises of money, and on the understanding that he should come back in six weeks and marry her, Alençon consented to depart. But it was the end of December; a great onshore gale sprang up and blew continuously, and the climax of leave-taking spun out into a long and agitating anticlimax. The queen sent for Sussex; while the winter winds raged, she told something of her secret to the man whose chivalry had protected and comforted her for thirty years. She hated the idea of marriage more every day, she said; she had reasons against it that she would not divulge to a twin soul, if she had one.

That such words were brought to Mendoza was due not only to his exceptional ability as an organizer of spies, but to the sixteenth-century fashion of living in public. In great houses one large room opened into another, and only at the end of the suite, in a small room a few yards square with one window and a small hearth, was it possible to hold a completely private conversation. Elsewhere, ushers and ladies- and gentlemen-in-waiting were always within sight, if not within earshot. With so many people to work upon, a great deal could be picked up, but Mendoza's system was remarkably clever; it moved from point to point up to the queen's very bedside, and back again to the Spanish embassy.

The gales which prevented Alençon from leaving the shore blew the French commissioners across the Channel in a trice. Henry III's secretary, Pinart, arrived in mid-January. His errand was a simple one. It was to say that if the English queen persisted in her present course, she would drive his master to seek alliance with the King of Spain.

At this threat, the nearest approach to mortal peril her diplomacy had yet encountered, the queen passed an entirely sleepless night. In the morning she was feverish and stayed in bed. After dinner she sent for Sussex to her bedside and told him she supposed she must sacrifice herself—she must marry Alençon. Sussex begged her not to discuss the matter with him anymore; let her only tell him her decision when she had made it.

But Burghley took a different course. After some members of the council had visited the queen, he stayed behind for a private interview. He told her that in face of the Franco-Spanish threat, Alençon must be gratified either by the marriage or by a large quantity of money. Both alternatives were distressing, but one or the other must be adopted immediately.

Once the necessity of it was admitted, the choice itself presented no difficulty. Thirty thousand pounds was made over to Alençon, with bills for twenty thousand pounds more, and a squadron prepared to take him to Flushing, where the Netherlanders were offering to make him duke of Brabant. The earl of Leicester was to sail with him, and the queen herself accompanied him as far as Canterbury. She besought him, in moving terms, to take the greatest care of himself. Nothing could exceed the sensibility, the elegance and the absurdity of her leave-taking. But while the party was at Rochester, an expedition was made to show Alençon the dockyards at Chatham. They presented a spectacle that took the Frenchmen's breath away. The masts of completed ships shaded the quays like groves, while in the yards vessels were building upon new and improved designs of which the world was presently to see the advantage. With enthusiastic courtesy the French exclaimed: Well might nations call Queen Elizabeth the Queen of the Sea! The queen assured Alençon that these ships should do him service if he needed it; but she was pleased with the opportunity to show the sight to foreigners.

Alençon embarked at the end of February. He wrote letters to Elizabeth full of desolation at leaving her, and she exclaimed she would give a million pounds to have her frog swimming in the Thames again.

Chapter 21

IN JUNE 1583 ELIZABETH had a terrible loss. Sussex died. His aid as a councillor could not compare with Burghley's, and she felt nothing for him to compare with what she felt for Leicester; but the quality of his loyalty was like no one else's. He died expressing it. Hatton was beside him, and Sussex knew that Hatton and Leicester were colleagues. He said: "Beware of the gipsy. He will betray you. You do not know the beast as well as I do."

Leicester was, indeed, deep in plans. He had approached Lady Shrewsbury to suggest a future marriage between the fated Arabella Stuart and his son by his wife Lettice, the child who was to die at six years of age, and whose tiny suit of armor is in Warwick Castle. But it was within the verge of possibility that Arabella Stuart, a descendant of Henry VIII's sister, might one day be Queen of England, and her redoubtable grandmother was in no hurry to afford yet another speculation to the house of Dudley. Leicester had another plan. His wife had presented him with two stepdaughters; he and Lettice thought one of the girls might be married to the young King of Scotland. This came to Elizabeth's ears, and to disapproval of a scheme so unsuitable in itself was added a passion of anger against the presumption of the countess. Elizabeth exclaimed that she would sooner see James stripped of his crown than married to one of that she-wolf's cubs. The matter was discreetly dropped.

Leicester, who had Mauvissière to dine at his house, and introduced him to his wife (of whom, Mauvissière said, he appeared extremely fond), told the ambassador sadly that he had now lost his favor with the queen. But the storms of the relationship showed only how enduring it was; by September it was said: "My Lord of Leicester groweth in great favour with her Majesty."

A comet appeared over London, and the general fear was that it boded the death of some great person. Elizabeth was at Richmond when it was seen, and the ominous supposition, unspoken, was felt by those around her. She braved it, "with a courage answering to the greatness of her state." She ordered the window to be opened on the sinister light and walked toward it, saying: *"Iacta alea est"*—"The die is cast."

The probability of attempts upon her life had been recognized since the Papal Bull of 1570. The pope had sanctioned her murder, provided it was undertaken in a proper spirit; it had been discussed in open council at Madrid, and now it formed a necessary feature of the invasion being planned by the duke of Guise, uncle of Mary Queen of Scots. This was to be paid for by the Spanish king, but launched in the pope's name, and it was believed that thousands of Catholics would rise all over the country to welcome the invaders. Guise and his brother Mayenne had at first considered having Elizabeth assassinated without waiting for the invasion, but somehow the design fell through. Philip's comment was: "If they had done it, it would have been no harm, though they should have made provision of certain things before-hand."

This extreme caution of the Spanish king's in fact assured the failure of the enterprise before it started. Walsingham got wind of the conspiracy, and the capture of Francis Throckmorton, a nephew of Elizabeth's old minister, placed a mass of incriminating documents in the council's hands. Throckmorton twice courageously withstood the agonies of the rack. The third time his resistance collapsed, and he revealed some extremely alarming information: the plans for the landing of Guise and his brother, the names of the Catholics who were expected to support him, the connivance of Mendoza, and finally that the Queen of Scots was conversant with the whole. When he had finished his confession the pitiable man rose from a seat beside the rack and exclaimed: "Now I have betrayed her who was dearest to me in this world." Now, he said, he wanted nothing but death.

The publication of the conspiracy aroused the fiercest passion in large numbers of the people, both of fury against the Queen of Scots and of love and protection for the English queen. On December 19 Mauvissière described to Henry III how he had ridden with Elizabeth from Hampton Court to London. The queen was riding a splendid horse and she and the ambassador were at some distance from the retinue. The roads were in their winter state but people knelt down in the mud as she passed, calling out blessings on her and wishing that her enemies and theirs might be punished. After one such demonstration the queen said to him, she perceived that not *everyone* wished her dead.

But the dangers of Mary Stuart and the Catholic powers, that had loomed from the day of Elizabeth's accession, were massing, and in spite of the people's love, there was treachery at home. Throckmorton's was less unnerving than Norfolk's had been, but it was more serious because the invasion it had tried to bring about had been far nearer success than Ridolfi's attempt.

The opening of the final act before the storm was the dismissal of Mendoza. The Privy Council received him, and as he did not speak English readily, Walsingham addressed him in Italian on behalf of the rest. Mendoza was told that he had abused his diplomatic privileges; therefore it was her Majesty's pleasure that he should leave the kingdom within fifteen days. Mendoza declared that he must first inform his master of her decision: whereupon the whole council rose to their feet and told him that he must depart without waiting.

The Queen of Scots was the center of this aspect of European politics, and also of the family situation of Lord Shrewsbury. The great earl had been chosen for her guardian not only for his enormous possessions, his castles and manors, and his influence in his own neighborhood, but for his character; he had sufficient breadth to be sympathetic to Mary while being inflexibly loyal to Elizabeth. The flaw was in his wife. Bess of Hardwick was much liked by people so long as she was on their side. Elizabeth had said she would always be glad to see Lady Shrewsbury at court, and in one of his early letters Shrewsbury had written: "My sweetheart, I give God thanks daily . . . that He hath sent you me in my old years to comfort me withal." When his long trial was over, he was to thank the queen for having delivered him from two devils, the Queen of Scots and his wife. The domestic situation was made difficult by the grasping and shrewish temper of the wife and the properties she had inherited from previous husbands, which absorbed money and attention that her present husband thought due to himself. Lady Shrewsbury had once been on very intimate terms with the illustrious prisoner: they had taken great pleasure in each other's society. But when the countess became the grandmother of a potential heiress to the English throne, her feelings toward the presumptive heiress underwent an alteration. An indiscreet intimacy was followed by a vindictive quarrel, and as the countess's feud with her husband was now raging, she and her sons William and Charles Cavendish put it about that the Queen of Scots was the earl's mistress and had borne him a child.

Mary had a long-pent-up torrent of anger and hatred to discharge; with deft economy, she wrote a letter to Elizabeth, detailing repulsive slanders against her and citing Lady Shrewsbury as the source of the information. The latter had told her, she said, that Elizabeth had lain with a man to whom she had promised marriage, she had lain with Alençon and with Simier, and to Simier she had betrayed the secrets of her councillors. She had so much embarrassed Hatton by the love she showed him, he had been obliged to leave the court. She swallowed such ludicrous flattery, her ladies dared not look at each other for fear of laughing; in her ungovernable ferocity, she had broken the finger of one and hacked another with a knife. Mary concluded by saying that she had many more things "in reserve," and would tell them to Elizabeth if a meeting could be arranged between them.

The passage about Hatton suffered from Lady Shrewsbury's not having had a sight of his letters to the queen, while the statement that Elizabeth had betrayed state secrets to Simier showed that neither lady had the artist's gift of knowing where to stop. As the letter was found with Lord Burghley's papers, it was assumed that with masculine discretion he kept it from Elizabeth's hands.

The accusation against the Queen of Scots and Lord Shrewsbury was, however, brought to the queen's ears by the earl himself, with a demand for retribution against his wife. The countess and her two sons were summoned before the Privy Council, and there they all admitted having repeated the slander, but only because they had heard it from other people; they said they themselves had never believed it. The queen said she hoped a reconciliation between husband and wife might now come about, but the Shrewsburys had so many and such varied causes of mutual recrimination, they had quarreled themselves to a standstill. Well, said the queen, would Shrewsbury accept her efforts at mediation? A grateful acceptance was returned and the family papers were made available to the queen's advisers. Deeds were scrutinized, settlements, expenses, contributions. The inventories of household stuff were examined, down to a very porringer which the countess had taken away while the earl kept hold of the lid. Then the queen invoked Walsingham's assistance, and between them they drew up a suggested scheme by which the countess was to receive three hundred pounds a year housekeeping money plus expenses for fuel and to have the wages paid for five servants.

The Queen of Scots had meanwhile been transferred to the keeping of Sir Ralph Sadler, a less sympathetic guardian.

THE GERMAN TRAVELER von Wedel, who visited England at this time, saw the queen at a Christmas dinner in 1584, in mourning for Alençon, whom disease had brought to a premature end the previous May. The queen wore black velvet, sumptuously embroidered in silver and pearls, and "a silver shawl of mesh, diaphanous like a tissue of gossamer, hung down to the hem of her skirt."

Ever-increasing prosperity had brought a degree of luxury that exasperated the moralists. The queen loved rich and precious objects. In Hampton Court Palace there was a small chamber called Paradise; it was indeed like the mystic's vision of heaven, for it was all color, transparency and light. Its walls were paneled with gold and silver; the chair of state stood under a canopy studded with pearls and precious stones, among which large diamonds, sapphires and rubies shone out "like the sun among stars." On one wall hung a crimson cloth, the royal arms emblazoned on it, in their center a table diamond of enormous size and luster. This small brilliant room contained a musical instrument of fairylike strangeness; except for its strings, it was made entirely of glass.

The reach of the river in front of Whitehall Palace was covered with swans, and in the palace garden were thirty-four columns, each surmounted by the effigy of a heraldic beast. In this palace was the great tilt yard; stands for spectators surrounded three sides of it, but the fourth was looked down upon by the windows of a long room in the palace.

On feast days the queen dined in public, and von Wedel saw her in the great hall at Greenwich. She sat at a table alone, and after she had sat down, five countesses took their seats at another table. The visitor saw in attendance Lord Leicester, Lord Howard of Effingham, who had succeeded Sussex as lord chamberlain, Lord Hertford and Sir Christopher Hatton. He described them as "handsome old gentlemen." The queen barely stayed till the second course was brought. The countesses, who had watched for her to move, rose just before she did and curtsied deeply twice. The queen turned her back to the hall while two bishops said grace; then a gold basin and a towel were brought her, and she took off a ring which she handed to the lord chamberlain. When she had washed her hands, she put it on again.

A stately dance was performed by ladies "slender and beautiful but no longer very young." This was followed by an extremely lively one by young men, who took off their cloaks and swords and danced with the young ladies. While this was going on, the queen held conversations, summoning young and old, and talking continuously. When she had finished, she waved her hand to the assembled company, and withdrew to her chamber.

Chapter 22

THE EVIDENCE against Mary Stuart discovered through Throckmorton was not pressed against her; but the Privy Council, who had always foreseen what would happen to them if Elizabeth were murdered, had been infuriated by it and they drew up what they called a Bond of Association by which they bound themselves, in event of the queen's murder, to pursue to death not only the persons who were guilty of the act, but the person in whose interests it had been done. Signatures were invited, and a mass of documents bearing signatures and seals were shown to the queen at Hampton Court.

A Parliament full of alarm and determination was opened in October 1584. The principal business was the matter of the queen's safety. The Houses adopted the Privy Council's Bond of Association, but the queen herself insisted on some modifications of it. She sent word by Sir Christopher Hatton that a claimant on whose behalf treason was undertaken must not be summarily put to death, but be tried before a committee of councillors, bishops and judges. Parliament wanted to make the heir to such a claimant also forfeit his right to the succession, but the queen demurred. If the Protestant James were to be excluded, the basis of her negotiations with Scotland would be lost. The matter finally stood that in the event of a rebellion or assassination of the queen, any claimant who, before a commission, could be proved to have had foreknowledge of the act, should be put to death. At the Christmas recess, the queen sent the House of Commons her thanks for their care of her, which she declared to be greater than she deserved. And when the members' thanks were returned for her gracious message, the queen sent again: "most hearty and loving thanks unto this whole House, yea, redoubling to them their thanks, to ten thousand, thousand fold." Hatton told the House he had a prayer in his pocket, written by a godly man for the queen's preservation. He asked if he should read it aloud. This he did, sentence by sentence, the House repeating it after him on their knees.

So far, the queen's preservation appeared miraculous, and she herself ascribed it to the protection of God. The Puritans, in the person of Walsingham, feared that her religious convictions were faint, and Cardinal Allen said she had no religion at all. But the English prayers written by herself show a poignant, unforced earnestness: "Thou has set me on high, my flesh is frail and weak. If I therefore at any time forget Thee, touch my heart, O Lord, that I may again remember Thee."

THE PRINCE OF ORANGE had already asked the English queen to accept the sovereignty of Holland, Zeeland and Utrecht, and she had refused it. When Orange was murdered in the same year that Alençon's death occurred, the states renewed the offer and Elizabeth refused it again. This was, perhaps, one of the most original acts performed by an English monarch. To accept would mean that England was inescapably committed to open war with Spain. Elizabeth did not even consider it. She promised armed assistance in exchange for holding the ports of Flushing, Brill and Rammikens, but the sovereignty of the provinces, bringing with it an invitation to a full-scale Spanish war, she would not have in any circumstances. An English force was to be sent and some English noble, who was prepared to spend a great deal of his own money on the enterprise, must be chosen to lead it. Though Lord Leicester was not a general, capable officers would be with him, and Burghley and Walsingham both considered that he had sufficient ability and experience to manage the administrative side of the task.

The necessity of helping the Netherlanders to hold the Spaniards in check so that they might be kept out of England was obvious, but the risk of Spanish reprisals, and the expense, caused Elizabeth so much uncertainty that she had worn down Walsingham to a state of grim endurance before she had made up her mind to it. At the very last moment, he received a letter from Leicester saying that the queen had been so low in her mind that evening "by reason of her oft-disease taking her of late, and this night worst of all," that she had "used very pitiful words" to him, he said, "of her fear that she shall not live, and would not have me from her." Walsingham might imagine how this had affected him; he had comforted her as well as he could and reminded her of how forward his preparations were. He admitted that he, too, was worn down by her varying purpose, "weary of life and all." However, he was at last embarked with his train, taking Philip Sidney with him, and arrived in the Netherlands in January 1586.

Hardly had he done so, when the states, thinking that a titular head would make easier the complicated task of unifying their separate, conflicting forces, and determined somehow to force the Queen of England to throw the whole weight of her alliance into their scale, offered the position which she had refused to Leicester. Inconceivable as it would appear that a man who understood Elizabeth's position should have accepted the offer, there was one thing yet more impossible: that the son of Northumberland should refuse it. Leicester was created governor-general of the United Provinces, and the letter in which he announced the fact to Elizabeth, with an explanation of his motives, did not reach her until she had already learned the fact itself.

She had been ailing, languishing, scarcely able to relinquish him when he left, but this news restored her to all her powers. She wrote a letter which she dispatched by Sir Thomas Heneage: "How contemptuously we conceive ourselves to have been used by you, you shall by the bearer understand. . . . We could never have imagined . . . that a man raised up by ourself, and extraordinarily favoured by us above any other subject of this land, would in so contemptuous a sort have broken our commandment." The description of the ceremonial festivities that had marked Leicester's inauguration had reached her, and with her unerring instinct for the effective, she announced that on the very spot where he had received the office, there, in the eyes of all, he must resign it. But Heneage, as well as others in the Netherlands and at home, could see that however ill judged Leicester's acceptance might have been, such a public humiliation would be disastrous, and advised a temporizing course.

The queen's anger was fanned by Lady Leicester's doings. Here, the countess thought, was a superb opportunity to assert and display herself, and the queen, already justly angry with

Leicester, heard that his wife was about to join him in the Netherlands "with such a train of ladies and gentlewomen, and such rich coaches, litters and side-saddles as her Majesty had none such, and that there should be a court of ladies as should far pass her Majesty's court here."

This project was decisively quashed; but Burghley and Walsingham made the strongest protests against Elizabeth's order to cancel the governor-generalship. They were in entire agreement with her as to the striking effect her plan would produce; and Burghley said the results would be so catastrophic that if she persisted in it, he must resign from the government. This powerful remonstrance and touching letters from Leicester, full of contrition and remorse, led the queen at last to concede that he might retain his honors. The passion of anger against him was succeeded, as always, by a relenting tenderness.

The campaign was a hopeless maze of administrative difficulties, and its only decided action was Leicester's attempt to take Zutphen, in which Philip Sidney was wounded in the thigh and carried off the field. His wife, Walsingham's beautiful daughter, came out to nurse him, but he died of blood poisoning three weeks later. The shock and the woe felt at the untimely death of a hero and a poet echo still in memorial verse. The present year, however, was to bring a crisis that overshadowed every other happening.

The Queen of Scots had been in close communication with Elizabeth's enemies for the past seventeen years; she had encouraged all their plans for invasion of England and used her money to pay their agents. From her point of view she was eminently justified in doing so, but the disclosures of Throckmorton determined the English government that she must not be allowed to do it any longer. She had been removed to Tutbury Castle, this time under the guardianship of Sir Amias Paulet, loyal, puritanical, and so efficient that when told by the Privy Council that he must prevent Mary or any of her servants from communicating with the outside world except through him, all private communication to and from the prisoner was completely checked.

But in 1586 Walsingham was extremely anxious to have an

insight into Philip's intentions toward England, for these must guide English policy in the Netherlands, and it was inconvenient that the Queen of Scots should be incommunicado. Walsingham therefore got Elizabeth's consent to an arrangement, but he confided it to none of the council, not even to Burghley. Mary and her household had been removed to Chartley in December 1585, and there Mary was betrayed by Walsingham's spy, Gifford, into resuming her secret correspondence through a medium Walsingham had devised. Her letters were sent out in a beer barrel, and the answers sent in to her in the same way. The brewer was in her pay but also in Walsingham's, and every letter that went to or from Chartley was deciphered by Walsingham's expert, Phillips, and then forwarded to its destination. Walsingham, having set up this elaborate machinery, now watched Mary's intrigues developing.

The crisis was not long delayed. In May there appeared under Walsingham's eye the last and most formidable of the plots for the queen's assassination. It had originated with Ballard, a Jesuit, and was concerted with Morgan, the Queen of Scots' agent in Paris who managed the payments to her of her dowry. It was discussed there with Mendoza, who told Philip it was the most hopeful of the plots yet undertaken because it was based on the murder of Elizabeth, without which it was now assumed that no plot could be expected to succeed. Morgan had drawn into it the rich young Catholic, Anthony Babington, who had long cherished a romantic devotion to the Queen of Scots; and Morgan, Ballard, Babington and Mary herself were all duped by Gifford, a sinister youth with an abnormal look of innocence. Babington had chosen six of what he called "noble gentlemen," all in positions about the court, who were only waiting the appropriate moment to shoot or stab Elizabeth, and in June, Morgan wrote to Mary's secretary Curle, saying: "There be many means in hand to remove the beast that troubles all the world."

Every word was noted by Walsingham before it reached Chartley: and in the last week in June, Mendoza's agent reported a strange thing of Queen Elizabeth. She was going to chapel, in full magnificence, when suddenly she was "overcome by a shock of fear." The pang was so severe she could not recover herself, but at once returned to her apartments, "greatly to the wonder of those present."

Mary meanwhile had heard that England and Scotland had signed a treaty, in which she herself was not once mentioned. In her rage and indignation she determined that her heretical son must never become King of England, and she informed Mendoza that she was bequeathing the English crown to the King of Spain.

She might, however, first wear it herself. A letter to her from Babington of July 12 outlined, in an almost final form, the plans for her release and for her ascending the throne. A harbor must be chosen for the landing of the Spanish troops Parma was expected to send, Babington himself would undertake to rescue her from her jailers, and then he mentioned the third, essential point: "the usurping competitor" must be "despatched." Six noble gentlemen, he said, were ready to undertake "that tragical execution."

Elizabeth sometimes gave the impression that she was insensible to fear, but she was not; she was terrified now, but she held on. In many respects she treated Walsingham badly, but in the supreme effort of his career, she supported him at the risk of her life. Babington and some of the conspirators could be seized on the strength of the letter; but the letter had not yet been answered. On the answer to the letter would depend the greatest catch of all. As Phillips wrote to Walsingham: "We attend her very heart at the next." Mary's reply was written on July 19, a long, detailed comment on the plans for her rescue, cautioning and encouraging, telling Babington to find out from Mendoza just when the Spanish help might be expected. Then she wrote: "When all is ready, the six gentlemen must be set to work, and you will provide that on their design being accomplished, I may be myself rescued from this place." This letter contained almost everything Walsingham wanted, but before he sent it on, he forged a postscript which was added to the cipher, asking for the names of the six gentlemen.

Babington was not at Lichfield, where he was expected to receive the letter, and the letter was eleven days in reaching him. During this time the queen came very close to death. The six had been chosen because they had means of coming into her presence, and could stab or shoot her as she sat on her dais, or went to chapel, or walked in the garden, for it was well known that she went about unguarded. Babington, in the height of elation, had had a picture painted of himself and his six accomplices; someone, possibly Gifford, had got possession of the picture long enough to show it to the queen and, it seemed, only just in time. She was walking in Richmond Park with her ladies and a few gentlemen, of whom Hatton was one, when, on the outskirts of the group, she saw Barnwell, an Irishman whose portrait was among the six. She gave him a long, penetrating stare, and as he slunk away he heard her say to Sir Christopher Hatton, "Am I not well guarded today, with no man near me who wears a sword at his side?" Barnwell repeated this in his trial, and Hatton, who was one of the commissioners, told him grimly that had anyone else recognized him he would not have got away as he did.

Walsingham began the rounding up of the conspirators by arresting Ballard in August, on the ostensible ground that he was a disguised seminary priest; the rest took fright and fled, precipitating their arrest. Fourteen in all were taken up, but these arrests were less important than the final bringing home to the Queen of Scots of being an accessory to the deed. Under pretense of a hunting expedition she was conducted from Chartley to Sir Walter Aston's park at Tixall; here she was arrested in the queen's name and detained while her rooms at Chartley were searched, and her papers, her letters from the Catholics abroad, the lists of those whom she relied upon to support her at home, and the keys to sixty different ciphers were collected, sealed and sent to London. The list of the English nobles who had tendered their allegiance to Mary as their future sovereign was shown to Elizabeth. She read the names and then burned the list, remarking: *"Video taceoque"*—"I see, and I say nothing."

The trials of Ballard, Babington and their twelve confederates resulted inevitably in the verdict of hanging and quartering, the sentence for treason. The severity of the sentence depended on whether the victim were, as it enjoined, cut down alive to be disemboweled, or allowed to remain hanging till he was dead so that the butcher's work was performed on a corpse.

Elizabeth had endured the submerged menace of assassination for fourteen years, since Ridolfi's attempt had failed. The anger she had felt at the rising in the north was renewed, while mounting rage against Mary Stuart's attempts to unseat her, and the severe fright of knowing herself exposed to hourly risk of murder during the last four months, had lashed her into a state of savage fury. She exclaimed to Burghley that she thought hanging and quartering was not terrible enough; something worse should be thought of, that the populace might take a lesson from the just vengeance on traitors. Burghley explained to her that to alter the penalty would be illegal; and secondly, there was no need to find anything worse. The victims were dispatched in batches of seven on succeeding days, Babington among the first. On him and his fellows the sentence was exactly carried out; but before the second day's work, Elizabeth had undergone a revulsion of feeling, and the second batch of victims were allowed to hang till they were dead.

The hundreds of letters removed from Chartley were deciphered, every translation being signed by Burghley, Walsingham, Shrewsbury, Cobham and Knollys. The contents showed that Mary had been in correspondence over every plan to invade England or stir up domestic rebellion over the last eighteen years; but only in Ridolfi's plot and Throckmorton's plot had it been capable of proof that she knew of the intended murder of Elizabeth and on both these affairs Elizabeth had refused to prosecute her. On the evidence of Babington's letter and Mary's reply, it was not possible to refuse any longer.

Mary was brought to Fotheringhay Castle in Northamptonshire to stand her trial, and a commission of thirty-four, consisting of councillors, peers and judges, was convened, and set off, along bad roads in the unfavorable autumn weather. Burghley and Walsingham were of course the two principal actors; Walsingham's undersecretary, Davison, remained with the queen, who, whatever just cause for complaint she might give to the lord treasurer and the principal secretary, did not like being parted from both of them, especially as Leicester was abroad in the final phase of the Netherland campaign.

Mary's behavior at the trial was what it had always been when she was called to account: emotional, dignified, full of self-justification and refusing to give a straight answer to a straight question. She was to be charged with being accessory to the attempted murder of Elizabeth; she herself declared that she was about to die in the cause of her religion, and wrote telling the duke of Guise not to fear that she would fail in the supreme test.

It was an opportunity of a sort for which she had longed ever since she came into England. She felt her powers called for some such occasion, and as a display of personal courage, energy and virtuosity her performance over the two days was arresting; the one effect it did not achieve was that of truth. Mary's method of dealing with the evidence was to make denials that contradicted themselves, and then to withdraw to the position that it was impious for ordinary mortals to challenge the word of a queen. Everyone else was lying, it seemed; she only had the right to be believed. She did not speak to the point, but she spoke with flaming eloquence. She accused Burghley of being her adversary. He replied: "I am the adversary of the adversaries of Queen Elizabeth."

After two days' hearing, Elizabeth, from whom Fotheringhay was separated by many slow leagues, ordered the commission to return and finish their process in the Court of Star Chamber. The verdict was a foregone conclusion; it pronounced the Queen of Scots guilty of being privy to conspiracy and of "imagining and compassing her Majesty's death."

At the end of October Parliament reopened, but in view of the business to be discussed, the queen was not present. A petition from both Houses "that just condemnation should be followed by just execution" was carried by a deputation to the queen at Richmond. Sitting in her canopied chair, she made them a speech, vivid, familiar, confidential, on her past difficulties, her present shrinking from what they had come to urge:

"I protest . . . for mine own life, I would not touch her. Neither hath my care been so much bent how to prolong mine as how to preserve both, which I am right sorry is made so hard, yea, so impossible. . . . I have not used over-sudden resolutions in matters that have touched me full near: you will say that with me, I think." Their care, their anxiety to preserve her, touched her deeply; she would try to be worthy of such subjects. "And as for your petition, your judgment I condemn not . . . but pray you to accept my thankfulness, excuse my doubtfulness, and take in good part my answer—answerless."

But this would not do, and Burghley now had all his faculties addressed to the last and hardest stage of the task. The queen remained at Richmond and he came and went, lamenting the expense of time in journeying. At last he got her to consent that the sentence should be drawn up, should be published. On December 4 the publication was greeted with wild enthusiasm; bells pealed, bonfires blazed, psalms were sung "in every street and lane in the City." The death warrant had been engrossed at the same time: a mere clerkly matter, that received no publicity; but until the queen's signature had been written on it, the sentence could not be carried out.

The French court had sent an ambassador, Bellièvre, to protest against cutting off the head of a crowned queen and a sister-in-law of French kings, and this formal remonstrance was based on a sound political consideration: since Mary had bequeathed the English crown to Philip, at her death Philip would consider himself King of England and might come to take possession of his property. Elizabeth on the throne, and Mary a prisoner, appealed to the French as a preferable alternative. James, who now learned that his mother had lost the English crown for him and had advised his being sent to Spain to be reeducated as a Catholic, was in a state of strong resentment. But the Scots' national pride was outraged at the idea of the queen they had themselves rejected being put to death by the English, and under pressure of a temporary revival of feeling for her, James said his honor required that he should demand his mother's life. Let her, he said, be shut up in solitary confinement "in some firm manse"; her life was his only stipulation.

The diplomatic situation with France and Scotland was not the real obstacle to the execution. On December 19 Mary had written a long letter to Elizabeth. It omitted any mention of the charge on which she had been convicted, merely saying that she had been unjustly condemned by those who had no jurisdiction over her, and that she had "a constant resolution to suffer death for upholding the obedience and authority of the apostolical Roman church." Perverse ingenuity could go no further, but the rest of the letter was a series of requests for her servants, the treatment her body should receive after death, and for her burial. It harrowed Elizabeth; she wept as she read it and Leicester reported to Walsingham in some alarm: "There is a letter from the Scottish Queen, that hath wrought tears, but I trust shall do no further herein: albeit, the delay is too dangerous."

By January the mounting impatience had found expression in an outbreak of false alarms. It was said the Queen of Scots had broken out of prison, that the City of London had been set on fire, that a Spanish army had landed at Milford Haven. The court was at Greenwich, and on February 1, the lord admiral, Lord Howard of Effingham, came to the queen. His father had been her great-uncle and protector, Lord William Howard, his wife was Kate Carey, one of her favorite cousins; from this privileged position Lord Howard spoke with severe plainness. The people would not tolerate much more of this suspense, he said; the public temper was becoming dangerous.

The queen listened to him, as she had once listened to his father. She would sign the warrant, she said: let Davison bring it. Davison was out walking in Greenwich Park, and a summons brought him hurriedly indoors. He collected the papers he had by him for the queen's signature, the warrant among them, and sent in his name by Mrs. Brooks, the lady-in-waiting. The queen had him shown in at once.

Elizabeth said, the morning was so fine, had he been out? When Davison said he had, she asked if Lord Howard had told him to bring the warrant for the Queen of Scots' execution? Yes, said Davison. Elizabeth took it, read it through, then called for pen and ink and signed it. This done, she dropped it on the floor beside her. Then she asked what else he had brought her and signed the remaining documents. Davison stooped to take up the long-hoped-for prize, and the queen told him to carry it to the lord chancellor for sealing but to get this done as secretly as might be; on his way, she said, he had better call in at Walsingham's house; the latter was ill, and the news, said the queen with weird gaiety, would go near to kill him outright. Then in all seriousness she told Davison she had delayed so long that people might not think her eager to put the Queen of Scots to death. Davison was bowing himself out, but Elizabeth had not finished. By the Bond of Association, its members had bound themselves "to prosecute to the death" anyone found guilty of attempting the queen's life, and Elizabeth thought that of so much spontaneous zeal—they had been obliged to bring the signatures to Hampton Court in a trunk—a little might surely be found to do her a real service in the matter. It was not a question of whether Mary Stuart were to live or die: her death was decided. It was a question of *how* she was to die. Elizabeth had twice before said in Davison's presence that she felt some way should be found of relieving her of the hateful burden of dooming her rival to death. Called back on the threshold, he now heard himself asked whether Sir Amias Paulet and his fellow commissioner Sir Drue Drury could not take the business upon themselves. The queen commanded that he and Walsingham should write to Fotheringhay and sound them on the matter.

Davison went off to Walsingham and told him the morning's doings, then he carried the warrant to the chancellor to be passed under the Great Seal. On his return with it, he found Walsingham had written the letter to Sir Amias Paulet. The reply was prompt and in the terms that had been foreseen. Paulet said his goods and his life were at her Majesty's disposal, but he would not "make so foul shipwreck of his conscience as to shed blood without law or warrant," and Sir Drue Drury agreed with him.

Next day the queen asked Davison if the warrant had passed the seal. He replied that it had. The queen, it was clear, was not pleased with the answer. "What needeth that haste?" she said.

Her instructions the day before had not been, it was true, to get the warrant sealed "at once," but that had been their implication. Davison began to feel the creepings of alarm. As soon as he could get away he went to Hatton and said he wanted the support of the Privy Council. Hatton agreed that he should have it and went with him to Burghley. The lord treasurer heard everything that Davison had to say; then he summoned the other available members of the Privy Council. Burghley said the queen had done her part in signing the warrant; she was asking to be spared the painfulness to herself of the final move; he said that in his view they should now act for her. The ten present decided that their numbers gave them sufficient protection. The warrant was directed to the earls of Shrewsbury and Kent, who were in the neighborhood of Fotheringhay. Burghley wrote letters to each of them and the council's secretary, Beale, was sent to deliver these and to show the warrant.

Next morning, February 5, Burghley was with the queen when she called in Davison. Smiling, she told him she had dreamed the night before that the Queen of Scots was executed, and this had put her into such a passion with him, she could have done she knew not what. Davison made a slight reply but then asked her earnestly if she meant the warrant to be executed. "Yes, by God," she answered, she did mean it, but she thought it should have been managed so that the whole responsibility did not fall upon herself. This was the crucial moment. Neither Burghley nor Davison said to her that the warrant was already on its way to Northamptonshire. Davison declared afterward that every word the queen had uttered made him believe she knew it.

On February 8, 1587, in the great hall of Fotheringhay, the awful deed was carried out. The power of Mary's personality over the minds of those who saw her was maintained to the last hour. The Stuarts did not know how to reign, but they knew how to die. Mary's behavior at the block was worthy of the traditions of martyrdom, and in the dreadful act of cutting off her head, those whom she had attempted to betray and kill were in the instant transformed into sacrilegious criminals.

Elizabeth knew that it would be so. To put to death by judicial sentence a crowned queen was something that appalled the world.

Shrewsbury's son set off from Fotheringhay to announce the

deed, rode all night and arrived at Greenwich on the morning of February 9. The queen was just going out to ride, and did not see him. When she came back, bells were ringing all over London, a pealing that lasted twenty-four hours. The news could not be kept back. Elizabeth received it calmly, then, in her own rooms, burst into a passion of weeping such as she had never given way to in her life. The following day she sent for Hatton, and told him that Davison had betrayed her. The day after that, a Saturday, she summoned the councillors and raged furiously at them all, especially Burghley and Davison. She declared that she had signed the warrant but had told Davison to keep it in his hands. She had not meant to have it executed then, perhaps never; they had stolen a march on her, they had wickedly encroached on her power, and made her an object of hatred and calumny to the world.

So much might perhaps have been expected, and the treatment of Davison followed a pattern that conformed to the expectation. He was tried in the Court of Star Chamber for having abused the queen's confidence, where, with weeping, he begged the commissioners not to ask him to say too much, and was committed to the Tower, deprived of his office and ordered to pay a fine of ten thousand marks. His conditions of imprisonment were exceptionally favorable, he was released a year later, his fine was remitted and though he was not reinstated, his salary was paid to him for the rest of his life. Had this been all, it would have borne out the view that the queen had used him in an elaborate deception for gaining her ends while appearing to reject the means. But this was not all.

Burghley had been banished from the queen's presence for two months, but he did not need to be at court to understand what was going on. To his utter dismay he heard that the queen had gained the opinion—as he said, "I know not how"—that by an exercise of her prerogative she could, without trial, have Davison hanged.

Burghley was not only forbidden to come to her; he could not have done so, for he was laid up by a fall from his horse; and in his state of helpless isolation, he heard that Elizabeth was seeking confirmation of this wild and shocking idea from the judges of the Queen's Bench. With unerring instinct she had laid her finger on the one who was going to agree with her. Burghley heard that Mr. Justice Anderson had given his opinion in her favor and that now she intended to hear what the other judges had to say. Burghley was aghast. He wrote in cipher to an unnamed correspondent, urging him to warn the judges secretly to be very careful how they replied. He said: "I would be loth to live, to see a woman of such wisdom as she is, to be wrongly advised, for fear or other infirmity . . . with an opinion gotten from the judges that her prerogative is above her law."

The queen's attempt came to nothing, but it showed that at one point her proceedings against Davison were no mere feint to conciliate the Scots and the French. She was acting on the conviction that Davison had betrayed her. Any review of the facts made such a conviction impossible; but an explanation of her attitude is supplied by the clinical description of hysteria. Hysterical phenomena, it is said, are the outcome of emotional distress, and of faulty reaction to situations of exceptionally exacting or distressing character. The patient either falls ill or disowns the memory of these situations.

Burghley's letters until he was recalled to his proper sphere were couched in terms of conventional abasement, but they were still the writings of a man of sense who had been deeply wounded. "To utter anything like a counsellor, as I was wont to do, I find myself debarred by your Majesty's displeasure." He could only, as one who loved her, "pray Almighty God to deliver your person, as He hath hitherto done, rather by miracle than ordinary means."

Chapter 23

IN THE YEAR 1587, it was plain that the Spanish invasion was coming at last.

Philip had not moved while Mary Stuart was alive and an expensive and perilous enterprise would result merely in putting the English crown on somebody else's head. But now the crown was his own, he thought. Mary had bequeathed it to him. He meant to take possession of England and give it to one of his daughters.

Mary's execution had brought the great menace over the horizon, but it had done something else. An invasion to put the Queen of Scots on the throne would have had the sympathy, at least, of the English Catholics; an invasion to make England into a Spanish province was not going to meet with sympathy from the English of any denomination.

Philip believed that the English Catholics were only waiting to welcome him. His mind was fixed upon what was to take place on English ground. The Armada that was being assembled carried tiers of guns, but it was built primarily for the transport of troops with their horses and stores. The ships were to sail up the Channel to the Flemish coast and convoy Parma and his seventeen thousand troops in their barges across to the Thames estuary. The fighting would be done on land; the expedition was to be essentially military.

Its setting out was delayed for a year because in April 1587 Drake made a lightning raid, burning the shipping in the harbors of Cadiz and Corunna. The bulk of the Spanish navy was lying in the mouth of the Tagus, but Drake was stopped in his design of burning these vessels also by a ship which brought him a message from the queen. She was still trying to make a treaty with Parma in the Netherlands. Drake came home disappointed, but bringing with him the vast and richly loaded *San Felipe*, one of the largest of the treasure ships ever to fall into English hands.

In spite of Walsingham's efforts to convince her that the task was hopeless and a waste of valuable time, Elizabeth, alone, kept the stubborn hope that war might be avoided by negotiation; the government meanwhile prepared as for a certainty.

The City of London, when called upon for their contribution to defense, asked how many men and ships they were expected to provide. The council told them five thousand men and fifteen ships. The aldermen asked for two days to consider, and then announced that they would provide ten thousand men and thirty ships. Lord Howard of Effingham, the lord high admiral, Vice-Admiral Drake and Hawkins, treasurer and comptroller of the navy, were all satisfied with the seaworthy condition of the queen's ships, thirty-four in number. Plymouth harbor was crowded and Hawkins had had four of the largest vessels riding in the Sound during "an extreme and continual storm" and they had felt it "no more than if they had ridden at Chatham." Howard wrote to Burghley: "I do thank God that they be in the state that they be in; there is never a one of them knows what a leak means."

Elizabeth's unfounded optimism over the prospects of a peace treaty with Parma had a result that Walsingham and the naval commanders found both dangerous and infuriating. She had allowed the whole naval strength to be made ready in December, but only for six weeks, by which time she hoped to have concluded a peace. She had had no experience of a full-scale war and of the methods it demanded, but her experience of the incompetence and the flagrant peculation during the campaign in the Netherlands had so alarmed and angered her that she determined not to see the like again. Instead of giving plenary powers to Howard and Hawkins, as she might safely have done, she kept the administration of supplies in her own hands, and would only allow crews to be taken on and stores brought in for very short periods at a time. Neither Howard nor Hawkins could make her see the dangers of keeping her ships without their full complement of men, munitions and stores. "Sparing and war have no affinity together," said Howard. Such words only increased her agonized resistance, and in the end the English sailors did their work on short rations and fell back on powder captured from the enemy.

The land forces were divided into an army of thirty thousand under Lord Hunsdon based on Windsor, whose task was to defend the queen, and sixteen thousand who were to prevent an attack on London. These were to be encamped at Tilbury under Leicester.

Mid-July of 1588 was fraught with storms, its nights were moonlit. On July 19 at three p.m. watchers on Lizard Head saw, at last, the great nightmare, rising above the horizon's rim and creeping over the sea toward them. "The Spanish Armada," wrote Camden, "built high like towers and castles, rallied into the form of a crescent whose horns were at least seven miles distant, coming slowly on, and though under full sail, yet as the winds laboured and the ocean sighed under the burden of it." The Spaniards anchored at nightfall outside Plymouth, and when the moon rose at two in the morning they saw that the English ships had come out behind them. The first engagement showed the amazing speed and maneuverability of the low-built English ships; the Spaniards said they had never seen ships so handled or that flew so fast. Three engagements on the 23rd, 24th and 27th inflicted heavy damage on the Spanish fleet, but by July 28th they had struggled up the Channel and were anchored in Calais roads not far from where Parma expected to embark. On the night of the 28th they were dislodged by fireships sent among them on a favoring wind, and the next day when they reassembled a fearful battle was fought off Gravelines. Sixty English were killed, but the slaughter of the close-packed Spanish soldiers under a fire they could not avoid or return was ghastly. The ships fled up the east coast of England and the pursuing English ships passed the bodies of the mules and horses the Spaniards had thrown into the sea. They made for the north of Scotland and on to the west coast of Ireland. Storms, wrecks and savage inhabitants continued the chain of their disasters and sufferings, and of thirty thousand men embarked for England, less than ten thousand returned to Spain.

The news, however, of their spectacular destruction was delayed, and England was waiting for the landing of Parma's troops. Elizabeth had said that she intended to come down to the coast, but Leicester in a letter of great good sense replied: "I cannot, most dear Queen, consent to that." But, he said, her courage and resolution would be a heartening sight for the troops, and he thought that if he took a house for her a mile from Tilbury, that would be reasonably safe and from there she might visit the camp. "So far, but no further, can I consent to adventure your person."

Elizabeth had made Leicester lieutenant-general of the forces and she accepted his decision. She came with her train to Tilbury on August 8, bringing with her a beautiful horse, white with dappled gray hindquarters, that had been given to her by Burghley's son Robert Cecil. On the 10th she was dining with

Leicester in his tent when a post arrived. Its intelligence was in fact false but it was highly alarming; it announced that Parma had embarked all his forces and was even then crossing the Channel. The troops were warned of imminent action and Elizabeth said she would review them.

It was now urged on the queen that she should not appear in the middle of an army without ample bodyguard, or a single shot might accomplish the purpose for which the whole invasion was designed. But Elizabeth knew that the effect she had in mind would be destroyed by any such accompaniment. A steel corselet was found for her to wear and a helmet with white plumes was given to a page to carry. Bareheaded, the queen mounted the white horse. The earl of Ormonde carried the sword of state before her, Leicester walked at the horse's bridle and the page with the helmet came behind. The ladies and footmen followed at a considerable distance. The queen rode through the lines to a piece of rising ground; there she dismounted and walked up and down the ranks, sometimes, said Camden, "like a woman, and anon with the countenance and pace of a soldier." She and the army believed that the terrible forces were within a few hours of the English coast. "Her presence and her words," Camden said, "fortified the courage of the captains and soldiers beyond all belief." Her message for them was written down and read out by the officers. It said that she had come to live or die amongst them: "I know I have the body but of a weak and feeble woman; but I have the heart and stomach of a king, and of a king of England too, and think foul scorn that Parma or Spain or any prince of Europe should dare to invade the borders of my realm." The men who heard it told each other that they would die for her.

The news came in at last of the tremendous victory and of the enemy's flight into the North Sea; but the burst of rejoicing and relief did not cause the queen a moment's relaxation from care. The expenses, she declared, must be stopped instantly: she allowed no margin to carry over from a state of war to a return to peace. Howard, Hawkins and Drake were faced with an epidemic of dysentery among their crews, who were carried on shore to die in the streets of Margate for lack of anywhere to receive them, and rather than spend time explaining to the queen what was needed, they supplied wine, arrowroot and other comforts for the sick out of their own money.

Walsingham was told by one of his agents: "Nothing so much displeased the King of Spain as the loyalty of the Catholics to their queen during the late enterprise." The most striking evidence of this loyalty was found in the English fleet itself, for Lord Howard of Effingham was a Catholic; but another sign was seen in an altogether unexpected place. When the news of the English victory was heard in the Jesuit college at Rome, some of the young English students burst out cheering.

LEICESTER HAD BEEN COMPETENT to discharge the duties of lieutenant-general at Tilbury; his care and affection for Elizabeth had been thoroughly proved, and the sense of having emerged with him from a mortal crisis had renewed all her old tenderness. She proposed to create him lieutenant-general of England and Ireland. This newly invented appointment would carry with it such enormous powers that, even left to herself, Elizabeth might, in the end, never have ratified it. As it was it met with strong resistance. The lord chancellor and the lord treasurer both besought the queen not to place such powers in the hands of a subject.

It was said that at this time Leicester dined with the queen, a thing hitherto unheard of. He was suffering from a low fever, caught perhaps on the Essex marshes; Elizabeth also was ailing; they discussed each other's symptoms and Elizabeth recommended him a specific. At the end of August he decided to try Buxton waters. On his journey he wrote to Elizabeth "to know how my gracious lady doth"; he himself was much better for her medicine, which, he said, had done him more good "than any other thing that hath been given me."

He came as far as Cornbury, and there his sickness, which the times could neither diagnose nor cure, overcame him, and on September 4, 1588, he died. He had made his will, in the form of a letter addressed to his wife, and by it he left Elizabeth a pendant of a great diamond set in emeralds, on a rope of six hundred "fair white pearls."

It was Elizabeth's habit to withdraw into herself in grief, and she did so now; but the loss was so severe, her reaction to it was alarming. She shut herself up, and allowed no one to come in for so long that at last Burghley took control; he ordered the door to be broken open. When the author Paul Hentzner visited Whitehall Palace he said that in the queen's bedchamber, beside her bed, was a casket ornamented all over with pearls, in which she put the earrings and bracelets she was wearing, and "other things of especial value." After her death, there was found in this casket Leicester's letter, and on the outside of it, written in Elizabeth's hand: *His last letter.*

The queen collected herself. The grimness of her loss did not alter her nature. The earl had died considerably indebted to the treasury and she ordered his goods to be seized for repayment of the sum. The dead could feel this no injury or unkindness, and if it were disagreeable to the widow, that could not be helped. In any case, Elizabeth's grief was not shared by the countess. Before Leicester's death, she had tormented him with jealousy of Sir Charles Blount, whom she now married without wasting time over formal mourning.

THE TREMENDOUS ACT of national thanksgiving for deliverance from the Spanish fleet was performed on November 24, in a state procession from Somerset House to a service at St. Paul's. For one day the great surge of national emotion carried all before it. The procession was headed by palace officials, aldermen and judges; the Lancaster, York, Somerset and Richmond heralds introduced the dukes, marquesses, earls and viscounts; behind these began the supremely exciting part of the spectacle; the lord treasurer of England, the lord chancellor of England, the archbishops, the French ambassador, the mayor of London; then the sword of state, the sergeants-at-arms, the gentlemen pensioners, and then "Her Majesty in her coach." This was a chariot, open on all sides, and the canopy was a gilded crown.

Arriving at the west door of the cathedral the queen stepped inside, knelt in the aisle and prayed silently. Then the procession re-formed and she was led to her seat in the choir, the litany chanted before her.

Robert Devereaux, earl of Essex.

Chapter 24

WIDESPREAD CHANGES were beginning and the dramatis personae were altering. Walsingham was to die in 1590, Hatton in 1591, and though Burghley himself, "the Atlas of the Commonwealth," supported his vast load till 1598, men who had made their mark before 1588 now assumed the positions of those who had brought Elizabeth so far, although the newer generation never replaced the old.

The early 1580's had seen the emergence of the new group. The earl of Oxford, after a long-standing quarrel, was at last reconciled to the queen, and the matter was helped on by Walter Raleigh. This dark, arrogant, brilliant man, so versatile that the English clergyman and author Thomas F. Fuller did not know whether to catalogue him as "statesman, seaman, soldier, learned writer or what you will," had served in Ireland under Lord Grey de Wilton, and being sent over with dispatches, gained the attention of the Privy Council by explaining to them the incompetence of his senior officers. The opening he took was characteristic and so was its success. "He had gotten the ear of the Queen in a trice, who loved to hear his reasons to her demands." Elizabeth was struck by his virility, his charm and his acute intelligence; they formed the combination she found irresistible.

It was soon Raleigh's turn to be jealous, not, like Hatton, from wounded affection, but with the furious, egotistical jealousy of a greedy, ambitious man who finds another sharing his advantages. Leicester had seen that the engrossing attraction Elizabeth felt for the young man as a cavalier could not be weakened by himself or Hatton, beloved and valued as they were; but his stepson, the twenty-year-old Robert Devereux, who had been earl of Essex since he was nine years old, would be a formidable rival to Raleigh. So it proved. Elizabeth, who had known him since he was a child, now found him presented to her as a courtier. The youth entirely charmed her. He was tall, powerful, with a stooping gait, a striding walk and carrying his head thrust forward. With his mother's auburn hair and black eyes he had inherited Lettice Devereux's vanity and her powerful egotism, but with these went the honesty that had been his father's.

When Essex's influence began, he was twenty-one and Elizabeth was fifty-four, but any affection that she felt for an attractive man was romantic affection, and no response gratified her unless it were in the romantic idiom. To have the entrée that countless other men would have given anything to gain, to have the intimate companionship of this legendary being of such talent, singularity and grandeur, and to find her generous, high-spirited and endlessly kind to himself, all produced in the imaginative young man a heady attraction, and at first the charm was mutual. In the summer of 1587 it was said: "When she is abroad, nobody near her but my Lord of Essex, and at night my Lord is at cards or one game or another with her, that he cometh not to his own lodging till the birds sing in the morning."

When the figures changed, the mood changed also. The tone among the men of Elizabeth's last circle was one of clamorous self-assertion, varied by a passionate sense of ill-usage amounting to stark tragedy, if their material ambitions were postponed or thwarted. This was notably so in Raleigh and Essex, and more discreetly expressed it was found in the third faction, the two sons of the late lord keeper, Anthony and Francis Bacon. One was exceedingly able and the other a genius, but their uncle by marriage, Lord Burghley, did not advance them. The lord treasurer wanted to keep all his benefits for his son Robert Cecil, clever, dearly loved of his father and a hunchback. The latter was eminently prudent and well-behaved; the rest eyed the queen like famished hounds and snarled if she gave something to anybody else.

"When will you cease to be a beggar, Raleigh?" she once exclaimed. "When your Majesty ceases to be a benefactor," was the cheerful, shameless answer. The powerful courtiers who were often patrons wanted favors for their dependents. Essex as a small boy had spent many years in Burghley's house; he disliked the lord treasurer, and as he wanted the defeat of the Armada to be followed by a vigorous policy of aggression against Spain, and Burghley still supported one of pacific caution,

Essex was able to regard the old man with contempt. The clever young Bacons attracted his attention; the astonishing ability of Francis drew out his admiration, their ill-usage at their uncle's hand aroused his quixotism. He became their patron and determined that the queen should be made to do something for them.

The new men looked upon advancement as their right. The queen was a generation older than themselves, they had not shared her dangers, her difficulties were hearsay to them. They were interested in her position rather than in her.

Elizabeth's fame in Europe in the years after 1588, her radiant splendor, her virginity, fitted her for the cult that developed in her later years, symbolizing her as Diana, as Cynthia, goddess of chastity and moonlight. The queen in her later years wore a great deal of white and silver. "All in white, sitting alone in her splendid coach, she looked like a goddess," said a foreign visitor. The French ambassador, de Maisse, noticed that her dresses were usually silver and white; cloth-of-silver slippers were in her wardrobe lists, and in 1589 Lady Walsingham's New Year's gift was a little cloth-of-silver muff, fastened with seed-pearl buttons and lined with carnation plush. The charming fashion of jewelry mounted in white enamel belongs to these years, and in 1589 the Swedish marchioness of Northampton gave the queen white enameled bracelets set with pearl daisies whose centers were rubies.

But the moon—radiant, remote, serene—was a symbol only in a farfetched sense. The heat and burden of the day had never lessened, and having been borne for so long, they had produced an effect of hardened endurance. Burghley said: "She knew all estates and dispositions of all Princes and parties," and now the dispositions were as complicated and dangerous as ever. In 1589 Henry III was assassinated, the Huguenot Henry of Navarre became Henry IV of France, and immediately, the secret league between the Guises and Philip of Spain came into open force to prevent a Protestant from holding the French throne. Elizabeth at once concluded an alliance with Henry IV, and four thousand English troops were sent to his assistance. The situation rapidly became extremely menacing; the Spaniards entered Brittany and it was understood that they would use it as a naval base from which to launch a second invasion of England. The Spanish threat was back again, nearer than before.

When Leicester died, the young Jesuit Robert Southwell had written: "I think now the Queen is freed from her slavery to this man she will adopt a milder policy towards us," and had she been left to herself Elizabeth would have fulfilled his hopes. But the Jesuits, unlike the English Catholics, were identified with Spain. Their order wished to see England forcibly reconverted by a Spanish invasion.

Chapter 25

IN 1593 ELIZABETH was sixty. The thirty-five years of the reign, so hard, so dangerous, so successful, had intensified and stabilized her character. Her health had improved, her minor ailments were less frequent, and she no longer gave way to hysterical collapse. But her nervous irritability had become a standing condition; a vast experience of this harsh world had imparted a roughness to her impatience.

Also the wonderful qualities of her intellect were unabated; she still found absorbing interest in presenting herself in clothes and jewels as a magical incarnation of sovereignty, and the assurance of the people's love was the deepest emotional satisfaction of her existence.

Her nose had slightly thickened, her eyes become sunken, and as she had lost several teeth on the left side of her mouth it was difficult for foreigners to catch her words when she spoke fast, but the impression she made in her last decade was one of astonishing energy for her years. She was erect and active as ever and though her face was wrinkled, her skin preserved its flawless white. The wigs she wore were a darker red than her own hair and made by her silkwoman Dorothy Spekarde. In 1602 the latter was paid for "6 heads of hair, 12 yards of hair curl and 100 devices made of hair."

Elizabeth had never had much appetite; she now ate less than ever; she mixed her wine with water for fear of its "clouding her faculties" and she "was not subject to love of sleep." Her routine was a strenuous one. Often she was at work before day-light with her secretaries. All orders in council, all measures relating to public affairs, were read over to her and she made notes on them. If anything left her undecided she summoned the available councillors, made them discuss the point with each other and then formed her own opinion. Burghley in a memo-randum he made for Robert Cecil's guidance warned him not to override the queen's judgment but to allow her to make up her own mind. When she had done so, the value of her opinion would be unique.

The national vigor and self-confidence, rising to its peak, expressed itself in a proliferation of ornament and a flamboyancy of dress such as had never been conceived. Men's and women's clothes achieved an air of visionary strangeness by combining grotesque exaggeration with the utmost delicacy of tint. The female bodice was elongated, the skirt of wide circumference was hung on a platelike frame encircling the hips, the sleeves swelled and rose nearly to the ears, and in addition to the small ruff a transparent muslin one stood like a nimbus behind the head. In the Ditchely portrait of 1592 Elizabeth's huge white silk dress is studded all over with aglets of black onyx, coral and pearl; she stands on a map of England in white shoes, she wears three ropes of milky, translucent pearls, and the fan she holds is tied to her waist by a coral-colored ribbon. Her face is wasted like the waning moon's, with eyes that look as if they never slept.

Her personal fastidiousness had not declined. In 1599 over seven hundred pounds was paid for "fine linen for her Majesty's own person" and the fame of her toilet preparations had been carried by English merchants to the Middle East. The mother of the Turkish sultan sent the English queen a set of oriental robes, a ruby necklace and a diamond wreath, asking in return for some English woolen cloth and some of the queen's "dis-tilled waters for the face and scented oil for the hands."

When Elizabeth had been shut up in the Tower, she had stood godmother to the son of a young couple there with her, John and Isabella Harington. Her godson John was now at court, and though his liveliness amused the queen, it sometimes got him into trouble. In 1597 he produced in three parts a satire on the times in the form of a discussion of the nastiness and indecorum of the privies in great houses. He called it *A Metamorphosis of Ajax*, punning on the word jakes. The queen suffered from a primitive sanitary system as much as anyone but she objected to these disgusting inconveniences being commented on with humorous gusto. She told Harington to go away and stay away—but then her mind reverted to something in his pages. In a welter of horrid descriptions and indelicate jokes he had introduced a plan with diagrams for a water closet; by this means, he said, a privy could be kept sweet all year. It was worth trying. The queen had his device installed at Richmond and found it worked. The delightful improvement "pacified her," Harington said, and she sent him "thanks for his invention."

Henry IV had checkmated the Catholic League by declaring himself a Catholic, but this had not got the Spaniards out of France; they were now waging war to gain the French crown for Philip's daughter, legal heir through her mother Elizabeth de Valois. The English supported the French king with men and money, and when the Spanish guns at the capture of Calais could be heard at Greenwich, Elizabeth finally authorized the departure of the expedition to attack Spanish bases. The Cadiz expedition of 1596 was a brilliant success, of which the chief honors went to Essex for his courage, initiative and his splendid chivalry. An expedition the following year to the Azores was a failure, but the English alliance was of the utmost importance to Henry IV, and a series of distinguished ambassadors kept him in close touch with the English court. In December 1597 de Maisse was accredited to St. James's and his journal gives a vivid, arresting view of Elizabeth at the age of sixty-four.

He saw her first in a large chamber where a great fire was burning. She wore a dark red wig decorated with jewels and though her face looked old and her neck was wrinkled, her bosom was delicate and white and her figure still beautiful in its proportions. She wore a white taffeta gown lined with scarlet, ornamented with pearls and rubies. She was most gracious and very talkative. She complained of the heat of the fire and had it damped down, and she was perpetually twisting and untwisting the long hanging ends of her red-lined sleeves. The queen's conversation when she got upon men and affairs held him spellbound, but on one occasion she startled him. At a private audience on December 15 he found her standing by a window in an Italian gown of black and gold; under it was a dress of white damask and under this a lawn chemise. These garments fastened in front and she held their edges in her hands, often as she spoke turning them back so that, he said, he could see her belly "even to the navel." Her intellect was otherwise functioning with its usual acuteness and she held a conversation with him of two hours or more.

De Maisse, however, showed a remarkable tolerance and sense of proportion in the face of this experience. The impression the queen's conversation made on him was so profound it counted for more than her aberration. His verdict was: "She is a very great Princess who knows everything."

Such was the view of an experienced ambassador, but it was not shared by the Devereux family. Essex in 1597 was thirty-one, and for ten years his rise in the sphere of court had been steady. On Leicester's death he was given the appointment of master of the horse, the first Leicester had ever received from Elizabeth. He had fought under Leicester in the Low Countries, he had commanded the English contingent sent to help Henry IV. He was a privy councillor at twenty-seven, and though the value of his advice, like the value of his generalship, was uncertain, it was sense that he lacked rather than ability. He could not banish the queen's other favorites, but it was plain that her fondness for him was greater than she had shown for any other man, and the thirty-three years' difference in their ages was an advantage that gave him almost unlimited power over a woman who loved him; so at least it seemed to every onlooker except one—but that one was Francis Bacon.

Essex had been at first dazzled and grateful but all that he really understood of Elizabeth was that she had a passionate affection for himself and that he could sometimes by a mixture of vehemence and sulking persuade her to do something she did not want to do. This made him boast of "doing the Queen good against her will." His tendency to underrate her was fatally encouraged by his mother, who was still not allowed to come to court, and by his favorite sister, Penelope. The latter had reacted with spirit against the tiresomeness of being married to Lord Rich and had formed a publicly accepted liaison with the discreet and elegant Lord Mountjoy. She had borne Rich seven children and was in process of bearing Mountjoy five more, but her radiance and ebullience were undimmed. She had been the adored of the celebrated Philip Sidney, she was a beauty, a toast, the sister of the incomparable Essex. Her self-confidence was natural but, as it turned out, it was unfortunate. Burghley's spies knew that she was corresponding with a member of the Douglas family at the Scots court. The correspondence was carried on under assumed names. "Writing for her brother," the spy reported, she described him as "always exceeding weary and longing for the change."

Since it was said that Essex could not dissemble, it may be that his sister did him an injustice, and that some at least of what he professed for Elizabeth he actually felt and that when he wrote: "It is not in your power, great Queen as you are, to make me love you less," the words owed something of their ring to an echo of genuine emotion. At all events when he wrote: "Since I was first so happy as to know what love meant, I was never one day nor hour free from hope and jealousy," this much at least was true: his jealousy of anyone who shared the queen's favor was devouring. He was a close friend of Mountjoy, but he had begun by violently insulting the latter when the queen gave him one of the queens out of a set of gold chessmen, for distinguishing himself in the tilt yard. "Now I perceive every fool must have a favour!" Essex snarled.

Lord Howard of Effingham, who had been commander in chief against the Armada, was created earl of Nottingham in 1597; but the patent, besides the Armada service, mentioned the Cadiz action. Essex was furious that anyone should be mentioned in this connection except himself; besides, whoever held the post of lord admiral took precedence of all his peers; therefore Howard as earl of Nottingham would now take precedence of the earl of Essex. Essex did his level best to force the queen to rescind the honor. He did not succeed but his explosions of fury over these two creations showed his influence to an ominous extent.

From his intolerable temper may be divined how great was the charm that outweighed it. In spite of his overbearing nature he could assume an enchanting courtesy and gentleness. The contrast entered into his physical makeup; despite his vigor he was subject to mysterious collapses, when he was too weak to rise from his bed. His appearance, too, with youth and height and auburn hair, was the more striking for a hint of melancholy. In the great tournament of 1591, when the other knights appeared in white and sky blue, green and silver, gold and orange tawny, Essex rode into the lists on a coal-black horse, armed in black, shaded with black plumage.

In 1596, after the triumph of Cadiz, Essex was in the height of the firmament, but Bacon, who had attached his own hopes to the fortunes of his splendid young patron, saw the state of things with alarm. In a letter of extraordinary penetration he begged Essex to realize how the queen must view him: "a man of a nature not to be ruled, that hath the advantage of my affection and knoweth it"; Essex should do his best to allay the misgiving she was bound to feel at his domineering ways and above all at the people's enthusiasm for him. He should accept civilian honors only, deprecate popularity and study to please her in every way he could. So far as this meant dissimulation Essex could not do it, and he saw no need to do it.

When in some dispute he had forced his will on the old woman, he would ask Bacon triumphantly which method of dealing with her was the right one, Bacon's or his? Bacon was very far from being reassured. He saw the desperate perils ahead in such a course. He began to withdraw from his close attendance on Essex.

Bacon was not alone in an estimate of Elizabeth's abilities that should have made Essex pause. When Henry IV sent over as his ambassador the future duke of Sully, Elizabeth said that she would give him her view of the European situation with reference to the House of Austria. She began her explanation, which built up in stroke after stroke a survey of the vast and complicated scene so masterly, so brilliant, that Sully gazed upon her with rapt astonishment. On the evidence of this conversation alone, Sully was convinced, he said, "that this great Queen merited the whole of that great reputation she had throughout Europe." This was the being whom Essex thought he could manage for her own good.

Meanwhile affairs in Ireland demanded immediate handling. The earl of Tyrone, who would have been friendly to the English Crown, had been driven into hostility by the misgovernment of succeeding deputies, and relying on Spanish aid he began a war of resistance in the northern province of Ulster. The queen proposed to send out Essex's uncle Sir William Knollys as deputy to deal with this critical situation. Essex was unwilling to lose his uncle's support in the balance of court factions and wanted the queen to send Sir George Carew, whose absence would be a disadvantage to the Cecils. It was June, the court was at Greenwich and the matter which had been under continuous debate was brought up again at a small conclave consisting only of the queen, Robert Cecil, Nottingham, Essex and the clerk to the council. Essex repeated his desire that Carew should go to Ireland and the queen said that Knollys was going. Essex saw he had lost the trick; anger and frustration possessed him; in vindictive contempt he turned his back on her. At this unheard-of insolence the queen flew at him, smacked his head and told him to go and be hanged.

The action by which Essex had provoked the cuff was extraordinary; his reaction to the cuff itself was almost unbelievable. Shouting that this was an outrage he would not have endured from Henry VIII, Essex clapped his hand to his sword and only the rushing forward of Lord Nottingham stopped him from drawing it. He dashed from the room and out of the palace and made his way at once to Wanstead.

He met with no reprisals from Elizabeth, but the utter silence with which she received his conduct did not reassure his wellwishers. For five weeks even Essex was not the first object of the queen's thoughts. Burghley was dying. Elizabeth prayed for him daily, sent every day to inquire for him, and frequently visited him herself. When the patient's food was brought and she saw that his gouty hands could not lift the spoon, she fed him.

Charmed and deeply touched, Burghley's mind went back to the only issue on which, in the long run, Elizabeth had ever disappointed him. He told his son of the queen's attentions and said though she would not be a mother, she showed herself a most careful nurse. He died at the end of August, 1598, and for months the Privy Council did their best not to mention him at council meetings when the queen was present: his name made her turn her face away and weep.

Chapter 26

ONCE IT had been seen that the queen would scarcely allow Essex out of her sight; now when people spoke to her about him she listened willingly, eagerly even, but she made no move to end the estrangement and Essex saw that if he wanted to return to court he must make the move himself.

In October he was at court again and the Irish question, still unsettled, was now of acute urgency. In Armagh, Tyrone had inflicted the heaviest defeat the English forces had ever experienced in Ireland, and at the news of his victory rebellion had broken out all over the country. The queen still proposed to send out Sir William Knollys, but now she had an alternative: with her astonishing gift for detecting ability before it had proved itself, she had singled out Mountjoy as a soldier who could handle this difficult situation. But Essex overbore both these suggestions on the ground that Knollys and Mountjoy had not the necessary vigor and initiative, and when the command was finally conferred upon himself, he spoke of it at first as a personal triumph.

But long before his forces were embarked, Essex was regarding his appointment with self-pitying bitterness. He had felt he owed it to himself to allow no one else to take it, but he foresaw that once he was over the Irish Sea, his enemies in council would undermine him. The choice of him as lord lieutenant, though not the queen's own, was ostensibly a sound one; Bacon said he was the best general of the day, he had the prestige necessary for the office and he was popular with the army.

He disembarked at Dublin on April 15 and from that hour he completely disregarded his instructions. He had been told to proceed north immediately and attack Tyrone with the full weight of his forces. Instead of this he agreed with the Irish Council that later in the year would be a better time, and he spent the next two months in marching over Leinster and Munster, putting down minor insurrections and receiving acclamations from the Anglo-Irish. The queen, who was increasingly annoyed by what she heard of his tactics, said she appeared to be paying him one thousand pounds a day to go on progresses. When she learned that three months after his landing, his army of over sixteen thousand had been reduced to four thousand and that, in spite of additional resources sent at his demand, he still had not marched against Tyrone, she wrote him a series of letters making a bitingly accurate criticism of his incompetence, his disobedience, and the stark failure in which they had resulted. The legend of a young man pursued by a shamefully infatuated old woman is exploded for anyone who reads them.

The results of his mismanagement did not inspire Essex either to admission or apology. "What talk I of victory or success? Is it not known that from England I receive only soul's wounds?" he wrote to the exasperated queen. Goaded by letters from her, he at last announced that he was going to march with his depleted forces into Ulster. The queen replied: "You have even to this hour, possessed us with expectation that you would proceed as we have directed you, but your actions always show the contrary though carried in such sort as we were sure to have no time to countermand them." She recapitulated the provision she had made of men, money and supplies, his persistent refusal to put them to the use for which they were intended and his making further demands, to which he attached the authority of the Irish Council: "There followed from you and the Council a new demand of two thousand men to which if we would assent you would speedily undertake what we had so often commanded. When that was granted and your going onward promised by diverse letters, we received by this bearer new fresh advertisement, that all you can do is to go to the frontiers and that you have provided only twenty days' victuals. In which kind of proceeding," the queen went on, working to a crescendo, "we must deal plain with you and that Council, that it were more proper for them to leave troubling themselves with instructing us by what rules our power and their obedience are limited," and to think over the calamitous results of their interference. Since neither the spring, nor the summer, nor the autumn, nor the winter had been considered a suitable time to march against Tyrone, "then surely we must conclude that none of the four quarters of the year will be in season for you."

When at last Essex and his dwindled forces came face-to-face with Tyrone, effective action was no longer possible. On September 14 the commanders held a parley on horseback, Essex on the riverbank, Tyrone in the water up to his horse's girths. The conversation lasted half an hour and there were no witnesses to it. The upshot was that Tyrone agreed to a truce of six weeks, terminable at a fortnight's notice, and issued to Essex a set of conditions which, when they were finally produced, amounted to home rule for Ireland. These conditions Tyrone said Essex must carry in his head; they must not be written down for fear the Spaniards should get at them.

Essex had lost twelve thousand men and spent three hundred thousand pounds, and this climax of his endeavors left the queen aghast. She did not, she emphasized, suspect him of treason, but she denounced his incompetence in the strongest terms, she forebade him to guarantee Tyrone a pardon and she demanded to hear at once what arrangements he was making with his garrisons. Her letter did not reach its destination.

Before he left England Essex had extracted from her a promise that he might return when he saw fit; when she saw affairs plunging to disaster Elizabeth had canceled this permission and ordered him to stay where he was and carry out his duties. But Essex decided to ignore the queen's command and come back to play what he thought was his strongest card, the old woman's absorbing fondness for himself. He had considered bringing the remains of the army with him, "four thousand choice men," to stand behind him while he made his points to the council. He was dissuaded from this desperate step; he brought two hundred men only, and with them and six officers he crossed to England, arriving in London very early in the morning of September 28. The queen was at Nonsuch, ten miles south of the Thames. Everything was now staked on her personal affection and on his gaining access to her in time to tell his own story first. He and his six friends crossed the river by ferry, landing at Lambeth, and there they seized some horses that were waiting for their riders on the bank. The wild ride began and ahead of them on the Nonsuch road they descried Lord Grey de Wilton, whom Essex declared was his enemy. Sir Thomas Gerard overtook Lord Grey and asked if he would allow the earl of Essex to ride on before him. Lord Grey said no, he had business with Mr. Secretary Cecil. Sir Christopher St. Laurence offered to kill Lord Grey there and then and the secretary when they got to Nonsuch. Essex declined these offers but they showed the mood of determination in which the party was arriving.

Grey was already with Cecil when Essex entered the palace and there was not an instant to lose. It was now ten o'clock. He had ridden so hard that his face was covered with splashes of mud, but he rushed upstairs to the presence chamber, through it to the privy chamber and, finding that empty too, pushed his way into the queen's bedchamber. Elizabeth, surrounded by her waiting women, was sitting at her dressing table, her gray hair "about her ears." Essex fell on his knees, seized her hands and covered them with kisses.

Elizabeth did not know he was in England until he was kneeling at her feet; taken by surprise, at the disadvantage of not being dressed and not knowing whether he had come with an army at his back or who there might be outside her bedroom door, in this annihilating moment she kept her head. Essex indeed thought he had succeeded. When presently he went to wash and dress he was heard to say "he thanked God that though he had suffered much trouble and storms abroad, he had found a sweet calm at home." The queen, fully dressed and in posses-sion of herself, received him after dinner. Her manner was now reserved. She said he must explain himself to the lords of the council. A meeting of the Privy Council was convened and a preliminary examination of Essex on his doings was opened that afternoon. By eleven at night the earl had been ordered to keep to his own room. Next day he was committed to the custody of Lord Egerton and lodged in York House, the great house that stood next to Essex House on the Strand.

It was understood that Essex was not to be charged with treason; the difficulties presented by the Irish and their terrain, a run of misfortune and the fact that the post had required administrative capacities which he did not possess, in the long run were accepted as explanations of his failure; but its overwhelming nature in a man supposedly able and receiving unlimited support from the Crown demanded very serious inquiry, particularly as it had been incurred while he was doing exactly the opposite of what he had been told to do.

In the past when Essex had jarred with Elizabeth, it had been as a rule because she was annoyed by some matter in his private life; she had resented his marriage to Walsingham's daughter and had disapproved violently of his carrying-on with four of her maids of honor. The very quarrels had served to enhance his power; he had been in the superior position of a young man contending with the jealousy of an old woman. He was now facing the formidable anger of a clever, exacting, arbitrary ruler whose costly enterprise had been thrown away by a policy that directly disobeyed her injunctions. Essex, however, did not acknowledge even a mistake, let alone a fault. His present situation he ascribed to the machinations of his enemies, but his chief danger he recognized in the fact that Elizabeth refused to see him.

The fierceness of his agitation and dismay brought on one of his attacks; he was declared to be almost at death's door and illness made its usual appeal to Elizabeth's feelings. With tears in her eyes she sent him a message that he should "comfort himself" and that she would come to see him "if it were consistent with her honour." Lady Essex, just out of childbed and dressed all in black, had come to court imploring to be allowed to visit her husband. She had been refused, but now permission was granted and the young wife was at York House by seven every morning and stayed till six at night.

But the queen's relenting mood was checked. The citizens

heard of Essex's illness and prayers were offered for him in all the churches in London. On "the very white walls" of Whitehall itself, abuse of Cecil was scrawled and an even more sinister sign appeared of the position the earl occupied in the public mind. A Latin history was published of the first year of the reign of Henry IV—the king who had landed with an army in Wales and gained the crown by the murder of his cousin Richard II. Twice in the Devereux line, females had married with the Plantagenets; there was a family connection however distant between Elizabeth and the man who had tried to draw his sword on her. The associations with Henry IV were sinister. She opened the book and found that it was dedicated to the earl of Essex. Such a demonstration added force to rumor. It was naturally asked what Essex had really been doing in Ireland; some said he had meant by compounding with Tyrone to make himself king of the island, and after that—who knew?

The queen made a courageous effort and to onlookers she seemed astonishingly calm. Harington had been with the army in Ireland, and when he came to pay his respects on his return, the queen had given him a furious berating that sent him off, he said, as if the Irish rebels were at his heels; but shortly afterward she sent for him and having frankly discussed his conduct she accepted his apologies and dismissed him graciously. He said: "Until I come to heaven I shall never come before a statelier judge again." The queen was not only self-possessed but cheerful. There was dancing at court every evening and Elizabeth still enjoyed her favorite pastime.

The indifference with which the queen appeared to bear the absence of Essex was the despair of his party. His mother and sister Penelope were next door to him in Essex House, from whose windows they could see him in the garden of York House walking with his wife. At the height of his influence Essex had succeeded on one occasion in persuading the queen to receive his mother, but after this, abhorrence had reasserted itself and Lettice Blount was not allowed to come again. Penelope Rich, however, had the entrée and she thought that a letter from herself to the queen would now be in season. The queen's avid fondness for gallantry was a byword and where her view of her own attractions was concerned she was a vain and foolish old woman; but it was a mistake to think that she was nothing else or that she could not recognize impertinence when she met it. Lady Rich's letter opened with a parody of the style in which letters to the queen were often couched, speaking of having her own eyes "blessed by your Majesty's beauties" and complaining that the earl should be sequestered—as though "his love, his life, his service to your beauties and the state had deserved no absolution after so hard prisonment." Essex, the letter said, was being sacrificed to "those combined enemies that labour on false grounds to build his ruin . . . only to glut themselves in their own private revenges."

The queen's reply was prompt. She conveyed by Robert Cecil her opinion of the "stomach and presumption" of Lady Rich and ordered her to keep to her own house until further notice. After a severe talking-to by the Privy Council, the ingenious letter writer "expressed sorrow for her Majesty's displeasure and her great desire to recover her Majesty's favour."

In May Essex was sent back to Essex House, but still as a prisoner. He had got over his illness, but he was in torments of frustration and bitterness. "Your Majesty" he wrote, "that hath mercy for all the world but me . . . your Majesty, I say hath now in the eighth month of my close imprisonment, as if you thought mine infirmities, beggary and infamy too little punishment, rejected my letters and refused to hear of me, which to traitors you never did." But the queen preserved her unnerving silence. In June he was heard before a special commission sitting in York House. He was charged with disobedience to the queen's commands and with grave misuse of her commission in his treatment of the rebel. He was suspended from all office and ordered to remain a prisoner in his own house till the queen's pleasure was known.

In August 1600 Essex was released; he might go where he would, but still he was not to come to court. The long, public humiliation of the queen's neglect was driving him frantic: "Till I may appear in your gracious presence time itself is a perpetual night and the whole world a sepulchre unto your Majesty's humblest vassal." Though Elizabeth had been generous to him, he was heavily in debt. At Michaelmas the chief source of his income, a monopoly tax on sweet wines, was due to expire. It was of the greatest financial importance to him that the queen should renew it. When the time came for renewing the grant, Elizabeth said: "An unruly beast must be stopped of his provender," and she returned it to the Crown.

Essex was now keeping open house for his sympathizers and his utterances were no longer private. One day in impotent rage he exclaimed that "the Queen's conditions were as crooked as her carcase," and the words were repeated to Elizabeth. It was Raleigh's opinion that if Essex had not said them, he need not have died. This view is contradicted by words of Elizabeth's own, but it shows the impression made by the insult on those who heard it.

Essex had never shown either understanding of his shortcomings or genuine repentance, or any reason at all why the queen should restore him to favor, and his conduct now proved that her judgment was sound in refusing to trust him. Mountjoy had been appointed lord deputy in his place and had sent on Essex's behalf a messenger to James, telling him that Cecil and his friends opposed the Scots king's succession. James's accession, it seemed, depended on the mediation of Essex. If James would send a body of troops to London to demand the reinstatement of Essex and the proclamation of his own right to the crown, Mountjoy would send the English army over from Ireland to ensure effective pressure on the queen. But when Mountjoy arrived in Ireland in February 1600 he vindicated the queen's judgment. The smooth, dapper young nobleman who took good care of himself with hot drinks and afternoon naps, proved a tireless, patient, brilliant organizer, an administrator of outstanding ability as well as a first-rate soldier in the field. Elizabeth had told him she knew he would settle Tyrone and bring her to her grave in peace, and Mountjoy received Tyrone's submission a few days before her death. By the time Essex sent to demand a renewal of his cooperation Mountjoy had relinquished any interest in treason.

But to Essex no other alternative commended itself. The galling sense of defeat where he had once enjoyed absolute supremacy was destroying his balance; he developed a persecution mania in which he actually believed that Cecil and Raleigh were planning his murder. Essex House became a magnet for disaffection; the earl's presence chamber was thronged with soldiers from Ireland, Puritans who disapproved of the queen, Catholics who sought toleration and adventurers who wanted opportunity. With the earl of Southampton and others, Essex determined that he must "surprise the court and the Queen's person." This done, he was to tell the queen she must dismiss his enemies; he would then put them on trial for their lives and afterwards summon a Parliament "and alter the government." This scheme caused such excitement among the crowds frequenting Essex House that the queen became aware of "a general churme and muttering," and on the afternoon of Saturday, February 7, 1601, Essex was summoned to the Privy Council. He declared himself too ill to go and it was determined that he and his party must move at once. They discussed whether they should first seize the Tower or surprise the court and determined on the latter, for Essex thought himself so beloved in the city that it was virtually his already. On Sunday morning the courtyard of Essex House was crammed with between two and three hundred swordsmen, but as ten o'clock struck, Lord Egerton, Sir William Knollys, Lord Worcester and the lord chief justice arrived at the gates demanding admittance. They were shown into the library, but the mob was already out of hand and Essex was borne on by them. He turned the key on the delegation and with two hundred men with drawn swords at his back came out of his gates into Fleet Street. It was plain that the court could not be surprised and the plans were hurriedly reversed. Instead of turning to the left toward Whitehall, the crowd turned right up Ludgate Hill. As Essex walked at their head he called out: "For the Queen!" telling the passersby to take up arms and follow him.

The government had already warned the citizens to arm themselves for fear of trouble, but there was no trouble. "There was not," said Bacon, "in so populous a city where he thought himself held so dear, one man from the chiefest citizen to the meanest artificer or prentice that armed with him." The dreadful silence of the Sunday morning streets reduced his cries to a theatrical absurdity. Heralds in the streets were proclaiming him a traitor; there had been a clash between his men and the queen's on Ludgate Hill and that road was closed to him. He dived down a side street leading to the river, took boat and was rowed upstream to the water gate of Essex House. Here he found that his captives had been let out. Penelope in his absence had endeavored to bring in the earl of Bedford, whom she had called for in her coach and obliged to leave his house in the middle of a sermon. His lordship had remained passive until he was set down at Essex House; he had then made the rest of his way to court and proclaimed himself at the queen's service.

At dusk Lord Nottingham and Sir Henry Sidney landed at the water gate and the latter came up the garden, shouting to Essex and Southampton to capitulate. Essex spoke to him from the roof, demanding as a condition of surrender to be allowed an audience of the queen. The lord admiral's reply was to send downstream to the Tower for ordnance and kegs of gunpowder. One hour he would grant, to let the ladies Essex and Rich with their shrieking gentlewomen get out of the house, then he would blow it up. The kegs were being landed on the lawn when Essex and Southampton came out, knelt to the lord admiral and presented their swords. They were lodged that night in Lambeth Palace and next day taken to the Tower.

Chapter 27

ESSEX'S ATTEMPT at rebellion had been futile. He and Southampton and five of their associates were charged with high treason, and on February 19, the two earls were sentenced to be beheaded.

Essex was thirty-five and his shining career had extinguished itself in utter desolation. He fell into a state of mind well known in such circumstances; under the eager, relentless ministrations of his chaplain, he poured out a hysterical confession, declaring himself "the greatest, the vilest, the most unthankful traitor that has ever been in the land." His defenses were broken down under a flood of remorse but he accepted the prospect of his death with a dignified and moving courage. To many, looking back, it was unbelievable that the queen should allow the sentence to be carried out. Those who thought so knew her as little as Essex had known her.

Elizabeth reprieved Southampton as a follower of Essex merely; for Essex there could be no reprieve; he had meant to come into her presence with armed men and force her to do his will. This offense admitted of no reconciliation, no pardon, no oblivion.

On the morning of February 25 the queen was sitting in the privy chamber playing the virginals, while several men, among them Oxford and Raleigh, stood about her. Admission was sought for a messenger who, on his knee, announced that sentence on the earl of Essex had been carried out. A dead silence filled the room. Then the twanging, plangent notes struck the air as the queen began to play again.

Almost at once melodramatic versions of the story were evolved, whose false and lurid coloring has never lost its popular appeal. The French ambassador, Beaumont, heard Elizabeth's version from her own lips. He could see that she was in deep grief and when she spoke of the matter she was almost in tears, but she said: "I had put up with but too much disrespect to my person, but I warned him that he should not touch my sceptre."

That Essex had meant to use his Plantagenet blood as an excuse actually to lay his hand on the crown had not been brought against him at his trial, but the rumor of it was prevalent, for he had sent to assure James that it was untrue. It had never been driven from Elizabeth's mind.

The response to life was vivid as ever, but the scene itself was changing. Admiration, gratitude, affection, she had them all, but her very success had resulted in bringing a new England into being. In her last years Elizabeth, weary and worn down, had to face situations she had never known before. Essex's attempt at a rebellion supported by Scots and Irish forces might have proved exceedingly formidable; it had collapsed in ignominy because the ordinary Englishman would not contemplate rebelling against the queen. Nevertheless Essex had enjoyed some of that magical popularity which up till then had been exerted only by Elizabeth herself, and in the mourning for his death—the popular ballad declared *"Sweet England's Pride is gone!"*—the queen's own grief was troubled by a still darker and colder shadow. In the last ten years she had not been able to keep pace with the inflationary tendencies of expanding prosperity. Aid to the French and Dutch had swallowed her painfully accumulated reserves; Mountjoy had the Irish position well in hand, but it required an increasing flow of money, for the Spaniards were about to launch another attempt at invasion from the Irish base. In her last years the queen had to sell Crown lands and her jewels. In 1601 a Parliament was summoned, for the need of a large subsidy was urgent.

Elizabeth was old: at the opening of the session her robes of velvet and ermine had proved too heavy for her; on the steps of the throne she had staggered and was only saved from falling by the peer who stood nearest catching her in his arms. But her royal instincts were not impaired. The queen had rewarded her servants by allowing them to tax articles of general use; now she told Robert Cecil she had not known how the monopoly tax was abused; the matter must be set right. He announced to the House of Commons that the offensive taxes were being removed forthwith: salt, brandy and starch were among the articles to be freed, and the restrictions were removed on the growing of woad, with the proviso that, as the vegetable had a nauseating smell, her Majesty hoped that people would not grow it near any of the palaces.

When a deputation waited on her at Whitehall at three in the afternoon of November 30, to tender the thanks of the Houses for this prompt and most substantial concession, the queen made in reply one of the most celebrated speeches of her life. She told them: "And though God has raised me high, yet this I count the glory of my crown, that I have reigned with your loves. . . . I do not," she said, "so much rejoice that God hath made me to be a queen as to be a queen over so thankful a people." In the simplest words she expressed the guiding motive of her existence: "I have cause to wish nothing more than to content the subject, and that is a duty which I owe. It is my desire to live nor reign no longer than my life and reign shall be for your good." As she drew to a close, she said: "Neither do I desire to live longer days than that I may see your prosperity, and that is my only desire. And I pray you, Mr. Comptroller, Mr. Secretary, and you of my council, that before these gentlemen depart into their countries, you bring them all to kiss my hand."

"We loved her," Harington said, "for she said she did love us."

The mutual love was inexhaustible, but it was mingled now with treasons, independencies, newfangledness. The situation she had driven off for forty-three years could be driven off no longer; hope and expectation were directed to the heir, and not to her. Behind the distractions, the labors of hour-to-hour existence, there was a vast darkness. Leicester was dead, Hatton was dead, Burghley was dead, and the last death of all was still an open wound. In 1602 Harington heard that there were times when the queen sat alone in the dark, lamenting the fate of Essex.

The energy of genius did not forsake her, it nearly wore her out. She rode still though it made her very weary; she refused help in stepping into the royal barge, stumbled and bruised her shin. She paid a visit to Sir Robert Sidney and his wife, who had exerted themselves to the utmost to make the occasion a success. Fanfares saluted the queen's arrival and departure, dances were performed, the family had put on their richest clothes, the children made speeches "very graciously received" by the glittering old lady whose velvet train was carried by four gentlewomen. But she called for a stick to help herself up the staircase; "she was wearied in walking about the house and said she would come another day."

For the first time she became forgetful, and her autocratic temper made these lapses difficult to explain to her, for "who dares say, your Majesty hath forgotten?" But the infirmities of age brought no numbing of her feelings. The coronation ring she had worn for forty-three years had now grown into her finger and they had to file it off. The nature of the act oppressed her with horror and desolation.

In January 1603 the queen had a bad cold. She decided to go

Elizabeth's funeral cortege.

to Richmond, the warmest of the palaces, and the court removed there on January 14, "being a filthy rainy and windy day." She was sixty-nine and the doctors said she might live for several years; they now considered her to have "a sound and perfect constitution." But by the end of February she was declining fast. It was put about that grief for Essex had deprived her of the wish to live, but as potent a reason was perhaps a perfect sense of timing. She had told the Houses she did not wish to live and reign after her life and reign could do them good. "She grew worse," said her cousin Robert Carey, "because she would be so." She refused all medicine, and when the archbishop of Canterbury and Cecil urged her to try some, she replied impatiently that she knew her own constitution better than they did.

Her symptoms increased, of fever, restlessness, sleeplessness, perpetual thirst and phlegm in the throat. When she was too much exhausted to walk about she sat on the floor cushions and once there she would not move. Cecil said, "Madame, to content the people you must go to bed." The queen gave a smile of indescribable scorn. "Little man, little man," she said, "the word *must* is not to be used to princes. If your father had lived ye durst not have said so much."

She remained silent for hours at a time and when one of the doctors ventured to ask "how she spent her time in so much silence: 'I meditate,' quoth she." For the last two days, Beaumont was told, she had had her finger almost always in her mouth, her eyes open and fixed upon the ground; in this awful trance she remained for four days on end, eating nothing and sitting upright on her cushions, except when she slept for an hour or so, and wasting visibly. At the end of the fourth day she was so faint they were able to carry her to bed. Here she revived a little, and asked for some meat broth. An abscess burst in her throat and she felt better. The privy councillors said they must speak with her; though every arrangement was made for the accession of James, opposition from rival claimants was possible and Cecil wanted Elizabeth's own word in support of the Scots king's claim.

She asked for something to rinse her throat and as it was still very sore they begged her, as they stood about her bed, only to sign with her hand if she agreed with their proposals. When they asked her if James should succeed her on the English throne, she made the sign that everyone expected.

Presently she asked for the archbishop of Canterbury, and at six in the evening Whitgift was brought to her bedside; when the archbishop entered the bedchamber her cousin Robert Carey came in too and knelt at a distance. Many people were in the room, and as the archbishop uttered prayers the bystanders gave the responses. The queen made no sound, but when, after half an hour, Whitgift blessed her and rose from his knees, she made a sign and Lady Scrope, who was her cousin Philadelphia Carey, interpreted it and asked the archbishop to go on praying. He prayed again, uttering exclamations of his own, fervently imploring mercy for her until at last she sank into unconsciousness.

Everyone now left the bedchamber except the ladies attending the queen. The palace was silent and a hush deeper than the tranquillity of night possessed the river, the fields and London itself. Midnight came and then it was March 24, the eve of the Feast of the Annunciation of the Blessed Virgin. At a quarter to three the watchers again approached the great bed.

Elizabeth was lying with her head on her right arm. Her warfare was accomplished.

WHEN THE GRIEF and lamentation of a national mourning had subsided and the cares and interests of a new era had begun, Camden's words enshrined the opinion of his own and of succeeding centuries:

"She was a Queen who hath so long and with so great wisdom governed her kingdoms, as (to use the words of her Successor who in sincerity confessed as much) the like hath not been read or heard of, either in our own time or since the days of the Roman Emperor Augustus."

DARWIN
AND THE
BEAGLE

A CONDENSATION OF

DARWIN
AND
THE
BEAGLE

by
ALAN
MOOREHEAD

It was an astonishing stroke of luck! With no more than an amiable disposition and a boyish passion for collecting flowers and rocks, twenty-two-year-old Charles Darwin, in the year 1831, was selected as ship's naturalist to H.M.S. *Beagle* for a prolonged exploration of the coast of South America.

At the outset Darwin did not question the objective of the *Beagle*'s austere captain, Robert Fitzroy— that his investigations should confirm the literal truth of the Book of Genesis: God had created the world in six days; it had not changed since. Everywhere he turned, however, the eager youth unearthed evidence that this extraordinary planet and its multiplicity of creatures had evolved over untold eons of turbulent change.

The wonder and excitement of the voyage itself and Darwin's growing awareness that he was on the track of a truth that would revolutionize men's thinking are here described in vivid prose and beautiful illustrations. Several of the latter were done by artists who sailed with the great naturalist and shared in his adventures.

Chapter 1

The Meeting

ONE OF THE fascinating things about Charles Darwin is that he really does seem to have been one of those men whose careers quite unexpectedly and fortuitously are decided for them by a single stroke of fortune. For twenty-one years nothing much happens, no exceptional abilities are revealed; then suddenly a chance is offered, things can go either this way or that, but luck steps in, or rather a chain of lucky events, and away he soars into the blue never to return. It all looks so inevitable, so predestined; yet the fact is that in 1831 no one in England, certainly not Darwin himself, had the slightest inkling of the extraordinary future that lay ahead of him, and it is next to impossible to recognize in the brooding, ailing figure of the later years this blithe young extrovert on the brink of his greatest adventure—the voyage of the *Beagle*.

Events moved so quickly that he could hardly take in what was happening. On 5 September 1831 he was summoned to London to meet Robert Fitzroy, captain of H.M.S. *Beagle*, a ship which the Admiralty was sending off on a long exploratory voyage round the world. The suggestion was that Darwin should be offered the post of naturalist on the voyage. It was an astonishing idea. He was only twenty-two years old. His youth, his inexperience, even his background, seemed all against him; yet against these odds he and Captain Fitzroy got on famously, and after their interview Fitzroy wrote to the Admiralty hydrographer: "I like what I see of him much, and I now request that you will apply for him to accompany me as naturalist."

The *Beagle*, Fitzroy explained to Darwin, was a small ship, but a good one. He had taken over her command on her previous voyage to South America. Now she was being entirely refitted at Plymouth and she had a splendid crew, many of whom had sailed in her before and had volunteered for this new voyage. They had two missions: they were to continue the charting of the South American coast, and they were to get a more accurate fixing of longitude by carrying a chain of chronological reckonings round the world. The ship would set off in a matter of weeks; they might be away for three or four years, but Darwin would be free to leave the ship and return home whenever he chose. He would have ample opportunities for getting ashore, and in the course of the voyage they would be doing many exciting things: exploring unknown rivers and mountains, calling at coral islands in the tropics and sailing far down towards the frozen south. To Darwin, it was all wonderful. "There is indeed a tide in the affairs of men," he wrote to his sister Susan, "and I have experienced it."

It was remarkably fortunate that he and Fitzroy should have got on as well as they did: at almost every point they were opposed. Whereas the Darwins were upper-class Whigs and Liberals, the Fitzroys were aristocrats and Tories. Charles Darwin was the son of a very successful country doctor—and the grandson of another, Dr. Erasmus Darwin, who had also made a great name as a writer of verse with scientific themes. The Fitzroys were descended from the illicit liaison between Charles II and Barbara Villiers, the Duchess of Cleveland. Robert Fitzroy himself was the son of Lord Charles Fitzroy, and a grandson of the Duke of Grafton.

He looked it. The head was proud and authoritarian, the expression disdainful, and although his figure was slight his whole bearing was that of a man accustomed to privilege. But, unlike Darwin, he had had the very opposite of an easy life; since the age of fourteen, when he entered the Royal Naval College, he had been recognized as a naval officer of exceptional ability. Even in an age when promotion was given very early to outstanding men, it was remarkable that he should have taken command of the *Beagle* when he was only twenty-three.

Fitzroy enjoyed authority. His values were fixed, and he was intolerant of all half shades of meaning. He believed every word in the Bible absolutely, and these certainties were transferred to his practical life; upon his quarterdeck he was a martinet. He was also brave, resourceful, efficient and just. But inside this tight outward sheath there was a restlessness, a yearning— perhaps for warmth and affection—and it broke through occa- sionally in acts of great generosity and contrition. There was no room for compromise in this nature, and he was already giving way to those manic-depressive tendencies that were to end in his suicide thirty-four years later.

Fitzroy was a little cool to Darwin when they first met. He had heard that Darwin was a Whig and when Darwin walked into the room he took a dislike to him, particularly his nose; it was not the nose of a man who could endure the rigors of a voyage around the world. But Darwin's natural easy enthu- siasm swept away all stiffness; before the interview was over Fitzroy was begging him not to be too hasty in giving a yes or no, and reassuring him about the terrors of the sea.

Darwin on his side had never met such a man before. Such perfect manners, such quiet power and authority, such under- standing, the very beau ideal of what a captain ought to be. One also gathers that Darwin sensed very clearly the doubts that were in Fitzroy's mind, the suggestion that the job would prove too much for him. A challenge was being offered. Well and good, he decided, he would accept it, he would show this splen- did man just what he could do.

Let us look back for a moment at Darwin's life as it had been up to the moment of this meeting. In 1831 he had just received his degree as Bachelor of Arts at Christ's College, Cambridge. He was a slim, tall figure, not really handsome but with a well-set head with a broad brow, direct and friendly brown eyes, no beard as yet (though there were sideburns), and the fresh complexion of a twenty-two-year-old who spends a good deal of his time out of doors. Christ's in those days had a reputation for "horsiness." Young Darwin loved to hunt and to shoot, and in his room he used to practice his marksmanship by throwing up his gun in front of a mirror. If he was giving a party, he might get one of his companions to wave a candelabra of lighted candles about while he snuffed out the flames with a blank cartridge. "At breakfast, wine or supper parties," wrote a contemporary, "he was ever one of the most cheerful, the most popular and the most welcome."

He was not a very diligent student; "I'm through, through, through," he exclaimed with relief and surprise when he scraped through his examinations. It was not thought remarkable that without being specially religious he was destined now to enter the Church as a country parson; lots of well-to-do young men did that. He was healthy, he was full of enthusiasms, and he enjoyed and did not want to change the world he lived in.

Upon just one count he was unusual, and that was in his exceptional interest in natural history. Everything in the fields delighted him. Flowers, rocks, butterflies, birds and spiders— from boyhood he had collected them all. Just now his passion was beetles. He had cases of specimens laid out in his room. One day he saw two rare beetles on a piece of bark and seized them both, one in each hand; then he saw a third which he could not bear to lose. In order to release his right hand he popped a beetle into his mouth. It instantly ejected a burning fluid which forced him to spit it out, but all he cared about was losing two valuable specimens.

This passion for collecting he regarded as a hobby; the true business of life was concerned with the classics, which he loathed, with mathematics, which he could not understand, and with the Church, though he privately doubted if he had a true vocation for it. Yet John Stevens Henslow, who lectured to him at Cambridge, was a clergyman and also professor of botany, and Henslow had greatly encouraged him in his interest in natural history. He had taken Darwin on botanizing walks and boating excursions along the river Cam, and even persuaded him to study geology. There was no reason why he should not continue with his collecting and his sports when he settled into his country vicarage.

Darwin was fortunate in his family background. His grandfather, Dr. Erasmus Darwin, had been a much respected if slightly controversial figure. He had worked on the idea of evolution, though he never brought it to a conclusion. Charles's father, Robert, had also gone in for medicine, and had done very well in practice at Shrewsbury, where he had built a fine house, The Mount, above the river Severn. Robert was a huge man, six feet two in height, 328 pounds in weight, and rather autocratic in his ways; his family used to say that when

Robert Fitzroy

Charles Darwin in 1840

he returned home in the evenings it was like the tide coming in. Charles's mother, born Susannah Wedgwood, had died when he was eight, and his three older sisters had brought him up devotedly. He was evidently a tough little boy for he always remembered awaiting some reproof from his sister Caroline and making himself "dogged" so as not to care what she might say.

Then there were his cousins, the Wedgwoods, the famous family of potters, who lived in a grand house, Maer Hall, only twenty miles away. Charles was forever riding over there, and he was a great fa-

Darwin's microscope and pistol

vorite of his Uncle Jos and Aunt Bessie and their four daughters, especially Emma. It was a world of well-staffed country houses, of coaches and grooms, of partridge shooting in the autumn and hunting in the winter, of dinner parties and elegant clothes, of the comfortable knowledge that he would come into a very adequate fortune later on.

School had not been much of a success; he had always been below average. He had gone on to study medicine at Edinburgh, which was a failure; among other things he could not stand the sight of blood. His father had let him abandon medicine and go on to Cambridge, and if he had frittered away his time there, at least he had enjoyed it.

Now in 1831 he had his degree in his pocket and the pleasant prospect of the summer vacation before him. "During midsummer geologised a little in Shropshire," he wrote in his diary. Then he went for a trip through Wales with a newfound scientific friend, Adam Sedgwick, the professor of geology at Cambridge. They spent some pleasant weeks studying rock formations and working on a geological map of the country, and it was not until 29 August that Darwin returned to his home in Shrewsbury. A letter from Professor Henslow awaited him. Enclosed with it was a letter from George Peacock, a Cambridge mathematician and astronomer, who made the completely unexpected offer of the post of unpaid naturalist aboard H.M.S. *Beagle*. Here was a bolt from the blue. Young Darwin had never thought of himself as a professional naturalist, eligible for a scientific job; he was to be a clergyman. After the partridge shooting he had hoped to make a journey down to the Canary Islands before taking holy orders. And yet he was inclined to accept this bizarre proposition.

Dr. Darwin, however, thought it was a wild scheme; Charles had already switched from medicine and now he was running away from the Church; he was not used to the sea and would be away for two years or more; he would be uncomfortable; he would never settle down after he got back; he would harm his reputation as a serious clergyman. It was, in short, a useless undertaking. Dr. Darwin did not absolutely forbid Charles to accept the appointment, but he made himself emphatic. "If," he said, "you can find any man of common sense who advises you to go I will give my consent."

Charles was in no position to argue. His allowance (which he had overspent at Cambridge) was his only source of income, and in any case he would never have dreamed of defying his father's authority. Reluctantly he wrote to Henslow saying that he could not go.

At least the partridge season was about to open, and on the following day he rode over to the Wedgwoods' house to be ready for the opening shoot. Unlike his brother-in-law, Josiah Wedgwood was a supple and humorous man. His house, Maer, was a light-hearted place, overflowing with guests—very unlike The Mount, where Dr. Darwin's overwhelming presence forced a certain gravity on his family. Uncle Jos was young Darwin's means of escape from his father; he had made journeys with him to Scotland, to Ireland and to France, he had confided in him, and now he told him about the offer of the *Beagle* post.

Wedgwood did not at all agree with Dr. Darwin. He thought it was a splendid opportunity and that it ought not to be turned down. He got Darwin to write out the list of Dr. Darwin's objections, and he had an answer to every one of them. Kindled by this Darwin decided to tackle his father again. He sent him a hesitant letter:

My dear Father

I am afraid I am going to make you again very uncomfortable. . . . The danger appears to me and all the Wedgwoods not great—The expence cannot be serious, and the time I do not think anyhow, would be more thrown away than if I staid at home—but pray do not consider that I am so bent on going, that I would for one single *moment* hesitate if you thought that after a short period you should continue uncomfortable.

This done, he was out with his gun and his dog soon after breakfast on the following morning, but it was barely ten o'clock when a servant brought a message from Uncle Jos saying that the *Beagle* offer was too important to be left in abeyance; they must drive over to The Mount together and get his father to change his mind.

235

On arrival at The Mount Uncle Jos took Dr. Darwin's objections one by one and demolished them. Charles, feeling guilty about his extravagance at Cambridge, dropped in a word about money: "I should have to be deuced clever to spend much money aboard the *Beagle*," to which his father replied, "They say you *are* very clever." But in the end the doctor was won round, and Charles, in a great state of excitement, dashed off a letter canceling his earlier refusal. He was now in a fever of anxiety that he was too late, that the job had already been offered to someone else, and at 3 a.m. on the following morning, 2 September, we find him aboard the express coach. When he arrived in Cambridge late that night, he sent a note round to Henslow asking if he could meet him first thing in the morning.

Henslow had bad news for him; a naturalist of some standing was also being considered for the post. All would depend on what sort of impression Darwin made upon Fitzroy, since he had made it clear that he would only take a man whom he personally liked—a not unreasonable condition since the naturalist was going to share his cabin throughout the voyage. On 5 September Darwin set off for London and managed to get an appointment with Fitzroy that same day. As we have seen, the interview went splendidly.

The two men met again next day. Fitzroy had been quite exceptionally frank and kind, Darwin wrote to his family. He had said: "Now your friends will tell you a sea captain is the greatest brute on the face of creation; I do not know how to help you in this case, except by hoping you will give me a trial." Their quarters on board would be cramped, and the captain had been very honest about it: "He asked me at once, 'Shall you bear being told that I want the cabin to myself, when I want to be alone. If we trust each other this way, I hope we shall suit; if not probably we should wish each other at the Devil.'"

The expenses would not be great; Darwin's mess bills would amount to only £30 a year, and a round sum of £500 ought to see him through the whole voyage. Would Susan get the servants at The Mount busy over his kit? "Tell Nancy to make me soon 12 instead of 8 shirts; tell Edward to send me up in my carpet-bag my slippers, a pair of lightish walking shoes—

my Spanish books, my new microscope which must have cotton stuffed inside . . . a little book, if I have got it in my bedroom—*Taxidermy*." Then there were firearms he must have—Fitzroy said that at many places it would not be safe to go ashore without a brace of pistols—but these he could get in London.

Next day he was off in a gig round the town with Fitzroy, shopping list in hand. Fitzroy, it turned out, was a mighty spender; he thought nothing of giving £400 for his personal firearms, and Darwin was sufficiently carried away by this extravagance to part with £50 for a "case of good strong pistols and an excellent rifle." There was so little time; they would sail in October. "I feel my blood run cold at the quantity I have to do."

On 11 September the two of them set off to see the *Beagle* in the dockyards at Plymouth.

Chapter II

The Departure

THEY TOOK three days to sail around from London, three days of talking. It was nothing unusual to take a naturalist on board a voyage such as this, but Fitzroy had also a religious object in view, and it is more than likely that he took this opportunity to explain the matter.

The voyage, he believed, would provide a grand opportunity to substantiate the Bible, especially the Book of Genesis. As a naturalist, Darwin might easily find many evidences of the Flood and the first appearance of all created things upon the earth. He could perform a valuable service by interpreting his scientific discoveries in the light of the Bible. Darwin was very ready to agree. He did not in the least doubt the literal truth of every word in the Bible at this time, and if he could be of use in this way, well then, that made the prospect of the voyage all the more exciting.

Of course other influences had already been at work upon him. It is reasonable to suppose that as Erasmus Darwin's

237

grandson he had read some of his work, notably the famous *Zoönomia*. "Would it be too bold to imagine that in the great length of time since the earth began to exist, perhaps millions of years ago, would it be too bold to imagine that all warm-blooded animals have arisen from one living filament?" Erasmus Darwin had written. At Cambridge Darwin had read Fleming's *Philosophy of Zoology*, Burchell's *Travels in the Interior of Southern Africa*, Scrope on volcanoes, Caldcleugh's *Travels in South America*, and he probably knew something of Lamarck's and Buffon's early theories of evolutionary change. He had read von Humboldt, the German naturalist, with enthusiasm, and Humboldt's *Personal Narrative* was one of the few books he took with him.

It seems quite certain, however, that at this point Darwin had not yet even begun to dream of the work he was to accomplish. He was barely more than a schoolboy, full of

YAWL AMIDSHIP

FORE HATCHWAY

MEN'S MESS TABLES

SICK BAY   LOCKER

COAL HOLE

BEEF AND PORK CASKS

SAIL ROOM

WATER TANKS

CHAIN LOCKER

adolescent enthusiasm. Writing to Fitzroy about the sailing date he said: "My second life will then commence, and it shall be as a birthday for the rest of my life."

But then everything pleased Darwin through these days. The *Beagle*, then lying dismasted in dry dock, was very small, a ten-gun brig of 242 tons, only 90 feet in length, into which seventy-four people would have to stow themselves. But "no vessel," he wrote, "has been fitted out so expensively and with so much care. Everything that can be is made of mahogany." The officers were evidently a "very intelligent, active, determined set of young fellows," though rather rough. The rest of the crew was made up of the master and his two mates, the boatswain, the carpenter, clerks, eight marines, thirty-four seamen and six boys. Finally there were three passengers, York Minster, Jemmy Button and a young girl, Fuegia Basket. These were three natives from Tierra del Fuego, the icy territory about Cape Horn. Fitzroy had picked them up on the previous voyage,

Top, Plymouth harbor. Bottom, cross section of the *Beagle*.

WHALEBOATS ON SKIDS

MEN'S   GUN ROOM   CAPTAIN'S CABIN   CAPTAIN'S STOREROOM

BREAD ROOM

had bestowed their whimsical names upon them (Jemmy had been bought for a few buttons), and for a year had had them educated at his own expense in England. He had showed them off to King William IV and Queen Adelaide; the Queen put one of her bonnets on Fuegia's head and a ring on her finger, and gave her a purse of money to buy clothes. Now, with a smattering of English, their European clothes and a stock of European goods and chattels, they were to be returned to their homes on the other side of the world to spread Christianity and civilization among their countrymen. A young missionary, Richard Matthews, had volunteered to go with them.

There was a round of farewells, with Charles coaching up to London and Cambridge to make his final arrangements. On 24 October 1831 he arrived back at Plymouth only to find that the *Beagle* was not ready. Repairs were taking much longer than had been expected.

The next two months were perfectly miserable. Darwin had nothing definite to do. "My chief employment," he wrote to his family, "is to go on board the *Beagle* and try to look as much like a sailor as ever I can." The combination of the winter weather, homesickness and the reaction from his first excitement filled him with misgivings and made him ill. A rash broke out on his hands and painful palpitations in his chest made him think he had heart disease. But he dared not go to a doctor lest he be told that he could not sail. He took rooms ashore and spent part of his days stowing and restowing his kit in his tiny cabin. Indeed there was very little room; Fitzroy, with his passion for exactness, had set up no less than twenty-two chronometers packed in beds of sawdust on shelves,

239

and Darwin's sleeping space was so confined that he had to remove a drawer from a locker so as to accommodate his feet.

Fitzroy continued to be very kind. There was just one odd little incident. They went into a shop in Plymouth one day to exchange a piece of crockery bought for the ship. When the dealer refused to make the exchange Fitzroy flew into a rage. He inquired the price of a very expensive set of china, and then said, "I should have purchased this if you had not been so disobliging." Then he stalked out of the shop. Darwin knew that Fitzroy never had any intention of making such a purchase, but he said nothing and they walked along in silence. Suddenly the captain's anger evaporated: "You do not believe what I said?" "No," Darwin replied, "I do not." Fitzroy said nothing for a few minutes and then burst out: "You are right. I acted wrongly in my anger at the blackguard."

By December the *Beagle* was ready. On 10 December and again on 21 December the vessel set out, only to be driven back into Plymouth. On each occasion Darwin was violently seasick. On Christmas Day the crew got drunk in port, and Midshipman King, the duty officer, was forced to put one sailor in chains for insolence. It must have been an uproarious spree since the men were not sufficiently recovered to man the sails on the following day. But by the afternoon of 27 December they were away, the men keeping time to the coxswain's pipe as they pulled away at the cables, and at dusk that night Darwin watched the Eddystone lighthouse drop below the horizon— his last view of England. As they headed through heavy seas out into the gray Atlantic, Fitzroy had the worst of the Christmas roisterers brought out on deck and flogged.

These early weeks were clouded over in Darwin's mind by illness. "The misery I endured from sea-sickness," he wrote sadly home, "is far beyond what I ever guessed at." Occasionally he dragged himself out on deck for a breath of fresh air, but the racing waves and the heaving deck were too much for him; most of the time he simply lay in his hammock or perched himself on Fitzroy's sofa, trying to read. He could eat nothing but raisins, and was too ill even to get up and see the coast of the island of Madeira as they sailed by.

There was an additional agony for Darwin in all this—the thought that Fitzroy was finding him too soft for the voyage. For the moment there was nothing to be done about it; he could only complain as little as possible, set his teeth and hold on, hoping for better days. Whatever happened he was not going to throw in his hand and go home as soon as they made a landfall. In the end he was rewarded. At the Cape Verde Islands there was a respite when they were at anchor for twenty-three days while Fitzroy fixed the exact position of the islands, and here Darwin got an inkling of what this voyage might mean to him. This was the first time he had seen a volcanic island; he had been deeply absorbed in Charles Lyell's first volume on *Principles of Geology*, and the thought now passed through his mind that *he* might one day write a book on geology.

Already Darwin was noting, collecting, recording, observing. Not a single item was allowed to get past his scrutiny: birds, the landscape, the natives, the dust, the plants. He observed in detail a sea slug, dissected it and found in its stomach several small pebbles. In his notes there is a drawing of a baobab tree, but this was probably done by Fitzroy; Darwin could not draw. He wrote to Henslow that only one thing worried him—whether he was noting the important facts; "in the one thing collecting, I cannot go wrong."

After the Cape Verde Islands they paused briefly at St. Paul's Rocks, a small archipelago about 600 miles off the coast of Brazil. They were astonished at the vast number of birds which rose in great circling flocks almost blacking out the sky. A boatload of sailors at once set off joyfully for the shore, and fell on the birds like schoolboys, knocking them out with the ends of their rifles or with their bare hands. The unfortunate birds were boobies and terns, and Darwin observed that "both are of a tame and stupid disposition." The sailors returned to the *Beagle* with a great heap of fresh meat, to find another boat's crew had started fishing and were pulling up enormous groupers as fast as they let their lines down.

As they went on across the equator, meeting blessedly calmer water as they approached Brazil, Darwin began to come to life again. He was a conspicuous figure on board; while the crew were in naval uniform he wore the civilian clothes of a gentleman of the early nineteenth century—the topcoat with its tails, the double-breasted waistcoat with its lapels and many buttons, the long trousers, the high-collared shirt with its cravat. His activities seemed to the crew very strange; he made himself a 4-foot townet of bunting, and by trailing it out astern was able to haul up myriads of tiny colored sea creatures that oozed and glistened on the deck.

The day's routine was simple and spartan. Breakfast was at eight, and Fitzroy and Darwin ate alone in the captain's cabin. They then went off to their work: Fitzroy to make his morning round of the decks, and Darwin, if the weather was calm, to deal with his marine animals, dissecting, classifying and making notes. If it was rough he went back to bed and tried to read. Dinner at 1 p.m. was a vegetarian meal, rice, peas and bread and water. No wine or liquor was ever served. At 5 p.m. they had supper, which might include meat and such antiscorbutics as pickles, dried apples and lemon juice. In the evening there was much slow talk, with the officers hanging over the rails under the tropical sky. "I find a ship a very comfortable house," he wrote to his father, "with everything you want, and if it was not for sea-sickness the whole world would be sailors."

Right, *Crossing the Equator.* Bottom, *Midshipman's Berth;* both by Augustus Earle

As the days went by Darwin found that his relations with Fitzroy were undergoing a change. He had been touched when he first came on board that Fitzroy himself showed him how to sling his hammock and stow his things, and the captain continued to show him every kindness. Still, Fitzroy was such a contradictory sort of man, so nervous, so touchy. Darwin was not becoming disillusioned about him, but there had been the incident in the crockery shop back at Plymouth, and then the flogging of the Christmas Day roisterers. Darwin had not thought it fair that the men should be allowed to drink if they were to be punished for it afterwards. But he had not dared to protest. It had not taken him long to realize that the captain of a naval vessel was a law unto himself. He could not be spoken to or argued with as an ordinary man. At the same time Fitzroy drove himself unnecessarily hard. "If he does not kill himself, he will during the voyage do a wonderful quantity of work," Darwin wrote home. "His ascendancy over everybody is quite curious. . . . Altogether he is the strongest marked character I ever fell in with."

Fitzroy's precarious temper was worst in the morning when he made his round of the ship. Junior officers coming on duty had a way of inquiring, "Has much hot coffee been spilled this morning?" meaning, "How is the Captain's temper?" But it was Fitzroy's "severe silences" that Darwin found hardest to bear; he would sometimes abandon himself to his black moods for hours at a stretch. All this did not make Fitzroy hated; everyone admired his wonderful seamanship, and generally his manners were courteous and charming. Still, one watched one's step aboard the *Beagle*. With the rest of his shipmates Darwin got on very well. To the crew he was known affectionately as "our flycatcher." The second lieutenant, who afterwards became Admiral Sir James Sulivan, wrote later: "I can confidently express my belief that

Jemmy Button in 1833

243

during the 5 years in the *Beagle* he (Darwin) was never known to be out of temper, or to say one unkind or hasty word to anyone . . . this, combined with the admiration of his energy and ability, led to our giving him the name of 'the dear old Philosopher.' " Wickham, the first lieutenant, railed against the mess made by Darwin's specimens on the decks, but he was gay and friendly, "by far the most conversible being on board." Benjamin Bynoe, the assistant surgeon, had become a special friend, and Darwin got on so well with Augustus Earle, the artist, that they decided they would share a house ashore when they got to Brazil.

Then there were the Fuegians. York Minster was a taciturn and moody character, but it was obvious that he was growing very fond of Fuegia Basket, and she of him. Jemmy Button, a boy of sixteen, was everyone's favorite. Darwin seems to have liked them all, but he was particularly attached to Jemmy, who was rather a dandy in his white kid gloves and highly polished boots.

As a landsman and a novice at sea Darwin naturally had his leg pulled from time to time. "A grampus bear to port," Sulivan shouted down to him in his cabin one day. Darwin rushed on deck to be met with a shout of laughter. It was 1 April. However, he scored a point in his favor when he managed to hook a large shark on a line trailed over the stern.

The ship made good time, averaging around 160 miles every twenty-four hours. Sixty-three days out from England they reached São Salvador, and landed at the beautiful ancient town of Bahia, set in a wild luxuriant greenness of oranges, bananas and coconuts. Darwin's first experience of a tropical forest was ecstatic.

"Delight," he wrote in his journal, "is a weak term to express the feelings of a naturalist who for the first time has wandered by himself in a Brazilian forest." He was, he felt, like a blind man who has just been given eyes, looking at a scene "like a view in the Arabian Nights." Then again, "A most paradoxical mixture of sound and silence pervades the shady parts of the wood. The noise from the insects is so loud that it may be heard even in a vessel anchored several hundred yards from the shore; yet within the recesses of the forest a universal silence appears to reign."

On 18 March 1832 they continued southwards down the Brazilian coast, and on the morning of 4 April they sailed into the beautiful harbor of Rio de Janeiro in bright sunshine. A squadron of British men-of-war was at anchor there, and long lines of half-naked Negro slaves were carrying cargo down to the trading ships. In the background the palace and the cathedral rose out of the maze of narrow streets, where priests in cone-shaped hats and Spanish ladies in carriages were going by, and the peak of Corcovado soared up into the clear blue sky. Elated with the prospect of getting off the ship and beginning his collecting, Darwin hurried ashore and took up quarters in the town. Now at last he could start to prove his usefulness as a scientist—perhaps even do something to please Fitzroy by relating his discoveries to the great religious truths of the Bible.

Chapter III

The Tropical Forest

WITHIN THREE days Darwin had arranged to join an Irishman named Patrick Lennon who was about to visit his coffee plantation 100 miles away to the north. They were a party of seven, all mounted on horseback. In hot sultry weather they followed the coast for the first few days, and then turned inland into the tropical rain forest. All round them vast trees and cabbage palms, as slender and tall as ships' masts, rose up and blotted out the sun. From the topmost branches Spanish moss and long rope-like lianas trailed down through the green light, and in the stillness of the midday heat the great blue morpho butterfly came sailing by. The air was filled with the scent of aromatic plants—camphor and pepper, cinnamon and clove. Then there were the monstrous anthills, 12 feet high, the parasitic orchids sprouting from the tree trunks and the incredibly brilliant birds: the toucans and the green parrots, the tiny humming-bird with its invisibly fluttering wings poised above a flower.

Darwin made quick ecstatic jottings in his notebooks as he rode along: "Twiners entwining twiners—tresses like hair—beautiful lepidoptera—silence—hosannah."

The bloodcurdling cry of the howler monkey erupted through the silence and this was followed by a distant roar like heavy surf falling on a beach—the approach of a storm. Great warm raindrops broke through the canopy of leaves above their heads and in a moment they were drenched. Fresh earthy smells came up into the washed air from the ground, and all the valleys about them were filled with billowing lakes of white mist. Then as the storm passed and it grew dark a tremendous commotion began: the nightly concert of the frogs, the cicadas and the crickets, and the flickering of the fireflies in the darkness.

Yet there was a terrifying ferocity in this abundance. One day Darwin got down from his horse to watch a fight to the death between a wasp and a large spider. The wasp made a sudden dart from the air, thrust home its sting and then flew off. Though badly wounded, the spider was just able to crawl into a tuft of grass and hide. When at last, by an involuntary movement, the spider gave its position away, the wasp came in for the kill with wonderful precision—two quick stings on the underside of the thorax. Then the victor alighted and began to drag the body away. Darwin did the irrational thing that most of us would have done; he drove the wasp away from its victim.

Further on they came upon one of the most devastating sights in the forest—a march of the army ants. As the shining, black, many-headed horde came on—it was a hundred yards long— every living thing in its path was thrown into panic. Lizards, cockroaches and spiders, driven mad by fear, were cut off by a fast encircling movement and then in an instant the ravening mass fell upon its prey.

So amid all this beauty there was a never-ending menace. Nothing was safe. To prey and to be preyed upon, that was the condition of existence, and the weak in order to survive had to camouflage themselves. Into Darwin's collecting jar went the phasmid stick, an insect that resembled a twig of dry wood, the harmless moth that disguised itself to look like a scorpion, the beetle that put on the colors of poisonous fruit to save itself from the birds, and some moths that had windowed wings to imitate dead leaves with holes.

And now abruptly Darwin was made aware that brutality in nature applied to human beings as well. They had entered a part of the forest where the track had become overgrown, and a Negro slave had been sent ahead to cut a way through. Darwin was trying to speak to him in broken Spanish, and was gesticulating to emphasize his meaning when he realized that the slave thought he was about to be struck. He cringed, dropped his hands and held up his face, waiting submissively for the blow to fall. Darwin was horrified. Were all the slaves as terrified as this? Presently they rode up to a steep-sided granite hill where for a time a group of runaway slaves had managed to hide themselves and to scratch a living from the soil. They had even built themselves a little group of grass huts. The huts were now deserted. A party of Brazilian soldiers had ambushed the place and had captured all the runaways with the exception of just one woman, who had preferred death to the prospect of being enslaved again; she had thrown herself off the summit of the hill and had been dashed to pieces on the rocks below.

As they approached Lennon's hacienda a cannon was fired, a bell began tolling to announce their arrival, and the plantation slaves came out to meet them. It was a delightful place, a quadrangle of thatched huts with the master's quarters on one side and on the other sides the stables, the plantation storehouses and the sleeping quarters of the slaves. Stacks of coffee beans were piled up in the center of the yard, and there was a great come-and-go of chickens and dogs, of horses and farm animals, of women gathered round their cooking fires and naked children playing in the sun.

A gargantuan meal was prepared for the guest—Darwin had hardly finished the turkey when he was confronted with roast pig—and all the while children, chickens and dogs strayed in through the open sides of the hut and had to be chased away by a slave who was specially kept for that purpose.

Lennon, the absolute ruler of this little feudalistic world, was something of an enigma in all this. During the ride up from Rio de Janeiro he had seemed to Darwin to be a reasonable and fair-minded man, but now suddenly, for no apparent reason at all, he flew into a violent rage with the English manager of the place. He announced that all his female slaves and their children were to be separated from their husbands and fathers and marched off to Rio to be sold at public auction. In particular he proposed to get rid of a mulatto child of whom the manager was very fond. It was at this stage that both men drew their pistols and might have opened fire had not Darwin and the others intervened.

The quarrel was forgotten by the morning. But the fact that Lennon could have broken up these families was to Darwin a shocking and a monstrous thing.

He had been brought up with a detestation of slavery—in England the Wedgwoods were among the earliest campaigners against it—and he was still brooding on what he had seen, and the hypocrisy with which it was overlaid, when he got back to Rio de Janeiro. Here his indignation was brought to the

A trogon of the tropical forest

boil again by the discovery that the old lady who lived opposite him kept screws to crush the fingers of her female slaves.

"I thank God," he wrote later, "I shall never again visit a slave country. To this day, if I hear a distant scream, it recalls . . . my feeling when, passing a house near Pernambuco, I heard the most pitiable moans, and could not but suspect that some poor slave was being tortured, yet knew that I was as powerless as a child to remonstrate. I have seen a little boy thrice struck with a whip for having handed me a glass of water not quite clean; I saw his father tremble at a mere glance from his master's eye."

It made one's "blood boil" to think that Englishmen and

Jungle river in Brazil

Female slaves with children

Americans were also involved in the slave traffic. He talked about it to Fitzroy when they were on board the *Beagle* one day. Fitzroy's views about slavery were what one might have expected: without actually condoning it he thought there was a good deal to be said in its favor. The system was a very old one and it should not be tampered with too readily, especially by idealists who had never had the responsibility of running an estate. Now, when Darwin began to recount his adventures, Fitzroy listened calmly enough at first. He said that he too had made a visit to one of the plantations while Darwin was away, and had found the slaves living in conditions that were every bit as good as those of the agricultural laborers in England. The owner of the plantation had called up a great many of his men, and he personally had asked them if they were unhappy and wished to be free. All had answered no.

Darwin was too angry to be prudent. What other possible answer, he demanded, could they have given in their master's presence? Fitzroy was infuriated. If Darwin doubted his word, then he had better get out of the cabin; it was impossible for them to live together any longer. Darwin thought that he would do better than that; he would get off the ship as well. And with that he walked out.

Directly the other officers heard of the quarrel they came to Darwin and said that he would be very welcome to move his belongings in with them. Meanwhile Fitzroy had sent for Wickham, the first lieutenant, and was working off his rage by pouring forth a tirade against Darwin and everything he stood for. But little by little he calmed down, and, as it always happened with that tense, wrought-up nature, remorse set in. He had gone too far. He had hurt Darwin's feelings. He must get him back.

Presently Wickham emerged on deck; the captain wished to present his apologies to Mr. Darwin and requested him to come back to his cabin. Darwin was very ready to accept. After all, the great adventure of the voyage was more important than any private quarrel.

Perhaps it was fortunate that in any case they were to be parted for the next few months; while Fitzroy went north with the *Beagle* to continue his survey of the coast, Darwin lived ashore at Rio with Augustus Earle and Midshipman King. They shared a pleasant cottage at the foot of Corcovado and he was soon engrossed in collecting spiders, butterflies, birds and sea-shells, and meticulously packing them up to send to Henslow.

"I think you have done wonders," Henslow wrote when he had received the specimens some six months later. But he urged Darwin to use more paper. One crab had lost all its legs, a bird had its tail feathers crumpled, two mice were rather moldy. The tiny insects were most excellent, but perhaps it was danger-ous to their antennae and legs to pack them in cotton. It must have been very tantalizing for Darwin to have to wait so long for news of his precious boxes. In one instance the letter of acknowledgment itself took seven months to reach him, making it a year or more since the package had been sent off.

When the *Beagle* got back it brought the calamitous news that a party had gone up the river from Rio snipe-shooting, all had got fever, and three of them had died. Everybody's spirits were low, and they were now all eager to get away on the next stage of the voyage, though Darwin was not so keen on the long days at sea. But already he referred to the *Beagle* as home; he took great pride in her and continually spoke of her beating other ships at maneuvers. "I find they all say we are now the no. 1 in South America," he wrote home with some pleasure.

Now they were off on the cruise down to the far south of the continent, the virtually unknown lands of Patagonia and Tierra del Fuego. "I long," Darwin wrote, "to set foot where no man has trod before."

Chapter IV

The Antediluvian Animals

DARWIN WAS SEASICK AGAIN as soon as they reached the open ocean. He was not one of those who grow used to the sea, and at the end of the voyage he was just as bad a sailor as when he first left Plymouth. But unless it was physically impossible he was never idle. He was up and out with his telescope whenever there was anything to see; he spent long days watching and thinking about the vast numbers of birds that he saw, and came to the conclusion that the instinct for migration takes precedence over all others. "Everyone knows how strong the maternal instinct is; nevertheless, the migratory instinct is so powerful that late in autumn some birds desert their tender young, leaving them to perish miserably in their nests."

Whales broke the surface and spouted alongside the ship, and once when they were traveling at 9 knots under full canvas hundreds of dolphins sported back and forth around the *Beagle*, crisscrossing in front of the bows and leaping clear out of the sea. Then, as the ship continued south, they saw barking or jackass penguins, a species that yaps like a dog. One night when they were anchored in the estuary of the Rio de la Plata, the blue flame of St. Elmo's fire lit up the mastheads and the rigging, and the penguins, darting through the water, left long trails of phosphorescence in their wake.

They were traveling now out of the tropics into the cool temperate zone, and in fresher, bluer seas the men put on heavier clothes. Darwin, along with the officers, began to grow a beard and looked, he says, "like a half-washed chimney-sweeper."

On Sunday mornings Fitzroy conducted divine service on the afterdeck with the men gathered before him. All around them were the things that had grown so familiar they hardly saw them anymore: the muskets, the pistols and the cutlasses clamped to the wall behind the wheel, the wheel itself with "England Expects Every Man To Do His Duty" engraved on the rim, and on the hub a drawing by Augustus Earle of Nep-

251

tune and his trident; and the never-ending sea beyond. With his passionate fundamentalism, Fitzroy can hardly have failed sometimes to have read the lesson from the Book of Genesis: *And God made the beast of the earth after his kind, and cattle after their kind, and every thing that creepeth upon the earth after his kind: and God saw that it was good.*

And God said, Let us make man in our image, after our likeness: and let them have dominion over the fish of the sea, and over the fowl of the air, and over the cattle, and over all the earth. . . .

One almost hears Fitzroy's clear authoritarian voice explaining: "But this man whom God had created became corrupt and filled the earth with violence. And so God flooded the earth for a hundred and fifty days and destroyed him. Yet in His great mercy God allowed Noah to build an Ark and take on board it his family and two each, a male and a female, of every living creature, and all these were saved. Thus the world as God created it in the beginning has been preserved to this present day. Let all of us then in this ship remember this divine providence and humbly ask for His blessing on our voyage into the uncharted seas that lie ahead. . . ."

Fitzroy was always at his best at sea. Here, in the narrow space of his ship, the complications and untidiness of life ashore were put away, things could be properly controlled and organized; a high polish on the brass cannon and the right set of the sails. Whatever else they thought of their captain, aboard the *Beagle*, no one ever doubted his courage: "I would sooner go with the Captain with 10 men than with anybody else with 20," Darwin wrote home to his sister Susan. "He is so very prudent and watchful as long as possible, and so resolutely brave when pushed to it."

And so they were all exhilarated when they ran into trouble in the Rio de la Plata. A twenty-eight-day cruise down from Rio had brought them up to the roadsteads of Buenos Aires, and they were about to sail into port when the Argentinian guard ship opened fire upon them. The first shot was a blank, the second was live and sent a splutter of bullets whistling over the *Beagle*'s rigging. Fitzroy sailed on to his anchorage, and at once dispatched two boats to the shore with a demand for an explanation. Before the men could land a customs officer came out and ordered them back on board again, saying that they must submit to a quarantine inspection. By now Fitzroy was in no mood to submit to anything. He ordered the ship to put about, ran out his guns and then sailed down close to the guard ship. He hailed her as they went by and said that if she dared to fire another shot he would send his whole broadside into her rotten hulk. With that he ran down the muddy tide of the Plata to Montevideo, where the British frigate *Druid* was at anchor. It was soon arranged that the *Druid*, with her guns ready, should sail at once for Buenos Aires to demand an apology from the governor. As with everybody else, Darwin's blood was up. "Oh I hope the guardship will fire a gun at the Frigate. If she does it will be her last day above water."

A day or two later the *Druid* got back with a handsome apology from Buenos Aires, and the news that the captain of the guard ship had been arrested. It had hardly been a famous victory; still, they had shown the Argentinians what was what, it had bound the *Beagle*'s company much closer to her captain, and they were all in good spirits as they sailed on down the barren coast to the south.

About this time Darwin had acquired an assistant named Sims Covington, who had formerly been listed on the *Beagle*'s books as "Fiddler and Boy to the Poop Cabin." Darwin had taught him how to skin and stuff birds and other creatures, and as time went by he let him do more and more of the practical work of collecting, even finally, a year or two later, giving him his precious gun and doing no more himself of the shooting he had once so passionately enjoyed. "My servant is an odd sort of person," wrote Darwin. "I do not very much like him; but he is perhaps from his very oddity very well adapted to all my purposes."

On 7 September they arrived at the little garrison township of Bahia Blanca, some 400 miles south of Buenos Aires, and here Fitzroy began his survey of the unmapped coastline of Patagonia. It was a desolate place. The wide, shallow bay was choked with reed-covered mudbanks, which were swarming with armies of crabs. Inland no trees grew—it hardly ever rained—and a bleak wind swept across the flat plains of the Pampas. The Argentinian garrison consisted of a little group of ragged gauchos got up as soldiers. Wild Indians (as distinct from those who had been "tamed") were roaming the interior, and it was not safe for anyone to stray far away from the settlement. The soldiers were suspicious of the *Beagle* at first—she might be smuggling arms to the tribes or perhaps spying for a foreign power—and they did not like the looks of *El Naturalista*, Don Carlos Darwin. What was a naturalist? They followed him along the beach and watched with distrust when he began to hack away at some old bones embedded in a cliff.

Punta Alta, the scene of some of Darwin's greatest discoveries, was a low bank on the shore some 20 feet in height, composed of shingle and gravel with a strata of muddy reddish clay running through it. The fossilized bones were found in the gravel at the foot of this cliff and were scattered over an area about 200 yards square. At first Darwin could not make out what it was he was unearthing: there was a tusk, a pair of huge claws, a hippopotamuslike skull, a great scaly carapace turned to stone. One thing these relics shared in common, apart from their strangeness; they were all much bigger than the bones of any similar animal alive today.

Up to this time—1832—very little research of this kind had been made in South America. As more and more fossilized skeletons came to light, Darwin began to realize that he was dealing here with creatures that were virtually unknown to modern zoology, and which had vanished from the earth many milleniums ago. There were parts of a giant sloth, the monster that had once reached up its claws to feed on the treetops; the *Toxodon*, an animal like a hippopotamus and "one of the strangest animals ever discovered"; the giant armadillo; a *Mylodon*, an extinct elephant; and a guanaco (or wild llama) as big as a camel. All these bones were embedded in a thick matrix of seashells, "a perfect catacomb for monsters of extinct races."

For Darwin the important thing about these creatures was that, being different species, they nevertheless closely resembled their much smaller counterparts alive in the world today. "This wonderful relationship in the same continent between the dead and the living will, I do not doubt, hereafter throw more light on the appearance of organic beings on earth and their disappearance from it." Where had these great beasts been at the time of the Flood? Perhaps most mysterious of all was the discovery of the bones of a horse. When the Spanish conquistadors arrived in the sixteenth century the horse was unknown in South America. Yet here was definite proof that the animals had existed in the remote past. Did all this mean that the various species were constantly changing and developing, that those which failed to adjust themselves to their environment died out? If this were so, then the present inhabitants of the world were very different to those that God had originally created; indeed, there could even be some doubt whether the Creation could have taken place within a single week; creation was a continuous process and it had been going on for a long time.

What had exterminated so many species? Darwin ruled out the possibility that changes in climate might have caused this extermination. After considering many theories, he came to the conclusion that the Isthmus of Panama might once have been submerged. He was right. For seventy million years South America was an island, and these great animals evolved in isolation. When the isthmus arose and North America was joined to South America the fate of these curious and largely helpless beasts was sealed: they could not defend themselves against other species, and so had been destroyed.

It must have been about this time that Darwin first began to argue with Fitzroy about the authenticity of the story of the Flood. How had such enormous creatures got aboard the Ark? Not *all* the animals had managed to get aboard the Ark, Fitzroy explained; for some divine reason these had been left outside and drowned. But, Darwin protested, *were* they drowned? There was much evidence—the seashells, for example—to prove that the coast here had risen above the sea, and that these animals had roamed across the Pampas in much the same way as the guanacos did at the present time. The land had *not* risen, Fitzroy contended; it was the sea that had risen and the bones of these drowned animals were an additional proof of the Flood.

At this early stage of the voyage Darwin was not prepared

to put his arguments too forcibly; he needed more evidence, more time for thought. He was even willing to be persuaded that his new and disturbing ideas were wrong. Certainly he had no wish to deny the truth of the Bible: "No one can stand in these solitudes (the great forests) unmoved," he had written, "and not feel there is more in man than the mere breath of his body." It was just a matter of interpreting its words in the light of modern science. Here Fitzroy was very ready to help. One can see the two of them in the tiny cabin, the lamp swinging above their heads, the twenty-two chronometers ticking away, and the books spread out before them: Fitzroy's well-thumbed Bible, Lyell's second volume on geology, which had just reached Darwin at Montevideo. Somehow, between them, they felt they would get at the truth.

The spring had arrived, and these were the pleasantest of days. Almost every morning Darwin was out with his new rifle getting fresh provisions for the ship. It was wonderful hunting; on some days he would bag as many as two or even three deer, and then there were the ostriches (not to speak of their huge and delicious eggs), the wild pigs, (he shot one weighing 98 pounds), the armadillos and the guanacos. The guanaco was a beast with an insatiable curiosity; Darwin found that if he lay on his back and kicked his legs in the air it would inevitably approach. Then he would jump up and take an easy shot. Ostrich dumplings and roast armadillo was a favorite meal on board, the one tasting like beef and the other like duck. Fitzroy bought a live puma from the Argentinian soldiers, and they skinned and ate that too. As for fish, they had all they wanted by dragging a net in the bay.

At the end of November 1832, well fed, and all things going well on board, they made another trip to the Rio de la Plata and then turned south once more to carry out the experiment on which Fitzroy had set his heart: the landing of Jemmy Button and his friends in their homes in Tierra del Fuego and the setting up of a new outpost of Christianity on that remote and lonely coast. In the Bay of Good Success Darwin decided once and for all to dedicate his life to natural history; he hoped to "add a little to it."

Chapter V

Tierra del Fuego

THE FUEGIANS on the whole had done very well on their year's voyage out from England. They had learned to speak English fairly fluently, they appeared to have absorbed Fitzroy's religious teachings, and they seemed to know what was expected of them. York Minster had announced that on getting ashore in his native territory he intended to marry Fuegia Basket. Latterly he had grown very jealous about her. He stood close by if any of the sailors talked to her and became sullen and morose whenever he was parted from her. Fuegia had a pretty little face, and among the native Fuegians might even have passed as a beauty. Jemmy Button was as cheerful as ever and was eagerly looking forward to returning home. Even Matthews, the missionary, seemed to be facing up resolutely to his lonely and devoted exile.

All this was very good. Yet what a bizarre undertaking it was and how typical of Fitzroy. On his own initiative he had picked up these waifs three years before, and had tamed them in England, much in the same way as a man might catch a wild animal and domesticate it. And now, with no other guide than an inexperienced young missionary, he was about to turn them loose in an unexplored region of howling gales and impossible cold where a few nomadic tribes scratched out a primitive living. Fitzroy had a theory that there were no such things as separate races of men in the world; we were all descended from Adam and Eve, who of course had sprung into existence fully grown and fully civilized. But Adam and Eve's descendants had deteriorated; the further they had drifted away from the Holy Land to the more primitive parts of the world the more they had lost touch with civilization. Hence these poor Fuegians. But they could be saved. All you had to do was to restore to them the civilization and the knowledge of God which their first ancestors had had in the Garden of Eden.

Tierra del Fuego had an appalling climate, one of the worst

in the world. Even though she arrived there in midsummer the *Beagle* had to battle for a month against mountainous seas as she tried to round the Horn. Once a great wave engulfed her, carrying away one of the boats, and the little ship would have foundered had they not opened the ports and let the sea gush out. Fitzroy, being a great sailor, at last got them into a safe anchorage at the entrance to the channel which had been named after the *Beagle* during her previous voyage. Glaciers reached down to the sea, and inland vast mountains covered with forests of beech and perpetual snow vanished into the swirling mists of a storm.

Darwin's first thought on catching sight of the native Fuegians was that they were much closer to wild animals than to civilized human beings. (This was a matter that was to strike him forcibly later on when he came to think and write about the descent of man.) They were huge creatures, with long matted hair and dark cadaverous faces which they painted in stripes of red and black, with white circles round their eyes. They shaved their eyebrows and beards with sharp shells. Except for a short mantle of guanaco skin thrown over their shoulders they went naked. The color of their skin was copper, and they coated themselves with grease. It was marvelous the way they could stand the cold: one woman who was suckling a baby came out to the *Beagle* in a canoe, and she sat there calmly in the tossing waves while the sleet fell and thawed on her naked breast. On shore these people slept on the wet ground while the rain poured through the roofs of their crude skin huts. They cultivated nothing; their diet was a mixed feast of fish, shellfish, birds, seals, dolphins, penguins, fungus and the occasional otter. Their language seemed to be made up of a series of guttural coughs. Yet they were not unfriendly and were not afraid. When Darwin went ashore with the sailors they clustered round him, patting his face and his body with great curiosity, and they were extraordinarily good mimics; every gesture he made and every word he uttered was perfectly imitated.

Jemmy Button was embarrassed by these antics, and Fuegia Basket ran away. These particular tribesmen, Jemmy explained, were not his own; they were a bad lot, very primitive. Fitzroy

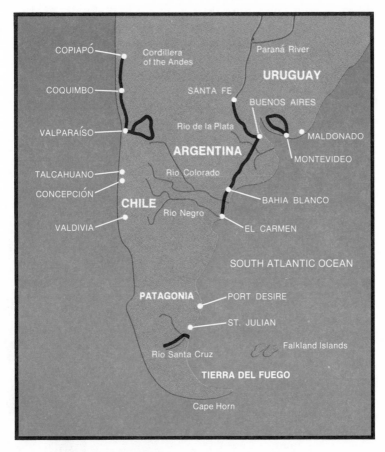

were. He was a little gloomy, but said that the savages were "no worse than he had expected."

So now they loaded the *Beagle*'s four boats with goods supplied by the London Missionary Society and set off up the quiet waters of the Beagle Channel for Jemmy's own country, Ponsonby Sound. Miraculously the weather cleared, and a bright sun shone on sparkling snowfields and forests. As they approached the sound they were loudly hailed from the shore, and a fleet of canoes came out to meet them. Presently they arrived at a snug cove, with a delightful meadow dotted with flowers running back into the forest, and here they decided to establish the new settlement. It must have been a strange and pleasant scene: the wild Fuegians, numbering a hundred or so, standing apart and watching intently as tents were put up to house the cargo, and the sailors falling to work erecting three wigwams, one for the missionary, another for Jemmy and a third for York Minster and Fuegia Basket. The women of the tribe were particularly kind to Fuegia.

Next the digging and planting of a vegetable garden was begun, and in the evening, when the sailors stripped to the waist to wash, the natives stood round them hardly knowing what to marvel at most—the act of washing or the whiteness of their skins. At night they all sat together round the campfires, the sailors shivering in the bitter cold, the Fuegians sweating in the heat of the fire.

After five days Fitzroy decided to leave Matthews and his charges to their own devices for a while, and he set off exploring the Beagle Channel. The scenery was inexpressibly grand. Glaciers reaching down to the indigo sea shone with a translucent blue, and the little boats crept along under vast mountain ranges and precipices of ice. They found a camping place on a spit of land under a peak that soared up some 7000

Fuegians hail approaching bo

Jemmy Button and his wife in 1834

feet directly from the sea, and here they beached their boats and lit a fire. There was a glacier close by with an overhanging cliff, and Fitzroy and Darwin walked up to it to admire the colors of the ice. As they did so a great chunk of ice split off and fell into the sea with a thundering crash. At once a great wave swept down the channel, dashing over the spit of land and tossing their boats about like bits of straw. They were 100 miles away from the *Beagle,* and if the boats and their stores had been washed out to sea they would have been utterly stranded. Darwin was very prompt. With a couple of sailors he ran across 200 yards of beach and secured the moorings while a second and a third wave crashed over them. Fitzroy was grateful; he named the peak under which they were encamped Mount Darwin.

Darwin had never thought that Fitzroy's experiment with the wild Fuegians had the ghost of a chance of success. After the first contact they had become more and more demanding; "yammerschooner" was their word when they wanted anything, a knife, a handkerchief, a blanket, and before long they had been "yammerschoonering" all the time and growing increasingly aggressive. Bynoe had witnessed an act of cruelty which had appalled him. A Fuegian child had dropped a basket of sea-gull eggs, and the wretched child's father, in a fit of rage, had dashed him against the stones again and again until, battered and bleeding, he was abandoned to die.

Jemmy Button had told Darwin that the Fuegians were cannibals—sometimes during a hard winter they would kill and eat their women—and Darwin repeats a conversation which the captain of a sealing ship had with a Fuegian boy. Why, the captain wanted to know, did the Fuegians not eat dogs? "Dog catch otter," the boy replied, "women good for nothing; men very hungry."

Thus it was not altogether a surprise when they got back to the camp and found that during the ten days they had been away the natives had overrun the place. Matthews came out to meet them in a state of great agitation. He had a terrible story to tell. Directly the *Beagle* party had gone off the natives had started to pilfer his belongings, and when he had tried to protect them he had been grabbed, knocked down and threatened with death. The vegetable garden had been trampled, and every day the situation had grown more menacing. Jemmy had been molested as well, but the taciturn York Minster had sided with the natives and had been left alone; little Fuegia Basket now refused even to come out of her hut and greet her friends from the *Beagle*. She wanted nothing to do with white men anymore.

Fitzroy was hurt, shocked and bewildered. He had meant these people no wrong, he had only wished to help. Why should they do this to him? Yet he would not give up hope just yet. Matthews, certainly, he would take back on board, but the others must remain and try to make their savage countrymen see the light. He distributed axes to the sullen groups of Fuegians who were standing about, commended Jemmy and York Minster to God, and sailed away, promising to return.

When the *Beagle* returned a year later the camp was derelict. York Minster and Fuegia had long since decamped with Jemmy's goods and had joined the wild Fuegians. Jemmy himself remained, but he had cast civilization away as though he had never known it existed; his European clothes had been replaced with a loincloth, he was terribly thin, and his once sleek hair fell in a coarse mat about his painted face. Yet he was friendly; he came out to the *Beagle* in a canoe with a gift of otter skins for Fitzroy and Bynoe and two spearheads for Darwin, and had a meal on board; "he ate his dinner as tidily as formerly." But no, he declared, he would not rejoin them. He had found a wife, this was his home, he was finished with civilization forever. Fitzroy pleaded with him, but Jemmy was adamant, and paddled back to the shore. The last they saw of him was a dark figure standing in the light of a campfire waving, as Darwin puts it, "a long farewell."

Whatever Fitzroy read into all this, to Darwin at least the facts were clear. Harm rather than good had been done by taking the Fuegians to England; their brief peep at civilization had merely made it more difficult for them to live in their own country. Primitive races could survive only if they were free to adjust themselves to their own environment. If you interfered with them they died. The Red Indians in America were dying, so were the aborigines in Australia; the turn of the Fuegians would come soon enough. And, indeed, by the end of the nineteenth century the three Fuegian tribes were almost extinct. The Alacaluf, canoe people of the western channels, numbered ten thousand at the time of Darwin's visit; by 1960 there were hardly a hundred.

Chapter VI

The Pampas

ONE BEGINS TO NOTICE an increasing tension in Fitzroy's nature from this point onwards. The more his plans miscarry, the greater the difficulties, the more determined he becomes. He does not lose touch with the feelings of his crew, but the generous, kindly side of his nature tends to become overshadowed in his persistent hunt for perfection. It was a fearfully difficult business trying to chart the South American coast in storms that hardly ever ceased, too much for one ship to accomplish. Well then, he decides, he will acquire additional vessels to help him carry out the work. No time to consult the Admiralty over this important step; he will take the money out of his own pocket and they can refund him later on.

And so he begins by chartering and manning two small boats and ends up by buying outright, for £1300, an American sealing vessel almost as big as the *Beagle* herself. He renames her the *Adventure*. He has to recondition this ship, he has to run the *Beagle* back and forth between Montevideo and the Patagonian coast in order to victual his little fleet, but nothing matters so long as the work progresses. Thus the next eighteen months were for Fitzroy a time of very great strain, and as he grows thin and nervous from overwork he retreats upon himself.

With Darwin it is altogether different. By now (the spring of 1833) he knows the ropes, and he becomes a very useful member of the expedition. The idea of his entering the Church grew fainter and fainter, and natural history possessed him entirely. In the journals which he kept up faithfully day by day one can see his confidence steadily increasing; his ideas form patterns and speculations begin to harden into theories.

In May, when the *Beagle* went off on survey, Darwin was landed at Maldonado, a forlorn little town at the entrance of the Rio de la Plata, and here he stayed for ten weeks making a collection of mammals, birds and reptiles which he parceled up to be sent home. In one of his notebooks he catalogued fifteen hundred and twenty-nine specimens, from fishes to fungi, sent home in spirits of wine. "My collection of the birds and quadrupeds of this place is becoming very perfect. A few Reales has enlisted all the boys in the town in my service, and few days pass in which they do not bring me some curious creature." It was not always easy for Henslow at the other end to know what he was getting. "For goodness' sake what is no. 233?" he wrote once. "It looks like the remains of an electric explosion, a mere mass of soot—something very curious I daresay."

At the end of July the *Beagle* picked Darwin up at Maldonado and sailed for El Carmen in Patagonia. He was now ready to set off on the first of his great inland journeys. El Carmen, about 18 miles upstream from the mouth of the Rio Negro, was the most southerly outpost inhabited by civilized people on the American continent. Buenos Aires lay some 600 miles to the north, and all the intervening plain—the Pampas—was unexplored territory over which tribes of wild Indians roamed and hunted. They were fierce and aggressive people when aroused, and great horsemen; they kept to their primitive beliefs and thought that the stars were old Indians, the Milky Way the field where the old Indians hunt ostriches and the Magellan clouds the feathers of the ostriches they kill. Just now they were fighting for their lives against the Argentinians who wanted their lands in order to graze their expanding herds of cattle. It was of course a losing battle; once there had been villages of two to three thousand Indians, but by the time of Darwin's visit the tribes wandered homeless across the Pampas.

General Rosas, the commander of the Argentinian forces, had established himself about 80 miles north of El Carmen on the Rio Colorado. From the Rio Colorado he had a string of lightly manned outposts leading all the way back to Buenos Aires. Apart from these outposts the whole vast region was a no-man's-land.

Darwin's plan was to ride overland from El Carmen to the Rio Colorado, make contact with Rosas and then push on, investigating the geology and the flora and fauna of the Pampas. It must have given Fitzroy some pleasure to see how the inexperienced young man he had recruited in London two years before had turned into this self-reliant campaigner. But there must be a few reasonable precautions; Darwin must have a guide and a few bodyguards. It was arranged that the *Beagle* should make a rendezvous with him at Bahia Blanca, 500 miles away. If all was well he could ride on again to Buenos Aires.

An escort of six gauchos was hired, and on 11 August Darwin set off. Their way at first lay across the desert, and it was astonishing that the waterless plain could support so many different birds and other creatures. An ostrich would start up in front of them, its wings outspread as it raced away, and off the gauchos would ride in pursuit.

Their hunting weapon was the *bolas,* two or three stones tied at the end of leather thongs which were whirled round the head and hurled at the animal they were pursuing in such a way that its legs became entangled and it was thrown to the ground.

The ostriches' nesting habits were unusual, Darwin noted. Several hens used the same nest, which sometimes had as many as seventy or eighty eggs in it. The cockbird did the sitting and hatching, and if it was disturbed on a nest could be very savage, and would chase a man on horseback. The males were easily distinguished from the females, not only by their darker color and bigger head, but by the noise they made, "a singular, deep-toned hissing note."

Once the gauchos ran down a puma and roasted its veal-like flesh over an open fire; and usually there were deer or guanacos to shoot. They were accompanied on their hunting forays by vultures and eagles, who were always attracted by the sight of blood, sometimes from many miles away. With claws outthrust and the hooked beak jutting out between two murderous eyes the birds would swoop down upon a carcass and within a few minutes pick it to the bones.

The smaller animals were fascinating; skunks or zorillos came wandering confidently by, casting out their outrageous smell on the evening air, a smell which can be perceived as far as a league away; the little molelike tuco-tuco emitted piercing disembodied screams from its burrow. Its name comes from the short repeated grunt which it makes underground; when angry or frightened the tuco-tuco's noise is incessant. The gentle armadillo was always too quick for Darwin; he could never get off his horse before it had dug itself into the sand. "It seems almost a pity to kill such nice little animals," said one of the gauchos as he sharpened his knife on the back of one, "they are so quiet." Armadillo was particularly good to eat if it was roasted in its shell.

All this time Darwin was taking intensely detailed notes on the birds and their habits. He was already getting that devotion to work which made him write later: "I trust that I shall act— as I now think—that a man who dares to waste one hour of time, has not discovered the value of life."

They stayed a night at an *estancia* belonging to an Englishman, and Darwin studied the curious method of rearing the sheep dogs which could be seen guarding large flocks of sheep at great distances from the house. These were trained by being separated from their mothers while still small puppies and put to live with the sheep. "An ewe is held three or four times a day for the little thing to suck, and a nest of wool made for it in the sheep pen; at no time is it allowed to associate with other dogs, or with the children of the family." Very often the puppy was castrated too, so once it was adult it had no desire to leave the flock, and just as an ordinary dog will defend its master, so would these dogs defend the sheep.

Generally by night the party camped around a fire on the open plain, their saddles for pillows and their saddlecloths for blankets. The scene for Darwin had a kind of magic: the horses tethered on the edge of the firelight, the men smoking cigars and playing cards, the dogs keeping watch. If an unfamiliar noise came to them out of the darkness, the gauchos would place their ears to the ground and listen intently; one never knew just how or when the Indians would attack.

Darwin loved the gauchos. They were as tough and leathery as old boots, and wildly picturesque to look at, with their mustachios and long black hair. They wore scarlet ponchos and wide riding drawers, white boots with huge spurs, and knives stuck into their waistbands. They were extremely polite and looked, Darwin said, "as if they would cut your throat and make a bow at the same time."

When the gauchos were not hunting they liked to play the guitar, to smoke, and occasionally engage in a little drunken brawling with their knives. They were superb horsemen; the idea of being thrown in any circumstances never entered their head. Like skaters on thin ice, they galloped at full speed over ground so rough that it would have been impassable at a slower pace. They forced their horses to swim great rivers; a man, naked, would ride his horse into the water, and once out of its depth he would slip off its back and catch hold of its tail. Each time the horse tried to turn back the man splashed water in its face and drove it on—thus he was towed across to the other side.

In the evening of the third day they arrived at General Rosas's camp. The place looked like the hideout of a band of brigands: guns, wagons and crude straw huts had been formed into a sort of compound, and within it the general's rough-and-ready cavalrymen were encamped. Many of them were of mixed Indian, Negro and Spanish blood, others were Indian tribesmen who had come over to the Argentinian side. In addition there were camp followers galore: rather splendid-looking Indian women who rode their horses with their knees hunched up high; theirs was the job of carrying the soldiers' kit on the baggage animals, of making camp and cooking the food. Dogs and cattle roamed about in the dust.

The general himself was as horsy and flamboyant as his men. He kept in his entourage a couple of buffoons for his amusement, and he was reputed to be most dangerous when he laughed; those were the moments when he was liable to order a man to be shot or perhaps tortured by being suspended by his arms and legs from four posts driven into the ground. However, he welcomed Darwin very courteously to his camp and Darwin was evidently charmed. He wrote that the general would use his influence for the prosperity of the country—a prophecy which, as he himself admitted ten years later, turned out "entirely and miserably wrong." Rosas was destined to be dictator of Argentina for many years and became a great tyrant.

The tactics of his campaign against the Indians were really quite simple; he was rounding up the stragglers on the Pampas, small tribes of a hundred or so who lived close to the *salinas*

or salt lakes, and when they had all been driven into one place
he proposed to massacre the lot.

The camp during Darwin's stay was in a continual uproar,
with news and rumors of skirmishes coming in by the hour.
One day it was reported that one of Rosas's outposts on the
route to Buenos Aires had been wiped out. A commandant
named Miranda was ordered to go
out with three hundred men and
take reprisals. Darwin heard later
that the raid was successful. A
party of Indians had been sighted
traveling across the open plain, and
Miranda's men had charged them at
the gallop. The Indians had had no time

The pichiciago, a
species of armadillo

to put up a concerted defense, they fled in different directions, each individual trying to save himself. Some of the
fugitives when cornered were very fierce; one dying man
had bitten his assailant's thumb and would not let go even
when his eye was forced out. In the end some hundred and
ten men, women and children were rounded up. All the
men who were not likely to be useful as informants were
shot. All the better-looking girls were set aside to be distributed among the soldiers later on, and the older women
and the uglier girls were then murdered. The children were
taken off to be sold as slaves.

Darwin was horrified. Yet everyone in Rosas's camp was
convinced that what they were doing was absolutely justified
and right. The Indians had resented the Argentinians overrunning their hunting grounds and had slaughtered the ranchers'
sheep and cattle. Therefore they were criminals and had to be
destroyed. It seemed to Darwin that this brutal war could only
end in one way: the retreat of the survivors to the more inacces-
sible mountains and eventually the extermination of the race—
in a very practical application of the theory of the survival of
the fittest.

The *Beagle* turned up in Bahia Blanca on 24 August and
Darwin went on board and spent the entire day relating his
adventures to Fitzroy. He had no difficulty in persuading

Fitzroy to allow him to continue on the second and longer leg of his journey, 400 miles through uninhabited country.

As Darwin rode on to Buenos Aires even the gauchos were astonished at his energy. If he saw a mountain he had to climb it—and he was probably the first European to ascend the 3500-foot Sierra de la Ventana. When he reached the top he found it broken in half by a valley. He crossed it, climbed again, and reached the second peak with great difficulty: "Every 20 yards I had the cramp in the upper part of both thighs, so

that I was afraid I should not have been able to have got down again." When one gaucho's horse went lame Darwin gave the man his own horse and walked. Gauchos, he explained later, could not walk. He smoked his cigar, drank his *maté*, and, like the gauchos, thrived on a diet of solid meat. Once he went twenty hours without water.

By the campfire at night he read a little from Milton's *Paradise Lost* which he always

Hunting ostriches with the *bolas*

carried with him and wrote up his notes on the day's adventures.

Found one little toad, most singular from its colour (black and vermillion) thinking to give it a great treat carried it to a pool of water; not only was the little animal unable to swim, but I think without help it would have drowned. . . . Many snakes with black patches in deep swamp, 2 yellow lines and red tail . . . lake enlivened by many black-necked swans and beautiful ducks and cranes . . . last night remarkable hailstorm (deer, 20 hides) already found dead and about 15 ostriches . . . hailstones as big as apples . . . slept at house of half madman . . . Indians going to *salinas* for salt—eat salt like sugar . . . women taken prisoners at 20 years never content . . . wife of old caique not more than 11 . . . ostriches lay eggs in middle of day . . . cranes carry bundles of rushes . . .

He never seems to be tired, never loses his curiosity or his sense of wonder. Finally after forty days in the wilderness we find him riding into Buenos Aires through orchards of quinces and peaches. With his beard, his wide hat, his worn clothes and his sunburnt face, he must have looked like some cowboy, or perhaps a gold prospector coming into town after a hard spell on the trail. He was leathery as the gauchos themselves.

Chapter VII

Buenos Aires

BUENOS AIRES had its charms. "Our chief amusement," Darwin wrote to his sisters, "was riding about and admiring the Spanish ladies. After watching one of these angels gliding down the streets, involuntarily we groaned out, 'How foolish English women are, they can neither walk nor dress.'"

Darwin returned to this theme later on when he reached Lima in Peru:

> The close elastic gown fits the figure closely and obliges the ladies to walk with very small steps, which they do very elegantly, and display very white silk stockings and very pretty feet. They wear a black silk veil which is fixed round the waist behind and brought over the head and held by the hands before the face, allowing only one eye to remain uncovered. But then that one is so black and brilliant and has such powers of motion and expression, that its effect is very powerful. . . . I could not keep my eyes away from them.

But this apparently was as far as he got. During the four months that he waited in Buenos Aires for the *Beagle* to complete her Patagonian survey he lived at the home of a Mr. and Mrs. Lumb, who were respectable English residents, and he was much too busy to get entangled. There were a number of English stores in the town and he shopped with abandon. One shopping list read: "Paper . . . scizzors, dentist, watch mended . . . spurs . . . French dentist . . . cigars . . . dentist . . . animal without tail . . . bookseller." Clearly he was suffering from toothache, but what was the animal without a tail?

Then there were his specimens to pack up and send to Henslow; two hundred skins of birds and other creatures, fish, insects, mice, stones, "a fine set of fossil bones" and many exotic seeds which he hoped could be made to grow in England. The question of money was a nagging business; his shore excursions were proving expensive and he had already overspent his allowance. Now, as he drew a bill for another £80, he winced at the thought of what Dr. Darwin was going to say; he trusted, he wrote to his sisters, that his father "after his first great growl" was over, would not grudge the money; surely he would understand that this voyage was changing his life, that he would never be able to return here, that he must see everything there was to be seen no matter what the cost. "I wish," he wrote home, "the same feeling did not act so strongly on the Captain. He is eating an enormous hole into his capital for the sake of advancing all the objects of the voyage . . . (he) asked me if I could pay a year in advance for my mess. I did so . . . for I could not refuse to a person who is so systematically munificent to everyone who approaches him."

There was another reason for Darwin to feel guilty when he thought of his father; sooner or later he would have to tell him that he would never now go into the Church. But for the moment he dodged this issue; in his letters home he never mentions his future.

Darwin did not really like Buenos Aires. Nor did he think much in general of its inhabitants (sixty thousand at this time). The wealthy Creole he openly detested: "He is a profligate sensualist who laughs at all religion; he is open to the grossest corruption; his want of principle is entire." Every official from the chief justice downwards was bribable.

Darwin was a fastidious man, an enthusiast with a fairly strict code of manners, and just now, when the world was opening up before him, he was impatient of all laziness and indifference in other people and furious at their active cruelty. The voyage had swallowed him up. It was all so new and desperately important.

A trip to Santa Fe was very nearly his undoing. He had arranged to rejoin the *Beagle* before she sailed from Montevideo late in October, and he estimated that this would give him ample time to make the 300-mile ride up to the Paraná River, where he had heard that fossil bones were to be found. On 27 September he rode out of Buenos Aires into the northern Pampas. At first all went well, though the journey was not without risk, since it was a popular route for Indian attacks. At one point they passed the skeleton of an Indian suspended from the branch of a tree, and Darwin's guides viewed the sight with "much satisfaction." Close to the pretty provincial town of Santa Fe he found a splendid deposit of fossil bones embedded in the riverbank. But then he went down with fever (probably it was malaria, for he describes how his hands were black with mosquitoes whenever he exposed them), and he was forced to lie in bed for a week. He was offered strange remedies, some harmless, such as a compress of split beans wound round the head, others "too disgusting to mention." "Little hairless dogs," he wrote, "are in great request to sleep at the feet of invalids."

When he felt better he decided that it would be quicker to return by river, and so he abandoned his horses and got on board a decrepit trading boat that was sailing to Buenos Aires. The Argentinian captain was so fearful of every breeze and current that they remained anchored to the shore for days on end, and crept downstream only for a few hours at a time. At last on 20 October they reached a village just outside the capital, and Darwin rushed ashore to find a horse—or canoe—anything to get him into the city. At once he found himself surrounded by armed men who refused to allow him to go on. Revolution had broken out and the city was blockaded.

A view of nineteenth-century Buenos Aires

General Rosas, it seemed, was not only interested in hunting down wild Indians; he was out to overturn the Argentinian government as well. All the countryside surrounding Buenos

Aires was up in arms. In the city itself the streets were cleared, the shops had pulled down their shutters, bullets were flying about and the general's forces were allowing no one to pass either in or out through the city gates. Frantic with anxiety that he would miss the *Beagle*, Darwin argued and protested, and in the end, after a long ride round the town, managed to reach the camp of Rosas's brother. He explained grandly that he was an intimate friend of the general. "Magic itself," Darwin says, "could not have altered circumstances quicker." He was told that he could go on foot to the city if he liked to take the risk of being shot. But he was forced to leave his assistant, Covington, outside the city, as well as his baggage and all the specimens he had collected on his trip.

For a fortnight Darwin fumed and fretted. The prospect of the *Beagle* sailing away and leaving him stranded in Buenos Aires was too horrible to be thought of. At last he succeeded in bribing a man to go out and bring Covington in. Together they managed to get aboard a ship that slipped through the blockade and down the river to Montevideo. Darwin's heart must have given a great bound of relief when at last he saw the *Beagle* placidly at anchor in Montevideo Bay.

Fitzroy all this time had been doggedly surveying, and never 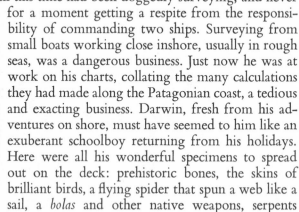 for a moment getting a respite from the responsibility of commanding two ships. Surveying from small boats working close inshore, usually in rough seas, was a dangerous business. Just now he was at work on his charts, collating the many calculations they had made along the Patagonian coast, a tedious and exacting business. Darwin, fresh from his adventures on shore, must have seemed to him like an exuberant schoolboy returning from his holidays. Here were all his wonderful specimens to spread out on the deck: prehistoric bones, the skins of brilliant birds, a flying spider that spun a web like a sail, a *bolas* and other native weapons, serpents bottled in alcohol and parcels of exotic seeds and flowers that were unknown in Europe. Then too there were all his exploits to recount.

Fitzroy must have been something less than human if he did not feel a pang of envy. He was entertained, no doubt, but one sees that aristocratic eye resting on Darwin a little coldly. Certainly he

The *Beagle* beached for repairs

was to be forgiven if with some curt phrase he turned away and told Darwin to get his junk out of the cabin and stow it, if he fell into one of his "severe silences," or even if he inquired of Darwin about just where all these exciting investigations were taking him—just how far had he succeeded in relating them to the fundamental truths of the Bible.

But Darwin, if we are to trust his notebooks, was not thinking of God at all through these days; he was beginning to entertain the notion that truth was not something imposed from above, but would be revealed bit by bit by man's own practical researches on this earth. So he might have been a little crestfallen when the *Beagle*'s discipline and austerity closed round him.

By the end of 1833 the Patagonian survey was all but done. The *Beagle*'s sailors had been more than a year among the storms and the cold of that arid coast, and they were all heartily sick of it. Augustus Earle, the artist, was so broken in health that he had to leave the ship. He was replaced by Conrad Martens, "an excellent landscape drawer . . . a pleasant person, and like all birds of that class, full up to the neck with enthusiasm." Darwin, for his part, soon parceled up the last of his Pampas collections for shipment to England and could think of one thing only: the day when they would round the Horn and sail out into the calm sunny waters of the Pacific. By now he had pretty well made up his mind about the geology of the eastern seaboard; it had been raised above the sea, he believed, in fairly recent times. But it was the Andes, with their great volcanoes, that held the real clue to the geology of the peninsula. To break through into the Pacific, to see the mighty Cordillera: that would be the climax of the whole voyage.

A year's provisions were taken on board the *Beagle* and her sister ship, the *Adventure*, at Montevideo. On 7 December they waved good-by to the Rio de la Plata for the last time and headed south, out of the muddy estuary into the clear blue sea.

Chapter VIII

The Andes

CHRISTMAS DAY, 1833, found them far down the coast in the estuary of the Desire River. It was the best Christmas they had in the whole voyage. Darwin had shot a 170-pound guanaco on the day before, so there was fresh meat for every man. In the afternoon the crews of both ships came ashore for a contest of wrestling, jumping and running: "Old men with long beards and young men without them were playing like so many children." Fitzroy, in a benign mood, presented prizes.

Physically Darwin was growing much stronger, stronger even than many of his shipmates, who were not able to climb mountains and stretch their legs on shore as he was. One day when they were anchored at St. Julian, a particularly arid stretch of the Patagonian coast, Fitzroy, Darwin and a party of men went ashore to search for a freshwater source which was marked on an old Spanish map. It was overwhelmingly hot, they were laden with instruments and guns, and after some hours of tramping all except Darwin were too exhausted to continue. From a hilltop they could see some lakes about two miles distant and Darwin went off to explore. They watched anxiously while he stooped down at the first lake, then got up and went to another. He at last came back with the news that the water was salt.

They were now in a serious situation. Fitzroy and one of the sailors were unable to move and seemed to be getting worse. Darwin did not much like leaving them with the vultures gathering ominously round, but there was nothing for it but to return with the others to the ship for help. By the time they reached the *Beagle* long after dark he had been on his feet continuously for eleven hours without water. A rescue party brought back Fitzroy and the sailor before morning.

Then they were away on their long sweep to the Falkland Islands, and down to Tierra del Fuego for a last call on Jemmy Button. They reached the Falkland Islands in March, and Darwin at once began to compare the insects and plants with those on the mainland. No detail escaped him. "Saw a cormorant catch a fish and let it go 8 times successively like a Cat does a Mouse or otter a fish." It was here that Hellyer, Fitzroy's clerk, was drowned while out alone duck shooting. When he did not return a party set out from the *Beagle* to look for him, and Bynoe found him dead, entangled underwater in the weeds of a creek about a mile away from the ship.

There was one final delay before they entered the Pacific; the *Beagle* had bumped her bottom on a rock at Port Desire—some of her false keel had come away— and so they turned back to the mouth of the Rio Santa Cruz where she could be beached for repairs. Seeing that all their lives depended on her and she was their only hope of getting home, it was a little disturbing to see her perched up there on the sand. But the carpenters found little damage and were soon at work.

Fitzroy, with Darwin eagerly supporting him, had a plan to pass the time while the refit was going on. The Rio Santa Cruz had never been explored. It was now decided that a party would go up the stream as far as it took them and perhaps get a glimpse of the Andes; better than that, they might even climb the mountains themselves. Three weeks' provisions were loaded into three boats, and twenty-five of them set off, with Fitzroy in command.

At first the going was easy; they sailed upstream on the incoming tide, with a cloud of seabirds circling above them and sea lions slithering down from the banks as they approached.

Then the wind and the tide failed; ropes fitted with collars were passed ashore, and every man took his turn at the heavy work of towing the boats upstream. By night it was bitterly cold, and sentries had to be posted in case of an Indian attack. Since Fitzroy felt bound to conserve his food supplies they were always hungry.

A treeless plain of black lava spread away on either side, but here the guanaco swarmed—Darwin saw a herd of a thousand one day—and once again it was the survival of the fittest. For reasons of protection, no doubt, the guanacos slept in groups, with their tails to the center, and changed their sleeping places each night. Let an animal go lame or perhaps fall ill and lag behind the rest, and the catlike puma was upon it. Then from the foothills of the Andes, where they perched "sultan-like" on the tops of the precipices, the condors would launch themselves into the air, marvelous fliers, hardly moving their wings. Directly the puma finished his meal, they came circling down to hack the carcass to pieces.

After ten days of toiling upstream the gleaming white crests of the Cordillera broke into view. But when they were 140 miles from the sea and the rations were running seriously low the mountains seemed as distant as ever. (In fact

Far left, a bromelia found in Chile. Left, traveling in the Andes. Bottom, a family of Araucanian Indians.

they were only 30 miles away.) For Fitzroy it was not too dis-appointing—there they were, the mighty works of God, un-changed since eternity—but to Darwin it was maddening; how did the mountains get there? How long had they been there? What were the rocks of which they were composed? But there was no help for it; they had to turn back without an answer. In four days the three boats shot downstream with a current at 10 miles an hour. On their return they found the *Beagle* "afloat, fresh painted and as gay as a frigate."

Now at last they set their course for the Pacific, and it would have been well at this stage if Fitzroy could have relaxed and taken things a little more easily. But they were tackling the icy straits of Tierra del Fuego in winter. Great masses of ice fre-quently fell from the cliffs, the rigging froze and the *Beagle*'s decks were covered with snow. "The sight of such a coast," wrote Darwin, "is enough to make a landsman dream for a week about shipwrecks, peril and death."

It took them a full month to get through, and even then the Pacific did not greet them well; storms followed them all the way up to the coast of Chile. Rowlett, the purser, who was the oldest man on board (he was in his middle-thirties) had been ill for some time, and this rough and uncomfortable passage was more than he could stand. It was only a few months since Hellyer had been drowned and it was a hateful thing to see another shipmate go, to stand bareheaded on the deck while Fitzroy read the service, and then lower the body with the Union Jack around it into the cold sea.

And so it was a gloomy and storm-battered little ship that arrived at last off Valparaíso (the Valley of Paradise) on 22 July 1834. But the sea was calm, the sun was shining at last, and after eight months of monotonous food, wet clothes and the perpetual heaving of the deck, it was an exhilarating thing for them to see a civilized town again, especially such a beautiful town as this. The white flat-topped houses straggled up the mountainside among trees and patches of green grass, and behind it rose up the tremendous backcloth of the Andes. Good country smells came out from the shore, and the smoke from the homestead chimneys was a promise of fresh food and the sight of women once again. Letters from home were awaiting them; Lyell's third volume on geology and even Darwin's walking shoes had arrived in packages from England. He lost no time in getting off the dank ship and taking up his quarters with Richard Corfield, an old schoolfellow he found living in the town. Then he was off on a mule to unravel the mystery of the Andes. He was away for six weeks.

There is something about Darwin's travels in the high Cordillera that is especially sparkling and fresh. The Andes lifted up his spirits to the highest pitch, ideas crowded into his mind, one discovery led to another. On the crag high above Valparaíso the clarity of the air is such that Chile spreads out below as though it were a map. Darwin can see the masts of the ships at anchor in the bay, 26 miles away. Behind him spreads a "fine chaos of mountains." It is sublime, "like hearing a chorus of the Messiah in full orchestra." They are so high up that their potatoes boil but will not cook, and he must huddle up to his two guides for warmth at night.

It is the geology of the mountains that engrosses him, and he makes two discoveries that rivet his attention: at 12,000 feet he comes on a bed of fossil seashells, and then somewhat lower down a small forest of snow-white petrified pine trees with marine rock deposits round them. Now at last the "marvellous story" was beginning to unfold. These trees had once stood on the shores of the Atlantic, now 700 miles away; they had been sunk beneath the sea, then raised 7000 feet. Clearly all this part of the South American peninsula was once submerged beneath the sea, and in quite recent geological times had been elevated again. As the Andes were pushed upwards they became at first a series of wooded islands and then a continuous chain of mountains whose cold climate killed off the vegetation as they rose. This movement had been accompanied by earthquakes and volcanic eruptions which acted like safety valves and "relieved the trembling ground."

Elated and excited, Darwin set out for Valparaíso. He got back to find that momentous things had been happening aboard the *Beagle* while he had been away, and that Fitzroy was in no condition to discuss anything reasonably. A letter had arrived from the Admiralty in London flatly refusing to take on the expense of the extra ship; Fitzroy had acted without instructions, must pay all the costs himself, must dismiss the additional sailors he had enlisted and must sell the ship at once.

To any normal commander this would have been a severe rebuke; to Fitzroy it was an unforgiveable blow at his pride. Perhaps he might have endured it had he been feeling well, but the strain of the last six months of danger and overwork showed clearly in his face. He had been brooding on the many things that had gone wrong with the voyage. Now this last blow was too much. The over-rigid self-control collapsed, hatred and rage took over, and he allowed his mind to go plummeting into complete despair. He was going insane, he declared, there was nothing to be done. He must resign; Wickham must take command and sail the ship directly to England.

It was Wickham who saved the day. He guessed correctly that what Fitzroy was really worrying about was his inability to complete the survey of Tierra del Fuego if he was left with only one ship. So now Wickham pointed out to Fitzroy that his instructions by no means obliged him to return to that dangerous coast. If he himself had command, Wickham went on, he would not return to Tierra del Fuego; he would carry out the original plan of returning to England on the much pleasanter Pacific route around the Cape of Good Hope. Thus there was every reason for Fitzroy to continue in command; he needed a respite on shore, and then he would feel much better when he got to sea again.

Little by little Fitzroy was pacified, and in the end he agreed to resume the command and to abandon the rest of the Fuegian survey. The *Adventure* was now sold for the surprisingly good price of £1400, and the *Beagle* made ready for sea again.

Darwin had become quite badly ill on his return from the Andes; he thought from the effects of drinking coarse red wine, but it must have been something much more serious, perhaps the bite of the poisonous Benchuga bug. Although he was carefully nursed at Corfield's home, and was looked after by Bynoe, it was over a month before he was on his feet again. Fitzroy delayed the departure of the *Beagle* for ten days on

Darwin's account, and then paradoxically provoked a quarrel with him.

It was an absurd incident. Fitzroy remarked that since he and all the officers had been so generously entertained in Valparaíso he would have to give "a great party to all the inhabitants of the place." Darwin demurred; it was not really necessary, he thought. Fitzroy burst into a fury; yes, Darwin was just the sort of man who would take any favors and make no return. Darwin without a word got up and left the ship. When he returned a few days later Fitzroy, already on the road to recovery, behaved as though nothing had happened. Wickham, however, had had enough; he drew Darwin aside and told him to stop making trouble with the captain. "Confound you, philosopher, I wish you would not quarrel with the skipper; the day you left the ship I was dead tired, and he kept me walking the deck till midnight abusing you all the time."

One wonders whether the mild Darwin was getting more aggressive as the voyage went on. Had his hero-worshipping gone? Certainly he was not prepared now to accept Fitzroy's flat pronouncements about the truth of the Book of Genesis. In Valparaíso for the first time since the voyage began he had found a group of educated and intelligent men who were prepared to discuss scientific matters in an open-minded way, and it had been a great relief. Fitzroy could go on thinking that the Andes had never risen from beneath the sea, that the mountains had always been there and that the Flood had simply come up and covered them, but he had positive proof that it was not so.

Chapter IX

The Earthquake

ON 20 FEBRUARY 1835, when the *Beagle* was anchored off the town of Valdivia on the south Chilean coast, Darwin went ashore with Covington for one of his usual forays in search of new specimens. They wandered for a time through the apple orchards, and then lay down on the ground to rest. Suddenly a breeze swept through the trees and at the same time the ground began to tremble. Darwin and Covington started to their feet, but although they managed to stand up they felt very giddy and insecure. "A bad earthquake," Darwin reflected afterwards, "at once destroys the oldest associations; the world, the very emblem of all that is solid, had moved beneath our feet like a crust over a fluid; one second of time had created in the mind a strange idea of insecurity, which hours of reflection would not have produced." On board the *Beagle* it was as though the ship for a moment had slipped her anchors and was bumping on the bottom.

The real center of the earthquake, however, was farther to the north, and it was only when they sailed into the port of Talcahuano that they realized the full horror of what had happened. All the shore was strewn with debris, and it was "as if a thousand great ships had been wrecked." Burst bales of cotton, dead animals, uprooted trees, chairs, tables, even the roofs of houses lay tossed about on every side, and great masses of rock had fallen onto the beaches.

The people had been given little warning; at 10 a.m. large flights of seabirds were seen moving inland, and the dogs in the port took to the hills. But no one had thought much of these things at the time, and in any case at 11 o'clock the usual sea breeze got up. Then at 11:40 a.m. the shocks began, and within a few seconds increased to an incredible violence. There was a curious twisting movement that made the ground rapidly open up into foot-wide fissures and then close again, and this was accompanied by a dry cracking sound. Meanwhile the sea was draining out of Talcahuano Bay. The sailing ships anchored there were left keeling over in a wet plain of mud and soggy seaweed. The people ashore had by now bolted for high ground, expecting a great wave would follow, and thirty minutes after the first shock it came. With an appalling roar an enormous wall of water—a moving hill—rose up out of the sea and swept into the bay. In the ships the sailors took to the rigging and there they hung on for dear life as the waves went by and burst upon the town. Here it carried everything before it, whole houses with their furniture inside, even the horses, sheep and cattle that were grazing in the fields. All these were floated out to sea as the wave fell back and once again the ships in the bay were bumping on the bottom.

And now a second, larger wave came on and this too receded, only to be followed by a third that was greater still. It was amazing the way most of the ships withstood this battering: they whirled around each other as if caught in a whirlpool, and, although some collided, their anchors held. A Chilean naval schooner was entering the bay at the time and safely rode the waves in deep water. So too did a number of smaller boats whose owners had managed to get out to sea before the waves had broken. Others were less lucky.

Out in the ocean the water turned black and seemed to be boiling; at two places columns of smoke were seen to be bursting through the surface, and they had a loathsome sulfurous smell, the smell, so it seemed to the inhabitants, of hell itself. Large numbers of fish were poisoned. Then a whirlpool developed, and it appeared as if the floor of the sea had cracked open and that the sea was pouring itself into a vast cavity below. For some days afterwards high and low tides occurred several times an hour.

Inland, the town of Concepción was demolished in a matter of six seconds. Here too there was some little warning; women washing clothes in the river were startled to find that the water became muddy and rose with great rapidity from their ankles to their knees. The first shocks were not severe, and most of the people had just enough time to rush outdoors before the real cataclysm began—a mad thrashing about and bucketing of the earth that lasted for two minutes. Some clung to trees, others who threw themselves onto the ground were turned over and over. Poultry flew about screaming, horses stood trembling with their heads down and their legs stretched stiff and were thrown to the ground with their riders on top of them. It was impossible to see clearly what was happening because of the dust and smoke that filled the air. The 6-foot-thick walls of the cathedral cracked and the roof fell in, whole streets of houses collapsed, and the people, running frenziedly through the dust and fires, kept calling to their families and friends who were buried under the heaving rubble. The heat was stifling, and each successive shock was preceded by a deep subterranean rumbling.

By the time the *Beagle* arrived at Talcahuano all was still, but a fearful stench of dead fish and animals and of decaying seaweed filled the air. Fitzroy and Darwin rode up to Concepción to find that not a house was left standing; many of the inhabitants were living in reed huts which had withstood the shock, and which the poor were now renting to the rich at excessive prices. This was no moment for petty triumphs, but as they walked about, Darwin—no doubt with a gleam in his eye—was able to point out to Fitzroy that the level of the land was higher than it had been before, not much, just a few feet, but enough to prove that the earth *could* rise up out of the sea; and if a few feet, why not 10,000? Why not whole mountains? What other possible explanation was there for the fact that he had found beds of seashells high up in the Cordillera?

This had been the worst earthquake that people could remember; it had run for 400 miles along the coast and it had been accompanied by the simultaneous eruption of a line of volcanoes. Could it not be, Darwin reasoned, that the center of the earth was a raging furnace of molten rock, and that from time to time this furnace burst through the earth's cold surface? Now finally he can say with confidence: "We can scarcely avoid the conclusion, however fearful it may be, that a vast lake of melted matter of an area (here in Chile) nearly double the extent of the Black Sea is spread out beneath a mere crust of solid land. . . . Nothing, not even the wind that blows, is so unstable as the level of the crust of the earth."

Darwin and Fitzroy were both shaken by what they had seen, and as they poked about among the ruins and talked to the survivors they learned many fascinating things not only about the earthquake itself but about human nature as well. In Concepción, the disaster had been a mighty leveler of social distinctions; since rich and poor alike had lost everything they possessed they were disposed to be much kinder to one another. Most of the people, like Fitzroy himself, believed that the disaster was caused by the will of God, probably as a punishment for human wickedness. Others spoke of an old Indian woman who was a witch; she had been offended when she had last passed through Concepción and had taken her revenge by plugging up the vents of the volcanoes; and thus the earthquake had occurred. The number of dead, less than a hundred, would have been infinitely greater, Darwin learned, had not the people been accustomed to rushing out of doors directly they felt even the slightest shock, and the doors themselves they always kept open in case they jammed during an earthquake. But even this precarious way of living had not made them want to live elsewhere; they intended now to rebuild their houses exactly as they had been.

The earthquake had its effects on board the *Beagle* as well. It cleared the air. Where before there had been gloom and talk of resignations and desertions now everyone from the captain downwards began to count his blessings and feel more cheerful.

Darwin was preoccupied with his geology. He stayed for a while with the hospitable Corfield when he got back to Valparaíso, and then in March 1835 set off again into the mountains. He planned to cross the Cordillera by the highest and most dangerous route, taking with him two guides, ten mules and a mare with a bell round her neck—a "sort of stepmother to the whole group." They rode for hour after hour in the icy wind, stopping only for Darwin to clamber up rocks, geological hammer in hand, fighting for breath at the high altitudes. On the ridges the atmosphere was so rarefied that even the mules were forced to stop every 50 yards. At night they slept on the bare earth. It is a proof of Darwin's extraordinary physical fitness (so sadly to be denied him for the rest of his life) that when he got back after twenty-four days, he said: "Never did I more deeply enjoy an equal space of time."

A couple of weeks later he was off again, this time along the coast road to Coquimbo and Copiapó, 500 miles away, where it was agreed that Fitzroy should pick him up in the *Beagle*. After a week of traveling along the coast road he got bored with the barren desert country and turned inland, up to the mining districts, where yellow pyrites were extracted under the most primitive and uneconomical conditions. Darwin was appalled by the conditions in the mines; the workers were truly beasts of burden. They carried loads of 200 pounds up notched poles placed in a zigzag line to the top of the shaft. There was a rule that the miner could halt for breath only if the mine were over 600 feet deep. In addition to carrying on an average twelve loads a day the miners were required to break up the ore when they had got it to the surface. Yet with all this Darwin was astounded to find them apparently healthy and cheerful. "Living for weeks together in the most desolate spots, when they descend to the villages on feast-days there is no excess or extravagance into which they do not run," he wrote.

By the beginning of June he was on his way down to Copiapó, traveling through country so sterile and arid that there was nothing at all for the horses to eat. One day they rode without stopping for twelve hours, but still found no possible fodder; the horses had had nothing for fifty-five hours and it was painful to listen to them gnawing at the hitching posts to which they were tied. In this part of the country rain only fell once in every two or three years, and the people depended entirely on snow-storms in the Andes above them; one good fall would give them water for a year. At last on 22 June Darwin reached Copiapó, and after one more short trip up into the mountains he joined up with the *Beagle* and they set off for Peru.

This time Fitzroy was not on board; he was off on an adventure of his own. While Darwin had been away in the Cordillera the *Beagle* had been pushing ahead with her survey of the Chilean coast. Several events had conspired to rejuvenate Fitzroy. He was busy, and he always felt better when he was at sea. Then the Admiralty, in London, thinking no doubt that they had hit him a little too hard, decided to make a gesture. When the *Beagle* got back to Valparaíso from her second trip to Concepción, Fitzroy got the news from London that he had been raised in rank from lieutenant to full captain. He of course showed no great elation, but it was clear that nothing on earth could have pleased him more.

And now followed the bracing incident of the *Challenger*. She was a British man-of-war that had become a wreck in a storm at Arauco, south of Concepción. Word had come through to Valparaíso that her commander, Captain Seymour, and his men were stranded in very wild country and having a rough time from the natives there. It was the business of H.M.S. *Blonde*, the senior British man-of-war on the station, to go to the rescue, but her commander, an elderly commodore, said he did not at all like getting onto a lee shore in the winter.

Now it happened that the stranded Captain Seymour was an old friend of Fitzroy's, and Fitzroy was not going to see him abandoned. He went aboard the *Blonde*, and argued hotly with the commodore, saying it was all rubbish about the danger of the coast. Fitzroy won the day; leaving Lieutenant Wickham to take the *Beagle* on to Copiapó he started off down the coast on the *Blonde* with himself as pilot. They anchored in Concepción Bay, and he set out overland to find the *Challenger*'s crew, nearly 100 miles away.

It was a hazardous trip and took some days; there were rivers with deceptive currents, there was little food and the constant danger of an attack from the Indians. When finally Fitzroy reached the shipwrecked crew he found that all but two were alive, but that many were sick and their provisions were low. A plague of mice had fallen on their encampment and hundreds had to be killed every hour. The men were getting mutinous. Fitzroy and Captain Seymour talked far into the night, and at dawn the next day Fitzroy set off back to the *Blonde* to get help. Finally the men were got back to Coquimbo, where a vessel was waiting to ship them back to England.

All this was very invigorating for Fitzroy. He returned in excellent spirits to the *Beagle*, which by then (August 1835) had arrived at Callao in Peru. "The Captain," Darwin wrote home, "is quite himself again."

It was now nearly four years since they had left England, and they were all longing for home. Already three months earlier—eighteen months before he would in fact reach home—Darwin had written to his sister Susan: "I have not quite determined whether I will sleep at the Lion, the first night when I arrive per 'Wonder,' or disturb you in the dead of night; everything short of that is absolutely planned. Everything about Shrewsbury is growing in my mind bigger and more beautiful." He chafed a little when Fitzroy went up to Lima to study some old charts and nautical papers which he thought might be of importance for the South American survey. Fitzroy to reassure him wrote a positively jaunty note: "Growl not at all. Leeway will be made up. Good has been done unaccompanied by evil— ergo, I am happier than usual."

By this time Darwin really had need of a spell of rest. He had driven himself very hard on his various journeys inland since the earthquake, sitting his mule from dawn to dark, cooking his meals by the campfire, sleeping on the ground in the open. Riding in the Cordillera he mentions that one night he suffered an "attack of the Benchuga." The Benchuga bug is now thought to be the carrier of Chagas' disease, and these bites might be one of the causes of ill health which was to bedevil Darwin for the rest of his life.

While waiting for Fitzroy to return from Lima, Darwin stayed on board the *Beagle* at Callao, working up his notes, packing his specimens and reading about the Pacific. "Living quietly on board the ship and eating good dinners," he wrote to Susan, "have made me twice as fat and happy as I have been for some months previously."

At last on 7 September 1835 they set sail, heading straight out into the open Pacific, where their first landfall was that strange little group of volcanic islands known as the Galápagos, or the Encantadas, the Enchanted Isles.

Chapter X

The Galápagos Islands

AFTER TAHITI the Galápagos were the most famous of all the tropical islands in the Pacific. They were not lush and beautiful like Tahiti; they were (and still are) far off the usual maritime routes, and nobody lived in them then except a handful of political prisoners. Their fame was founded upon one thing; they were infinitely strange, unlike any other islands in the world. No one who went there ever forgot them. For the *Beagle* the Galápagos were just another port of call, but for

Darwin they were much more than that. In his own words: "Here, both in space and time, we seem to be brought somewhat near to that great fact—that mystery of mysteries—the first appearance of new beings on the earth."

At first sight the islands were not earthly at all; they looked more like hell. When the *Beagle* came up to Chatham Island, the most easterly of the group, the crew saw a shore of hideous black lava that had been twisted and tossed about as though it were a petrified stormy sea. Hardly a green thing grew, and on the crumbling rocks repulsive lizards crawled about. A lowering sultry sky hung overhead and a forest of little volcanic cones stuck up like chimney pots. There was even a smell of burning. "The Infernal Regions . . ." Fitzroy commented.

The *Beagle* cruised for just over a month in the Galápagos, and whenever they reached an interesting point Fitzroy dropped off a boatload of men to explore. Darwin, Covington, Bynoe and two sailors were landed for a week's stay on James Island with a tent and provisions.

The marine lizards, on closer inspection, turned out to be miniature dragons, several feet in length. They had great gaping mouths with pouches under them and long flat tails; "imps of darkness," Darwin called them. They swarmed in thousands; everywhere Darwin went they scuttled away before him, and they were even blacker than the forbidding black rocks on which they lived. Everything about these iguanas was odd. They never went more than 10 yards inland. Either they sunned themselves on the shore, or dived into the sea where at once they became expert swimmers, holding their webbed feet close to their sides and propelling themselves along with strong swift strokes of their tails. And yet, like some sailors, these marine beasts hated the sea. Darwin took one by the tail and hurled it into a big pool that had been left in the rocks by the ebbtide. At once it swam back to the land. Again Darwin caught it and threw it back, and again it returned. No matter what he did the animal simply would not stay in the sea, and Darwin was forced to conclude that it feared the sharks and instinctively, when threatened by anything, came ashore where it had no enemies.

The other creatures on the coast were also strange in different ways: flightless cormorants; penguins and seals, both cold-sea creatures, unpredictably living here in these tropical waters; and a scarlet crab that scuttled over the lizards' backs, hunting for ticks. Walking inland with Covington, Darwin arrived among some scattered cactuses, and here two enormous tortoises were feeding. They were quite deaf and did not notice the two men until they had drawn level with their eyes. Then they hissed loudly and drew in their heads. These animals were so big and heavy that it was impossible to lift them or even turn them over on their sides—Darwin and Covington tried— and they could easily bear the weight of a man. Darwin got aboard and found it a very wobbly seat, but he in no way impeded the tortoise's progress. He calculated that it managed 60 yards in ten minutes, or 360 yards an hour, which would be roughly four miles a day—"allowing a little time for it to eat on the road."

The tortoises were headed towards a freshwater spring on higher ground, and from many directions broad paths converged upon the spot. Darwin and Covington soon found themselves in the midst of a strange two-way procession, some of the animals going up, others coming down, all of them pacing deliberately along and occasionally pausing to browse on the cactus along the way. This procession continued all through the day and night, and appeared to have been going on for countless ages.

As they went higher the two men found themselves in quite different country; clouds filled the air with moisture and there were tall trees covered with ferns, orchids, lichens and mosses. At the spring itself one line of tortoises was quietly leaving, having drunk its fill, and another line was eagerly traveling towards the water, with outstretched necks. "Quite regardless of any spectator, the tortoise buries his head in the water above his eyes, and greedily swallows great mouthfuls, at the rate of about ten in a minute." They drank and drank as though they were not drinking for one day but for a month, as indeed they were.

The males were easily distinguished from the females by

their greater size and their longer tails; during the mating season the male utters a hoarse bellow which can be heard a hundred yards away. "The female," says Darwin briskly, "never uses her voice."

The huge beasts were quite defenseless. Whalers took them by the hundred to provision their ships, and Darwin himself had no difficulty in catching three young ones which were later put on board the *Beagle* and taken back alive to England. Natural hazards beset them too, of course; the carrion-feeding buzzards swooped on the young tortoises as soon as they were hatched, and occasionally Darwin would come upon the body of some monster who in his old age had missed his footing and fallen down a precipice. Everywhere through the islands discarded shells lay about. Roast tortoise, Darwin discovered, was good eating, especially if you cooked it as he had seen the gauchos cook the armadillos—in the shell.

Another phenomenon was the land iguana. These were almost as big as the marine iguana—a 4-foot specimen was nothing unusual—and even uglier; they had a ridge of spines along the back and a Joseph's coat of orange yellow and brick red that looked as though it had been splashed upon them in blotches by a clumsy hand. They fed upon the 30-foot cactus trees, climbing up quite high to get at the more succulent bits, and always seemed to be ravenous. Their burrows were so numerous that Darwin was constantly putting his foot into them as he walked along, and they could shift the earth with astonishing rapidity, one quick scrape with the front paws and then another with the back. They had sharp teeth and a general air that was menacing, yet they never seemed to want to bite.

On James Island Darwin counted twenty-six species of land birds, all unique. They were incredibly tame. Having never learned to fear man they regarded Darwin simply as another large harmless animal, and they sat unmoved in the bushes whenever he passed by. He brushed a hawk off a bough with the end of his gun. A mockingbird came down to drink from a pitcher of water he was holding in his hand. "We may infer," wrote Darwin, "what havoc the introduction of any new beast of prey must cause in a country, before the instincts of the indigenous inhabitants have become adapted to the stranger's craft or power."

An enchanted week went by, and Darwin's jars were filled with plants, seashells, insects, lizards and snakes. The Garden of Eden presumably was not quite like this, nevertheless the island had a quality of timelessness and innocence, nature was in a state of balance with itself. Darwin saw a finch unconcernedly eating one end of a bit of cactus while a lizard ate the other, and in the upper, greener regions lizards and tortoises fed together on the same bush of berries. The only real intruder here was man. One day they walked around the coast to a crater which contained a perfectly circular lake. The water was only a few inches deep, and it rested on a floor of sparkling white salt. The shore was covered with a fringe of bright green plants. In this idyllic spot the mutinous crew of a whaling ship had murdered their captain a short time before, and the dead man's skull was still lying on the ground.

The *Beagle* could not linger, much as Darwin longed to. Back on board he began to sort out his specimens, and was soon struck by an important fact: the majority of them were unique species which were to be found in these islands and nowhere else, and this applied to the plants as well as to the reptiles, birds, fish, shells and insects. It was true that they resembled other species in South America, but at the same time they were very different. "It was most striking," Darwin wrote later, "to be surrounded by new birds, new reptiles, new shells, new insects, new plants, and yet by innumerable trifling details of structure, and even by the tones of voice and plumage of the birds, to have the temperate plains of . . . Patagonia, or the hot dry deserts of northern Chile, vividly brought before my eyes."

He made another discovery: the species differed from island to island, even though many of the islands were only 50 or 60 miles apart. Thus the tortoises of Albemarle Island had a different sort of shell from those on Chatham, and both differed

again from those on James. With the little finches these effects were still more marked. It was the variety of their beaks that amazed Darwin. On one island they had developed strong thick beaks for cracking nuts and seeds, on another the beak was smaller to enable the bird to catch insects, on another again the beak was adjusted to

Top, giant Galápagos tortoises. Right, land iguana. Left, large-beaked finches drawn by John Gould. Bottom, comparative sizes of the beaks of finches.

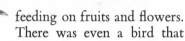

feeding on fruits and flowers. There was even a bird that had learned how to use a cactus spine to probe grubs out of holes.

Clearly the birds had found different foods on different islands, and through successive generations had adjusted themselves accordingly. The fact that they differed so much among themselves suggested that they had got to the Galápagos Islands first; for a period, possibly quite a long one, they were probably without competitors for food and territory, and this had allowed them to evolve in directions which would otherwise have been closed to them. Isolation had encouraged the origin of new species.

Somewhere here a great principle was involved. Naturally Darwin did not grasp the full implications of it all at once, but by this time he must have realized that he was on the edge of a remarkable and disturbing discovery. Until this point he had never openly objected to the current belief in the creation of unchangeable species, though he may well have had secret doubts. But now here on the Galápagos, faced with the existence

293

of different forms of mockingbirds, tortoises and finches on different islands, he was forced to question the most fundamental contemporary theories. More than that; if the ideas that were now buzzing round in his head were proved correct then all the accepted theories of the origin of life on this earth would have to be revised, and the story of Adam and Eve and the Flood would be exposed as nothing more than a superstitious myth. It might take years of research and investigation to prove anything, but in theory at least all the pieces of the jigsaw puzzle seemed to be coming together.

He can hardly have failed to have put his ideas to Fitzroy, and if we follow the two men's later writings it is not impossible to reproduce their argument, not impossible to envisage them in their narrow cabin or out on the poop deck as they sailed away from the Galápagos, putting forth their ideas with all the force of young men who passionately want to persuade one another and to get to the absolute truth.

Darwin's thesis was simply this: the world as we know it was not just "created" in a single instant of time; it had evolved from something infinitely primitive and it was changing still. There was a wonderful illustration of what had happened here in these islands. Quite recently they had been pushed up out of the sea by a volcanic eruption, and at first there was no life at all upon them. Then birds arrived, and they deposited seeds from their droppings, possibly even from mud clinging to their feet. Other seeds which were resistant to seawater floated across from the South American mainland. Floating logs may have transported the first lizards across. The tortoises may have come from the sea itself and have developed into land animals. And each species as it arrived adjusted itself to the food—the plant and animal life—that it found in the islands. Those that failed to adjust and defend themselves from other species became extinct. That is what had happened to the huge creatures whose bones they had discovered in Patagonia; they had been set upon by enemies and destroyed. All living things had been submitted to this process. Man himself had survived and triumphed because he was more skillful and aggressive than his competitors, even though in the beginning he was a very primitive creature, more primitive even than the apes. Indeed, it was possible that all forms of life on earth had started from one common ancestor.

Fitzroy must have thought that all this was blasphemous rubbish; man, it was definitely stated in the Bible, was created perfect, the image of God Himself, and all the different species were created separately and had not changed. Some had simply died out, that was all. He even went so far as to turn the question of the finches' beaks to support his own theories: "This appears to be one of those admirable provisions of Infinite Wisdom by which each created thing is adapted to the place for which it was intended."

Fitzroy as the voyage progressed had become more and more rigid in his biblical views. He believed that there were some things that we were not meant to understand; the explanation of the original source of the universe must remain a mystery which defied all scientific investigations. But by now Darwin had gone too far to be able to accept this. Civilized man was bound to go on asking the most vital of all questions, Where have I come from? and to follow his inquiries wherever they took him. Perhaps they would lead him nearer to God than any act of blind faith could ever do.

There was to be no end to this argument. For the moment, however, the two men could do no more than agree to disagree; Darwin certainly did not push his ideas too hard, and there still remained a great deal of personal liking between the two young men. The future was to carry them far apart, but just now the voyage itself conspired to put aside their differences.

Chapter XI

Homeward Bound

THE *Beagle* now was a happy ship. She was homeward bound. In the swell of the tropical Pacific she bowled along at the rate of 150 miles a day. With great good luck just before she sailed from the Galápagos she had fallen in with a little schooner from

Guayaquil, and there had been a bag of mail for them aboard the vessel. They had fresh meat; eighteen live turtles were lying on their backs on the afterdeck. Darwin was busy in his cabin, by now a miniature laboratory; every cranny was stuffed with snakes and insects in jars, the skins of birds and other creatures, and he sat at his table, pretty much as he was to sit for the rest of his life, with his microscope, his dissecting instruments and his notebooks before him.

Darwin, now twenty-six, had changed in appearance since they had left Plymouth four years before; he had filled out, his head had become a little heavier, and in his manner there was more assurance and authority. His studies possessed him absolutely. "I literally could hardly sleep at night for thinking over my day's work," he had written to Susan. He did not even bother to shoot or fish for specimens any more—all that was left to Covington.

The bulk of the *Beagle*'s work was done—she had merely to complete her chain of chronological reckonings round the world—and so there was a less purposeful atmosphere on board. Long uneventful weeks at sea were punctuated by pleasant landfalls at Tahiti, New Zealand and Australia.

It took them twenty-five days, running before the steady tradewind, to cover the 3200 miles from the Galápagos to Tahiti. When they landed at Point Venus they were greeted by a crowd of happy, laughing men, women and children. "Charming Tahiti!" exclaimed Darwin. He found the island beautiful and the inhabitants hospitable, but both Darwin and Fitzroy were disappointed in the appearance of the women of Tahiti, and Darwin thought they were in great need of a becoming costume. "Their personal appearance . . . is far inferior in every respect to that of the men. . . . Most of the men are tattooed . . . so gracefully that they have a very elegant effect," Darwin wrote.

At daybreak next morning the ship was hemmed in by canoes, and at least two hundred natives eagerly swarmed on board. Every one of them had brought something to sell. Most of the men knew a few English words, so that "a lame sort of conversation could be carried on." One of the Tahitians to whom Darwin had given some trifling gift brought him a present of hot roasted bananas, a pineapple and some coconuts, and Darwin was so pleased with this "adroit attention" that he engaged the man and a companion to accompany him as guides on a three-day trip into the mountains.

It would be hard to imagine anything less like his perilous and carefully planned excursions into the mountains in South America. Darwin had told his two guides to bring food and clothing with them, but they replied that there was plenty of food in the mountains, and for clothing their skin was sufficient. And indeed they lived off the land with the greatest ease and comfort. When they stopped for the night the two Tahitians in a few minutes built an excellent hut of bamboos thatched with banana leaves and cooked delicious meals of fish and bananas wrapped up in small green parcels of leaves which they roasted between two layers of hot stones.

Darwin had been told that the Tahitians had become a gloomy race, living in fear of the missionaries, but this he found to be decidedly untrue. "It would be difficult in Europe," he wrote, "to pick out of a crowd half so many merry and happy faces." Yet there was one revealing little incident. Up in the mountains he offered his guides a drink from his flask of spirits; "they could not resolve to refuse; but as often as they drank a little, they put their fingers before their mouths and uttered the word 'Missionary.'" A sort of incantation, one imagines, to soothe their consciences.

On 26 November the *Beagle* set sail and steered a course for New Zealand. They were at sea for more than three weeks. "It is necessary to sail over this great ocean to comprehend its immensity," wrote Darwin; "for weeks together . . . nothing but the same blue, profoundly deep ocean."

The first sight of the Bay of Islands, up in the northwest corner of the North Island, was not impressive. Little villages of tidy-looking houses came down to the water's edge; they belonged to the English settlers who had tried to re-create English cottage gardens in this alien soil. There were three whalers at anchor in the bay, but there was an air of dullness and inactivity; only one canoe came alongside the *Beagle*—"a

not very pleasing contrast with our joyful and boisterous welcome at Tahiti." In every way the native New Zealanders
compared badly with the Tahitians; Darwin even goes so far
as to say "one is a savage, the other a civilised man." The idea
of washing never seemed to enter their heads; most of them
were dressed in a couple of blankets, black with dirt, and their
faces were entirely covered by a complicated design of tattooing
which gave them a disagreeable expression. They were surly
and inhospitable. Only one thing about them took Darwin's
fancy: their habit of rubbing noses when they met. The rubbing
lasted rather longer than a cordial shake of the hand, and was
accompanied by "comfortable little grunts."

While in New Zealand Darwin learned of the onetime existence of the giant prehistoric bird, the moa. Little was known
about this terrifying creature which stood 10 to 12 feet high, but
it was thought to have become   extinct in comparatively re-
cent

times. It was one of those
strange anomalies in nature,
a flightless bird; remembering the cormorants in the Galápagos, Darwin concluded later
that the use of wings could be a
disadvantage in the case of birds
and insects living on oceanic
islands, where a sudden
storm might catch
their wings
and blow
them out
to sea.

After nine days in New Zealand, the *Beagle* set off for Australia. "I believe we were all glad to leave New Zealand," Darwin noted in his journal. "It is not a pleasant place. Among the natives there is absent that charming simplicity which is found at Tahiti, and the greater part of the English are the very refuse of society."

On 12 January 1836 a light air carried them towards the entrance of Port Jackson. They were astounded by the size of the town of Sydney, the large white stone houses, the windmills, the general air of prosperity. Following his usual custom, Darwin hired a man and two horses and set off inland. The roads were excellent, due largely to the iron gangs—parties of convicts working in chains under the guard of armed sentries —but there were few travelers except for the occasional bullock wagon piled up with bales of wool. He found the eucalyptus woods, with their pale foliage and shredding bark, desolate and untidy after the tropical forests of South America. They gave no shade, a great disadvantage since he was riding in a temperature of 119°, in a wind which felt "as though it had passed over a fire." On his way back there was a pleasant interlude at a large country house outside Sydney, where he met a bevy of "pretty, ladylike Australian girls—deliciously English-like."

But Australia did not really interest him; he thought the scenery monotonous and disliked the state of society, supported by convict labor; how odious, he felt, to be waited on by a man who perhaps the day before had been flogged for some trifling misdemeanor and had no redress. He saw

Far left, Australian aborigine. Left, a native kangaroo dance. Bottom, diagrams showing stages of coral development.

SEA LEVEL

SEA LEVEL

the convicts' lives being passed away with discontent and unhappiness, while the settlers were only bent on acquiring wealth.

The New World was not for Darwin, but the old world, the primeval world of darkness of the aborigines and the prehistoric animals—that was a different matter. Far from being such utterly degraded beings as they had been represented, he found the aborigines to be good-humored and pleasant, admirable in their own arts of tracking and throwing spears. He realized well enough that they had no future. "Wherever the European has trod," he wrote, closely echoing Captain Cook, "death seems to pursue the aboriginal." Their numbers were already rapidly decreasing and they were becoming outcasts in their own country. "It is very curious to see in the midst of a civilised people, a set of harmless savages wandering about without knowing where they shall sleep at night." Even more disturbing was the fact that the aborigines seemed to accept this treatment without protest; they were all too grateful for the small help they got from the white man: the occasional use of his dogs for hunting, offal from his slaughterhouse, a little milk from his cows.

It was the same with the animals. He went kangaroo-hunting, riding for hours in the raging heat, but all the day long saw never a kangaroo nor even a wild dog. "A few years since this country abounded with wild animals; but now the emu is banished to a long distance, and the kangaroo is become scarce; to both the English greyhound has been highly destructive. It may be long before these animals are altogether exterminated, but their doom is fixed." He had one bit of luck; he saw several platypuses at play in a river: "a most extraordinary animal."

Darwin was not sorry to leave Australia. By now homesickness had begun to overwhelm him; he only longed for England. He had been bitterly disappointed to find no letters awaiting him in Sydney; the last direct news he had had from his family was thirteen months old. He wrote to his sisters: "I confess I never see a Merchant Vessel start for England, without a most dangerous inclination to bolt . . . I have a constant longing, a feeling a prisoner would have . . . I feel inclined to keep up one steady deep growl from morning to night."

The spring of 1836 found the *Beagle* pushing up through the Indian Ocean to the Cocos (or Keeling) Islands. If the Galápagos in appearance had been a kind of hell, then the Cocos were heaven; the dark ocean swell was breaking on the coral reef, boobies, frigate birds and terns were wheeling over the coconut palms and the white sand beaches, and in the emerald-green water in the lagoons they could see gardens of brilliantly colored coral. In bright moonlight the Malay women danced and sang for the sailors on the beach. By day the crew bathed and fished. They jumped on top of turtles swimming in the lagoon and rode them to the shore, and they dragged up from the ocean floor great clams that were big enough to grasp a man's leg and hold him until he drowned. Darwin made several little excursions ashore with Fitzroy, and even the prosaic Fitzroy marveled at the curiosities they saw: a coral-eating fish, dogs which caught fish, shells which became dangerous mantraps, rats making their nests at the top of high palm trees. There were huge crabs that fed on fallen coconuts. They were equipped with two strong pincers for tearing away the fibers of the bark covering the three eyeholes of the nut. This being done the crab would hammer open one of the holes and with the aid of a secondary pair of narrow pincers extract the meat: a marvelous example of a species adapting itself to its environment.

It was in the Cocos Islands that Darwin resolved a matter which had been on his mind for a long time. Back on the Chilean coast he had conceived the notion that if the crust of the earth could be elevated then it could also be depressed, that in fact while the Andes had been rising the floor of the Pacific Ocean had been gradually sinking. Already in October 1835, while they were on their way from the Galápagos to Tahiti, he had made a note on coral islands. "These low hollow coral islands bear no proportion to the vast ocean out of which they abruptly rise; and it seems wonderful, that such weak invaders are not overwhelmed, by the all-powerful and never-tiring waves of that great sea, miscalled the Pacific."

Now was the time to test Lyell's theory that coral atolls represent coral-encrusted rims of submerged volcanic craters.

Darwin believed that the coral polyp, the little animal that built up the reefs in tropical waters, would throw some light on the matter. The polyp could not live at a greater depth than 120 feet, and it had always been said that it had to perch itself close to a mainland shore or around volcanic islands. But suppose, he had asked himself, it was found that these reefs went down a very long way, and that all the coral below the 120-foot mark was dead—would not that be a proof that the floor of the ocean had been gradually sinking, and that the coral polyp had kept pace with this sinking by building the reefs up to the surface? This was a theory he could now put to the test.

He went out with Fitzroy in a small boat to the outer reef and carefully took numerous soundings on the steep outside of Keeling atoll. They found that up to the 120-foot mark the prepared tallow of the lead came up marked with the impression of living corals, but perfectly clean; as the depth increased the impressions became fewer, until at last it was evident that the bottom consisted of a smooth sandy layer. This suggested to Darwin that coral formations were the end products of eons of slow reciprocal processes: the uplifting of an island by submarine volcanic action, the colonizing of its slopes by myriad coral polyps and finally the gradual subsiding of the island into the sea. He worked out that there were three different varieties of coral formations: atolls, barrier reefs and fringing reefs, all part of the same evolutionary process stretching over millions of years. The growth of the coral must keep pace with the subsidence beneath it, and so form first a barrier reef and then an atoll: "Mountains of stone accumulated by the agency of various minute and tender animals." He reckoned that the birth of an atoll required not less than a million years. As evidence of the subsidence of these reefs he noted the coconut trees falling in on all sides of the lagoon. "In one place the foundation posts of a shed which the inhabitants asserted had stood 7 years just above high-water mark, was now daily washed by every tide." It was a dramatic and brilliant demonstration of his theory of the instability of the earth.

It was now late in the spring of 1836, and at last they could truly feel they were homeward bound. "There never was a ship so full of homesick heroes as the *Beagle*. . . . The Captain continues to push along with a slack rein and an armed heel." When the weather was fine Darwin was busy getting his notes in order, and for the first time he was discovering the difficulties of expressing his ideas on paper. But he was in good spirits. Fitzroy too was busy all day writing, and the crew were well pleased with the good store of coconuts, poultry, pumpkins and turtles which the *Beagle* had taken on board at the Cocos Islands. On 29 April they reached Mauritius, an island "adorned with an air of perfect elegance." Darwin stayed for a couple of days with the surveyor general, who rather surprisingly sent him back to the ship on the back of his personal elephant, the only one on the island.

For the next two months they were rounding the Cape of Good Hope; they ran into rough weather and it became evident that their chances of reaching England before the end of the summer were receding; they put in only briefly at Cape Town but did not reach St. Helena until 8 July. Darwin now had to face the fact that it would be October at the earliest before he got home. He found it hard to tolerate traveling anymore; "there is no country which has now any attractions for us, without it is seen right astern." The five days they spent at St. Helena were only made endurable for him by the walks which he took over the island from morning to night. At Ascension Island he got letters from home at last, and one of them told him that Professor Sedgwick had said that Charles Darwin "should take a place among the leading scientific men." This news, together with the sight of the volcanic rocks of Ascension, fired him again with all his old enthusiasm for geology. "After reading this letter I clambered over the mountains with a bounding step, and made the volcanic rocks resound under my geological hammer."

It was a bitter blow when towards the end of July Fitzroy decided that in order to complete his circle of chronological measurements he must return home by way of South America. "This zig-zag manner of proceeding is very grievous; it has put the finishing touch to my feelings. I loathe, I abhor the sea, and all ships which sail on it. But yet I believe we shall reach England the latter half of October." In fact things went better than this. They paused only a few days at Bahia and Pernambuco, and then on 19 August they left South America for the last time. The wind favored them, and six weeks later the battered little *Beagle* sailed up the English Channel to her journey's end.

It was a Sunday, and in drenching rain Fitzroy held his last service on board to give thanks to God for their safe return. In this at least Darwin could fervently join him; he was frantic to get home to his family and his cousins in

A Bible-reading on board ship, painted by Augustus Earle

Maer Hall. "On the 2nd of October we made the shores of England; and at Falmouth I left the *Beagle*, having lived on board the good little vessel nearly five years."

Chapter XII

The Oxford Meeting

As SOON AS the *Beagle* was tied up in the harbor at Falmouth, Darwin hurried ashore and took the first coach for Shrewsbury, where he arrived two days later, on 4 October. But it was quite late in the evening when the coach got into the town, and he was too kindhearted to think of disturbing his family at such an hour. He slept the night at an inn, and the next morning walked into The Mount, unannounced, just as his father and sisters were sitting down to breakfast. Amid all the cries of welcome Dr. Darwin turned to his daughters and said: "Why, the shape of his head is quite altered."

One incident pleased Charles immensely. He went into the yard and called for his dog, as he had been accustomed to do every morning in the past. The dog came out and set off ahead on their usual walk, showing no more emotion or excitement

than if it had been yesterday, instead of five years ago, that they had last walked together. Almost immediately Darwin wrote off to his uncle Josiah Wedgwood: "My head is quite confused with so much delight," and his cousin Emma wrote, "We are getting impatient for Charles's arrival."

When Darwin saw the *Beagle* once more, in May 1837, he wrote, "She sails in a week for Australia. It appeared marvellously odd to see the little vessel and to think that I should not be one of the party. If it was not for seasickness, I should have no objection to start again."

He never did start again, however; Darwin, though he lived till the age of seventy-three, never again left the shores of England. This was largely due to the fact that from 1838 onwards the life of this adventurous and seemingly robust young man, still only twenty-nine years old, was dominated by ill health. In 1842 he made a trip to Wales: "This excursion . . . was the last time I was ever strong enough to climb mountains or to take long walks." The nature of his illness has never been clearly established; the terrible bouts of seasickness he suffered on the voyage may have played a part. Some doctors, leaning on the rather critical and authoritarian character of Darwin's father, have suggested that the illness was psychosomatic; others thought he must indeed have caught Chagas' disease from the Benchuga bug in South America. Whatever it was, we cannot doubt Darwin's words when he said in 1871, "I never pass 24 hours without many hours of discomfort."

But in 1836, freshly released from the confined spaces of the *Beagle*, he threw himself into such a passion of activity that he had no time to think of his health. These were the two most active years of his life. He set to work to classify his enormous collection of specimens, hurrying between Cambridge and London and Shrewsbury. Henslow and Lyell were endlessly encouraging, and through their influence he got a grant of

Down House

£1000 towards a five-volume work on the zoology of the *Beagle*, which he edited, and he was made secretary of the Geological Society of London. He was also busy writing his *Journal of Researches*, which was first published in 1839 as Volume III of the three-volume *Narrative of the Surveying Voyages of H. M. Ships Adventure and Beagle*.

In 1837 Darwin took rooms in London near his brother Erasmus and at the end of January 1839 he married his cousin Emma, youngest daughter of Josiah Wedgwood. When Darwin was making up his mind whether to marry or not, he wrote to himself on a scrap of paper: "Only picture to yourself a nice soft wife on a sofa with good fire, and books and music perhaps—compare this with the dingy reality of Grt Marlboro' St. (where he had lodgings) Marry—Marry—Marry."

Emma was a charming woman, a year older than Darwin, intelligent and gay and very musical; she had had piano lessons from Chopin. She was clearly an excellent wife. Few husbands would write as Darwin did, thirty years later: "I can declare that in my whole life I have not heard her utter one word which I had rather have been unsaid." She on her side described him as "the most open, transparent man I ever saw, and every word expresses his real thoughts. He is particularly affectionate and very nice to his father and sisters, and perfectly sweet-tempered, and possesses some minor qualities that add particularly to one's happiness—such as being humane to animals." She found it impossible to enter into his work, and did not even find it interesting to watch his experiments, but she never made any pretense about it. Once when they attended a scientific lecture together he said to her, "I am afraid this is very wearisome to you." "Not more than all the rest," she said. He used to quote this with pleasure; they evidently understood one another perfectly.

When they were first married the Darwins lived in London, but by 1842 Charles could not take the strain of a city life, and

they moved to Down House in Kent, sixteen miles outside London. At first he visited London every two or three weeks, hoping "not to turn into a Kentish hog," but soon he found even this too much for him, and gradually he settled down into a routine which was not to alter for the rest of his life. His hours of scientific work were invariable: 8 to 9:30 a.m., and 10:30 to midday; by then he considered his "work" for the day done. The writing up of his material was for him the worst part; he found it an exacting and painful labor. The rest of his time was spent in walking, riding, resting, thinking, answering letters

Darwin's study

Emma Darwin

and long hours of reading. "When I see the list of books of all kinds which I read and abstracted," he wrote later, "I am surprised at my industry." His library became large, but above all it was a working library; for books in themselves he had no feeling, and when studying a heavy book would sometimes tear it in half to make it easier to handle. Weekdays and Sundays passed by alike, each with their stated intervals of work and rest.

This period of his life was occupied with immediate matters: editing the five volumes of *Zoology of the Voyage of the Beagle*, working on a paper on coral reefs, which took him twenty hard months, and endlessly revising his material from the voyage of the *Beagle*. John Murray, the publisher, read the *Journal* when it came out in 1839, and realized at once that, apart from its scientific value, it was one of the best books of travel and adventure ever written. He bought up the unsold copies and sent them round to some influential friends. When he found that they were as enthusiastic as he was he bought the copyright for £150 and put the book out again in 1845. From then on it had a steadily increasing sale, and was finally translated and published all over the world. Darwin was delighted: "The success of this my first literary child always tickles my vanity more than that of my other books."

By 1846 he thought he was finished with the *Beagle*. In October he wrote to Henslow: "You cannot think how delighted I am at having finished all my *Beagle* materials . . . it is now 10 years since my return, and your words, which I thought preposterous, are come true, that it would take twice the number of years to describe, that it took to collect and observe." In fact there was one item left over from the voyage, a tiny barnacle, not much bigger than the head of a pin, and the study and classification of this species took up the next eight years of Darwin's life.

Now his work stretched before him with ever wider horizons. He had so many ideas; he was interested in everything. He studied sheep, cattle, pigs, dogs, cats, poultry, peacocks, canaries, goldfish, earthworms, bees and silk moths, as well as flowers and vegetables. He particularly experimented with pigeons and joined two pigeon fanciers' clubs; the men called him "Squire" and he sat at their meetings in a cloud of tobacco smoke. "Pigeon raising is a majestic and noble pursuit and beats moths and butterflies, whatever you say to the contrary," Darwin wrote.

He had a great love for experiment—"I shan't be easy till I've tried it"—and much enjoyed what he called fools' experiments; once, for instance, he asked his son Francis to play his bassoon close to the leaves of a sensitive plant; he fancied it might vibrate to the chords.

One does not readily believe that the pleasures of Victorian family life were as idyllic as biographers make out. But in the Darwins' case there is no doubt whatever; parents, children, relations, friends, acquaintances—all have left undisputed evidence of a genuine happy family. Maria Edgeworth described

Charles's "radiantly cheerful countenance." Another visitor wrote that "when Charles is most unwell he continues sociable and affectionate." "More than any woman I ever knew, she *comforted*," said Mrs. T. H. Huxley about Emma. Darwin had an altogether exceptional devotion to his children, treating them with an affection and kindness which they never forgot. The Darwins had ten children, seven of whom survived childhood, and he treated them from the first as independent human beings, a rare approach to children in those days. One of them at four years old tried to bribe him with sixpence to play with them during his working hours. If a child was ill it might easily be found tucked up on the sofa in his study "for comfort and company."

He wrote the most charming, warmhearted letters; when his eldest son Willy got a good place at Rugby: "My dear old Willy, I have not for a very long time been more pleased than I was this morning at receiving your letter with the *excellent* news. . . . We are so very glad to hear that you are happy and comfortable . . . I go my morning walk and often think of you." To his son George when he was appointed second wrangler at Cambridge: "My dear old fellow . . . Again and again I congratulate you. . . . You have made my hand tremble so I can scarcely write." He was present at the death of his second daughter Annie when she died in Malvern at the age of ten (Emma could not be there because she was about to have her ninth child) and still twenty-five years afterwards tears would come into his eyes when he thought about her.

The Darwins were a comparatively wealthy family; when his father died Charles inherited £5000 a year. He was most liberal with money to all his children; he balanced his accounts at the end of each year and divided the surplus among them.

As his work took a deeper and deeper hold on Darwin other interests faded, and became even actively irritating. Writing in 1876 he said that he "could not endure to read a line of poetry . . . found Shakespeare intolerably dull, and music merely drove his thoughts to worry about his work." The one thing that really entertained him was listening to a book being read aloud, preferably a novel with a happy ending. This was the man who had taken the greatest pleasure in listening to Mozart and Beethoven and had invariably carried a volume of Milton's poems on his inland expeditions in South America. He himself found this "curious and lamentable loss of the higher aesthetic tastes" very odd. But there it was; "My chief enjoyment and sole employment throughout life has been scientific work."

This way of life naturally did not bring him into much contact with Fitzroy, and in fact the two men did not meet again often once the voyage was over. In 1843 Fitzroy was appointed governor and commander in chief of New Zealand, but his obvious partiality for the aborigines—no doubt his missionary instincts at work—made him unpopular with the settlers and the Admiralty soon recalled him. It was not long before he retired from the Navy, though he was moved up to vice admiral on their books. But while the course of Darwin's life—with the exception of his health—was a steady upward progression, poor Fitzroy's circumstances and character combined to depress him. His first wife died in 1852, and four years later his eldest daughter also, a beautiful girl of sixteen. In 1857 he applied for the post of chief naval officer in the Board of Trade's maritime department, but it was given instead to Sulivan—the man who twenty-five years before had been his second lieutenant in the *Beagle*. For a man of Fitzroy's pride this must have been hard to accept. He became a great expert on weather prediction; in fact he was the originator of all the weather forecasting on which shipping now depends. But here again he came in for criticism, *The Times* going so far as to refer to "the singularly uncouth and obscure dialect employed by the Admiral in his explanations."

Gradually Darwin and Fitzroy became less than friends. Their last meeting in 1857, when Fitzroy went to stay at Down House for two nights, was not a success; Fitzroy was a man, Darwin wrote to his sister, "who has the most consummate skill in looking at everything and everybody in a perverted manner."

But now the great crisis—and glory—of Darwin's life was coming upon him. All these years, ever since he had seen the Galápagos Islands and had started classifying and correlating his materials from the voyage of the *Beagle*, he had been "haunted" by the conviction that the various species of life on earth had diverged from ancestral lines; they had not been created complete and unchanging, heredity and environment had produced new forms. Far back in 1837 he had started his first notebook on the mutation of species. He felt so certain that he was on the track of an idea of great importance that a few years later he made a rough outline of his theory and left it with a letter to his wife asking her to publish it in the event of his sudden death.

He took no steps towards publishing it himself, however; he must have realized what a storm these heretical ideas would arouse. He tells us in his autobiography that as a young man, before going to Cambridge, he did not "in the least doubt the strict and literal truth of every word in the Bible." It cannot have been easy for him to accept his own discoveries; his religious upbringing must have put up a great fight against the conclusions he was forced to draw. But he knew he was right. "Thus disbelief crept over me at a very slow rate, but was at last complete. The rate was so slow that I felt no distress, and have never since doubted even for a single second that my conclusion was correct."

His conclusion, as he expanded it later, was briefly this:

As many more individuals of each species are born than can possibly survive, and as consequently there is a frequently recurring struggle for existence, it follows that any being, if it vary however slightly in any manner profitable to itself... will have a better chance of surviving, and thus be naturally selected.... This preservation of favourable individual differences and variations, and the destruction of those which are injurious, I have called Natural Selection, or the Survival of the Fittest.

The idea that the accumulation of favorable variations over long periods of time must result in the emergence of new species and the extinction of older ones was heresy. In Britain Archbishop Ussher and Dr. John Lightfoot of Cambridge University by a series of mystical calculations had fixed the actual date of the creation of the world—it was at 9 a.m. on Sunday 23 October in 4004 B.C. The facts of the Book of Genesis were sacrosanct: the world had been created by God in six days, man had been made in His image, all the creatures of the earth had sprung into existence at the same instant, and had survived the Flood only because Noah had taken a male and a female of each species aboard the Ark.

In Victorian England these thoughts were at the very heart of nearly everyone's consciousness; if you took these foundations away you destroyed society, you mocked God Himself. No wonder Darwin had delayed for more than twenty years before publishing his heretical theories; in England he faced social ostracism, on the Continent he might have been arrested.

He would have waited even longer had he not been in danger of being forestalled by another naturalist, Alfred Russel Wallace, who was thinking upon the same lines as himself. In June 1858 there had arrived out of the blue a letter to Darwin from Wallace, enclosing an essay and asking Darwin, if he thought it good enough, to send it on to Lyell. The essay was entitled *On the Tendency of Varieties to Depart Indefinitely from the Original Type.*

Darwin, as usual, behaved admirably. Faced with the prospect of his years of work being rendered worthless, his brilliant new theory anticipated, he did not hesitate for a moment. He sent the essay on to Lyell with a warm recommendation. "So all my originality," he could not help adding, "will be smashed."

Fortunately both Lyell and the botanist Joseph Hooker knew of all the work he had already done on the subject, and had read his outline of his theories. They persuaded him that he must not step aside; he and Wallace must act together. It was arranged that a joint paper should be presented to the Linnaean Society the following month.

A year later Darwin published his book, *On the Origin of Species by Means of Natural Selection, or the Preservation of Favoured Races in the Struggle for Life.* The first edition of 1250 copies sold out on the day of publication, but surprisingly there was not a great deal of fuss at first. Most scientists sniffed at the theory cautiously, and preferred to reserve their judgment; as Hooker said later, "the interest aroused was intense, but the subject was too novel and too ominous for the old school to enter the lists unarmed."

But it was too revolutionary an issue to lie dormant, it pushed at men's minds everywhere. What Darwin was suggesting was that the world had not been created in a week, and certainly not in the year 4004 B.C. It was inconceivably older than this, it had changed out of recognition and was still changing, all living creatures had changed as well, and man, far from being made in God's image, may have begun as something much more primitive. The story of Adam and Eve, in brief, was a myth.

This was intolerable. People were furious at the idea that they might share a common lineage with animals. They thought, wrongly, that Darwin was saying that man had descended from an ape; in fact, what he did believe was that modern man and modern apes had diverged in prehistory from a common line of ancestors.

It was not possible any longer for the Church to stand aside. By 1860, when Darwin's book had run through three editions, the clergy were thoroughly aroused. They chose to come out and do battle at that famous meeting of the British Association for the Advancement of Science which was held at Oxford in June that year, the meeting which was to bring together the great exponents of science and religion to debate the theory of the origin of the species.

The clergy arrived at the meeting in strength; they were led by the formidable figure of Samuel Wilberforce, the Bishop of Oxford, a man whose impassioned eloquence was a little too glib for some people (he was known as "Soapy Sam"), but whose influence was very great indeed. Wilberforce announced beforehand that he was out to "smash Darwin." He was supported by the anatomist Richard Owen, who was a rabid anti-Darwinist, and who probably supplied the bishop with scientific ammunition for his speech. Darwin was ill and could not come, but his old teacher, Professor Henslow, was in the chair, and he had two ardent champions in T. H. Huxley and Joseph Hooker.

Things got off to a slow start. Through Thursday, 28 June, and Friday, the discussion droned on among minor scientists in a desultory way. By a coincidence Fitzroy had come to the meeting to read a paper on *British Storms*, and this he did on the

Friday. But by the Saturday it was known that Soapy Sam was ready, and many undergraduates as well as the clergy and the scientists and their wives crowded into the meeting.

The proceedings opened quietly, not to say dully. For an hour or more Professor Draper from America rambled on about the "intellectual development of Europe considered with reference to the views of Mr. Darwin and others," and he was followed by three other speakers who were hardly more inspired. The last of them, a man with an odd accent, began making diagrams on the blackboard. "Let this point A be a man," he declared, and "let that point B be the mawnkey." This was too much for the bored undergraduates. They had come to be entertained and entertainment they were going to have, even if they had to generate it themselves. "Mawnkey, Mawnkey," they roared, and refused to allow the unfortunate speaker to continue.

By now Wilberforce had entered the hall with his attendant clergy about him, and he created something of a stir with his priestly clothes and his air of confident episcopal authority. Henslow called on him to speak, and he plunged at once with a fine flow of words into ridicule of Darwin's "Casual theory." Where were the proofs? Darwin was merely expressing sensational opinions, and they went flatly against the divine revelation of the Bible. This was no more than had been expected, but the bishop on rising to the height of his peroration went too far. He turned to Huxley, who was sitting on the platform—an arresting figure in his topcoat, his high wing collar and his leonine black hair—and demanded to know if it was through his grandmother or his grandfather that he claimed to be descended from the apes.

It was not really the moment for heavy sarcasm, and Huxley was not a man to provoke lightly. It was by chance that he was at the meeting at all; he had met a friend in the street that morning who had persuaded him to go. Now when he heard how ignorantly the bishop presented his case, ending with his "insolent question," he said in an undertone, "The Lord hath delivered him into my hands." He got up and announced that he would certainly prefer to be descended from an ape rather than from a man like Wilberforce who prostituted the gifts of culture and eloquence to the service of prejudice and falsehood. The bishop in short did not know what he was talking about.

One did not lightly insult the clergy in the 1860's. Uproar ensued. The undergraduates clapped and shouted, the clergy angrily demanded an apology, and the ladies from their seats under the windows fluttered their handkerchiefs in consternation. One of them collapsed from shock.

And now amid the hubbub a slight gray-haired man got to his feet. His thin aristocratic face was clouded with rage, and he waved a Bible aloft like an avenging prophet. Here was the truth, he cried, here and nowhere else. Long ago he had warned Darwin about his dangerous thoughts. Had he but known then that he was carrying in his ship such a . . . He was shouted down and the rest of his words were lost.

There were those in the audience who recognized Vice Admiral Robert Fitzroy, and it must have been a disturbing thing to hear him so passionately denouncing his old shipmate. Indeed, it was both disturbing and a little shocking, for it carried the memory back to the beginning of this whole affair, to the days when Fitzroy and Darwin were eager young men in their twenties, both delighting in one another's company, both utterly engrossed in their great adventure—the five years' voyage of the *Beagle*.

It was on that voyage that Darwin had first begun to explore his ideas about evolution, and Fitzroy, unconsciously, had helped him by arguing with him. Stage by stage as they had traveled round the world young Darwin had pitted his notions against the blank wall of Fitzroy's uncompromising faith. By that very opposition Darwin had been encouraged to persist in his inquiries, to embark on that other long, hard, speculative journey of the mind.

Now, thirty years later, it must have been a bitter experience for Fitzroy to stand up in this noisy crowded room and hear Darwin's name acclaimed. It was turning white into black. How had it happened? How had these satanic thoughts prevailed? Hurt, bewildered and furious, he went out, and it was less than five years later that in a spasm of despair he committed suicide.

Darwin lived on for another twenty-two years after the Oxford meeting, and his health somewhat improved. The *Origin of Species* was published all over the world, and he wrote eight more major works, including the preeminently important *The Descent of Man*. His reputation grew steadily; he was given an honorary doctor's degree at Cambridge, and when he attended a lecture at the Royal Institution the whole assembly rose to their feet and applauded him. Down House is now a museum, and there are Darwin museums and libraries all over the world; a mountain range, the Cordillera, has taken his name. On the Galápagos Islands there is a biological research station maintained by the Charles Darwin Foundation.

Charles Darwin is now recognized as the man who, as Julian Huxley says, "provided a foundation for the entire structure of modern biology," but during his lifetime he received no official honor from the State. The Church was strong enough to see to that. He never stopped working. "When I am obliged to give up observation and experiment," he said, "I shall die." He was working on 17 April 1882; he died two days later. He was buried at Westminster Abbey, with Huxley, Hooker and Wallace among the pallbearers.

MARTIN LUTHER

Oak of Saxony

A CONDENSATION OF

MARTIN LUTHER

Oak of Saxony

by
EDWIN P. BOOTH

ILLUSTRATED BY
FRITZ KREDEL

Except for the university and its cathedral there was little to distinguish Wittenberg from other medieval German towns. But on the eve of All Saints' Day in the year 1517 an event occurred that made Wittenberg the center of a storm that first shook and then split the Christian world. For on that night a young priest and university professor named Martin Luther nailed to the door of the castle church a manifesto that challenged the power of the Roman Catholic Church.

What had brought Martin, the son of simple and God-fearing parents, to such "heresy"? What devil had compelled this dedicated servant of the Lord openly to attack the institution to which he had sworn obedience? His superiors were determined to find the answer—even if it cost Luther his life.

Here is a dramatic human portrait of the great revolutionary, an unswerving idealist who was also a loving father, author of the tenderest of children's hymns.

I

PLANTING

ON THE MORNING OF NOVEMBER 11, 1483, the parish priest of the Church of St. Peter and St. Paul in Eisleben, in the German province of Thuringia, baptized the day-old son of Hans and Margaret Luther. It was St. Martin's Day and the devout father and mother offered the name Martin for their firstborn. The priest took the baby in his arms, touched his fingertips in holy water, and laid them gently on the boy's head. ". . . in the name of the Father and of the Son and of the Holy Ghost, Amen." The sign of the Cross, ancient symbol of glory and humility, he marked on the little forehead to ward off the devil and all his works. The service over, Hans carried the baby home again, and as Margaret Luther looked at her boy she knew that their life as a family had now begun in earnest.

Hans Luther, strong and determined, but not ungentle, had come up from the land, son and grandson of peasants. By the custom of his people the family land would fall to the youngest, not the eldest, son, so he had known for a long time that he must cut his own path. In journeys to Eisenach, the town of Margaret Ziegler's birth and girlhood, he had met and courted her. The Zieglers were burghers and had not been sure that a

321

marriage with a peasant was a good one for her. But she had
not been afraid of life with Hans, for they had talked often of
the way in which, forsaking the land for the mines, they would
work their way steadily up in life.

Now they knew the fruition of their love in marriage, a home,
and a son. Hans was working daily in the mines of Eisleben,
and they were living in a small, dark house on a narrow street
near the great church. They were comparative strangers in
Eisleben, having no relatives here, and few friends, but Hans
honored the Church, was devout in his religious practices, and
kept his courage stout. The devil would do strange and unexpected things, the mines were treacherous, plagues would
come—but, in firm spirit, Hans was laying the foundation of
his family security. They would stay a while now in Eisleben
until the little fellow was more ready for traveling and then
they would move to Mansfeld, the center of the mining area,
and set up their home.

Through the winter months of 1483–1484 Hans worked, Margaret kept house, and the baby grew. Then, in the early summer months, they moved to Mansfeld, where Hans hoped someday to lease a mine of his own. But the early years in Mansfeld were not easy. Economic competition does not yield its fruits easily, and the newcomers had hard struggles. But Margaret had rightly gauged Hans in the days when he came courting, for now she saw his hold on work and reward grow steadily stronger, and the future held some promise as she carried on her daily work.

After Martin, brothers and sisters came to share the family love. The father and mother early instituted a rigorous but fair discipline. Obedience was exacted, and in righteous earnestness offenses were punished severely. Hans desired good things from the family and good things he would have. But the love that lighted the home in Eisleben at Martin's birth never was absent from the home in Mansfeld as the years went by. The newer children were as well beloved as Martin, and the whole atmosphere was one that carried into the opening lives of the children a sense of protection and affection.

Long afterward Luther would say that the fear of punishment inculcated in him in his boyhood drove him into the monastery. But the fact behind this boyhood fear was the strangely lovely experience of a father and a mother throwing their entire earnestness into the corrective rearing of their boy. The love of Hans Luther would follow his boy Martin through such vicissitudes as few fathers face, and would never falter.

Hans and Margaret were building well in Mansfeld. The long winter evenings around the great, highly decorated porcelain stove and the long summer evenings sitting through the twilight brought realization to their youthful dreams and set marks of family love on little hearts gathered around them.

From his mother Martin learned the Lord's Prayer, wondering often what it was all about, waiting for the years to give it meaning. The Ten Commandments he slowly mastered, reciting them to father and mother, who showed him how in the breaking of any of them he would be earning for himself a terrible eternal punishment. The Apostles' Creed, too, they taught him.

323

They told him of the God who creates and governs, who watches, rewards, and punishes. They told him of the Christ who came for his salvation, and they sang with him the infinitely tender Christmas songs of Thuringian tradition.

Song and picture brought him alike the little Christ of Love and the supreme Christ of Judgment. They taught him that Christ sits to judge the quick and the dead, that He will exact from His people the Holy Life, and that dreadful is His wrath. When they took Martin to church each week, he looked with growing intelligence upon the sword-holding Christ on the rainbow in the great stained-glass window.

Not all at once, but slowly did these strong teachings become fixed in his mind. Perhaps, being the first, he was given more attention than his brothers and sisters, and his mind was early sensitized to the existence of the world of spirits. He knew that the otherwise self-sufficient Hans, his father, was strangely sure of the work of the devil and aware of the need for intercession by the saints. He saw his mother's face when she knelt before the crucifix, and he felt it must be indeed some holy power to bring such strange beauty to her whom he knew so well. He heard both father and mother appeal with fervor and sincerity to Saint Anne, protectress of the miners, and in his own little way he breathed many a prayer to her, too.

When Martin was eight his father was elected to the town council, and was to serve with distinction in this capacity until his death. Also the burden of poverty began to lighten, for Hans was now leasing mines and smelting furnaces to operate for himself. So the family prospered and Martin entered his first year in the common school in Mansfeld as the son of a family independent and respected.

On that morning in 1490 when Martin Luther walked down the narrow crooked street to enter the school, he walked into a different world. Latin was the object of the school's existence. The methods were strict and brutal, the teachers stupid and unsympathetic, the entire atmosphere one to charge any boy's mind with thorough dislike and even hatred. To memorize slowly and without interest the rules of Latin grammar; to be beaten by the assistant for faulty memory as well as for breaks in discipline; to be forced to talk in Latin instead of German; this was to be his lot. There were great days of excitement and interest as the Church festivals came around and the whole town turned out to celebrate, but the burden of the school was always on the boys. Neither stupid nor rebellious, Martin moved in a fair way through the first few years. He sang in the custom of Mansfeld with the sons of the rich and poor alike in many a street serenade and many a church choir.

Martin was content. But Mansfeld school was not the place of interest; interest was where brothers and sisters were growing up, where his father, warmed by strong Mansfeld beer, would sing to him and tell him stories. Lovely indeed is the picture, drawn long afterward by Martin, of his father "in his cups"— Hans laughing, good-humored, everybody loving him. Here is revealed the true Hans Luther with the burden of the day removed and the sternness of discipline relaxed, while friendship, family life, and deep good humor lighten up the evening.

The rhythm of life was unbroken for the schoolboy of Mansfeld in 1492, his ninth year, but the world into which he had been born was passing away, events of almost unbelievable importance were happening. While he conned the old familiar declensions, the sailors of Columbus looked in mingled terror and hope at the endless miles of water ahead. While Martin gathered wood from the forest nearby and set the yard in order, Rodrigo Borgia ascended St. Peter's throne to bring to a climax the deadly secularization of the Church these northern peasants loved so well. While he watched his mother taking care of a little brother, another mother was taking care of two little sons, named Arthur and Henry, while her husband, Henry VII, was making a strong successful effort to nationalize his England. And toward the close of the year Martin might have heard some neighbor tell his father that Maximilian was to be the new emperor of the Holy Roman Empire to which his people owed allegiance. The world was fixed and stable for him and his Mansfeld elders, yet while they taught its flatness and its immobility to the little Luther, the eyes of Copernicus were poring over his books at the University of Cracow. Little ships and great men were moving, thrones were rising, ancient truths were falling, while in Mansfeld nine-year-old Martin learned his Latin, sang his folk songs, loved his family, dreamed the dreams of boyhood.

THROUGH THE WINTER of 1496–1497 Hans Luther talked often with a friend, Reinicke, about their sons. Martin was now thirteen and Reinicke's oldest son, John, was nearly the same. The boys had been together through the Mansfeld schools and now they should either go to school in some larger town or go to work. Hans wanted Martin to continue in school, and on into one of the professions, possibly law.

In the neighboring larger town of Magdeburg were good schools, and there, too, was a mutual friend, Paul Mosshauer, who could receive the boys. Educational custom called for a change of school every so often, and it was time for the boys to go out for themselves. So the fathers agreed to send their sons off to school there together. They would have to test their courage and ability in competition. Martin and John heard the news gladly. They were to remain close friends through life, and they looked forward eagerly to the interests of Magdeburg.

Some money was available, but not too much, and it would be the task of the boys to help as best they could with begging and with street singing. Both of these were accepted as the normal activities of "wandering students." Special laws protected students and gave them certain freedoms. Their clothes were arranged in the lightest possible bundle to be strapped on their backs; shoes were set in order for the long walk; letters to Paul Mosshauer written; and they were ready.

Martin was strong and well grown when he started out for Magdeburg in the Easter season of 1497. Naïve, spontaneous, his laugh was hearty and free. He enjoyed life and moved through it with unconscious happiness. He lived in honorable fear of his father's judgment and with firm assurance of his family's support.

The walk to Magdeburg was not long, and the boys were strong and enthusiastic. They found shelter in the home of Mosshauer, and they sang on the streets for their bread that year. Martin's voice and his feeling for music were exceptionally good. Yet there is ground for the belief that in Magdeburg the boy learned, as he never had at home, what poverty and hunger could mean.

Magdeburg had a fine, large cathedral, built toward the opening of the thirteenth century. It was the seat of an arch-bishopric and was prominent in affairs of Church and state. Attached to the cathedral was a well-known and popular cathedral school, and here Martin became a regular scholar. He took his place in the choir of the cathedral, and absorbed without conscious education the mighty liturgy of his Church.

More important than all else, after the harshness of the Mans-feld teachers, was a new emphasis from the well-loved Brethren of the Common Life, who were intent on the growth of their pupils in Christian character even more than in the acquisition of learning. These brethren touched and trained more of the leaders of the Reformation period than any other teaching group—Erasmus, Calvin, Ignatius of Loyola, and a host of others.

The brethren taught Martin the pure Catholic faith. They set in his life, by example and precept, the precious essence of the historic piety of the Church. To live in sincere simplicity, to avoid sin, to take duty and obligation seriously, to serve incessantly and without fear the commands of conscience, to refuse wealth and position, to scorn sin in high places, to feel for the mystic satisfaction available in prayer—these marked their daily life. In doctrine, simple and obedient; in life, quiet, controlled, sincere; such were the brethren. And into Luther's nature this quiet goodness and firm peace sank deeply. But there was no relative near to keep a family touch with him.

Magdeburg was filled, too, with other orders of the Church, and the boy became familiar with the devotion of the ascetics who, scorning the world, sought the discipline of self-denial. With his family ambition and respect for social superiors, Luther found cause for disturbing thought in seeing one day in the streets of Magdeburg a prince from the house of Anhalt humiliating himself by begging, struggling to create the "good deeds" of penitence. What a strange world, indeed, when princes walked at the behest of conscience in the pathways of the beggar! The picture stayed in his mind.

Summer came and Martin Luther went home. Hans and Margaret saw that he had grown, his Latin was better, and he was still the unspoiled boy. When they talked of further schooling, his eyes lit up and he spoke with great enthusiasm of study and of the men who had been his teachers in Magdeburg. But Margaret remembered her own home in Eisenach and suggested that he go there for a year. In Eisenach her people could keep an eye on her oldest son, and he could roam the streets she loved so well. There were three fine churches, many monasteries, and so much religious activity that one in every ten persons was in the business of the Church. The Luthers were not dissatisfied with Martin's year at Magdeburg, but Eisenach seemed to them a better place for him.

Thus, to the school attached to the Church of St. George in Eisenach, Martin Luther came. John Trebonius, the headmaster, taught in the old accustomed style of the late medieval spirit, with lecture and question, textbook and memorized recitation, but he possessed the great teaching gift which overrides all method to bring its mighty inspiration to the student. In recognition of the future greatness that was in his students, Trebonius would lift his master's hat from his head when entering the older classes. Under him Luther found new life and enthusiasm in the old world of grammar, rhetoric, dialectic of the medieval Latin school.

Eisenach also brought him many things outside of school. As in Magdeburg, he sang on the streets and accepted bread in return, but he did not depend upon singing and begging for his living, nor was he a homeless, hungry boy. His relatives were not unkind to him, and other families now entered into his life. The Schalbes, wealthy, prominent, and greatly interested in religious activity, took him unto themselves. The Cotta family also captured his heart. Frau Cotta, so the story goes, heard him sing in the church choir, and, taking a fancy to him, invited him, in proper Eisenach fashion, to her home. Here he learned the grace of Thuringian custom. Here he sang the traditional folk songs of his people. Here he laughed and drank and danced, and knew the open freedom of a beloved circle of friends.

On every side in Eisenach there was evidence of one great tradition. Saint Elizabeth had marked this whole countryside as her own, and these people spoke her name with reverence and love. Born to rank and wealth, she had heard the high call of Christian poverty as retold and relived in the blessed Francis of Assisi. Forsaking all the possibilities of her social station she had donned the robe of the Third Order of St. Francis and had spent her life in a superbly beautiful service to the sick and needy.

In youthful, idealistic fashion the chivalric mind of Martin Luther was captivated by the otherworldly beauty of Saint Francis. He thought often of the superior quality of the consecrated life and the inferior quality of the normal life. But the warmhearted Ursula Cotta wouldn't let him get too far away from the normal. She told him many a time of the equally lovely value of the life of love and marriage.

One other friend touched his life deeply during his three years in Eisenach. John Braun, vicar of St. Mary's Church, was a man of rich and flexible experience. Many years older than Luther, he was in the habit of cultivating the friendship of the students in Eisenach. At his rooms they would gather for long evenings of conversation and singing. Braun was a man of deep religious experience and must have told young Luther many times of the struggles that preceded and the peace that followed his decision to take holy orders. And Martin must have walked home through the gentle quiet of the night turning over in his mind the all-important question of his own profession. His heart stood still within him as he sensed the possibilities that he, too, might be a priest. And on occasion when he reached a temporary decision to serve the Church and God, he must have walked with exultant, light step and singing heart. Then the morning would come and he would put off once more the day of decision. His father had his heart set on the law, and that was enough for the present.

Into the valley under the great gray castle of Wartburg he would walk, and drink again and again of its powerful earthly beauty. He knew here all the flowers and the animals that made this valley their home. His mind and heart were steadily growing, yet the strange superstitions of the countryside were to him as real as to the humblest peasant. Deep into his nature these Thuringian beliefs were set, never to be ousted. And the Eisenach of Luther's day held some strange ideas. A splinter of wood from a bed in which Saint Elizabeth had slept healed the toothache. Cripples were made whole by the power of her relics. An indulgence could be had if one visited the grave of Heinrich Raspe, a man of unusual holiness. These religious superstitions were mixed with the regulation "old wives' tales," countless in number. It was a strange dark world, and the devil moved through it with surprising secrecy. One was secure only through the intervention of the saints and the means of salvation provided in the Church and in her traditions. Luther's mind was none too flexible, rather was it solid and terrifically honest. Once the beliefs of his childhood and boyhood were confirmed in serious study, as they were now at Eisenach, not all the years of the future could wholly eradicate them. He was to remain the child of the light and darkness.

Happy were his days there, and when they came to end, he did not easily see the breaking of daily contact with the Schalbes, the Cottas, John Braun, and many another friend. But Erfurt and its universities lay just ahead, and he, in his eighteenth year, was ready to go.

II

SPRINGTIME

NEARING ERFURT, walking from Eisenach, Martin watched for the first sight of the city spires. With its more than one hundred major buildings devoted to religion, Erfurt had earned the title "Little Rome." Luther stepped jubilantly into this new world.

Here was located what was in the early sixteenth century one of Germany's greatest universities. The old scholastic interests were well represented on the faculty, but there had also grown up a fine center of the newer humanistic studies, and the combination had brought renown to the school. Attached to the major department of arts were the schools of law and theology. Hans Luther had prospered in the mines and was now able to pay Martin's full expenses, so, some time in May of 1501, Martin came to live at the student dormitory called the Burse of St. George.

Registering in the faculty of arts, he set himself for the bachelor's degree. Luther's studies now introduced him into philosophy, and to the normal lectures in rhetoric and its kindred arts were added those in arithmetic, the natural sciences, ethics, and metaphysics. In leisure hours among his fellow students, he heard the exaltation of humanism and became familiar with the mood of the poets who were bringing renown to Erfurt. But his training in dialectic was sharp and precise, and he never quite shook it off, remaining through life somewhat of a master in that art. There is no question of Luther's success in his university studies. At his promotion to the bachelor's degree in 1502 he held a respectable place in rank, and three years later at his master's graduation he was second in a class of seventeen. His Catholicity was unquestioned, his philosophy that of his teachers, his use of Latin and of the processes of dialectic thoroughly commendable.

But other and deeper currents were moving in his soul. The line that seemed to run securely through his experience was that formed by his father's desire and strength of will. That will had held the family secure in the hard years of poverty; it had reared Martin through the years of boyhood in a strict discipline; it had furnished the incentive and the money for the great privilege of Erfurt University; it had destined him for the law and seemed able to hold all other problems to its high intent. But now young Luther was seeing things a little differently.

Without too much thought of conflict he had lived those earlier years. But by the time he came to Erfurt, he had been away from the direct influence of his home since his fourteenth year. His maturity was on him, and the call of other interests, unknown to Hans, was disturbing. His native religious sensitivity began to assert itself. There was a great preacher in the Erfurt Cathedral, and many a day Luther left his presence with the divine restlessness upon him. In the cathedral, too, the mighty organ, wonder of Thuringia, spoke to him with an unnamed and hitherto unknown power. Slowly through these student days came the vision of the eternal calling. He was happy, carefree, enjoying student fellowship, and singing as always, but the problem was forming.

As the months of study drew to a close Martin faced the possibility of professional school. It seemed to Hans that the climax of long planning was almost at hand, but to Martin the air was charged with uncertain terror. Definitely he felt the religious calling, definitely he followed his father's will for him; and these two things were warring in his mind when he received his master's degree in the spring of 1505.

In spite of his apprehension and native dislike for law, Martin, in accordance with the wishes of Hans, entered the faculty of law in May of this year. Hans was now proud of his boy and addressed him with the formal and not the familiar personal pronoun. He sent as his gift at the commencement of study a copy of the expensive but necessary *Corpus Juris*. In June, for some unknown reason, Martin left school for a visit to his home;

possibly because the plague was raging at Erfurt, possibly because he wanted to talk with Hans about his distaste for law.

We do not know any detail of the visit. But long afterward Martin wrote that it was on the return from this visit as he came near the village of Stotternheim that he was caught in a thunderstorm, knocked from his horse by lightning, and, in fear of instant death, vowed his life to the monastic calling if Saint Anne would save him. Reared in sincere and simple belief in the intercession of the saints, in the terror of hell, in the value of the monastic life, in the efficacy and obligatory quality of vows, face-to-face with an instant decision, prepared by long months if not years of indecision, with a nature intensely religious and intensely quick, Martin Luther, now nearly twenty-two, took the logical result of known causes when he took the impetuous vow.

Yet the decision was already made when the lightning of July, 1505, surprised him into its acknowledgment. Through years of training he had been moving this way. The lightning and the nearness of the eternal judgment but broke the power of his father's will. Perhaps it substituted another and a greater will than his father's when it set the will of the Church over his own.

Continuing his journey, Luther rode finally into Erfurt, intent on an immediate ending of his studies and an immediate entrance into the monastery. What he thought those first few days after his return we cannot tell, nor can we tell why he chose the monastery that he did. The Augustinian order, founded in the middle of the thirteenth century, had been split by the well-known quarrel between lax and strict observants, and the house in Erfurt was the stricter branch. The vicar-general in the Saxon province, in which Erfurt belonged, was John Staupitz, a man known for gentle piety and ordered life. Also, the order had a highly reputed theological school to which Luther would certainly be attracted. To study theology in the peace of the monastic life was to him a vision of paradise. He decided to ask permission to enter the order. It was given.

On the evening of July 16 he called some of his men and women friends to his rooms. They feasted, drank, and sang.

Luther was the happy, warm spirit they had always known. Then he told them that on the morrow he was to enter the Augustinian monastery. In tears, and with strong argument, they pleaded with him to stay in the normal life. They must have spoken of the hopes of Hans and Margaret, of the promise of usefulness in teaching, of the happy fellowship of the years of life, of the probability of wife and family, of the fact that one could gain his hope of salvation in the world—but all to no avail; his heart was set. The next day, July 17, friends accompanying him, he walked down the familiar streets of Erfurt to the long high wall that enclosed the buildings of his chosen home and quietly knocked on the wooden gate.

It was no easy task now to write his father. Martin knew that Hans would be heartbroken over the change of plans that he had nursed for many years. And heartbroken he was; heartbroken in emotion, but furious in mind and will.

Hans was not one to let the main line of life be thus easily broken. He refused with definiteness and temper to give his permission. Martin pleaded with him; Hans came to see the boy and found him immovable. For many months the break between father and son seemed severe and permanent. But in the late fall the plague came again to Erfurt, and rumor drifted up to Mansfeld that it had claimed Martin Luther. Poor Hans could readily believe it, for he was struggling night and day to hold two other sons in life, the plague having come to Mansfeld too. Hans, now in middle life, heart bowed down by the defection of his oldest son, stood by the bedsides of his younger sons and saw them each in turn enter the dark eternal realms. Crushed by grief, it brought him some relief to be told the report of the death of Martin had been false. Neighbors came to plead that he allow God the honor of the service of his eldest. Feeling the strange inevitability of fate, Hans consented with his mind, but his deep approval he withheld.

Yet Luther's mind and heart fixed themselves with high devotion on the object of his desire—the holy life. And in the monastery in Erfurt the newcomer to the ranks of Augustinians submitted himself willingly and with intensity to the disciplines of his novitiate. Like the prince of Anhalt, seen long ago in

Magdeburg, the master of arts now begged bread in the streets of Erfurt. And not for bread's sake did he beg, but for the sake of sweet humility. So, too, for the sake of character, was he taught how to walk, how to sit at table, how to rise, how to understand the sign language of the daily routine, how to wear his clothes, and how to do all the other little things that make the monastic day an ordered existence. There was no undue severity here, only the well-known movement of life in a monastic order devoted to its regulations.

The long discipline well endured, his father's permission gained, and his own mind at ease, Luther was ready for the final vows by September, 1506. In accordance with the ritual of his order, he vowed his life to the service of God in the monastic calling, the *militia Christi* (warfare of Christ). He was tonsured. He received the habit of the order, and when he knelt before his prior for the taking of the vows, he heard this prayer offered for him:

"Know, Lord Jesus Christ, Thy servant among Thy sheep, that he may know Thee, and denying himself may not follow a strange shepherd, nor hear the voice of strangers, but Thine, who sayest, 'Who serveth me, let him follow me.' "

So the first long phase of life, the epoch controlled by the will of father and home, passed, and he entered the period when his will was at the absolute command of his superiors in the warfare of Christ.

MARTIN LUTHER was a marked man in the order. His fine record in the university was known, his personality made itself felt throughout Erfurt, and he showed promise of great usefulness when he entered the monastery. His superiors were attentive to him. They set him to study and destined him to teach theology. The deep trouble was not between Luther and his superiors, nor between Luther and his order, but within Luther's own mind.

Increasingly, Luther's thought turned to the problems of religion. His life in the monastery was moving steadily forward toward the subjugation of fleshly desires. In behalf of inner purity he and his comrades fought persistently against the encroachment of wordly thought. The idealistic quality of this his first devotion to the religious life called forth from him heroic efforts. He examined his conscience with severity, and, with that relentless honesty which is one of his most outstanding characteristics, found again and again that the desires of the world still found a home within his mind. Day after day, in prayer and work, his whole nature was concentrated on the cleansing of his mind. But the mind does not cleanse easily.

So Luther drove himself still harder, and in the years afterward referred to this experience as his "martyrdom" in the monastery. He fasted until the hours seemed unreal and strength was so far gone that he could hardly move. In this weakened condition his thoughts came to have unnatural reality. They loomed large and intensely real. He locked himself into his unheated cell and remained there to pray until exhaustion overcame him, and his brethren had to break in the door to rouse him. Before the altar in the church attached to the monastery, he spent long hours in supplication to the God whose presence filled that place with dread, and once, at least, he slipped unconscious to the cold stone floor before the altar.

This was not the order abusing Luther; this was Luther following to the extreme the counsels of his order and his Church and seeking to win the consciousness that his life was well accepted in the sight of God.

This inner concentration increased as the day drew near for his ordination and for the saying of his first mass. The superiors had well instructed him in the meaning of ordination. He had moved step by step in the regular custom of the Church, becoming subdeacon and deacon, and now was to be made a priest. With confidence unshaken in the glories of the Church's sacraments, Luther approached these events with mingled terror and exaltation. He was deeply conscious of his high calling and fervent in his acceptance of the Church's major doctrines.

His whole heart went out in love and adoration at the thought of the mass, but when he turned the thought to himself and considered how unworthy he was for such a task, the world seemed to fall in blinding light around him, while his own strength failed.

Some time in April, 1507, when he was twenty-three years old, Martin Luther knelt at the feet of his superiors to be made one in the long succession of priests in the western Catholic Church. He sang his first mass on May 2, a few weeks after his ordination. On the appointed day Mansfeld friends showed no lack of interest. Hans Luther, now prosperous, rode into Erfurt at the head of twenty horsemen. He presented himself at the monastery, was well received by the monks, and gave them a gift in money large enough to pay for all expenses. They visited and talked until the hour for service and then silently took their places in the church.

Martin Luther had been preparing for this hour for many months, yet it seemed now that his will would fail. The kindly words of a superior just before he entered had steadied him some, but hardly enough. At the thought of addressing God personally he was terror-stricken, the words almost stopped in his throat, his tongue clove to the roof of his mouth, and he felt an almost uncontrollable desire to turn and run from the altar.

Yet the words came slowly and with difficulty from his lips. And Hans Luther bowed his heart in prayer in the cool, silent church and heard the voice of his boy fill the house with the presence of God.

Later, at the table in the refectory, Hans and Martin, who had not seen each other since July, 1505, talked over all the affairs of life. Hans told of the health and activity of Margaret and the family, and of the general condition of the mines. They talked of the plague and of the deaths of Martin's brothers. Life seemed suddenly serious and quiet then, and the talk turned to Martin and his affairs. Hans was still unhappy over the religious calling. Martin argued that it was the will of God and told again of the divine call that came to him on the road near Stotternheim. But Hans was not sure.

"God grant that it was not a mere illusion and deception of the devil," he said.

This disturbed Martin, but he argued from the ground of his happiness in the cloister that the call must have been valid, and suggested that this was sufficient justification for his action. Still Hans's mind moved a little wistfully in the realm of his broken dreams, and he called Martin sharply on his disobedience, saying, while all around the table listened:

"Have you not read in Scripture that one shall honor one's father and mother?"

So the conversation ended, but Martin never forgot his father's appeal to Scripture, and felt himself more than once tempted by his father's suggestion that the vision at Stotternheim could have come from the devil as well as from God.

But when the visit was over, and Hans started home at the head of his party, riding out from the courtyard of the monastery back to the active life, Martin returned to his study and his prayer.

THE ERFURT MONASTERY, which took its task of study faithfully, furnished the teachers for the theological faculty at the university. Under one of these teachers, John Nathin, Martin Luther studied systematically, laying the foundation of his philosophic thought. Nathin was not a particularly good teacher, but he was teaching in the reigning tradition, which held that man could by his own will and action attain righteousness. So Luther went from study to prayer and action, striving to find therein the peace of God. Yet all the while he knew the immovable righteousness of God, which he, in his humble human life, was utterly unable to gain.

A happy counterbalance, and a suggestion of hope, he found in biblical studies, carried on simultaneously with philosophical studies. The rules of the Augustinian order required biblical study, and Luther was given a red-bound Bible for his personal use when he entered the order. This book was precious to him and remained in his memory through life. He read in it so steadily and so thoroughly that he could quote whole passages by heart. The Bible began to dominate in his thinking and he used it as a criterion for all judgments.

The medieval Church had ample cause to beware of the independent study of the Scriptures, for this was the food of heresy as well as that of the lovely piety of a Bernard or a Francis. Luther immersed himself in the Bible thoughout his twenty-third to twenty-fifth years. His mind and heart sought and found great refreshment in its exhaustless well. What came later to public expression in the lectures at the University of Wittenberg is here in its beginning.

The Christ in the Gospels, and the Christ in the letters of Paul, began slowly to supplant in Luther's mind the Christ of stern, severe judgment, upon which his steady fear had been based. But it is no wonder that he found his mind in constant upheaval as he turned from philosophy to Scripture and back to philosophy again. The one taught him to answer the terror of his personal religious sense of insufficiency with more stringent efforts of the will and action; the other constantly held up the open acceptance of the free love of God, unearned and undeserved, but real and historic in Christ.

His study broadened now, and in the fathers of the Church he began to find the central stream of piety, the source of assurance as other men had possessed it, the sense that he was God's. The great insatiable desire of Christianity for the perfect life was upon him, and Luther's elemental honesty refused to let the cry of his conscience be stilled until it knew the lasting sense of fulfillment.

In the sacrament of penance he hoped to find relief, but this relief was hindered by the fact that the beauty of this sacrament rests upon the heart's belief in the forgiving goodness of God But Luther did not believe. He argued it out with his confessor, saying that God must of necessity be angry with him for his sins. But the gentler, older man told him to go and read his Apostles' Creed again and find that he was commanded to believe in the "forgiveness of sins," and finally point-blank told Luther:

"It is not God who is angry with you. It is you who are angry with God."

And in the discussion that followed on this point, the confessor told Luther to read the works of Bernard of Clairvaux, pointing out that Bernard found the grace of God to be the source of peace.

So Martin Luther sat in his cell in Erfurt, and the centuries disappeared while Bernard spoke to him. For Bernard, too, had felt the strong hold of the sense of sin, and he, too, in the twelfth century had fled the world to make in the monastic life the mighty effort for redemption. The winters passed over his head and the sense of sin still remained within him, but in the historic work of Christ he found the proof of God's everlasting affection. He led Luther into a vision of the crucifixion from which the riches of the love of God could be understood. And soon Luther felt the hold of sin weakening, and terror of death lessening, the nearness of God a little more discernible.

Eager in the pursuit of study, Luther turned to Saint Augustine, whose name his order bore. Luther read his works to find what he knew of the way to God. No father of the Church could speak more directly and more strongly on the very points at which he felt himself lost—the issues of personal religion. The difficulties of Luther's speculative thought began to disappear in the presence of Augustine's historical piety; metaphysics clothed with dignity the humble human experience. A strong and new conception of Christ began slowly to establish itself in his heart.

"To believe is to believe in his humanity which is given for us in this life for life and salvation. For He, himself, through our faith in his Incarnation is our life, our justification, and our resurrection."

There stands Martin's own handwriting on the margin of a page of Augustine's essay on the Trinity.

Luther was not alone in his return to Augustine's Christ of faith and experience as the great liberating agent of the whole scriptural story. There was at the end of the fifteenth century a general return to the fundamental position of Augustine on grace exclusive. Thus Luther is seen to be in the movement of his age and to be appropriating the best tradition of thought to which he was heir.

At this point in his development, Luther was greatly troubled by the specter of eternal damnation involved in the doctrine of predestination. Here, in Augustine, he had the chance to study the master of the doctrine of predestination, who is at the same time the master of the doctrine of the free grace of God in Christ. So predestination lost its terror and passed over into the larger doctrine of the dependability of the human will on that of God. Augustine was indeed a great rock in a weary land, and Luther temporarily rested.

THE MAN WHO WAS most influential in Luther's development was John Staupitz, the Augustinian vicar of the Saxon province, and dean of the theological faculty at the University of Wittenberg. Staupitz, visiting the Erfurt monastery, became interested in the young monk who had so suddenly left the university for the cloister. He watched Luther's inner spiritual struggle, which was so thoroughly reflected in his external appearance. Luther had come to the monastery a strong, enthusiastic young man of twenty-two, and Staupitz watched him grow thin and tired, nervous and overwrought.

Eager to help and to conserve this brilliant new member of the order, Staupitz engaged him in friendship, and as the months of the first two severe years went by, Luther began to feel that in Staupitz he had a sympathetic, understanding superior. He unburdened his soul time after time to Staupitz; told him how he was unable to achieve in his own life the sense of assurance that he had done sufficient to win the mercy of Christ. The advice of Staupitz was always gentle; always to the point. With keen insight he tried to make Luther see the introspective quality of his meditation and to direct him to historic and actual things.

One day he said: "Look not on your own imaginary sins, but look at Christ crucified, where your real sins are forgiven, and hold with deep courage to God." Luther never forgot this and throughout his entire life he acknowledged his indebtedness to Staupitz for teaching him to center the conception of forgiveness of sins around the crucifixion of Christ. They spent a great many hours together, and the older man grew increasingly fond of the younger.

It was not entirely a surprise, then, when in 1508 Staupitz moved Luther from the Erfurt monastery to that at Wittenberg. Luther was ready for active work. The change came suddenly, and he found himself at Wittenberg with hardly opportunity to bid good-by to friends at Erfurt.

He was definitely committed now to biblical studies, chafing under the philosophical emphasis. The whole desire of his life focused more and more around the Bible. He could not teach it, however, until he had earned his doctor's degree. He was therefore lecturing on Aristotle's ethics, scholastic philosophy having been his major study in the B.A. and M.A. courses at Erfurt.

On March 9, 1509, he took his first degree in theology at the University of Wittenberg. Staupitz now insisted that Luther continue in studies for his doctor's degree in theology, so that he could proceed to a professorship in the theological faculty. Staupitz said to him one day at Wittenberg, in a half-serious, half-joking manner, "You should take the degree of doctor so as to have something to do." Luther objected; said that his strength was already used up in his regular duties and that he was sure he could not survive if the duties of a professorship were laid upon him. Staupitz answered, "Do you not know that the Lord has a great deal of business to attend to in which he needs the assistance of clever people? If you should die you might be his counsellor."

Luther laughed and agreed to follow Staupitz's advice, taking up his studies for the doctorate. Accordingly in the fall of 1509 he returned to Erfurt and began his work. Staupitz supervised this move, too, and kept in close touch with his protégé.

The notes which Luther made that winter bear witness to a vast reading. He continually emphasized faith against reason, tradition against speculation, theology against philosophy. A keen consciousness of the fact and power of sin was evidenced and there was a tendency to bring every problem around the person of Jesus. Luther expressly asserts that Christ and not "wisdom" was the first creation. Christ is the "son of God," and "our Redeemer," the way by which sin is overcome and forgiven, and grace is received.

There were strength and independence of thought in his notes. Luther was growing, becoming master of his own mind, and he was ready for increased responsibilities.

III

GROWTH

THE EXPERIENCES OF ERFURT in this second residence were broken by the great opportunity to visit the city of Rome. It is a tribute to the position which Luther had already attained within the order, that when a dispute arose which necessitated a representation at Rome, Luther was chosen to accompany the messenger whom the order sent to the papal see. Staupitz was, of course, involved in the difficulty. It was an administrative problem and a minority group in the order was protesting against a decision of the vicar-general. So it was a great comfort to Staupitz that Martin Luther was the second member of the commission.

In October, 1510, John von Mecheln and Martin Luther, wearing the black robes of the Augustinian order, left Erfurt on their long walk to Rome. Down through the verdant valleys of central and southern Germany they journeyed. Gone was the quick, elastic, joyous step of Luther's late boyhood.

Yet as day after day passed, he found the strength of youth returning to him. Descending the Alps onto the rich plains of northern Italy, the brothers came finally to Florence.

A quarter of a century past the height of her renaissance, Florence yet possessed rich treasures unsurpassed in the world of art. Raphael, Leonardo da Vinci, Michelangelo, and many another mighty creative genius was at work in Italy, but not to these things did Martin Luther turn his attention. Oblivious of the beauty in stone and on canvas that Florence possessed, Luther visited the hospitals and the churches of that queenly city. Long years afterward he described in detail the fine work of the Florentines in their hospitals. He remembered the cleanliness, the efficiency, the courtesy, the intelligence of their hospital work, but all the great world of the humanistic Renaissance apparently had no interest for him.

In Florence, also, he heard with amazement stories of the papal court at Rome, and saw in the city itself lives of churchmen of such quality as to bring a thorough shock to his quick consciousness of sin. He felt through all the spiritual atmosphere of Florence the tremendous memory of Savonarola, and the monks whom he visited in the city told him of those terrible experiences just twelve and a half years ago when the great Dominican, after his conscience had weakened under torture, reasserted his real convictions and was hanged and burned in the public square. What the mysterious movement of destiny suggested in Luther's mind as he stood, the devout son of the Church, on streets made holy with the reforming work of Savonarola, we shall never know. Whether he caught his breath and saw dimly and for an instant the hour when he, too, should face the same accusers, we do not know. But into his mind and life, destined to be the meeting place of all the mighty forces of his age, was poured the mood of the courageous monk who had brought moral defiance to a sinful Church.

Down from Florence the brothers journeyed, under the quiet skies of Umbria. Past towns made blessed by the presence of Francis of Assisi, and churches immortalized by the works of Giotto, they moved toward Rome.

The night before they arrived in sight of the holy city, Luther's religious devotion rose to almost ecstatic heights. He believed thoroughly in the remission of sins which he should win at the holy places in the city of his faith. His mind was fastened on the great traditions of his fathers in Christian history as he spent the last night behind the hills that separated the north from Rome. Journeying on the next day, as he came over the top of Mount Mario, he saw spread out before him the central city of western Christendom. Overcome with joy and exaltation, he fell on his knees and cried out, "Hail, holy Rome! Thrice blessed in the blood of the martyrs!"

Luther was a real pilgrim. He sought anxiously, and with joy, the great shrines of the Church. The catacombs, just recently rediscovered and the object of great interest, he visited, and felt the strange influence that comes from the memories of the martyrs buried there. He went, as was the custom with Roman pilgrims, to the great sacred stairs. Up near the Lateran church, real mother church of Roman Catholicism, these stairs were set, leading to a room containing relics of the saints. Roman tradition told Luther that the steps were those up which Jesus had walked the night he appeared before Pilate. Pope Leo IV had granted an indulgence of nine years for every step, and there were twenty-eight steps. For centuries the devout in the Catholic faith have climbed these steps on their knees, with the proper prayers in their hearts and on their lips. Luther was of these devout. He had walked the great pathway of penitence for five years now, and this was a kind of climax.

Yet all the while that he had walked the way of penitence another way had been appearing to him as superior. He had read of it many times in the Bible, in Bernard, in Augustine, and Staupitz had pointed it out to him: *The just shall live by faith.* The whole trend of purest Catholic tradition was toward prayers of faith and away from the superstitious confidence in "good works." Preaching in Wittenberg the year before his death, Martin related how as he reached the top of the stairs a doubt regarding the efficacy of the practice came into his mind. Who knows whether this be true? he thought.

Luther did not come down these steps a rebel against his Church. He did not from this moment forsake the great comforts and assurances of his Church's sacraments and works. His mind and soul were forming themselves in tremendous, moving experiences. The holy steps were not crucial, but only one more movement in the experience. A child of Rome he was when he came and a child of Rome he was when he left.

But the Rome of Luther's dream and ideal was broken and forever shattered. The Rome of the apostles and of the Vicar of Christ, so precious in his mind, became the Rome of reality, where the popes of the Renaissance had steadily centered their policy around the secularization of the Church, while the moral life of Rome had steadily degenerated. With each pope setting the example in defiance of every one of the ten commandments, Rome had steadily become a place of notorious anti-Christian life. Innocent VIII had seen his own daughter married in a hall of the Vatican Palace, and sat at the wedding banquet in company with his mistress. Alexander VI had given the Church a powerful, worldly dictatorship. The whole family of the

Borgias—Calixtus III, Alexander VI, Cesare, and Lucrezia—had marked Rome with such scandal and immoderate living that the Church seemed unable to recover. Now Julius II, after seven years in office, was at the height of his reign. For him Raphael was painting in the Vatican, and Michelangelo was finishing the Sistine Chapel. For Julius, too, Michelangelo was to carve his great *Moses*. But in Julius no vestige of the moral grandeur of Moses could be found.

Luther saw and felt a Rome utterly abandoned to money, luxury, and all kindred evils. Stunned and unable to understand it, he yet did not stay long enough in Rome to rebel against it. One cannot hear scandal enough in four or five weeks, nor see sufficient evil in that length of time, to unseat a devotion held since birth. Yet as the years went by for Luther and as other things in theology and Church organization became clear to him, then he remembered the Rome of his visit and could see far more clearly how utterly corrupt was the leadership offered the great Church in 1510. This is what was in his mind in later years when he thought of Rome:

> Rome is a harlot. I would not take a thousand gulden not to have seen it, for I never would have believed the true state of affairs from what other people told me had I not seen it myself. The Italians mocked us for being pious monks, for they hold Christians fools. They say six or seven masses in the time it takes me to say one, for they take money for it and I do not. The only crime in Italy is poverty. They still punish homicide and theft a little, for they have to, but no other sin is too gross for them. . . . So great and bold is Roman impiety that neither God nor man, neither sin nor shame, is feared. All good men who have seen Rome bear witness to this; all bad ones come back worse than before.

Returning to Erfurt sometime in February, 1511, Luther was glad again to pick up his books and the routine of his study. But life was not the same to him. He had been to Rome. In the journey he had gained some confidence, some assurance, some command of himself which in the days of steady introspection he had never known. Now Rome would hear from him.

LUTHER RESUMED HIS WORK in the Erfurt monastery, continuing there as a teacher until Staupitz called him again to Wittenberg in the autumn of 1511. Wittenberg was now to be his home until his death.

It was a small, mean town of some three thousand people. The Elbe River, upon which Wittenberg is situated, is at this point shallow and slow-moving. No commerce of any kind is possible upon it. The soil of the countryside is sandy and poor. The entire area is flat and uninviting. The townspeople were unlettered, coarse, and generally uncultured.

The town possessed two churches: one, the cathedral church attached to the university, a church of particular interest to Elector Frederick of Saxony, who filled it with relics and generally supported it; the other, a smaller, less conspicuous parish church for the inhabitants of the town. The Augustinian monks owned a cloister here, which, because of the black robes always worn by the monks, was known as the Black Cloister. To this Black Cloister Martin Luther came to live.

His duties for the first year of his Wittenberg residence were largely duties of personal study, following the plans laid by himself and Staupitz for his doctor's degree in expectation of the professorship in biblical interpretation. But his life was considerably varied, and he found himself deeply interested in the affairs of his order.

His mission to Rome the previous year had been only the beginning of a rise to recognition from his brother monks. In May, 1512, he and Staupitz journeyed to Cologne to attend the district meeting. Here Luther was elected subprior of the monastery at Wittenberg. On his return from Cologne he assumed a good many of the administrative functions under the prior.

In October, 1512, he received the degree of doctor of theology; not long afterward he was admitted to the university senate, which gave him, finally, full rights in the teaching profession. He accepted these obligations with his usual intensity and sincerity.

When Wittenberg, then but ten years old as a university, admitted Martin Luther to its staff of professors, it placed itself in line for a leadership of all the universities of western Europe. Strong men already on the faculty, such as Nikolaus Amsdorf and Andreas Bodenstein (known in history as Carlstadt), soon succumbed to the intellectual leadership and moral vigor of their new colleague. Around Luther there grew a Wittenberg tradition; he became the acknowledged leader in a new movement, and men began to speak within a few years of "the Wittenberg theology."

Sometime during this year, 1512–1513, Martin Luther brought to a focus the conflicting elements of his thought, and saw them temporarily in such clarity and in such harmony that he named this experience as the birthday of his faith. In the tower of the Black Cloister where Luther often studied, he kept his attention on the great text in Romans 1:17, *The just shall live by faith*. The whole problem of his life, since first he felt the call of religion, from boyhood days, was the problem of sin and the acceptance of his life in the sight of God. He believed so thoroughly in the perfect righteousness and perfect justice of God, and he felt so thoroughly his own sinfulness, that he could not understand how anyone could be just or justified in the sight of God.

What, then, did Paul mean by *The just shall live by faith*— Paul, who above all other men pointed out the sinfulness of the human race; Paul, who cried out, as Luther himself so often cried out, *O wretched man that I am! who shall deliver me from the body of this death?* Paul, who talked of the warfare between the flesh and the spirit; Paul, who believed in the immovable and eternal will of God operating in human life?

Luther recalled how in countless places this same Paul centered his whole thought around the crucifixion. By belief in the crucifixion, could he, Luther, find release from this burden of sinfulness? Could even he, Martin Luther, find that mighty gulf between himself and God bridged? Was it true that God's righteousness was not the righteousness of condemnation but the righteousness transferred from Christ to him?

He, then, could feel the whole mighty rhythm of the Pauline thought, wherein his sinfulness was ever present, yet God's justification, likewise, was ever present. It was now no longer a

349

battle with God to force God's recognition of his good deeds, but God was on his side. He saw, as it were, in one great vision, all the tremendous movement in the human race, from its sin in Adam through to its redemption in Christ, and he, Martin Luther, could stand steadfast by faith in Christ and the endless mercy made possible in Christ.

This was the hour of his freedom, and the hour of his great "illumination." From this day forth all his teaching began, centered, and ended in the history of redemption. He came from the tower room, not with his whole theology clearly wrought, but with its basis immovably fixed, secure in the conviction that he had found the key to the understanding of the Scriptures. Through all the wars into which his life carried him, he held steadfast to his understanding that *the just shall live by faith.*

He lectured in the university from 1513 to 1515 on the Psalms. His heart had been troubled for many years over the mighty problems of religious peace, and now his students heard as though they listened to an autobiography all the spiritual depth of the Psalms come to life. He lectured in Latin. But if his Latin came to him in too stereotyped scholastic form he would break over into German, sometimes changing in the midst of a sentence. Soon students were flocking to his classroom. "We students heard him gladly, for he spoke to us in our mother tongue," wrote one of his scholars.

So, too, when the old forms so well known in university lectures were insufficient to hold the fullness of his message, he created new and striking illustrations. For example, "As the meadow is to the cow, the house to the man, the nest to the bird, the rock to the chamois, and the stream to the fish, so is the Holy Scripture to the believing soul." When Martin Luther spoke to his students on the Twenty-third Psalm, or on the Fifty-first Psalm, they could feel that they were listening to one who spoke with authority.

In 1515, continuing into 1516, he lectured on Paul's Epistle to the Romans, and as he set forth before his students the mind of Paul through chapter after chapter, they saw once again the whole drama of heavenly redemption unveiled before them. Just before he began his lectures on the ninth chapter of Romans,

Erasmus's edition of the Greek New Testament came into his hands, and from that point on was his lecture book. Here, in the lectures on Psalms and Romans, his conception of theology was formulated in a systematic way. Although his interest was never in system, as such, but always in practical piety, he did in these lectures bring his thoughts into ordered shape. He was jubilant as he found, month after month, all the great problems of his life falling into relationship, one with the other.

As he lectured on Romans he brought before the judgment bar of this mighty book the society of his own day. Julius II and the frightful immorality of Rome he bitterly attacked. He denounced the Curia and all the hierarchy for the corruption and vileness which were so widespread. Luxury and avarice, pride and selfishness were rampant in the city of the Pope. Romans 13:13 now gave Luther a vocabulary for the describing of Rome: "rioting"—"drunkenness"—"chambering"—"wantonness"—"strife"—"envying." And in severe language he arraigned the clergy for thinking their task was to defend the Church instead of to preach the Gospel.

He had said to Staupitz a few years before that he could not survive the duties of the doctorate many months, but he found to his amazement that strength added to strength as his life organized itself in his new field. Staupitz had known the caliber of Luther, and now saw with great joy the steady progress of the teacher.

Luther's days were not confined at Wittenberg to the professorship, for his elevation to the doctor's degree involved preaching to his brother monks. At first he preached only to the monks in their little wooden chapel attached to the cloister, but his sermons developed a distinctive quality and attracted such attention that the town council of Wittenberg petitioned him to preach in the parish church. He therefore took up the duties of parish preacher. The earliest sermon extant is one he preached, in all probability, in 1514. His text was *Whatsoever ye would that men should do to you, do you even so to them*; and the sermon showed what was to be the major quality of his preaching. He talked simply and in straightforward fashion. He named the areas of life in which his hearers lived, talked about the things they knew in daily contact and analyzed them in the light of Christian principles, and exhorted his people to walk in Christian ways.

Added to the burdens of the professorship and the preaching office came election in May, 1515, as district vicar of the monasteries in Meissen and Thuringia. There were ten monasteries in the district when he was first elected, with the addition later of Eisleben, the town of his birth, bringing the number to eleven. He had, by the rules of his office, to visit each of these monasteries once a year. This visitation involved, of course, time and effort and strength. His correspondence increased tremendously with this election.

He now found all the hours of his day filled with tasks of importance. He had to preach to monk and to villager; he had to lecture to his students; and he had to exercise discipline in administration over distant monasteries. He ceased to be the introspective, troubled monk that he had been in Erfurt days, and became the strong, assured, confident leader, enjoying the respect and confidence of his entire circle. Humble in personal thought, he lost himself completely in public action, in professional responsibility.

When the plague came to Wittenberg in the fall of 1516, many of the town's citizens left immediately and many of the monks were transferred temporarily to other cloisters. But Martin Luther stayed in Wittenberg. Here his task was set; here his superiors had placed him; and here he would stay. Throughout his entire life this stalwart courage is discernible. Neither plague nor emperor nor pope were ever able to move him from his chosen course.

LUTHER IN 1516, the year before his public appearance in controversy, was a well-recognized, self-controlled, intelligent leader. But the pressure of his many duties was so great that day after day went by without sufficient time for prayer or sleep. Evening of the day brought him to his rest so worn out and tired that he was not even able to unclothe himself before falling asleep on his narrow cot in the cell in the cloister. He tried to catch up sometimes on his omitted prayers by reciting them all at once, when a break would come in his week's routine. He was truly in the "warfare of Christ," to which he had vowed himself when he entered the Erfurt monastery.

He found he was in a life strangely adapted to bring him information, almost as though fate were preparing him to be the focus for the problems of his age. In pastoral work, in student direction, in biblical study, in philosophic speculation, in private devotional life, and in the many cares, personal and impersonal, of the administration of eleven monasteries, Martin Luther gathered experience which day by day formed within him a broad, sensitive, accurate understanding of the life around him. And all the interests aroused by the deep intensity of his personal religious struggles were accentuated by his experience in the parish church.

Not the least of the things that disturbed him was the veneration of relics; the belief that the relics carried spiritual power. The elector of Saxony, Luther's own civil lord, was particularly active in the collection of relics, having assembled hundreds in the cathedral in Wittenberg. Many of the claims for the relics were preposterous. Luther had himself seen several exhibits, in widely scattered places, of the whole seamless robe of our Lord. These, and other things of an equally incredulous nature, disturbed the Wittenberg preacher greatly, and a note of protest occurred again and again in sermon and lecture. He was in no sense a rebel. A devout son of the visible Church, his protest was not against the thought or history of Catholicism, but against abuse.

He was not alone. Throughout western Christendom the cry of scandal had been heard so steadily for fifty years that the oncoming tide of reform was gathering. Rome could not hold the lid on Europe's disaffection much longer. Sir Thomas More and others in England had steadfastly called for a higher, cleaner administration throughout the Church. Erasmus's pen had been insistent in some of the finest criticism in Christian history that the Church reform itself. Leaders of the Church in Italy had banded themselves into a society dedicated to reform.

What was needed, longed for, waited for, was an accurate, consecrated, intelligent leadership. And here in far-off Wittenberg was being formed a religious experience strong enough, intelligent enough, courageous enough to bring it.

But Martin Luther, in the tremendous driving activity of his many fields of interest, was unaware of anything except that he had discovered the source of the early piety of the Church, and that his voice could not be silent in the face of abuse.

He would protect his people. The oppression of the under classes by overlords both civil and ecclesiastical moved him to fury and he spoke out openly against it. He pleaded in lecture and sermon the cause of the common man. He championed the peasant, challenging the right of the nobility to enact and enforce the terrible laws whereby they reserved the game for themselves and punished severely, often with death, the poor man for shooting one rabbit. He called the great civil lords "robbers" or "sons of robbers." The immemorial greed and avarice which lie behind all war received severe condemnation. He even named Pope Julius II, Duke George of Saxony, Elector

Frederick, and other princes as guilty in this devastating petty warfare. He was a gloriously eloquent spokesman in the name of religion for all the mighty causes which uplift mankind. The lords and rulers must answer to the written word of Scripture for their unchristian exploitation of the sons of God.

Rome, with the abuses she created and lived upon, was the heretic! Martin Luther was the Catholic.

IV

LORD OF THE FOREST

ONE EVENING toward the middle of November, 1517, Hans Luther was sitting by his home in Mansfeld when a close friend came and handed him a long, closely printed, double-columned, single-sheet tract from Wittenberg. Hans read:

> Out of love for the truth and from a desire to elucidate it, the Reverend Father Martin Luther, Master of Arts in Sacred Theology, and ordinary lecturer therein at Wittenberg, intends to defend the following statements and dispute on them in that place.
>
> Therefore he asks that those who cannot be present to dispute with him orally shall do so in their absence by letter.
>
> In the name of our Lord Jesus Christ. Amen.

1. Our Lord and Master Jesus Christ in saying, *"Penitentiam agite,"* meant that the whole life of the faithful should be repentance.
2. And these words cannot refer to penance—that is confession and satisfaction.
5. The Pope does not wish, nor is he able, to remit any penalty except what he or the Canon Law has imposed.
6. The Pope is not able to remit guilt except by declaring it forgiven by God—or in cases reserved to himself. . . .
11. The erroneous opinion that canonical penance and punishment in purgatory are the same assuredly seems to be a tare sown while the bishops were asleep.
28. It is certain that avarice is fostered by the money clinking in the chest, but to answer the prayers of the Church is in the power of God alone.

The paper shook in Hans's hand, and great excitement possessed him as he realized with stunning force that his son was challenging the mightiest institution on earth. To Hans, Martin was still a boy, only thirty-four. Yet those sentences spoke from the anvils of experience. His eye turned to the page again:

50. Christians are taught that if the Pope knew exactions of the preachers of indulgences he would rather have St. Peter's Church in ashes than have it built with the flesh and bones of his sheep.
60. The treasury of the Church is the power of the keys given by Christ's merit.
71. Who speaks against the apostolic truth of indulgences, let him be anathema.
72. But who opposes the lust and license of the preachers of pardons, let him be blessed.
82. Why does not the Pope empty purgatory from charity?

This sharp and incisive reasoning took Hans off guard. Martin was right! The sale of indulgences to remit purgatorial or temporal punishment had become widespread. But if the Pope could help those in purgatory, then charity *should* move him so to act. Hans closed his eyes for a moment and felt intuitively the approach of an hour when Martin would be called to answer for this. The Church would not brook such exposure. But it *was* abuse in the Church to do these things, he thought, and he felt a thrill of exaltation as he knew his flesh and blood so courageous.

92. Let all those prophets depart who say to the people of Christ, Peace, peace, where there is no peace.
93. But all those prophets do well who say to the people of Christ, Cross, cross, and there is no cross.

Hans read slowly and thoughtfully through the ninety-five propositions. He asked his neighbor what information the messenger who brought this news from Wittenberg had given. He heard that Martin had set this statement on the bulletin board of the university at noon on All Saints' Day; that the original had been in Martin's own handwriting, but that the

Wittenberg printers had rapidly published both Latin and Greek texts which were being broadcast throughout Germany.

Hans did not know the full background of the situation, nor did he know Martin's final intention, but this much he did know: that for a long time he and his fellow citizens in the Church and state had been restive under the financial pressure and abuses of the Church. If now his boy, grown to manhood, could successfully wage a defense of a more ancient and worthy practice, then the name of Luther would be brought to a higher distinction than ever he had dreamed for it when he had visioned Martin for the law.

IN HIS OWN SEARCH for a sincere and honest piety Luther had long discounted the penitential customs of the Church. But then, in his ordinary pastoral work in the Wittenberg parish late in the summer of 1517, his people had come to him with letters of indulgence which they had bought, and on the basis of these letters argued the release from certain consequences of sinning.

Luther could not believe that what his people told him was true. He knew that the Church believed that Christ had stored up great benefits for the human race by means of his passion. He knew that the Church believed that the heroic Christian activity of the saints was of benefit to the common Christian. He knew that the Church believed that the Bishop of Rome possessed the "power of the keys." He believed these things, too, but this sale was different. Hardly willing to credit the stories told him by his own parishioners, he procured the letter of instructions given by Albert, archbishop of Magdeburg, to the commissioner who sold the indulgences. How long could he hold his peace?

He knew that Albert, a prince of Brandenburg, archbishop of Magdeburg, and acting bishop of Halberstadt, had secured likewise his election to the archbishopric of Mainz. But he did not know that in order to secure himself in these three bishoprics, which canon law forbade him to hold, Albert had made a financial bargain with the papacy. Luther did not know that the house of Fugger, bankers of Augsburg, had loaned Albert the money for the bribe and fees which he paid to Leo X for confirmation in these offices. Nor did he know that the representatives of Albert and the representatives of Leo met and discussed the price which should be paid. The representatives of Leo had said twelve thousand ducats, for the twelve apostles. The representatives of Albert had said seven thousand ducats, for the seven deadly sins. They had compromised on ten thousand ducats. Luther did not know that in order to make sure the financial transaction would be carried through, Leo had granted to Albert the privilege of selling an indulgence. He did not know that one-half of the proceeds of this sale was to go to Albert, himself, from which he would pay his debts to the Fuggers; the other half to go to Leo. He did know that the whole proceeds of the sale of the indulgence was supposed to go to the rebuilding of St. Peter's Church. The inner workings of this—one of the most scandalous operations in the history of the Church—were unknown to Luther. All he knew was that the clear and expressed intention of Christian piety was brutally and inexcusably broken by this particular indulgence sale.

He sat in his study in the Black Cloister and argued with himself through August, September, and October, while the sale went on. Luther's own prince, the elector of Saxony, too wise to allow his subjects to be bled for Rome, had refused permission for the selling of the indulgences in his territory. He knew well the old proverb, "When Rome comes by, draw your purse strings tight." Wittenberg itself, therefore, did not see the indulgence seller, but Luther's people walked just a few miles to the west and bought their indulgence tickets at the town of Zerbst, or a few miles to the east at Jüterbog. Both of these towns, outside the dominions of the elector, were visited by the commissioner for the indulgence.

The prior of the Dominican convent at Leipzig, Johann Tetzel, was selling these indulgences, and when he entered Jüterbog, where Luther's people went to see him and to hear him, he had the papal bull announcing the indulgence carried on velvet cloth at the head of a procession, and with great pomp and ceremony he marched through the streets of the town to the place of preaching. There, in unbelievable boldness, he promised to the Saxons that they could buy release from all punishment imposed by Church law; that they could also buy release from the penances which they must do in purgatory for their sins. More than this, with mock pathos and brutal hypocrisy, he painted for the benefit of his hearers the sufferings of their dead relatives in purgatory and told them point-blank that they could release their loved ones from suffering by the payment of a little money.

The Black Cloister became the scene of a furious battle in Luther's heart and mind. How could the heads of the Church act like this? Did they not understand how far the papal power went, and what its limits were? Did they not know that the mercy of Christ was not for sale, or was everything for sale in Rome? Furious in spirit at the way the sacred things of life were thus destroyed, but cool and determined in mind, he quietly wrote out ninety-five distinct sentences, each of which was a debatable point in the whole question of the office of penance, particularly the indulgence phase. These things, he thought, ought to be cleared up, and he, as a teacher of theology, and possessor of the sacred right of clarifying Scripture, was in a position to express himself.

So it had come about that on the thirty-first of October, when Wittenberg was crowded because it was the anniversary of the consecration of the cathedral church, he attached his ninety-five sentences with a brief preamble to the bulletin board of the university. The wooden doors of the cathedral church, since the church was attached to the school, were used as the bulletin board, and on these doors the theses appeared.

He did not even print his statement, as two months before he had printed and sent to most of his friends a similar list of theses on the weaknesses of scholastic theology. He was totally unprepared for the torrential fashion with which these theses on indulgences swept through Europe. "As though carried by angelic messengers" they appeared in every language and in every place in Christendom.

The strong, sturdy, quiet teacher in Wittenberg now found himself the rallying leader for the disaffection of half a century. The son of Hans Luther was forced to direct a campaign for the clarification of the Gospel and the reform of the Church.

LUTHER HAD NO INTENTION that any of this work should be done under cover. With the publication of his theses he wrote a letter to Albert, who had to bear the responsibility for the indulgence sale. The letter is dated the same day that the theses were posted, October 31, 1517, and, after formal greetings, it says:

Papal indulgences for the building of St. Peter's are hawked about under your illustrious sanction. . . . I regret that the people have conceived about them the most erroneous ideas. Forsooth these unhappy souls believe that if they buy letters of pardon they are sure of their salvation; likewise that souls fly out of purgatory as soon as money is cast into the chest; in short, that the grace conferred is so great that there is no sin whatever which cannot be absolved thereby, even if, as they say, taking an impossible example, a man should violate the mother of God. They also believe that indulgences free them from all penalty and guilt.

360

My God! thus are the souls committed, Father, to your charge, instructed unto death, for which you have a fearful and growing reckoning to pay. . . .

What else could I do, excellent Bishop and illustrious Prince, except pray your Reverence for the sake of the Lord Jesus Christ to take away your Instructions to the Commissioners altogether and impose some other form of preaching on the proclaimers of pardons. . . .

Your unworthy son,
Martin Luther, Augustinian, Dr. Theol.

It was Albert who, on receipt of this letter, first brought the matter of Martin Luther to the attention of Rome. Luther had been so successful in diminishing the confidence of the people in the indulgences that the sales had been seriously curtailed. But when Albert appealed to Rome for guidance, the head of the Church was in no mood to give serious consideration to a question of the practice of piety.

Luther, himself, still intent on working in the open, wrote to the Pope in May of 1518. He told him that he had always accepted the authority of the papacy and was in no sense desirous of moving in the fields of heresy, but that the recent papal indulgence had spread grave scandal and mockery and that he had been driven to protest against the abuse. He desired now only that the Pope should understand his position and that he should give careful attention to the matters at issue. But careful attention was not what Leo X was prepared to give.

The son of Lorenzo the Magnificent, tonsured at seven, made a cardinal at fourteen, given voting power in the Curia at seventeen, Giovanni de' Medici was elected to the papacy in February, 1513, taking the name of Leo X. He is reported to have said to his brother when informed of his election, "Let us now enjoy the papacy, since God has given it to us."

Cultured, refined, agreeable, and exceptionally clever, Leo was well equipped to bring the papacy to new Renaissance heights in the arts. In affairs of finance, however, he was a tremendous spender and not a successful gainer. Therefore his papacy was always troubled. Supposed to be a kindly man, he was nevertheless equal to the ruthless execution of several cardinals suspected in a plot of poisoning. Completely immersed in secular affairs, he was not able to understand the religious issue of this northern quarrel.

The attempt to control Luther began through his order. Leo thought that the theses had been composed by a drunken monk who would see things clearer when he was sober, and so he instructed the general of the Augustinian order to quench these fires of rebellion. Accordingly the issue was brought up at the meeting of the order at Heidelberg in May, 1518. Luther was present, as was also his friend Staupitz. There the brothers discussed quietly and without violence the position of the accused. Luther spoke in explanation and defense of his theses. He found some brothers in agreement and some in disagreement. He thought the issue was serious and he did not desire to involve his order, so he resigned as district vicar. There was no indication at the Heidelberg chapter that Luther's mind had changed. One young, enthusiastic conservative at the meeting challenged Luther that he dare not teach such doctrines to the peasants or they would stone him to death. But Luther had more rightly read the temper of the peasants. Even then Luther was not in danger of his life, but Tetzel, who had sold the indulgences, was afraid to move outside his cloister at Leipzig.

Returning to Wittenberg, Martin Luther awaited the next move.

ON AUGUST 25, 1518, twenty-two year old Philipp Melanchthon entered Wittenberg. He came to teach Greek. Luther had urged the appointment of another candidate and now looked on the thin, unprepossessing Melanchthon with considerable anxiety. But this anxiety vanished when four days later Melanchthon delivered his installation address to the faculty at the university. Luther sat in his academic robes and listened to the impassioned pleas of this boy for an orientation of the curriculum around the humanities and the New Testament.

Luther was thirty-five and in possession of his greatest strength. Melanchthon was twenty-two and at the very beginning of his career. Between them there sprang up instantly a steadfast friendship, never to be broken until death. The ability and devotion of Melanchthon became daily more important to Luther. Now he had at his elbow, bound to him in close friendship, the finest humanist Germany had yet produced. The fine, sensitive, accurate, grammatical scholarship of Melanchthon was now joined to the powerful, emotional dynamic of Luther.

Throughout the remainder of their lives, during the fiercest days of public battle, Luther and Melanchthon were accustomed to meet in the little garden behind Melanchthon's home. There, at a stone table, with beer and laughter and relaxation, they enjoyed the fruits of fellowship.

ROME WAS NOT TO LET the case rest. Soon Luther was forced to appear in defense of his action before a representative of the papacy in Augsburg. Luther had received earlier, on the seventh of August, 1518, a communication ordering him to appear in person at Rome. The message was sent to his elector, but, after considerable anxious debate, the request to appear at Rome was withdrawn and his summons to Augsburg substituted. The substitution was a tremendous relief—Luther knew that to step within the control of his enemies now was to meet death.

He journeyed to Augsburg in October and there met the general of the Dominican order, Cardinal Cajetan. The cardinal, true to the Dominican type, was earnest, zealous, hard driving for papal rights. He was not willing that Luther should even talk. Martin, on the other hand, had come to Augsburg expecting to defend himself. Before the cardinal he accorded him the respect due his rank. But they could get nowhere. In a memorable description of the meeting Luther stated how he had tried to interrupt the cardinal's steady flow of contradiction and abuse, and how the cardinal shouted louder and louder, until he himself finally lost his moderation and shouted likewise. The conference ended in thorough misunderstanding. The cardinal insisted on recantation. Luther insisted on a discussion of the issue. The cardinal claimed heresey. Luther challenged him to prove any statement of the theses heretical. The cardinal was unable to do so.

Friends tried to effect a reconciliation after a definite break at a second meeting. Luther wrote an apology for his conduct in the argument. The cardinal accepted the apology, and they met for a third and last time, but it was the same story—the call for recantation and a refusal.

Luther withdrew from the audience and waited a few days in Augsburg, all the while hearing rumors that a trap was laid for his arrest. So by night he quietly left Augsburg, riding steadily to the north and home. Horse and rider alike were thin and haggard.

On his return he wrote a description of his meeting with Cardinal Cajetan for public reading, and a letter to Pope Leo, which he called "An appeal from the Pope ill informed to the Pope well informed."

The next attempt at reconciliation was conducted by a papal ambassador to the Elector Frederick, named Karl von Miltitz. This entire attempt was greatly colored by the political necessities. The Diet of the Holy Roman Empire was soon to meet for the election of an emperor, and the Pope was anxious to hold the favor of the Elector Frederick so that he could control his vote in the coming election. The Elector Frederick, while a devout Catholic, not then nor ever to be in sympathy with Luther's theology, was nevertheless a staunch defender of the rights of his subjects. He would not be a party to any intrigue which would surrender Martin Luther without fair defense. But in January, 1519, Miltitz won from Luther the promise to write the Pope a letter of apology, agreeing to support indulgences in their proper sense, and urging steady reverence for the holy see. But the mission of Miltitz was disowned by his superiors and came to naught.

The next stage in the controversy was far more dramatic and eventful than any that had yet occurred. Johann Eck, professor of theology at the University of Ingolstadt, a Dominican monk, and a man of considerable ability in debate, challenged Martin Luther and his Wittenberg colleague, Andreas Bodenstein, to public discussion in Leipzig. Luther was not a heretic, and could not be classed with the heretics, but if Eck could be successful in wringing from either Luther or Bodenstein heretical statements, then Rome could silence both men. Eck was masterful at this. Leipzig was in the unfriendly territory of Duke George of Saxony. The University of Leipzig was jealous of the growing prestige of the University of Wittenberg. Everything looked bad for Luther.

The faculty and students of Wittenberg would not let him go alone. The professors rode in two carts, while two hundred armed students walked beside and behind them. In Leipzig there was the constant menace of rioting. At the inns where they lodged they kept guards placed. They went in groups, well armed, from inn to church and to the council chamber where the debate was to be held. Leipzig itself furnished extra police to keep order.

After a preliminary debate between Eck and Bodenstein, Martin Luther entered the lists on the fourth of July, 1519. They were assembled in the largest hall of Duke George's own palace, and the duke was present at the debate. Johann Eck was the dominant figure.

> He had a huge square body, a full strong voice coming from his chest; fit for a tragic actor or a town crier, more harsh than distinct; his mouth, eyes and whole aspect gave one the idea of a butcher or a soldier rather than of a theologian . . . a man striving to overcome his opponent rather than to win a victory for the truth. . . . He was continually misquoting his opponent's words or trying to give them a meaning they were not intended to convey.

When Luther rose to speak he appeared as:

> . . . of medium height; his body is slender, emaciated by study and by cares; one can count almost all the bones; he stands in the prime of his age; his voice sounds clear and distinct—however hard his opponent pressed him he maintained his calmness and his good nature, though in debate he sometimes used bitter words. . . . He carried a bunch of flowers in his hand, and when the discussion became hot he looked at it and smelled it.

Eck's desire clearly was to drive Luther into the admission of a position similar to that held by the heretical groups in the history of the Church. If this could be done, then he could set the name of heretic on the Wittenberger. So he tried, but to no avail. He called forth the activity of the Waldenses, and of John Wycliffe, but Luther was not caught. Finally he brought into the discussion the work of Jan Hus.

After a particularly vigorous expression of opinion on the part of Eck, Luther interrupted him saying, "But, good Dr. Eck, every Hussite opinion is not wrong."

At this Duke George, who had good cause to look with distrust upon everything Hussite, was heard to whisper with an oath, "That's the plague."

Eck was jubilant. He countered Luther with the challenge that the Church had denounced the Hussite opinions; that the Council of Constance had condemned them; that the Pope had declared them heretical. Luther was driven finally with remorseless logic to the damning admission that popes and councils could err.

The Leipzig debate ended. Eck started southward to Rome, triumphant. He had unmasked another heretic. Martin Luther had come to Leipzig a reforming, protesting voice within the historic Church. He was leaving Leipzig branded "heretic, rebel, a thing to flout."

Luther sensed deeply as he rode home over the rough roads of Saxony that dark days were ahead for him. But he felt strength too. The days of indecision were over. Now he was out in the open. He could move quite clearly now.

THE WINTER OF 1519–1520 passed uneventfully in Wittenberg while the opposing forces gathered their strength. Luther, Melanchthon, and their colleagues talked steadily, corresponded at length with friends all over Europe, and prepared themselves for the next meeting.

It came in the early summer of 1520. On the fifteenth of June, 1520, Leo signed the bull *Exsurge Domine*. This was the work of the belligerent Johann Eck, not of Leo himself. It called upon Luther to recant within sixty days or be excommunicated. It affirmed the heretical quality of Luther's position in opposing the sale of the indulgences, it did so in open defiance of the finest thought of the historic Catholic Church, and it was the cause of further disaffection rather than for the healing of the Church. In many of the northern provinces and cities, people were now so thoroughly on Luther's side that they refused to allow the bull to be published. It was often torn into bits and scattered through the streets of the towns. When it came to Wittenberg it met a royal reception. For after long consideration Martin Luther had decided to handle this thing directly, and as though it were in reality open warfare.

Early in the morning of December 10, the students in Wittenberg read the following notice on their bulletin board:

> Let whosoever adheres to the truth of the Gospel be present at nine o'clock at the Church of the Holy Cross outside the walls, where the impious books of papal decrees and scholastic theology will be burnt according to ancient and apostolic usage, inasmuch as the boldness of the enemies of the Gospel has waxed so great that they daily burn the evangelic books of Luther. Come, pious and zealous youth, to this pious and religious spectacle, for perchance now is the time when the Antichrist must be revealed!

A few hours later Luther headed a march of the students and faculty out through a gate in the city wall to a nearby field. There a huge bonfire was prepared and one of the university professors set the fire. In quietness and with dignity Martin Luther himself placed the books of the canon law on the fire, in token of his refusal to be bound by them. Then, taking the bull that called for his recantation, he placed it on the fire too.

The summer of 1520 also saw Martin Luther present his reasoned opinions on the entire question to the Christian public. In three famous pamphlets he drew up his offensive and defensive position. In August he published *To the Christian Nobility of the German Nation on the Improvement of the Christian Estate.* Here, with clear, forceful logic and powerful emotion he attacked the sole and arbitrary authority of the papacy. In the growing spirit of nationalism he appealed to the German people to free themselves from the tyranny of the papal power. He contradicted the famous Roman positions that the clergy are superior to the laity in the control of the Church; that only the

Pope may interpret Scripture authoritatively. In the light of the great essential doctrine of the priesthood of all believers, he said, there is no essential distinction between priest and people. Each Christian is in spiritual reality a priest.

To German ears this was a glorious appeal for freedom from Italian control, and even his bitter antagonist, Duke George, admitted a thrill of exaltation as he read this call to Germany.

Hardly had Europe caught its breath from this powerful attack when Luther published in October a work entitled *On the Babylonian Captivity of the Church*. This is a consideration of the sacramental system of the Roman Church, a system built up in the same few centuries preceding Luther which had seen the rise of the autocratic power of the papacy. Luther maintained that Christian people were in a captivity like the captivity of the Jews of old in Babylon, and the seven sacraments of Rome were the chains by which the captor, Rome, held them in slavery. He argued that no sacrament was valid which could not find its justification in the New Testament. Starting from the New Testament premise, Luther could justify wholly only the Eucharist and baptism. There was partial justification also, he admitted, for the sacrament of penance. But as for confirmation, marriage, holy orders, and extreme unction, while they might be great customs of the Christian people, worthy of the Church's blessing, they were not sacraments.

In November of the same year he followed these attacking documents with that sensitive, lovely presentation of the center of his own belief, *The Freedom of the Christian Man*. Here he stated the paradox:

> A Christian man is the most free lord of all,
>   subject to no one.
> A Christian man is the dutiful servant of all,
>   subject to everyone.

And from this he wrung a glorious presentation of the free spiritual life of the Christian believer. The grace of God accepted in his life by faith makes the Christian lord of the universe. He may starve in a dungeon or reign from a prince's throne, and still possess within himself the glorious freedom of the sons of God. All this is free gift made possible by faith in Christ. But because he is thus free, he is bound by the great law of Christian love and by the indwelling spirit of Christ to serve in perfect charity all mankind.

Remembering his pledge to Miltitz, he sent this document to Leo X. He wrote a letter to accompany the little tract.

> Of your person, excellent Leo, I have heard only what is honorable and good . . . but of the Roman See, as you and all men must know, it is more scandalous and shameful than any Sodom or Babylon, and, as far as I can see, its wickedness is beyond all counsel and help, having become desperate and abysmal. It made me sick at heart to see that under your name and that of the Roman Church, the poor people in all the world are cheated and injured, against which thing I have set myself and will set myself as long as I have life. . . . I offer you this little treatise, dedicated to you as an augury of peace and good hope. . . . I am poor and have nothing else to send you, nor do you stand in need of any but my spiritual gifts.

This letter and pamphlet had been sent to Rome two months before the bonfire in Wittenberg which signaled the open rebellion.

THROUGH THE WINTER OF 1520–1521, Luther was active in all his regular work. He preached every day, often twice a day. He taught his regular classes in the university. He wrote commentaries on Genesis and the Psalms. He answered the polemics of his enemies with harsh invective and biting sarcasm of his own. The division was becoming daily more severe and men were being called on for decision.

It saddened Luther tremendously to find his beloved Staupitz not willing to take to the open rebellion. Staupitz was well along in years now and had retired to Salzburg. He had been unable to go the whole way along which he had started Martin.

Finally the old vicar wrote an open letter in which he tried to be conciliatory, but which bore evidence of his allegiance to Rome. But this was not an hour for hesitation and Luther gently wrote him:

Wherefore as much as you exhort me to humility, I exhort you to pride. You are too yielding. I am too stiff-necked.

Indeed it is a solemn matter. We see Christ suffer. Should we keep silence and humble ourselves? Now that our dearest Saviour, who gave himself for us, is made a mock in the world, should we not fight and offer our lives for him? Dear father, the present crisis is graver than many think. . . . The word of Christ is not the word of peace, but the word of the sword. But why should I, a fool, teach a wise man?

I write this more confidently because I fear you will take a middle course between Christ and the Pope, who are now, as you see, in bitter strife. . . .

Truly your submission has saddened me not a little, and has shown me that you are different from that Staupitz who was the herald of grace and of the cross.

Intimation that he would be called to the imperial Diet came to Luther throughout the winter. Charles V, newly elected head of the Holy Roman Empire, was holding his first Diet at Worms, a German town on the Rhine. It opened on January 25, 1521, to consider all the affairs of the empire.

The question of how to handle the Luther issue had been discussed before the arrival of the imperial party at Worms. The Elector Frederick had met Charles and his retinue at Cologne in October and November, 1520. The elector carried a letter from Luther to the emperor asking for protection and a fair trial. The two men talked over the possibilities, and the emperor promised Frederick that Luther should be given a safe-conduct and be lawfully treated. But the papal representatives to the court of Charles demanded that all Luther's work be burned and that Luther be delivered up bound. The elector sent for Erasmus, then in Cologne, and asked:

"Has Luther erred?"

"Yes, he has erred in two points, in attacking the crown of the Pope and the bellies of the monks," answered the greatest of the humanists.

"What is to be done?" asked Frederick.

Erasmus drew up twenty-two axioms, proving that the Pope should appoint an impartial tribunal for the consideration of

Luther's propositions. So Frederick decided to stand by Luther and see him through the Diet.

The bull *Exsurge Domine*, meanwhile, had only threatened excommunication. But Luther's burning of it had brought an end to the matter, and on January 3, 1521, Leo X signed the final bull demanding complete excommunication. So when the Roman party acted at Worms they acted on the principle that Luther was already condemned. He should not be heard. He should be executed as a heretic. The civil authority was not bound to keep faith with a heretic. He should either recant or die. Even recanting, it was not certain that he should live.

The representatives of Rome were Girolamo Aleandro and Marino Caracciolo. Aleandro, the chief representative, was, by temperament, an inquisitor. It was easy for him to light bonfires for books or men. He could see men die for the glory of God without troublings of conscience. He had killed five peasants because of the loss of his favorite dog. And now at Worms he hews to one line—Luther is to die! On February 13 he spoke to the Diet for three hours demanding that Luther be condemned without a hearing. But to Luther, working in Wittenberg, the cause was the great issue. It was to be explained and defended. The quarrel was not concluded. The question was open. He was a spokesman for a living, growing movement.

On March 26 Luther received the summons from Charles V to appear in order "to obtain information about certain doctrines originating with you and certain books written by you." Luther was no coward, but he knew the game he played now. Despite all assurances of safe-conduct and lawful treatment, the sensitive balance could break at any moment and he would be in the hands of the enemy. But he would not stay away. For this hour he was born.

On April 2 he left for Worms. Melanchthon wanted to go, but Luther would not have it, saying: "Dear brother, if I do not come back, if my enemies put me to death, you go on teaching and standing fast in the truth; if you live, my death will matter little."

Crowds waved Luther and his companions off. The magistrates of the city hired a driver and horses for the open country wagon, half-filled with straw, in which they rode. Caspar Sturm, the imperial herald, rode ahead on horseback, carrying the royal coat of arms, a square yellow banner with a black two-headed eagle. Martin carried his lute, to while away the long hours in the inns.

Over the old familiar road they traveled to Leipzig, where townspeople, magistrates, and students gave them cordial welcome. From Leipzig to Weimar, then on toward Erfurt. As they rode Luther wondered how Erfurt would receive him— Erfurt where his happy student days had led him steadily toward the high calling of God—Erfurt where vows were taken. He remembered the vow now—the warfare of Christ—and knew indeed its deep fulfillment.

Luther was anxious as they neared the city. Great joy welled up in his heart as he saw a long procession of students and faculty headed by the rector come to meet him. The magistrates gave a banquet in his honor, and Erfurt knew its distinguished son returned in fame. He slept in his old convent of the Augustinians. Sunday morning, April 7, he preached in the cathedral where his youthful heart had once been stirred.

As he came nearer the danger zone, stopping to visit schools and preach in Frankfurt, not far from Worms, again and again friends interceded to stop his coming. Caspar Sturm, the herald, pointed out the emperor's edict of March 10, to seize all Luther's books, and asked if he should proceed to Worms. Luther's reply was yes.

Just before ten in the morning of Tuesday, April 16, the watchman on the tower of the cathedral at Worms blew his horn loudly to announce the arrival. Thousands gathered along the road and Martin Luther rode in his humble wagon in triumph into Worms. The papal legate wrote to Rome that Luther stepped from his carriage saying, "God will be with me," and looking around with "demoniac" eyes on the people.

He was put up at the house of the Knights of St. John. There the crowd gathered rapidly and kept him busy with visitors until late into the night. The next day at four in the afternoon the herald and the imperial marshal came for him.

Martin was dressed in his black Augustinian gown. He was

sturdy, large boned, but not stout. His eyes were set deep and glowed as always with exceptional brightness. Tonsure newly shaved, he was crowned with a circle of thick, black hair. He was in his thirty-eighth year, with heart still unsoiled by the terrors of public warfare, mind still in its mature vigor, and spirit undampened by the long vicissitudes of defeat and compromise. Peasant strength, monastic training, personal piety, elemental honesty, and courage were all in him.

The crowds were so thick in the main streets that the men went through the gardens from house to house and so gained the entrance to the hall in the bishop's palace. He waited about two hours, and finally at six o'clock he was ushered into the meeting of the Diet. It was dark outside and great smoking lamps lit the hot, stuffy room, overcrowded with dignitaries. Charles V was the central figure. Only twenty years of age, pale, quiet, he was surrounded by all his counselors. Six electors of the empire were there, including the Elector Frederick, Luther's own civil lord. The papal legates were there, unable to control events completely. Bishops, princes, deputies, ambassadors filled the hall. Spanish and German soldiers were on guard. Thousands of persons jammed the passageways and doors. Before Charles V in person, and Leo X in representation, Luther stood a moment quietly.

Looking around, he saw the chief papal representative glaring at him.

So the Jews must have looked at Christ, he thought.

His gaze finally came to rest on the youthful emperor. Their eyes met, but not their spirits. Each failed to read the strength in the other. Luther saw Charles, now surrounded by the court, and, it seemed to him, like "some poor lamb amid swine and hounds."

His reveries were broken by a movement before him, and he watched an official rise and turn to him. He was told that his case was now before the Diet and he was to say nothing except in answer to questions. He thought this admonition strange, and waited anxiously.

Then Dr. Eck, not the debater of Leipzig fame, but the representative of the archbishop's court, pointed to a group of books on a central table and asked Luther if these books were his and if he would recant the positions set forth in them.

This was too sudden for Luther. He had thought this was to be a hearing, not a demand. Charles's summons had so read. He seemed powerless to answer. Jerome Schurf, his friend and lawyer, stepped to his rescue, crying out, "Let the titles of the books be read."

They were read. *To the Christian Nobility of the German Nation! On the Babylonian Captivity of the Church! The Freedom of the Christian Man!* etc., etc., etc.

By the time the reading was over Luther had recovered his presence; he was not to be driven too quickly. This was his hour. Slowly he spoke:

"His Imperial Majesty asks me two things, first, whether these books are mine, and secondly, whether I will stand by them or recant part of what I have published. First, the books are mine, I deny none of them. The second question, whether I will reassert all or recant what is said to have been written without warrant of Scripture, concerns faith and the salvation of souls and the Divine Word, than which nothing is greater in heaven or in earth, and which we all ought to reverence; therefore it would be rash and dangerous to say anything without due consideration, since I might say more than the thing demands or less than the truth, either of which would bring me in danger of the sentence of Christ. *Whosoever shall deny me before men, him will I also deny before my Father which is in heaven.* Wherefore, I humbly beg your Imperial Majesty to grant me time for deliberation, that I may answer without injury to the Divine Word, or peril to my soul."

Confusion followed for a moment, in the midst of which Charles conferred with his counselors and then with Dr. Eck. Finally Eck addressed Luther:

"Although, Martin, you knew from the Imperial mandate why you were summoned and therefore do not deserve to have a longer time given you, yet his Imperial Majesty of his great clemency, grants you one day more, commanding that you appear tomorrow at this time and deliver your answer orally and not in writing."

He withdrew from the hall and returned to his rooms. The experience was exacting. For a moment it had looked bad for him. His enemies had been almost successful in the attempt to force too hasty a statement. Now he knew the question—and he would be ready. That night he wrote, in great excitement, to a friend. "This hour I have stood before the Emperor and the Diet, asked whether I would revoke my books. . . . Truly, with Christ's aid I shall not retract one jot or tittle."

He was often in prayer throughout the night. In the morning, friend after friend came to visit. Luther was in the best of spirits. He was well and strong, laughed heartily, and was in constant good humor. With his intimate associates he planned the work of the afternoon and was ready when at four o'clock the herald came. Again through gardens they gained the entrance to the palace. There they stood in a hot, pressing crowd. His mind kept itself rigidly fastened to its one great task. Life was precious to him. His enemies were strong. They might march him easily from the hall of the Diet to the stake of Hus. He knew that Rome had pleaded with Charles not to keep the promise of safe-conduct. But here was his real and valid opportunity to confess his truth before the world. Strange mingling of faith, fear, strength, exaltation possessed him. There was for the moment a singular clarity to the problem. He would be honest!

At six the emperor and court entered. Aleandro and Caracciolo would not come. They said they would not listen to a heretic! Luther came in, cheered by many encouragements from German knights and soldiers.

The session was again in the charge of Dr. Eck. He turned to Luther, both men standing, and said:

> "His Imperial Majesty has assigned this time to you, Martin Luther, to answer for the books which you yesterday openly acknowledged to be yours. . . . Do you wish to defend all of your books or to retract part of them?"

Luther was self-possessed. He had gained the hour of his life. He spoke to the greatest assembly of princes Germany could muster. This was no persecuted one, pleading, but a clear appeal, in ancient prophetic fervor.

"Most Serene Emperor, Most Illustrious Princes, Most Clement Lords! At the time fixed yesterday I obediently appear, begging for the mercy of God, that your Most Serene Majesty and your Illustrious Lordships may deign to hear this cause, which I hope may be called the cause of justice and truth, with clemency. ... Two questions were asked me yesterday. To the first, whether I would recognize that the books published under my name were mine, I gave a plain answer, to which I hold and will hold forever, namely, that the books are mine, as I published them, unless perchance it may have happened that the guile or meddlesome wisdom of my opponents has changed something in them. For I only recognize what has been written by myself alone, and not the interpretation added by another.

In reply to the second question I beg your Most Sacred Majesty and your lordships to be pleased to consider that all my books are not of the same kind.

In some I have treated piety, faith, and morals so simply and evangelically that my adversaries themselves are forced to confess that these books are useful, innocent, and worthy to be read by Christians. Even the bull, though fierce and cruel, states that some things in my books are harmless, although it condemns them by a judgment simply monstrous. If, therefore, I should undertake to recant these, would it not happen that I alone of all men should damn the truth which all, friends and enemies alike, confess?"

Luther spoke calmly, in complete command of himself, but his deep intensity stilled every noise in the hall, and he was being heard clearly.

"The second class of my works inveighs against the papacy as against that which both by precept and example has laid waste all Christendom, body and soul. No one can deny or dissemble this fact, since general complaints witness that the consciences of all believers are snared, harassed, and tormented by the laws of the Pope and the doctrines of men, and especially that the goods of this famous German nation have been and are devoured in numerous and ignoble ways. Yet the Canon Law provides ... that the laws and doctrines of the Pope contrary to the Gospel and the Fathers are to be held erroneous and rejected. If, therefore, I should withdraw these books, I would add strength to tyranny and open windows and doors to their impiety, which would then flourish and burgeon more freely than it ever dared before. It would come to pass that their wickedness would go unpunished, and therefore would become more licentious on account of my recantation, and their government of the people, thus confirmed and established, would become intolerable, especially if they could boast that I had recanted with the full authority of your Sacred and Most Serene Majesty and of the whole Roman Empire. Good God! In that case I would be the tool of iniquity and tyranny."

The sound of his voice uplifted in rebuke to high sin brought a welcome thrill to many a heart. Men forgot the heat and smoke, while the defense continued:

"In a third sort of books I have written against some private individuals who tried to defend the Roman tyranny and tear down my pious doctrine. In these I confess I was more bitter than is becoming to a minister of religion. For I do not pose as a saint, nor do I discuss my life but the doctrine of Christ. Yet neither is it right for me to recant what I have said in these, for then tyranny and impiety would rage and reign against the people of God more violently than ever by reason of my acquiescence."

Luther paused a moment, then picked up a triumphant strain, moving, in prophetic humility, from rebuke to proof and calling on all present to rise and answer him.

"As I am a man and not God, I wish to claim no other defense for my doctrine than that which the Lord Jesus put forward when he was questioned before Annas and smitten by a servant: he then said, 'If I have spoken evil, bear witness of the evil.' If the Lord himself, who knew that He could not err, did not scorn to hear testimony against His doctrine from a miserable servant, how much more should I, the dregs of men, who can do nothing but err, seek and hope that someone should bear witness against my doctrine? I therefore beg by God's mercy that if your Majesty or your illustrious Lordships, from the highest to the lowest, can do it, you should bear witness and convict me of error and conquer me by proofs drawn from the Gospels or the

Prophets, for I am most ready to be instructed and when convinced will be the first to throw my books into the fire.

From this I think it is sufficiently clear that I have carefully considered and weighed the discords, perils, emulation, and dissension excited by my teaching. . . . To me the happiest side of the whole affair is that the Word of God is made the object of emulation and dissent. For this is the course, the fate, and the result of the Word of God, as Christ says: 'I am come not to send peace, but a sword, to set a man against his father and the daughter against her mother.' We must consider that our God is wonderful and terrible in his counsels. If we should begin to heal our dissensions by damning the Word of God, we should only turn loose an intolerable deluge of woes."

He spoke now to the heads of the empire. From authority born in Scripture and conscience, he called on the lords of Germany in terms no underling could use:

"Let us take care that the rule of this excellent youth, Prince Charles (in whom, next God, there is much hope), does not begin inauspiciously. For I could show by many examples drawn from Scripture that when Pharaoh and the King of Babylon and the kings of Israel thought to pacify and strengthen their kingdoms by their own wisdom, they really only ruined themselves. For He taketh the wise in their own craftiness and removeth mountains and they know it not. We must fear God. I do not say this as though your Lordships needed either my teaching or my admonition, but because I could not shirk the duty I owed Germany. With these words I commend myself to your Majesty and your Lordships, humbly begging that you will not let my enemies make me hateful to you without cause. I have spoken."

In proper custom he spoke in Latin. But many of the northerners did not understand it, and there were cries for it in German. The hall was hot, Luther perspiring. He seemed on the point of collapse. A Saxon, Frederick von Thun, called out, "If you can't do it, Doctor, you've done enough." Luther repeated it in German. But Charles V, in whose hands was the destiny of Europe, understood neither Latin nor German! And

Leo X, master of the Church, who alone had power sufficient for this healing, was far away! Eck rose, amazed that Luther would dare so to speak, and said:

"Luther, you have not answered to the point. You ought not to call in question what has been decided and condemned by councils. Therefore I beg you to give a simple, unsophisticated answer without horns. Will you recant or not?"

And then, Luther, realizing the point had been sharply called for, said briefly and exactly:

"Since your Majesty and your Lordships ask for a plain answer, I will give you one without either horns or teeth. Unless I am convinced by Scripture or by right reason, for I trust neither in popes nor in councils, since they have often erred and contradicted themselves—unless I am thus convinced, I am bound by the texts of the Bible, my conscience is captive to the Word of God. I neither can nor will recant anything, since it is neither right nor safe to act against conscience. God help me. Amen."

Eck was furious, and called again for recantation. Luther replied, while the tumult increased. Charles V rose abruptly and left the room, signifying an end of the audience. So the marshal took Luther quickly from the hall, while the Germans cheered and the Spaniards hissed.

Fearing an attempt on his life, friends gathered in a marching circle around him. And with hands held high in an old Saxon sign of victory, they escorted him through the crowds that jammed the palace court and streets. Back in his rooms Luther clapped his hands and shouted happily, "I am through! I am through!" But he wasn't.

Friends gathered around Luther in the inn that night, overjoyed with his strong stand at the Diet. One staunch old German patriot placed before him with his compliments a stein of the finest wine obtainable. The Elector Frederick was greatly pleased and remarked to his secretary, Georg Spalatin, about how well his Dr. Martin had spoken at the Diet that day.

Affairs in the political realm were so tense that the counselors, both of Frederick and of the emperor, tried hard to arrive at a compromise. They called on Luther several times during the succeeding few days, but he was adamant. If any compromise involved the surrender of his position, taken in public on his conscience, then it was impossible. The authority upon which that conscience based its decision was the written word of God, as he saw it. In this field compromise was out of the question, and so in despair the intermediaries gave it up.

Feeling that the need for his remaining in Worms was over, and wanting to get far away before the safe-conduct would expire, Luther silently slipped out on the morning of April 26 in the company of the same few friends with whom he had come.

V

STORM

THE JOURNEY HOME was more leisurely and not fraught with the same anxiety that the journey southward had known. But riding along a narrow road through the forest, Luther was suddenly surprised by the approach of a company of armed horsemen. They stopped his carriage forcibly, assured his companions that no harm was meant, and whispered something to Luther. He turned to his friends and told them he had to leave, but that all was well and he would write soon about it. Then he mounted, and galloped off through the forest. After a hard ride through the day and well into the night, he arrived at the castle of the Wartburg and was turned over to the commandant.

Word spread rapidly through the whole area that Luther had been kidnapped, but no man knew who the kidnappers were, or why the deed had been done. Suspicions that the Elector Frederick had had a hand in it could not be proved. To reassure some of his most intimate friends Luther wrote them after a few weeks to tell them of his health and safety, but did not divulge his hiding place. The Elector Frederick was afraid that Luther would meet the fate by assassination which the Romanists had wished for him at the council.

At the castle of the Wartburg, Luther was treated as a guest,

with due respect and honor. Hidden now from the world of turmoil, he lived as one set apart from that world. He dressed as a knight and was spoken to by everyone in the Wartburg as "Sir George." Thick black hair appeared over his tonsure, and a full beard covered his chin.

The first few weeks of his hiding passed quickly and quietly, and then the old restlessness possessed him again. He had been born, it seemed, for battle, and for ten long years now he had been steadily moving in public warfare. The great desire of his mind and heart was to give what he called "evangelical leadership" to the people of Saxony. And so, in his room in the Wartburg, he set his fine abilities to a task that he had long anticipated. He would bring his beloved New Testament forth in the German tongue. He would set forth in strength and vigor the blessed stories in idioms chosen for the general understanding. Throughout the long summer months and well into the winter he labored at these chosen tasks. There came from his pen not only the New Testament translation but also tract after tract on all the major issues of the controversy. He wrote sermons to be used in the churches in the regular cycle of the church year. He wrote on the mass and on monastic vows.

While he wrote, with much time for reflection, the old controversy between himself and his father when first he took his own vows came with freshness to his mind. He could see, as he could not then see, that there was something intrinsically wrong in the Roman practice with regard to vows. The deep piety of his father was clearer to him. He could understand now how piety and resistance to the organization could be united in one person. When the book was ready for the public in November, 1521, Martin wrote to Hans:

> This book, dear father, I wish to dedicate to you. . . .
>
> It is now sixteen years since I became a monk, having taken the vow without your knowledge and against your will. You were anxious and fearful about my weakness, because I was a young blood of twenty-two . . . and you had learned from numerous examples that monkery made many unblessed and so were determined to marry me honorably and tie me down. This fear, this anxiety, this nonconsent of yours were for a time simply irreconcilable. . . .
>
> Dear father, will you still take me out of the cloister? If so, do not boast of it, for God has anticipated you and taken me out himself. What difference does it make whether I retain or lay aside the cowl and the tonsure. Do they make the monk? . . . My conscience is free and redeemed; therefore I am still a monk but not a monk, and a new creature not of the Pope, but of Christ, for the Pope also has creatures and is a creator of puppets and idols and masks and straw men, of which I was formerly one, but now have escaped by the Word. . . .
>
> The Lord bless you, dear father, with mother, your Margaret, and all our family. Farewell in the Lord Christ.

He handled the problem of vows as he did everything else, asking only one question: What does Scripture say? From Scripture he argued vows were hostile to the good of Christianity. With strong argument he cut away the basis for the great monastic emphasis on celibacy. The Bible encourages marriage, does not place a premium on virginity, destroys the distinction between clergy and laity.

The book which was made of these writings was widely read and very influential. Again Luther touched a source of income for Albert, archbishop of Mainz, for he sold licenses to priests to permit them to keep concubines. Marriage of the clergy assumed an important phase of the struggle against the papacy after the appearance of this book.

During Luther's Wartburg stay, the hills around the castle were the scene of many walks. He tried to live the life of knight and hunter, and took part in the chase, but his heart was too tender and too gentle to enjoy the snared rabbit. But the same flowers and the same fields which had delighted the eye of his childhood were now his joy.

The deep intensity of his life, however, was centered in the moments in his room when all the strength of his nature was concentrated on religious study. Superstitious as always, he now had time to nurse this superstition. Not called away to routine duty, he could hear through the long hours of silence strange noises throughout the old castle, and as always when a direct cause could not be seen for action, he associated the action with the devil, or the Holy Spirit. So he heard the devil in strange noises in his room, under his bed, outside the door. It is no wonder that with his strong impetuous nature, so active in the past five years and now so forced to inaction, concentrating on Greek and Hebrew grammar, and wrestling with the New Testament phrases, he should imagine that the devil plagued him, leered at him from the opposite wall, and laughed at him when the Greek would not respond.

No wonder, either, is it that anger, furious enough to dissolve the coherence of his personality, would take possession of him when he thought of the way Rome had handled the precious Gospel, and himself, its proclaimer! Even that very day, as he sat in the Wartburg, the Archbishop Albert was displaying at Halle nine thousand relics, including manna from the wilderness, the burning bush of Moses, jars from the wedding at Cana, with the promise of indulgence for those who attended! Albert was also opening the indulgence sale again. Luther wrote a powerful letter to Albert, demanding once again that he withdraw the abusive practices. His mind worked clearly and quickly. His sentences cut through to the issue every time:

> I humbly pray your Grace, therefore, to leave poor people undeceived and unrobbed, and show yourself a bishop rather than a wolf. It has been made clear enough that indulgences are only knavery and fraud, and that only Christ should be preached to the people, so that your Grace has not the excuse of ignorance. Your Grace will please remember the beginning, and what a terrible fire was kindled from a little despised spark, and how all the world was surely of the opinion that a single poor beggar was immeasurably too weak for the Pope, and was undertaking an impossible task. But God willed to give the Pope and his followers more than enough to do, and to play a game contrary to the expectation of the world . . . so that the Pope will hardly recover, growing daily worse. . . . Let no one doubt that the same God yet lives and knows how to withstand a cardinal of Mainz even if four emperors would support him.

Strange things had been done by the power of God, and Martin was certain that in this cause emperors were no match for the Holy Spirit. He took upon himself the prophet's authority, and in its power the monk delivered an ultimatum to the cardinal:

> Wherefore I write to tell your Grace that if the idol is not taken down, my duty to godly doctrine and Christian salvation will absolutely force me to attack your Grace publicly as I did the Pope, and oppose your undertaking, and lay all the odiums which Tetzel once had, on the Archbishop of Mainz, and show all the world the difference between a bishop and a wolf. . . . Moreover, I beg your Grace to leave in peace the priests who, to avoid unchastity, have betaken themselves to marriage. Do not deprive them of their God-given rights. Your Grace has no authority, reason, nor right to persecute them. . . . If you do not take care, the Evangelic party will raise an outcry and point out that it would become a bishop first to cast the beam out of his own eye and put away his harlots before he separates pious wives from their husbands. . . .

I beg and expect a right speedy answer from your Grace within the next fortnight, for at the expiration of that time my pamphlet against the Idol of Halle will be published unless a proper answer comes. . . . God give your Grace His grace unto a right mind and will.

Your Grace's obedient, humble servant,

Martin Luther

Luther's letter was dated December 1, 1521. Before the end of the month a messenger brought to the Wartburg a letter addressed to "Martin Luther." Luther opened it and read:

My dear doctor, I have received your letter and I take it in good part and graciously, and will see to it that the thing that moved you so be done away, and I will act, God willing, as becomes a pious, spiritual, and Christian prince, as far as God gives me grace and strength, for which I earnestly pray and have prayers said for me, for I can do nothing of myself, and know well that without God's grace there is no good in me, but that I am as much foul mud as any other, if not more. I do not wish to conceal this, for I am more than willing to show you grace and favor for Christ's sake, and I can well bear fraternal and Christian punishment. I hope the merciful, kind God will give me herein more grace, strength, and patience to live in this matter and in others by His will.

Albert, with his own hand

IT WAS NOT EASY for Luther to remain out of the leadership in the most crucial days of the new movement. He thought with mingled bitterness and scorn of the tricks to which Aleandro and Charles V had descended at Worms. When he read the Edict of Worms calling on the people of Germany to surrender him for his proper condemnation, placing under the interdict all who gave him any shelter, food, or clothes, or who read, bought, sold, or printed any of his books, he paced the halls of the Wartburg, impatient at the elector's continued demand for his seclusion. There were days when his gifts of clear exposition were at their height, and he felt himself working with the highest efficiency, but other days he knew, too, when all the distractions and all the balked fury of these years of quarreling got the better of him. Impatient, restless, he was finally summoned out of his seclusion by the course of events at Wittenberg.

Here, in his absence, colleagues like Andreas Bodenstein were moving too rapidly. They wanted to throw over the whole of the ancient organization and faith. Luther was by nature and by training thoroughly conservative. He had been driven by the severest experiences of life to open up the abuses in his Church, but the Church itself he devoutly loved and all its ancient customs he would keep. Not so with the more radical men, who had welcomed his leadership. Wittenberg needed him badly. So finally, in the spring of 1522, the Elector Frederick permitted him to slip away from the Wartburg.

Still in beard and full head of hair, dressed as a knight and with sword by his side, he journeyed incognito through the territory of Duke George of Saxony, who would willingly have turned him over to the proper authorities and who had kept constant pressure on the Elector Frederick to do so. When warned of the duke's intention, Luther had written that he would come through Leipzig to Wittenberg even "though it should rain Duke Georges for nine days in succession, each fiercer than the other."

In an inn at Jena one night two students noticed a strange contradiction between the sword by the side of the knight and the book that he was reading, the Psalms in Hebrew. Well informed on the movements of the Reformation, as Luther's movement was now being called, the two students talked with the knight and surmised that he was Luther. One of them described him in a letter and noted that he was "somewhat stout, yet upright, bending backward rather than stooping, with deep, dark eyes and eyebrows, twinkling and sparkling like stars, so that one could hardly look steadily at them."

No others than the two Swiss students suspected his identity, and safely he arrived at Wittenberg. He talked with Melanchthon and his other friends and analyzed the situation with them. Then for eight successive days he preached in the village church against the fanatical activities which had resulted in the destruction of pictures and images and in the breakdown of organizational morale. At the close of the week he was once again the leader of the Wittenberg movement. The radical wing of the Reformation was henceforth to locate its center elsewhere.

Luther, with the help of Melanchthon, now concentrated on the clear formulation of the Wittenberg position. Throughout 1520 and 1521 Melanchthon had worked on an outline of theology constructed from Paul's letter to the Romans. He had sent a copy, in proof, to Luther at the Wartburg. Now, with Luther's approval, he published it in Wittenberg, calling it *Theological Commonplaces*. It moved in the evangelical circle of ideas, beginning with the doctrine of the Trinity and then setting forth the idea of "Man, Sin, The Law, The Gospel, Grace, Faith, The Sacraments, The Magistracy, Church Government, Condemnation, and Blessedness." There was need of such a logical and systematic presentation, and Melanchthon's detailed skillfulness was equal to the task. The proofs of argument were all scriptural and the book marked a tremendous advance for the Luther forces.

Far away in his retreat at Salzburg, Staupitz, Luther's old vicar-general, watched with mingled sorrow and joy the progress of Luther, as the young monk, come to maturity, battled for piety in the open world. The last exchange of letters between the two old friends was after the great crisis in the battle had been passed. Luther wrote in September, 1523:

> Reverend Father in Christ, your silence is most unjust, and you know that we are obliged to think of it. But even if you are no longer pleased with me, it is not fitting that I should forget you, who first made the light of the Gospel to shine in my heart.

This called forth the last letter from Staupitz, dated Salzburg, April 1, 1524:

> My love to you is most constant, passing the love of women, always unbroken.... But as I do not grasp all of your ideas, I keep silence with them.... But we owe much to you, Martin, for having led us back from the husks which the swine did eat to the pastures of life and the words of salvation.

Staupitz died in December, 1524.

THE SEVEREST TEST THAT LUTHER ever had to face came in the years 1524 and 1525 during the so-called Peasants' War. The causes of the peasants' revolt lay deep in history, completely disconnected from the Reformation.

For centuries in central Europe the peasant class had been strictly held in leash by the nobles, both civil and ecclesiastical. The long story of uprisings in an attempt to gain and hold their birthright is discernible throughout western European history. In the German area, these uprisings had become increasingly severe and frequent in the one hundred fifty years preceding 1525. The princes of the Church were more at fault than those of the laity. For centuries the bishops and the other high officials of the Church had held serfs in severe oppression. The genesis of the peasant rebellion throughout these years is found in two sources: first, in the native refusal of the oppressed classes to bear oppression beyond a certain point; and, second, in the preaching of the New Testament. For the same Church that nurtured ecclesiastical princes, preserved in others of its priests the strange gospel message of equality.

Long before Luther, these two streams of rebellion and the gospel had met in the forests of central Germany. Such organizations as the Bundschuh, a secret society dedicated to social rebellion, bear witness to the long effort of the peasants. Its symbol was a peasant's shoe, tied, in token of servility, instead of buckled, as were the shoes of the nobility. The peasants seemed to gather strength for a century and break out into rebellion, only to be beaten back by superior technique and superior equipment. Then they would nurse their wrath through many generations until once again, sorely pressed, they stormed the castles of the princes.

Now in the tremendous moving days of the late fifteenth and early sixteenth centuries, there was a ground swell of rebellion through all of central Europe. The papacy, ancient symbol of autocratic strength, was weakening and fighting for its hold on Europe. The empire was no longer the source of strength that it once had been, and many were the princes of the empire refusing allegiance to their chief. Feudalism was in the last stages of existence. Francis I in France, Henry VIII in England,

Charles V in Spain, Cesare Borgia in Italy, Leo X in Rome, all acted as personal will dictated, in violent disregard of the rights of humanity and of the accepted law of the medieval world. Wealth was increasingly concentrated in the hands of the few. Luxury and its ever-present companions, immorality and brutality, spread through the armed classes of Europe. Hundreds of the finest minds of Christendom attacked from a thousand angles the abuse in every recognized authority.

The day after Luther left Worms, Magellan was killed in the Philippine Islands, and during the early months of Luther's stay in the Wartburg, Cortez was accomplishing his dastardly conquest of Mexico, which involved the death of Montezuma. With this breaking, transforming, and re-forming world, the peasants moved in perfect rhythm. This, too, was their hour to strike. The ever-restless movement grew steadily toward the tragic days of 1524 and 1525. The chief misfortune was that the leadership fell to men unequipped for the task.

Late in 1524 the crisis came. The countess of Lupfen, whose estate bordered on Lake Constance, attempted to force her serfs to gather snail shells for some guests at the castle. It was a church holiday on which the serfs were under no obligation to work. In response to her whim they rose in rebellion. The entire Swabian peasantry joined the outbreak. Northward it spread, and terror took possession of the people.

In the opening of the rebellion, during the summer of 1524, the peasants were everywhere successful. When they captured a castle or an estate of the wealthy they robbed, pillaged, and murdered without restraint. The torch and the sword, with all the accompanying hideousness of brutality to which a human mob can descend, rose menacingly over Germany.

Thomas Münzer, who had organized a fanatical sect dedicated to the reform of Church and state, now assumed a precarious leadership of the peasants. Speaking from the German town of Mühlhausen, Münzer claimed that he had divine right and that this was the hour when the Holy Spirit should lead the peasants to their rightful world. He was himself unbalanced, hasty, ignorant, but he was moved by a fiery spirit. And Thomas Münzer offered the peasants of Germany the most brutal advice that could possibly have been given:

"Arise! Fight the battle of the Lord! The wicked tremble when they hear you. Be pitiless! Rouse up the towns and villages! On! On! On! while the fire is burning. On while the sword is yet reeking with the slaughter! Give the fire no time to go out, the sword no time to cool! Kill all the proud ones. While they reign over you it is no use to talk of God!"

As the movement spread in strong violence northward into Saxony it became increasingly clear that Luther had to speak.

His mind was clear. He had never in his life sanctioned the use of force except by the civil magistrate. He would have died nonresistant at Worms had they led him to the stake. He would never have sanctioned an armed defense by the Elector Frederick and the Saxon warriors in his behalf.

On his return from Wartburg to Wittenberg in 1522, in the memorable week of preaching in which he had stilled the fanatical activities there, he had said:

"I will preach, speak, write, but I will force no one; for faith must be voluntary. Take me as an example. I stood up against the Pope, indulgences, and all the papists, but without violence or uproar. I only urged, preached, and declared God's Word, nothing else. And yet while I was asleep, or drinking Wittenberg beer with my Philipp Melanchthon and Amsdorf, the Word inflicted greater injury on popery than prince or emperor ever did. I did nothing, the Word did everything. Had I appealed to force, all Germany might have been deluged with blood; yea, I might have kindled a conflict at Worms, so that the Emperor would not have been safe. But what would have been the result? Ruin and desolation of body and soul. I therefore kept quiet, and gave the Word free course through the world. . . . The Word is almighty, and takes captive the hearts."

But his heart was ever a peasant's heart. The blood in his veins, it was his boast, was peasant blood. No man in Europe had spoken more directly against the abuses of the ruling class than he. And now he faced a terrible conflict between his native, idealistic sympathy for the peasants and his strong belief in the divine order of civil government. The princes whom he had

known in Saxony, chiefly the great Elector Frederick, had been men wise and well controlled. In this hour when the uprising was at its height, Frederick was on his deathbed, and could not organize his followers to the defense.

With the demands of the peasants, too, Luther was in hearty sympathy. The leaders of the peasants had stated their position in the famous Twelve Articles drawn up some time during the winter of 1524–1525 and adopted in a council at Memmingen on March 7. Luther read these carefully:

1. The right to choose their own pastors.
2. They would pay tithe of corn, out of which the pastors should be paid, the rest going to the use of the parish. But small tithes (i.e., of the produce of animals, every tenth calf, or pig, or egg, and so on) they would not pay.
3. They would be free, and no longer serfs and bondmen.
4. Wild game and fish are to be free to all.
5. Woods and forests belong to all for fuel.

6. No services of labor to be more than were required of their forefathers.
7. If more service required, wages must be paid for it.
8. Rent, when above the value of the land, to be properly valued and lowered.
9. Punishments for crimes to be fixed.
10. Common land to be given up again to common use.
11. Death gifts (i.e., the right of the lord to take the best chattel of the deceased tenant) to be done away with.
12. Any of these articles proved to be contrary to the Scriptures or God's justice, to be null and void.

This, he thought, was clear and honorable. He left Wittenberg, journeyed down through the insurrection area, visited the camps of the peasants, and in Eisleben wrote his *Exhortation to Peace on the Twelve Articles of the Swabian Peasants.*

In this he spoke to the nobles:

> We need thank no one on earth for this foolish rebellion but you, my lords, and especially you blind bishops, parsons, and monks, for you, even yet hardened, cease not to rage against the holy Gospel, although you know that our cause is right and you cannot controvert it. Besides this, in civil government you do nothing but oppress and tax to maintain your pomp and pride, until the poor common man neither can nor will bear it longer. The sword is at your throat, and yet you still think you sit so firm in the saddle that no one can hoist you out. You will find out that by such hardened presumption you will break your necks. . . . If these peasants don't do it, others will; God will appoint others, for He intends to smite you and will smite you.

and to the peasants:

> It is my friendly and fraternal prayer, dearest brothers, to be very careful what you do. . . . Those who take the sword shall perish by the sword and every soul should be subject to the powers that be, in fear and honor. . . . If the government is bad and intolerable, that is no excuse for riot and insurrection, for to punish evil belongs not to everyone, but to the civil authority which bears the sword. . . . Suffering tyranny is a cross given by God.

He believed firmly in the rights of the peasants. With equal firmness he believed in the rights of civil government, and he hoped for arbitration. But it was too late for arbitration. Not even Luther's powerful spirit could check the rising fury of the suicidal struggle.

He saw with increasing anguish his country broken, her fields destroyed, cloisters and castles burned, all types of violence and anarchy. His mind dwelt on the progress of his own great cause. He remembered again the Diet of Worms and saw the evangelical faith defended by the princes of northern Germany. He knew how terrible and how unchecked was the license of Münzer and the radicals. He knew the hopelessness and helplessness of destructive civil war. He preached in town after town and in the camps of the peasants, gathered for warfare, against this violence. He pleaded for peace. He visited the wounded and the plague-stricken in the gathering places of the peasant army.

Throughout March and April the situation grew increasingly serious. Both Frederick and his brother, who was to succeed him as elector of Saxony, were unable to cope with the uprising. The staunch old elector, ever loyal to his subjects, weakened while Luther was preaching against the revolution. Word came to Luther that he was wanted at the deathbed, but it was too late. Frederick died, and Luther knew deep sorrow. His strong protector was gone, and rioting was everywhere.

In final desperation, in what was to him a frightful and bitter hour, Luther was driven to choose between two evils. Sensing the destruction of his native land by anarchy, he wrote early in May the pamphlet entitled *Against the Thievish, Murderous Hordes of Peasants*.

> In my former book [*Exhortation to Peace*] I dared not judge the peasants, since they asked to be instructed, and Christ says *Judge not*. But before I could look around they . . . betake themselves to violence—rob, rage, and act like mad dogs, whereby one may see . . . that their pretense to speak in the name of the Gospel in the Twelve Articles was a simple lie. They do mere devil's work, especially that Satan of Mülhausen does nothing but rob, murder, and pour out blood.

The peasants deserved death for three reasons: (1) because they have broken their oath of fealty; (2) for rioting and plundering, and (3) for having covered their terrible sins with the name of the Gospel.

> Wherefore, my lords, free, save, help, and pity the poor people; stab, smite, and slay all ye that can. . . . I implore everyone who can to avoid the peasants as he would the devil himself. I pray God will enlighten them and turn their hearts. But if they do not turn, I wish them no happiness for ever more. . . . Let none think this too hard who considers how intolerable is rebellion.

Luther knew the leadership of the peasants was thoughtless, impractical, without hope of salvation, and he had confidence in his Saxon princes. His leadership had never been accepted by the peasants. His gospel had never undergirded the revolution. They had followed the broken, brutal, insane leadership of men like Münzer, whom Luther called "that Satan of Mühlhausen."

The decisive battle of the revolution was fought near Frankenhausen on the fifteenth of May. It was a terrible event. The peasants were equipped with all manner of rude weapons—pitchforks, wood axes, scythes, spears, bows. Across a long open field they barricaded themselves—behind overturned farm wagons and such other impediments as they could find, and, exhorted by Münzer's promises that a miracle would be wrought, they awaited the attack. Under the able leadership of Landgrave Philip of Hesse the charge came. Well-armed knights on armored horses, with stout lances and keen swords, swept all before them, and no peasant was alive when the sun went down unless he had saved his life in hiding or in flight. Thomas Münzer was executed.

Social darkness settled over Germany. A great cause had been so miserably led that it promised worse consequences in victory than in defeat. The peasants felt bruised and hurt that the lion of Wittenberg had not fought with them. All over Europe the conservative class, ever the home of men who rationalize their own desires, blamed Luther for this rebellion. They could not see that their miserable, selfish exactions over the centuries had stirred up this fury.

Luther was no coward. He stood his ground. For the peasants he had worked. Until his death a peasant he would be, but in intellectual and moral honor he hewed to his well-defended line. Physical violence was not his to command. Nevertheless against his will and by the force of circumstances the Church that bears his name moved from that day closer and closer to the princes, with disastrous consequences.

VI

COLORING LEAVES

LUTHER'S LIFE AS A BOY in Mansfeld had given him a deep affectionate appreciation of a Christian home. His friendship with the Cotta family in Eisenach had strengthened in him a belief in the essential piety of the family life. All the thoughts of a wife and family that might have gathered in his mind through these early years had, by an effort of will, been set into the background of his life when he took the vows in the Erfurt monastery in 1505.

There is no authentic record that Luther loved and courted in the days of his young manhood. That he was happy, free, and joyous, and often in mixed company through his student days at Erfurt, is well known. But no man may say, unless he moves into a realm of pure speculation, anything about Luther's life of affection in his youth.

In the Erfurt monastery the great struggle was not against desire for sexual experience or indulgence. He lived then in one of the highest fields of experience known to humanity, wherein he tried to purge his mind of the thoughts which he considered unworthy of his Christian calling. It was a long, hard fight, but it was not a fight against action, nor the effort of a powerful will to control an over-strong passion.

Back again in Wittenberg after the Wartburg seclusion, he found that as a consequence of his attack upon the vows, men and women were leaving monastery and convent. Some of them probably from nonevangelical motives, but the great majority left in clear and honorable choice. The problem took on serious consequences when from the convents to Wittenberg came nuns, without economic security, expecting guidance.

Luther defended the marriage of the clergy on the grounds that in the first picture of humanity presented in the opening chapters of Genesis, God had himself created them man and wife and had called for their life together, and all through the Scriptures the married appears as the ideal life. Nowhere in Luther's reading of the Old Testament could there be found any justification for the suspension of this relationship. By the laws of nature and by the laws of God the married life is justified. The Roman Catholic position, a position not shared by its older Christian neighbor, the Greek Catholic Church, based the celibate ideal upon the separation of the clergy and laity. This separation Luther had steadfastly denied, setting forth in opposition to it his famous doctrine of the priesthood of all believers.

So now he found no cause for complaint, but only cause for joy when his friends in Wittenberg and other north German towns, released from their vows by their allegiance to the Reformation, began to marry. Philipp Melanchthon, Justus Jonas, and other leaders in the movement were by 1525 established in homes of their own.

Among several groups of nuns who had sought refuge in Wittenberg was a group of nine who had come in early April, 1523. On April 10 Luther wrote to a friend as follows:

> Nine fugitive nuns, a wretched crowd, have been brought to me by honest citizens of Torgau. . . . I pity them much, but most of all the others who are dying everywhere in such numbers in their cursed and impure celibacy. This sex, so very, very weak, joined by nature or rather by God to the other, perishes when cruelly separated. O tyrants! O cruel parents and kinsmen in Germany. O Pope and bishops, who can curse you enough? Who can sufficiently execrate the blind fury which has taught and enforced such things? But this is not the place to do it.
>
> You ask what I shall do with them? First I shall inform their relatives and ask them to support the girls; if they will not I shall have the girls otherwise provided for. Some of the families have already promised me to take them; for some I shall get husbands

if I can. Their names are Magdalene Staupitz, Elsa von Canitz, Ave Gross, Ave von Schonfeld and her sister Margaret, Laneta von Goltz, Margaret and Catharine Zeschau, and Katharina von Bora. Here are they, who serve Christ, in need of true pity. They have escaped from the cloister in miserable condition.

Luther must have talked with great interest to Magdalene Staupitz, thinking of the long affection between her brother and himself. One after another, the nuns in this group were taken care of by friends, or married to suitors. All except Katharina von Bora.

KATHARINA VON BORA was born in a little village twenty miles south of Leipzig in January, 1499. Her mother's early death and her father's remarriage combined to place her at five years of age in a convent school. At first in a Benedictine convent, she was later transferred to the Cistercian convent at Nimbschen. Katharina received the veil at sixteen years of age, when Martin Luther was lecturing on Romans in Wittenberg.

In the general exodus from the monasteries some of the young nuns at Nimbschen attempted to escape. They were disciplined and guarded. Through a conspiracy with a businessman in Torgau, near Nimbschen, who had access to the convent, twelve of the nuns, including Katharina, succeeded in making their escape on the night of April 4, 1523. They met in Katharina's rooms, escaped through the window to the garden, thence over the wall to the street. Hidden in empty beer barrels, they rode away from Nimbschen. Katharina was twenty-four years old and had been in the monastic life since childhood. Arriving in Wittenberg, Katharina was settled in the home of one of the wealthy citizens named Reichenbach, where for two years she assisted in the housework. Toward the close of 1523 she fell in love with Jerome Baumgärtner, a student guest in Melanchthon's home. They were engaged to be married, and it looked as though Katharina's future was secure. But when Baumgärtner left Wittenberg he neglected Katharina, neither writing to her nor coming to see her. Luther interceded and wrote him that he would like to see them married as soon as possible, but

Jerome did not accept the doctor's advice, announcing, early in the following year, his engagement to the daughter of a very wealthy family.

Not long afterward, another friend of Luther, named Dr. Glatz, courted Katharina and desired to marry her, but when the subject was broached to Katharina, she refused Dr. Glatz and laughingly said that she would marry only Dr. Amsdorf or Dr. Luther. The old companions who had journeyed to Worms together were thus once again coupled in warfare!

Luther suddenly, and with very little warning to his friends, decided to marry. For a long while his father, Hans, had been urging him to do so. Luther, of course, connected his marriage, as he did everything else, with the cause of his gospel. He wrote to one friend that he would marry to "please his father, tease the pope, and spite the devil." This, in his regular semihumorous vein, nevertheless sets forth the state of his mind. He loved and honored his father, and the marriage would please him. He held the Pope as his mortal enemy, and it would give further evidence of the irreconcilable breach. So, in reality, he did not marry for youthful, idealistic affection, but for the heroic, mature consummation of the evangelical life he now professed. Katharina von Bora held for him no charms like the charms of youth. He was forty-two and she was twenty-six. His mind and heart had been exposed for ten years, at least, to public life, and were somewhat toughened. The long years of the monastic discipline had given him complete control over himself. This was a choice, not an emotion.

Katharina von Bora was of a good family. She was capable in the duties that would fall on the wife of Martin Luther, and had demonstrated that capability in the home of Luther's friend. She was strong, rugged, healthy. She possessed a marked degree of vitality and good humor.

In the spring of 1525 in Wittenberg Martin talked to her of his hopes. It was not easy. They had both known the monastic life. He knew what would be said of them. But Martin's heart was gentle and his honor unassailable. They were immediately in harmony with one another, and, when once the gentle words had been said, the supposed differences in age and temperament dissolved. Katharina held him in high respect—he was the "great doctor," but he was, also, her lover. The mind and tongue equal to the task of awakening Europe did not fail in this immemorial persuasion, so on the evening of June 13, they were married in Luther's home by Johann Bugenhagen, a colleague on the faculty. The quiet wedding accomplished, Luther sent invitations for a public announcement and celebration, and on June 27 Hans and Margaret Luther, and many other friends, gathered in Wittenberg to celebrate the marriage of Martin and Katharina.

Europe was in a turmoil with the report. The scandal they had heard in other years was nothing to that which flooded Wittenberg now. The bitter and unscrupulous tongues of his more violent Catholic opponents lashed at him in frenzy. Rumor was, of course, spread that the marriage was a marriage of necessity. Rome said the Antichrist would result from the union, since popular tradition expected it to come from the marriage of a monk and a nun. Erasmus silenced the enemy with the remark that if such were the case Antichrist had had plenty of opportunities before this.

Still, with rumor unchecked and the sources of information so thoroughly partial, it was impossible that Luther's marriage should be properly represented throughout Europe. Many a sincere and sensitive Catholic mind won to Luther in the earlier years was now lost to him by what appeared a thoroughly improper relationship. Many could not forget that Martin and Katharina had each in youth taken what were supposed to be irrevocable vows. They did not feel the might and power of the evangelical faith which for Martin and Katharina had been sufficient to break obedience to the vows.

Martin Luther married with clear and open consciousness of what would follow. But he was not prepared for the strange and quiet happiness that slowly came into his life, as his home now fell into normal routine. Katharina von Bora brought to him a strong and willing service, a loyal and sympathetic heart, a keen, delightful sense of humor, and was to him through all the rest of life increasingly a joy and a source of peace. The highest tribute he ever paid to her was when he spoke one day of St. Paul's

Epistle to the Romans as, "This is my Katharina von Bora." In St. Paul's Epistle to the Romans his heart had first found its religious peace.

WITH THE YEAR 1526 Luther's life settled into activity in three major shares. He had, first, to carry on the great battle with the papacy and the state. Simultaneously he must construct the Evangelical Church in all its branches; and, thirdly, his home began increasingly to call for his attention and strength.

In the first of these fields he was technically an outlaw and had always to be on the lookout lest he unwarily step into traps set for his capture. The Edict of Worms was supposed to be in force. Under its provisions any citizen of Germany was, by the allegiance he owed his emperor and the head of his Church, to deliver Luther alive or dead to the proper authorities. This being so, his friends were careful not to allow strangers around his home or the university lest perchance an assassin, motivated by deep loyalty to the ancient Church, should take his life. Because of the edict Luther was unable to appear in person at any of the great meetings held in the fifteen years following Worms in the unsuccessful attempt to heal the schism.

At home in Wittenberg, while the Diet gathered for the first such meeting in 1526 at the German town of Speyer, Martin Luther watched anxiously the work of Katharina, his Katie, and watching her knew the beauty of the stirring life that brought the *Magnificat* to Mary's lips. Early in June they knew the wait would soon be over, and great was the rejoicing when, on the sixth, Martin looked on his firstborn son. The desire of life was knowing some fulfillment and old Hans Luther, in Mansfeld, was notified that he had a grandson, a namesake. While he waited for news from the Diet, Martin Luther heard through the once quiet Black Cloister, where they had come to live, the cries of little Hans.

Meanwhile the long rivalry between France and Spain had been greatly increased by the elevation of the Spanish Charles V to the imperial throne, and Francis I of France was keeping European politics in turmoil. Thus, Charles did not protest too strongly against the inconclusive action of the Diet when it finally permitted the reforming units in the empire to continue their evangelic work. For a strange spectacle was about to take place. In Rome, a new pope had been installed and Charles V, standard-bearer of the Catholic faith in the north, had ordered his army in the south to invade Italy and march on the holy city. Leo X had died in December, 1521, while Luther was in the Wartburg. He was succeeded by Adrian VI, who had been Charles's private chaplain. Adrian's election had been dictated by the emperor, but his health was not equal to the strain, and in less than a year the cardinals convened again for an election. They had had enough of Adrian's reform policies and joyfully welcomed another Medici. Pope Clement VII, the nephew of Leo X, was shrewd, luxury-loving, and secular, as his uncle had been. And to Charles V, Clement seemed overfriendly to the French cause.

The army of Charles was composed both of Spanish and German soldiers, and the very men who had hissed and cheered Luther at the Diet of Worms now found themselves marching together under a German general to the attack on Rome. Benvenuto Cellini was in Rome at the time, doing work for Clement VII. On the approach of the northern army the papal party took refuge in the impregnable Castle of St. Angelo. They were in such a hurry to get in the castle that Cellini carried the train of the Pope's robes as they ran for the quickly closing doors. One cardinal was hoisted by his retainers through a window. The Germans and the Spaniards took the city on May 6, 1527, and thoroughly sacked it. Inside the castle, Cellini cleverly picked the jewels, and melted the gold from papal ornaments in order that Clement VII might, in dire necessity, have the wherewithal to pay his ransom.

While Charles and the Pope were thus engaged, Luther was carrying on an heroic life in Wittenberg. He preached and taught daily, but his health began to show signs of weakening under the long strain. As early as 1521, in the Wartburg, he had experienced severe digestive disturbances. By 1523 this had increased to such an extent that throughout the month of March he had been afflicted with constant nausea and vomiting. Nervous headaches appeared in the same month, never to leave him throughout life, and now in 1527, on July 6, starting up from the dinner table for his room, he fainted before he could reach it and was for days seriously ill. Before his recovery was complete, the plague had come once again to Wittenberg. Upon its appearance the university moved to Jena, but not Luther, who never fled the plague. Katharina was carrying her second child. Little Hans, now over a year old, fell desperately ill and for eleven days could neither eat nor drink. Martin, himself weak and exhausted, summoned up the strength to carry the burdens of home and Church.

Out of this depth of misery and uncertainty, with death around him and with the great authorities of his childhood, in Church and state, on the field of battle against each other, Luther's mind dwelt constantly on the strength that was his through his faith in God. Poring over the Forty-sixth Psalm, he brought its rich and glorious lesson to the hour of his need. He knew the strength of the castle walls that crowned his Teutonic hills. He knew how, in the hour of battle, his people were safe behind these majestic fortresses, and so, he thought, was he safe, when death and destruction were all around him, in God. He remembered how secure he had been from violence in the castle above Eisenach. God was his protection against the devil, and from this, his hour of deep stress, came the triumphant song of victory:

> *A mighty fortress is our God,*
> *A bulwark never failing;*
> *Our helper he, amid the flood*
> *Of mortal ills prevailing.*
> *For still our ancient foe*
> *Doth seek to work us woe,*
> *His craft and power are great;*
> *And armed with cruel hate*
> *On earth is not his equal.*
>
> *And though this world with devils filled*
> *Should threaten to undo us;*
> *We will not fear, for God hath willed*
> *His truth to triumph through us.*

The prince of darkness grim,
We tremble not for him
His rage we can endure,
For lo, his doom is sure,
One little word shall fell him.

That word above all earthly powers,
No thanks to them abideth;
The spirit and the gift are ours
Through him who with us sideth.
Let goods and kindred go,
This mortal life also;
The body they may kill—
God's truth abideth still,
His kingdom is forever.

The cadenced, solemn music, too, he wrote for this, his march-ing song. And while he hummed the melody into form he watched Hans recover, and rejoiced to see him strong again. Katharina also weathered the plague, and entered the last few weeks of her second confinement in fair health. A daughter was born on December 10. They named the little girl Elizabeth, but strength was not allotted to her, and before a year had passed they buried her.

Luther, writing to a friend, just after her death, said: "Little Hans thanks you for the rattle of which he is inordinately proud. . . . My little daughter, Elizabeth, is dead. She has left me wonderfully sick at heart and almost womanish, I am so moved by pity for her. I could never have believed how a father's heart could soften for his child."

As though his work was not enough, Luther turned his attention to the condition of the parishes in the section of Germany now accepting the Reformation. In company with Melanchthon and others, he journeyed throughout the Saxon province visiting town after town and examining its educational system and its church practices. This was tremendously hard work, with rough travel, uncomfortable lodging, and irregular food, but Luther felt keenly the great necessity for education if his new Church was to support itself. On his return from the visitation he called attention to the miserable condition of instruction throughout the whole province and insisted that the pastors begin a thorough reconstruction of this phase of their work.

The troubles in Italy and France finally quieted, Charles V turned his attention again to his rebellious Germany, and in 1529 called a second Diet to meet at the city of Speyer. Controlling this Diet in person, the emperor succeeded in obtaining by a majority vote a prohibition of the reformed worship. In answer to this action, the delegates from the Lutheran areas presented to the Diet a formal protest, signed by the representatives of Saxony, Brandenburg, Brunswick, Hesse, Anhalt, and fourteen of the free cities. From this point on the party of non-Catholic adherence was called "Protestant." Some of the signers of the protest were non-Lutheran, and the term Protestant carried, therefore, a broad connotation. The emperor was unable to heal the breach and the Diet closed with the two parties well defined.

At home in Wittenberg, Luther received the news of the proceedings of the Diet and saw a political party grow out of his religious reform, himself unable to control it. Family life continued its course in Wittenberg regardless of actions in the political world, and on May 4, almost a year after her little sister had died, Magdalene Luther was born.

THE BEST EFFORT Charles V made to reconcile the religious differences in Germany was at Augsburg in 1530. Thomas Lindsay in his *History of the Reformation* describes the entrance of Charles into Augsburg:

> The summons to the Diet, commanding the Electors, princes, and all the Estates of the Empire to meet at Augsburg on the 8th of April, 1530, had been issued when Charles was at Bologna. No threats marred the invitation. The Emperor announced that he meant to leave all past errors to the judgment of the Saviour; that he wished to give a charitable hearing to every man's opinions, thoughts, and ideas; and that his only desire was to secure that all might live under the one Christ, in one Commonwealth, one Church, and one Unity.

In response to this summons John, the Saxon elector, in company with Luther and Melanchthon, had waited at Coburg, the most southern town in his province, for a safe-conduct from the emperor. When the safe-conduct arrived, it omitted the name of Luther. While the elector and Melanchthon and the rest of the company journeyed on to Augsburg, Luther took refuge in the great castle overlooking the town of Coburg, where he remained from April 25 through October 4. These were bitter days for him. He was sick and discouraged, yet he kept himself busy.

All the while he received messages from Augsburg where the Diet was in session. They told him how the evangelical princes had refused to march in the Corpus Christi procession through the streets of Augsburg; how stalwart George of Brandenburg had told the emperor, whom he loved, that rather than deny his God he would kneel then and allow his head to be cut off; how steadfastly his friends were maintaining the faith. But he grew anxious as they brought him news that Melanchthon was drawing up the great Augsburg Confession. Melanchthon was a bit too conciliatory for Luther, who feared he would concede too much to the papists; Melanchthon was anxious above all else to heal the break. But the loyalties conflicting in Melanchthon's mind were overpowered by his tremendous belief in Martin Luther. The Augsburg Confession of the Protestant princes written by Melanchthon was read in the Diet on the twenty-fifth of June by Christian Bayer, chancellor of Saxony. It was a clear, concise statement, containing the religious views of the Lutherans, and listing the abuses which must be corrected.

Luther rejoiced when word came that they had been permitted to read their confession before the Diet, but his rejoicing was short-lived, for the Emperor Charles asked a group of papal theologians, headed by Luther's longtime adversary, Johann Eck, to prepare an answer. Here is seen once again the deadly fault in the imperial policy. For Eck was embittered. Five distinct times Eck's report was returned to the committee for softening and revision, and when finally brought forth was still too hard and too bitter for the Lutherans. John, the elector of Saxony, called by his people John the Steadfast, refused to remain at the Diet under such conditions, and departed after a difficult scene with the emperor. Charles V and John the Steadfast held each other in affection and the elector honored his emperor with the ancient civil loyalty of the German, but this was a case where his emperor required the surrender of his conscience. He told Charles that he must stand by his faith and withdrew from the Diet. Charles's final words to him were: "Uncle, uncle, I did not expect this from you." Tears were in the elector's eyes as he turned his back on his sovereign and started northward.

Meanwhile Luther continued anxious, high in the lovely castle. In the midst of a week of sickness a messenger arrived from Wittenberg bringing little gifts from Katharina and the family, among them a picture painted by Lucas Cranach of the twelve-month-old Magdalene. Martin hung it on the wall in his study, where it was a constant source of joy. Luther was unhappy in separation from his family and was faithful in correspondence. Hans was now four years old and Luther's memory re-created the laughing, playing boy. That June he wrote him:

Grace and peace in Christ, dear little son. I am glad to hear that you are studying and saying your prayers. Continue to do so, my son, and when I come home I will bring you a pretty present.

I know a lovely, pleasant garden where many children are; they wear golden jackets and gather nice apples under the trees and pears and cherries and purple plums, and sing and run and jump and are happy and have pretty little ponies with golden reins and silver saddles. I asked the man who owned the garden whose children they were. He said: "They are the children who say their prayers and study and are good." Then said I: "Dear man, I also have a son whose name is Hans Luther; may he come into the garden and eat the sweet apples and pears and ride a fine pony and play with these children?" Then said the man: "If he says his prayers and is good, he can come into the garden, and . . . shall have whistles and drums and fifes and dance and shoot little crossbows." Then he showed me a fine large lawn in the garden for dancing, where hang real golden whistles and fine silver crossbows. But it was yet too early and the children had not finished eating and I could not wait to see them dance, so I said to the man: "My dear sir, I must go away and write at once to my dear little Hans about all this. . . ."

Your loving father,
Martin Luther

While his heart was entranced and his mind happy with meditations on the life of little Hans, John Reinicke, the friend of his school days, brought him news that old Hans was dead. Luther had left Wittenberg for Coburg knowing of his father's sickness; had written that he was unable to come to Mansfeld; had gently recalled to old Hans, in this his last letter, the faith in which they lived. The pastor at Mansfeld read the letter to Luther's father and asked him if he believed this faith and the old man replied: "Aye, he would be a knave who didn't."

Gone. Life over. His father's spirit at the last great judgment. He rose, took his psalter, and entered the study, where he stayed for almost two days in unnerved sorrowing. But prayer and faith were always to Luther the source of strength and toward the close of the second day he returned again to normal control and picked up the routine of life.

A few days later his friend Wenzel Link opened a letter from Luther and read:

> Now I am sorrowful, for I have received tidings of the death of my father, that dear and gentle old man whose name I bear, and although I am glad for his sake that his journey to Christ was so easy and pious and that, freed from the monsters of this world, he rests in peace, nevertheless my heart is moved to sorrow. For under God, I owe my life and bringing up to him.

THE DIET OF AUGSBURG closed unhappily for the Protestants, and Luther returned to Wittenberg in the fall of the year knowing that imperial pressure would be more severe than ever. From this point on it is a battle of political alliances, with Luther more and more in the background. He watched through the succeeding years the riotings in Münster and the overthrow, with murderous cruelty, of the Anabaptists gathered there. He saw the death of Clement VII and the election of Paul III, and knew the Catholic Church now controlled by a strong and able pope. He watched with strange interest the long game of chess between Henry VIII and the papacy, resulting in the severance of England's loyalty to Rome. He read in 1539 a book by the young John Calvin and wrote him a letter of commendation, but he did not sense that under Calvin's control the Swiss city of Geneva would rise to a prominence equal to that of Wittenberg. He heard of the formation of the Society of Jesus, but he did not know that moving that society was a spirit equal in intensity and devotion to his own, and superior in organizational ability. He mourned the death of John the Steadfast but rejoiced that the successor, John Frederick, was of staunch Protestant adherence. And through all this troubled time, he was but seldom called into actual leadership.

On one of these occasions he journeyed, in 1537, to Schmalkalden, and struggled there to draw up a confession of faith emphasizing the differences of the Protestants and Catholics in stronger fashion than had the Augsburg Confession. Luther's health broke while there, and he was in despair of recovery. With the severe and painful affliction known as "the stone" he suffered intensely. He longed, as he had at Coburg, for his wife and children, and thought that he should never see them again.

John Frederick ordered him carried home and sent word ahead for Katharina von Bora to come from Wittenberg to meet him. The jolting of the carriage caused such pain that they could only take him two miles the first day. During that night relief came. And so happy was the messenger who rode back with the news of Luther's returned health, that he stopped by the papal legate's window and shouted: "Luther lives!" before he carried the word to John Frederick.

Luther felt rather uncertain of life even after the recovery, and on the way home, at Gotha, wrote his first will, beginning: "God be praised, I know I did right to attack the papacy which injures the cause of God, Christ, and the Gospel" and closing: "Now I commend my soul into the hands of my Lord Jesus Christ whom I have preached and confessed on earth."

He returned to Wittenberg to carry on his labors there, but life was increasingly painful. The severity of his headaches, the presence of severe rheumatism, the recurrent digestive disturbances, neuritis in his chest, and a disease in the middle ear which caused giddiness and dizziness, all plagued him steadily.

In 1539 Duke George of Saxony, the fairest as well as the staunchest of Catholic defenders in the north, died. His successor was an admirer of Luther's and an adherent of the reformed faith. To attend the installation of the new duke, Martin Luther rode from Wittenberg to Leipzig, and once again stood in the hall of the ducal palace where twenty years before he had debated with Johann Eck. He had a deep and quiet sense of victory now as he stood to proclaim in this room the evangelical faith. His appearance at Leipzig in 1519 had been the prelude to a long and stern warfare. That warfare was not over, but he could already see some lasting consequences, and he was glad to add Leipzig to his inheritance.

But all this rejoicing was quickly turned to trouble when Philip of Hesse brought to Luther for advice the question of his unhappy marriage. Philip had married at nineteen the daughter of Duke George. They had never been happy. They were repugnant to each other and had not lived together as man and wife for years. Philip had at first taken the conventional escape out of his difficulties and kept a mistress. But his conscience troubled him so greatly that he was unable to feel comfortable about his life. Having long since dismissed his mistress, he had lately fallen in love with one of the young ladies of the Leipzig court. Her mother refused her consent to the marriage unless Philip was either divorced or obtained permission from the great Protestant preachers for this second marriage without the dissolution of the first. Philip represented his case with clarity and decision. He did not tell Luther and Melanchthon that he had ever had a mistress, and Luther thought the case was one in clearer honor than it really was. The question of a man's having two wives at the same time was not a closed question in European thought. Cardinal Campeggio had actually suggested this same thing to Clement VII in the discussion of Henry VIII's request.

Luther believed firmly that the Church had the right of dispensation in special cases for the protection of morals and character. This was a practice of the ancient Church from which he did not depart, and he was now operating in the belief that as Protestant pastors they had the right to grant departure from the normal moral law. For example, the Church had often argued that when a man's wife was stricken with leprosy or with insanity it was quite within the realm of moral law that without deserting her he should be granted the privilege of marrying a second wife.

All parties to the agreement were willing, and in consideration of the exigencies of life, and under their rights as pastors, they granted Philip of Hesse permission to marry. They did this under what they called the seal of the confessional, requiring from all parties secrecy. Part of the agreement was that if it should become public information the marriage was by that fact dissolved and reverted to concubinage.

This was their great error. It was as impossible to keep this secret as it was anything else in that generation, and before many months had passed Luther was once again the center of a storm of protest. He had given his sanction to the breaking of the moral law; he had defied all the accepted canons of Christianity. All this attack he accepted, and defended his course with the honesty which he had always shown. But the damage was irreparable. Philip was hurt desperately by the abuse heaped on him from the other Protestant princes, and his fine leadership was no longer available for agressive Lutheranism.

MEANWHILE THE STEADY ADVANCE in the inner life of the Lutheran Church continued. Himself a man of deep historic piety, Luther was constantly struggling to impart this feeling to his people. The translation of the Bible was finally completed in 1534, the last edition to have his personal supervision coming in 1545. Since the Bible was read in this century with feverish anxiety by hundreds of thousands of Germans, the imprint of Luther's style and phrases was ineradicable from the German language.

The great services of the Catholic Church in which Luther had been reared came likewise over into the German under his direction. The service of the mass, the central point in Lutheran worship, was set in the familiar tongue under Luther's own editorship, and for the use of public worship he produced a series of noble hymns, furnishing music as well as words for the rhythm of his movement. Loveliest, perhaps, of all his hymns are those he wrote for his own children. Many were the evenings in the Luther home when father, mother, and children sang their Christian faith. Luther was ever conscious of the gentleness, beauty, and simplicity of a child's understanding, and when the family entered the Christmas season together, he brought the story of Bethlehem to the understanding of his German sons and daughters. He who had sung so lustily in the streets of Magdeburg and Eisenach now sang from new experiences the gentle songs of Christian childhood.

Meanwhile, Katie von Bora had plenty to do in these hectic years. Managing a household without sufficient finances was task enough, but she had many others. Luther's salary was not sufficient for his needs, even though he received many presents, including a pension from the King of Denmark, granted to him

411

for the services he had rendered the Church. There were always friends, visitors, guests, to be given lodging and food. As his own children grew, he brought to live with them orphan nephews and a niece. In the course of the years eleven orphaned relatives found support in Luther's home.

Martin was himself thoroughly unsystematic in the use of money. He never sold a book or manuscript in his life, refusing steadfastly to do so, although the printers offered him a good many hundred gulden a year for his written works. These, he said, were the gifts of God and were not for sale. Nor did he ever receive a salary for teaching. He was supported after the break from the monastic order by an annual gift from the elector, which was steadily increased until it reached a maximum of four hundred gulden. But even with this he wrote a pathetic letter one day to a friend who had asked him for money, in which he said there was no money to be had and they were even pawning their wedding gifts. Lucas Cranach, ever a friend in need, loaned him money steadily. For the support of the family they had cattle, a large garden, and a fish pond. They owned a farm a few miles out from Wittenberg on the road to Zulsdorf, and this farm Katie, likewise, managed.

Privacy was denied them. His tremendous reputation and the insatiable curiosity of his followers kept them constantly in public notice. But underneath the stress and storm of this visible life was a very quiet, gentle current. Katie and Martin loved each other more dearly as the years passed. Their conversation around the home and their correspondence reveals a steady banter based on happy affection. She never lost her high respect for him, but never surrendered either her independent will, and Luther often laughingly told Melanchthon and other friends that he had only changed one authority for another when he married. Katie was not backward about the expression of her own opinion even with guests present, and Luther, calling these expressions "sermons," often said to her that he wished she would preface the sermon with a prayer, for then he knew she would pray so long she would never get to the sermons!

With the smallest children in the house Luther was always particularly happy. He was constantly holding his youngest child in his lap, talking and playing. Having lost one daughter in her early babyhood, Luther watched the growth of his second daughter, Magdalene, with tender, sensitive affection. He knew the heights of a father's love as she grew nearer and dearer to him. And then in September, 1542, Magdalene took seriously ill. One who was with Martin Luther wrote:

As his daughter lay very ill, Dr. Luther said: "I love her very much, but, dear God, if it be Thy will to take her, I submit to Thee." Then he said to her as she lay in bed: "Magdalene, my dear little daughter, would you like to stay here with your father, or would you willingly go to your Father yonder?" She answered: "Darling father, as God wills." Then said he: "Dearest child, the spirit is willing but the flesh is weak." Then he turned away and said: "I love her very much; if my flesh is so strong, what can my spirit do? God has given no bishop so great a gift in a thousand years as he has given me in her. I am angry with myself that I cannot rejoice in heart and be thoughtful as I ought."

Now as Magdalene lay in the agony of death, her father fell down before the bed on his knees and wept bitterly and prayed that God might free her. Then she departed and fell asleep in her father's arms.

THE CONSTANT PRESSURE of twenty-five years of public life was breaking Luther. He grew touchy and sensitive. He felt Wittenberg no longer honored him properly and no one paid any attention to him. The stern ethics of his preaching were disregarded by the villagers. On a trip in the late spring of 1545 to the town of Zeitz, south of Leipzig, he gave his full expression to his satiety with Wittenberg. His son Hans was with him, and Luther decided to stay away forever from the town which, he thought, was repudiating his leadership. He sent this letter back by messenger to his wife:

Dear Katie:
. . . I should like to arrange not to go back to Wittenberg. My heart has grown cold so that I do not care to live there, but wish you would sell garden and the farm, house and buildings, except the big house, which I should like to give back to my gracious

lord. . . . Day after tommorrow I am going to Merseburg, for Prince George has pressed me to do so. I will wander around here and eat the bread of charity before I will martyr and soil my poor old last days with the disordered life of Wittenberg, where I lose all my bitter, costly work. You may tell Melanchthon and Bugenhagen this, if you will, and ask the latter to give Wittenberg my blessing, for I can no longer bear its wrath and displeasure. God bless you. Amen.

Martin Luther

Wittenberg was not to let such a tragedy occur and sent Melanchthon, Bugenhagen, the burgomaster, and the elector's physician to bring Luther home. They met him at Merseburg, paid him due honor, and brought him home in triumph.

The evening of life had come.

VII

WINTER

ON NOVEMBER 10, 1545, there was a birthday celebration in the Luther home. Friends of long standing came to do honor to the man they loved. Katie, as ever, was efficient and thoughtful. Hans, home from school, was now nineteen years old. Martin was fourteen, Paul twelve, and Margaret ten. Song and laughter rang through the rooms. But Martin's heart did not rejoice. The infirmities of age weighed heavily on him. Like the stranger in a foreign land he longed for the sweet visitation of death. Peace and quiet he had wanted these past few years, but the world would not permit. And now with the certainty of approaching death he lived as it were in two worlds. In the present world he loved and enjoyed Katie, children, friends. But in the world of the spirit he could almost commune with his Lord and Master. There was a strong sense of companionship between him and the dead. Hans, his father, and Margaret, his mother, were there. Elizabeth, darling of ten months' life, was there. And his heart warmed as he thought of Magdalene, now three years in that sweet land.

He looked at Katie across the room filled with friends. Older, stouter now than when first she came to live in his home, twenty years ago. Time had taken heavy toll from her, too. He thought of the iron will which had carried her and her family through many a hard hour. He saw her hands, roughened by the work of house and farm, and in his heart thanked God for her life and love. Her eyes caught his, and quickly she was at his side to touch his hand and ask his slightest wish. Friends departed and the night settled over them. The world that saw his birth was not now looking on his sixty-second celebration. He had been an instrument in the hands of God, he believed. He had followed his conscience through all circumstances. Staunchly in the written word of God his mind was set. But not the Word, rather his conscience, had been his guide. God had been merciful. Tomorrow he would finish his present lecture series and then be through. So, tired and anxious for his home-going, he slept.

The next day, November 11, he lectured on the Book of Genesis. His students saw him close his notebook, look up gently, and say quietly: "This is dear Genesis; God grant that others do better with it after me; I am weak. Pray God to grant me a good, blessed hour." And so he left the lecture hall.

In Mansfeld, home of his childhood, the counts, Albert and Gebhardt, were in dispute, and none could solve the difficulty but Luther. In December he left for Mansfeld, and there he spent Christmas; his heart in Wittenberg; Katie alone. In January he returned home, the dispute unsettled.

On January 23 he left home once again. Katie begged him not to go. She pleaded for his health in this bitter weather. But Martin had too long known only duty, and he could not spare himself. In tears, wrung from honest love and the presentiment of death, he kissed his "Lord Katie" good-by. The three boys, Hans, Martin, Paul, went with him. Melanchthon remained in Wittenberg. Two days' journey brought them to Halle. There a flood of the Saale River delayed them. Crossing the flood, they moved toward Eisleben from which point he again wrote home describing the journey:

I wish you grace and peace in Christ, and send you my poor, old, infirm love. Dear Katie, I was weak on the road to Eisleben, but that was my own fault. . . . As I drove through the village such a cold wind blew from behind through my cap on my head that it was like to turn my brain to ice. This may have helped my vertigo, but now, thank God, I am so well that I am sore tempted by fair women and care not how gallant I am. . . . I drink Neunberger beer of just that flavor which you praised so much at Mansfeld. It pleases me well and acts as a laxative.

Your little sons went to Mansfeld day before yesterday, after they had humbly begged Jack-an-apes to take them. I don't know what they are doing; if it were cold they might freeze, but as it is warm they may do or suffer what they like. God bless you with all my household and remember me to my table companions.

Your old lover,

M.L.

The negotiations were carried on in Eisleben. Luther was for solving the whole problem by brotherly love and affection. But the lawyers, he said, made it hard for him.

Three days later the counts signed an agreement settling their dispute. Luther's work was done, and preparations for the homeward journey were made. But Luther was sick. Faintness that would not now leave so easily. Tightness in the chest, around the heart, hurt him. Hot towels and hot brandy helped, and he tried to sleep. But the mystery kept its grip on him—he could not rest quietly—and at two o'clock in the morning of the eighteenth, he roused his friends, and lay down on a couch. Martin and Paul stood by their father's bed. Hans was not present.

Terrific pain seized him, but it could not quite unseat his mind. The ever-blessed phrases of Scripture were heard from his lips. Three times he repeated, *"God so loved the world that he gave his only begotten Son, that whosoever believeth on him should not perish but have everlasting life."* And again his boys heard him whisper, *"Father, into Thy hands I commend my spirit."*

The agony would not subside. In one clear vision, time and space obliterated, he saw the whole of his life. His mighty will held off the suspended stroke. In the final moment, faith transparent, his halting senses whispered the glorious message:

"Who . . . hath . . . my word . . . shall . . . not . . . see . . . death. . . ."

Then darkness.

Eisleben bore him and in Eisleben he died, but back over the beloved road to Wittenberg he journeyed now.

On February 22 they buried him in the cathedral church. Melanchthon preached.

Katie gathered her children around her that night in the Black Cloister.

VIII

SPRING COMES AGAIN

THE WORLD WOULD NOT let Luther rest. He had set a mighty force in motion. Men possessed by his vision carried on the battle for their freedom.

He had risen in strength to protest against *abuse* within a *system*. The defenders, by refusing to consider the correction of the abuse, had brought the attack directly against the institution itself. Luther understood the abuse to be within the *Roman*, not the *Catholic*, phase of the system. But men had too long been accustomed to think in terms of Roman authority to be able to follow this new leadership easily.

The real contradiction between the Roman and the Lutheran concepts of Catholicism fought itself out in political warfare. With a sort of dreadful necessity, battle and conflict raged over central Europe for all too long a time. The pure religious issue was early lost, and the long struggle was dynastic, national, economic, religious—all confused.

What, then, shall we claim for Luther's greatness?

It is foolish to say he is the first "modern" man, or to claim for Luther the consummation of Christian thought. Not in all things can he furnish us leadership. Gone forever is the world into which he was born and in which he worked. He was studying Paul's epistles while the Americas were being mapped. The Americas are mapped long since—and Paul's letters still call for study.

Devils, witches, and all the world of superstition, were his native environment. But the devils in character were his chief concern—and these abide. In the Wartburg he may have thrown an inkwell at an imagined devil; but shall we, then, forget that in the Wartburg he translated the New Testament into German for the first time?

In all the fields of time, Luther is tremendously of his own day. Rough, strong, boisterous, he knew that he and his Germans were unlettered and uncultured. But he knew also the sweet gentleness of friendship and affection, the strong attachment of hill and valley, the haunting comfort of music. The hatreds, prejudices, sciences, philosophies, habits, and pleasures of six-teenth-century Saxony were all in him.

But in the fields of the eternal, he lived a free man. Here he transcended all things constricted by epoch and custom. He wrestled with the moral law and came to understand the first great principle of all ethics, that *man* and not *law* itself is the objective. The story of the human life of Jesus was the founda-tion of his faith, and the "humanity of Christ" was a key to all Luther's theology.

Is it not enough to watch him win the heroic personal faith of Christian experience; to be present, while in lecture hall, con-fessional, and pulpit he feeds the sheep of his pasture; to see him battle for the honor of the faith and the purity of its practice through the long and bitter night; to know him standing in quiet, stubborn peace, as the martyrs of early days stood, affirm-ing the sufficiency of his faith; to walk with him through the long years after the glamour and the shouting; to hear his cradle songs of Christian beauty; and then to see him die, heart un-shaken—is this not enough for our humanity?

Eternal validity is not given to men. Yet in a world of swiftly moving change, he sought and held steadfast the ancient truth.

The
Autobiography of
MARK
TWAIN

The
Autobiography of
MARK
TWAIN

Mark Twain was seventy-five years old when
he died in 1910. He had lived exuberantly,
nothing ever happening to him in a small way, his
adventures invariably fraught with drama.
He summed it up himself: while others toiled he
spent "a lifetime of delightful idleness"; for he
lived so vigorously that work was indistinguishable
from pleasure.

Some of this he told in books like *Tom Sawyer*
and *Huckleberry Finn* and *Life on the Mississippi*.
It was his *Autobiography*, however, that was to tell
the whole story, and this he wrote in bits and pieces
over a period of forty years, as memory moved
him and without regard to chronological sequence.

From the bulky and uncoordinated manuscript
Mark Twain left, Charles Neider has fashioned the
first edition of the *Autobiography* that is
both complete and arranged in life's normal
sequence. Of it the New York *Herald Tribune*
said, "a book filled with richnesses of
humor and tragedy, of disappointment and
triumph, of sweetness and bitterness, and all
in that unsurpassed American prose."

In this autobiography I shall keep in mind the fact that I am speaking from the grave. I am literally speaking from the grave, because I shall be dead when the book issues from the press.

I speak from the grave rather than with my living tongue for a good reason: I can speak thence freely. When a man is writing a book dealing with the privacies of his life—a book which is to be read while he is still alive—he shrinks from speaking his whole frank mind. The frankest and freest and privatest product of the human mind and heart is a love letter; the writer gets his limitless freedom of statement and expression from his sense that no stranger is going to see what he is writing. It has seemed to me that I could be as frank and free and unembarrassed as a love letter if I knew that what I was writing would be exposed to no eye until I was dead, and unaware and indifferent. *Mark Twain*

CHAPTER I

I was born the 30th of November, 1835, in the almost invisible village of Florida, Monroe County, Missouri. My parents removed to Missouri in the early 1830's; I do not remember just when, for I was not born then and cared nothing for such things. The village contained a hundred people and I increased the population by one percent. It is more than many of the best men in history have done for a town. It may not be modest in me to refer to this but it is true. Recently someone in Missouri sent me a picture of the house I was born in. Heretofore I have always stated that it was a palace but I shall be more guarded now.

The village had two streets, each a couple of hundred yards long; the rest of the avenues were mere lanes, with cornfields on either side. Both the streets and the lanes were paved with the same material—tough black mud in wet times, deep dust in dry.

Most of the houses were of log—all of them, indeed, except three or four; these were frame. There were none of brick or stone. There was a log church, with slab benches and a puncheon floor. A slab bench is made of the outside cut of a sawlog, with the bark side down; it is supported on four sticks driven into holes at the ends. A puncheon floor is

The Clemens house, Florida, Missouri

made of logs whose upper surfaces have been chipped flat with the adze. The cracks between the logs were not filled; consequently, if you dropped anything smaller than a peach it was likely to go through. The church was elevated two or three feet from the ground. Hogs slept under there, and whenever the dogs got after them during services the minister had to wait till the disturbance was over. In winter there was always a refreshing breeze up through the puncheon floor; in summer there were fleas enough for all.

There were two stores in the village. My uncle, John A. Quarles, was proprietor of one. It was very small, with a few rolls of calicoes on half a dozen shelves; a few barrels of salt mackerel, coffee and sugar behind the counter; stacks of brooms, axes and rakes here and there; cheap hats, bonnets and tinware strung on strings. At the other end of the room was another counter with bags of shot on it and a cheese or two; and behind it a barrel of molasses and native corn whiskey. If a boy bought five or ten cents' worth of anything he was entitled to a handful of sugar from the barrel; if a woman bought a few yards of calico she was entitled to a spool of thread; if a man bought a trifle he was at liberty to swallow as big a drink of whiskey as he wanted.

Everything was cheap: apples, potatoes and corn, ten cents a bushel; chickens, ten cents apiece; butter, six cents a pound; eggs, three cents a dozen; whiskey, ten cents a gallon. The ordinary cigar cost thirty cents a hundred, but most people did not try to afford them, since smoking a pipe cost nothing in that tobacco-growing country.

At first my father owned slaves but by and by he sold them and hired others by the year from the farmers. For a Negro woman of twenty-five, as general house servant, he paid twenty-five dollars a year and gave her a pair of shoes and two linsey-woolsey frocks; for an able-bodied man he paid from seventy-five to a hundred dollars a year and gave him two suits of jeans and two pairs of shoes—an outfit that cost about three dollars.

I used to remember my brother Henry walking into a fire outdoors when he was a week old. It was remarkable in me to remember a thing like that and still more remarkable that I should cling to the delusion for thirty years that I *did* remember it—for of course it never happened; he would not have been able to walk at that age. For years I believed that I remembered helping my grandfather drink his whiskey toddy when I was six weeks old but I do not tell about that anymore. When I was younger I could remember anything, whether it had happened or not; but my faculties are decaying now and soon I shall be able to remember only the things that never happened. It is sad to go to pieces like this but we all have to do it.

MY UNCLE, John A. Quarles, was also a farmer, and his place was in the country four miles from the village of Florida. He had eight children and fifteen or twenty Negroes and was also fortunate in other ways, particularly in his character. I have not come across a better man than he was. I was his guest for two or three months every year, from the fourth year after we removed to Hannibal till I was eleven or twelve years old. I have never consciously used him or his wife in a book but his farm has come very handy to me in literature once or twice. In *Huck Finn* and in *Tom Sawyer, Detective* I moved it down to Arkansas. It was all of six hundred miles but it was no trouble; it was not a very large farm—five hundred acres, perhaps—but I could have done

425

it if it had been twice as large. And as for the morality of it, I cared nothing for that; I would move a state if the exigencies of literature required it.

It was a heavenly place for a boy, that farm of my uncle's. The house was a double log one, with a spacious floor (roofed in) connecting it with the kitchen. In the summer the table was set in the middle of that shady floor, and the meals—well, it makes me cry to think of them. Fried chicken, roast pig; turkeys, ducks and geese; venison; squirrels, pheasants, prairie chickens; biscuits, hot battercakes, hot buckwheat cakes, hot rolls, hot corn pone; watermelons, muskmelons, cantaloupes; apple pie, peach pie, pumpkin pie—I can't remember the rest. The way that the things were cooked was perhaps the main splendor—particularly a certain few of the dishes. For instance, the corn bread, the hot biscuits and the fried chicken. The North thinks it knows how to make corn bread but this is gross superstition. Perhaps no bread in the world is quite so good as Southern corn bread and perhaps no bread is quite so bad as the Northern imitation of it.

The farmhouse stood in the middle of a very large yard and the yard was fenced on three sides with rails and on the rear side with high palings; against these stood the smokehouse; beyond the palings was the orchard; beyond the orchard were the Negro quarters and the tobacco fields. The front yard was entered over a stile made of sawed-off logs of graduated heights; I do not remember any gate. In a corner of the yard were a dozen hickory and walnut trees, and in the nutting season riches were to be gathered there.

Down a piece, abreast the house, stood a little log cabin against the rail fence; and there the woody hill fell sharply away, past the barns, to a limpid brook which sang along over its gravelly bed and curved and frisked here and there in the shade of overhanging foliage and vines—a divine place for wading, and it had swimming pools, too, which were forbidden to us and therefore much frequented by us. For we were little Christian children and had early been taught the value of forbidden fruit.

In the little log cabin lived a bedridden white-headed slave woman whom we visited daily and looked upon with awe, for we believed she was upward of a thousand years old and had talked with Moses. The younger Negroes credited these statistics and had furnished them to us in good faith; and so we believed that she had lost her health in the long desert trip coming out of Egypt and had never been able to get it back again. She had a round bald place on the crown of her head and we used to creep

around and gaze at it in reverent silence and reflect that it was caused by fright through seeing Pharaoh drowned. We called her "Aunt" Hannah, Southern fashion. She was deeply religious; also superstitious. Whenever witches were around she tied up the remnant of her hair in little tufts, with white thread, and this promptly made the witches impotent.

All the Negroes were friends of ours, and with those of our own age we were in effect comrades. I say in effect, for we were comrades and yet not comrades; color and condition interposed a subtle line which both parties were conscious of and which rendered complete fusion impossible. We had a faithful and affectionate good friend and adviser in "Uncle Dan'l," a middle-aged slave whose sympathies were wide and warm and whose heart was honest and simple. I have not seen him for more than half a century and yet spiritually I have had his welcome company a good part of that time and have staged him in books under his own name and as "Jim." It was on the farm that I got my strong liking for his race and my appreciation of certain of its fine qualities. This feeling has suffered no impairment. The black face is as welcome to me now as it was then.

427

In my schoolboy days I had no aversion to slavery. I was not aware that there was anything wrong with it. No one said anything against it in my hearing; the local pulpit taught us that God approved it, and that the doubter need only look in the Bible if he wished to settle his mind. If the slaves themselves had an aversion to slavery they were wise and said nothing. In Hannibal we seldom saw a slave misused; on the farm never.

There was, however, one small incident of my boyhood days which touched this matter, and it must have meant a good deal to me or it would not have stayed in my memory, clear and sharp, all these slow-drifting years. We had a little slave boy whom we had hired from someone in Hannibal. He was from Maryland and had been brought away from his family halfway across the continent and sold. He was a cheery spirit, innocent and gentle, and the noisiest creature that ever was. All day long he was singing, whistling, yelling, laughing—it was maddening. At last, one day, I lost all my temper and went raging to my mother and said Sandy had been singing for an hour and I couldn't stand it and *wouldn't* she please shut him up. The tears came into her eyes and her lip trembled and she said something like this:

"Poor thing, when he sings it shows that he is not remembering and that comforts me; but when he is still I am afraid he is thinking and I cannot bear it. He will never see his mother again; if he can sing I must not hinder it, but be thankful for it. If you were older you would understand; then that friendless child's noise would make you glad."

It was a simple speech and made up of small words but it went home, and Sandy's noise was not a trouble to me anymore. My mother never used large words but she had a natural gift for making small ones do effective work. She lived to reach the neighborhood of ninety years and was capable with her tongue to the last—especially when a meanness or an injustice roused her spirit. In my books, she figures as Tom Sawyer's Aunt Polly. I fitted her out with a dialect and tried to think up other improvements for her but did not find any. I used Sandy once, also; it was in *Tom Sawyer*. I tried to get him to whitewash the fence but it did not work.

I CAN SEE THE FARM yet, with perfect clearness. I can see all its belongings, all its details; the family room of the house, with a trundle bed in one corner and a spinning wheel in another—a wheel whose rising and falling wail, heard from a distance, was the mournfullest of all sounds to me and made me homesick and low-spirited; the vast fireplace, piled high on winter nights with flaming hickory logs from whose ends a sugary sap bubbled out but did not go to waste, for we scraped it off and ate it; the lazy cat spread out on the rough hearthstones; the drowsy dogs braced against the jambs and blinking; my aunt in one chimney corner, knitting; my uncle in the other, smoking his corncob pipe; the slick oak floor faintly mirroring the dancing flame tongues; half a dozen children romping in the background twilight; split-bottomed chairs here and there; a cradle—out of service but waiting with confidence; in the early cold mornings a snuggle of children in shirts and chemises occupying the hearthstone and procrastinating—they could not bear to go out on the windswept floor space between the house and kitchen, where the general tin basin stood, and wash.

Along outside of the front fence ran the country road, dusty in the summertime and a good place for snakes—they liked to lie in it and sun themselves; when they were rattlesnakes or puff adders we killed them; when they were house snakes or garters we carried them home and put them in Aunt Patsy's work-basket for a surprise; when she took the basket in her lap and they began to climb out of it, it disordered her mind; she never could seem to get used to them. She was always cold toward bats, too, and yet I think a bat is as friendly a bird as there is. My mother was Aunt Patsy's sister and had the same wild superstitions. A bat is beautifully soft and silky; I do not know any creature that is pleasanter to the touch or is more grateful for caressings, if offered in the right spirit. I know all about them because our great cave, three miles below Hannibal, was multitudinously stocked with them and often I brought them home to amuse my mother with. She was not a suspicious person but full of trust; and when I said, "There's something in my coat pocket for you," she would put her hand in. But she always took it out again, herself; I didn't have to tell her. It was remarkable the way she couldn't learn to like bats.

I think she was never in the cave in her life; but everybody else went there. Many excursion parties came from considerable distances to visit the cave. It was miles in extent and was a tangled wilderness of narrow clefts and passages. It was an easy place to get lost in; I got lost in it myself, along with a lady, and our last candle burned down to almost nothing before we glimpsed the search party's lights in the distance.

"Injun Joe," the half-breed, got lost in there once and would have starved to death if the bats had run short. But there was no chance of that; there were myriads of them. He told me all his story. In the book called *Tom Sawyer* I starved him entirely to death in the cave but that was in the interest of art; it never happened. "General" Gaines, who was our first town drunkard before Jimmy Finn got the place, was lost in there for a week and finally pushed his handkerchief out of a hole in a hilltop, several miles down the river from the cave's mouth, and somebody saw it and dug him out. There is nothing the matter with his statistics except the handkerchief. I knew him for years and he hadn't any. But it could have been his nose. That would have attracted attention.

The cave was an uncanny place, for it contained a corpse—the corpse of a young girl of fourteen. It was in a glass cylinder enclosed in a copper one which was suspended from a rail which bridged a narrow passage. The body was preserved in alcohol and it was said that loafers and rowdies used to drag it up by the hair and look at the dead face. The girl was the daughter of a surgeon of wide celebrity. He was an eccentric man and did many strange things. He put the poor thing in that forlorn place himself.

Beyond the road where the snakes sunned themselves was a dense thicket and through it a dim-lighted path led a quarter of a mile; then out of the dimness one emerged abruptly upon a level prairie which was covered with wild strawberry plants, vividly starred with prairie pinks and walled in on all sides by forests. The strawberries were fragrant and fine, and in the season we were generally there in the freshness of early morning, while the dew beads still sparkled upon the grass and the woods were ringing with the first songs of the birds.

Down the forest slopes to the left were the swings. They were made of hickory bark. When they became dry they were dangerous. They usually broke when a child was forty feet in the air and this was why so many bones had to be mended every year. I had no ill luck myself but none of my cousins escaped. There were eight of them and at one time or another they broke fourteen arms among them. But it cost next to nothing, for the doctor worked by the year—twenty-five dollars for the whole family.

I remember two of the Florida doctors, Chowning and Meredith. They not only tended an entire family for twenty-five dollars a year but furnished the medicines themselves. Good measure, too. Only the largest persons could hold a whole dose. Castor oil was the principal beverage. The dose was half a dipperful, with half a dipperful of New Orleans molasses added to help it down and make it taste good, which it never did. The next standby was calomel; the next rhubarb; and the next jalap. Then they bled the patient and put mustard plasters on him. It was a dreadful system and yet the death rate was not heavy. The calomel was nearly sure to salivate the patient and cost him some of his teeth. There were no dentists. When teeth became touched with decay or were otherwise ailing, the doctor knew but one thing to do—he fetched his tongs and dragged them out. If the jaw remained, it was not his fault.

Doctors were not called in cases of ordinary illness; the family grandmother attended to those. Every old woman was a doctor and gathered her own medicines in the woods and knew how to compound doses that would stir the vitals of a cast-iron dog. And then there was the "Indian doctor"; a grave savage, remnant of his tribe, deeply read in the mysteries of nature and of herbs; and most backwoodsmen had high faith in his powers and could tell of wonderful cures achieved by him.

We had the "faith doctor," too, in those early days—a woman. Her specialty was toothache. She was a farmer's old wife and lived five miles from Hannibal. She would lay her hand on the patient's jaw and say, "Believe!" The cure was prompt. Mrs. Utterback. I remember her very well. Twice I rode out there on horseback, behind my mother, and saw the cure performed. My mother was the patient.

Dr. Meredith removed to Hannibal and was our family physician there. He saved my life several times. Still, he was a good man and meant well. Let it go.

I was always told that I was a sickly, tiresome and uncertain child during the first seven years of my life. I asked my mother about this—she was then in her eighty-eighth year—and said:

"I suppose that during all that time you were uneasy about me?"

"Yes, the whole time."

"Afraid I wouldn't live?"

After a reflective pause, ostensibly to think, "No—afraid you would."

It sounds like plagiarism but it probably wasn't.

THE COUNTRY SCHOOLHOUSE was three miles from my uncle's farm. It stood in a clearing in the woods and would hold about twenty-five boys and girls. We attended the school once or twice a week in summer, walking to it in the cool of the morning by the forest paths and back in the gloaming at the end of the day. All the pupils brought their dinners in baskets—corn dodger, buttermilk and other good things—and sat in the shade of the trees at noon and ate them. It is the part of my education which I look back upon with the most satisfaction.

My first visit to the school was when I was seven. A strapping girl of fifteen, in the customary sunbonnet and calico dress, asked me if I "used tobacco"—meaning did I chew it. I said no. It roused her scorn. She reported me to the crowd and said:

"Here is a boy seven years old who can't chaw tobacco."

By the looks and comments which this produced I realized that I was a degraded object; and I determined to reform. But I only made myself sick; I was not able to learn to chew tobacco. I learned to smoke fairly well but that did not conciliate anybody and I remained a poor thing and characterless.

As I have said, I spent some part of every year at the farm until I was twelve or thirteen. The life which I led there with my cousins was full of charm, and so is the memory of it yet. I can call back the solemn twilight and mystery of the deep woods, the earthy smells, the faint odors of the wild flowers, the sheen of rain-washed foliage, the far-off hammering of woodpeckers and the drumming of wood pheasants in the remoteness of the forest. I can call it all back and make it as real as it ever was, and as blessed. I can call back the prairie, and its loneliness and peace, and a vast hawk hanging motionless in the sky, with his wings spread wide. I can see the woods in their autumn dress, the oaks purple, the hickories washed with gold, the maples luminous with crimson fires, and I can hear the rustle made by the fallen leaves as we plowed through them.

I can see the blue clusters of wild grapes hanging among the foliage, and I remember the taste of them and the smell. I know how the wild blackberries looked, and how they tasted, and the same with the pawpaws, the hazelnuts and the persimmons; I can feel the thumping rain, upon my head, of hickory nuts and walnuts when we were out in the frosty dawn to scramble for them with the pigs, and the gusts of wind loosed them and sent them down.

I know how a prize watermelon looks when it is sunning its fat rotundity among pumpkin vines and simblins; I know how to tell when it is ripe without plugging it; I know how inviting it looks when it is cooling itself in a tub of water, waiting; I know how it looks when it lies on the table in the sheltered floor space between house and kitchen, and the children gathered for the sacrifice, their mouths watering; I know the crackling sound it makes when the carving knife enters its end, and I can see the split fly along in front of the blade as the knife cleaves its way to the other end; I can see its halves fall apart and display the rich red meat and the black seeds; I know how a boy looks behind a yard-long slice of that melon, and I know how he feels, for I have been there. I know the taste of the watermelon which has been honestly come by, and I know the taste of the watermelon which has been acquired by art. Both taste good, but the experienced know which tastes best.

I know the look of green apples and peaches and pears on the trees, and I know how entertaining they are when they are inside of a person. I know how ripe ones look when they are piled in pyramids under the trees, and how pretty they are. I know the look of an apple that is roasting and sizzling on a hearth on a winter's evening, and I know the comfort that comes of eating it hot, along with some sugar and a drench of cream. I know the delicate art of cracking hickory nuts and walnuts on a flatiron with a hammer, and I know how the nuts, taken in conjunction with winter apples, cider and doughnuts, make old people's old tales sound fresh and crisp and enchanting, and juggle an evening away before you know what went with the time. I know the look of Uncle Dan'l's kitchen as it was on the privileged nights, when I was a child, and I can see the white and black children grouped on the hearth, with the firelight playing on their faces, and I can hear Uncle Dan'l telling the immortal tales which Joel Chandler Harris was to gather into his Uncle Remus books and charm the world with; and I can feel again the creepy joy which quivered through me when the time for the ghost story of the "Golden Arm" was reached—and the sense of regret, too, which came over me, for it was always the last story and there was nothing between it and the unwelcome bed.

I can remember the bare wooden stairway in my uncle's house, and the turn to the left above the landing, and the rafters and the slanting roof over my bed, and the squares of moonlight on the floor, and the white cold world of snow outside, seen through the curtainless window. I can remember the howling of the wind on stormy nights, and how snug and cozy one felt, under the blankets, listening; and how the powdery snow used to sift in, around the sashes, and lie in little ridges on the floor and make the place look chilly in the morning and curb the wild desire to get up—in case there was any.

I can remember how very dark that room was, in the dark of the moon, and how packed it was with ghostly stillness when one woke up by accident away in the night, and forgotten sins came flocking out of the secret chambers of the memory; and how dismal was the hoo-hooing of the owl and the wailing of the wolf, sent mourning by on the night wind.

I remember the raging of the rain on that roof, summer nights, and how pleasant it was to lie and listen to it, and enjoy the white splendor of the lightning and the majestic crashing of the thunder. It was a very satisfactory room, and there was a lightning rod which was reachable from the window, an adorable and skittish thing to climb up and down, summer nights, when there were duties on hand of a sort to make privacy desirable.

I remember the coon and possum hunts, nights, and the long marches through the black gloom of the woods, and the excitement which fired everybody when the distant bay of a dog announced that the game was treed; then the wild scramblings through briers and bushes to get to the spot; then the lighting of a fire and the felling of the tree, the joyful frenzy of the dogs, and the weird picture in the red glare—I remember it all well, and the delight that everyone got out of it, except the coon.

I remember the pigeon seasons, when the birds would come in millions and cover the trees and by their weight break down the branches. They were clubbed to death with sticks; guns were not necessary. I remember the squirrel hunts, and wild-turkey hunts; and how we turned out, mornings, while it was still dark, to go on these expeditions, and how chilly and dismal it was. A toot on a horn brought twice as many dogs as were needed, and in their happiness they raced about, and knocked small people down, and made no end of noise. At the word, they vanished away toward the woods, and we drifted silently after them in the gloom. But presently the gray dawn stole over the world, the birds piped up, then the sun rose, everything was fresh and dewy, and life was a boon again. After three hours of tramping we arrived back wholesomely tired, overladen with game, very hungry, and just in time for breakfast.

CHAPTER 3

My father was John Marshall Clemens of Virginia; my mother Jane Lampton of Kentucky. Back of the Virginian Clemenses is a dim procession of ancestors stretching back to Noah's time. According to tradition, some were pirates in Elizabeth's time. But this is no discredit to them; it was a respectable trade then. In my time I have had desires to be a pirate myself. The reader, if he will look deep in his secret heart, will find—but never mind what he will find. I am not writing his autobiography but mine.

Later, according to tradition, one of the ancestors was ambassador to Spain in the time of James I, or of Charles I, and married there and sent down a strain of Spanish blood to warm us up. Also, according to tradition, this one or another—Geoffrey Clement, by name—helped to sentence King Charles to death. I have not examined into these traditions myself; but the other Clemenses claim they have made the examination and that it stood the test. Therefore I have always taken for granted that I did help Charles out of his troubles, by ancestral proxy.

My mother, as I have said, was a Lampton of Kentucky. She married my father in Lexington in 1823, when she was twenty years old and he twenty-four. Neither of them had an overplus of property. She brought him two or three Negroes but nothing else, I think. They removed to the secluded village of Jamestown, in the mountain solitudes of East Tennessee. There their first crop of children was born, but as I was of a later vintage I do not remember anything about it. I was postponed—postponed to Missouri. Missouri was an unknown new state and needed attractions.

My eldest brother, Orion, was ten years older than I. I think that he, my sisters Pamela and Margaret, and my brother Benjamin were born in Jamestown. There may have been others but as to that I am not sure. It was a great lift for that little village to have my parents come there. It was hoped that they would stay, so that it would become a city. But by and by they went away and it was many years before Jamestown got another start.

My father left a fine estate behind him in the region round about Jamestown—above 100,000 acres. When he died in 1847 he had owned it about twenty years. The taxes were almost nothing (five dollars a year) and he had paid them regularly and kept his title perfect. He had always said that the land would not become valuable in his time but that it would be a commodious provision for his children some day. It contained coal, copper, iron and timber, and he said that in the course of time railways

Opposite page, top to bottom, Mrs. Clemens; Clemens House, Hannibal, Missouri; Orion; Pamela; Sam; Henry

would pierce to that region and then the property would be property in fact as well as in name. It also produced a wild grape of a promising sort. He had sent some samples to Nicholas Longworth of Cincinnati and Mr. Longworth had said that they would make as good wine as his Catawbas. The land contained all these riches; and also oil, but my father did not know that. I wish I owned a couple of acres of that land now, in which case I would not be writing autobiographies for a living.

My father's dying charge was, "Cling to the land and wait; let nothing beguile it away from you." He had bought the enormous area at one purchase. The entire lot must have cost him in the neighborhood of four hundred dollars. That was a good deal of money to pass over at one payment in those days—at least it was considered so way up there in the pineries and "Knobs" of the Cumberland Mountains of Fentress County, East Tennessee. When my father had paid down that sum and looked abroad over his vast possessions, he said, "Whatever befalls me, my heirs are secure; I shall not live to see these acres turn to silver and gold but my children will." Thus with the very kindest intentions he laid the heavy curse of prospective wealth upon our shoulders. He went to his grave in the full belief that he had done us a kindness. It was a woeful mistake but fortunately he never knew it.

My eldest brother was four or five years old when the great purchase was made, and my eldest sister was an infant. The rest of us came afterward and were born during the next ten years. Four years after the purchase came the great financial crash of 1834, and in that storm my father's fortunes were wrecked. From being envied as the most opulent citizen of Fentress County—for outside of his great land possessions he was considered to be worth not less than three thousand five hundred dollars—he suddenly woke up and found himself reduced to less than one-fourth of that amount.

He was a proud man, a silent, austere man, and not a person likely to abide among the scenes of his vanished grandeur and be a target for public commiseration. He gathered his household together and journeyed through wilderness solitudes toward what was then the Far West, and at last pitched his tent in the little town of Florida, Missouri. He "kept store" there several years but had no luck, except that I was born to him.

He presently removed to Hannibal and prospered somewhat; rose to the dignity of justice of the peace and had been elected to the clerkship of the Surrogate Court when the summons came which no man may disregard. He had been doing tolerably well during the first years of his residence in Hannibal, but ill fortune tripped him once more. He did the friendly office of "going security" for a friend named Ira Stout, and Ira walked off and took the benefit of the new bankrupt law—a deed which enabled him to live easily and comfortably till death called for him, but a deed which ruined my father, sent him poor to his grave and condemned his heirs to a long and discouraging struggle for a livelihood. But my father would brighten up and gather heart, even upon his deathbed, when he thought of the Tennessee land. He said that it would soon make us all rich and happy. And so believing, he died.

We straightway turned our waiting eyes upon Tennessee, and through all our wanderings and our ups and downs they gazed thitherward, over intervening continents and seas, with the hope of old habit.

After my father's death we reorganized the domestic establishment but on a temporary basis, intending to arrange it permanently after the land was sold. My brother borrowed five hundred dollars and bought a worthless weekly newspaper, believing, as we all did, that it was not worthwhile to go at anything in earnest until the land was disposed of. We rented a large house to live in, at first, but we were disappointed in a sale we had expected to make (the man wanted only a part of the land and we decided to sell all or none) so we were obliged to move to a less expensive one.

As I have said, that vast plot of Tennessee land was held by my father twenty years—intact. When he died in 1847 we began to manage it ourselves. Forty years afterward we had managed it all away except 10,000 acres and gotten nothing to remember the sales by. About 1887 the 10,000 went. My brother found a chance to trade it for a house and lot in the town of Corry, in the oil regions of Pennsylvania. About 1894 he sold this property for two hundred and fifty dollars. That ended the Tennessee land.

If any penny of cash ever came out of my father's wise investment but that, I have no recollection of it. Yet that land influenced our life in one way or another during more than a generation. Whenever things grew dark it rose and put out its hopeful hand and said, "Do not be afraid—trust in me—wait." It kept us hoping and hoping during forty years and forsook us at last. It put our energies to sleep and made visionaries of us. We were always going to be rich next year—no occasion to work. It is good to begin life poor; it is good to begin life rich—these are wholesome; but to begin it poor and *prospectively* rich! The man who has not experienced it cannot imagine the curse of it.

WHEN MY MOTHER died in October 1890 she was well along in her eighty-eighth year, a mighty age, a well-contested fight for life for one who at forty was so delicate of body as to be accounted a confirmed invalid and destined to soon pass away. I knew her well during the first twenty-five years of my life; but after that I saw her only at wide intervals, for we lived many days' journey apart. I am proposing to write merely flashlight glimpses of her character, not a processional view of her career. Technically speaking, she had no career; but she had a character and it was of a fine and striking and lovable sort.

What becomes of the multitudinous photographs which one's mind takes of people? Out of the million which my mental camera must have taken of this first and closest friend, only a strongly defined one of early date remains. She was forty years old then, and I was eight. She held me by the hand and we were kneeling by the bedside of my brother, two years older than I, who lay dead. The tears were flowing down her cheeks. And she was moaning. That dumb sign of anguish was perhaps new to me, since it made a very strong impression.

She had a slender, small body but a large heart—a heart so large that everybody's grief and everybody's joys found welcome in it and hospitable accommodation. The greatest difference which I find between her and the rest of the people whom I have known is this: those others felt a strong interest in a few things, whereas to the day of her death she felt a strong interest in the whole world and everything and everybody in it. She never knew such a thing as a halfhearted interest in affairs and people, or an interest which drew a line and left out certain affairs or people. The invalid who takes a strenuous interest in everything and everybody but himself, and to whom a dull moment is an impossibility, is a formidable adversary for disease. I am certain that it was this feature of my mother's makeup that carried her so far toward ninety.

Her interest in people and other animals was warm, personal, friendly. She always found something to excuse, and as a rule to love, in the toughest of them. She was the natural friend of the friendless. It was believed that, Presbyterian as she was, she could be beguiled into saying a soft word for the devil himself, and so the experiment was tried.

The abuse of Satan began; one conspirator after another added his bitter word, his pitiless censure, till at last, sure enough, the unsuspecting subject of the trick walked into the trap. She admitted that the indictment was sound, that Satan was utterly wicked and abandoned; *but* would any claim that he had been treated fairly? A sinner was but a sinner; Satan was just that, like the rest. What saves the rest? Their own efforts alone? No—to their feeble efforts is added the mighty help of prayers that go up daily out of all the churches in Christendom. But who prays for Satan? Who, in eighteen centuries, has had the common humanity to pray for the one sinner that needed it most?

This friend of Satan was a most gentle spirit, and when her indignation was stirred by hurt or shame inflicted upon some defenseless person or creature, she was the most eloquent person I have heard speak. It was seldom eloquence of a fiery or violent sort, but gentle, pitying, persuasive; fears that belonged to her sex and small stature retired to the rear and her soldierly properties came promptly to the front.

One day in our village I saw a vicious devil of a Corsican, a terror in the town, chasing his grown daughter past cautious male citizens with a heavy rope in his hand, declaring he would wear it out on her. My mother spread her door wide to the refugee and then stood in it and stretched her arms across it, barring the way. The man swore, cursed, threatened her; but she only stood straight and fine and defied him in tones not audible to the middle of the street; and he asked her pardon and said with a blasphemous oath that she was the bravest woman he ever saw; and so went his way and troubled her no more. He and she were always good friends after that, for in her he had found a long-felt want—somebody who was not afraid of him.

Once in St. Louis she greatly surprised a burly cartman who was beating his horse over the head with the butt of his whip; for she took the whip away from him and then made such a persuasive appeal in behalf of the horse that he was tripped into volunteering a promise that he wouldn't ever abuse a horse again.

That sort of interference in behalf of abused animals was a common thing with her. All animals had a friend in her. By some subtle sign the homeless, bedraggled and disreputable cat recognized her at a glance as the born champion of his sort—and followed her home. His instinct was right, he was as welcome as the prodigal son. We had nineteen cats at one time, in 1845. And there wasn't one in the lot that had any character, nor any merit, except the cheap merit of being unfortunate. They were a vast burden to us all—including my mother—but they were out of luck and that was enough; they had to stay.

CHAPTER 4

MY SCHOOL DAYS BEGAN when I was four years and a half old. There were no public schools in Missouri in those days but there were two private schools—terms twenty-five cents per week per pupil and collect it if you can. Mrs. Horr taught the children in a small log house at the southern end of Main Street. Mr. Sam Cross taught the young people of larger growth in a frame schoolhouse on the hill.

I was sent to Mrs. Horr's school and I remember my first day there with perfect clearness. I broke one of the rules and was warned not to do it again and was told that the penalty for a second breach was a whipping. I presently broke the rule again and Mrs. Horr told me to go out and find a switch and fetch it.

I was glad she had appointed me, for I believed I could select a switch suitable to the occasion with more judiciousness than anybody else. In the mud I found a cooper's shaving, oak, two inches broad, a quarter of an inch thick, and rising in a shallow curve at one end. There were nice new shavings of the same breed close by but I took this one, although it was rotten. I carried it to Mrs. Horr, presented it and stood before her in an attitude of meekness and resignation which seemed to me calculated to win favor and sympathy, but it did not happen. She divided a look of strong

disapprobation equally between me and the shaving; then she called me by my entire name, Samuel Langhorne Clemens, and said she was ashamed of me. I was to learn later that when a teacher calls a boy by his entire name it means trouble. She said she would try and appoint a boy with a better judgment than mine in the matter of switches, and it saddens me yet to remember how many faces lighted up with the hope of getting that appointment. Jim Dunlap got it and when he returned with the switch of his choice I recognized that he was an expert.

Mrs. Horr was a New England lady of middle age with New England ways and she always opened school with prayer and a chapter from the New Testament; also she explained the chapter with a brief talk. In one of these talks she dwelt upon the text, *Ask, and ye shall receive*, and said that whosoever prayed for a thing with earnestness need not doubt that his prayer would be answered.

I was so forcibly struck by this information and so gratified by the opportunities which it offered that I thought I would give it a trial. I had no doubts as to the result. I prayed for gingerbread. Margaret Kooneman, the baker's daughter, brought a slab of gingerbread to school every morning; she had always kept it out of sight before, but when I finished my prayer and glanced up, there it was in easy reach and she was looking the other way.

In all my life I believe I never enjoyed an answer to prayer more than I enjoyed that one; and I was a convert, too. I had no end of wants, and I meant to supply them and extend them now that I had found out how to do it. But this dream was like almost all the other dreams we indulge in in life. I did as much praying during the next two or three days as anyone in that town, I suppose, but nothing came of it. I found that not even the most powerful prayer was competent to lift that gingerbread again.

Something about my conduct and bearing troubled my mother and she took me aside and questioned me. At last I confessed, with tears, that I had ceased to be a Christian. She was heartbroken and asked me why.

I said it was because I had found out that I was a Christian for revenue only and I could not bear the thought of that, it was so ignoble. She gathered me to her breast and comforted me. I gathered from what she said that if I would continue in that condition I would never be lonesome.

My mother had a good deal of trouble with me but I think she enjoyed it. She had none at all with my brother Henry, who was two years younger than I, and I think that the monotony of his goodness would have been a burden to her but for the relief which I furnished in the other direction. I was a tonic. I never thought of it before but now I see it. I never knew Henry to do a vicious thing toward me or anyone else—but he frequently did righteous ones that cost me as heavily. It was his duty to report me, when I needed reporting and neglected to do it myself, and he was very faithful in discharging that duty. He is Sid in *Tom Sawyer*. But Sid was not Henry. Henry was a very much finer and better boy than ever Sid was.

It was Henry who called my mother's attention to the fact that the thread with which she had sewed my collar together to keep me from going in swimming had changed color. My mother would not have discovered it but for that, and she was manifestly piqued when she recognized that that prominent bit of circumstantial evidence had escaped her eye. That detail probably added a detail to my punishment—but no matter. I took it out on Henry. I often took it out on him—sometimes as an advance payment for something which I hadn't yet done. These were occasions when the opportunity was too strong a temptation, and I had to draw on the future.

There was a stairway outside the house, which led up to the rear part of the second story. One day Henry was sent on an errand and he took a tin bucket along. I knew he would have to ascend those stairs, so I went up and locked the door on the inside and came down into the garden, which had been newly plowed and was rich in choice, firm clods of black mold. I gathered a generous supply of these and waited till Henry had climbed the stairs and was near the landing and couldn't escape. Then I bombarded him with clods, which he warded off with his bucket the best he could, but without much success, for I was a good marksman. The clods smashing against the boarding fetched my mother out to see what was the matter and I tried to explain that I was amusing Henry. Both of them were after me in a minute but I knew the way over that fence and escaped.

After an hour or two, when I ventured back, there was no one around and I thought the incident was closed. But it was not so. Henry was ambushing me. With an unusually competent aim for him, he landed a stone on the side of my head which raised a bump that felt like the Matterhorn. I carried it to my mother straightway for sympathy but she was not moved. It seemed to be her idea that incidents like this would reform me if I harvested enough of them. So the matter was only educational. I had had a sterner view of it than that.

The incident of the "Pain-Killer" is in *Tom Sawyer*. It was not right to give the cat the pain-killer; I realize it now. But in those days it was a great and sincere satisfaction to me to see Peter perform under the influence of that detestable medicine.

Those were the cholera days of 1849. The people along the Mississippi were paralyzed with fright. Those who could run away did. Those who couldn't flee kept themselves drenched with preventives. My mother chose Perry Davis's

Perry Davis's Pain-Killer

Pain-Killer for me. She made me promise to take a teaspoonful of pain-killer every day. She didn't watch Henry's bottle—she could trust Henry. But she marked my bottle with a pencil on the label every day, and examined it to see if the teaspoonful had been removed. The floor was not carpeted. It had cracks in it and I fed the pain-killer to the cracks with very good results— no cholera occurred down below.

It was upon one of these occasions that that friendly cat came waving his tail and supplicating for pain-killer—which he got—and then went into those hysterics which ended with his colliding with all the furniture in the room and finally going out of the open window, carrying the flowerpots with him, just in time for my mother to arrive and in petrified astonishment say, "What in the world is the matter with Peter?"

That was about 1849, as I have said. Tom Nash was a boy of my own age—the postmaster's son. The Mississippi was frozen across that winter and he and I went skating one night, probably without permission. There could be no considerable amusement to be gotten out of skating at midnight if nobody was going to object to it.

About midnight, when we were more than half a mile out toward the Illinois shore, we heard some ominous rumbling and crashing going on between us and the home side of the river, and we knew what it meant—the river was breaking up. We started for home, badly scared. We flew along at full speed whenever the moonlight sifting between the clouds enabled us to tell which was ice and which was water. In the pauses we waited, started again whenever there was a good bridge of ice, paused again when we came to naked water, and waited in distress until a floating vast cake should bridge that place.

It took us an hour to make the trip—a trip made in a misery of apprehension. But at last we arrived within a very brief distance of the shore. We waited again. There was another place that needed bridging. All about us the ice was plunging and grinding along, piling itself up on the shore. The dangers were increasing, not diminishing. We grew impatient to get to solid ground, so we started too early and went springing from cake to cake. Tom made a miscalculation and fell short. He got a bitter bath but he was so close to shore that he only had to swim a stroke or two—then his feet struck bottom and he crawled out. I arrived a little later, without accident.

We had been in a drenching perspiration and Tom's bath was a disaster for him. He took to his bed, sick, and had a procession of diseases. The closing one was scarlet fever and he came out of it stone-deaf. Within a year or two speech departed. But some years later he was taught to talk, after a fashion—for he could not modulate his voice, since he couldn't hear himself talk. When he supposed he was talking low and confidentially, you could hear him in Illinois.

In 1902 I was invited by the University of Missouri to come out there and receive the honorary degree of LL.D. I took that opportunity to spend a week in Hannibal—a city now, a village in my day. It had been fifty-five years since Tom Nash and I had had that adventure. When I was at the railway station ready to leave Hannibal, there was a great crowd of citizens there. I saw Tom Nash approaching me across a vacant space. I recognized him at once. He was old and white-headed, but the boy of fifteen was still visible in him. He came up to me, made a trumpet of his hands at my ear, nodded his head toward the citizens and said confidentially—in a yell like a fog-horn—"Same damned fools, Sam."

IN 1849 we were still living in Hannibal, on the banks of the Mississippi, in the new "frame" house built by my father five years before. That is, some of us lived in the new part, the rest in the old part back of it. In the autumn my sister gave

Mark Twain revisits Hannibal

a party and invited all the marriageable young people of the village. I was too young for this society and too bashful to mingle with young ladies, anyway; therefore I was not invited—at least not for the whole evening. Ten minutes of it was to be my whole share. I was to do the part of a bear in a small fairy play. I was to be disguised all over in brown hairy stuff proper for a bear.

About half past ten I was told to go to my room and put on this disguise and be ready in half an hour. I started but changed my mind, for I wanted to practice a little and that room was very small. I crossed over to the large unoccupied house on the corner of Main Street, unaware that a dozen of the young people were also going there to dress for their parts.

I took the little black boy, Sandy, with me and we selected a roomy and empty chamber on the second floor. We entered it talking and this gave a couple of half-dressed young ladies an opportunity to take refuge behind a screen undiscovered. That was a rickety screen with many holes in it but as I did not know there were girls behind it I was not disturbed by that detail. If I had known, I could not have undressed in the flood of cruel moonlight that was pouring in at the curtainless windows; I should have died of shame.

Untroubled by apprehensions, I stripped to the skin and began my practice. I was full of ambition, I was determined to make a hit; so I threw myself into my work with abandon. I capered back and forth from one end of the room to the other on all fours, Sandy applauding with enthusiasm; I walked upright and growled and snapped and snarled, I stood on my head, I flung handsprings, I danced a lubberly dance with my paws bent and my imaginary snout sniffing from side to side, I did everything a bear could do and many things which no bear could ever do and no bear with any dignity would want to do; of course I never suspected that I was making a spectacle of myself to anyone but Sandy. At last, standing on my head, I paused in that attitude to take a rest. There was a moment's silence, then Sandy spoke up with excited interest and said:

"Mars Sam, has you ever seed a dried herring?"

"No. What is that?"

"It's a fish."

"Well, what of it? Anything peculiar about it?"

"Yes, suh, you bet you dey is. Dey eats 'em innards and all!"

There was a smothered burst of feminine snickers from behind the screen! All the strength went out of me and I toppled forward like an undermined tower and brought the screen down, burying the young ladies under it. In their fright they discharged a couple of piercing screams—and possibly others—but I did not wait to count. I snatched my clothes and fled to the dark hall below, Sandy following.

I was dressed in half a minute and out the back way. I swore Sandy to eternal silence, then we went and hid until the party was over. The ambition was all out of me. I could not have faced that giddy company after my adventure, for there would be two there who would be privately laughing at me. I was searched for but not found, and the bear had to be played by a young gentleman in his civilized clothes.

The house was still and everybody asleep when I finally ventured home. Pinned to my pillow I found a slip of paper which bore a line which made my face burn. It was written in a laboriously disguised hand and these were its mocking terms:

> You probably couldn't have played bear but you played bare very well—oh, very <u>very</u> well!

We think boys are rude, unsensitive animals but it is not so in all cases. Each boy has one or two sensitive spots and if you can find where they are located you can scorch him as with fire. I suffered miserably over that episode. I expected that the facts would be all over the village in the morning but it was not so. The secret remained confined to the two girls and Sandy and me.

That was some appeasement of my pain but it was far from sufficient. During several weeks I could not look any young lady in the face; I dropped my eyes in confusion when any one of them smiled upon me and gave me greeting; I said to myself, "That is one of them," and got quickly away. When I left Hannibal four years later the secret was still a secret; I had never guessed those girls out.

One of the dearest and prettiest girls in the village at the time of my mishap was one whom I will call Mary Wilson. She was twenty years old, dainty and sweet, gracious and lovely in character. I stood in awe of her, for she seemed to me to be made out of angel clay and unapproachable by any unholy ordinary kind of boy like me. I probably never suspected *her*. But—

The scene changes to Calcutta—forty-seven years later. It was in 1896. I arrived there on a lecturing trip. As I entered the hotel a vision of glory passed out of it—the Mary Wilson of my long-vanished boyhood! It was a startling thing. I thought maybe I had seen an apparition but it was not so, she was flesh—the granddaughter of the other Mary.

The other Mary, now a widow, was upstairs and presently sent for me. She was old and gray-haired but she looked young and handsome. We sat and talked. We steeped our thirsty souls in the reviving wine of the past, the dear and lamented past; we uttered names that had been silent upon our lips for fifty years and it was as if they were made of music; we searched our memories and dragged forth incident after incident, episode after episode, folly after folly, and laughed till the tears ran down; and finally Mary said, suddenly, without any leading up:

"Tell me! What is the special peculiarity of dried herrings?"

It seemed a strange question. And yet I was aware of a stir of some kind away back in the deeps of my memory. Dried herrings? Dried herrings? The peculiarity of . . . I glanced up. Her face was grave, but there was a twinkle in her eye and all of a sudden I remembered, "Dey eats 'em innards and all!"

"At—last! I've found one of you, anyway! Who was the other girl?" But she drew the line there. She wouldn't tell me.

But a boy's life is not all comedy; much of the tragic enters into it. A drunken tramp who was burned up in the village jail lay upon my conscience a hundred nights afterward and filled them with hideous dreams—dreams in which I saw his appealing face as I had seen it in the pathetic reality, pressed against the window bars, with the red hell glowing behind him—a face which seemed to say to me, "If you had not given me the matches this would not have happened; you are responsible for my death." I was *not* responsible for it, for I had meant no harm but only good, when I let him have the matches; but no matter, mine was a trained Presbyterian conscience and knew but the one duty—to hunt and harry its slave upon all pretexts and on all occasions; and so I suffered for months.*

The shooting down of a poor old man named Smarr in the main street at noonday supplied me with some more dreams;

---

*Mark Twain tells this story in more detail in *Life on the Mississippi*.

and in them I always saw again the grotesque closing picture—
the great family Bible spread open on the old man's breast by
some thoughtful idiot and rising and sinking to the labored
breathings and adding the torture of its leaden weight to the
dying struggles. An anvil would have been in better taste there
than the Bible, swifter in its atrocious work. In my nightmares
I gasped and struggled for breath under the crush of that vast
book for many a night.

All within the space of a couple of years we had two or three
other tragedies and I had the ill luck to be too near by on each
occasion. There was the slave man who was struck down with
a chunk of slag for some small offense; I saw him die. And the
young Californian emigrant who was stabbed with a bowie
knife by a drunken comrade; I saw the red life gush from his
breast. And then there was the case of the young Californian
emigrant who got drunk and proposed to raid the "Welsh-
man's house" all alone one dark and threatening night.

This house stood halfway up Holliday's Hill and its sole occupants were a poor but respectable widow and her blameless
daughter. The ruffian woke the whole village with his yells and
obscenities. I went up there with a comrade—John Briggs, I
think—to look and listen. The figure of the man was dimly visible; the women were on their porch, not visible in the shadow,
but we heard the elder woman's voice.

She had loaded an old musket with slugs and she warned the
man that if he stayed where he was while she counted ten it
would cost him his life. She began to count, slowly; he began to
laugh. He stopped laughing at "six"; then through the stillness,
in a steady voice, followed: "seven . . . eight . . . nine"—a long
pause, we holding our breaths—"ten!"

A red spout of flame gushed out into the night and the man
dropped with his breast riddled to rags. Then the rain and the
thunder burst loose and the waiting town swarmed up the hill
in the glare of the lightning like an invasion of ants. Those people saw the rest; I had had my share and went home to dream.

My teaching and training enabled me to see deeper into these
tragedies than an ignorant person could have done. I knew what
they were for. I tried to disguise it from myself but down in the

secret deeps of my heart I knew—and I *knew* I knew. They were inventions of Providence to beguile me to a better life.

I took all the tragedies to myself and tallied them off in turn as they happened, saying to myself in each case, "Another one gone—and on my account; this ought to bring me to repentance; the patience of God will not always endure." And yet privately I believed it would. That is, I believed it in the daytime; but not in the night. With the going down of the sun clammy fears gathered about my heart. It was then that I repented.

Those were awful nights, nights of despair, nights charged with the bitterness of death. After each tragedy I recognized the warning and repented and begged like a coward, like a dog. My repentances were very real, very earnest; and after each tragedy they happened every night for a long time. But as a rule they could not stand the daylight. They faded out and disappeared in the glad splendor of the sun. In all my boyhood life I am not sure that I ever tried to lead a better life in the daytime—or wanted to. But at my age, as in my youth, night brings me many a deep remorse. I realize that from the cradle up I have been like the rest of the race—never quite sane in the night.

BACK IN THOSE far-distant days there was a time when Jim Wolf came to us. He was from Shelbyville, a hamlet thirty or forty miles back in the country. He was approaching seventeen, a grave and slender lad, trustful, gentle and honorable. And he was incredibly bashful. He was with us a good while but he could never conquer that peculiarity; he could not be at ease in the presence of any woman, not even my mother; and as to speaking to any girl, it was wholly impossible.

It is to this kind that untoward things happen. My sister gave a candy pull on a winter's night. I was too young to be of the company and Jim was too diffident. I was sent up to bed early and Jim followed of his own motion.

His room was in the new part of the house and his window looked out on the roof of the L annex. That roof was six inches deep in snow which had an ice crust upon it, slick as glass. Out of the comb of the roof projected a short chimney, a common resort for cats on moonlight nights—and this was a moonlight night. Down at the eaves, below the chimney, a canopy of vines spread away to some posts, making a cozy shelter, and after an hour or two the rollicking crowd of young ladies and gentlemen grouped themselves in its shade, with their saucers of piping-hot candy disposed about them on the frozen ground to cool. There was joyous joking and laughter—peal upon peal of it.

About this time a couple of old, disreputable tomcats got up on the chimney and started a heated argument. I gave up trying to get to sleep and went visiting Jim's room. He was awake and fuming about the cats and their yowling. I asked him, mockingly, why he didn't climb out and drive them away. He was nettled and said overboldly that for two cents he *would*.

It was a rash remark and probably repented of before it was out of his mouth. But it was too late. I knew him; and I knew he would rather break his neck than back down, if I egged him on. "Oh, of course you would! Who's doubting it?"

It galled him and he burst out, "Maybe *you* doubt it!"

"I? Oh no! You are always doing wonderful things, with your mouth."

He was in a passion now. He snatched on his socks and began to raise the window, saying, "*You* think I dasn't—you do! I'll show you!"

The window made him rage; it wouldn't stay up.

I said, "Never mind, I'll hold it."

Indeed, I would have done anything to help. I was only a boy and was already in a heaven of anticipation. He climbed carefully out, then began to pick his perilous way on all fours along the glassy comb, a foot and a hand on each side of it.

The frosty breeze flapped his shirt about his lean legs; the crystal roof shone in the glory of the moon; the unconscious cats sat upon the chimney, alertly watching each other, lashing their tails and pouring out their grievances; and cautiously Jim crept on, flapping as he went, while the frolicsome young creatures under the vine canopy, unaware, were laughing.

Every time Jim slipped I had a hope; but always on he crept. At last he was within reaching distance. He paused, raised himself carefully, measured his distance, then made a frantic grab at the nearest cat—and missed it. Of course he lost his balance. His heels flew up, he struck on his back, and like a rocket he darted down the roof feet first, crashed through the vines and landed in a sitting position in fourteen saucers of red-hot candy in the midst of all that party—and dressed as *he* was—this lad who could not look a girl in the face with his clothes on. There was a wild scramble and a storm of shrieks and Jim fled up the stairs, dripping broken crockery all the way.

Eighteen or twenty years later I arrived in New York from California, and by that time I had failed in all my other under-takings and had stumbled into literature without intending it. This was early in 1867. I was offered twenty-five dollars to write something for the *Sunday Mercury* and I answered with the tale of "Jim Wolf and the Cats."

A year or two later "Jim Wolf and the Cats" appeared in a Tennessee paper in a new dress—it was masquerading in South-ern dialect. The appropriator of the tale had a wide reputation in the West and was exceedingly popular. His name has passed out of my memory.

A couple of years went by; then the original story cropped up again and went floating around in the original spelling and with my name to it. Soon, first one paper and then another fell upon me vigorously for "stealing" "Jim Wolf and the Cats" from the Tennessee man. I got a merciless basting but I did not mind it. It's all in the game. Besides, I had learned, a good while before that, that it is not wise to keep the fires going under a slander unless you can get some large advantage out of keeping it alive. Few slanders can stand the wear of silence.

CHAPTER 5

AN EXCITING EVENT in our village was the arrival of the mesmer-izer. I think the year was 1850. As to that I am not sure but I know the month—it was May.

The mesmerizer advertised his show and promised marvels. Admission as usual: twenty-five cents, children and Negroes half price. Not many people attended the first night but next day they had so many wonders to tell that everybody's curiosity was fired and after that for a fortnight the magician had prosperous times. I was fourteen or fifteen years old, the age at which a boy is willing to suffer all things short of death by fire if thereby he may be conspicuous and show off before the public; and so, when I saw the "subjects" perform and make the people laugh and shout I had a burning desire to be a subject myself.

Every night for three nights I sat in the row of candidates on the platform and held the magic disk in my hand and gazed at it and tried to get sleepy, but it was a failure; I remained wide-awake, like the majority. Also, I had to sit there and be gnawed with envy of Hicks, our journeyman; I had to see him scamper and jump when Simmons the enchanter exclaimed, "See the snake!" and hear him say, "My, how beautiful!" in response to the suggestion that he was observing a splendid sunset; and so on. I couldn't applaud; it filled me with bitterness to have people make a hero of Hicks and crowd around him when the show was over and ask him for more particulars of the wonders he had seen in his visions. Hicks—the idea! I couldn't stand it.

On the fourth night temptation came and I did not resist. When I had gazed at the disk a while I pretended to be sleepy. Straightway came the professor and made passes over my head to discharge the surplus electricity; then he began to "draw" me with the disk, holding it in his fingers and telling me I could not take my eyes off it; so I rose slowly and followed that disk all over the place, just as I had seen the others do. Then on suggestion I fled from snakes, passed buckets at a fire, kissed imaginary girls, fished from the platform and landed mud cats that outweighed me—and so on, all the customary marvels. But not in the customary way. I was cautious at first and watchful, being afraid the professor would discover that I was an impostor; but as soon as I realized that I was not in danger, I set myself the task of terminating Hicks's usefulness and of usurping his place.

It was an easy task. Hicks was born honest, I without that incumbrance. Hicks saw what he saw and reported accordingly, I saw more than was visible and added details to it. Hicks had no imagination; I had a double supply.

At the end of my first half hour Hicks was a thing of the past, a fallen hero. I knew it and was glad and said in my heart, "Success to crime!" Whatever Hicks had failed in, I made it a point to succeed in. For instance, if the magician asked, "What do you see?" and left him to invent a vision for himself, Hicks was dumb and blind; whereas the magician soon found out that when it came to seeing visions of a stunning and marketable sort I could get along better without his help than with it.

Then there was another thing: Hicks wasn't worth a tallow dip on mute mental suggestion. Whenever Simmons stood behind him and tried to drive a mental suggestion into the back of his skull, Hicks sat with vacant face. If he had been noticing he could have seen by the rapt faces of the audience that something was going on behind his back that required a response.

Inasmuch as I was an impostor I dreaded to have this test put upon me, for I knew the professor would be willing me to do something, and as I couldn't know what it was, I should be exposed and denounced. However, when my time came, I took my chance. I perceived by the tense faces of the people that Simmons was behind me willing me with all his might. I tried my best to imagine what he wanted but nothing suggested itself. I believed then that the hour of my disgrace was come. I am ashamed to confess it but my next thought was not how I could win compassion by going out humbly and in sorrow for my misdoings, but how I could go out most sensationally and spectacularly.

There was a rusty and empty old revolver lying on the table among the properties employed in the performances. Two or three weeks before I had had a quarrel with a big boy who was the school bully and I had not come out of it with credit. That boy was now seated in the house. I crept impressively toward the table, with a murderous scowl on my face, seized the revolver suddenly, flourished it, shouted the bully's name, jumped off the platform and made a rush for him and chased him out of the house before the paralyzed people could interfere to save him. There was a storm of applause, and the magician, addressing the house said, most impressively—

"That you may know how really remarkable this is and how wonderfully developed a subject we have in this boy, I assure you that without a spoken word to guide him he has carried out what I mentally commanded him to do, to the minutest detail."

So I was not in disgrace. I returned to the platform a hero. As regards mental suggestion, my fears of it were gone. I judged that in case I failed to guess what the professor might be willing me to do, I could count on putting up something that would answer just as well. I was right, and exhibitions of unspoken suggestion became a favorite with the public. Whenever I perceived that I was being willed to do something I got up and did something—anything that occurred to me—and the magician always ratified it. When people asked me, "How *can* you tell what he is willing you to do?" I said, "It's easy," and they always said admiringly, "Well, it beats *me* how you can do it."

Hicks was weak in another detail. When the professor made passes over him and said, "His whole body is without sensation now—come test him, ladies and gentlemen," the ladies and gentlemen always complied and stuck pins into Hicks, and if they went deep Hicks was sure to wince. Then that poor professor would have to explain that Hicks "wasn't sufficiently under the influence." But I didn't wince; I only suffered and shed tears on the inside. The miseries that a conceited boy will endure to keep up his "reputation"!

After that night, that triumphant night, I was the only subject. Simmons invited no more candidates to the platform. I performed alone every night the rest of the fortnight. Up to that time a dozen wise old heads, the intellectual aristocracy of the town, had held out as unbelievers. That handful of overwise gentlemen kept on shaking their heads all the first week and saying they had seen no marvels there that could not have been produced by collusion; and they were pretty vain of their un-belief too—particularly old Dr. Peake. Dr. Peake was the ring-leader of the irreconcilables and very formidable; for he was an F.F.V., learned, white-haired and stately. His opinion upon any matter was worth much more than that of any other person in the community. When I conquered him at last, I knew I was undisputed master of the field; and now after more than fifty years I acknowledge with a few dry old tears that I rejoiced without shame.

IN 1847, PERHAPS three years before the mesmerizer came to town, we had been living in a large white house on the corner of Hill and Main streets. My father died in it in March of the year mentioned but our family did not move out of it until some months afterward. Ours was not the only family in the house; there was another, Dr. Grant's.

The Grants were Virginians, like Peake, and one day when they were all sitting around in the parlor the conversation fell upon Virginia and old times. I was present but the group were probably unconscious of me, I being only a lad and a negligible quantity. Two of the group—Dr. Peake and Mrs. Crawford, Mrs. Grant's mother—had been of the audience when the Rich-mond theater burned down thirty-six years before, and they talked over the frightful details of that memorable tragedy. These were eyewitnesses, and with their eyes I saw it all with an intolerable vividness; I saw the black smoke rolling toward the sky, I saw the flames burst through it, I heard the shrieks of the despairing, I glimpsed their faces at the windows, I saw them jump to their death or to mutilation. The picture is before me yet and can never fade.

In due course they talked of the colonial mansion of the Peakes, with its stately columns and spacious grounds, and by odds and ends I picked up a clearly defined idea of the place. One detail hit my imagination hard. In the wall by the great front door there was a round hole as big as a saucer—a British cannonball had made it in the war of the Revolution.

Very well, three or four years later, as already mentioned, I was king bee and sole subject in the mesmeric show; it was the beginning of the second week; the performance was half over; just then the majestic Dr. Peake with his ruffled bosom and his gold-headed cane entered and took a seat. This happened while I was trying to invent something fresh in the way of vision, in response to the professor's remark—

"Concentrate your powers. Look—look attentively. There—don't you see something? Now—describe it."

Without suspecting it, Dr. Peake, by entering the place, had reminded me of the talk of three years before. I began on a vision, a vague and dim one (that was part of the game at the beginning of a vision). The vision developed by degrees and gathered momentum. It was the Richmond fire.

Dr. Peake was cold at first and his fine face had a trace of scorn on it; but when he began to recognize that fire, that expression changed and his eyes began to light up. As soon as I saw that, I turned on all the steam and gave those people a supper of fire and horrors that was calculated to last them one while! When I got through they were petrified. Dr. Peake had risen and was standing—and breathing hard. He said, in a great voice:

"My doubts are ended. No collusion could produce that miracle. It was totally impossible for him to know those details, yet he has described them with the clarity of an eyewitness—and with what truthfulness God knows I know!"

I saved the colonial mansion for the last night and solidified and perpetuated Dr. Peake's conversion with the cannonball hole. He explained to the house that I could never have heard of that small detail, which differentiated this mansion from all other Virginian mansions; therefore the fact stood proven that I had *seen* it in my vision. Lawks!

It is curious. When the magician's engagement closed there was but one person in the village who did not believe in mesmerism and I was the one. All the others were converted but I was to remain an implacable and unpersuadable disbeliever in mesmerism. And in afterlife, the subject revolted me. Perhaps it brought back to me a passage in my life which for pride's sake I wished to forget; though I thought, or persuaded myself I thought, I should never come across a "proof" which wasn't thin and cheap and probably had a fraud like me behind it.

The truth is I did not have to wait long to get tired of my triumphs. Not thirty days, I think. The glory which is built upon a lie soon becomes a most unpleasant incumbrance. No doubt for a while I enjoyed having my exploits wondered over in my presence, but I distinctly remember that there presently came a time when the subject was odious to me.

How easy it is to make people believe a lie and how hard it is to undo that work again! Thirty-five years after those evil exploits of mine I visited my old mother; and being moved by what seemed to me a rather heroic impulse, I thought I would confess my ancient fault. It cost me a great effort; I dreaded the sorrow that would rise in her face. But to my astonishment there were no sentimentalities, no dramatics; she was not moved in the least; she simply did not believe me and said so!

I was not merely disappointed, I was nettled to have my costly truthfulness flung out of the market in this placid and confident way. I asserted, with rising heat, that every single thing I had done on those long-vanished nights was a lie and a swindle; and when she tranquilly said she knew better, I put up my hand and *swore* to it—adding a triumphant, "*Now* what do you say?"

It did not affect her at all; it did not budge her an inch from her position. She refused to believe that I had invented my visions myself; she said that I was only a child at the time and could not have done it. She cited the Richmond fire and the colonial mansion and said they were quite beyond my capacities. I said she was right—I didn't invent those, I got them from Dr. Peake. Even this great shot did no damage; she said Dr. Peake had said in plain words that it was impossible for me to have heard about those things.

I realized with shame that I was defeated all along the line. I had but one card left and I played it. It was the pin-sticking. I said solemnly, "I give you my honor, a pin was never stuck into me without causing me cruel pain."

She only said, "It is thirty-five years. I believe you do think that now, but I was there and I know better. You never winced."

"Oh, my goodness!" I said, "let me *show* you that I speak the truth. Here is my arm; drive a pin into it—I shall not wince."

She only shook her gray head. "You are a man now and could

dissemble the hurt; but you were only a child then and could not have done it." And so the lie which I played upon her in my youth remained with her as an unchallengeable truth to the day of her death. Carlyle said "a lie cannot live." It shows that he did not know how to tell them.

I RECEIVED this morning* a letter from a man who dealt in names familiar to me in my boyhood. The writer enclosed a newspaper clipping, and he wanted to know if his brother, Captain Tonkray, was really the original of "Huckleberry Finn."

I replied that "Huckleberry Finn" was Tom Blankenship. As this writer evidently knew the Hannibal of the 1840's he will easily recall Tom Blankenship. Tom's father was at one time Town Drunkard, an exceedingly well-defined and unofficial office of those days. In *Huckleberry Finn* I have drawn Tom exactly as he was. He was ignorant, unwashed, insufficiently fed; but he had as good a heart as ever any boy had. His liberties were totally unrestricted. He was the only really independent person—boy or man—in the community, and by consequence he was continuously happy and was envied by all the rest of us. And as his society was forbidden us by our parents, therefore we sought and got more of his society than of any other boy's. I heard, four years ago, that he was justice of the peace in a remote village in Montana and was a good citizen and greatly respected.

Now I will quote a brief paragraph from this letter:

You no doubt are at a loss to know who I am. I will tell you. In my younger days I was a resident of Hannibal, Mo., and you and I were schoolmates attending Mr. Dawson's school along with Sam and Will Bowen and Andy Fuqua and others whose names I have forgotten. I was then about the smallest boy in school, for my age, and they called me little Aleck Tonkray.

I don't remember Aleck Tonkray but I knew those other people. I remember Dawson's schoolhouse perfectly. I described it in *Tom Sawyer*. I can remember the drowsy and inviting summer

---

*Written March 8, 1906.

sounds that used to float in through the open windows from that distant boy-Paradise, Cardiff Hill, and mingle with the murmurs of the studying pupils. I remember Andy Fuqua, the oldest pupil —a man of twenty-five. I remember the youngest pupil, Nannie Owsley, a child of seven. I remember George RoBards, eighteen or twenty years old, the only pupil who studied Latin. I remember vaguely the rest of the twenty-five boys and girls. I remember Mr. Dawson very well. I remember his boy, Theodore, who was as good as he could be. In fact he was detestably good—and he had popeyes—and I would have drowned him if I had had a chance.

In that school we were all about on an equality and, so far as I remember, the passion of envy had no place in our hearts except in the case of Arch Fuqua—Andy's brother. Arch Fuqua was about my own age—ten or eleven. He was a bitterness to us, for he could double back his big toe and let it fly and you could hear it snap thirty yards. There was not another boy in the school that could approach this feat. He had not a rival—except in Theodore Eddy, who could work his ears like a horse. But he was no real rival, because you couldn't hear him work his ears; so all the advantage lay with Arch.

I am talking of a time sixty years ago and upward. I remember the names of some of those schoolmates and, by fitful glimpses, even their faces rise dimly before me. I catch glimpses of George RoBards, the Latin pupil—slender, studious, bending over his book, his long straight black hair hanging down below his jaws like a pair of curtains on the sides of his face.

John RoBards was the little brother of George. When he was twelve years old he crossed the plains with his father amid the rush of the gold seekers of 1849. I remember the departure of the cavalcade when it spurred westward. We were all there to see and to envy. And I can still see that proud little chap sailing by on a great horse, with his long locks streaming out behind. We were also all on hand to gaze and envy when he returned two years later in unimaginable glory—*for he had traveled!* None of us had ever been forty miles from home. But he had crossed the continent. He had been in the gold mines, that fairyland of our imagination. And he had been in ships—in ships on the actual ocean; for he had sailed down the Pacific and round the Horn among icebergs and through snowstorms and wild wintry gales and flown northward in the trades and up through the blistering equatorial waters—and there in his brown face were the proofs of what he had been through. We would have sold our souls to Satan for the privilege of trading places with him.

I saw him when I was out in Missouri on a trip four years ago. He was old then—and the burden of life was upon him. He said his granddaughter, twelve years old, had read my books and would like to see me. It was a pathetic time, for she was a prisoner in her room and marked for death. Twelve years old—just her grandfather's age when he rode away on that great journey. In her I seemed to see that boy again. It was as if he had come back out of that remote past and was present before me in his golden youth. Her malady was heart disease and her brief life came to a close a few days later.

Another of those schoolboys was John Garth. And one of the prettiest of the schoolgirls was Helen Kercheval. They grew up and married. He became a prosperous banker; and a few years ago he died, rich and honored. *He died.* It is what I have to say about so many of those boys and girls.

I recall Mary Miller. She was not my first sweetheart but I think she was the first that furnished me a broken heart. I fell in love with her when she was eighteen and I nine—but she scorned me. I believe I was as miserable as even a grown man could be. But I think that this sorrow did not remain with me long. As I remember it I soon transferred my worship to Artimisia Briggs, who was a year older than Mary Miller. When I revealed my passion to her she did not scoff at it. She was very kind and gentle about it. But she was also firm, and said she did not want to be pestered by children.

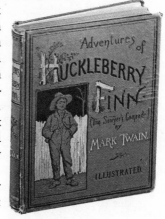

Jimmie McDaniel was another schoolmate. His age and mine about tallied. His father kept the candy shop and he was the most envied little chap in the town—after Tom Blankenship—for, although we never saw him eating candy, we supposed that it was, nevertheless, his ordinary diet. He was the first human being to whom I ever told a humorous story, so far as I can remember. This was Jim Wolf and the cats; I gave him that tale the morning after the memorable episode. I thought he would laugh his teeth out. I had never been so proud and happy before and I have seldom been so proud and happy since.

For a little while Reuel Gridley attended that school of ours. He was an elderly pupil, twenty-two or twenty-three. Then came the Mexican War and he volunteered. A company of infantry was raised in our town and Mr. Hickman, a tall, handsome athlete of twenty-five, was made captain and had a sword and a broad yellow stripe down the leg of his gray uniform pants. When that company marched through the streets in its smart uniform—which it did several times a day for drill—its evolutions were attended by all the boys whenever school permitted. I can see that marching company yet and I can almost feel again the consuming desire that I had to join it. But they had no use for boys of twelve and thirteen, and before I had a chance in another war, the desire to kill people to whom I had not been introduced had passed away.

There was George Butler, whom I remember as a child of seven wearing a blue leather belt with a brass buckle, and hated and envied by all the boys on account of it. He was a nephew of General Ben Butler and fought gallantly at Ball's Bluff and in several other actions of the Civil War.

In 1845, when I was ten years old, there was an epidemic of measles in the town and it made a most alarming slaughter among the little people. There was a funeral almost daily and the mothers of the town were nearly demented with fright. My mother worried over Pamela and Henry and me and took constant pains to keep us from coming into contact with the contagion. I cannot remember now whether I was frightened about the measles or not but I clearly remember that I grew very tired of the suspense I suffered on account of being continually under the threat of death. I remember that I got so weary of it that I made up my mind to end the suspense and settle this matter one way or the other.

Will Bowen was dangerously ill with the measles and I thought I would go down there and catch them. I entered the house and slipped along through halls, keeping sharp watch against discovery. At last I reached Will's bedroom on the second floor and got into the bed uncaptured. I don't know how long I was in the bed. I only remember that Will, as society, had no value for me, for he was too sick to even notice that I was there. When I heard his mother coming I covered up my head, but that device was a failure. Anybody could see that there were two of us under the blanket. It didn't remain two very long. Mrs. Bowen snatched me out of that bed and conducted me home herself, with a grip on my collar which she never loosened until she delivered me into my mother's hands along with her opinion of that kind of a boy.

It was a good case of measles that resulted. It brought me to where I no longer felt any interest in anything, but, on the contrary, felt a total absence of interest—which was most tranquil and delightful and enchanting. I have never enjoyed anything in my life any more than I enjoyed dying that time. I was, in effect, dying. The family even assembled around the bed to see me off. They were all crying, but that did not affect me. I took but the vaguest interest in it and that merely because I was gratified by all this attention.

When Dr. Cunningham had made up his mind that nothing more could be done for me he put bags of hot ashes all over me. He put them on my breast, my wrists, my ankles; and so—very much to his astonishment—he dragged me back into this world and set me going again.

CHAPTER 6

I WAS EDUCATED not only in the common school at Hannibal but also in my brother Orion's newspaper office, where I served in all capacities. My literature attracted the town's attention "but not its admiration" (my brother's testimony).

Orion Clemens was born in Tennessee, in 1825. He was the

465

family's firstborn, ten years older than I. Between him and me came a sister, Margaret, who died aged nine in 1839; and Pamela, who was an invalid all her life; she married William A. Moffett and died in New York in 1905. Also there was a brother, Benjamin, who died in 1842, aged ten.

The family had moved to Hannibal when Orion was ten years old. When he was fifteen or sixteen he was sent to St. Louis and there he learned the printer's trade.

One of Orion's characteristics was eagerness. He woke with an eagerness about some matter or other every morning; it consumed him all day; it perished in the night and he was on fire with a fresh new interest next morning before he could get his clothes on. He exploited in this way three hundred and sixty-five red-hot new eagernesses every year of his life—until he died, in 1898, sitting at a table with a pen in his hand, in the early morning, jotting down the conflagration for that day and preparing to enjoy the fire and smoke of it until night should extinguish it. But he also had deep glooms, despondencies, despairs; these had their place in each day along with the eagernesses. Thus his day was divided from sunrise to midnight with alternating brilliant sunshine and black cloud.

During his apprenticeship in St. Louis, Orion joined a number of churches, one after another, and taught in the Sunday schools —changing his Sunday school every time he changed his religion. He was correspondingly erratic in his politics—Whig today, Democrat next week, and anything fresh that he could find in the political market the week after. I may remark here that throughout his life he was always trading religions and enjoying the change of scenery. I will also remark that his sincerity was never doubted; in matters of business and money his honesty was never questioned. Notwithstanding his forever-recurring changes, his principles were always high and absolutely unshakable. Everything he did he did with conviction and enthusiasm—though you could break his heart with a word of disapproval.

He had an intense lust for approval. He was so eager to be approved that he was commonly ready to forsake his opinions at a moment's notice in order to get the approval of any person who disagreed with them. I wish to be understood as reserving his fundamental principles all the time. He never forsook those to please anybody. Born and reared among slaveholders, he was yet an abolitionist from his boyhood to his death. But in light matters—matters of small consequence, like religion and politics and such things—he never acquired a conviction that could survive a disapproving remark from a cat.

He was always dreaming; he was a dreamer from birth and this characteristic got him into trouble now and then. Once when he was twenty-three or twenty-four and was become a journeyman he conceived the romantic idea of coming to Hannibal without giving us notice, in order that he might furnish the family a pleasant surprise. If he had given notice he would have been informed that we had changed our residence and that gruff old bass-voiced Dr. Meredith, our family physician, was living in the house which we had occupied and that Orion's former room in that house was now occupied by Dr. Meredith's two ripe old-maid sisters.

Orion arrived at Hannibal by steamboat in the middle of the night and started with his customary eagerness on his excursion. When he arrived at the house he slipped off his boots and crept upstairs and arrived at the room of those old maids without having wakened any sleepers. He undressed in the dark and got into bed and snuggled up against somebody. He was a little surprised, but not much, for he thought it was our brother Ben. It was winter and the bed was comfortable and the supposed Ben added to the comfort. So he began to drop off to sleep well satisfied with his progress and full of happy dreams of what was going to happen in the morning.

But something else was going to happen sooner than that, and it happened now. The old maid that was being crowded squirmed and presently came to a half-waking condition and protested. That voice paralyzed Orion. He couldn't move a limb; and the crowded one began to paw around, found Orion's whiskers, and screamed, "Why, it's a man!"

This removed the paralysis; Orion was out of bed in a fraction of a second, clawing around in the dark for his clothes. Both old maids began to scream, so Orion did not wait to get his whole outfit. He started with such parts of it as he could grab. He flew to the head of the stairs and started down. He was paralyzed again at that point, because he saw the yellow flame of a candle soaring up the stairs from below. Dr. Meredith was behind it, and he had a butcher knife in his hand.

Orion shouted to him and this saved his life, for the doctor recognized his voice. Then, in those deep bass tones of his that I used to admire so much when I was a little boy, he explained to Orion the change that had been made, told him where to find the Clemens family, and closed with some quite unnecessary advice about posting himself before he undertook another adventure like that—advice which Orion probably never needed again as long as he lived.

WHEN MY FATHER DIED, in 1847, the disaster happened just at the very moment when our fortunes had changed and we were about to be comfortable once more after several years of grinding poverty. My father had just been elected clerk of the Surrogate Court. This modest prosperity was not only quite sufficient for us and for our ambitions, but also he was so esteemed now that his occupancy of that dignified office would, in the opinion of everybody, be his possession as long as he might live.

He went to Palmyra, the county seat, twelve miles away, to be sworn in about the end of February. While he was returning home on horseback a storm of sleet and rain assailed him and he arrived at the house in a half-frozen condition. Pleurisy followed and he died on the 24th of March.

Thus our splendid new fortune was snatched from us and we were in the depths of poverty again.

Orion did not come to Hannibal until two or three years after my father's death. He remained in St. Louis, a journeyman printer. Out of his wages he supported my mother and my brother Henry, who was two years younger than I. My sister Pamela helped in this support by taking piano pupils. Thus we got along, but it was hard sledding. I was not one of the burdens, because I was taken from school at once upon my father's death and placed in the office of the Hannibal *Courier* as printer's apprentice. Mr. Ament, the proprietor of the paper, allowed me the usual emolument of the office of apprentice—that is to say, board and clothes but no money. The clothes consisted of two suits a year but one of the suits always failed to materialize and the other suit was not purchased so long as Mr. Ament's old clothes held out. I was only about half as big as Ament, consequently his shirts gave me the uncomfortable sense of living in a circus tent, and I had to turn up his pants to my ears to make them short enough.

There were two other apprentices. One was Wales McCormick, seventeen or eighteen years old and a giant. He was a reckless, hilarious creature; he had no principles and was delightful company. At first we three apprentices had to feed in the kitchen with the old slave cook and her very handsome daughter. We got but little food at that kitchen table, so we apprentices used to keep alive by arts of our own—that is to say, we crept into the cellar every night and we robbed the cellar of potatoes and onions and carried them downtown to the printing office, where we slept on pallets on the floor, and cooked them at the stove and had very good times.

By and by, we apprentices were promoted from the basement to the ground floor and allowed to sit at the family table, but the economies continued. Mrs. Ament did not trust the sugar bowl to us but sweetened our coffee herself; that is, she seemed to put one heaping teaspoonful of brown sugar into each cup but, according to Wales, that was a deceit. He said she dipped the spoon in the coffee first to make the sugar stick and then scooped the sugar out of the bowl with the spoon upside down, so that the effect to the eye was a heaped-up spoon, whereas the sugar on it was nothing but a layer. This all seemed perfectly true to me and yet that thing would be so difficult to perform that I suppose it really didn't happen but was one of Wales's lies.

I have said that Wales was reckless, and he was. It was the recklessness of ever-bubbling good spirits flowing from the joy of youth. Among his shining characteristics was his limitless irreverence. There didn't seem to be anything serious in life for him; there didn't seem to be anything that he revered.

Once the celebrated founder of the Campbellite sect arrived

in our village and made a prodigious excitement. Farmers and their families drove or tramped from miles around to hear the illustrious Alexander Campbell. He preached a sermon on one of these occasions which he had written especially for that occasion. All the Campbellites wanted it printed, so they drummed up sixteen dollars, which was a large sum then, and for this great sum Mr. Ament contracted to print five hundred copies of that sermon and put them in yellow paper covers.

It was a sixteen-page duodecimo pamphlet and it was a great event in our office. We set it up eight pages to a form and by help of a printer's manual managed to get the pages in their apparently crazy but really sane places in the imposing stone. We printed that form on a Thursday. Then we set up the remaining eight pages, locked them into a form and struck a proof.

Wales read the proof and presently was aghast, for he had struck a snag. And it was a bad time to strike a snag, because it was Saturday; it was approaching noon; Saturday afternoon was our holiday and we wanted to get away and go fishing. Wales showed us what had happened. He had left out a couple of words in a page of solid matter and there wasn't another break line for two or three pages ahead. What in the world was to be done? Overrun all those pages in order to get in the two missing words? Apparently there was no other way. It would take an hour to do it. Then a revise must be sent to the great minister; if he encountered any errors we must correct them. It looked as if we might lose half the afternoon before we could get away.

Then Wales had one of his brilliant ideas. In the line in which the "out" had been made occurred the name Jesus Christ. Wales reduced it in the French way to J.C. It made room for the missing words but it took ninety-nine percent of the solemnity out of a particularly solemn sentence. We sent off the revise, meaning to get out and go fishing before that revise should get back, but we were not speedy enough. The great Alexander Campbell appeared at the far end of that sixty-foot room. He strode down to our end and what he said was brief, but it was very stern and to the point. He said to Wales, "So long as you live, don't you ever diminish the Saviour's name again. Put it all in." Then he went away.

This admonition intruded itself into Wales's incorrigible mind. It offered him an opportunity for a momentary entertainment which seemed to him to be more valuable than even fishing and swimming could afford. So he imposed upon himself the long and weary task of overrunning all those three pages in order to improve upon his former work. He enlarged the offending J.C. into Jesus H. Christ. Wales knew that that would make prodigious trouble and it did. But it was not in him to resist it. He had to succumb to the law of his make.

ABOUT 1849 OR 1850 Orion severed his connection with the printing house in St. Louis and came up to Hannibal and bought a weekly paper called the Hannibal *Journal*, together with its plant, for the sum of five hundred dollars. He borrowed the cash at ten-percent interest from an old farmer named Johnson. Then he reduced the subscription price of the paper from two dollars to one dollar. He reduced the rates for advertising in about

the same proportion and thus he created one absolute certainty— to wit: that the business would never pay him a single cent of profit.

He took me out of the *Courier* office and engaged my services in his own at three dollars and a half a week, which was an extravagant wage, but Orion was always generous. It cost him nothing in my case, for he never was able to pay me a single penny as long as I was with him. By the end of the first year he found he must make some economies. The office rent was cheap but it was not cheap enough, so he moved the whole plant into the house we lived in, and it cramped the dwelling place cruelly.

He kept that paper alive during four years but I have no idea how he accomplished it. Finally he handed it over to Mr. Johnson and went up to Muscatine, Iowa, and acquired a small interest in a weekly newspaper there.

It was not a sort of property to marry on—but no matter. He came across a winning and pretty girl who lived in Quincy, Illinois, a few miles below Keokuk, and they became engaged. He was always falling in love with girls but by some accident or other he had never gone so far as engagement before. And now he achieved nothing but misfortune by it, because he straightway fell in love with a Keokuk girl. The first thing he knew he was engaged to her; and he was in a great quandary. He didn't know which to marry, or whether to try to marry both of them and suit everyone concerned. But the Keokuk girl soon settled that for him. She was a master spirit and she ordered him to write the Quincy girl and break off that match, which he did. Then he married the Keokuk girl and they began a struggle for life which turned out to be a difficult enterprise.

To gain a living in Muscatine was plainly impossible, so Orion and his new wife went to Keokuk to live, to be near her relatives. He bought a little job-printing plant—on credit, of course —and at once put prices down to where not even the apprentices could get a living out of it, and this sort of thing went on.

I had not joined the Muscatine migration. Just before that happened (which I think was in 1853, when I was eighteen years old) I disappeared one night and fled to St. Louis. There I worked in the composing room of the *Evening News* for a time and then started on my travels to see the world. The world was New York City and there was a little World's Fair there. I arrived in New York with two or three dollars in change and a ten-dollar bank bill in the lining of my coat. I got work at villainous wages in the establishment of Gray & Green in Cliff Street and found board in a mechanics' boardinghouse in Duane Street. By and by I went to Philadelphia and worked there some months as a "sub" on the *Inquirer* and the *Public Ledger*. Finally I made a flying trip to Washington to see the sights, and in 1854 I went back to the Mississippi Valley, sitting upright in the smoking car two or three days and nights. When I reached St. Louis I went to bed on board a steamboat that was bound for Muscatine. I fell asleep at once, and didn't wake again for thirty-six hours.

After Muscatine, I went to Keokuk and worked in that little job office as much as two years, I should say, without ever collecting a cent of wages, for Orion was never able to pay anything. Then one winter day in 1856 I was coming along the main street of Keokuk in the forenoon. It was bitter weather. Dry snow was blowing here and there, swirling this way and that and making all sorts of beautiful figures. The wind blew a piece of paper past me and it lodged against a wall of a house. Something about it attracted my attention and I gathered it in. It was a fifty-dollar bill, the largest assemblage of money I had ever seen in one spot.

I advertised it in the papers and suffered more than a thousand dollars' worth of fear during the next few days lest the owner should see the advertisement. Four days went by without an applicant; then I could endure this misery no longer. I felt that I must take that money out of danger. So I bought a ticket for Cincinnati and went to that city. I worked there several months in the printing office of Wrightson & Company.

Our boardinghouse crew was made up of commonplace people of various ages. They were good-natured and full of bustle, chatter and joy; but they were oppressively uninteresting—with one exception. This was Macfarlane, a Scotchman. He was forty years old—double my age—but we were comrades from the start. I always spent my evenings by the fire in his room, listening to his talk and to the dulled complainings of the winter storms until the clock struck ten. At that hour he grilled a smoked herring. This herring was his nightcap and my signal to go.

He was six feet high and rather lank, a serious and sincere man.

The desk and typecase from Keokuk

He had no humor, and if I ever heard him laugh, the memory of it is gone from me. He had two or three dozen weighty books—philosophies, histories and scientific works—and at the head of this procession were his Bible and his dictionary. After his herring he always read two or three hours in bed.

Diligent talker as he was, he seldom said anything about himself. To ask him a personal question gave him no offense—nor the asker any information; he merely turned the matter aside. He told me once that he had had hardly any schooling and that such learning as he had, he had picked up for himself. That was his sole biographical revelation. Whether he was bachelor or widower remained his own secret. He left our boardinghouse at six, mornings, and returned to it toward six, evenings; his hands were not soft, so I reasoned that he worked at some mechanical calling ten hours a day for humble wages—but I never knew.

There was another noteworthy feature about him: he seemed to know his dictionary from beginning to end. He claimed that he did, and he said I would not find it possible to challenge him with a word he could not spell and define. I lost much time trying to hunt up a word which would beat him but I finally gave it up; which made him so proud and happy that I wished I had surrendered earlier.

He seemed to be as familiar with his Bible as he was with his dictionary. It was easy to see that he considered himself a philosopher and a thinker. His talk always ran upon grave and large questions. Of course his philosophizings were those of a partly taught and untrained mind, yet he hit by accident upon some striking things. For instance. The time was early 1856—fourteen or fifteen years before Mr. Darwin's *Descent of Man* startled the world—yet here was Macfarlane talking the same idea to me, there in the boardinghouse in Cincinnati.

CHAPTER 7

IN TIME I READ Lieutenant Herndon's account of his explorations of the Amazon and I was mightily attracted by what he said of coca. I made up my mind that I would go to the headwaters of the Amazon and collect coca, trade in it and make a fortune.

I left Cincinnati for New Orleans in the steamer *Paul Jones* with this great idea filling my mind. One of the pilots of that boat was Horace Bixby. Little by little I got acquainted with him and soon I was doing a lot of steering for him in his daylight watches. When I got to New Orleans I inquired about ships leaving for Pará and discovered that there weren't any and probably wouldn't be any during that century. It had not occurred to me to inquire about these particulars before leaving Cincinnati, so there I was. I couldn't get to the Amazon. I had no friends in New Orleans and no money to speak of.

I went to Horace Bixby and asked him to make a pilot out of me. He said he would do it for five hundred dollars, one hundred dollars in advance. So I steered for him up to St. Louis and borrowed the money from my brother-in-law, Mr. William A. Moffett, who had married my sister Pamela.

Mark Twain's pilot certificate

Within eighteen months I became a competent pilot, and I served that office until the Mississippi River traffic was brought to a standstill by the breaking out of the Civil War.

In 1858 I was a steersman on board the swift and popular New Orleans and St. Louis packet, *Pennsylvania*, Captain Klinefelter. I had been lent to Mr. Brown, one of the pilots of the *Pennsylvania*, by my owner, Mr. Bixby, and I had been steering for Brown about eighteen months. Then in the early days of May 1858 came a tragic trip—the last trip of that fleet and famous steamboat. I have told all about it in one of my books, called *Life on the Mississippi*. But I did not tell about the dream in that book. I never wanted my mother to know about that dream, and she lived for several years after I published that volume.

I had found a place on the *Pennsylvania* for my brother Henry. It was not a place of profit, it was only a place of promise. He was mud clerk. Mud clerks received no salary but they were in the line of promotion. They could become, presently, third clerk and second clerk, then chief clerk—that is to say, purser.

The dream begins when Henry had been mud clerk about three months. We were lying in port at St. Louis. Pilots and steersmen had nothing to do during the three days that the boat lay in port in St. Louis and New Orleans, but the mud clerk had to begin his labors at dawn and continue them into the night by the light of pine-knot torches. Henry and I, moneyless and unsalaried, had billeted ourselves upon our brother-in-law, Mr. Moffett, as night lodgers while in port. We took our meals on board the boat. No, I mean *I* lodged at the house, not Henry. He spent the *evenings* at the house, from nine until eleven, then went to the boat to be ready for his early duties.

On the night of the dream he started away at eleven, shaking hands with the family, and said good-by according to custom. I may mention that handshaking as a good-by was not merely the custom of that family but the custom of the region—of Missouri. In all my life up to that time I had scarcely ever seen one member of the Clemens family kiss another one. Henry's good-bys were always executed in the family sitting room on the second floor, and he went from that room and downstairs without further ceremony. But this time my mother went with him to the stairs and said good-by again. As I remember it, she was moved to this by something in Henry's manner and she remained at the head of the stairs while he descended. When he reached the door he hesitated and climbed the stairs and shook hands good-by again.

In the morning, when I awoke, I had been dreaming, and the dream was so vivid that it deceived me and I thought it was *real*. In the dream I had seen Henry a corpse. He lay in a metallic burial case dressed in a suit of my clothing, and on his breast lay a great bouquet of flowers, mainly white roses, with a red rose in the center. The casket stood upon a couple of chairs. I dressed and moved toward that door, thinking I would go in there and look at it, but I changed my mind. I thought I could not yet bear to meet my mother. I thought I would wait awhile and make some preparation for that ordeal. The house was in Locust Street, a little above Thirteenth, and I walked to Fourteenth before it suddenly flashed upon me that there was nothing real about this—it was only a dream. I returned to the house, flew up the stairs and rushed into that sitting room, and was made glad again, for there was no casket there.

We made the usual eventless trip to New Orleans—no, it was not eventless, for it was on the way down that I had the fight with my superior officer, Mr. Brown,* which resulted in his requiring that I be left ashore at New Orleans. In New Orleans I always had a job watching the freight piles from seven in the evening until seven in the morning. It was a three-night job. Henry always joined my watch about nine in the evening, when his own duties were ended, and we often walked my rounds and chatted together until midnight.

This time we were to part and so the night before the boat sailed I gave Henry some advice. I said: "In case of disaster to the boat, don't lose your head—leave that unwisdom to the passengers—they'll attend to it. But you rush for the hurricane deck, and to the lifeboat aft the wheelhouse, and obey the mate's orders—thus you will be useful. When the boat is launched, give such help as you can in getting women and children into it, and don't try to get into it yourself. The river is only a mile wide as a rule, and you can swim ashore without trouble."

Two or three days afterward the boat's boilers exploded at Ship Island, below Memphis, early one morning—and what happened afterward I have already told in *Life on the Mississippi*. As related there, I followed the *Pennsylvania* about a day later on another boat, and we began to get news of the disaster at every port we touched, and so by the time we reached Memphis we knew all about it.

I found Henry stretched upon a mattress on the floor of a great building, along with thirty or forty other scalded and wounded persons, and was promptly informed by some indiscreet person that he had inhaled steam, that his body was badly scalded and that he would live but a little while; also, I was told that the physicians and nurses were giving their whole attention to persons who had a chance of being saved. They were short-

*See *Life on the Mississippi*, Chapters 18, 19 and 20.

477

handed, and Henry and others considered to be fatally hurt were receiving only such attention as could be spared from the more urgent cases. But Dr. Peyton, a physician in the community, gave me his sympathy and took vigorous hold of the case and in about a week he had brought Henry around.

He never committed himself with prognostications which might not materialize, but at eleven o'clock one night he told me that Henry would get well. Then he said, "At midnight these poor fellows lying all over this place will begin to mourn and make outcries and if this commotion should disturb Henry it will be bad for him; therefore ask the physicians on watch to give him an eighth of a grain of morphine, but this is not to be done unless Henry shall show signs that he is being disturbed."

Oh, well, never mind the rest of it. The physicians on watch were young fellows and they made a mistake—they had no way of measuring the eighth of a grain of morphine, so they guessed at it and gave him a vast quantity on the end of a knife blade, and he died about dawn. He was carried to the dead-room and I went away to a citizen's house and slept off some of my accumulated fatigue. Meantime something was happening.

The coffins provided for the dead were of unpainted white pine, but in this instance some of the ladies of Memphis had made up a fund and bought a metallic case. When I came back and entered the dead-room Henry lay in that open case and he was dressed in a suit of my clothing. I recognized instantly that my dream of several weeks before was here exactly reproduced, so far as these details went—and I think I missed one detail, but that one was immediately supplied, for just then an elderly lady entered with a large bouquet consisting mainly of white roses, and in the center of it was a red rose and she laid it on his breast.

I have not told the entire dream; I mean I have not told all that happened in the dream's fulfillment. But I may mention one more detail, and that is this. When I arrived in St. Louis with the casket, my brother-in-law had it conveyed out to his house. I hastened thither and when I arrived and went upstairs there

Opposite page, Mark Twain as a pilot; Captain Bixby; the "Edward J. Gay," said to have been piloted by Mark Twain

stood the two chairs which I had seen in my dream, and by two or three minutes later the casket was resting upon those two chairs, just as in my dream of several weeks before.

CHAPTER 8

I WAS IN New Orleans when Louisiana went out of the Union, January 26, 1861, and I started North the next day. Every day on the trip a blockade was closed by the boat, and the batteries at Jefferson Barracks below St. Louis fired two shots through the chimneys the last night of the voyage. In June I joined the Confederates in Ralls County, Missouri, as a second lieutenant under General Tom Harris and came near having the distinction of being captured by Colonel Ulysses S. Grant. I resigned after two weeks' service in the field, explaining that I was "incapacitated by fatigue" through persistent retreating.

Meantime Orion had been sweating along with his little office in Keokuk. On account of charging nothing for the work done in his office he had almost nothing to do there. He was never able to get it through his head that work done on a profitless basis deteriorates and is presently not worth anything and that customers are obliged to go where they can get better work, even if they must pay better prices for it. He had plenty of time and he took up studying law. He also put up a sign which offered his services to the public as a lawyer. He never got a case in those days, nor even an applicant, though he was quite willing to transact law business for nothing.

By this time I was beginning to earn two hundred and fifty dollars a month as pilot and so I supported him. Then in 1861 an ancient friend, Edward Bates, a member of Mr. Lincoln's Cabinet, got him the place of Secretary of the new Territory of Nevada. Orion and I cleared for that country in the overland stagecoach, I carrying with me what money I had been able to save—eight hundred dollars, I should say—and it was all in silver coin and a nuisance because of its weight. And we had another nuisance, which was an unabridged dictionary. It weighed about a thousand pounds and was a ruinous expense, because the stage-coach company charged for extra baggage by the ounce—and it wasn't even a good dictionary—didn't have any modern words—only obsolete ones they used when Noah Webster was a child.

The government of the new Territory of Nevada was an interesting menagerie. Governor Nye was an old and seasoned politician from New York—politician, not statesman. He had white hair, a friendly face and deep lustrous brown eyes. He was a shrewd man, and a very remarkable talker.

The Governor's official menagerie had been drawn from the humblest ranks of his constituents at home—harmless good fellows who had helped in his campaigns, and now they had their reward in petty salaries payable in greenbacks that were worth next to nothing. Those boys had a hard time to make both ends meet. Orion's salary was eighteen hundred dollars a year and he couldn't even support his dictionary on it. But an Irishwoman who had come out on the Governor's staff charged the menagerie only ten dollars a week apiece for board and lodging. Orion and I were among her boarders and lodgers; and so, on these cheap terms the money I had brought from home held out very well.

At first I roamed about the country seeking silver. I have written about those days in my book *Roughing It*, and I have told in that book the tale of how my old mining comrade Calvin Higbie and I discovered a rich blind lead in the Wide West Mine in Aurora. Due to a misunderstanding Higbie and I failed to make our ownership permanent by doing work on the claim. It reads like a wild fancy sketch, but for ten days we were absolutely and unquestionably worth a million dollars. Then on the stroke of midnight on the tenth day we lost our fortune to jumpers. That would be in 1862.

I parted from Higbie about the end of 1862, and went to Virginia City, for I had been invited to come there and work as a reporter on the *Territorial Enterprise*. I was presently sent down to Carson City to report the legislative session. I wrote a weekly letter to the paper; it appeared Sundays, and on Mondays the legislative proceedings were obstructed by the complaints of members as a result. They rose to questions of privilege and answered the criticisms of the correspondent with bitterness, customarily describing him with elaborate uncomplimentary phrases, for lack of a briefer way. To save their time, I presently began to sign the letters, using the Mississippi leadman's call, "Mark Twain" (two fathoms—twelve feet), for this purpose.

Orion by now had become very popular with the members of the Nevada legislature because they found that whereas they couldn't usually trust each other they could trust him. He easily held the belt for honesty in that country but it didn't do him any good in a pecuniary way because he had no talent for either persuading or scaring legislators. But I was differently situated. I was there every day in the legislature to distribute compliment and censure and spread the same over half a page of the *Enterprise;* consequently I was an influence. I got the legislature to pass a law requiring every corporation in the territory to record its charter in full, in a record to be kept by the Secretary of the Territory—my brother. For this service he was authorized to charge forty cents a hundred words for making the record; five dollars for furnishing a certificate of each record, and so on. Everybody had a toll-road franchise but no toll road. But the franchise had to be recorded and paid for. Everybody was a mining corporation and had to have himself recorded and pay for it. Very well, we prospered. The record service paid an average of one thousand dollars a month.

Governor Nye was often absent from the Territory. He liked to run down to San Francisco every little while and enjoy a rest. Nobody complained, for he was prodigiously popular. The whole population, of twenty thousand persons, were his personal friends. Whenever he was absent from the Territory Orion served his office in his place, as Acting Governor, a title which was easily shortened to Governor. Mrs. Governor Clemens enjoyed being a Governor's wife. No one on this planet ever enjoyed a distinction more than she enjoyed that one.

When Governor Nye's four-year term was drawing to a close, the mystery of why he had ever consented to leave the great State of New York to inhabit that sagebrush desert was solved. He had gone out there in order to become a United States Senator. All that was now necessary was to turn the Territory into a State. He did it without difficulty. That patch of sand and that sparse population were not well fitted for the heavy burden of a state government but no matter, the people were willing to have the change and so the Governor's game was made.

Orion's game was made too, apparently, for he was as popular because of his honesty as the Governor was for more substantial reasons. But at the critical moment the inborn capriciousness of his character rose up and disaster followed.

There were several candidates for all the offices in the new State of Nevada save two—United States Senator (Governor Nye) and Secretary of State (Orion Clemens). Nye was certain to get a Senatorship, and Orion was so sure to get the Secretaryship that no one but him was named for that office. But he was hit with one of his spasms of virtue on the very day that the Republican party was to make its nominations in the convention. Orion refused to go near the convention. He said his presence there would be an improper influence and that if he was to be nominated the compliment must come to him as a free and unspotted gift. He also had another spasm of virtue on the same day; he suddenly changed from a friendly attitude toward whiskey—which was the popular attitude—to uncompromising teetotalism.

The paper next morning contained the list of chosen nominees. His name was not in it. He had not received a vote.

ORION'S RICH INCOME ceased when the state government came into power. He was without an occupation. Well, it seemed to me that our society was no longer desirable in Nevada; so I left. Orion stayed on for a while in Carson City, but I went on to San Francisco.

There I became a reporter on the *Morning Call*. I was more than that—I was *the* reporter. There was no other. There was enough work for one and a little over, but not enough for two—according to Mr. Barnes, and he was the proprietor.

By nine in the morning along with reporters from other papers I had to be at the police court for an hour and make a brief history of the squabbles of the night before. They were usually between Irishmen and Irishmen, and Chinamen and Chinamen, with now and then a squabble between the two races for a change. Next we visited the higher courts and made notes of the decisions which had been rendered the day before. During the rest of the day we raked the town from end to end, gathering such material as we might, wherewith to fill our columns—and if there were no fires to report we started some.

At night we visited the six theaters, one after the other: seven nights a week, three hundred and sixty-five nights in the year. We remained in each of those places five minutes, got a glimpse of play and opera, and with that for a text we "wrote up" those plays and operas, as the phrase goes, torturing our souls every night to find something to say about the performances which we had not said a hundred times before.

After having been hard at work from nine or ten in the morning until eleven at night scraping material together, I took the pen and spread this muck out in words and made it cover as much acreage as I could. It was fearful drudgery, awful slavery for a lazy man, and I was born lazy. I am no lazier now than I was forty years ago, but that is because I reached the limit forty years ago. You can't go beyond possibility.

Finally there was an event. One afternoon I saw some hoodlums chasing and stoning a Chinaman, and I noticed that a policeman was observing this performance with an amused interest—nothing more. He did not interfere. I wrote up the incident with considerable indignation. Usually I didn't want to read in the morning what I had written the night before; it had come from a torpid heart. But this item had come from a live one. There was fire in it and I believed it was literature—and so I sought for it in the paper next morning with eagerness.

It wasn't there. It wasn't there the next morning, nor the next. I went up to the composing room and found it tucked away among condemned matter. The foreman said Mr. Barnes had found it in a galley proof and ordered its extinction. And Mr. Barnes furnished his reasons. They were commercially sound. He said that the *Call* was the paper of the poor. It gathered its livelihood from the poor and must respect their prejudices or perish. The Irish were the poor. Without them the *Morning Call* could not survive a month—and they hated the Chinamen. Such an assault as I had attempted could rouse the whole Irish hive and seriously damage the paper. The *Call* could not afford to publish articles criticizing the hoodlums for stoning Chinamen.

I was lofty in those days, loftier than I am now, and I felt a deep shame in being slave of such a journal as the *Morning Call*. If I had been still loftier I would have thrown up my berth and gone and starved, like any other hero. But I had never had any experience. I had *dreamed* heroism, like everybody, but I had had no practice and I didn't know how to begin. I couldn't bear to begin with starving. I had already come near to that once or twice in my life and got no real enjoyment out of remembering it. I knew I couldn't get another berth if I resigned. Therefore I swallowed my humiliation and stayed where I was.

But whereas there had been little enough interest attaching to my industries before, there was none at all now. I continued my work but I took not the least interest in it, and naturally I got to neglecting it. As I have said, there was too much of it for one man. Even Barnes now noticed that, and told me to get an assistant, on half wages.

There was a great hulking creature down in the counting room—good-natured and unintellectual—and he was getting little or nothing a week. A graceless boy of the counting-room force was always making fun of this beachcomber, and he had a name for him which somehow seemed apt. He called him Smiggy McGlural. I offered the berth of assistant to Smiggy and he accepted it with alacrity.

Smiggy went at his work with ten times the energy that was left in me. He was not intellectual but mentality was not needed in a *Morning Call* reporter. I gradually got to leaving more and more of the work to McGlural. I grew lazier and lazier and within thirty days he was doing almost the whole of it.

Now in those ancient times the counting room of the *Morning Call* was on the ground floor; the office of the Superintendent of the United States Mint was on the next floor above, with Bret Harte as private secretary of the Superintendent. The quarters of the editorial staff and the reporter were on the third floor, and the composing room on the fourth floor. I spent a good deal of time with Bret Harte in his office after Smiggy McGlural came. Harte was doing a good deal of writing for the *Californian*—contributing "Condensed Novels" and sketches to it and also acting as editor, I think. I was a contributor. We had very good times together—very social and pleasant times.

It was Mr. Swain, Superintendent of the Mint, who discovered Bret Harte. Harte had arrived in California in the 1850's, twenty-three or twenty-four years old, and had wandered up into the surface diggings of the camp at Yreka. He taught school in that camp several months. He also edited the weekly rag which was the newspaper. He spent a little time also in the pocket-mining camp of Jackass Gulch. It was at Yreka and Jackass Gulch that Harte learned to observe and put with photographic exactness on paper the scenery of California and its general country aspects—the stagecoach; its driver and passengers; the miner, the gambler and their women. By and by he came to San Francisco. He was a compositor by trade and got work in the *Golden Era* office at ten dollars a week. Harte was paid for setting type only but he entertained himself by contributing literature to the paper, uninvited.

The *Golden Era* was ostensibly a literary paper, but its literature was pretty feeble. Mr. Swain, the Superintendent of the Mint, noticed a new note in that *Golden Era* orchestra—a fresh and spirited note that was recognizable as music. He asked Joe Lawrence who the performer was and Lawrence told him. It seemed to Mr. Swain a shame that Harte should be wasting himself in such a place so he took him away, made him his private secretary on a good salary, and told him to develop his talent. Harte was willing and the development began.

Bret Harte was one of the pleasantest men I have ever known. He was also one of the unpleasantest men I have ever known. He was showy, meretricious, insincere; and he constantly advertised these qualities in his dress. He was distinctly pretty, in spite of the fact that his face was pitted with smallpox. His clothes always exceeded the fashion; he was always conspicuously a little more fashionable than the fashionablest of the community. His clothes invariably had a single smart little accent. Oftenest it was his necktie. Perhaps it was crimson—a flash of flame under his chin; or it was indigo blue and as hot and vivid as if one of those luminous Brazilian butterflies had lighted there.

He hadn't a sincere fiber in him. I think he was incapable of emotion, for he had nothing to feel with. His heart was merely a pump and had no other function. I knew him in the days when he was private secretary on the second floor and I a fading and perishing reporter on the third. I knew him when he came east five years later in 1871 to take the editorship of the *Lakeside Monthly* in Chicago, and crossed the continent in a prodigious blaze of national interest.

I knew him pretty intimately thenceforth until he crossed the ocean to be consul, first at Crefeld in Germany and afterward in Glasgow. He never returned to America. When he died in London, he had been absent from America and from his wife and daughters twenty-six years.

Harte told me once, when he was spending a fortnight in my house in Hartford, that his fame was an accident—an accident that he much regretted for a while. He said he had written "The Heathen Chinee" for amusement; then had thrown it into the wastebasket; that presently there was a call for copy to finish out the *Overland Monthly*. He had nothing else, so he fished the "Chinee" out of the basket and sent that. It created an explosion of delight, and Harte's name, from being obscure in one week, was as notorious and as visible in the next as if it had been painted on the sky in letters of astronomical magnitude. He regarded this fame as a disaster, because he was already at work on such things as "The Luck of Roaring Camp," a loftier grade of literature, a grade which he had been hoping to presently occupy with distinction in the sight of the world.

"The Heathen Chinee" did obstruct that dream, but not for long. It was presently replaced by the finer glory of "The Luck of Roaring Camp," "Tennessee's Partner," and those other felicitous imitations of Dickens.

It is a pity that we cannot escape from life when we are young. When Bret Harte started east in his newborn glory thirty-six years ago, with the eyes of the world upon him, he had lived all of his life that was worth living. He had lived all of his life that was to be respectworthy.

There was a happy Bret Harte, an ambitious Bret Harte, a cheerful, easy-laughing Bret Harte, to whom it was a bubbling and effervescent joy to be alive. That Bret Harte died in San

Francisco. It was the corpse of that Bret Harte that swept in splendor across the continent; that refused to go to the Chicago banquet given in its honor because a carriage had not been sent for it; that resumed its eastward journey with the grand scheme of the *Lakeside Monthly* in sorrowful collapse; that undertook to give all the product of its brain for one year to the *Atlantic Monthly* for ten thousand dollars—furnished nothing worth speaking of for the great pay, but collected and spent the money before the year was out and then began a dismal death-in-life of borrowing from men and living on women which was to cease only at the grave.

But all of that was to happen later. Meanwhile, in San Francisco, as I have said, while I was having good times with Bret Harte and others, I got to leaving more and more of my work to Smiggy McGlural.

Smiggy was a great advantage to me—during thirty days. Then he turned into a disaster, for Mr. Barnes discharged me.

I WAS on the world now, with nothing to do. It was at that time that I went and spent three months in the log-cabin home of Jim Gillis and his "pard," Dick Stoker, in Jackass Gulch, in Calaveras County.

Jim Gillis was a remarkable person. He had a bright and smart imagination and it was of the kind that can turn out an impromptu story and do it well. Every now and then he would have an inspiration and he would stand up before the great log fire, with his back to it, his hands crossed behind him, and deliver himself of an elaborate impromptu lie—a fairy tale, an extravagant romance—with Dick Stoker as the hero of it as a general thing. Jim always soberly pretended that what he was relating was strictly history, not romance. Dick Stoker, gray-headed and good-natured, would sit smoking his pipe and listen with a gentle serenity to these monstrous fabrications and never utter a protest.

In more than one of my books I have used Jim's impromptu tales. One which he called "The Tragedy of the Burning Shame" I had to modify considerably to make it proper for print, and this was a great damage. As Jim told it, inventing it as he went along, it was one of the most outrageously funny things I have ever listened to. How mild it is in the book; and how extravagant and how gorgeous it was in its unprintable form!

I used another of Jim's impromptus in a book of mine called *A Tramp Abroad*, a tale of how the poor innocent and ignorant blue jays tried to fill up a house with acorns. It is a charming story, full of happy fancies. Jim stood before the fire and reeled it off with the easiest facility, claiming as usual that it was all straight fact, history pure and undefiled. I used another of Jim's inventions in my book *Roughing It*, the story of Jim Baker's cat, the remarkable Tom Quartz. Jim Baker was Dick Stoker, of course; Tom Quartz had never existed; there was no such cat, at least outside of Jim Gillis's imagination.

From Jackass Gulch I returned at last to San Francisco. I wrote letters to the Virginia City *Enterprise* for a while and was then sent to the Sandwich Islands by the Sacramento *Union* to write about the sugar interests.

While I was in Honolulu the survivors of the clipper *Hornet* (burned on the line) arrived, mere skin and bone, after forty-three days in an open boat. I worked all night and produced a complete account of the matter and flung it aboard a schooner which had already cast off. It was the only full account that went to California, and the *Union* paid me tenfold the current rates for it.

After about four or five months I returned to California to find myself about the best-known honest man on the Pacific Coast. Thomas McGuire, proprietor of several theaters, said that now was the time to make my fortune—strike while the iron was hot—break into the lecture field! I did it. I announced a lecture on the Sandwich Islands, closing the advertisement with the remark: "Admission one dollar; doors open at half past seven, the trouble begins at eight." A true prophecy. The trouble certainly did begin at eight, when I found myself in front of the only audience I had ever faced. The fright which pervaded me from head to foot was paralyzing. It lasted two minutes and was as bitter as death; the memory of it is indestructible but it had its compensations, for it made me immune from timidity before audiences for all time to come.

I LECTURED IN ALL the principal California towns and in Nevada, then lectured once or twice more in San Francisco, then retired from the field rich—for me—and laid out a plan to sail from San Francisco and go around the world. The proprietors of the *Daily Alta California* engaged me to write an account of the trip for that paper—fifty letters, about two thousand words per letter, and the pay to be twenty dollars per letter.

I went east to St. Louis to say good-by to my mother and then I was bitten by the prospectus of the *Quaker City* Holy Land excursion and I ended by joining it. During the trip I wrote and sent the fifty letters. Then I put together a lecture on the trip and delivered it in San Francisco at great profit; then I branched out into the country and was aghast at the result: I had been entirely forgotten, I never had people enough in my houses! I inquired into this curious condition of things and found that the thrifty owners of that rich *Alta* newspaper had *copyrighted* all those twenty-dollar letters and had threatened with prosecution any journal which should venture to copy a paragraph from them!

So there I was! I had contracted to furnish a large book to the American Publishing Company of Hartford, and I supposed I should need those letters to fill it out with. I was in an uncomfortable situation—if the proprietors of this stealthily acquired copyright should refuse to let me use the letters.

That is just what they did; Mr. MacCrellish said his firm was going to make a book out of the letters in order to get back the thousand dollars which they had paid for them. I said that if they had acted fairly and honorably and had allowed the country press to use the letters or portions of them, my lecture skirmish on the coast would have paid me ten thousand dollars, whereas the *Alta* had lost me that amount. Then Mr. MacCrellish offered a compromise: he would publish the book and allow me ten-percent royalty on it. The compromise did not appeal to me and I said so. The book sale would be confined to San Francisco, and my royalty would not pay me enough to board me three months, whereas my eastern contract, if carried out, could be profitable to me.

In the end Mr. MacCrellish agreed to suppress his book, on certain conditions: in my preface I must thank the *Alta* for waiving its "rights." I objected to the thanks. After considerable debate my point was conceded and the thanks left out.

After all the fuss, I did not levy heavily upon the *Alta* letters. I found that they were newspaper matter, not book matter. I used ten or twelve. I wrote the rest of *The Innocents Abroad* in sixty days. I was very young in those days, marvelously young, younger than I am now by hundreds of years. I worked every night from eleven or twelve until broad day, and as I did two hundred thousand words in sixty days, the average was more than three thousand words a day—nothing for Sir Walter Scott, nothing for plenty of other people, but quite handsome for me.

I wrote *The Innocents Abroad* in March and April 1868 in San Francisco. It was published in August 1869. But to go back: for my experiences as an author began early in 1867.

I had come to New York from San Francisco in the first month of that year and presently Charles H. Webb, whom I had known in San Francisco as editor of the *Californian*, suggested that I publish a volume of sketches. I had but a slender reputation to publish it on but I was excited by the suggestion and quite willing to venture it.

What reputation I did have in the Atlantic states rested upon the story of "The Jumping Frog." When Artemus Ward had passed through California on a lecturing tour in 1865 or 1866, I had told him the "Jumping Frog" story and he had asked me to write it out and send it to his publisher, Carleton, in New York, to be used in padding out a small book which Artemus had prepared for the press.

When the story reached Carleton he didn't think much of it and was not willing to add it to the book. He did not put it in the wastebasket but made Henry Clapp a present of it and Clapp used it in his literary journal, *The Saturday Press*. "The Jumping Frog" appeared in that paper, and was at once copied in the newspapers of America and England. It had a wide celebrity at the time that I am speaking of—but I was aware that it was only the frog that was celebrated. It wasn't I. I was still an obscurity.

Webb undertook to collate the sketches. He handed the result to me and I went to Carleton's establishment with it. I approached a clerk and he bent over the counter; but when he found that I had come to sell a book and not to buy one, his temperature fell sixty degrees. I meekly asked the privilege of a word with Mr. Carleton and was coldly informed that he was in his private office. Discouragements followed, but after a while I got by the frontier and entered the holy of holies. Carleton rose and said brusquely, "Well, what can I do for you?"

I told him that I was there to offer him my book for publication. He began to swell and went on swelling until he had reached the dimensions of a god of about the second or third degree. Finally he made a sweep with his hand which comprehended the room and said, "Books—look! Every one of those shelves is loaded with books that are waiting for publication. Do I want any more? I don't. Good morning."

Twenty-one years elapsed before I saw Carleton again. I was then sojourning with my family in Lucerne. He called on me, shook hands and said at once, "I am substantially an obscure person but I have a couple of such colossal distinctions to my credit that I am entitled to immortality—to wit: I refused a story and then a book of yours and for this I stand without competitor as the prize ass of the nineteenth century."

It was a most handsome apology and I told him so and said it was a long-delayed revenge but was sweeter to me than any other that could be devised.

I reported my adventure to Webb and he bravely said that not all the Carletons in the universe should defeat that book; he would publish it himself on a ten-percent royalty. And so he did. He brought it out and made a very pretty little book of it.

I think he named it *The Celebrated Jumping Frog of Calaveras County, and Other Sketches,* price $1.25. He printed the book through a job-printing house and published it through the American News Company.

In June I sailed in the *Quaker City* excursion to the Holy Land. I returned in November and in Washington found a letter from Elisha Bliss of the American Publishing Company of Hartford, offering me five-percent royalty on a book which should recount the adventures of the excursion. In lieu of the royalty I was offered the alternative of ten thousand dollars cash upon delivery of the manuscript. I consulted A. D. Richardson and he said, "Take the royalty." I followed his advice and closed with Bliss.

But I must go back to Webb. When I got back from the *Quaker City* excursion in November 1867, Webb told me that *The Jumping Frog* book had been favorably received by the press and that he believed it had sold fairly well, but that he had found it impossible to get a statement of account from the American News Company. He said the book had been something of a disaster to him, since he had manufactured it with his own funds and was now not able to get any money back because of the dishonest ways of the News Company.

I was sincerely sorry for Webb, sorry that he had lost money by befriending me, also in some degree sorry that he was not able to pay me my royalties.

I meanwhile made my contract for *The Innocents Abroad* with the American Publishing Company. Then it occurred to me that perhaps I was violating that contract, there being a clause in it forbidding me to publish books with any other firm during a term of a year or so. Of course that clause could not cover a book which had been published before the contract was made; anybody else would have known that. But I didn't know it. It was my ignorant opinion that I was violating the Bliss contract and that I was in honor bound to suppress *The Jumping Frog* book. So I went to Webb with the matter.

Webb was willing to accommodate me upon these terms: that I should surrender to him such royalties as might be due me; that I should also surrender to him, free of royalty, all copies which might be in the News Company's hands; also that I should hand him eight hundred dollars cash; also that he should superintend the breaking up of the plates of the book, and for that service should receive such bounty as the typefounders pay for the broken plates as old type metal. Type metal was worth nine cents a pound and the plates weighed about forty pounds. One may perceive by these details that Webb had some talent as a trader.

After this Webb passed out of the field of my vision for a long time. But meantime chance threw me in the way of the manager of the American News Company, and I asked him about Webb's difficulties with the concern. He said he didn't know of any difficulties. I then explained to him that Webb had never been able to collect anything from the company. In turn, he explained to me that my explanation was not sound. He said the company had always furnished statements to Webb at the usual intervals and had accompanied them with the company's check to date.

By his invitation I went to his office and by his books and accounts he proved to me that what he had said was true. Webb had collected his dues and mine from the beginning and had pocketed the money. At the time that Webb and I had settled, he owed me six hundred dollars on royalties. The *Jumping Frog* copies which he had inherited from me at that time had since been sold and the result had gone into his pocket—including six hundred more that should have come to me on royalties.

To sum up, I was now an author, I was an author with some little trifle of reputation, I was an author who had published a book, I was an author who had not become rich through that publication, I was an author whose first book had cost him twelve hundred dollars in unreceived royalties, eight hundred dollars in blood money, and three dollars and sixty cents smouched from old type metal. I was resolved from that moment that I would not publish with Webb anymore—unless I could borrow money enough to support the luxury.

In the meantime, being out of money, I went down to Washington to see if I could earn enough there to keep me in bread and butter while I wrote *The Innocents Abroad*.

In Washington I came across William Swinton, brother of the historian, and together we invented a scheme for our mutual sustenance; we became the originators of what is a common feature in the newspaper world now, the syndicate. It was on a small scale but that is usual with new enterprises. We had twelve journals on our list; they were all weeklies, all obscure and poor. It was a proud thing for those little newspapers to have a Washington correspondent and a fortunate thing for us that they felt in that way about it. Each of the twelve took two letters a week from us, at a dollar per letter; each of us wrote one letter per week and sent off six duplicates of it to these benefactors, thus acquiring twenty-four dollars a week to live on, which was all we needed in our humble quarters.

Swinton was one of the loveliest human beings I have ever known, and we led a charmed existence together. He was highly educated; he was of a beautiful spirit; he was pure in heart and speech. He was a Scotchman and a Presbyterian. He hadn't a vice, unless a large sympathy with Scotch whisky may be called by that name. I didn't regard it as a vice, because he was a Scotchman, and Scotch whisky to a Scotchman is as innocent as milk is to the rest of the human race. In Swinton's case it was a virtue and not an economical one. Twenty-four dollars a week would really have been riches to us if we hadn't had to support that jug; because of the jug we were always sailing close to the wind, and any tardiness in the arrival of any part of our income was sure to cause some inconvenience.

I remember a time when a shortage occurred; we had to have three dollars and have it before the close of the day. Swinton told me to go out and find it and he said he would also go see what he could do. He told me to give myself no uneasiness; and said in a simple, confident way, "The Lord will provide." Before he was done with me his strong faith had had its influence and I went forth almost convinced that the Lord really would provide.

I wandered around the streets for an hour, trying to think up some way to get that money. At last I lounged into the big lobby of the Ebbitt House and sat down. Presently a dog came loafing along. He glanced at me and said with his eyes, "Are you friendly?" I answered with my eyes that I was. He gave his tail a grateful wag and came forward and rested his jaw on my knee and lifted his brown eyes to my face in a winningly affectionate way. He was a lovely creature, beautiful as a girl, and made all of silk and velvet. I stroked his smooth brown head and fondled his drooping ears and we were a pair of lovers right away.

Soon Brigadier General Miles, the hero of the land, came strolling by in his blue-and-gold splendors. He saw the dog and stopped, and there was a light in his eye which showed that he had a warm place in his heart for dogs like this gracious creature; then he came forward and patted the dog and said, "He is very fine; would you sell him?"

I was greatly moved; it seemed a marvelous thing to me, the way Swinton's prediction had come true. I said, "Yes."

The General said, "What do you ask for him?"

"Three dollars."

The General was surprised. He said, "Only three dollars? Why that dog can't possibly be worth less than fifty. Reconsider your price if you like, I don't wish to wrong you."

I responded with the same quiet decision as before. "No, three dollars. That is his price."

"Very well," said the General, and he gave me three dollars and led the dog away upstairs.

In about ten minutes a gentle-faced, middle-aged gentleman came along and began to look here and there, and I said to him, "Is it a dog you are looking for?"

His face lit up and he answered, "Yes—have you seen him?"

"Yes," I said, "he was here a minute ago and I saw him follow a gentleman away. I think I could find him for you if you would like me to try."

I have seldom seen a person look so grateful, and he conceded that he would like me to try. I said I would do it with great pleasure but that as it might take a little time I hoped he would not mind paying me something for my trouble. He said, "Most gladly"—and asked me how much.

I said, "Three dollars."

He looked surprised, and said, "Dear me, it is nothing! I will pay you ten, quite willingly."

But I said, "No, three is the price," and I started for the stairs without waiting for further argument, for Swinton had said that that was the amount that the Lord would provide and it seemed to me that it would be sacrilegious to take a penny more than was promised.

I got the number of the General's room, and when I reached the room I found the General there caressing his dog. I said, "I am sorry, but I have to take the dog again."

He seemed surprised and said, "Take him again? Why, you sold him to me."

"Yes," I said, "it is true—but I have to have him, because the man that owns him wants him again."

For a moment the General couldn't seem to find his voice; then he said, "Do you mean to tell me that you were selling another man's dog—and knew it?"

"Yes."

"Then why did you sell him?"

I said, "Well, that is a curious question to ask. I sold him because you wanted him. You offered to buy the dog; you can't deny that. I was not anxious to sell him—I had not even thought of selling him—but it seemed to me that if it could be any accommodation to you—"

He broke me off, and said, "*Accommodation* to me? It is the most extraordinary spirit of accommodation I have ever heard of—the idea of your selling a dog that didn't belong to you—"

I broke him off there and said, "There is no relevancy about this kind of argument; you said yourself that the dog was probably worth fifty dollars. I only asked you three; was there anything unfair about that?"

"Oh, what in the world has that to do with it! The crux of the matter is that you didn't own the dog—can't you see that?"

I said, "Please don't argue about it anymore. You can't get around the fact that the price was perfectly fair—considering

May 11 - 1922

that I didn't own the dog—so arguing about it is only a waste of words. I have to have him back again because the man wants him; don't you see that? Put yourself in my place. Suppose you had sold a dog that didn't belong to you; suppose you—"

"Oh," he said, "don't muddle my brains anymore with your idiotic reasonings! Take him along and give me a rest."

So I paid back the three dollars and led the dog downstairs and passed him over to his owner and collected three for my trouble. I went away then with a good conscience, because I had acted honorably; I never could have used the three that I sold the dog for, because it was not rightly my own, but the three I got for restoring him to his rightful owner was righteously and properly mine, because I had earned it. That man might never have gotten that dog back at all, if it hadn't been for me.

Now then, that is the tale. Some of it is true.

CHAPTER 10

I HAD BEGUN as a lecturer in 1866 in California; in 1867 lectured in New York and in the Mississippi Valley; in 1868 made the whole western circuit; and in the two or three following seasons added the eastern circuit to my route.

The "lyceum system" was in full flower in those days and James Redpath's Bureau in School Street, Boston, had the management of it throughout the northern states and Canada. Redpath farmed out the lectures in groups of six or eight to the lyceums all over the country at an average of about one hundred dollars for each lecture. His commission was ten percent; each lecture appeared about one hundred and ten nights in the season. There were a number of good drawing names in his list: Henry Ward Beecher; Horace Greeley; Petroleum Nasby; Josh Billings; *et al.* He also had in his list twenty or thirty men and women of light consequence who wrought for fees ranging from twenty-five to fifty dollars. All the lyceums wanted the big guns— wanted them yearningly. Redpath granted their prayers—on

Top, opposite, Jim Gillis; bottom, left to right, Petroleum Nasby,
Mark Twain, Josh Billings; Bret Harte

this condition: for each house filler allotted them they must hire several of his house emptiers. This arrangement permitted the lyceums to get through alive for a few years, but in the end it killed them and abolished the lecture business.

The chief ingredients of Redpath's makeup were honesty, sincerity, kindliness and pluck. When I became a public lecturer he was my agent.

I had pleasant company on my lecture flights out of his bureau in Boston and plenty of good talks and smokes after a lecture was finished and the committee had escorted me to the inn to make their good-night. There was always a committee; they received me at the station and drove me to the lecture hall; they sat behind me on the stage, and in the earliest days their chief used to introduce me to the audience; but these introductions were so grossly flattering that they made me ashamed; therefore after the first season I always introduced myself—using, of course, a burlesque of the timeworn introduction.

Now and then I had a mild little adventure. Once I arrived late at a town and found no committee in waiting. I struck up a street in the moonlight, found a tide of people flowing along, judged it was on its way to the lecture hall—a correct guess—and joined it. At the hall I tried to press in, but was stopped by the ticket taker: "Ticket, please."

I bent over and whispered: "It's all right. I am the lecturer."

He closed one eye impressively and said, loud enough for all the crowd to hear: "No you don't. Three of you have got in, up to now, but the next lecturer that goes in here tonight *pays*."

Of course I paid; it was the least embarrassing way out of the trouble.

Those of us who were lecturers for Redpath had to bring out a new lecture every season, and expose it in the "Star Course," Boston, for a first verdict, before an audience of twenty-five hundred in the old Music Hall; for it was by that verdict that all the lyceums in the country determined the lecture's commercial value. The campaign did not really *begin* in Boston but in the towns around. We did not appear in Boston until we had rehearsed about a month in those towns and made necessary corrections and revisings.

This system gathered the whole tribe of lecturers together in the city early in October and we had a lazy and sociable time for several weeks. We lived at Young's Hotel; we spent the days in Redpath's Bureau, smoking and talking shop; and early in the evenings we scattered out among the towns and made them indicate the good and poor things in the new lectures. The country audience is the difficult audience; a passage which it will approve with a ripple will bring a crash in the city. A fair success in the country means a triumph in the city. And so, when we finally stepped onto the great stage at the Music Hall we already had the verdict in our pocket.

As opposed to a "lecture," what is called a "reading" was first essayed by Charles Dickens. He brought the idea with him from England in 1867. He made the idea so popular in America that his houses were crowded everywhere, and in a single season he earned two hundred thousand dollars.

I heard him once during that season; it was in Steinway Hall in New York, in December, and it made the fortune of my life— not in dollars, I am not thinking of dollars; it made the real fortune of my life in that it made the happiness of my life; on that day I called at the St. Nicholas Hotel to see my *Quaker City* excursion shipmate, Charley Langdon, and was introduced to a sweet and lovely young girl, his sister. The family went to the Dickens reading and I accompanied them. It was forty years ago; from that day to this the sister has never been out of my mind nor heart.

MR. DICKENS read scenes from his books. From my distance he was a small, slender figure, rather fancifully dressed, and striking in appearance. He wore a black velvet coat with a large and glaring red flower in the buttonhole. He stood under a red upholstered shed behind whose slant was a row of strong lights. He read with great force and animation. It will be understood that he did not merely read but also acted. His reading of the storm scene from *David Copperfield* in which Steerforth lost his life was so vivid and so full of energetic action that his house was carried off its feet, so to speak.

Dickens had set a fashion which others tried to follow, but no one was more than temporarily successful in it. The public reading was discarded after a time and was not resumed until more than twenty years after Dickens had introduced it. Lecturing and reading were quite different things; the lecturer didn't use notes or book, but got his lecture by heart and delivered it night after night during the whole lecture season of four winter months. The lecture field had been a popular one all over the country for many years when I entered it in the late 1860's; it was then at the top of its popularity.

I remained in the lecture field three seasons—long enough to learn the trade; then domesticated myself in my new married estate after my weary life of wandering and remained under shelter at home for fourteen or fifteen years.

IN FEBRUARY 1870 I was married to Miss Olivia L. Langdon, and I took up my residence in Buffalo, New York. Tomorrow* will be the thirty-sixth anniversary of our marriage. My wife passed from this life one year and eight months ago in Florence, Italy, after an illness of twenty-two months' duration.

I saw her first in the form of an ivory miniature in her brother Charley's stateroom in the steamer *Quaker City* in the Bay of Smyrna, in the summer of 1867, when she was in her twenty-second year. I saw her in the flesh for the first time in New York, as I have already indicated, in the following December.

She was slender, beautiful and girlish—and she was both girl and woman. She remained both girl and woman to the last day of her life. Under a grave and gentle exterior burned inextinguishable fires of sympathy, energy, devotion and affection. She was *always* frail in body and lived upon her spirit.

She became an invalid at sixteen through a partial paralysis caused by falling on the ice and was never strong again while her life lasted. After that fall she was not able to leave her bed during two years, nor was she able to lie in any position except upon her back. All the great physicians were brought to Elmira one after another during that time, but there was no helpful result.

In those days the world was well acquainted with the name of

---

*Written February 1, 1906.

Dr. Newton, a man who was regarded as a quack. He moved through the land in state; like a circus. Notice of his coming was spread upon the dead walls in vast colored posters several weeks beforehand.

One day Andrew Langdon, a relative of the Langdon family, came to the house and said: "You have tried everybody else; now try Dr. Newton, the quack. He is downtown at the Rathbun House. *I saw him* wave his hands over Jake Brown's head, take his crutches away, and send him about his business as good as new. *I saw him* do the like with some other cripples. *They* may not have been genuine. But Jake is genuine. Send for Newton."

Newton came. He found the girl upon her back. Over her was suspended a tackle from the ceiling. It had been put there in the hope that by its motion she might be lifted to a sitting posture, at intervals, for rest. But it had proved a failure. Any attempt to raise her brought nausea and exhaustion.

Livy, as a young girl

Newton delivered a short fervent prayer; then he put an arm behind her shoulders and said, "Now we will sit up, my child." The family, alarmed, tried to stop him, but he raised her up. She sat several minutes without nausea or discomfort. Then Newton said, "Now we will walk a few steps, my child." He took her out of bed and supported her while she walked several steps; then he said: "I have reached the limit of my art. She is not cured. It is not likely that she will *ever* be cured. She will never be able to walk far, but after a little daily practice she will be able to walk one or two hundred yards, and she can depend on being able to do *that* for the rest of her life."

From the day that she was eighteen until she was fifty-six she was always able to walk a couple of hundred yards without stopping to rest; and more than once I saw her walk a quarter of a mile without serious fatigue. I met Newton once, in afteryears, and asked him what his secret was. He said he didn't know but thought perhaps some subtle form of electricity proceeded from his body and wrought the cures.

Perfect truth, perfect honesty, perfect candor, were qualities of my wife's character. Her judgments of people and things were sure and accurate, and her charity never failed. I have compared her with hundreds of persons and my conviction remains that hers was the most perfect character I have ever met. And she was the most winningly dignified person I have ever known. Her character and disposition were of the sort that not only invite worship but command it.

She was always cheerful, and during the nine years that we spent in poverty and debt she was always able to reason me out of despair. In all that time I never knew her to utter a word of regret concerning our altered circumstances, nor did I ever know her children to do the like, for she had taught them and they drew their fortitude from her.

It was a strange combination which was wrought into one individual, so to speak, by marriage—her disposition and character and mine. She poured out her prodigal affections in caresses and in a vocabulary of endearments whose profusion was always an astonishment to me. I was born *reserved* as to endearments of speech, and caresses, and hers broke upon me as the summer waves break upon Gibraltar.

Tomorrow will be the thirty-sixth anniversary. We were married in her father's house in Elmira, New York, and went next day by train to Buffalo, along with the whole Langdon family. We were to live in Buffalo, where I was to be an editor and a part owner of the Buffalo *Express*. I knew nothing about Buffalo but I had made my household arrangements there through a friend, by letter. I had instructed him to find a boardinghouse of as respectable a character as my light salary as editor would command.

We were received at about nine o'clock at the station in Buffalo and were put into several sleighs and driven all over America, as it seemed to me—turning all the corners in the town—I freely scolding that friend of mine for securing a boardinghouse that apparently had no definite locality. But there was a conspiracy—my bride's father, Jervis Langdon, had bought and furnished a new house for us in a fashionable street, and had laid in a cook and maids and a brisk young coachman, Patrick McAleer—and we were being driven all over the city in order that one sleighful of these people could have time to go to the house and see that the gas was lighted and supper prepared.

We arrived at last, and when I entered that fairy place my indignation reached high-water mark, and I delivered my opinion to my friend for being so stupid as to put us into a boardinghouse whose terms would be far out of my reach. Then Mr. Langdon brought forward a box and took from it a deed of the house. So the comedy ended pleasantly and we sat down to supper.

The company departed about midnight and left us alone. Then Ellen, the cook, came in to get orders for the morning's marketing—and neither of us knew whether beefsteak was sold by the barrel or by the yard. We exposed our ignorance and Ellen was full of Irish delight over it. Patrick McAleer, that brisk young Irishman, came in to get his orders for next day—and that was our first glimpse of him.

It sounds easy and swift and unobstructed but that was not the way of it. It had not happened in that smooth and comfortable way. There had been a deal of courtship. There had been three or four proposals of marriage and just as many declinations.

I was roving far and wide on the lecture beat but I managed to arrive in Elmira every now and then and renew the siege. Once I dug an invitation out of my friend Charley Langdon to come and stay a week. It was a pleasant week but it had to come to an end. I was not able to invent any way to get the invitation enlarged. So at last I got ready to leave for New York.

A wagon stood outside the main gate with my trunk in it, and Barney, the coachman, in the front seat. It was eight or nine in the evening and dark. I bade good-by to the grouped family on the front porch, and Charley and I climbed into the wagon. We took our places back of the coachman on the remaining seat, which was aft toward the end of the wagon and was only a temporary arrangement and not fastened in its place; a fact which—most fortunately for me—we were not aware of. Charley was smoking. Barney touched the horse with the whip. He

made a sudden spring forward. Charley and I went over the stern of the wagon backward.

In the darkness the red bud of fire on the end of Charley's cigar described a curve through the air which I can see yet. I struck exactly on the top of my head and stood up that way for a moment, then crumpled down to the earth unconscious. It was a very good unconsciousness for a person who had not rehearsed the part. My head had struck in a dish formed by the conjunction of four cobblestones. That depression was half full of sand and this made a cushion. I got not a bruise. I was not even jolted. But I managed to be such a deadweight that it required the combined strength of Barney and Mr. Langdon and Charley to lug me into the house.

When the old family doctor arrived, he said that if I would go to bed I would be all right. I got a good three days' extension out of that adventure and it pushed my suit forward several steps. A subsequent visit completed the matter and we became engaged conditionally; the condition being that the parents should consent.

In a private talk Mr. Langdon called my attention to something I had already noticed—which was that I was an almost entirely unknown person; that no one around knew me except his son Charley, and he was too young to be a reliable judge; that I was from the other side of the continent and that only those people out there would be able to furnish me a character, in case I had one—so he asked me for references. I furnished them, and he said we would now suspend our industries and wait until he could write to those people and get answers.

In due course answers came. I was sent for and we had another private conference. I had referred him to six prominent men, among them two clergymen (these were all San Franciscans), and he himself had written to a bank cashier who had in earlier years been a Sunday-school superintendent in Elmira and whom he knew. The results were not promising. All those men were frank to a fault. They not only spoke in disapproval of me but

Opposite page, Mark Twain at his writing desk; the Hartford house; the Clemenses of Hartford

they were quite unnecessarily enthusiastic about it. One clergy-man (Stebbins) and that ex-Sunday-school superintendent (I wish I could recall his name) added to their black testimony the conviction that I would fill a drunkard's grave.

The reading of the letters being finished, there was a good deal of a pause. I couldn't think of anything to say. Mr. Langdon was apparently in the same condition. Finally he raised his hand-some head, fixed his candid eye upon me and said: "What kind of people are these? Haven't you a friend in the world?"

I said, "Apparently not."

Then he said: "I'll be your friend myself. Take the girl. I know you better than they do."

Thus dramatically and happily was my fate settled.

OUR FIRST CHILD, Langdon Clemens, was born the 7th of November, 1870, and lived twenty-two months. I was the cause of the child's illness. His mother trusted him to my care and I took him for a long drive in an open barouche for an airing. It was a raw, cold morning but he was well wrapped about with furs. No harm should have come to him. But I dropped into a reverie and forgot about my charge. The furs fell away and exposed his legs. By and by the coachman noticed this and I arranged the wraps again, but it was too late. The child was almost frozen. I hurried home with him, aghast at what I had done. I have always felt shame for that morning's work and have not allowed myself to think of it when I could help it. I doubt if I had the courage to make confession at that time. I think it most likely that I have never confessed until now.

Susy was born the 19th of March, 1872. The summer seasons of her childhood were spent at Quarry Farm on the hills east of Elmira, New York; Quarry Farm was the home of my wife's sister, Mrs. Theodore Crane, and we visited there a great deal. The other seasons of the year were spent at our home in Hartford, Connecticut. (We removed to Hartford in October 1871 and presently built a house.)

Like other children, Susy was blithe and happy, fond of play; *un*like the average of children, she was at times much given to retiring within herself and trying to search out the hidden meanings of human existence. As a child aged seven she was oppressed and perplexed by the maddening repetition of the stock incidents of our race's fleeting sojourn here, just as the same thing has oppressed and perplexed maturer minds from the beginning of time. A myriad of men are born; they labor and struggle for bread; they squabble and scold and fight; then age creeps upon them; and at length they die, and vanish from a world where they were of no consequence. "Mamma, what is it all for?" asked Susy, preliminarily stating the above details in her own halting language, after long brooding over them in the nursery.

A year later she was groping her way alone through another sunless bog. For a week, her mother had not been able to go to the nursery at the child's prayer hour. She spoke of it—was sorry for it and said she would come tonight and hear Susy pray, as before. Noticing that the child wished to respond but was evidently troubled, she asked what the difficulty was. Susy explained that Miss Foote (the governess) had been teaching her about the Indians and their religious beliefs, whereby it appeared that they had not only a god, but several. This had set Susy to thinking. As a result of this thinking she said she could not now pray "in the same way" as she had formerly done.

"Mamma," she said, "the Indians believed they knew, but now we know they were wrong. By and by it can turn out that we are wrong. So now I only pray that there may be a God and a heaven—or something better."

I wrote down this pathetic prayer at the time in a record which we kept of the children's sayings. My reverence for it has grown with the years. Its untaught grace and simplicity are a child's, but the wisdom and the pathos of it are of all the ages.

I will throw in a note or two here touching the time when Susy was seventeen. She had written a play modeled upon Greek lines, and she and Clara and Margaret Warner and other young comrades had played it to a charmed houseful of friends in our house in Hartford. Charles Dudley Warner and his brother, George, were present. They were full of praises of the workmanship of the play, and George came over next morning to talk with Susy. The result of it was this verdict: "She is the most interesting person I have ever known, of either sex."

From her earliest days, as I have indicated, Susy was given to examining things and thinking them out by herself. She was not trained to this; it was the make of her mind. In Munich, when she was six years old, she was harassed by a recurrent dream, in which a ferocious bear figured. She came out of the dream each time sorely frightened and crying. She set herself the task of analyzing this dream. The reasons of it? The purpose of it? No—the moral aspect of it. Her verdict, arrived at after candid and searching investigation, exposed it to the charge of being one-sided and unfair: for (as she worded it) *she* was "never the one that ate, but always the one that was eaten."

Susy backed her good judgment in matters of morals with conduct to match. When she was six and her sister Clara four, the pair were quarrelsome. Punishments were tried to break up this custom—these failed. Then rewards were tried. A day without a quarrel brought candy. The children were their own witnesses—each for or against her own self.

Once Susy took the candy, hesitated, then returned it with a suggestion that she was not fairly entitled to it. Clara kept hers, so here was a conflict of evidence—one evidence *for* a quarrel and one against it. But the better witness of the two was on the affirmative side and the quarrel stood proved and no candy due to either side. There seemed to be no defense for Clara—yet there was and Susy furnished it. She said, "I don't know whether she felt wrong in *her* heart. I didn't feel right in *my* heart."

There was no way to convict Clara now, except to put her on the stand again and review her evidence. Then she was given the benefit of doubt and acquitted; which was just as well, for in the meantime she had eaten the candy anyway.

Sometimes while Susy was still a child her speech fell into quaint and strikingly expressive forms. Once—aged nine or ten—she came to her mother's room when her sister Jean* was a baby and said Jean was crying in the nursery. Her mother asked, "Is she crying hard?"—meaning cross, ugly.

"Well, no, Mamma. It is a weary, lonesome cry."

It is a pleasure to me to recall various incidents which reveal

---

*Jean Clemens, born in 1880, was eight years younger than Susy.

A child's crib
in the nursery at Hartford

the delicacies of feeling which were so considerable a part of Susy's budding character. Such a revelation came once in a way which, while creditable to her heart, was defective in another direction. She was in her eleventh year then. Her mother had been making Christmas purchases and she allowed Susy to see the presents for Patrick's children. Among these was a handsome sled for Jimmy, on which a stag was painted; also in gilt capitals the word DEER. Susy was joyous over everything until she came to this sled. Then she became silent—yet the sled was the choicest of all the gifts. Her mother was surprised and disappointed, and said: "Why, Susy, doesn't it please you? Isn't it fine?"

Susy hesitated. Then being urged, she said haltingly:

"Well, Mamma, it *is* fine and of course it *did* cost a good deal—but—but—why should that be mentioned?"

Seeing that she was not understood, she reluctantly pointed to the word DEER. It was her spelling that was at fault, not her heart. She had inherited both from her mother.

CHAPTER II

When Susy was thirteen and was a slender little maid with plaited tails of copper-tinged brown hair down her back and was perhaps the busiest bee in the household hive, by reason of the manifold studies, exercises and recreations she had to attend to, she secretly and of her own motion added another task to her labors—the writing of a biography of me.

She did this work in her bedroom at night and kept her record hidden. After a little her mother discovered it, filched it and let me see it; then told Susy what she had done and how pleased I was and how proud. I remember that time with a deep pleasure. I had had compliments before but none that touched me like this. As I read it *now*, after all these many years, it is still a king's message to me and brings me the same dear surprise it brought me then—with the pathos added of the thought that the eager and hasty hand that scrawled it will not touch mine again.

It is quite evident that several times, at breakfast and dinner, in those long-past days, I was posing for the biography. In fact, I clearly remember that I *was* doing that—and that Susy detected it. I remember saying a very smart thing, with a good deal of an air, at breakfast one morning and that Susy later observed privately to her mother that Papa was doing that for the biography.

I cannot bring myself to change any line or word in Susy's sketch of me but will introduce passages from it now and then just as they came in. The spelling is frequently desperate but it was Susy's and it shall stand. I love it and cannot profane it.

She began the biography in 1885, when I was in my fiftieth year, and she in her fourteenth. She begins in this way:

> We are a very happy family. We consist of Papa, Mamma, Jean, Clara and me. It is papa I am writing about, and I shall have no trouble in not knowing what to say about him, as he is a *very* striking character.
>
> Papa's appearance has been described many times, but very incorrectly. He has beautiful gray hair, not any too thick or any too long, but just right; a Roman nose, which greatly improves the beauty of his features; kind blue eyes and a small mustache. His complexion is very fair, and he doesn't ware a beard. He is a very good man and a very funny one. He *has* got a temper, but we all of us have in this family. He does tell perfectly delightful stories. Clara and I used to sit on each arm of his chair and listen while he told us stories about the pictures on the wall.

I remember the storytelling days vividly. They were a difficult and exacting audience—those little creatures.

Along one side of the library, in our Hartford home, there were bookshelves joining the mantelpiece on both sides. On these shelves and on the mantelpiece stood various ornaments. At one end of the procession was a framed oil painting of a cat's head; at the other end was the head of a beautiful young girl, life size—called Emmeline, an impressionist watercolor. Between the one picture and the other there were twelve or fifteen bric-a-brac things. Every now and then the children required me to construct a romance—not a moment's preparation permitted—and into that romance I had to get all that bric-a-brac and the pictures. I had to start always with the cat and finish with Emmeline, and it was not permissible to introduce a bric-a-brac ornament into the story out of its place in the procession.

As romancer to the children I had a hard time. If they brought me a picture in a magazine and required me to build a story to it,

A drawing by one of the Clemens children

they would cover the rest of the page with their pudgy hands to keep me from stealing an idea from it. The stories had to be absolutely original. Sometimes the children furnished me simply a character or two, or a dozen, and required me to start out at once on that basis and deliver those characters up to a vigorous life of crime. If they heard of an unfamiliar animal or anything like that, I was pretty sure to have to deal with those things in the next romance. Once Clara required me to build a tale out of a plumber and a "bawgun strictor." She didn't know what a boa constrictor was until he developed in the tale.

Papa's favorite game is billiards, and when he is tired and wishes to rest himself he stays up all night and plays billiards, it seems to rest his head. He smokes a great deal almost incessantly. He has the mind of an author exactly, some of the simplest things he can't understand. Our burglar alarm is often out of order, and papa had been obliged to take the mahogany room off from the alarm, because the burglar alarm had been in the habit of ringing even when the mahogany-room window was closed. At length he thought that perhaps the burglar alarm might be in order, and he decided to try and see; accordingly he put it on and then went down and opened the window; consequently the alarm bell rang. Papa went despairingly upstairs and said to mamma, "Livy the mahogany room won't go on. I have just opened the window to see."

"Why, Youth," mamma replied. "If you've opened the window, why of course the alarm will ring!"

"That's what I've opened it for, why I just went down to see if it would ring!"

Mamma tried to explain to papa that when he wanted to go and see whether the alarm would ring while the window was closed he *mustn't* go and open the window—but in vain, papa couldn't understand, and got very impatient with mamma for trying to make him believe an impossible thing true.

Mark Twain's billiard table, Hartford

This is a frank biographer; she uses no sandpaper on me. I have to this day the same dull head in the matter of conundrums. Complexities annoy me. I cannot get far in the reading of the simplest contract—with its "parties of the first part" and "parties of the second part"—before my temper is all gone. Susy is right in her estimate. I can't understand things.

That word "Youth," as the reader has already guessed, was my wife's name for me. It was gently satirical but also affectionate. As for that burglar alarm which Susy mentions, it led a gay and careless life. All the windows and doors in the house were connected with it, and it was generally out of order. However, we quickly found out that it was fooling us, buzzing its bloodcurdling alarm; then we would send for the electrician. When the repairs were finished we would set the alarm again and reestablish our confidence in it. It never did any real business except once. Just that time it performed admirably. It let fly about two o'clock one black March morning and I turned out promptly. The bathroom door was on my side of the bed. I stepped in there, turned up the gas, looked at the annunciator, turned off the alarm—so far as the door indicated was concerned—thus stopping the racket. Then I came to bed. Mrs. Clemens opened the debate:

"What was it?"

"It was the cellar door."

"Was it a burglar, do you think?"

"Yes," I said, "of course it was."

"What do you suppose he wants?"

"I suppose he wants jewelry, but he is not acquainted with the house and he thinks it is in the cellar. If he had had sagacity enough to inquire, I could have told him we kept nothing down there but coal and vegetables. Still, it may be that what he really wants *is* coal and vegetables. On the whole, I think it is vegetables he is after."

"Are you going down to see?"

"No. I could not be of any assistance; I don't know where the things are."

"But suppose he comes up to the ground floor!"

"That's all right. We shall know it the minute he opens a door on that floor. It will set off the alarm."

Just then the terrific buzzing broke out again. I said: "He has arrived. I told you he would. I know all about burglars and their ways. They are systematic people."

I went into the bathroom to see if I was right, and I was. I shut off the dining room on the annunciator and stopped the buzzing and came back to bed. My wife said:

"What do you suppose he is after now?"

I said, "I think he has got all the vegetables he wants and is coming up for napkin rings and odds and ends for the wife and children. They all have families—burglars have—and they are always thoughtful of them. And then he is probably after ceramics and bric-a-brac and such things. If he knows the house he knows that that is all that he can find on the dining-room floor."

She said, with strong interest, "Suppose he comes up here!"

I said, "It is all right. He will give us notice."

"What shall we do then?"

"Climb out of the window."

She said, a little restively, "Well, what is the use of a burglar alarm for us?"

"You have seen, dear heart, that it has been useful up to the present moment, and I have explained to you how it will be useful after he gets up here."

That was the end of it. He didn't ring any more alarms.

Presently I said, "He is disappointed, I think. He has gone off with the vegetables and the bric-a-brac."

We went to sleep and at a quarter before eight in the morning I was out and hurrying, for I was to take the 8:29 train for New York. I found the gas burning brightly all over the first floor. My new overcoat was gone; my old umbrella was gone; my new patent-leather shoes were gone. A large window at the rear of the house was standing wide. I passed out through it and tracked the burglar down the hill without difficulty, because he had blazed his progress with imitation-silver napkin rings and my umbrella, and other things he had disapproved of; and I went back in triumph and proved to my wife that he *was* a disappointed burglar. I had suspected he would be, from the start, and from his not coming up to our floor to get human beings.

> Papa has a peculiar gait we like, it seems just to sute him, but most people do not; he always walks up and down the room while thinking and between each coarse at meals.

A lady distantly related to us came to visit us once in those days; she came to stay a week, but left the next morning. Later we found out what the trouble was. It was my tramping up and down between the courses. She conceived the idea that I could not stand her society.

> Papa is very fond of animals particularly of cats, we had a dear little gray kitten once that he named "Lazy" (papa always wears gray to match his hair and eyes) and he would carry him around on his shoulder, it was a mighty pretty sight! the gray cat sound asleep against papa's gray coat and hair. The names that he has given our different cats, are realy remarkably funny, they are namely Stray Kit, Abner, Fraeulein, Lazy, Bufalo Bill, Soapy Sall, Sour Mash, and Pestilence and Famine.

At one time when the children were small we had a very black mother cat named Satan, and Satan had a small black offspring named Sin. Pronouns were a difficulty for the children. Little Clara came in one day, her black eyes snapping with indignation, and said, "Papa, Satan ought to be punished. She is out there at the greenhouse and there she stays and stays, and his kitten is downstairs, crying."

> Papa uses very strong language, but I have an idea not nearly so strong as when he first married mamma. He said the other day, "I am a mugwump and a mugwump is pure from the marrow out." (Papa knows that I am writing this biography of him, and he said this for it.) He doesn't like to go to church, why I never understood, until just now, he told us the other day that he couldn't bear to hear any one talk but himself, but that he could listen to himself talk for hours without getting tired, of course he said this in joke, but I've no dought it was founded on truth.

Susy's remark about my strong language troubles me. All through the first ten years of my married life I kept a constant watch upon my tongue while in the house, and went outside when circumstances were too much for me. I prized my wife's respect and approval above all the rest of the human race's respect and approval. I dreaded the day when she should discover that I was but a whited sepulcher partly freighted with suppressed language.

But of course in due time accident exposed me to her. As for the children, once they were present at breakfast—Clara, aged six, and Susy, eight—and the mother made a remark about not using such strong language; guarded because she did not wish the children to suspect anything. Both children broke out in one voice with this comment: "Why, Mamma, Papa uses it!"

I was astonished. I asked, "How did you know, you little rascals?"

"Oh," they said, "we often listen over the balusters when you are explaining things to George."

A caricature by Max Beerbohm

One of papa's latest books is "The Prince and the Pauper" and it is unquestionably the best book he has ever written, some people want him to keep to his old style, some gentleman wrote him, "I enjoyed Huckleberry Finn immensely and am glad to see that you have returned to your old style." That enoyed me greatly, because it trobles me to have so few people realy know papa, they think of Mark Twain as a humorist joking at everything; and I have wanted papa to write a book that would reveal something of his kind sympathetic nature, and "The Prince and the Pauper" partly does it. The book is full of lovely charming ideas, and oh the language! It is *perfect*.

The children always helped their mother to edit my books in manuscript. She would sit on the porch at the farm and read aloud, with her pencil in her hand. The children would keep an alert and suspicious eye upon her, for the belief was well grounded in them that whenever she came across a particularly satisfactory passage she would strike it out. Their suspicions were well founded. The passages which were so satisfactory to them always had an element of strength in them which sorely needed modification or expurgation, and was always sure to get it at their mother's hand.

For my own entertainment and to enjoy the protests of the children, I often abused my editor's innocent confidence. I often interlarded remarks of an atrocious character purposely to achieve the children's brief delight and then see the remorseless pencil do its work, and I often joined my supplications to the children's for mercy. They were deceived and so was their mother. It was three against one and most unfair. But it was very delightful. Now and then we gained the victory and there was much rejoicing. Then I privately struck the passage out myself. It had served its purpose; it had furnished three of us with good entertainment.

Clara and I are sure that papa played the trick on Grandma, about the whipping, that is related in "The Adventures of Tom Sawyer": "Hand me that switch." The switch hovered in the air, the peril was desperate—"My, look behind you Aunt!" The old lady whirled around. The lad fled on the instant, scrambling up the high fence and disappeared over it.

Susy and Clara were quite right about that.

Then Susy says:

> And we know papa played "Hookey" all the time. And how readily would papa pretend to be dying so as not to have to go to school!

These exposures are searching but they are just.

> Grandma couldn't make papa go to school, so she let him go into a printing-office to learn the trade. He did so, and gradually picked up enough education to enable him to do about as well as those who were more studious in early life.

It is noticeable that Susy does not get overheated when she is complimenting me but maintains a proper judicial and biographical calm. It is noticeable also that she distributes compliment and criticism with a fair and even hand.

CHAPTER 12

ABOUT 1872 I WROTE another book, *Roughing It*. I had published *The Innocents Abroad* on a five-percent royalty, which would amount to about twenty-two cents per volume. Proposals were coming in now from several other good houses. One offered fifteen-percent royalty; another offered to give me *all* of the profits and be content with the advertisement which the book would furnish the house.

I sent for Elisha Bliss from the American Publishing Company, and he came to Elmira. If I had known as much about book publishing then as I know now, I would have required of Bliss seventy-five or eighty percent of the profits above cost of manufacture. But I knew nothing about the business. I told Bliss I did not wish to leave his corporation and that I did not want extravagant terms. I said I thought I ought to have half the profit above cost of manufacture and he said with enthusiasm that that was exactly right, exactly right.

He went to his hotel and drew the contract and brought it to the house in the afternoon. I found a difficulty in it. It did not name "half profits," but named a seven-and-a-half-percent royalty instead. I asked him to explain that. He said he had put in a royalty to simplify the matter—that seven-and-a-half-percent royalty represented fully half the profit and a little more, up to a sale of a hundred thousand copies, that after that the publishing company's half would be a shade superior to mine.

I was a little doubtful, and asked him if he could swear to that. He promptly put up his hand and made oath to it.

It took nine or ten years to find out that that was a false oath and that seven and a half percent did not represent one-fourth of the profits. In the meantime I had published several books with Bliss and had been handsomely swindled on all of them.

In 1879 I came home from Europe with a book ready for the press, *A Tramp Abroad*. Bliss came to the house to discuss the book. I said that I was not satisfied about those royalties, that this time he must put the half profit in the contract and make no mention of royalties—otherwise I would take the book elsewhere. He said he was perfectly willing to put it in, and that if his directors opposed it he would withdraw from the concern and publish the book himself—and he pointed out a detail which I had overlooked, to wit: the contract was with Elisha Bliss, a private individual, and the American Publishing Company was not mentioned in it.

He told me afterward that he took the contract to the directors and said that he would turn it over to the company for one-fourth of the profits of the book together with an increase of salary for himself, and that if these terms were not satisfactory he would leave the company and publish the book himself, whereupon the directors granted his demands. Six weeks before the book was issued Bliss told the truth once, to see how it would taste, but it overstrained him and he died.

When the book had been out three months there was an annual meeting of the stockholders of the company and I was present, as a half partner in the book. A statement of the company's business was read and to me it was a revelation. Sixty-four thousand copies of the book had been sold. In 1872 Bliss had made out to me that a seven-and-a-half-percent royalty, a trifle over twenty cents a copy, represented one-half of the profits, whereas it hardly represented a sixth of the profits.

Well, Bliss was dead and I couldn't settle with him for his swindlings. He has been dead a quarter of a century now. My bitterness against him has faded away. I feel only compassion for him and if I could send him a fan I would.

When the balance sheets exposed to me the rascalities which I had suffered at the hands of the American Publishing Company I delivered a lecture to the conspirators—meaning the directors.

My opportunity was now come to level up matters with the publishing company but I didn't see it, of course. I knew all about that house now and I ought to have remained with it. But I didn't. I removed my purity from that atmosphere and carried my next book to James R. Osgood of Boston. That book was *Life on the Mississippi*. Osgood was to manufacture the book at my expense, publish it by subscription and charge me a royalty for his services.

Osgood was one of the dearest human beings to be found on the planet, but he knew nothing about subscription publishing and he made a mighty botch of it. He was a sociable creature and we played much billiards and daily had a good time. In the meantime his clerks ran our business for us. That book was a long time getting built; and when at last the final draft was made upon my purse I realized that I had paid out fifty-six thousand dollars. It took a year to get the fifty-six thousand back into my pocket, and not many dollars followed it. So this first effort of mine to transact that kind of business on my own hook was a failure.

Osgood tried again. He published *The Prince and the Pauper*. He made a beautiful book of it but all the profit I got out of it was seventeen thousand dollars. I should have continued with Osgood after his failure with *The Prince and the Pauper* because I liked him so well, but he failed and I had to go elsewhere.

MEANTIME I HAD been having an adventure on the outside. An old friend of mine unloaded a patent on me, price fifteen thousand dollars. It was worthless and he had been losing money on it, but I did not know those particulars because he neglected to mention them. He said that if I would buy the patent he would do the manufacturing for me. So I took him up.

Then began a cash outgo of five hundred dollars a month. That raven flew out of the Ark regularly every thirty days but it never got back with anything and the dove didn't report for duty. After a time I relieved my friend and put the patent into the hands of Charles L. Webster, who had married a niece of mine and seemed a capable young fellow. At a salary of fifteen hundred a year he continued to send the raven out monthly, with the same old result to a penny.

At last, when I had lost forty-two thousand dollars on that patent I gave it away to a man whom I had long detested and whose family I desired to ruin. Then I looked around for other adventures. That same friend was ready with another patent. I spent ten thousand dollars on it in eight months. Then I tried to give that patent to the man whose family I was after. By this time he was experienced. He wouldn't take it and I had to let it lapse. Then I took some stock in a Hartford company which proposed to revolutionize everything with a new kind of steam pulley. The steam pulley pulled thirty-two thousand dollars out of my pocket in sixteen months, then went to pieces and I was alone in the world again, without an occupation.

But I found one. I invented a scrapbook—and if I do say it, it was the only rational scrapbook the world has ever seen. I patented it and put it in the hands of that old friend who had originally interested me in patents and he made a good deal of money out of it. But by and by, just when I was about to begin to receive a share of the money myself, his firm failed.

There were other speculations as the months drifted by, but by the spring of 1877 I was the burnt child. I wanted nothing further to do with speculations. General Hawley sent for me to come to the *Courant* office. There was a young fellow there who said that he had been a reporter but that he was in another business now. He was with a man named Graham Bell and was agent for a new invention called the telephone. He wanted me to take some stock in it. I declined, I said I didn't want anything more to do with wildcat speculation. Then he offered the stock to me at twenty-five. I said I didn't want it at any price. He became eager—insisted that I take five hundred dollars' worth. He said he would sell me as much as I wanted for five hundred dollars—offered to let me gather it up in my hands and measure it in a plug hat. But I was the burnt child and I resisted all these temptations, resisted them easily, and went off.

About the end of the year I put up a telephone wire from my house down to the *Courant* office, the only telephone wire in town, and the *first* one ever used in a private house in the world.

That young man couldn't sell *me* any stock but he sold a few hatfuls of it to an old dry-goods clerk in

Hartford for five thousand dollars. That was that clerk's whole fortune. He had been half a lifetime saving it. It is strange how foolish people can be and what ruinous risks they can take when they want to get rich in a hurry. I was sorry for that man when I heard about it. I thought I might have saved him if I had had an opportunity to tell him about my experiences.

We sailed for Europe on the 10th of April, 1878. We were gone fourteen months and when we got back one of the first things we saw was that clerk driving around in a sumptuous barouche with liveried servants all over it—and his telephone stock was emptying greenbacks into his premises at such a rate that he had to handle them with a shovel. It is strange the way the ignorant and inexperienced so often and so undeservedly succeed when the informed and the experienced fail.

CHAPTER 13

As I HAVE already remarked, I had imported my nephew-in-law, Charles L. Webster, from the village of Dunkirk, New York, to conduct that original first patent-right business for me, at a salary of fifteen hundred dollars. That enterprise had lost forty-two thousand dollars for me, so I thought this a favorable time to close it up. I proposed to be my own publisher now and let young Webster do the work. He thought he ought to have twenty-five hundred dollars a year while he was learning the trade. I took a day or two to consider the matter. Then early in 1884 I erected Webster into a firm—a firm entitled Charles L. Webster & Co., Publishers—and installed him in a couple of offices on the second floor of a building below Union Square in New York.

For assistants he had a girl and a masculine clerk of about eight-hundred-dollar size, and for a while he had another helper. This was a man who had long been in

I GATE SCENE.
II INTERVIEW.
III GATE SCENE II.
IV Lady Jane Grey & Taupy
V Guild Hall.
VI. The Prynce & Miles Hendon
VII. Coronation

Above, a program printed on the back of ticket for the production of "The Prince and the Pauper"; right, a scene from the play performed in the house at Hartford, Clara, left, Susy, right.

the subscription-book business, and who was able to teach it to Webster. I handed Webster a competent capital and along with it I handed him the manuscript of *Huckleberry Finn*. Webster's function was general agent. It was his business to appoint subagents throughout the country. At that time there were sixteen of these subagencies. They had canvassers under them who did the canvassing.

Before ever any of these minor details that I am talking about had entered into being, the careful Webster had suggested that a contract be drawn before we made any real move. That seemed sane, though I should not have thought of it myself. So Webster got his own lawyer to draw the contract. I was coming to admire Webster and at this point one of those gushing generosities surged up in my system, and I tried to confer upon Webster a tenth interest in the business in addition to his salary. Webster declined—with thanks, of course. That raised him another step in my admiration. I knew perfectly well that I was offering him a partnership interest which would pay him two or three times his salary within the next nine months, but he didn't know that. He was coldly discounting all my prophecies about *Huckleberry Finn*'s high commercial value. And this was new evidence that in Webster I had found a jewel, a man who would not get excited; a man who would not lose his head; a cautious man.

The contract was drawn by a young lawyer from Dunkirk, New York, which produced him as well as Webster and has not yet gotten over the strain. Whitford was good-natured, obliging and endowed with a stupidity which by the least little stretch would go around the globe four times and tie.

That first contract was all right. There was nothing the matter with it. It placed all obligations, all expenses, all liability, all responsibilities upon *me*, where they belonged.

That autumn I went off with George W. Cable on a four months' reading campaign in the East and West—the last platform work which I was ever to do in my own country. Meanwhile Webster was successful with *Huckleberry Finn* and a year later handed me the firm's check for fifty-four thousand five hundred dollars, which included the fifteen thousand dollars capital which I had originally handed to him.

Once more I experienced a new birth. I have been born more times than anybody except Krishna, I suppose.

Webster conceived the idea that he had discovered me to the world but he was reasonably modest about it. He did much less cackling over his egg than Webb and Bliss had done.

IT HAD NEVER BEEN my intention to publish anybody's books but my own. An accident diverted me from this wise purpose. That was General Grant's memorable book. One night in November 1884 I had been lecturing in Chickering Hall, in New York City, and was walking homeward. It was a rainy night and, in the midst of a black gulf between lamps, two dim figures stepped out of a doorway in front of me. I heard one of them say, "Do you know General Grant has determined to write and publish his memoirs? He said so today."

That was all I heard—just those words—and I thought it great luck that I heard them.

In the morning I went and called on General Grant, whom I had originally met in Washington in 1866. I found him in his library with Colonel Fred Grant, his son. The General said in substance this: "Sit down and keep quiet until I sign a contract" —and added that it was for a book he was going to write.

Fred Grant was reading the contract. He found it satisfactory and his father took up the pen. It might have been better for me, possibly, if I had let him alone but I didn't. I said, "Don't sign. Let Colonel Fred read it to me first."

Colonel Fred read it and I said I was glad I had come in time to interfere. The Century Company was proposing to pay the General ten-percent royalty. This was nonsense—but the proposal had its source in ignorance, not dishonesty. The great Century Company knew all about magazine publishing. But at that time they had had no experience of subscription publishing.

I explained that these terms would never do; that they were unfair. I said, "Strike out the ten percent and put twenty in its place. Better still, put seventy-five percent of the net returns in its place." The General demurred. He said they would never pay those terms.

I said that that was a matter of no consequence, since there was not a reputable publisher in America who would not be very glad to pay them. The General still shook his head. He challenged me to name the publisher that would be willing to have this deed perpetrated upon him. I named the American Publishing Company of Hartford. He asked if I could prove my position. I said I could furnish the proof by telegraph in six hours.

The General still stood out. But Fred Grant was beginning to be persuaded. He proposed that the Century contract be laid on the table for twenty-four hours and that the situation be examined. He said that this thing was not a matter of sentiment; it was a matter of business. His remark about sentiment had a bearing. The reason was this. The broking firm of Grant and Ward had swindled General Grant out of every penny he had in the world. And at a time when he had not known where to turn for bread, Roswell Smith, head of the Century Company, had offered him five hundred dollars per article for four magazine articles about the Civil War. The offer had come to the despairing old hero like the fabled straw to the drowning man. He had accepted it with gratitude. The articles were easily worth ten thousand dollars apiece but he didn't know it.

He was now most loath to desert these benefactors of his. If I remember rightly, his first article lifted the Century's subscription list from a hundred thousand copies to two hundred and twenty thousand. This made the Century's advertisement pages, for that month, worth more than double the money they had ever commanded. And the doubled subscription list established in that month was destined to continue for years.

I began to tout for the American Publishing Company. I argued that the company had been first in the field as applicants for a volume of Grant memoirs and that perhaps they ought to have a chance at a bid. This seemed to be news to General Grant. But I reminded him that once during more prosperous days I had called upon him in his private office one day and begged him to write his memoirs and give them to the American Publishing Company. He had declined at the time, saying he was not in need of money and that he was not a literary person.

I think we left the contract matter to stew for that time and took it up again the next morning. At our second conference, the General exhibited some of the modesty which was so large a feature of his nature. General Sherman had published his *Memoirs* with Scribner's, and that publication had been a notable event. General Grant said: "Sherman told me that his profits on that book were twenty-five thousand dollars. Do you believe I could get as much out of my book?"

I said I not only believed but I *knew* that he would achieve a vastly greater profit than that.

The General had his doubts. He said he had already applied a test. He said he had offered to sell his memoirs out-and-out to Roswell Smith for twenty-five thousand dollars and that the proposition had so frightened Smith that he hardly had breath enough left to decline with.

Then I had an idea. It suddenly occurred to me that I was a publisher myself. I said, "Sell *me* the memoirs, General. I am a publisher. I will pay double price. Take my check for fifty thousand dollars now and let's draw the contract."

General Grant said he wouldn't hear of such a thing. He said if I should fail to get the money back out of his book— He stopped there and said he simply would not consent to help a friend run any such risk.

Then I said, "Give me the book on the terms which I have already suggested that you make with the Century people. I know it to be a perfectly safe guess that your book will sell six hundred thousand volumes. At that rate the clear profit to you will be half a million dollars and the clear profit to me a hundred thousand."

We had a long discussion over the matter. Finally General Grant telegraphed for his particular friend, George W. Childs of the Philadelphia *Public Ledger*, to come and furnish an opinion. Childs came. I convinced him that Webster's publishing machinery was ample and in good order. Then Childs delivered the verdict, "Give the book to Clemens." Colonel Fred Grant endorsed the verdict. So the contract was drawn and signed and Webster took hold of his new job at once.

BY MY EXISTING CONTRACT with Webster he merely had a salary of twenty-five hundred dollars a year. He had declined to accept, gratis, an interest in the business. I now offered him again, gratis, a tenth share in the business—the contract as to other details to remain as before. Then, as a counterproposition, he modestly offered this: that his salary be increased to thirty-five hundred dollars a year; that he have ten percent of the profits accruing from the Grant book, and that I furnish all the capital required at seven percent.

I said I should be satisfied with this arrangement.

Then he called in his pal, Whitford, who drew the contract. I couldn't understand the contract—I never could understand any contract—and I asked my brother-in-law, General Langdon, a trained businessman, to understand it for me. He read it and said it was all right. So we signed it. I was to find out later that the contract gave Webster ten percent of the profits on the Grant book *and* ten-percent interest in the profits of the whole business—but not any interest in such losses as might occur.

The news went forth that General Grant was going to write his memoirs and that the firm of Charles L. Webster & Co. would publish them. The announcement produced a sensation throughout the country. On the one day, young Webster was as unknown as the unborn babe. The next day his name was in every paper in the United States. He was young, he was human, and he naturally mistook this transient notoriety for fame. His juvenile joy in his new grandeur was a pretty spectacle to see. The first thing he did was to secure quarters better suited to the most distinguished publisher in the country.

His new quarters were on the second or third floor of a tall building which fronted on Union Square, a commercially aristocratic locality. His previous quarters had consisted of two good-sized rooms. His new ones occupied the whole floor. What Webster really needed was a cubbyhole; this cubbyhole for office work. He needed no storage rooms, no cellars. The printers and binders of the great memoir took care of storage for us. Conspicuous quarters were not needed for that mighty book; you couldn't have hidden General Grant's publisher where the agent and the canvasser could not find him. However, these were impressive quarters—as impressive as nakedness long drawn out could be, and I suggested that we put up a protecting sign inside the door: "Come in. It is not a rope walk."

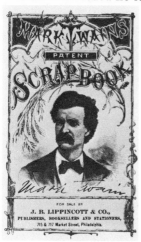

Mark Twain's scrapbook

It was a mistake to deal in sarcasms with Webster. He hadn't a single intellectual weapon and could not fight back.

He had one defect which particularly exasperated me, because I didn't have it myself. When a matter was mentioned of which he was ignorant, he not only would not protect himself by remarking that he was not acquainted with the matter, but he would say something intended to deceive the hearers into the notion that he knew something about that subject himself. Once in a drawing-room company some talk sprang up about George Eliot and her literature. Soon Webster uttered with tranquil complacency: "I've never read any of his books, on account of prejudice."

Before we had become fairly settled in the new quarters, Webster had suggested that we abolish the existing contract and make a new one. Very well, it was done. Under the preceding contracts Webster had been my paid servant; under the new one I was his slave, and without salary. I owned nine-tenths of the business, I furnished all the capital. I shouldered all the losses, I was responsible for everything, but Webster was sole master. This new condition and my sarcasms changed the atmosphere. I could no longer give orders as before. I could not even make a suggestion with any likelihood of its acceptance.

General Grant was a sick man but he wrought upon his memoirs like a well one and made steady and sure progress.

Webster throned himself in the rope walk and issued a summons to the sixteen general agents to come from the sixteen quarters of the United States and sign contracts. They came. Webster delivered the law to them as from Mount Sinai. They kept their temper wonderfully, signed contracts and departed. Ordinarily they would have resented the young man's arrogance but this was not an ordinary case. The contracts were worth to each agent a good many thousands of dollars.

Whitford was always at Webster's elbow. Webster was afraid to do anything without legal advice. He could have all the legal advice he wanted, because he had now hired Whitford and was paying him ten thousand dollars a year out of my pocket.

This is not a time nor a place to damn Webster, yet it must be done. It is a duty. Let us proceed. I am not alive. I am dead. If I were alive I should be writing an autobiography on the usual plan. I should be feeling just as malicious toward Webster—but instead of expressing it honestly I should be trying to conceal it: trying to swindle the reader, who would still read the malice between the lines. Nothing worse will happen if I let my malice have frank and free expression. I am expecting my future editors to suppress all such chapters in early editions of this book, until all whom they could pain shall be in their graves. But after that, let them be published. It is my desire, and at that distant date they can do no harm.

MEANWHILE, AS I HAVE SAID, General Grant made steady progress upon his memoirs. Whenever galley proofs or revises went to the General a set came also to me. General Grant was aware of this. Sometimes I referred to the proofs casually but entered into no particulars concerning them. By and by I learned through a member of the household that he was disturbed because I had never expressed an opinion as to the literary quality of the memoirs. It was also suggested that a word of encouragement from me would be a help to him.

I was as much surprised as Columbus's cook would have been to learn that Columbus wanted his opinion as to how Columbus was doing his navigating. It could not have occurred to me that General Grant could have any use for anybody's assistance or encouragement in any work which he might undertake. He was the most modest of men and this was another instance of it. It was a great compliment that he should care for my opinion and I took the earliest opportunity to diplomatically turn the conversation in that direction.

By chance, I had been comparing the memoirs with Caesar's "Commentaries" and was qualified to deliver judgment. I was able to say in all sincerity that the same high merits distinguished both books—clarity of statement, directness, unpretentiousness and fairness toward friend and foe alike. I placed the two books side by side upon the same high level and I still think that they belonged there. I learned afterward that General Grant was pleased with this verdict. It shows that he was just a man, just a human being, just an author. An author values a compliment even when it comes from a source of doubtful competency.

General Grant wrought heroically with his pen while his disease made steady inroads upon his life, and at last his work stood completed. He was moved to Mount McGregor, near Saratoga, New York, and there his strength passed gradually away. Toward the last he was not able to speak, but used a pencil and small slips of paper when he needed to say anything.

I went there to see him once toward the end, and he asked me with his pencil, and evidently with anxiety, if there was a prospect that his book would make something for his family.

I said that the canvass for it was progressing vigorously, that subscriptions were coming in fast, that the campaign was not half completed yet—but that if it should stop where it was there would be two hundred thousand dollars coming to his family. He expressed his gratification, with his pencil.

General Grant died at Mount McGregor on the 23rd of July, 1885. In September or October the memoirs went to press. The book was in sets of two volumes—priced nine dollars in cloth. It was issued on the 10th of December and I turned out to be a competent prophet. In the beginning I had told General Grant that his book would sell six hundred thousand single volumes and that is what happened. It sold three hundred thousand sets. The first check that went to Mrs. Grant was for two hundred thousand dollars; the next one, a few months

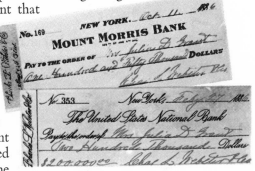

Royalty checks issued to Grant's widow

later, was for a hundred and fifty thousand. In the aggregate the book paid Mrs. Grant something like half a million dollars.

Webster was in his glory. In his obscure days his hat was number six and a quarter; in these latter days he was not able to get his head into a barrel. He loved to descant upon the wonders of the book. He liked to go into the statistics. Of course he thought it was *he* that sold the book; he thought that General Grant's great name helped but he regarded himself as the main reason of the book's prodigious success.

LET ME TRY to bring this painful business to a close. One of the things which poisoned Webster's days and nights was the aggravating circumstances that whereas he, Charles L. Webster, was the great publisher—the greatest of publishers—and my name did not appear anywhere as a member of the firm, the public persisted in regarding me as the substance of that firm and Webster the shadow. Everybody who had a book to publish offered it to me, not to Webster. I accepted several excellent books but Webster declined them every time, and he was master. But if anybody offered *him* a book, he was so charmed with the compliment that he took the book without examining it. He was not able to get hold of one that could make its living.

Joe Jefferson, the famous actor, wrote me and said he had written his autobiography and he would like me to be the publisher. Of course I wanted the book. I sent his letter to Webster and asked him to arrange the matter. Webster did not decline the book. He simply ignored it. He accepted and published two or three war books that furnished no profit. He accepted still another one, distributed the agency contracts for it and named its price. One day in the office I asked Webster how many thousand words it contained. He said he didn't know. I asked him to count the words, by rough estimate. He did it. I said, "It doesn't contain words enough for the price and dimensions, by four-fifths. You will have to pad it with a brick. We must start a brickyard, and right away, because it is much cheaper to make bricks than it is to buy them in the market."

It set him in a fury. Any little thing like that would have that effect. He had several books on hand—worthless books which he had accepted—and I found that he had never counted the words in any of them. Webster was a good general agent but he knew nothing about publishing and he was incapable of learning anything about it. By and by he kept back a book of mine, *A Connecticut Yankee in King Arthur's Court*, as long as he could and finally published it so surreptitiously that it took two or three years to find out that there was any such book. He suppressed a compilation made by William Dean Howells and me, *The Library of Humor*, and finally issued it so clandestinely that I doubt if anybody in America ever did find out that there was such a book.

Webster was the victim of a cruel neuralgia in the head. He eased his pain with the new German drug, phenacetine. The physicians limited his use of it but he found a way to get it in quantity, and he took this drug with increasing frequency. It stupefied him and he went about as one in a dream. He ceased from coming to the office except at intervals, and when he came he was pretty sure to exercise his authority in ways perilous for the business. In his condition, he was not responsible for his acts.

Something had to be done. Whitford, the lawyer, explained that there was no way to get rid of this dangerous element except by buying Webster out. But what was there to buy? Webster had always promptly collected any money that was due him. He had squandered, long ago, my share of the memoir's profit—a hundred thousand dollars. The business was gasping, dying. The whole of it was not worth a dollar and a half. Then what would be a fair price for me to pay for a tenth interest in it? After much consultation, it transpired that Webster would be willing to put up with twelve thousand dollars and step out. I furnished the check.

Webster's understudy and business manager had now been for some time a young fellow named Frederick J. Hall. Poor Hall meant well but he was wholly incompetent for the place. He carried it along for a time with the heroic hopefulness of youth, but there was an obstruction which was bound to defeat him sooner or later. It was this:

Stedman, the poet, had made a compilation, several years earlier, called *A Library of American Literature*—nine or ten octavo volumes. A publisher in Cincinnati had tried to make it succeed. It swallowed up that publisher, family and all. If Stedman had offered me the book I should have said, "Such a book requires a cash capital of several hundred thousand dollars and we haven't a hundred thousand." But Stedman didn't bring the book to me. He took it to Webster. Webster, delighted and flattered, accepted the book on an eight-percent royalty and thereby secured the lingering suicide of Charles L. Webster & Co.

We struggled along two or three years under that deadly load. After Webster's time, poor little Hall struggled along with it and got to borrowing money of a bank—borrowing on notes endorsed by me and renewed from time to time. These notes used to come to me in Italy for renewals. I endorsed them without examining them and sent them back.

At last I found that additions had been made to the borrowings, without my knowledge. I began to feel troubled. I wrote young Mr. Hall and said I would like to have an exhaustive report of the condition of the business. The next mail brought that report, whereby it appeared that the concern's assets exceeded its liabilities by ninety-two thousand dollars. I felt better. But there was no occasion to feel better, for the report ought to have read the other way. Poor Hall soon wrote that we must have more money right away or the concern would fail.

I sailed for New York. I emptied into the till twenty-four thousand dollars which I had earned with the pen. I looked around to see where we could borrow money. This was in the midst of the fearful panic of 1893. I went up to Hartford to borrow—couldn't borrow a penny. I offered to mortgage our house. The property had cost a hundred and sixty-seven thousand dollars. Henry Robinson said, "Clemens, I give you my word, you can't borrow three thousand dollars on that property."

Charles L. Webster & Co. failed. The firm owed me about sixty thousand dollars, borrowed money. It owed Mrs. Clemens sixty-five thousand dollars, borrowed money. Also it owed ninety-six creditors an average of a thousand dollars apiece. The panic had stopped Mrs. Clemens's income. It had stopped my income from my books. We had but nine thousand dollars in the bank. We hadn't a penny wherewith to pay the Webster creditors. Henry Robinson said, "Hand over everything belonging to Webster and Company to the creditors and ask them to accept that in liquidation of the debts. They'll do it. They are aware that you are not individually responsible for those debts."

I didn't think much of that way out of the difficulty and Mrs. Clemens wouldn't hear of it at all. She said, "This is my house. The creditors shall have it. Your books are your property—turn them over to the creditors. Reduce the indebtedness in every way you can think of—then get to work and earn the rest of the indebtedness, if your life is spared. And don't be afraid. We shall pay a hundred cents on the dollar yet."

It was sound prophecy. Our friend, Mr. Henry H. Rogers, stepped in about this time and preached to the creditors. He said they could not have Mrs. Clemens's house—that she must be a preferred creditor and would give up the Webster notes for sixty-five thousand dollars, money borrowed of her. He said they could not have my books, that they were not an asset of Webster & Co., that the creditors could have everything that belonged to Webster & Co., that I would wipe from the slate the sixty thousand dollars I had lent to the company, and that I would now make it my task to earn the rest of the Webster indebtedness, if I could, and pay a hundred cents on the dollar— but that this must not be regarded as a promise.

MR. ROGERS has by now passed from life. But I do not believe I will ever find myself competent to put into words my feelings for him and my estimate of him.

Mr. Rogers was a great man. He was great in more ways than one. But what I am trying to place before unfamiliar eyes is the heart of him.

When the publishing house of Webster & Co. failed, in the early 1890's, I was morally bound for the debts, though not legally. Old business friends of mine said: "Business is business, sentiment is sentiment—and this is business. Turn the assets over to the creditors and compromise on that; other creditors are not getting thirty-three percent."

But Mr. Rogers had a clear eye for the situation and could see that it differed from other apparently parallel situations. He sided with my wife. In substance he said this: "Business has its laws and customs and they are justified; but a literary man's reputation is his life; he can afford to be money poor but he cannot afford to be character poor; you must earn the cent per cent and pay it."

So it was decided. I must cease from idling and take up work again. I must write a book; also I must return to the lecture platform. My wife said I could clear the debt in four years. Mr. Rogers was more cautious. He said I could have as many years as I wanted—seven to start with. That was his joke. Privately I was afraid his seven might be nearer the mark than Mrs. Clemens's four.

One day I got a shock—a shock which disturbed me a good deal. I overheard a brief conversation between Mr. Rogers and a couple of seasoned men of affairs.

First Man of Affairs: How old is Clemens?

Mr. Rogers: Fifty-eight.

First Man of Affairs: Ninety-five percent of the men who fail at fifty-eight never get up again.

Second Man of Affairs: You can make it ninety-eight percent and be nearer right.

Those sayings troubled me with melancholy forebodings. However, the depression did not last, because Mrs. Clemens took her pencil and paper, when she learned my trouble, and convincingly ciphered out the intake of the four years and the resultant success. I could see that she was right. Indeed, she was always right. In foresight, wisdom and good judgment, she had no match among people I have known, except Mr. Rogers.

Necessarily it took a good while to arrange the details for a lecture trip around the globe, but this labor was completed at last and we made our start in July 1895, for twelve months.

Meantime Mr. Rogers was in command, in the matter of the creditors. There were ninety-six of them. He had meetings with them, discussions, arguments, but no quarrels. Mrs. Clemens wanted to turn over to the creditors the house she had built in Hartford and which stood in her name, but he would not allow it. Neither would he allow my copyrights to go to them.

I am grateful to his memory for many a kindness and many a good service he did me but gratefullest of all for the saving of my copyrights—a service which in later days saved me and my family from want and assured us permanent comfort and prosperity.

Mr. Rogers was endowed with many great qualities; but the one which I most admired was his unselfishness where a friend or a cause that was near his heart was concerned. He never shirked anything, but kept his master brain and his master hands going all day long and every day.

Meanwhile Mrs. Clemens and Clara and I started, on the 15th of July, 1895, on our lecturing raid around the world. We lectured and robbed and raided for thirteen months. I wrote a book and published it.* I sent the book money and lecture money to Mr. Rogers as fast as we captured it. He banked it

---

Following the Equator, 1897.

and saved it up for the creditors. At the end of 1898 or the beginning of 1899 Mr. Rogers cabled me, at Vienna, "The creditors have all been paid a hundred cents on the dollar. There is eighteen thousand five hundred dollars left. What shall I do with it?"

I answered, "Put it in Federal Steel"—which he did, all except a thousand dollars, and took it out again in two months with a profit of a hundred and twenty-five percent.

There—thanks be! A hundred times I have tried to tell this intolerable story with a pen but I never could do it. It always made me sick before I got halfway to the middle of it. But this time I have held my grip and walked the floor and emptied it all out of my system, and I hope to never hear of it again.

CHAPTER 14

THERE HAS NEVER BEEN a time in the past thirty-five years* when my literary shipyard hadn't two or more half-finished ships on the ways, neglected and baking in the sun. This has an un-businesslike look but it was not purposeless. As long as a book would write itself I was a faithful and interested amanuensis and my industry did not flag, but the minute that the book tried to shift to *my* head the labor of contriving its situations and inventing its adventures, I put it away and dropped it out of my mind. Then I examined my unfinished properties to see if among them there might not be one whose interest in itself had revived through a couple of years' restful idleness and was ready to take me on again as amanuensis.

It was by accident that I found out that a book is pretty sure to get tired along about the middle. It was when I had reached the middle of *Tom Sawyer* that I made this invaluable find. At page four hundred of my manuscript the story made a sudden halt and refused to proceed. Day after day it still refused. I was

---

*Written August 30, 1906.

Opposite page, H. H. Rogers; Charles L. Webster; Sam, Clara, and Livy on world tour

NOTICE
ALL STOWAWAYS WILL
BE PROSECUTED AT HONOLULU,
AND RETURNED TO THIS PORT.
BY ORDER

distressed, for I knew that the tale was not finished and I could not understand why I was not able to go on with it. The reason was very simple—my tank had run dry; the stock of materials in it was exhausted; the story could not go on without materials.

When the manuscript had lain in a pigeonhole two years I took it out one day and read its last chapter. It was then that I made the great discovery that when the tank runs dry you've only to leave it alone and it will fill up again in time, while you are asleep—also while you are at work at other things. There was plenty of material now and the book went on and finished itself without any trouble.

Ever since then, when I have been writing a book I have pigeonholed it without misgivings when its tank ran dry. *The Prince and the Pauper* struck work in the middle, and I did not touch it again for two years. A dry interval of two years occurred in *A Connecticut Yankee in King Arthur's Court*. A like interval has occurred in the middle of other books. Two similar intervals have occurred in a story of mine called "Which Was It?" It is now four years since that second interval intruded itself. I am sure that the tank is full again now and that I could take up that book and write the other half of it without a break—but I shan't do it. The pen is irksome to me. Dictating has spoiled me. I am sure I shall never touch a pen again; I am tired of it.

In Rouen in 1893 I destroyed fifteen thousand dollars' worth of manuscript, and in Paris in the beginning of 1894 ten thousand dollars' worth—I mean, estimated as magazine stuff. I was afraid to keep those manuscripts on hand lest I be tempted to sell them, for I was fairly well persuaded that they were not up to standard. Ordinarily I would never think of publishing doubtful stuff—but I was heavily in debt then and the temptation to mend my condition was so strong that I burnt the manuscript to get rid of it. My wife encouraged me to do it, for she cared more for my reputation than for any other concern of ours.

Mark Twain's pigeonholes

There are some books that refuse to be written. They stand their ground year after year and will not be persuaded. It isn't because the book is not worth being written—it is only because the right form for the story does not present itself. There is only one right form for a story and if you fail to find that form the story will not tell itself. In *The Personal Recollections of Joan of Arc* I made six wrong starts and each time that I offered the result to Mrs. Clemens she responded with the same deadly criticism—silence. When at last I found the right form I recognized at once that it was the right one and I knew what she would say. She said it, without doubt or hesitation.

In the course of twelve years I made six attempts to tell a simple little story which I knew would tell itself in four hours if I could ever find the right starting point. I scored six failures; then one day in London I offered the text of the story to Robert McClure and proposed that he publish the text in his magazine and offer a prize to the person who should tell it best. I became interested and went on talking for half an hour; then he said, "You have told the story yourself. You have nothing to do but put it on paper just as you have told it."

I recognized that this was true. At the end of four hours it was finished, and quite to my satisfaction. So it took twelve years and four hours to produce that little bit of a story, which I called "The Death Wafer."

THERE IS A MAN whose name and whose words always stir me, stir me more than do any other living man's. That man is Kipling. But I remember a time, seventeen or eighteen years back, when the name did not suggest anything to me and only the words moved me. At that time Kipling was beginning to be known in India but not outside of that empire. He came over and traveled about America, maintaining himself by correspondence with Indian journals. He wrote dashing, brilliant letters but no one outside of India knew about it.

On his way through the State of New York he stopped off at Elmira and made a tedious and blistering journey up to Quarry Farm in quest of me. He ought to have telephoned the farm first; then he would have learned that I was at the Langdon homestead, hardly a quarter of a mile from his hotel. But he was only a lad of twenty-four and properly impulsive and he set out without inquiring on that dusty and roasting journey up the hill. He found Susy Crane, my wife's sister, and my own little daughter Susy there, and they came as near making him comfortable as the weather and the circumstances would permit.

The group sat on the veranda and while Kipling rested and refreshed himself he refreshed the others with his talk. They often spoke wonderingly of Kipling's talk afterward and they recognized they had been in contact with an extraordinary man. His was an unknown name and was to remain so for a year yet, but Susy kept his card and treasured it as an interesting possession. Its address was Allahabad.

Quarry Farm

No doubt India had been to her an imaginary land up to this time, a fairyland, a dreamland, a land made out of moonlight for the Arabian Nights to do their gorgeous miracles in; and doubtless Kipling's flesh and blood and modern clothes realized it to her for the first time and solidified it. I think so because she more than once remarked upon its incredible remoteness from the world that we were living in, fourteen thousand miles away, or sixteen thousand, whichever it was. Kipling had written upon the card a compliment to me. This gave the card an additional value in Susy's eyes, since as a distinction it was the next thing to being recognized by a denizen of the moon.

Kipling came down that afternoon and spent a couple of hours with me, and at the end of that time I had surprised him as much as he had surprised me. I believed that he knew more than any person I had met before, and I knew that he knew I knew less than any person he had met before—though he did not say it. When he was gone, Mrs. Langdon wanted to know about him. I said, "He is a most remarkable man—and I am, too. Between us, we cover all knowledge; he knows all that can be known and I know the rest."

He was a stranger to me and to all the world and remained so for twelve months. Then about a year after his visit, George Warner came into our library one morning in Hartford with a book in his hand and asked me if I had ever heard of Rudyard Kipling. I said, "No."

He said I would hear of him very soon. The book was *Plain Tales from the Hills* and he left it for me to read, saying it was charged with a new fragrance and would blow a refreshing breath around the world. A day or two later he brought a copy of the London *World*, which had a sketch of Kipling in it. According to this sketch Kipling had traveled in the United States and had passed through Elmira. This fact attracted my attention—also Susy's. She went to her room and brought his card from its place in the frame of her mirror, and the Quarry Farm visitor stood identified.

I am not acquainted with my own books but I know Kipling's—at any rate I know them better than I know anybody else's books. They never grow pale to me; they keep their color; they are always fresh. Certain of the ballads have a peculiar and satisfying charm for me. To my mind, the incomparable *Jungle Books* must remain unfellowed permanently. It was worth the journey to India to qualify myself to read *Kim* understandingly. The deep and fascinating charm of India pervades no other book as it pervades *Kim*. I read *Kim* every year and in this way I go back to India without fatigue—the only foreign land I ever daydream about or deeply long to see again.

CHAPTER 15

We LIVED FOR A YEAR in a Florentine villa in 1892. This was the Villa Viviani. Among random diaries I find some account of that pleasantly remembered year and will make some extracts from the same and introduce them here.

The situation of the villa was perfect. It was three miles from Florence, on the side of a hill. The flowery terrace on which it stood looked down upon sloping olive groves and vineyards; to the right, beyond some hill spurs, was Fiesole, perched upon steep terraces; in the distant plain lay Florence, pink and gray and brown, with the huge dome of the cathedral dominating its center like a captive balloon; and all around the horizon was a billowy rim of blue hills. After nine months of familiarity with this panorama I still think that this is the fairest picture on our planet, the most enchanting. To see the sun sink down, drowned on his pink and golden floods, and overwhelm Florence with tides of color that make all the sharp lines dim and turn the solid city to a city of dreams, is a sight to stir the coldest nature.

Here are some of my notes:

Sept. 26, 1892—Arrived in Florence. Got my head shaved. This was a mistake. Moved to the villa in the afternoon. Some of the trunks brought up in the evening by the *contadino*—if that is his title. He is the man who lives on the farm and takes care of it for the owner, the marquis. He is middle-aged, handsome, good-natured, and courteous. He charged too much for the trunks, I was told. My informant explained that this was customary.

Sept. 27—The rest of the trunks brought up this morning. The contadino charged too much again but I was told that this also was customary. It is all right, then. I do not wish to violate the customs. Hired landau, horses and coachman. The landau has seen better days and weighs thirty tons. The horses are feeble and object to the landau; they stop and turn around every now and then and examine it with surprise and suspicion. This causes delay. But it entertains the people along the road.

I will insert in this place some notes made in October concerning the villa:

This is a two-story house, said to be two hundred years old. It is a very fortress for strength; the main walls are about three feet thick; and the ceilings of the rooms on the ground floor are more than twenty feet high. I have several times tried to count the rooms in the house but the irregularities baffle me. There seem to be twenty-eight. The ceilings are frescoed, the walls are papered, and the whole place has a roomy, spacious look. There is a tiny family chapel on the main floor, with benches, and over the little altar is an ancient oil painting which seems to me to be as beautiful and as rich in tone as any of those old-master performances down yonder in the galleries of the Pitti and the Uffizi.

The curious feature of the house is the salon. This is a spacious and lofty vacuum which occupies the center of the house; it extends forty feet up through both stories and its roof projects some feet above the rest of the building. That vacuum is very impressive. The sense of its vastness strikes you the moment you step into it. I have tried many names for it: the Skating Rink, the Mammoth Cave, the Great Sahara and so on, but none exactly answer. There are five divans distributed along its walls; but they make little or no show. A piano in it is a lost object. We have tried to reduce the sense of space and emptiness with tables and things but they have a defeated look. Whatever stands or moves under that soaring painted vault is belittled.

Sept. 29, 1892—I seem able to forget everything except that I have had my head shaved. No matter how closely I shut myself away from draughts it seems to be always breezy up there. But the main difficulty is the flies. They like it up there better than anywhere else; on account of the view, I suppose. They walk over my head all the time. It is their park, their club. They have garden parties there and conventions and all sorts of dissipation. And they fear nothing. All flies are daring but these are more daring than those of other nationalities. These cannot be scared away by any device. But there are compensations. The mosquitoes are not a trouble. There are very few of them, and they are not much interested in their calling. A single unkind word will send them away; if said in English, which impresses them, they come no more that night. There also seem to be no fleas here. This is the first time we have struck this kind of an interregnum in fifteen months. Everywhere else the supply exceeds the demand.

Oct. 6—I find myself at a disadvantage here. Four persons in the house speak Italian and nothing else, one person speaks German and nothing else, most of the rest of the talk is in French, and Angelo speaks a French which he could get a patent on, because he invented it himself; a French which no one can understand. It makes no difference what language he is addressed in, his reply is in his peculiar, grating French, which sounds like shoveling anthracite down a coal chute.

Oct. 27—The first month is finished. We are wonted now. It is agreed that life at a Florentine villa is an ideal existence. The weather is divine, the outside aspects are lovely, the days and nights are tranquil and reposeful. There is no housekeeping to do, no marketing to superintend—all these things do themselves, apparently; each servant minds his or her own department. There is no noise or quarreling or confusion—upstairs. I don't know what goes on below. Late in the afternoons friends come out from the city and drink tea in the open air and tell what is happening in the world; and when the great sun sinks down upon Florence and the daily miracle begins, they hold their breaths and look. It is not a time for talk.

THE CERRETANI FAMILY, of old and high distinction, have lived on this property during many centuries. Along in October we began to notice a pungent odor which gave us some apprehension. I laid it on the dog, but privately I believed it was our adopted ancestors, the Cerretanis. I believed they were preserved under the house somewhere, and that it would be a good scheme to get them out and air them. But I was mistaken. I made a secret search and had to acquit the ancestors. It turned out that the odor was harmless. It came from the wine crop, which was stored in a part of the cellars. This discovery turned a disagreeable smell into a pleasant one. But not until we had so long and lavishly flooded the house with disinfectants that the dog left and the family had to camp in the yard. It took two months to disinfect the disinfectants. When they were finally all gone and the wine fragrance resumed business at the old stand we welcomed it with effusion and have had no fault to find with it since.

MY DAUGHTER SUSY passed from life in our Hartford home the 18th of August, 1896. With her when the end came were my youngest daughter Jean, our old servant Katy Leary, and John and Ellen, the gardener and his wife.

My other daughter, Clara, and her mother and I had arrived in England from around the world on the 31st of July and had taken a house in Guildford. A week later, when Susy, Katy and Jean should have been arriving from America, we got a letter instead. It explained that Susy was slightly ill—nothing of consequence. But we were disquieted and began to cable for later news. This was Friday. All day no answer—and the ship to leave Southampton next day at noon. Clara and her mother began packing, to be ready in case the news should be bad. Finally came a cablegram saying, "Wait for cablegram in the morning."

This was not satisfactory—or reassuring. I cabled again, asking that the answer be sent to Southampton, for the day was now closing. I waited in the post office that night till the doors were closed, toward midnight, in the hope that good news might still come, but there was no message. Then we took the earliest morning train and when we reached Southampton the message was there. It said the recovery would be long but certain. This was a great relief to me but not to my wife. She was frightened. She and Clara went aboard the steamer at once and sailed for America to nurse Susy. I remained behind to search for another and larger house in Guildford.

That was the 15th of August, 1896. Three days later, when my wife and Clara were halfway across the ocean, I was in our dining room when a cablegram was put in my hand. It said, "Susy was peacefully released today."

It is one of the mysteries of our nature that a man, all unprepared, can receive a thunderstroke like that and live. There is but one explanation of it. The in-

Mark Twain's luggage

547

tellect is stunned by the shock and but gropingly gathers the meaning of the words. The mind has a dumb sense of vast loss —that is all. It will take mind and memory months and possibly years to gather together the details and thus learn and know the whole extent of the loss.

The 18th of August brought me the awful tidings. The mother and the sister were in mid-Atlantic, ignorant of what

Susy's bedroom at Hartford

was happening, flying to meet this calamity. All that could be done to protect them from the shock was done by relatives and friends. They met the ship, and then showed themselves only to Clara. When she returned to the stateroom she did not speak and did not need to. Her mother looked at her and said, "Susy is dead."

At half past ten that night Clara and her mother drew up at Elmira by the same train which had borne them and me westward from the town one year, one month and one week before. And again Susy was there—not waving her welcome as she had waved her farewell thirteen months before, but lying white and fair in her coffin in the house where she was born.

The last thirteen days of Susy's life had been spent in our house in Hartford, the home of her childhood and always the dearest place in the earth to her. About her she had had faithful old friends—her pastor, Mr. Twichell, who had known her from the cradle; her uncle and aunt, Mr. and Mrs. Theodore Crane; Patrick, the coachman; Katy, who had begun to serve us when Susy was a child; John and Ellen. Also Jean was there.

At the hour when my wife and Clara set sail for America,

Susy was in no danger. Three hours later there came a sudden change for the worse. Meningitis set in. That was Saturday, the 15th of August.

"That evening she took food for the last time." (Jean's letter to me.) The next morning the brain fever was raging. She walked the floor in her pain and delirium, then succumbed to weakness and returned to her bed. Previously she had found hanging in a closet a gown which she had seen her mother wear. She thought it was her mother, dead, and she kissed it and cried. About noon she became blind (an effect of the disease) and bewailed it to her uncle.

From Jean's letter I take another sentence:

"About one in the afternoon Susy spoke for the last time."

It was only one word that she said. She groped with her hands and found Katy and caressed her face and said, "Mamma."

How gracious it was that in that forlorn hour, with the night of death closing around her, she should have been granted that beautiful illusion—that the latest emotion she should know in life was the joy and peace of that dear imagined presence.

About two o'clock she composed herself as if for sleep and she never moved again. She fell into unconsciousness and so remained two days, until the release came. She was twenty-four years and five months old.

On the 23rd her mother and her sisters saw her laid to rest— she that had been our wonder and our worship.

CHAPTER 16

TOMORROW WILL BE the 5th of June,* a day which marks the disaster of my life—the death of my wife. It occurred two years ago, in 1904, in Florence, Italy, whither we had taken her in the hope of restoring her broken health.

The dictating of this autobiography, which was begun in Florence in the beginning of 1904, was soon suspended because of the anxieties of the time, and I was never moved to resume the work until January 1906, for I did not see how I was ever

*Written June 4, 1906.

going to bring myself to speak in detail of the mournful experiences of that desolate interval and of the twenty-two months of distress which preceded it. I wish to bridge over that hiatus now with an outline sketch. I can venture nothing more.

Mrs. Clemens had never been strong, and when we planned in 1895 to go lecturing around the world, a thirteen months' journey seemed a doubtful experiment for such a physique as hers. But it turned out to be a safe one. When we—Mrs. Clemens, Clara and I—took the train westward bound at Elmira on the 15th of July, 1895, we moved through blistering summer heats. This for twenty-three days—I lecturing every night. Notwithstanding these trying conditions, Mrs. Clemens reached Vancouver in as good health as she was when she began the journey.

From that day her health seemed improved, although the summer continued thereafter for five months without a break. It was summer at the Sandwich Islands, summer in Australia, New Zealand and Tasmania, summer in Ceylon, and summer to us, of course, all over India. We sweltered along till we finally took ship for South Africa. Still Mrs. Clemens's health had steadily improved, and she and Clara went with me all over my lecturing course in South Africa.

We finally finished our lecture raid on the 14th of July, 1896, sailed for England and landed at Southampton on the 31st. A fortnight later Mrs. Clemens and Clara sailed for home to nurse Susy through her reported illness.

After Susy's death the diminished family presently joined me in England. We lived in London, in Switzerland, in Vienna, in Sweden, and again in London, until October 1900. And when at that time we took ship, homeward bound, Mrs. Clemens's health was in better condition than it had ever been since she was sixteen years old and met with her accident.

We took No. 14 West Tenth Street, just out of Fifth Avenue, in New York, for a year, and there the overtaxing of Mrs. Clemens's strength began. The house was large; housekeeping was a heavy labor but she would not have a housekeeper. Social life was another heavy tax upon her strength. In the hurly-burly of the New York season my correspondence grew beyond my secretary's strength and mine, and I found that Mrs. Clemens was trying to ease our burden for us. One day I wrote thirty-two letters with my own hand, and then found to my dismay, that Mrs. Clemens had written the same number. She had added this labor to her other labors and they were already too heavy for her.

By the following June this kind of life began to exhibit effects. Three months' repose in the Adirondacks did her good. Then we

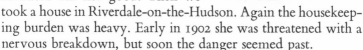

took a house in Riverdale-on-the-Hudson. Again the housekeeping burden was heavy. Early in 1902 she was threatened with a nervous breakdown, but soon the danger seemed past.

At the end of June we secured a house in York Harbor, Maine, for the summer. Mr. Rogers brought his yacht *Kanawha* and cast anchor at our riverfront in Riverdale. Mrs. Clemens and Jean and I went down to embark. I found, then, that Mrs. Clemens was not taking a servant along because she was afraid of inconveniencing Mr. Rogers. It was too bad. Jean's health was poor, and she would need attention. This service would fall upon Mrs. Clemens. She had arranged to ship the entire household and all the baggage by rail to York Harbor.

It was lovely weather and we sped over the sparkling seas like a bird. But these delights were not for Mrs. Clemens. She had to stay below and take care of Jean during the whole voyage.

Once again, here was opportunity to rest, but she would not rest. She had the spirit of a steam engine in a frame of flesh. Her heart soon began to alarm her. She began to dread driving out; anything approaching swift motion terrified her. She was afraid of descending grades, even slight ones. She would implore the coachman not only to walk his horses down imperceptible hills, but she watched him with fear, and if the horses stepped out of a walk for only a moment she would seize me in an ecstasy of fright. This was the condition of things through July.

York Harbor consists of a scattered cluster of independent little villages called York, York Harbor, York Village, West York—I think those are the names. About the 6th of August a celebration broke out among these hives—a celebration in commemoration of the two hundred and fiftieth anniversary of the institution of municipal government on the continent of America. For two or three days there were quaint back-settlement processions, orations and so on, by day, and fireworks by night.

Mrs. Clemens was always young and these things had a strong interest for her. During three days she went about, seeing and enjoying all that was going on and overtaxing her strength. With difficulty I persuaded her to forgo the grand performances of the closing night, and we observed the fireworks from our piazza. But my interference had come too late. The overtaxing of her strength had already been oversufficient.

The next afternoon was the last she ever spent in this life as a person intimately connected with this world's affairs. It was the last time she was to entertain a visitor. The visitor was a lady, American-born, who had married a Russian nobleman. She had forwarded to us a letter of introduction and now she came, upon our invitation, and spent the afternoon and dined with us.

At seven the next morning I was wakened by a cry. I saw Mrs. Clemens standing on the opposite side of the room, leaning against the wall, and panting. She said, "I am dying."

I helped her back to bed and sent for Dr. Leonard, a New York physician. He said it was a nervous breakdown and that nothing but absolute rest and careful nursing could help her. That was the beginning. During the twenty-two succeeding months she had for society physicians and trained nurses only.

The next sixty days were anxious ones for us. By October it was a question if we could get her back to Riverdale. At last we resolved to try the contrivance called an invalid's car. We secured a special train to take this car to Boston. Then we hitched it to a regular express train which delivered us at Grand Central Station in New York. A locomotive stood ready, and in fifteen minutes it delivered us at our home—Riverdale.

The burly English butler carried Mrs. Clemens upstairs to her bed and left her there with the nurse. When he closed that bedroom door he shut the truth out from that bedchamber forevermore. The physician, Dr. Moffat, came once or twice a day and remained a few minutes. If any doctor lies were needed he faithfully furnished them. When the nurse was on duty she furnished such lies as were needful. Clara stood a daily watch of three or four hours, and hers was a hard office indeed. Daily she sealed up in her heart a dozen dangerous truths and thus saved her mother's life and happiness with holy lies.

Clara had never told her mother a lie in her life before, and I may almost say that she never told her a truth afterward. It was fortunate for us all that Clara's reputation for truthfulness was so well established in her mother's mind. The mother never doubted Clara's word. Clara could tell her large improbabilities, whereas if I had tried to market even a small and simple one the case would have been different. I furnished no information in the bedchamber. But my protection lay in the fact that I was allowed in the bedchamber only once a day, then for only two minutes. The nurse stood at the door with her watch and turned me out when the time was up.

My room was next to Mrs. Clemens's, with a bathroom between. I could not talk with her, but I could correspond by writing. Every night I slipped a letter under the bathroom door that opened near her bed—a letter which contained no information about current events and could do no harm. She responded, with pencil, once or twice a day—at first at some length, but as the months dragged along and her strength grew feebler, she put her daily message of love in trembling characters upon little scraps of paper, and this she continued until the day she died.

I have mentioned that Clara's post was difficult. Several times, in letters written to friends in those days, I furnished illustrations of the difficulties of her position. One of these letters was written to Susy Crane at the end of 1902, two months after we had come back from York Harbor. Some days before Christmas,

Mark Twain's writing tools

Jean came in from a long romp in the snow, in the way of coasting, skiing and so on, and was presently struck with a violent chill. By Christmas Eve she was very ill. The disease was double pneumonia.

From that time onward her case was alarming. During all this time her mother never suspected that anything was wrong. She questioned Clara every day concerning Jean's health and employments; and Clara furnished information in minute detail— every word of it false, of course. Every day she had to tell how Jean dressed; and in time she got so tired of using Jean's existing clothes over and over that finally, as a relief, she got to adding imaginary clothes to Jean's wardrobe, and would probably have trebled it if a warning note in her mother's comments had not admonished her that she was spending more money on these spectral gowns than the family income justified.

Of course Jean had to have a professional nurse, and a woman named Tobin was engaged. Jean's room was at the other end of the house from her mother's; and so, doctors and nurses could come and go without their presence being detected by Mrs. Clemens. By the end of January, Jean had become able to be about, and the doctor ordered a change of scene for her. Our servant Katy and Miss Tobin accompanied her south to Old Point Comfort, and she remained there several weeks.

During the whole of Jean's absence Mrs. Clemens was happy in the thought that she was on the premises; that she was in blooming health and having as joyous a time as any girl in the region. On one day Clara would report Jean as being busy with her wood carving; the next day, as being at work at her language studies; the day after, as busy typewriting literature for me.

I will here insert the Susy Crane letter.

Clara's Day

Riverdale, Dec. 29, 1902, 9 p.m.

Susy dear, two hours ago Clara was recounting her day to me. Of course I can't get any of it right, there's so much detail; but with your York Harbor experience of the hardships attendant upon sickroom lying, you will get an idea, at any rate, of what a time that poor child has every day, picking her way through traps and pitfalls, and just barely escaping destruction two or three times in every hour.

[Today. Jean's other lung attacked; a crisis expected tonight. Our doctor is to stay all night.]

Of course Clara does not go to her Monday lesson in New York today, on Jean's account—but forgets that fact, and enters her mother's room toward train time, *dressed in a wrapper*.

LIVY: Why Clara, aren't you going to your lesson?

CLARA: (Almost caught) Yes.

LIVY: In that costume?

CL: Oh, no.

L: Well, you can't make your train, it's impossible.

CL: I know, but I'm going to take the other one.

L: Indeed *that* won't do—you'll be *much* too late for your lesson.

CL: No, the lesson time has been put an hour later. (sic)

L: (Satisfied. Then suddenly) But Clara, that train and the late lesson together will make you late to Mrs. Hapgood's luncheon.

CL: No, the train leaves fifteen minutes earlier than it used to. (sic)

L: (Satisfied) Tell Mrs. Hapgood etc., etc. (which Clara promised to do). Clara dear, after the luncheon—*could* you do two or three little errands for me?—it is a pity to send Miss Lyon* all the way to New York for so little.

CL: Oh, it won't trouble me a bit. (Takes a list of the things she is to buy—a list which she will presently hand to Miss Lyon and send her to New York to make the purchases.)

L: (Reflectively) What is that name? Toby—no, it's Tobin—Miss Tobin.

CL: (Turning cold to the marrow—Miss Tobin is Jean's nurse.) What about Tobin—Miss Tobin? Who is it?

L: A nurse. They say she is very good. Have you seen her?

CL: (Desperately) Seen her? A Miss Tobin? No. Who is it?

L: (To Clara's vast relief) Oh, *I* don't know. The doctor spoke of her—praised her. I suppose it was a hint that we need another nurse. But I didn't respond, and he dropped the matter. I think it is time you were dressing, dear—remember and tell Mrs. Hapgood what I told you.

This is a rude sketch, Aunt Sue, and all the *fine* things are left

---

*Mark Twain's secretary.

out. Clara is constantly getting into close places and then slipping out *just* alive by a miracle of impromptu fraud. The whole thing would be funny, if it were not so heartbreakingly tragic.

I have the strongest desire to call you to us, but the doctor wouldn't let you see Livy; and if he did—but he wouldn't.

Dec. 30, 6 a.m. (which is about dawn)—I have been up to Jean's room, and find all quiet there—Jean sleeping. Miss Tobin whispered, "She has had a *splendid* night." The doctor (and Clara) had put in an appearance a couple of times in the night and gone back to bed, finding things going well.   SLC

When one considers that Clara had been practicing these ingenuities for two months and that she was to continue to practice them daily for a year and a half longer, one gets something of a sense of the difficulties of the office she was filling.

TOWARD THE END of October 1903 we carried Mrs. Clemens aboard ship, her excellent nurse, Miss Sherry, accompanying us. We reached Florence on the 9th of November. We conveyed our patient to the Villa di Quarto.

Mrs. Clemens was doomed but she never suspected it—*we* never suspected it. She had been ill many times but her recuperative powers had always brought her safely out of peril. We were full of fears but I do not think we ever really lost hope. At least, not until the last two or three weeks. It was not like *her* to lose hope—and so at last when she looked me pathetically in the eyes and said, "You believe I shall get well?" it was a form which she had never used before and it was a betrayal. Her hope was perishing and I recognized it.

During five months I had been trying to find another satisfactory villa, in the belief that if we could get Mrs. Clemens away from the Villa di Quarto, which was an odious place, happier conditions would improve her health. I found many villas, but always lacking one or two essentials—features necessary to the well-being of the invalid. But at last I heard of a villa which promised to meet all requirements. Sunday Jean and I examined it and came home delighted. The purchase price was thirty thousand dollars and we could have possession at once.

We got back home at five in the afternoon and I waited until seven with my news. At this time I was allowed to have fifteen minutes in the sickroom two or three times a day—the last of these occasions being seven in the evening—and I was also privileged to step in for a single moment at nine in the evening and say good night. At seven that evening I was at the bedside. I described the villa and said we would buy it tomorrow if she were willing. She was pleased, and her face—snow white, marble white, these latter weeks—was radiant.

Sunday Evening, June 5, 11:15 o'clock—She has been dead two hours. It is impossible. The words have no meaning, but they are true. She was my life, and she is gone; she was my riches, and I am a pauper. How sudden it was, how wholly unexpected! Only this afternoon Clara and Jean and I were talking blithely about her, and Clara said "She is better today than she has been for three months"—then, half frightened, she said, *"Unberufen!"** and we echoed it hastily, superstitiously.

Only four hours ago I sat by her bedside while Clara and Jean were at dinner, and she was bright and cheerful—a rare thing these last weeks—and she *would* talk, although it was forbidden because she was so easily exhausted. She was full of interest in the calls which Jean and I had been making, and asked all about the people, and was like her old self. And smiled! It was sunshine breaking through weeks of cloud and gloom. It lifted me up and made me believe the impossible—that she would walk again, be our comrade again!

I was deceived by her inspiriting life and animation, and far overstayed my privilege. Only a word and a kiss were permissible, but I stayed a half hour. Then I blamed myself and said I had done wrong; but she said there was no harm, and lavished caresses upon me in her old natural way, the way which has been hers for thirty-four years, and she said, "You will come back?" and I said, "Yes, to say good night"—meaning at nine, as usual these many months. As usual, I stood a minute in the door, throwing kisses, she throwing kisses in response, and her

---

*A German expression meaning "May no evil befall us."

face all bright with that newfound smile—I not dreaming that I was looking upon that dear face for the last time in life. Yet so it was.

For a time I sat in my room, musing, my heart burdens strangely gone, my spirit at peace for the first time in many months. Then under the influence of that uplift I did a thing which I have hardly done since we lost our Susy eight years ago—I went to the piano and sang the old songs, the quaint Negro hymns which no one cared for when I sang them, except Susy and her mother.

When I sang them Susy always came and listened; when she died, my interest in them passed away; I could not put force and feeling into them without the inspiration of her presence. But now the force and feeling were all back, and it was as if eight years had fallen from me. In the midst of *"My Lord He call me! He call me by the thunder!"* Jean crept into the room, to my astonishment and—embarrassment; and I stopped, but when she asked me to go on, only the astonishment remained, and it was pleasant and inspiring.

With great difficulty I brought up little by little the forgotten words of many songs, and Jean remained until a servant came and called her out. After a little I went to my room, and it was now getting toward time to go downstairs and say good night; for it was a quarter of nine, and I must not go later than nine. At that moment Livy was breathing her last!

At the head of the stairs I met Miss Lyon, who had come for me. I thought nothing of that; I merely supposed our old Katy thought Livy was tired and ought to be quieting down for the night. She was already sleeping—and I never suspected!

Livy was sitting up in bed, with her head bent forward—Katy was on one side of the bed and the nurse on the other, supporting her; Clara and Jean were standing near the foot of the bed, looking dazed. I bent over and looked into Livy's face, and I think I spoke to her; but she did not speak to me, and that seemed strange. I kept looking and wondering—and never dreaming of what had happened! Then Clara said, "But is it *true?* Katy, it can't be true!" Katy burst into sobs, and then for the first time I knew.

It was ten minutes of nine. Only five minutes before, she had been speaking. She had heard me and had said to the nurse, "He is singing a good-night carol for me." She was happy and was speaking—and in an instant she was gone from this life. How grateful I was that she had been spared a struggle. Five times in the last four months she had spent an hour and more fighting violently for breath, and she had lived in fear of death by strangulation. Mercifully she was granted the gentlest and swiftest of deaths—by heart failure—and she never knew.

She was the most beautiful spirit, and the highest and the noblest I have known. And now she is dead.

CHAPTER 17

A CABLEGRAM HAS ARRIVED from England* inviting me to come to Oxford and receive an honorary degree on the 26th of next month. Of course I have accepted. During the past two years I have been saying with great decision that my traveling days were over and that nothing would ever induce me to cross the ocean again, yet I was not surprised at the alacrity with which I put that resolution behind me. I could have declined an invitation to come over and accept a London town lot, but a university degree is a quite different matter; that is a prize which I would go far to get at any time.

I remember the time that I found a battered old-time picayune in the road, when I was a boy, and realized that its value was vastly enhanced to me because I had not earned it. I remember the time, ten years later, in Keokuk, that I found a fifty-dollar bill in the street, and that the value of that bill also was vastly enhanced to me by the reflection that I had not earned it. I remember the time in San Francisco, after a further interval of eight years, when I had been out of work and out of money for three months, that I found a ten-cent piece at the junction of Commercial and Montgomery streets, and realized that that dime gave me more joy, because unearned, than a hundred earned dimes could have given me.

---

*Written May 23, 1907, three years after the death of his wife.

Now then, to me university degrees are unearned finds, and they bring the joy that belongs with property acquired in that way. It pleased me beyond measure when Yale made me a Master of Arts, because I didn't know anything about art; I had another convulsion of pleasure when Yale made me a Doctor of Literature, because I was not competent to doctor anybody's literature but my own. I rejoiced again when the University of Missouri made me a Doctor of Laws, because it was all clear profit, I not knowing anything about laws except how to evade them. And now at Oxford I am to be made a Doctor of Letters—all clear profit, because what I don't know about letters would make me a multimillionaire if I could turn it into cash.

In England he was asked why he always carried a cheap cotton umbrella. He answered: "Because that's the only kind of umbrella that an Englishman won't steal"

Oxford is healing a secret old sore of mine which has been causing me sharp anguish for many, many years. Privately I am quite well aware that for a generation I have been as widely celebrated a literary person as America has ever produced, and I am also privately aware that I have stood at the head of my guild during all that time, and so it has been an annual pain to me to see our universities confer an aggregate of two hundred and fifty honorary degrees upon persons of small and temporary consequence—and never a degree offered to me! In these past thirty-five or forty years I have seen our universities distribute nine or ten thousand honorary degrees and overlook me every time. This neglect would have killed a less robust person than I am, but it has not killed me; it has only shortened my life; but I shall get my strength back now. Out of those decorated and forgotten thousands not more than ten have been decorated by Oxford, and I am quite well aware—and so is America—that an Oxford decoration is a loftier distinction than is conferrable by any other university on either side of the ocean, and is worth twenty-five of any other, whether foreign or domestic.

Now then, having purged myself of this thirty-five years' accumulation of bile and injured pride, I will smooth my feathers down and drop the matter.

TWO OR THREE WEEKS AGO* Elinor Glyn called on me one afternoon and we had a long talk, of a distinctly unusual character. It may be that by the time this chapter reaches print she may be less well known to the world than she is now, therefore I will insert here a word of information about her. She is English. She is an author. The newspapers say she is visiting America to find a hero for a romance she is purposing to write. She has come to us upon the storm wind of a vast and sudden notoriety. The source of this notoriety is a novel of hers called *Three Weeks*. In this novel the hero is a fine and gifted young English gentleman. He goes to the Continent on an outing and there he happens upon a beautiful young lady of foreign extraction, with a deep mystery hanging over her. It transpires later that she is the childless wife of a king or kinglet, a coarse and unsympathetic animal whom she does not love. She and the young Englishman fall in love with each other at sight. So the pair flit away privately to the mountains and take up quarters in a remote house—and then business begins. They recognize that they were highly created for each other and that their passion is a sacred thing, that its commands must be obeyed. They get to obeying them at once and they keep on obeying them and obeying them, to the reader's intense delight and disapproval.

The unstated argument of the book is that the laws of nature are paramount and take precedence over the interfering restrictions obtruded upon man's life by man's statutes.

Madam Glyn called, as I have said, and she was a picture! Slender and beautiful—with blue eyes, English complexion and a glory of ravishing red hair. There she is, just a beautiful girl; yet she has a daughter fourteen years old. I talked to her with daring frankness, frequently calling a spade a spade instead of coldly symbolizing it as a snow shovel; and on her side she was equally frank. It was one of the damnedest conversations I have ever had with a stranger of her sex, if I do say it myself. She

---

*Written January 13, 1908.

wanted my opinion of her book and I furnished it. I said its literary workmanship was excellent and that I quite agreed with her view that in the matter of the sexual relation man's statutory regulations of it were a distinct interference with the law of nature. I went further and said that nature's laws were in my belief plainly the laws of God, since He instituted them. I said that her pair of indelicate lovers were obeying the clearly enunciated law of God, and in His eyes must manifestly be blameless.

Of course what she wanted of me was support and defense for her book. She said I was very brave (gross flattery which could have beguiled me when I was very very young), and she implored me to publish these views of mine; but I said, "No. Such a thing is unthinkable." I said that if I, or any other intelligent and experienced person, should suddenly throw down the walls that protect and conceal his *real* opinions, it would be perceived that he had lost his intelligence and ought to be sent to the asylum. I said I had been revealing to her my private sentiments, *not* my public ones; that I, like all other human beings, expose to the world only my trimmed, perfumed and carefully barbered public opinions and conceal, wisely, my private ones.

DUBLIN
NEW HAMPSHIRE

This series of 7 photographs registers with scientific precision, stage by stage, the progress of a moral purpose through the mind of the human race's Oldest Friend.
SLC
Aug. 29/06. 2

Shall I learn to be good? . . . I will sit here and think it over

The lady was young enough and inexperienced enough to imagine that whenever a person has an unpleasant opinion in stock which could be of educational benefit to Tom, Dick and Harry it is his *duty* to come out in print with it and become its champion. I was not able to get that juvenile idea out of her head. I was not able to convince her that we never do *any* duty for duty's sake but only for the mere personal satisfaction we get out of doing that duty. Take it all around, it was a very pleasant conversation and glaringly unprintable, particularly those considerable parts of it which I haven't had the courage to more than vaguely hint at in this account of our talk.

Some days afterward I met her again for a moment and she gave me the startling information that she had written down every word I had said, just as I had said it, and that it was "just splendid." She said she had sent it to her husband in England. Privately I didn't think that was a very good idea, and yet I believed it would interest him. She begged me to let her publish it and said it would do infinite good in the world, but I said it would damn me before my time and I didn't wish to be useful to the world on such expensive conditions.

LAST MONDAY* Albert Bigelow Paine** personally conducted me to Boston, and the next day to Portsmouth, to assist at the dedication of the Thomas Bailey Aldrich Memorial Museum.

As text and basis I will here introduce a few simple statistics. *And yet if I should really try . . . .*

The late Thomas Bailey Aldrich was born in his grandfather's house in the little town of Portsmouth, New Hampshire, seventy-two or seventy-three years ago. His widow lately bought that house and stocked it with odds and ends that once belonged to Tom Aldrich, and has turned the place into a memorial museum in honor of him. She has instituted an Aldrich Memorial Museum Corporation and has turned the museum

There do seem to be so many diff. . . .

---

*Written July 3, 1908.
**Albert Bigelow Paine was later to write Mark Twain's official biography. Twain helped him gather material for this work and in time the two men became fast friends. Paine came to live in the Clemens household as a member of the family.

over to this corporation, which is acting for the City of Portsmouth, the ultimate heir of the benefaction. A strange and vanity-devoured, detestable woman! I do not believe I could ever learn to like her except on a raft at sea with no other provisions in sight.

The justification for an Aldrich Memorial Museum for pilgrims to visit may exist, but to me it seems doubtful. Aldrich was never widely known, though he wrote half a dozen small poems which are not surpassed in our language for exquisite grace. A sprinkling of people would reverently visit the memorial museum if it were situated in a handy place, such as Boston or New York; but it isn't —it is in Portsmouth, New Hampshire, an hour and three-quarters from Boston by the Boston and Maine Railway. For the protection of the reader I must confess

. . . and just put my whole heart in it . . .

that I am perhaps prejudiced; it is possible that I would never be able to see anything creditable in anything Mrs. Aldrich might do. I conceived an aversion to her the first time I ever saw her, thirty-nine years ago. She is one of those people who are profusely affectionate, and whose demonstrations dis-

. . . But then I couldn't break the Sab . . . . .

order your stomach, for you never believe in them. Aldrich was delightful company, but we never saw a great deal of him because we couldn't have him by himself.

If anything was ever at any time needed to increase my aversion to that lady, that lack was made up three years ago, at a time when I was to spend six days in Boston and could invent no plausible excuse for declining to visit the Aldriches at Ponkapog, their estate a few miles out of Boston. I did not want to go to Ponkapog, but I could think of no good excuse, so I accepted an urgent invitation and went. There the guest room turned out to be spacious and judiciously furnished, with a noble big bed in it. I was given that room and was properly thankful and said so. But a girl of twenty arrived unexpectedly in midafternoon and I was moved out of it and she into it. I was transferred to a remote room which was so narrow and small that one could hardly turn around in it; it had in it a table, a chair, a small kerosene lamp, a cylindrical sheet-iron stove, and no other furniture. It was the meanest cell I had ever been in since I got out of jail. The month was October, the nights were cool; the little stove fed on white pine fragments, and it would turn red-hot in three minutes and be empty and cold again in ten. The little kerosene lamp filled the cell with a vague and gentle light while it was going, and with a cordial and energetic stench when it wasn't.

The reason I was transferred to that unsavory closet was soon apparent. Young Aldrich was a bachelor of thirty-seven; that young girl was daughter to an ex-Governor of *. . . and there's so many other privileges, that. . . perhaps . . . . .* the state and was high up in "society." The matchmaking Madam was setting traps to catch her for her son. She was quite frank about the matter and was feeling sure she was going to succeed in her designs. But she didn't; the girl escaped. *Oh, never mind, I reckon I'm good enough just as I am.*

I have at last disgorged that rankling incident. It makes me angry every time I think of it. That that woman should jump at me and kiss me on both cheeks, unsolicited, when I arrived, and then throw me down cellar, seventy years old as I was, to make room for a mere Governor's daughter, seemed to me to be carrying insult to the limit.

As to the memorial function in honor of Aldrich, let us take that up again.

I had not inquired into the amount of travel which would be

required. It came near being very great.* Paine and I reached Boston at two in the afternoon after a dusty and blistering journey. We were to go to Portsmouth next day, June 30th. Printed cards had been mailed to the invited guests, containing information. Whereby it appeared that the nine-o'clock express for Portsmouth would have a couple of special cars sacred to the guests.

To anybody but me, to any reasonable person, the providing of special cars by the rich Aldriches would have seemed a natural thing. But I was full of prejudice. I resented this special train. I said to myself that it was out of character; it was not for Mrs. Aldrich to do such a thing: to squander money on politeness. It irritated me to see her rising above herself, and in my animosity I said to myself that I would not allow her to collect glory from me at an expense to her of two dollars and forty cents, so I made Paine buy tickets to Portsmouth and return. That idea pleased me; indeed there is more real pleasure to be gotten out of a malicious act, when your heart is in it, than out of thirty acts of a nobler sort.

But Paine and I went into one of the two special cars in order to chat with their occupants, male and female authors—friends, some of them, the rest acquaintances. It was lucky that we went in there; the result was joyous. I was sitting where I could carry on a conversational yell with all the males and females at the northern end of the car, when the conductor came along, austere and dignified as is the way of his breed of animals, and began to collect tickets.

Several of the guests in my neighborhood I knew to be poor, and I saw—not with any pleasure—a pathetic look of distress exhibit itself in their faces. They pulled out of their pockets the handsomely engraved card of invitation, along with the card specifying the special train, and offered those credentials to the

---

*Mark Twain was by now living in Redding, Connecticut, in a new house called Stormfield which he had built after his wife died. In that house he did his final work on this *Autobiography*—work which consisted largely of recounting his memories to his friend Paine while a stenographer took down his words.

conductor to explain that they did not have to pay. The unsympathetic conductor said with his cold Boston and Maine Railway bark that he hadn't any orders to pass anybody, and he would trouble them for cash.

The incident restored my Mrs. Aldrich to me undamaged, undeodorized, and not a whiff of her missing. Here she was, rich, getting all the glory of indulging in the grandeur of a special train, and then stepping aside and leaving her sixty hardworked breadwinners to pay the bill for her.

At a way station the Governor of Massachusetts came on board with his staff. At Portsmouth we all went on to the Opera House. About three-fourths of the special-train guests were sent to seats among the general audience, while the Governor and staff and several more or less notorious authors were marshaled into the green room to wait. The Mayor of Portsmouth was there too, the ideal municipal Mayor, a big, hearty, muscular animal. Presently we marched in onto the stage

A letter from Rogers with a gift of a watch

and sat down in a row. William Dean Howells and I sat together near the center in a short willow sofa. Howells glanced down the line and murmured, "What an old-time, pleasant look it has about it!"

After a time the Mayor stepped to the front and thundered forth a vigorous speech in which he said many fine things about Aldrich. Governor Guild next made a graceful and animated speech. But then the funeral began. Mourner after mourner crept to the front and meekly read a poem he had written for the occasion. Pretty soon I was glad I had come in black clothes; at home they had fitted me out in that way, warning me that the occasion was not of a festive character, but mortuary.

Poet after poet got up, crawled to the desk, pulled out his manuscript and lamented; this went on and on and on, till the very solemnness of the thing began to become ludicrous. Howells' speech was brief, and felicitously worded; and he had it by heart and delivered it well; but he too read his poem from manuscript. Adding it to the pile, he came back to his seat, glad it was over and looking like a pardoned convict.

Then I abolished my prepared and memorized solemnities and finished the day's performance with twelve minutes of lawless, unconfined and desecrating nonsense.

The memorial function was over. There were two sweltering hours of it, but I would not have missed it for twice the heat and exhaustion and Boston and Maine travel it cost, and the cinders I swallowed.

CHAPTER 18

Mark Twain's daughter Jean Clemens, then in her twenty-ninth year, died December 24, 1909. Two days later Mark Twain showed the following account to Albert Bigelow Paine and said, "If you think it worthy, some day—at the proper time—it can end my autobiography. It is the final chapter."

Stormfield, Christmas Eve, 11 a.m., 1909

Jean is dead!

Has anyone ever tried to put upon paper all the little happenings connected with a dear one—happenings of the twenty-four hours preceding the sudden and unexpected death of that dear one? Would a book contain them? They pour into the mind in a flood. They are little things that have been always happening every day, and were always so unimportant and easily forgettable before—but now! Now, how different! How precious they are, how dear, how unforgettable, how pathetic, how sacred!

Last night Jean, all flushed with splendid health, and I the same, from the wholesome effects of my Bermuda holiday, strolled hand in hand from the dinner table and sat down in the library and chatted and planned and discussed, cheerily and happily (and how unsuspectingly!) until nine—which is late for us—then went upstairs, Jean's friendly German dog following. At my door Jean said, "I can't kiss you good-night, Father: I have a cold and you could catch it." I bent and kissed her hand. She was moved—I saw it in her eyes—and she impulsively kissed my hand in return. Then with the usual gay "Sleep well, dear!" from both, we parted.

At half past seven this morning I woke and heard voices outside my door. I said to myself, "Jean is starting on her usual horseback flight to the station for the mail." Then Katy, our old servant, entered, stood quaking at my bedside a moment, then found her tongue:

"*Miss Jean is dead!*"

Possibly I know now what the soldier feels when a bullet crashes through his heart.

In her bathroom there she lay, the fair young creature, stretched upon the floor and covered with a sheet. And looking so natural, as if asleep. We knew what had happened. She was an epileptic: she had been seized with a convulsion and heart failure in her bath. When the doctor came, his efforts, like our previous ones, failed to bring her back to life.

It is noon, now. How lovable she looks, how sweet and how tranquil! It is a noble face and full of dignity; and that was a good heart that lies there so still.

In England, thirteen years ago, my wife and I were stabbed to the heart with a cablegram which said, "Susy was mercifully released today." I had to send a like shock to Clara, in Berlin, this morning. With the peremptory addition, "You must not come home." Clara has been nursing her husband day and night for four months. She and her husband sailed from here on the eleventh of this month. How will Clara bear it? Jean, from her babyhood, was a worshiper of Clara.

I LOST Susy thirteen years ago; I lost her mother—her incomparable mother!—five and a half years ago; Clara has gone away to live in Europe; and now I have lost Jean. How poor I am, who was once so rich! Seven months ago Mr. Rogers died—one of the best friends I ever had, and the nearest perfect man I ever met. Gilder has passed away, and Laffan—old, old friends. Jean lies yonder, I sit here; we kissed hands good-by at this door last night—and it was forever, we never suspecting it. She lies there, and I sit here—writing, busying myself, to keep my heart from breaking. How dazzlingly the sunshine is flooding the hills around! It is like a mockery.

Seventy-four years old, twenty-four hours ago. Seventy-four years old yesterday. Who can estimate my age today?

I have looked upon her again. I wonder I can bear it. She looks just as her mother looked when she lay dead in that Florentine villa. The sweet placidity of death! It is more beautiful than sleep.

I saw her mother buried. I said I would never endure that horror again; that I would never again look into the grave of anyone dear to me. I have kept to that. They will take Jean from this house tomorrow and bear her to Elmira, New York, where lie those of us that have been released, but I shall not follow.

Jean was on the dock when the ship came in with me from Bermuda only four days ago. She was at the door, beaming a welcome, when I reached this house the next evening. We played cards and she tried to teach me a new game called "Mark Twain." We sat chatting cheerily in the library last night and she wouldn't let me look into the loggia, where she was making Christmas preparations. She said she would finish them in the morning and then her little French friend would arrive from New York—the surprise would follow; the surprise she had been working over for days. While she was out for a moment I disloyally stole a look. The loggia floor was clothed with rugs and furnished with chairs and sofas; and the uncompleted surprise was there: a Christmas tree that was drenched with silver film in a most wonderful way; and on a table was a prodigal profusion of bright things which she was going to hang upon it. What desecrating hand will ever banish that unfinished surprise from that place? Not mine, surely. All these little matters have happened in the last four days. "Little." Yes—*then*. But not now. Nothing she said or thought or did is little now. And all the lavish humor!—what is become of it? It is pathos, now. Pathos, and the thought of it brings tears.

I have been to Jean's parlor. Such a turmoil of Christmas presents for servants and friends! They are everywhere; tables, chairs, the floor—everything is occupied. It is many and many a year since I have seen the like. In that ancient day Mrs. Clemens and I used to slip into the nursery at midnight on Christmas Eve and look the presents over. The children were little then. And now here is Jean's parlor looking just as that nursery used to look. Jean's mother always worked herself down with her Christmas preparations. Jean did the same yesterday and the preceding days, and the fatigue has cost her her life. The fatigue caused the convulsion that attacked her this morning. She had had no attack for months.

JEAN WAS so full of life and energy that she was constantly in danger of overtaxing her strength. Every morning she was in the saddle by half past seven and off to the station for her mail. She examined the letters and I distributed them: some to her, some to Mr. Paine, the others to the stenographer and myself. She dispatched her share and then mounted her horse again and went around superintending her farm and her poultry the rest of the day. Sometimes she played billiards with me after dinner, but she was usually too tired to play and went early to bed.

Yesterday afternoon I told her about some plans I had been devising while absent in Bermuda, to lighten her burdens. We would get a housekeeper; also we would put her share of the secretary work into Mr. Paine's hands. No—she wasn't willing. The matter ended when I submitted. I always did. Jean was pleased and that was sufficient for me. She was proud of being my secretary, and I was never able to persuade her to give up any part of her share in that unlovely work.

In the talk last night I said I found everything going so smoothly that if she were willing I would go back to Bermuda in February and get blessedly out of the clash and turmoil again for another month. She was urgent that I should do it, and said that if I would put off the trip until March she would take Katy and go with me. We struck hands upon that and said it was settled. I was to write to Bermuda and secure a furnished house. I meant to write the letter this morning. But it will never be written now.

For she lies yonder and before her is another journey than that.

Night is closing down; the rim of the sun barely shows above the skyline of the hills.

I have been looking at that face again that was growing dearer and dearer to me every day. I was getting acquainted with Jean in these last nine months. She had been long an exile from home when she came to us three-quarters of a year ago. She had been in exile two years with the hope of healing her malady—epilepsy. She had been shut up in sanitariums, many miles from us. How glad and grateful she was to cross her father's threshold again!

Would I bring her back to life if I could do it? I would not. If a word would do it, I would beg for strength to withhold the word. In her loss I am almost bankrupt, and my life is a bitterness, but I am content: for she has been enriched with the most precious of all gifts—that gift which makes all other gifts mean and poor—death. I have never wanted any released friend of mine restored to life since I reached manhood. I felt in this way when Susy passed away; and later my wife, and later Mr. Rogers. When Clara met me at the station in New York and told me Mr. Rogers had died suddenly, my thought was, "Oh, favorite of fortune!" The reporters said there were tears of sorrow in my eyes. True—but they were for *me*, not for him. He had suffered no loss. All the fortunes he had ever made before were poverty compared with this one.

There was never a kinder heart than Jean's. From her childhood up she always spent the most of her allowance on charities of one kind and another. She was a loyal friend to all animals and she loved them all, birds, beasts and everything—even snakes—an inheritance from me. She became a member of various humane societies even when she was still a little girl, both here and abroad, and she founded two or three societies for the protection of animals, here and in Europe.

Her dog has been wandering about the grounds today, comradeless and forlorn. I have seen him from the windows. She got him from Germany. He has tall ears and looks exactly like a wolf. He was educated in Germany and knows no language but German. Jean gave him orders in that tongue. And so, when the burglar alarm made a clamor at midnight a fortnight ago, the butler, who is French and knows no German, tried in vain to interest the dog in the supposed burglar. Jean wrote me, to Bermuda, about the incident. It was the last letter I was ever to receive from her.

THE TELEGRAMS of sympathy are flowing in from far and wide now, just as they did in Italy five years and a half ago, when this child's mother laid down her life. They cannot heal the hurt, but they take away some of the pain.

"Miss Jean is dead!"
It is true. Jean is dead.
A month ago I was writing bubbling and hilarious articles for magazines yet to appear, and now I am writing—this.

Christmas Day, noon—Last night I went to Jean's room at intervals and looked at the peaceful face and kissed the cold brow. About three in the morning, while wandering about the house in the deep silences, as one does in times like these, when there is a dumb sense that something has been lost that will never be found again, yet must be sought, I came upon Jean's dog in the hall downstairs, and noted that he did not spring to greet me, according to his habit, but came slow and sorrowfully; also I remembered that he had not visited Jean's apartment since the tragedy. Poor fellow, did he know? I think so.

Always when Jean was abroad in the open he was with her; always when she was in the house he was with her. Her parlor was his bedroom. Whenever I happened upon him on the ground floor he always followed me about, and when I went upstairs he went too—in a tumultuous gallop. But now it was different: after patting him a little I went to the library—he remained behind; when I went upstairs he did not follow me, save with his wistful eyes. He has wonderful eyes—big and kind and eloquent. He can talk with them. I do not like dogs, because they bark when there is no occasion for it; but I liked this one from the beginning, because he belonged to Jean and because he never barks except when there is occasion—which is not oftener than twice a week.

In my wanderings I visited Jean's parlor. In a closet I found she had hidden a surprise for me—a thing I have often wished I owned: a noble big globe. I couldn't see it for the tears. She will never know the pride I take in it, and the pleasure. Today the mails are full of loving remembrances for her: full of those old, kind words she loved so well, "Merry Christmas to Jean!" If she could only have lived one day longer!

Christmas Night—This afternoon they took her away from her room. As soon as I might, I went down to the library and there she lay in her coffin, with the dignity of death and the peace of God on her face.

They told me the first mourner to come was the dog. He came uninvited and stood up on his hind legs and rested his forepaws upon the trestle and took a last long look at the face that was so dear to him, then went his way as silently as he had come. *He knows.*

At midafternoon it began to snow. The pity that Jean could not see it! She so loved the snow.

The snow continued to fall. At six o'clock the hearse drew up to the door. As they lifted the casket, Paine began playing on the orchestrelle Schubert's *Impromptu*, which was Jean's favorite.

From my windows I saw the hearse wind along the road and gradually grow vague and spectral in the falling snow and presently disappear. Jean was gone out of my life and would not come back anymore.

December 26—The dog came to see me at eight this morning. He was very affectionate, poor orphan! My room will be his quarters hereafter.

The storm raged all night. It has raged all the morning. The snow drives across the landscape in vast clouds, superb, sublime —and Jean not here to see.

2:30 p.m.—It is the time appointed. The funeral has begun, four hundred miles away, but I can see it all just as if I were there. The scene is the library in the Langdon homestead. Jean's coffin stands where her mother and I stood, forty years ago, and were married; and where Susy's coffin stood thirteen years ago; where her mother's stood five years and a half ago; and where mine will stand, after a little time.

Five o'clock—It is all over.

When Clara went away two weeks ago to live in Europe, it was hard but I could bear it, for I had Jean left. I said *we* would be a family. We said we would be close comrades and happy—just we two. That fair dream was in my mind when Jean met me at the steamer last Monday; it was in my mind when she received me at the door last Tuesday evening. We were together; *we were a family!* The dream had come true—oh, preciously true, contentedly true, satisfyingly true! And remained true two whole days.

And now? Now Jean is in her grave!

In the grave—if I can believe it. God rest her sweet spirit!

Four months after the death of Jean, Mark Twain himself died, on April 21, 1910.

ACKNOWLEDGMENTS

The condensations in this volume have been created by The Reader's Digest Association, Inc., and are used by permission of and special arrangement with the publishers and the holders of the respective copyrights.

ELIZABETH THE GREAT, copyright 1958, renewed © 1986 by Elizabeth Jenkins, is reprinted by permission of Curtis Brown, Ltd. and Victor Gollancz, Ltd.

DARWIN AND THE BEAGLE, copyright © 1969 by Alan Moorehead, is reprinted by permission of The Rainbird Publishing Group, Ltd.

MARTIN LUTHER: OAK OF SAXONY, copyright 1933, renewed © 1961 by Edwin P. Booth, is reprinted by permission of Abingdon Press.

THE AUTOBIOGRAPHY OF MARK TWAIN, edited by Charles Neider, copyright © 1959 by the Mark Twain Company; copyright © 1959 by Charles Neider, is reprinted by permission of Harper & Row, Publishers, Inc. and Curtis Brown, Ltd.

ILLUSTRATION CREDITS

COVER: top, illustration by Charles Raymond; bottom left, Mark Twain Memorial, Hartford, Connecticut; bottom center, George Richmond, Down House; bottom right, illustration by Fritz Kredel.

DARWIN AND THE BEAGLE: *Page 226:* The *Beagle* in Murray Narrow, Beagle Channel, by Conrad Martens, Down House. *233* top left: by Francis Lane, Royal Naval College, Greenwich. *233* top right, *307* bottom: by George Richmond, Down House. *233* center, bottom: Royal College of Surgeons, England. *238-239* center, *307* center, *316:* Down House. *239* top, *242* bottom, *304-305:* National Maritime Museum, Greenwich. *242-243* center, *243* bottom, *260-261, 274:* from *Narrative of the surveying voyages of HMS Adventure and Beagle, 1826-1836* by King, FitzRoy and Darwin, 1839. *248-249* top: from *Travels in Brazil, 1815, 1816, 1817,* by Prince Maximilian of Wied-Neuwied, 1820. *248* bottom: from *A Monograph of the Trogonidae* by John Gould, 1838. *249* right, *298-299* center: from *Voyage dans les deux océans* by E. Delessert, 1848. *268* top: from *The U.S. Naval Astronomical expedition to the Southern hemisphere,* 1855. *268-269* center, *272-273:* from *Picturesque illustrations of Buenos Ayres and Montevideo* by E. E. Vidal, 1820. *276, 277* right: from *Historia física y política de Chile* by Claudio Gay, 1854. *277* left, *292-293* center, *299* bottom: from *Journal of researches into the Natural History and Geology of the countries visited during the voyage of HMS Beagle round the world* by C. Darwin, 1890. *292* top, *293* top right: from *Zoology of the voyage of HMS Beagle* by C. Darwin, 1840. *293* top left: from *Merveilles de la Nature—Les Reptiles et les Batraciens* by A.E. Brehm, *1885. 298:* from *Voyage de découvertes aux terres australes* by F. Peron, 1807-16. *306-307* top: Mansell Collection. Photographed by Derrick Witty: pages *226, 233, 242* bottom, *277* right, *293* top left, top right, *299* bottom, *306, 307, 316.* Photographed by John Freeman: pages *248* bottom, *268-269* center, *272-273, 276, 298.* All photos courtesy of George Rainbird Ltd., London, England.

MARK TWAIN: Pages *421, 463, 473, 490, 511, 513, 514, 523, 524* left, *532, 540, 547, 548, 553, 567:* photos by Harry Seawell/Mark Twain Memorial, Hartford, Connecticut. *423, 424, 437* top, middle, bottom right, *447, 479* top left and right, *491, 498* bottom left and right, *506* top left and right, *524* right, *529, 539* top left and right, *560, 562, 563, 564, 566:* Mark Twain Memorial, Hartford, Connecticut. *445:* photo by William Sonntag. *475:* The Mariners' Museum, Newport News, Virginia. *479* bottom: U.S. Information Agency. *498* bottom right, *539* bottom, *575:* Brown Brothers. *437* bottom left, *503, 506* bottom: Mark Twain Papers, Bancroft Library, University of California. *517:* courtesy Wadsworth Atheneum, Hartford, Connecticut. *542:* U.S. Office of War Information. *498* top, *551:* Bettmann Archive. *561:* Yale Collection of American Literature. *427, 443, 457, 471, 496:* illustrations by John Falter.